THE DUTCH IN THE CARIBBEAN

AND ON THE WILD COAST

1580-1680

CORNELIS CH. GOSLINGA

UNIVERSITY OF FLORIDA PRESS

GAINESVILLE / 1971

A University of Florida Press Book

The publication of this book was made possible through a grant from the Netherlands Organization for the Advancement of Pure Research (Z.W.O.)

PUBLISHED SIMULTANEOUSLY IN THE NETHERLANDS BY
ROYAL VANGORCUM LIMITED, ASSEN

Library of Congress Catalog Card Number 72-93193

International Standard Book Number 0-8130-0280-X

PRINTED IN THE NETHERLANDS BY
ROYAL VANGORCUM LTD.

To my wife

CONTENTS

LIST OF ILLUSTRATIONS

LIST OF MAPS

PREFACE

In spite of the important role the Dutch played in the Caribbean during the seventeenth century, no study has ever been published which deals specifically with this topic, not even in the Dutch language. While the Spanish, French, English, and even the Danish activities in that area have been dutifully recorded in well-known scholarly works, accounts of Dutch achievements are not available except in the accounts of their foes; consequently they are seen not only from a particularly hostile point of view, but also to a very limited extent. Numerous wrong notions about their performances were the inevitable result, from statements that their most famous "sailor of fortune" Pieter Pieterszoon Heyn had a wooden leg and was knighted by his merchant-government—a comparatively small error—to allegations that breathe venomous anti-Dutch sentiments like Robert Southey's assertion that "there is no nation whose colonial history is so inexcusably and inexpiably disgraceful to human nature," an idea still to some degree prevailing in Anglo-Saxon historiography. The achievements of the Dutch in the Caribbean escape denigration only in a few exceptions. The reasons are understandable: because of a language barrier which is hard to overcome, their national point of view never entered the picture. This study is, more than anything else, an attempt to show that there is another side to the case.

Thus the importance of the Dutch presence in the Caribbean during the seventeenth century, because of the limited quantity of information, has not yet been fully realized. English and French accounts of contemporaneous chroniclers were, understandably, tainted with hostile feelings. Without claiming to be a paragon of the unbiased approach—who is?—I have tried hard to avoid the pitfalls of chauvinistic exaltation and have made a serious effort to describe the Homeric epic of the Dutch struggle for power against odds which soon proved to be overwhelming. This struggle had a glorious beginning, and yet it meant an unavoidable defeat for the Dutch. It is closely interrelated with the intricacies of the European involvements of the United Netherlands, with the government's evaluation of the Dutch West India Company as a useful and valuable war tool, and with the costs and profits of this institution's possessions on Africa's West coast, in Brazil, on the Wild Coast, and in New Netherland. I have tried to give a cool and balanced account of this contest, which was fought with extreme bitterness on all sides, although with a variation on a seventeenth-century saying, I must add: "Mon coeur était pour les Hollandais." I am afraid this was inevitable: there is just too much Dutch blood in my veins.

The dynamic quality of the Dutch presence in the Spanish *mare clausum* makes its history extremely fascinating. In my efforts to reconstruct their performances in an era which was their Golden Age, I leaned heavily on documentary information in Dutch and Spanish archives. French, English, and Portuguese sources have also been used, and in a few cases I have had to refresh my rusty knowledge of Latin, especially in the use of pamphlets, for which there were no translations available. For whatever knowledge or information that I have received for bringing this study to completion I am indebted to the many helpful and understanding functionaries in Dutch and Spanish archives and in other institutions for research. To them I give my thanks. Their courtesy, patience, and efficiency will not be forgotten. I wish to acknowledge also my indebtedness to *Zuiver Wetenschappelijk Onderzoek* at The Hague which provided me with a grant, and to the personnel of the Bancroft Library of the University of California, Berkeley, for the use of their excellent collection of microfilms. I am also indebted to the Metropolitan Museum of Art in New York, the New York Historical Society in New York City, the Atlas van Stolk at Rotterdam, the Rijksmuseum at Amsterdam, the Provinciale Bibliotheek van Zeeland, and the El Prado Museum in Madrid for supplying me with photographs of many paintings and engravings together with permission for their reproduction. I am particularly indebted to my daughter Marian who read the rough draft of this study and rewrote large parts of it. It is almost as much her book as it is mine. I freely give my thanks to Dr. Butler H. Waugh of the University of Florida for the delicate task of editing this work. I give my sincere thanks to the Division of Sponsored Research of said University, where the manuscript was typed and made ready for publication. Finally, I thank the University of Florida for its cooperation in making this publication possible, and the Prince Bernhard Foundation, Netherlands Antilles, for including it in its *Anjerpublikaties*.   *Cornelis Ch. Goslinga*

INTRODUCTION

There is a legend that Dutch ships, after defeating the fleet of the competing Hanseatic League in the middle of the fifteenth century, returned home carrying a broom in their masts as a symbol that they had swept the sea clean. Their action inaugurated a proud tradition of Dutch victories over competitors and enemies alike in the ensuing two centuries. More importantly, perhaps, that symbol inspired Dutch self-awareness during their long struggle for independence from a tyrannical Spanish rule, a self-consciousness that had been expressed earlier by Celsus: "The use of the sea is free for everyone." This idea was to be more poetically defined by de Buzanval, the French ambassador to The Hague: "The sea is a common element and its use as free as that of the air,"[1] and it would be crystallized in the sublime philosophical thesis *Mare Liberum*,[2] that eloquent defense of the principle of a free sea composed by Grotius in opposition both to the Spanish and Portuguese thesis of *mare clausum*[3] and to the British arrogance that found its formula in the phrase "Britannia rules the waves."

The *mare clausum* thesis was challenged and ultimately wrecked in 1588 when the mighty Armada was destroyed by storms and cliffs along the Scottish and Irish coasts, and again in 1639 when the Dutch Admiral Maarten Harpertszoon Tromp ruined a second Spanish armada under the very eyes of the British at the Downs. Portuguese claims were swept away when the Dutch, under the aegis of their East India Company, opened up the Indian Ocean—formerly a Portuguese sea—in the first quarter of the seventeenth century. The British premise, which was instigated by the first two weak and vainglorious Stuarts, was comprised of furtive gestures against Dutch fishermen along the British coast, and the challenge was met, though not always successfully for the Dutch, by the first, second, and third Anglo-Dutch wars. Thereafter, the Dutch were finally outnumbered and driven from the sea by the English, but only then, and that was after 1700. For some hundred years the Dutch broom had kept the sea clean and theoretically free.

It was a wonderful principle—the free sea. The Spaniards had denied it with the Cross and with the sword, in spite of the insistence of their earliest philosophers in this field, that the Spanish "right to the sea" pretensions were absurd. Even more absurd, however, is that the Dutch really believed that they were defending the principle of an open sea. Grotius explored and elaborated the free sea thesis into a philosophy. The Dutch historian Emanuel van Meteren accepted Grotius' hypothesis, but his narrative also reveals the practical implications of the thesis: "The United Provinces have gotten a free government; their inhabitants, consequently, can reckon themselves freed from the papal bulls which closed the navigation of the world's sea to all other nations. They are the richest in ships of the whole world."[4] Van Meteren's words, written not in Latin but in the vernacular, were easily accepted by Dutch businessmen. Most of them were Calvinists in whose opinion "...the donation of the Pope [was] vain, and against the teachings of Christ and the Christian religion."[5] But even Catholic Dutch merchants found favorable results in a free sea and free trade policy.

The Dutch colonial empire, built in the first half of the seventeenth century, began with a broom in the mast, i.e., with the principle of a free sea. As soon as the sea was cleaned, however—as soon as Spanish sea power was no longer a real danger for the Dutch—the latter lost interest in the high principles expounded by their finest philosopher and, not even reluctantly, accepted the Iberian thesis of a *mare clausum*. Once Dutch supremacy had been established in the formerly Spanish and Portuguese controlled East Indian archipelago, the area proved to be an unhealthy place for Englishmen as well.

Intolerance is almost always, sadly enough, victorious over more lenient and humane approaches to problems. As long as the Dutch had to fight, to struggle, and to risk their lives and goods against overwhelming odds—and Spain was Europe's greatest power—they fought for freedom, for free trade, and for a free sea. This course was in their best interests. They could not have survived without it. When they, in turn, became a world power, i.e. when they could dictate terms, they forgot the ideals that Grotius had defended for them.[6] Nor was that all: they went on to use two contending philosophies of business in dealing with their colonies and with other European powers. With others, they continued to uphold commercial freedom, unhampered competition, distrust of monopoly, and the free sea principle. Toward the colonies which they established in the East and West, however, their position is illustrated in the two powerful companies which they built on the principle of an exclusively monopolistic policy.

Even the great apostle of *mare liberum*, praised as an *ingenium tam pacatum*, became confused and twisted.[7] Such weakness of character may be explained by the fact that he was a paid propagandist for the East India Company and a member of several committees charged with negotiating with "the wisest fool in Christianity"—as James I of England was called by the French King Henry IV. He thus had to fight the very principles he had once defended. In London Grotius was forced to insist that a free sea—and free trade—never be applied to a sale that had already been closed or to a settlement that was already fortified. This argument signified his acceptance of the policies of monopoly and exclusive rights which were to find their finest expression in the mercantilism of the seventeenth and eighteenth centuries.

The *mare clausum* doctrine led directly to a refusal to submit to any sea law or to any recognition of rights at sea—except one's own. As soon as the Dutch felt themselves capable of protecting their navigation and trade, and at the same time saw possibilities to practice a profitable piracy far from home waters, they favored this thesis and made it theirs.

It is, however, a fact that until 1609, the year of the Twelve Years' Truce with Spain, Hollanders and Zeelanders both rejected the *mare clausum* principle. Moreover, the men who carried the Dutch banner to the farthest corners of the earth tried for at least three decades to apply the free sea thesis in practice, and to defend it. Even in 1638, when the Stadhouder Frederick Hendrik laid siege to Antwerp, a Dutch merchant who provided the town with war materials and food shouted presumptiously, "Commerce must be free and acts of war may not interfere with it."[8] The principle was duly honored when it agreed with the interests of the purse.

It was, perhaps, impossible to maintain this ideal and at the same time put it into practice. No other power was inclined to honor it; as soon as any one of them dominated an area, it chose to make it exclusive. The Romans had done so with the Mediterranean. Later the Venetians exercised complete control over the Adriatic, and found philosophers to defend their pretensions. The Genoese followed with pretentions to exclusive rights on the Ligurian Sea.

And, too, the growing power of the Netherlanders made the *mare liberum* principle a useless tool in their diplomacy: guns are more convincing than ideals. But it had given the young nation, in those first three or four decades when it was struggling for its existence, a unifying motive. At least in European waters the Dutch claim for some time kept a balance between the Spanish, French, and English fleets. For a moment the keys to the Sound lay in Amsterdam, and the Dutch sailed up the Thames to show the "merry old king" that they meant business about the free sea principle.

The Dutch activities in the Caribbean and the Guianas are only a small part of the far-flung exploits of those years. For a time they held good positions in Brazil and New Netherland, too, but they were never able to dominate the Caribbean and make it their *mare clausum*. The Dutch West India Company, after an amazing start, soon abandoned her aggressive pose, and the Dutch were compelled—in the West Indies at least—to concur with Grotius and Celsus: the Caribbean was indeed a free sea.

The history of the Dutch activities in this sea is the subject of this book.

THE BEGGARS AND THE BROOM

Fidèle au Roi jusqu'à la besace.

"War is the father of all things," wrote Karl von Clausewitz when Napoleon conquered Europe, but the observation applies as fully to the terrible eighty-year struggle which the Dutch undertook against Spain from 1568 to 1648. It is not our concern whether this revolt against Spanish absolutism and Catholic intolerance began *religionis* or *libertatis causa*. The seeds were planted long before the "Prudent King," as Philip II was called, succeeded his more diplomatic, though no more tolerant, father in 1555. Indeed, one can argue that the growing prosperity of the Low Countries, paralleled by the increasing sense of self-confidence, made independence only a matter of time, that it was speeded up by the lack of understanding in the Spanish approach to the problems of these countries. The long years of this war of independence pushed the young nation forward to a Golden Age. War was the father of that age, the father of the Dutch colonial empire in the East and in the West, and of Dutch naval pre-eminence.

A Dutch sea-power had existed as early as the fifteenth century when the Hanseatic League was defeated. It was, of course, not the fleet of an independent nation since the Low Countries were then a part of the Burgundian realm and later the "Tenth or Burgundian Circle," a province of the Holy Roman Empire. When, under the Burgundian dukes, a merchant marine came into existence and a code of laws was drawn up to regulate navigation, it meant, at the same time, that a potential war navy was founded. The difference between trading and war vessels, in those days, was almost nil. It is true that a few warships were built; this fleet was supplemented, in time of need, by merchantmen and put under the command of men with the title of admiral.

The "merchant shipping act," if we may call the Burgundian navigation code by this modern term, required that every ship leaving port have a letter of permission. Some of these were called "letters of marque"; the Dutch terminology reveals what these permits really were—*kaperbrieven*, permits for privateering. The Burgundians soon realized that the core of a good navy was experience in sailing and fighting. Seamanship, then, was still a rare commodity. Piracy provided the much valued experience.

The House of Austria succeeded the Burgundians and followed the same policy. An "Admiralty Board" with the purpose of administering naval affairs was created;[1] the institution still functioned when the Dutch revolted against Philip. The board provided the prototype for the United Provinces' organization for their war navy with administrative sites at Amsterdam, Rotterdam, Zeeland, West Friesland, and Friesland. The Prince of Orange became the admiral, and the members of the various boards took their oaths from him. Although the Dutch admirals commanded the fleets *de facto*—the princes of Orange never sailed with the fleet—they were only lieutenant-admirals. The admiralty boards, despite their decentralized organization and their consequent rivalry, functioned very well in the early years of the revolt. Efforts to centralize this institution were frustrated by the sudden death of William the Silent and were regularly opposed by Zeeland because of her fear of possible domination by Holland.

This decentralization, although born out of a strong feeling of provincialism and local autonomy, later prevented fast action and cooperation in cases of emergency and was one cause of the downfall of Dutch sea-power. The organization of these admiralty boards served as models, however, for the organization of the Dutch East and West India Companies.

The series of crises which the Low Countries passed through during the course of the sixteenth century culminated in the abjuration of Philip II in 1581. We have suggested that the tensions already existed under Charles V who, because he was not only sire of the Low Countries but also emperor of the Holy Roman Empire of the German nations and king of Spain, often followed a policy contrary to the interests of the provinces in the northwestern part of his realm and many times involved them in affairs which were not their concern. Warships belonging to the Low Countries, for instance, were used by Charles V against his Turkish and French adversaries. These and other enterprises caused the creation of a small standing fleet which was stationed in the Zeelandian town of Vere. From Vere the warfleets of the Seventeen Provinces which formed the Low Countries— mostly transformed trading vessels—sailed out under Dutch command.

Dissatisfaction with Charles' rule continued to increase, however, and his firm stand on the religious question augmented the unrest.

The placard of 1535, described as "one of the most terrible that were ever carried out against heretics,"[2] caused more agitation and disappointment. After all, Charles was born in the Netherlands and the Flemings, Hollanders, and Zeelanders could not understand so much intolerance in a fellow countryman. The placard was even directed against repentants, totally contrary to accepted medieval tradition.

In the political field, as in the religious, Charles' policy caused annoyance, even though he succeeded in uniting the Seventeen Provinces into a semi-political reality with a lessened bond of union between the Low Countries and the rest of the Holy Roman Empire. Under his rule national unity began; national feeling, however, grew more slowly. Philip II continued the policy his father had begun. But Charles had made two mistakes. In the first place, he reduced somewhat the many ties the Low Countries had had with the German Empire, and consequently he brought the provinces into relations with Spain, a power with which there was no common tradition, language, or commercial interest. Secondly, Charles did not realize that his son was the last man in the world to entrust with the Low Countries and their growing sense of independence. Given the character of this prince and his political and religious aims, the personal union with Spain may be certainly called, according to one historian, an "unmixed evil."[3]

Much has been written about that intransigent "Catholic Calvin" of the Escorial, and the evaluations vary from the purest white to the deepest black. Spanish and Catholic historians consider Philip II a great king. One of the explanations for his greatness, according to Santiago Nadal, was in his "complete adaptation to the time in which he lived."[4] He is called an exceptional figure and the most Spanish king of the House of Hapsburg, a man who carried the preservation and maintenance of the Catholic Church on his shoulders.[5] Admirers see him as a peace-loving and affectionate man who abhorred violence. Against contrary Protestant accusations, a bishop-historian maintained that he "was not the Nero of his century." Did he not write once to his half-sister Margaret: "God knows that I avoid nothing more than the shedding of human blood?"[6] Protestant views are different, of course. One Protestant historian calls him "a crowned Inquisitor";[7] another, milder or perhaps better balanced in his judgment, observes that Philip only followed the example of his father.[8] Emanuel van Meteren, certainly not impartial in his evaluation since he had to suffer under Philip and leave his own country, the Southern Netherlands, because of his Protestantism, argues that he could not be compared with his father and was "inclined to melancholy, jealousy, envy and hypocrisy."[9]

Perhaps Philip's character was too complex to be analyzed accurately. There are two aspects, however, which there is no question about: first, Philip did not like the Flemings, as he called the Dutch-speaking Netherlanders; and second, the religious basis of Philip's policy made him completely unable to understand or to respect any religious conviction that differed from his own. He seemed, moreover, to have been entirely indifferent to the enormity of human suffering which was caused by his Inquisition.[10] He identified opponents of the Roman Catholic Church as enemies of Christ. The Netherlanders, although still largely Catholic, had little of their king's horror of heresy: their Catholicism, though pure, was colored with humanism, and Erasmus was, in this respect, their prophet.

It is certainly true that Philip's policy lay in a direct line of descent from his father's, but he lacked Charles' camouflaging caution. In addition, Philip II was a complete stranger to the inhabitants of the Low Countries, a prince who did not even speak their language—be it Dutch or French.[11] Add to this the horrors of the Spanish Inquisition and the outrages against the numerous local privileges and charters. A Spanish historian might see him as the first modern statesman, but he was still completely wrapped up in the medieval concept that diversity in religious convictions would injure the political unity of the state.[12] Instead of being adapted to his time, he was a stranger, not only for the Low Countries but also for the entire non-Iberian world: he lived, indeed, in *la gran soledad*.

Could Philip have done differently? Could he have separated his strong religious prejudices from his policy? His rule in Spain was a joint Church-State affair, and he tried to apply the same formula to his northern dependencies. This policy not only caused the decline of his own country and that of the southern part of the Low Countries but also led to successful revolt in the north, an area which became independent. Throughout the Middle Ages Rome had insisted that heresy had to be persecuted; Philip's intransigent Catholicism certainly accepted that position. Further, Charles V had no tolerance for heresy, and the dependents in the Netherlands obeyed Charles. In the meantime, however, a religious peace had been concluded at Augsburg which gave northwestern Europe a solution for the problem of dissidents which—although not ideal—was for some time a workable one. Philip's blindness in this matter was, if possible, only surpassed by his insistence upon confounding political issues with Catholic glory. This and more led the Low Countries to rebellion.

Calvinism was also an obvious factor in the revolt. Although Calvin's followers in the Netherlands formed only a small minority, they knew how to arouse the majority and it was they who provided the leadership that the rebellion needed. The value of Calvin's teaching in the Low Countries, among a population long unhappy under foreign domination, lay in the fact that it sanctified all human action. Calvin's awestricken consciousness of God carried with it no indifference to mundane matters; it demanded instead the most intense participation in the common affairs of men. Within the limits of reason this teaching meant that commercial policies were as important as prayers; privateering on an enemy who endangered the "true religion"—Calvinism—as edifying as a Contra Remonstrant sermon. Were not all men's actions always in the Great Taskmaster's eyes?[13] This was the point which Philip missed entirely. The theses of the rigid reformer of Geneva became the focus of a rebellion against the *roi-bureaucrate* and the *roi paperassier* who, with pathological accuracy, always made his decisions in the huge rooms of the Escorial without regard for the irrevocable facts.[14]

A new spirit took possession of northwestern Europe, inspired it, and affected even those who thought themselves to be pure Catholic.[15] The heretics destroyed the churches, the Catholics did nothing against this, thus all must suffer, a medal struck in 1568 announced.[16] This new spirit did not, of course, appreciate the Dutch Catholic position: "My heart is for Rome, my arm is for liberty."[17] It fed itself, instead, if we may use this dangerous metaphor, from three sources: the religious unrest of the Reformation, the change in economic structure, and the beginning of a new national consciousness.

The bonds of religious and economic control, characteristic for the Middle Ages and accepted in earlier days, began to gall. Though Calvinism, in its principles, was as intolerant as Roman Catholicism, practice still differed widely. The burning of Michael Servetus in Geneva, Mary Dyer in Boston, and the hanging of some priests in the Dutch town of Brielle were exceptions to a *Realpolitik* which made the United Provinces of the Northern Netherlands a haven for religious refugees. No Catholic was ever burned there, and although they lacked some of the rights enjoyed by the orthodox Dutch Reformed, life for everybody, no matter what religion they professed, was possible and bearable. The same cannot be said for Spain.

The circulation of new ideas was also stimulated by the freedom the Low Countries enjoyed before the Hapsburgs had inherited that area, and this freedom was, at least partly, the result of commercial activities. But the revolt against Philip II occurred not only because of the fact that he wanted absolute religious and political control. In a country of businessmen and merchants, economic problems served to strengthen considerably the intellectual and moral reasons in favor of religious freedom.[18]

The Spanish king, who did not understand the changing world, could not see that economic, political, and religious monopolies were causing unrest. Instead, he saw in the revolt what his governors Alva and Requesens also saw: a purely political rebellion of the Prince of Orange and his followers. They soon discovered how wrong they were. Philip's too rigid policy, always oriented toward Spanish and Catholic interests, did not have the elasticity to include a *diesseits* orientation toward the new spirit which was conquering the Germanic world; it was continuously dictated by the king's *jenseits* convictions. Because of this myopia Philip was the chief cause of Spain's decline as a world power.

With these observations the longitude and latitude of the conflict between the King of Spain and his subjects in the Low Countries have been taken. It was the Duke of Alva, "tyrant and bloodhound" as he was called by the Sea-Beggars, "a nobleman of elegant affability" in the words of others,[19] burdened with the same concept of the revolution as Philip, who bore the primary responsibility for dealing with people whose recent deeds so clearly expressed their yearnings for freedom. "One has to exterminate them or give in to their fantasy," wrote a historian.[20] Alva chose the first solution.

His arrival in the Netherlands caused alarm, even terror. Many inhabitants felt guilty, including the Catholics. If one had not listened, once in a while, to the hedge-sermons, one had at least criticized the placards, or the Inquisition, or the reorganization of the Church, or the taxes. In the words of the seventeenth-century Dutch historian Johan van den Sande, no one was so innocent or so Catholic that he could not be accused of the *crimen omissionis*.[21] The heretics, as every one knew, would be punished, and especially those who had participated in the image-breaking while yelling *Vive les Gueux*! But even those who had remained faithful were likely to feel Alva's fist because they had been too tolerant, too moderate, too lenient.[22] It was under Alva that a priest was heard to exclaim from the pulpit: "Oh, you Spaniards, you Spaniards, will make us all Beggars."

New professions arose out of Alva's terror. Many people, with or without guilty consciences, left the country where they no longer felt safe. One of these was William of Orange, Philip's lieutenant in Holland, Zeeland, and Utrecht, who became the leader. Most of those who fled called themselves Beggars—Sea-Beggars—for, as exiles, the only safe outlet was the sea.[23] They pretended to fight for the king against his bad representatives. Dutch historians have rightly pointed out that from the start, in 1568, Philip's subjects fought against the Spanish in the name of the king. The national anthem written then began: "I have always honored the King of Spain."

Not all who called themselves Beggars, however, were criminals, outcasts, fugitives, adventurers, and image-breakers. The best of them, if not most, writes Conrad Busken Huet, were martyrs of the Spanish terror.[24] There were Englishmen, Scots, Germans, too. Dutchmen, however, because of their number and their stronger anti-Catholic and anti-Spanish feelings, became the natural leaders and certainly represented the core of nationalistic consciousness—at that time—if this were already born.

Perhaps it was French Admiral Gaspar de Coligny who advised William the Silent to incorporate these men into his program to break away from Spanish rule.[25] Although roaming the sea, in those days, was the natural outlet for malcontents, the Prince of Orange seems to have been slow to realize the potential of these Beggars for the cause of freedom. In due time, however, he discovered that they were the only force then resisting Spanish domination which could stand its ground; they would soon grow into his most efficient and formidable force.[26] They harrassed the Spanish, of course, but also those in the Low Countries who stayed loyal to the king. And very soon they shook off the pretension of "faithful to the king down to beggary" and accepted a new battle-cry: "Better Turkish than popish." There were pirates and adventurers among them, robbers and murderers. But the best were more than this: they became champions of freedom, the only ones who continued to fight against Spanish forces when the country lay trampled under Alva's feet.

Reinforced after the defeats suffered by the Prince of Orange and his brothers in 1568 and in the following years, the Beggar-fleet grew continuously and became a formidable force that made the North Sea, already swarming with French and English pirates, even more unsafe. They became the men who gave form to a new, aggressive Dutch fleet. It may be doubted, however, whether there existed, then, a national party.[27] Certainly there was no national army. But a national navy was in the making and its organization became, after 1570, a cause of real concern for the Prince of Orange. It fell to these "Sea-Beggars," vagabonds, to provide the impetus for the liberation of the Low Countries.

Privateering furnished a training ground of experience in seamanship which was of vital importance to the Dutch as a revolting power. William of Orange gave the Beggars letters of marque with a triple purpose: to create a fleet which would help him in the revolt against Spain; to strengthen his war chest with the revenue from their prizes; and to create, by their piracy, such discontent in the Low Countries that the rebellion would succeed.

An incredible and unpardonable carelessness led Alva to neglect the defence of the sea towns. The disdain in which he held the Sea-Beggars may be responsible for this attitude; it became apparent in his name for their cannons: "wooden pumps" he called them. He had no understanding of the war at sea, and he underestimated its importance. It was not the only mistake of this "beloved son of Pius V."[28] None of the important Spanish leaders seemed to realize its role in the rebellion, but then, many were not well-informed. Alva had no such excuse.

Another mistake the Spanish governor made was his attempt to use what may be called "total force." It is undoubtedly much better, he wrote, to have, "through a war for God and His Majesty," an impoverished and even ruined country than, without the war, to see it become "a prey of the devil and the heretics, his followers."[29] The revolt, however, did not ruin that part of the Low Countries which was successful and which became independent; the other part, however, which returned to Spanish control, returned to impotence.

But Alva's worst mistake was in supposing that his repressive measures would really be effective. They were not. It was an era in which many believed that the Day of the Lord was coming and that Jesus' prediction, made in Matthew 24, was on the point of being fulfilled. The Sea-Beggars were inspired to repay the Anti-Christ—by whom they meant the pope and the Catholic Church—sevenfold for the hardship they had caused the faithful. The papal impositions and the new taxes had been deeply felt; the common people, too, were deeply offended by the many deaths resulting from Alva's terror. "Their beautiful white bodies were seen floating on the water," says one of the popular Beggar-songs of four housewives who were killed by Alva's hangmen.[30] Many were beheaded, strangled, burned, sometimes for political disturbances, sometimes for divergent religious opinions, many times for both. "They will pay dearly for it," Philip had said, "I swear it by the soul of my father."[31]

Faith is everything; skepticism does not lead anywhere. The days of philosophical doubt had not yet arrived; the spirit of Bacon and Descartes had not yet been introduced to the world. Calvin and

Loyola fought against each other with their respective Christs, and the Christian world saw, with paralyzing stupor, "with the grumbling of the storm, in the glimmer of sinister lightning, two armed Christs, one against the other."[32] Each man had the only true faith and hurled his anathemas against any other; each had the true Christ. Bad omens were seen in the skies that predicted misery and bloodshed. Terrible signs caused Gemma Frisius and his son to publish their predictions based on the appearance of the comet of 1556. Hunger and plague would come, and unusual monsters would be born. They had seen, in a sky red like blood, armies fighting each other; the great flood of 1570 did not come unexpectedly. A new star, seen below the sign of Cassiopea, frightened even Alva. Comets were predicted and seen; it was generally believed that they represented the rod of an approaching angry God. *Cometa venturi Dei virga* was the prevalent belief in those days.[33]

Fiercely and pitilessly Spain carried the war against her rebels; fiercely and pitilessly the Dutch answered it. No quarter was given from either side. The *buena guerra* of the later years did not yet exist. The accounts of the Sea-Beggars are frightening. It may be true that the best had become Beggars out of their beliefs in the teaching of Calvin, but their appearance was terrifying: raw, wild people, "hardened in the war and in piracy," sang Onno Zwier van Haren, one of the few Dutch poets who composed an epic to their glory.[34] Many lacked ears or noses and were branded "carved" or "chopped" by these wounds—or in the more poetic description of the contemporary Dutch historian Pieter Corneliszoon Hooft: "their skin was sewn together with scars of endured battles."[35]

The aggressive power developed by this type of fierce fighters was increased by effective leadership. True, William of Orange, in his first two appointments, picked the wrong men. Fortunately Alva was no more successful with admirals. The prince, however, found in Lumey—an accidental choice in 1572—a man of action, even if he was later to be notorious for his intolerance and cruelty. Lumey knew how to maintain order and discipline among the riff-raff under his command, and he had good lieutenants. One of them was Jan de Moor, from Flushing, the father of a proud family that would soon be known in the West Indies. Another was Blois van Treslong, a Dutch nobleman from Brielle "with his whole soul attached to the cause of freedom." Huguenots from La Rochelle reinforced their ranks, like Odet de Châtillon, older brother of the well-known Admiral de Coligny, who once said mass in the Calvinist rite, dressed in cardinal's purple, in the Cathedral of Beauvais.[36]

There was also the Prince of Orange. Opinions about him differ as greatly as they do about Philip II. Avermaete calls him a "banner used by others to justify all kind of actions and doctrines unknown to him and his time."[37] The Belgian historian Henri Pirenne, while not praising William the Silent too loudly, nevertheless saw two dominating characteristics in him that were worth observing: "vigor of intelligence" and "stubbornness of the will."[38] In addition, Pirenne admits his "genius," although he was, in that historian's opinion, a Machiavellian politician, compared with whom the diplomacy of Philip "did not seem more than a coarse and naïve tactic."[39] Catholic historians, full of praise for the Spanish king, close their eyes to Orange's merits. Dutch historians have, of course, a different approach. Van Meteren calls him "an able instrument of the Almighty,"[40] and Hooft: "No Prince was ever more loved by his subjects than His Illustriousness by the Hollanders and Zeelanders."[41] Even Johan de Witt, the well-known grand pensionary of a century later, and a rabid anti-Orangist, praised William the Silent: "He seems to be free of most shortcomings that predominate in princely houses."[42]

Although circumstances beyond his control forced Orange into the leadership of the revolt against Spain, the same circumstances were also the main cause of the evolution of a governmental system in which, lacking a king—after the abjuration of Philip II—the *stadhouder* or king's lieutenant remained an anomaly. Between the fanatical, intolerant, and orthodox Calvinists striving after a kind of totalitarianism, and the tolerant, particularistic, and more liberal groups who formed the ruling class, William and his descendants posed both as advocates of a strongly centralized government and of the tolerance that would soon make the United Provinces famous.

The history of an independent Dutch navy really begins only after the Prince of Orange was able to organize the Sea-Beggars under his immediate command. This navy not only cooperated in the liberation of the northern Netherlands but became, *de facto*, the foundation for that new and independent state. William's procedure in organizing the Sea-Beggars was to limit some activities and to bring discipline to the various separated groups. He issued letters of marque which legalized the robberies and piracies then being committed; he appointed an admiral to organize the fleet into a positive asset for the revolt; he forbade privateering on neutrals or friends; and he ordered one-third of all booty claimed set aside to finance the war on land. Careful watch was kept to see to it that good crews were engaged; nobody could enlist who was wanted for some crime or who was in general bad repute. Naval chaplains were appointed to maintain a high spirit: they brought the Word of God to the men, persuaded them to prayer, and tried to keep them within the limits of Christian modesty.[43]

It was time to keep them under control because their continuous attacks along the coast had aroused the population of those areas, Catholic or not. There was now, moreover, a danger that the revolt would not be popularly supported. The new regulations handed down by William not only provided the nucleus for a very successful war navy but created also a fleet which, after hostilities in the home waters ended, was available to swarm out into the seas of the world and make the Dutch flag known everywhere. The rules of the Sea-Beggar fleet became, later, the basis of conduct for the several boards of admiralty and for the great companies in the organization of their fleets.

Philip II and his Spanish councillors and governors held the letters of marque given out by William in utter contempt: the Beggars, with or without letters, were to them so many robbers and pirates. But the Spanish would soon learn what their reorganization meant. In the spring of 1572 the Sea-Beggars made their historic conquest of Brielle, a small Dutch town at the mouth of the river Maas. The town, which surrendered without a fight, was taken "in the name of the Prince of Orange." Flushing soon followed. "No es nada," said Alva contemptuously, "Brielle y Pisselingas es nada." But it was as if the country had been waiting for just such an event. Suddenly, on all sides, rebellion against Spain broke out. The real and successful movement for independence now began.[44]

Some Dutch historians maintain that when the Sea-Beggars organized as a war navy their identity as Beggars ended.[45] Others do not agree with this opinion, however, and think that this organization meant only a phase in the development of an official fleet. True, their rapacity was moderated. Under the Prince of Orange as admiral, and with the supervision of the sea towns and the commissars of the prince, all their actions were now directed toward one goal: the liberation of the Netherlands.

But their story continued. The same men continued to play an important role. Now, instead of Calvinist *sansculottes*, however, they became the guard "which does not surrender." They fought on the Zuydersea; their cannons thundered over the Haarlemmermeer; they struggled to relieve Leyden; they rescued Flushing, and they isolated Spanish Middelburg. Lumey was replaced by Louis de Boisot, who had, long before, signed the Compromise of the Noblemen which asked for more religious tolerance. He was a brave man who had lost an eye in a battle against the Spanish fleet at Middelburg where his vice-admiral, courageous Jan de Moor, was killed.

After the violent Lumey, who died from a dog-bite, and the valiant Boisot, Willem Blois van Treslong from Brielle, "the last of the Sea-Beggars" as he is called, became admiral of their fleet. In those days there were in fact two Sea-Beggar fleets, one of Hollanders and one of Zeelanders. The competition between the two provinces is evident again and again, in their navies, in the Chambers of the West India Company, and in their trade.

In 1576 the rebellious provinces concluded the Pacification of Ghent. While negotiations were under way, the Beggars played their role: Treslong sailed up the river Scheldt toward Antwerp to exert pressure, perhaps with the additional intention of attacking the Spanish. The Pacification was confirmed by Alva's second successor, Don Juan of Austria. He was a half-brother of Philip II, the "last of the Crusaders" and the "last of the knights."[46] Handsome, elegant, and a fluent orator with great military talents, his arrival in the Netherlands aroused expectations and misgivings. "There was a man sent from God, whose name was John,"[47] but he died, perhaps poisoned, before having realized his beautiful dreams. Crushing the Dutch heretics proved more of a problem than crushing the Turks, and his proud words, "In this sign I defeated the Turks, in this sign I will defeat the heretics," died with him. His successor was Alexander Farnese, the duke of Parma and son of the former governess Margaret.

Parma could probably have saved the Low Countries for Spain if Philip had trusted him more and had given him better support. Although he was called Holophernes after the bloody capture of Maastricht, he was not cruel, and he managed to bring the southern provinces back under Spanish rule. "The Low Countries won't submit to a heretic yoke," wrote a priest many years later, but he forgot to add: with the help of the Inquisition and the Spaniards, and only half of the Low Countries.

During the governorships of Don Juan and Parma the Beggars were everywhere: in the North to aid Delfzijl against Spanish attacks; in the South, under Treslong, to escort the Duke of Anjou, brother of the French king, called by William of Orange to get French support in the revolt, to Antwerp. The future was dark for the rebels in those years. Philip II had put a price on William's head, and murderers were hired who tried to kill him. Parma, tough and flexible at the same time, was very successful not only because of his wise statesmanship but also because of the excesses of some Calvinist fanatics who, when they had taken hold of Flanders and its most important towns, tried to establish a Calvinist theocracy which manifested all the terror of fanaticism and intolerance.[48] He did not go so far as Alva's immediate successor, Requesens, when during his negotiations with William of Orange, the Spanish governor openheartedly confessed to the king that "everyone is convinced that the rebels are right,"[49] or as Don Juan who wrote: "They all want freedom of conscience," meaning Catholics as well as Protestants.[50] Parma had, in addition to his rare military qualities, the *souplesse du diplomate*, and he saw opportunities for negotiations where they escaped the eyes of his predecessors. Instead of continuing a policy which would ruin and depopulate the country by bringing it to the brink of famine and desperation through religious terror, Parma tried to help it back on a road toward normalcy and prosperity through a government of justice, clemency, and goodness, even though, of course, no freedom of religion could be granted. He succeeded in the southern provinces.

The North, however, rejected Parma's proposals and concluded the Union of Utrecht. The most important initiator of this treaty was William's well-known brother, John of Nassau. Perhaps those historians are right who accuse Holland and Zeeland of destroying any possibility of uniting the seventeen provinces.[51] The fact remains, however, that the Union of Utrecht, which was concluded in 1579, when the situation for the North was very dark, not only became a document of faith in the future, but also appeared to be an anti-Catholic league, perhaps more so than an anti-Spanish one. It was also a defensive union among the signators. *Concordia res parvae crescunt* became their device, symbolized by a lion with seven arrows in one of its claws and a sword in the other.

How dark were those days for those revolutionary Calvinists! They had faith in God, but kept their powder dry. They offered the French king, Henry III, sovereignty over their tiny country. Afraid of mighty Spain, he refused, despite his hatred of Philip, although he sent his brother, the Duke of Anjou. But the latter's intervention ended in the "French fury," a miscarried attack by the duke on Antwerp that brought an end to French influence. It also brought the withdrawal of those Catholics who had joined the Union of Utrecht in hopes of a Catholic sovereign. They returned to Spanish allegiance in preference to being ruled by a Protestant republic.

It was just at this moment, when things were darkest—in 1584—that the worst happened: William of Orange was killed by a paid assassin in Spanish service. One after the other of the Flemish rebellious towns now fell into Parma's hands. The siege of Antwerp was memorable. Parma succeeded in blockading the Scheldt in spite of attempts by the Sea-Beggar fleet, now under the command of Justinus of Nassau, William's natural son. Zeeland had nothing to gain from an Orangist Antwerp, nor had Amsterdam, and thus their support of the Beggars was weak. The river Scheldt was closed after the fall of the town. Parma gave the Protestants in Antwerp ample time to leave the town; their ministers exhorted the people to leave Babylon rather than give up their faith. Many did leave, some more motivated by commercial interests than by religious convictions, and Antwerp remained a dead city for two centuries.

Although the rudder of the ship was gone, the rebellion continued. William's second son Maurits—the oldest was a prisoner in Spain receiving a Catholic education—was too young to replace his father. The States General of the rebellious provinces, in its desperation, offered the crown to Elizabeth. She refused, but she made a treaty. English interests would also be served by removing Spain from the North Sea. The queen promised to send help under the Duke of Leicester, who would then serve as governor of the provinces. His appointment was certainly a *problème de femme*. The duke, writes Stern, had no other merits than his agreeable face.[52] He was ignorant, insolent, inconstant, and vain about talents he did not possess.

The Leicester interlude had two advantages: it gave young Maurits time to grow up, and it gave the States General a taste of what foreign help meant. Elizabeth, shrewd and practical, had taken over three important fortresses in the rebellious provinces as a guarantee for the repayment of her expenses: Brielle, Flushing, and Rammekens. When Leicester left, in 1588, after he had made himself impossible, these towns stayed under English control, leaving England in control of trade and navigation along the two rivers Rhine and Scheldt. The rebels grouped themselves around Maurits, who soon developed into a military genius.

The times were still dark. Philip was building a huge armada; the pope had given England to the Catholic king. The frequent interventions of the popes in the political developments of Northwestern Europe—bulls against Henry of Navarre, against Elizabeth, against William of Orange and the heretics in the Low Countries—are a remarkable proof of the source of information which they had. Philip saw to it that they received only Spanish reports. They could not even get permission to send a nuncio to Brussels, and consequently they saw as Catholic victories what were, in reality, victories of Spanish despotism.

Spain had many reasons to complain about English activities. The audacity of English pirates, especially Hawkins and Drake, went beyond Spanish limits. They acted as though the Caribbean Sea were not a *mare clausum*, a gift of the papacy to its faithful servants the Catholic Spanish kings. England was a country of heretics. A crusade against them would bring them back under papal authority. Such a victory would also doom the Dutch attempts for independence. The spirit of Sixtus V brought back to Philip all the intrepidity of his earlier dreams and again encouraged in him the delusion of a divine mission. Parma, more practical and realistic, warned his king, but in vain. He was too far from Madrid to be heard.

Indulgences were offered for all who went with the Armada. Drake had the audacity to attack Cádiz and to destroy there a number of Spanish ships which were to participate in the planned expedition against England. What a man! He was worthy of the fame of the Sea-Dogs, worthy too of the Sea-Beggar tradition. Elizabeth made him a knight and Lope de Vega composed a jubilant poem to celebrate his death. For many years small children in the West Indies trembled when they heard this sailor's name, this man who had no use for friars and who spit at the images of the Holy Virgin.

Elizabeth, now concerned over the Spanish plans, asked her Parliament for help, and also the States General of the rebels, in accordance with the treaty of 1585. The States General sent part of their navy—the old Sea-Beggar fleet—under Admiral Cornelis Loncq, to assist the English. Another part, supplemented with hired merchantmen under the command of Justinus of Nassau, protected the Zeelandian estuaries and controlled the Flemish seaports where Parma was assembling an army that had to be brought over to England by the Armada. There was much fear in England and in the rebellious provinces. Spain was powerful; her fleet had never been defeated. Although the Sea-Beggars operated during this crucial period in several squadrons, cooperation between the rebels and England, under the pressure of necessity, was remarkably smooth.

What happened is well known.[53] The Armada approached England with crucifixes on the sterns and relics in the cabins, while England and the United Provinces trembled. Parma, locked in the Flemish ports by the Sea-Beggars, could not move. The Spanish galleons were too big, drew too much water to cross the sand banks and fight with the much smaller ships of the Beggars. Skirmishes with the English, assisted by Loncq's squadron, deterred the Spanish, and their incompetent admiral chose to retire in the wrong direction: around Scotland and Ireland where storms and cliffs ruined most of the ships.

Not more than one third saw Spanish ports again. *Tu, Deus Magnus, et Magna facis*, and *Flavit Deus et dissipati sunt* exulted the victors.[54] "Insolence" was the Spanish comment regarding the medals struck by the English and Dutch.

Philip II took the loss stoically, but he continued to face grave problems. Where did God stand? The great rejoicing in England and the Low Countries found its counterpart in the deep consternation that occurred in Spain, and in the scandal that arose when it became known that fifteen hundred Spaniards who had escaped death by drowning and had been stranded on the Irish coast were killed there in cold blood. Forgetting altogether that Spain did not recognize any law at sea and treated English sailors as pirates, the very pro-Spanish and Catholic historian Pfandl wrote: "Thus England treated shipwrecked persons and defenseless enemies in the days of Queen Elizabeth."[55]

When the remnant of the Armada sailed home, it went to a different Spain. The world had changed. Spain seemed already to have begun her decline. Soon her *mare clausum* in the East and the West would be invaded systematically and would be opened by the English and Dutch. The latter, their home seas cleared—there the broom had done its work—would now look for a wider horizon. Together with the English, they sailed into Spanish waters, visiting the enemy on his own coasts. After Maurits' many successes on land and the conclusion of an alliance with the French and the English, a combined Anglo-Dutch fleet was sent to Cádiz. The Dutch squadron was under the command of Johan van Duivenvoorde, who grew up in a good Sea-Beggar tradition. Many of his captains had also been Beggars or had learned their profession from the Beggars. At Cádiz the combined fleet attacked and sank many of the ships in the harbor and took the town. The United Provinces were not yet strong enough to operate on their own and had to tolerate van Duivenvoorde's subordination to the English admiral. But their fleet carried, for the first time, something new and unknown in Spain: a national banner and a new emblem, the lion with the arrows.

The year 1588 marked a turning point for more than Spain. For the rebellious provinces a new era began, called by a nineteenth-century Dutch historian "The Ten Years."[56] The first two decades of the revolt may be defined as the defensive period. Now the Dutch, under the military leadership of Prince Maurits and the political guidance of Johan van Oldenbarnevelt, advocate of the States of Holland and of West-Friesland, who acted as a kind of prime minister and secretary of state, took the offensive against Spain, the *erf-vijand* or hereditary enemy. These ten years were, for the Dutch, extreme-ly successful, and culminated in the official recognition of their independence by France and England in the Triple Alliance of 1596.

Now, comparatively immune from damaging Spanish naval attack in the North Sea, the Dutch, as a consequence, were ready to expand hostilities against Spain by carrying the war to the home waters of the enemy. It is, however, true that these independent Netherlands were not yet in a position to operate independently from English sea power. They were in debt to Elizabeth, and she controlled considerable Dutch trade and navigation through the towns she occupied. These con-ditions dictated continued cooperation, but fear of English domination hampered truly effective joint naval operations. Thus, in 1597, both countries again fitted out an expedition against Spain, but it failed, defeated by the elements in a great storm.

Undeterred, the States General, the executive and legislative power in the United Provinces, decided two years later to fit out another powerful fleet in order to attack the enemy again on his own coasts and in his own seas. It was the first appearance of an independent Dutch fleet outside of home waters, a sure sign that Spain was now on the defensive. Somewhat later she would learn that her *guerra defensiva* was, in reality, a *guerra consumiente*, but that realization would come to her the hard way.

The secret of the Dutch expedition of 1599 was not kept very well. Early in the year the French ambassador, Buzanval, wrote that sixty ships would be outfitted and added: "That whole race of sailors burns with desire to resume their trade." Shortly thereafter Buzanval revised his figures: now there would be eighty ships and eight thousand sailors.[57] Later he reported that there would be one hundred and five ships. *Fama crescit eundo.*

There were at least seventy-two ships in that fleet of rebels "hungry for fame." Their admiral was Pieter van der Does—in most Spanish accounts called Bandordues or Wanderdoes—son of a famous father who had distinguished himself in the earlier days of the Sea-Beggars when they freed his hometown of Leyden. The son had acquired fame in the battles against the Invincible Armada. Under his red banner was the white of Vice-Admiral Jan Gerbrantsz of Enkhuizen, also a pupil of the Sea-Beggar's school, and the blue banner of Zeelandian Rear-Admiral Cornelis Geleynsz, with the same back-ground. It was a mighty fleet under capable command, trained in the Sea-Beggar's fashion, but the Spaniards knew weeks in advance what the Dutch were planning and were well prepared. They sailed from

La Coruña just four days before the arrival of the Dutch fleet which thus encountered its first great disappointment.[58]

Subsequently, van der Does turned to the Canaries. Perhaps he intended to conquer those islands in order to control Iberian trade to the East and West Indies and Brazil. Arriving there, he attacked the main island. Its fortresses surrendered. The population fled to the woods. But the Dutch soldiers in their reconnoitering ventures fell into an ambush and were defeated. And then, advised by his engineers that the fort was in bad repair and not worth keeping, van der Does decided to withdraw from the islands.

Disappointed a second time, the Dutch admiral divided his fleet before continuing the offensive against Spanish possessions. Over thirty-five sails were sent home with booty under Vice-Admiral Gerbrantsz. The admiral himself continued his voyage to the island of São Thomé, perhaps to see what could be done there to avenge the defeat of Balthazar de Moucheron's audacious expedition of 1595. But fate seemed to be stalking the Dutch fleet. The murderous climate killed a thousand men; the plans to continue on to Brazil had to be abandoned. Only some seven ships, under Captain Hartman, crossed the Atlantic and returned later with sugar prizes taken on the Brazilian coast.[59]

Despite their inauspicious beginnings, the Dutch assumed their offensive war against Spain in 1606, when they launched two expeditions under the Zeelandian Admiral William Haultain. The first of these expeditions had some success; the second experienced a defeat because most of the ships—and their commanders—fled before a Spanish fleet. Only Vice-Admiral Reynier Claessen held his own valiantly, setting a spark to the tinder after two days of fierce fighting. In those days the Zeelanders also fought bravely in their own waters against Spanish efforts to regain at least some of the lost power in the North. Zeelandian Admiral Legier Pietersz and Vice-Admiral Joos de Moor maintained the glorious tradition of the Sea-Beggars. "The galleys defeated by the ships," exulted a contemporary medal.

Before the conclusion of the Twelve Years' Truce with Spain—the negotiation dragged on for some time—the States General authorized one more attack along the Spanish coast to avenge the bad impression left by Haultain. They equipped a fleet under Jacob van Heemskerk, well known for his exploits in the north when the Dutch were seeking another sea route to East India. The Dutch fleet under this fine commander maintained the best traditions of the Sea-Beggars. Composed of twenty-six ships and two yachts it sailed against the Spanish fleet at Gibraltar in spite of the fact that this fleet was protected by the artillery of the fortresses. "No battlefield ever showed a more terrifying scene," wrote a Dutch naval historian, "than the Bay of Gibraltar at the moment of his attack. Forty-seven warships fought against each other within the narrow bay. The thundering of the guns, the burning of the ships, the exploding of some bottoms, the shouting of the combatants, the wailing of the wounded and dying, the cheering of the victors, resulted in a picture that cannot be described by any pen nor painted in sufficient colors by the most experienced brush."[60] Van Heemskerk was killed, but the attack was a perfect success for the Dutch fleet and the Beggars who led it.

That was the last battle at sea against the Spanish before the conclusion of the Truce. It ended a period of fighting in which the Dutch had made a national fleet from the ragged Sea-Beggars' ships, a fleet which made Spain willing to treat with them when they could not be defeated in European waters and the East Indies. Prince Maurits could smile and ask the Spanish negotiators: "So you came to bargain with the Beggars?"[61]

They came to make a treaty with the Beggars. The seas of Europe already knew their banner—red, white and blue—and it was swarming over other seas, in the East and West Indies, and in Brazil, where it made a startling appearance. Brave and self-confident—the bravado and self-confidence of a young nation—the Dutch were now prepared to carve out an empire that would amaze the world.

2

DREAMERS AND REALISTS

Palma sub pondere crescit.

"Imagine," wrote Busken Huet, a nineteenth-century Dutch historian, man of letters, and art-critic,

a young State that, properly speaking, is a church... Its shield is a divine revelation, worded in holy books. The only true doctrine of salvation for this and future time, the only behavior agreeable to God, is clearly written down in those sacred pages. To have this recognized they have taken up arms against their worldly ruler, against the supreme father of the Church. Everything was faced for it: poverty, exile, prison, death. Through a succession of undeserved and transcendent divine blessings they were victorious in that conflict. To the astonishment of Europe little Holland not only tore itself loose from mighty Spain, but succeeded very soon in standing on its own legs.

This the Calvinists explained as something that had happened because of the Lord. "And it has been a miracle in our eyes," they added.[1]

Even if this were an exaggeration, it was nevertheless the prevailing belief. Pieter Bor, a contemporary historian, gave eloquent testimony of it: God has saved and helped these countries always, in their most pressing distress, in their greatest difficulties, when human help was lacking.[2] The same disposition caused Prince Maurits, after the victory of Newport, to kneel on the beach and to thank God; it inspired van Oldenbarnevelt to write to the Dutch ambassador in Paris: "We must pray to God, our Lord, and do all our best, to let this all be conducive to His honor and glory and the welfare of our country."[3] The same thought characterizes the writings of the first chronicler of the Dutch West India Company, Ioannes de Laet. It appears in the minutes of the Heren XIX, the directors of that company, and in the correspondence of the time. Stubborn Peter Stuyvesant refused to surrender New Amsterdam to the English, even in spite of the overwhelming odds against him, until a minister read Luke 14: 31-32 to him. He then hoisted the white banner. Pieter Pieterszoon

Heyn, after the greatest act of privateering in history, thanked the Almighty humbly for his catch in the Bay of Matanzas.

It was not only the peculiarity of the Calvinists to see everything from a theocentric angle. "God," writes Irene Wright, "was invoked from both sides." "Blessed be the Lord who favored our arms," exulted the Spaniards at the reduction of the Zeelandian town of Zierikzee. "God, bring the silver galleons home safely," prayed Philip; and if a storm or enemies interfered with the granting of this prayer, His Catholic Majesty was divided between surprise and resentment.[4] When his desires were granted, he accepted it as an indication of divine favor.

It was the language of the century, and it was no empty language. Man was not yet the rational being of later times. Born on the threshold between the Middle Ages and the Modern World, he stood with one foot in the age of religious and commercial revolution, and the other in medieval tradition. In spite of the fact that with Dutch Protestantism, Catholic liturgy had atrophied into sermons highlighted in only a few cases by the beautiful psalms of Petrus Dathenus, and in spite of the fact that their Calvinism rejected the magisterial grace of symbolic action and compelled the faithful to listening and singing, man in the Low Countries was no less sensitive to mysticism. And although very busy with profit and war, he lived under the mystic influence of the Word of God, of election and predestination. His was "the great century of Calvinist orthodoxy" of which Chaunu writes,[5] and it collided with the great century of Spanish Counter-Reformation: the century of the Word which had inspired Calvin and Loyola.

It was a great century. The people lived close to the principles of the Reformation and the Counter-Reformation. The Word of God was probably nowhere more alive than in the United Provinces. It may be true, as a priest was said to have remarked to William the Silent, "When the Calvinist pot is as long on the fire as the Catholic, it will look as black,"[6] but in that century the Calvinist pot still gleamed, thanks to the two thousand Dutch Reformed preachers who taught, held catechism, and defended their doctrines with all the enthusiasm of a young faith and with all the elation inspired by their anti-papism. Many of them certainly had the genius of piety. Their task was to show people the only true road to heaven. In this vocation it was a continuous comfort to know that they were protected—but also controlled—in their divine work by the High and Mighty Lords of the States General of the Seven United Netherlands.

It was a century of faith without doubt. Life was a struggle between good and evil, and God had placed man on one side or on the other. The Dutch war for independence proves this spiritual atmosphere. The rebels thought, of course, that they were on the right side, and that the Spaniards were on the wrong one. It was simply a question of election. The *Geuzenliedtboeck*, a collection of songs of the Sea-Beggars, is drenched with this vision of destiny. Election found expression too in the words of the Dutch leaders: *Tandem fit surculus arbor* (the twig finally becomes a tree) was the device of Prince Maurits, while Jan Pieterszoon Coen, of the Dutch East India Company, hailed her destiny in that famous slogan: "Something great may be done in the East Indies."

Although the Word of God ruled all their lives, the God of Love and Infinite Grace was absent. On the contrary, theirs was a God of revenge, the God of the Maccabees. Retaliation was permitted and even agreeable to that God when the victim was the hereditary enemy, the Spaniard. Piracy and privateering on the enemy were not objectionable since he had threatened the True Church. For more than a century—the period in which the Calvinist faith grew and blossomed—a theological thread twined through the ropes of the Dutch ships that sailed over the seven seas of the world.

The history of their explorations all over the globe before, during, and after their war for independence, is one of Homeric alloy. It may be difficult today to remember that in the seventeenth century the Dutch were a great power, that they were the best businessmen in the world, that they out-competed every other nation, and that they had the finest war navy with the most outstanding admirals. Dutch merchants became the organizers of the most daring expeditions and explorations to the four corners of the earth. Dutch sailors—worthy sons of the Sea-Beggars—followed the traces of the Spanish and Portuguese voyages of the previous centuries, and went in all directions. They crossed unbelievable distances, over unknown seas, through stormy straits. They plodded through oceans and hurricanes, and they survived cannibals and treacherous enemies. They performed the most courageous actions, gained the most amazing victories, and suffered the most crushing defeats. These adventurers went through hunger and thirst, and they died like rats. Scurvy decimated them. And in between they founded settlements and baptized diverse areas of the world with the names of their native towns, rivers, and provinces, often, in spite of their rigid Calvinism, sprinkled with Catholic leaven: New Amsterdam, New Holland, New Netherland, Brooklyn, New Walcheren, Staten Island, Oranjestad, Willemstad, Fort Zeelandia, Waaigat, Saint Lawrence Bay (at Nova Zembla), Strait Le Maire, Cape Horn, and many others.

The story of their discoveries and adventures has many famous names worthy of the best Sea Beggars' tradition: Jan Pieterszoon Coen, that profound hater of perfidious Albion; Olivier van Noort, who paraded with his crew through Rotterdam in clown outfits just before he set sail to circumnavigate the globe; Simon de Cordes, who in the dangerous Strait of Magellan founded the crazy Brotherhood of the Unchained Lion; Cornelis Corneliszoon Jol, alias "Wood-leg" or "Peg-leg," who dressed his men like monks and priests when he sailed into the port of Santiago de Cuba. Piet Heyn was such a man, a cool organizer and a reckless sailor. To this same daring breed belonged Balthazar de Moucheron, whose ships sailed under his own banner, and that other refugee from the Southern Netherlands, Isaac le Maire, who made a million or more and then lost it: The Lord gives and the Lord takes away, praised be the Lord. All these and many more played a role in a drama which levied heavy tolls; on their expeditions, sometimes less than one-third came back. The Low Countries, in its Golden Age, was full of widows and orphans.

The Dutch, who were emerging from their struggle with Spain as the victors, as the elect of God, suddenly seemed to be the most gifted people on earth: a race of *Übermenschen*. They founded five universities within one century; their religious tolerance was not only extended to Catholics, but also to Jews, who had come from Spain or Portugal and strongly supported the House of Orange. The material power of these tolerant and freedom-loving bourgeois became, in the second half of the seventeenth century, an object of jealousy for France and England.

Perhaps most amazing of all, the achievements of the Dutch in this century were performed by a mere handful of men.[7] It has been estimated that the total population of the United Provinces, at the height of their Golden Age, was not more than one and one-half million people, which was three or four times less than England, and perhaps eight times less than France or Spain. This factor is important in the eventual decline of the Dutch, since the sheer reality of being outnumbered escaped those visionaries and merchants.

Long before the rebellion against Spain, Hollanders, Zeelanders, and Frieslanders had signed on Spanish and Portuguese ships bound for Africa, Brazil, and even mysterious India. Though the Spanish and the Portuguese, for understandable reasons, tried to keep their courses secret, it proved impossible, in spite of rigid and strict regulations. In the beginning, the Dutch, nevertheless, had no intention of visiting other continents. They were only interested, in the sixteenth century, in establishing good commercial relations with other European countries, especially with the Iberian peninsula and with the Baltic. The Dutch wanted to act as carriers between them.

In a certain way the English had paved the road for the Dutch. Long before the latter appeared, the English had been seen both in the East and West Indies, and far to the north where Willoughby— later a well-known name in the Caribbean—had sought a strait to Cathay. That was long before the famous hibernation of Dutch explorers on Nova Zembla. It was long, too, before van Noort sailed through the Strait of Magellan: Drake had already made the perilous voyage twice before. John Hawkins, Francis Drake, and George Clifford, Duke of Cumberland, were known and feared throughout the West Indies, and they had fought against the Spaniards long before the first Beggars dared to thrust their noses beyond the Channel and into the Atlantic.

But soon the Netherlanders were contaminated with the sickness of the century. Discovery and exploration became the passwords of a new generation, one which, though inspired by the Word of God in its Calvinist version, had not suffered the persecution of the Spanish Inquisition, had not experienced the tyranny of Alva, the massacres of towns, and the starvation in besieged cities. This new generation was possessed by a more active vocation sucked in with mother's milk: to fight and damage the hereditary enemy, who was everywhere in the world, for the glory of God and for the prosperity of their country. Especially after 1588, the lust for adventure spread quickly; the Beggars and their heirs swarmed off in all directions—to the untrodden coasts of the Eastern world or to the white beaches of the Western. Or, as Dutch historian Blok says in his more official and less romantic way: "The new roads were in the direction of the Oriental and Occidental Indies."8

Though unwillingly, Philip II actually stimulated this urge among the Dutch by his infamous "arrests." The first of these seizures of Dutch ships in Iberian ports by Spanish authorities occurred in 1585. Velius, the well-known historian of West Frisian town Hoorn concluded: "This arrest was the cause for our people to start to seek for new routes,"9 an observation repeated more or less literally after the third arrest of 1598. Bor, already quoted, reports that merchants dealing with Spain and Portugal, as a result of the vexations, began to try other far and foreign routes.10 The testimony of contemporaries is unambiguous: since 1577 the Dutch had lived with the fear of not knowing what Philip might do with their ships when they visited his ports. They continued, however, to drop anchor in Spanish ports.

This commerce with the enemy is one of the strangest phenomena in the rebellion. It continued, in spite of regulations against it, and in spite of Philip's repeated arrests. But at the same time, the Dutch had to find some remedy. They did.[11]

In the United Provinces, geography became the most popular field of study, after religion of course. History and ethnography were a close second and third. Numerous books were published to meet the growing demand, and these, in turn, stimulated imagination and lust for adventure. The nation—not known for its imaginative qualities, although it produced a Rembrandt, but with a good sense of reality, and of phlegmatic character—digested the truths, half-truths, and outlandish lies published about faraway countries, wild tribes, and unbelievable events. Sailors sailed over the ocean dependent upon unreliable maps that had been produced by dozens of mapmakers with unlimited fantasy. It would be fair to ask how they ever found their way, since longitude was still a mystery, and there was virtually no information on winds, currents, and reefs. To sail from the Caribbean Antilles to Brazil seamen had to cross the Atlantic twice: first to the African coast and then back again. It was entirely possible, even then, to miss Pernambuco.

During the first years of the revolt against Spain, the Dutch had not dared to sail along the Iberian coast, although they had been known in the Mediterranean and in the Levant before the war. In 1584 a *Mirror of Navigation* made public all the known facts for navigating along the European coast to Portugal. The author was Lucas Janszoon Wagenaer, a printer in the well-known house of Plantijn at Leyden. There were, of course, sea maps before Wagenaer's publication, but these were hand-sketched.[12] Wagenaer's work was, moreover, probably the first in the Dutch vernacular; the earlier *Cosmographia Petri Apiani* of Gemma Frisius, although much in use between 1560 and 1600, was written in Latin.[13] A second volume concerning the Baltic and Scandinavian waters followed in 1585. Five years later a resolution of the States General gave Cornelis Claesz the exclusive six-year publishing patent for another of Wagenaer's books called the *Treasure of Navigation*. Claesz or Wagenaer had probably acquired the maps through bribery. They were of Portuguese origin, and their export was forbidden by Iberian authorities on pain of death. The new publication included maps and descriptions of the countries and peoples with whom trade could be conducted.

Two other works on navigation were not so well known as those above. One was the posthumous *Navigation and Teaching of the Whole Eastern and Western Waters* by Adriaen Gerritsz of Haarlem in 1588. In the same year Nicolaes Pietersz of Deventer and Herman Jansz of Amsterdam obtained a patent from the States General authorizing the publication of a book entitled *Globe*.[14]

These, together with some smuggled English, Spanish, and Portuguese descriptions, were about all Dutch sailors had at their disposal until 1590. It was not much, and worse, it was unreliable. It was enough, nevertheless, to push the new breed of Dutchmen—worthy heirs of the Sea-Beggar tradition—out of the home ports and away from their own coasts.

This new breed of Dutchmen, however, had not come exclusively from the northern part of the country. When, in 1585, Philip joyously exulted that Antwerp was his once more—and with Antwerp, the southern part of the Netherlands—he did not realize that he had won an empty basket. The very pith of the southern provinces was driven out. Given a few years to settle its affairs, the Protestant population just left the town and the country. The most notable citizens, the richest merchants, the most industrious artisans were predominantly Protestant. Many Flemings had taken refuge in the North with the coming of Alva; many more left now. Belgian refugees had been well represented among the Beggars; they now became prominent among the merchants as well, and they were to push the Dutch forward toward a Golden Age.

Although most of the refugees from the South left their country for religious reasons—because of "popish superstition and Catholic intolerance"—many, and especially the businessmen, simply saw more possibilities for their purses in the North.[15] Thousands upon thousands left the South; between 1585 and 1587 it is said that more than twenty thousand emigrated to the North, a drastic purge of intellect and money from which the southern provinces were not to recover for more than two centuries. They remained Spanish and Catholic, but they paid a high price for it. In Antwerp, five years after its fall to Spain, one-third of the houses were for sale. International firms closed, and either reopened in the North or went bankrupt. Silence prevailed in the once noisy Bourse. In 1648 the building which had heard the babble of every European tongue was transformed into a library. There was no business any longer.[16]

Clear advantages accrued to the refugees in going to the North rather than to other countries. They shared the same language, and the Pacification of Ghent had guaranteed privileges to all the provinces which were signatories. The refugees received citizen rights in the North; all official positions stood open to them unless their own provinces prohibited the same openings to Hollanders. But, however tempting it may be to attribute the Golden Age of the North to the forced exodus from the South—and this has been tried—it was but a factor. Even before Antwerp fell, Amsterdam had become a growing competitor.

Some of the refugees played a crucial role in the early stages of the Golden Age—that age of expansion, discovery, conquest, and knowledge. There was Balthazar de Moucheron, merchant and shipowner; William Usselinx, a fervent Calvinist and planner; Simon de Cordes, who risked his capital and his life in an enterprise around the world; Sebald de Weert, a Latin poet at age thirteen, who was murdered on the island of Ceylon; Petrus Plancius, *theologus et mathematicus* says the legend on his engraving, one of the few who was not a merchant; Isaäc le Maire, eternal recalcitrant against monopolies, whose son found the Strait named after the father; Johan van der Veken, who furnished the money that van Oldenbarnevelt needed to pay James Stuart for the redemption towns; and there were hundreds more.

Petrus Plancius, who served God—according to Calvin's persuasion—for more than fifty faithful years, came from Flanders and deserves some attention. He was more than a preacher of the Gospel: he had been a student of Gerard Mercator and soon became an expert in geography and astronomy. On Sundays he showed his flock the road toward heaven; during the week he opened the roads to the East and West for sailors. Thanks to his efforts and to the invention of his great teacher, the Dutch soon had more reliable sea maps when they set forth on their expeditions to the East Indies. He was busy, too, with the difficult problem of finding the longitude. Although already Gemma Frisius knew that a time element was the decisive factor, no one had solved the problem. Plancius seems to have made a partial contribution to its solution. His involvement in Dutch achievements in the late sixteenth and early seventeenth century cannot be easily evaluated; it was certainly in the mind of the poet who said of him:

> That great zealot, promotor of God's church,
> Who died, ten times seven years old,
> Has caused more damage to the Pope and Spain
> With his sermons and lessons, than a great army....[17]

In the center of Amsterdam's harbor quarter—in the Oudezijds-chapel—he offered lectures on latitude and longitude, and on currents and winds. He corrected the astrolabe, that primitive predecessor of the sextant—although he met with much opposition from experts. "What the deuce does a minister know of longitude?" his fellow refugee, the well-known cartographer and geographer Jodocus Hondius must have exclaimed. Another expert on navigation, Albert Heyes, stubbornly continued to use the old astrolabe in his lectures.

But Plancius received the powerful support of Prince Maurits, and the valuable recommendation of fortress engineer Simon Stevin. In practice his correction of the astrolabe seems to have been of little importance: Jacques Mahu and Simon de Cordes, who used the new instrument during their voyage around the world, discovered somewhere that they had been drawn more than 250 miles off their course.

Although it is true that Plancius focused almost all his attention on East Indies, he was also involved in the foundation of the West India Company, though he did not live long enough to see it actually started. He had compiled a rich archive that was later bought by the Amsterdam Chamber of the company. His collaborator, Hessel Gerritsz,[18] sketched and engraved the excellent sea maps included in the work of de Laet. These were presumably based on dates given by the theo-geographer or geo-theologian. Gerritsz was rightly called one of the most distinguished mapmakers of his time, and was chosen as the official cartographer of the Dutch East India Company.[19]

Not only cartography and geography became popular sciences. There were many other bestsellers in those days. It was an age in which adventurous young men left their homes and countries to travel around the world. They came back with stories to delight their fellow countrymen and to stimulate them further to satisfy their own curiosity. Books of travel, published as popular books, were edited by the dozens in the United Provinces. Some were translations from English or from Spanish; many were written in Dutch. Some of the accounts bore the ponderous style of the rhetoricians; many were written in the simple, sometimes clumsy style of sailor's diaries.

One of the first travelers whose adventures were published was Dirck Gerritszoon Pomp, also called Dirck China, probably the first Dutchman to visit Japan and China. He was originally from West Friesland, that cradle of famous men, whose towns today are deserted, but whose buildings still recall the glorious past. Lucas Wagenaer had a very high opinion of his work. He interviewed him more than once and incorporated what he learned in the popular *Treasure*.[20]

Indeed, the United Provinces were flooded in the 1590's with travel accounts. A list of those works would not add anything here, but one example—by Jan Huygen van Linschoten, the forerunner of the modern itinerary—will illustrate the kind of work being produced. As were virtually all Dutch adventurers of that era, van Linschoten was mainly concerned with the East. The author was a "plain burgher of West Friesland," the son of a notary-barkeep from

Enkhuizen. In his father's tavern, Jan heard sailors' stories and soon took to traveling himself. He learned Spanish and Portuguese and traveled around the world. When he returned he wrote an *Itinerario* which became an immediate bestseller. The superiority of van Linschoten's work lies in his research. He read everything he could on his subject, and he consulted with a young Leyden professor, Berent ten Broeke—Paludanus[21]—but like others of his time, he did not always distinguish between fact and fable. The *Itinerario* included a number of copies of good Portuguese maps, which were obtained from the government on the recommendation of Plancius.

Van Linschoten did much more than simply satisfy curiosity. He provided a complete handbook for sailors: the courses they had to take and information about winds and currents. Little wonder that his book inspired the Dutch who were burning with energy. And they understood Linschoten's device *Souffrir pour parvenir*, to be unafraid to fight for a place in the sun—to include the sun of the tropics. "Because of you the Dutch now shine in the Indian skies," wrote an enthusiastic fellow countryman.[22]

Similar to the itineraries were the numerous ship's journals which soon appeared. Pieter van der Does' *True Story*, Joris van Spilbergen's *Historical Journal*, and Hendrick Ottsen's *Journal* were the best known. They were preceded by the *First Navigation* of William Lodewijksz, one of the most important ship's journals published at that time.[23] They satisfied the curiosity and interest in foreign countries and dangerous voyages while at the same time they stimulated young men to follow in those tracks.

Most of these books had little value for anyone interested in the Caribbean area, although they did inspire the adventurous spirit. Van Linschoten included many dates on the Caribbean in his work, but he had never been there and was forced to rely on other works for his figures. The lack represented in his work and in the studies listed above was filled by Dierick Ruyters' *Torch of Navigation*.[24]

"Dierick Ruyters," writes a Dutch historian in his introduction to the modern edition of the *Torch*, "belonged to that rare species of sailors who handled the pen with the same skill as the steering-wheel, the derrick, rapier or musket."[25] His fame as a soldier has been preserved for posterity in the work of de Laet. He has himself insured his fame as a scientific sailor and navigator and concurrently as a lover of astronomy and mathematics. Ruyters was one of the breed which made the foundation of the Dutch West India Company possible.

We know that he actually visited the areas he described. In 1618, for instance, he was a prisoner of the Portuguese in Brazil. He escaped and returned to Zeeland. In 1619 he sailed from that province, probably licensed as a captain, bound for the West Indies.

The *Torch of Navigation* appeared in 1623. The title page explains the scope of the work: it provided information "to sail the coasts south of the Tropic of Cancer." Ruyters supplemented his own observations with Portuguese accounts which make his work highly reliable. For some unknown reason, however, the directors of the West India Company returned to Ruyters the six copies he had sent to them: "any director wishing to read the work should pay for it," or so the minutes of the Heren xix say.[26] But it was regarded as a *bequaem boeck*—an efficient book.

While a great part of Ruyters' work was concerned with Africa, he devoted some time to Brazil and a few pages to "the great Gulf Occidentalis, formerly the New World and now the West Indies." He made his readers aware of the three possible routes the Spaniards followed to the Caribbean: the first from Cádiz; there ships loaded with textiles and everything that "was necessary for the support of human life" left Spain to cross the Atlantic; the second route started in the Canary Islands from whence wine was brought to the West; the third began on the West coast of Africa—especially the coast of Guinea—where slaves were transported to the Caribbean area. Ruyters gave concise information about navigation along the coast of Venezuela, Colombia, and the passage from Honduras to Santo Domingo; he also discussed the trade in hides between Guadeloupe, Puerto Rico, and Hispaniola, and the trade with New Spain. The records of the early voyages of the West India Company immediately reveal their dependence on Ruyters' information on both sailing and types of cargo.

Ruyters chose to publish his work at a most inopportune moment. The *Torch of Navigation* appeared just shortly before the *New World* or *Description of West India* by Ioannes de Laet,[27] a director of the West India Company. De Laet combined a commercial spirit with religious zeal and a vast knowledge of many subjects. He was an upright Contra-Remonstrant, had been a member of the famous Synod of Dordrecht which had set the record straight concerning the true religion; he was later to become the first chronicler of the West India Company. Thus de Laet's work had a much wider scope than Ruyters. The former had read José de Acosta and Antonio de Herrera, together with many other sources. Ruyters was only a sailor who had written a manual for sailors, de Laet was a man of great cultural attainments who even dared to argue with Grotius on the origin of the Indians in America.[28]

He copied the best part of Ruyters' work in his *New World*, with Ruyters' blessing, but the result was that this work overshadowed the *Torch*.

It is generally understood that de Laet's *New World* was less captivating than Linschoten's *Itinerario* and de Laet's own later *Iaerlijck Verhael*—his account of the first sixteen years of the Dutch West India Company. But the earlier work did not do badly; it appeared in a second edition in 1630 and was soon translated into French and Latin. Like the *Itinerario*, the *New World* included many historical dates and the excellent maps of Hessel Gerritsz. The author was praised by Their High Mightinesses for his efforts. On first reading it, though, they had been dismayed that de Laet admitted French and English pretensions to first discoveries in the New World. They later realized, however, that he had only acknowledged French and English allegations, and he was allowed a twelve-year patent for publishing the book in the United Provinces.[29]

In addition to the dreamers of the era—if thus we may call the ones who wrote books and sailed to foreign lands more for adventure than for profit—we have the merchants, the ones who made money and prayed for more, the ones who risked everything, except their lives, in any enterprise that looked favorable. Two centers were most important in these mercantile ventures: Amsterdam, the capital, which enjoyed more business than all the other Dutch towns put together, and the province of Zeeland, with its two important towns, Middelburg and Flushing. Sailors from the latter town, called *pichelingues* by the Spaniards, were well known and feared by the Iberians.[30]

Throughout the seventeenth century, Amsterdam played such an important and central part in the history of the United Provinces and Europe that definition of its precise role becomes difficult. Grotius called it "our only Amsterdam, without parallel, without comparison." The town had already begun its rise to fame before Antwerp fell. In the revolt against Spain, Amsterdam had started as pro-Catholic, and only force drove it to support the rebellion. Its conservative burghers were adverse to anything that smacked of popular rule. The town gained enormously, however, when Antwerp was taken by the Spanish with the consequent exodus of brains and purses that migrated north. After its conversion from pro-Spanish to pro-Calvinist—a policy change called the "Alteration"—most refugees from the South found a welcoming environment there. But merchants still controlled the destiny of the capital, and they were too motivated by profit to be intolerant. These men were typically realistic, an aspect which has been well captured in their portraits by the best of the Dutch school of painters, and even those by Rembrandt the dreamer. They were businessmen who stood with both feet on solid ground and risked their money where others risked their lives. They were also steady churchgoers; their convictions may be defined as humanistic Calvinist. Some of them, eminent as they were, were too lukewarm to be martyrs, too honest to be hypocrites. Religion was not the only important thing in their lives. There were some men, certainly, with deep religious convictions. Reynier Pauw, for example, was such a man, but he was also one of the most industrious, one of the most plotting and scheming burgomasters of Amsterdam. He was an outstanding businessman and a member of the town council when he was only twenty-seven years old. His passionate Contra-Remonstrant convictions and his devotion to the foundation of a West India Company forced him to a seat on the tribunal which convicted Johan van Oldenbarnevelt, the landsadvocate. He was also a director of the East India Company, and one of his sons became a director of the West India Company when that institution was founded.[31]

Another important businessman of Amsterdam, who was interested in the West Indies, was Pieter van der Haghen. Although he was a textile merchant primarily, he also had business relations with that financial genius so appropriately named Hendrick Anthoniszoon Wissel.[32] Like Pauw, van der Haghen did not get along with van Oldenbarnevelt and consequently found himself imprisoned at one time. With Johan van der Veken, Joris Joosten, and Vincent Bayaert, he traded in Brazil; with Wissel he fitted out ships for Hispaniola and Puerto Rico.[33] Shrewdly, he and Wissel staffed their fleet with Spanish and Portuguese sailors because they thought they could thus legitimately trade in the Spanish possessions. Their admiral, however, was Dutch: Melchior van den Kerckhove. Van der Haghen seems also to have established some commercial relations on the African coast.

It is undoubtedly true that during the sixteenth century Amsterdam's main interest was in the Levant and the Mediterranean; later, it shifted to the East Indies and the North. The directors of the East India Company, men like Pieter de Graeff, Johannes Hudde, and Gilles Valckenier, were Amsterdammers. The West Indies, New Netherland, and Brazil attracted fewer men. There was, however, a proto-West India Company already as early as 1597, which was started by a merchant of Amsterdam. Another small company with similar interests was founded by a merchant of Enkhuizen. Neither of these companies was important, and both prove the rule that other global regions were subject to more attention. Even the Dutch expeditions to the North had an Eastern orientation since they sought a strait to the East Indies that would afford passage without encountering the dangers of the Iberian coast.

The situation, however, was quite different in Zeeland. There, as soon as the threat of a Spanish invasion of the islands was eliminated, their merchants looked to the West and especially to the Guianas, the estuaries of the Orinoco and the Amazon, and the West Indies. The divergence of commercial interests represented by Amsterdam and Zeeland should thus be seen within the framework of the constant rivalry between the two most important provinces in the United Netherlands.[34]

In the first forty years of the war for independence, Zeeland was a frontier territory. Nationally and religiously it belonged to the northern provinces, but economically and linguistically it could not deny its close relationship with Flanders. If the Zeelanders were obliged to follow the political leadership of The Hague, they were not willing to submit to Amsterdam's commercial supremacy. The resultant tensions appear regularly in the documents of the West India Company and they extend themselves into the West Indies and the Guianas. The rivalry was a constant problem for the directors of the company as well as for Their High Mightinesses, the States General of the United Provinces.[35]

Well-known Zeelanders with interests in the West were the brothers Adriaen and Cornelis Lampsins. Although they called themselves the "New Beggars," they were in fact wealthy merchants from Flushing. They went as far as to outfit a private war navy of twelve ships and one hundred and eighty pieces of artillery specifically for privateering. Their defeat of the Dunkirk pirates at one point was so decisive that insurance rates dropped from eight to three per cent. Both men were of incorruptible faithfulness to their given word, of great ability, and "burning with zeal to increase the glory and fame of the fatherland."[36] In Dutch national history their role in connection with Admiral Michiel Adriaenszoon de Ruyter is well known.

Another famous Zeelandian house interested in the West was that of de Moor. Vice-Admiral Jan de Moor, founder of this dynasty of explorers and merchants, had also played an important role in the liberation of Zeeland from Spanish oppression. His son further enhanced the reputation of the family in an encounter with the Spanish fleet under Admiral Federigo Spinola. The grandson of the Vice-Admiral, together with Abraham van Pere and Pieter van Rhee, two other Zeelandian merchants, was very interested in a colonization plan for the Guianas and Lesser Antilles. Another Zeelander interested in the West was burgomaster Geleyn ten Haeff of Zeeland's capital, Middelburg.

Perhaps the most famous of the Zeelandian businessmen was Balthazar de Moucheron, a man who, in the words of his only biographer, "combined the lust for profit of the Dutch merchants with the adventurous spirit of his Norman ancestors."[37] Like many others, and for the same reasons, he had fled the southern provinces for the freedom of the North. According to a Dutch historian, his plans were "more grandiose and broader in concept than those of anyone else." One remarkable tribute to de Moucheron appeared in a van Linschoten publication which honors him as a pioneer of many intrepid Dutch explorations.[38]

De Moucheron settled in Zeeland's capital, Middelburg, and there worked out the schemes which made him famous. Through him, other merchants were stimulated to cooperation, as was the pensionary of this province, Christoffel Roeltius, who was very interested in de Moucheron's plans.[39] He became a principal instigator of Dutch discovery trips in the North and organized navigation in the Caribbean and along the coast of Africa, where his ships sailed under a personal banner: a Burgundian cross on a green field.

And then there was William Usselinx, another refugee from the South, who was full of grandiose dreams and whose strategic importance in the foundation of the West India Company merits him more attention in this account. Although Usselinx' ostracism, which was imposed on him by narrow-mindedness, prevented his actual participation in the direction of the company, he alone had done the groundwork for it for many years. Jameson rightly calls him its "originator."[40]

Born in the Southern Netherlands and soon a refugee, almost nothing is known of his early years. His writings show the antipathy toward Spanish rule and Catholic beliefs which he may well have acquired in his youth. He sought, however, an education in commerce in Spain, Portugal, and the Azores. In Seville he witnessed the arrival of the treasure fleet which made a deep and lasting impression. In Portugal he saw the exports from Brazil arrive: sugar, brazilwood, and many other products. In the Azores he met many of his countrymen; these islands, en route between East and West, were sometimes called the Flemish Isles. As everyone knew, they were a service depot for the silver fleet. Perhaps Usselinx was there when Grenville sacked the islands in 1586, when Drake seized there a Spanish *carraca*, or when Cumberland took Fayal.

Young William settled in the Low Countries in 1591, and he was already a rich man. He did not return to Antwerp, however, since his Calvinism made that place dangerous. In Amsterdam he found a more tolerant environment and a better audience for his ideas. He was soon respected there, writes van Meteren, as "a man well informed of trade and conditions in the West-Indies,"[41] and knew the first families in the capital. He became acquainted with Plancius and knew the councillor of the High Court, François Francken, who, from the very start, saw in a West India Company an excellent tool with which to fight Spain in the New World.

In 1600, just as the first flourish of Dutch enterprise abroad began, and while the hope of recapturing Flanders still lingered in the hearts of her refugees, Usselinx put into writing what had been in his mind and what he had spoken of to a few of his intimate friends. His plan, it appeared, had two aspects: first, he proposed a colonization program to teach natives the techniques of European agriculture in order to exploit the rich soil in the New World, and, second, he intended their conversion to Calvinism. He hoped to activate this program on the Wild Coast which the Spanish had claimed. Usselinx maintained that Spain was weak in that area because she had no defenses there.

The realization of this program, however, required a company, since only a powerful organization, supported by the government, had any hope of successfully attacking Spanish possessions. A company alone could organize immigration on a grand scale in order to divert the war from the homeland to the Spanish king's domains in America. According to the plan, the Dutch colonists would convert the Indians to Calvinism, arm them, teach them the use of horses, and initiate them in the techniques of modern warfare. The plan did not envision the use of slaves or the prospect that colonists would wear themselves out looking for gold and silver. The real treasure of America was its soil according to Usselinx. Agriculture and trade on a barter basis should become the economic bases for these colonies. They might, of course, tap the Spanish stream of gold and silver as a sideline.

Usselinx' project lost favor, though, on the unsuccessful return of an expedition under Pieter van Caerden to Brazil. Until van Caerden's failure many merchants had seemed enthusiastic and willing to put up huge sums for the project. He had been sent to Brazil with six ships to build the first Dutch stronghold on the coast. Though he returned with three thousand chests of sugar and some gold and silver, he failed in his primary goal, and the total profit was not enough to sharpen the right appetites.

Despite this setback, however, and partly because of the influence of Plancius and Francken, Usselinx' plan was discussed in the July,

1606, meeting of the Provincial States of Holland. A committee was appointed to examine the plan more thoroughly and to draft a patent for it. Although Usselinx was a member of this committee, the project which emerged bore little resemblance to his own. Not colonization and trade but war and profit by war were the primary goals developed in the first draft. It was, Usselinx said, "not conceived according to his ideas."[42]

Even more disastrous to Usselinx' hopes for the realization of his ideas was the fact that peace negotiations with Spain had started. Van Oldenbarnevelt, for one, was anxious that peace come, and he was the political leader of the most important province of the free Netherlands. It would have been contrary to the peace policy he pursued to accept a program which, in the form drafted by the committee, was clearly directed toward war.

By that time it became increasingly apparent that there was a strong peace party in the Netherlands and that Usselinx was not a part of it. Van Oldenbarnevelt was its leader. Since he knew how desperately the treasury needed peace, he intended to bring an end to the war. Because he was, therefore, ready to abandon the Southern Netherlands on that point, as he was on the proposed company, the landsadvocate and Usselinx became bitter enemies. But the Flemish refugee found the tide for peace nearly overwhelming. True, van Oldenbarnevelt went to the negotiation table spouting talk about a West India Company but only, as van Meteren observes, "as a bugbear to scare them."[43] This policy dismayed Francken, Usselinx' friend and supporter, to such a degree that he seriously considered resigning and entering the service of Henry IV of France, who was very eager to hire Dutch experience to implement his own plans for a French colonial empire.

Usselinx, however, was not a man who gave up easily. When the peace negotiations focused on the exclusion of the Dutch from the East and West, he sent to the States General a series of pamphlets which pled the cause of free navigation for the Dutch in both the East and West Indies. One of these pamphlets, the *Remonstrance*, belongs, as Asher rightly observes, to the most remarkable productions of that kind of literature.[44] All his pamphlets were written in a powerful and convincing style; their effect, however, seemed only to accelerate the conclusion of a truce.[45]

Usselinx claimed in the *Remonstrance* that the articles of the Truce permitted his type of company—an agricultural and trading corporation with missionary overtones. His voice, in those days, however, was the *vox clamantis in desertis*. Other problems attracted attention just then. Philosophers, ministers, pamphleteers, and poets vied with each other to bring the new issues before the public eye: predestination or free will, monopoly or free trade. Such famous men as Grotius, Hendrik Boxhorn, Pieter de la Court, and even Spinoza displayed a vivid interest in these burning questions. The most inflammatory of the issues was that of predestination and free will, a dispute which had started between two Leyden professors, Arminius and Gomarus. The entire country took positions in the theological controversy. Curiously, one's decision about it determined one's partisanship on one side or the other in the dispute about the war with Spain. The majority of the population, i.e., the lower classes in the towns, headed by the Dutch Reformed ministers and supported by the Flemish refugees, were strongly orthodox and Gomarian or Contra-Remonstrant. This majority favored predestination and war. Their opponents were the liberals, the Arminians or Remonstrants, who were the rich merchant and regent classes. Although they were a distinct minority, they held the power and the money. The ruling class assumed, as any ruling class, that its interests were the interests of the country. Some years before this same class had decided that the country could best be served by creating a monopolistic institution to trade in the East. It then urged the foundation of the East India Company. Now it would oppose a Dutch West India Company because such an institution would imply support for the House of Orange and its war policy. These were the complexities which hindered Usselinx' project for almost two decades.[46]

During the Truce, which was concluded in 1609 to last for twelve years, Usselinx continued his propaganda for a company. He became, in those years, what Laspeyres calls "the most energetic representative of the warparty."[47] In spite of the conclusion of the Truce, he was not discouraged, and by 1614 things seemed to be less black. His consultations with important people in Holland and Zeeland began to yield results. Amsterdam, which had always opposed the Truce, had enough influence to bring Usselinx' project before the States of Holland once more. After that hearing Usselinx was told to bring his proposals before the States General. This body discussed the plan at a meeting on August 25, 1614, but the results of the discussion are unknown.[48] Obviously, van Oldenbarnevelt and the East India Company, for quite different reasons, both opposed it, and this opposition may provide some reason for the silence.

In 1616 Usselinx once more submitted a request to the States General in which he proposed to prove that:

1. The United Provinces, by creating a Dutch West India Company, would be strengthened and secured against the hereditary enemy, the King of Spain.

2. When peace came the Netherlanders would reap as many profits from the Indies as Spain had.

3. If war with Spain were renewed, the Netherlands would gain not only the profits stipulated in Point 2 but also what could be taken from Spain as prizes of war.

4. All the inhabitants of the United Provinces would profit from this company.[49]

At the same time Usselinx proposed ways to raise the necessary operating expenses for his plan: ten million guilders raised on a voluntary basis.[50]

This request became the subject of discussions in the States General meeting of June 24, 1617. A committee, which included van Oldenbarnevelt, was appointed to hear Usselinx. Although Usselinx had a favorable response, generally, van Oldenbarnevelt was once more able to block any progress. Other requests were ignored by Their High Mightinesses on the advice of the landsadvocate.

Usselinx' personal situation was now most uncomfortable. He had lost money in bad investments, and his creditors were persecuting him. He was simply in debt for more thousands than he could ever hope to pay. "That bankrupt merchant," van Oldenbarnevelt called him contemptuously. Usselinx' temperament did not make things any easier. He was not a forbearing man; and his fulminations against Catholics and Jews—and against other Protestants not adhering to the Dutch Reformed Church—together with his abuse of the Arminians, were not calculated to win him much support among the Remonstrant members of the States of Holland.[51]

It should be mentioned here, however, that there was some reason for his unpleasant outbursts. Usselinx was a Fleming, and he was fiercely proud of it. In his eyes, the North had been insignificant until the Flemish immigrated. In a pamphlet of 1627 he pointed out that before the exodus of 1567 the northern provinces barely had the funds to keep their dykes intact, while the southern provinces had enjoyed a prosperous trade with Spain and were acquainted with navigation to the East and West Indies, Africa, and the Levant. Of course his point of view was exaggerated; even worse, it was without tact, and it prejudiced warm relations with those authorities whose cooperation was a *sine qua non* for the realization of his plans.

In those years the Arminian-Gomarist dispute reached its climax. In the bitter struggle van Oldenbarnevelt lost and was beheaded. The war party, orthodox and centralist, took over under Maurits: Force was for the Gomarists.[52] With the removal of the old landsadvocate, strong opposition to a renewal of hostilities was gone. The States of Holland soon heard once more from Usselinx on the matter of a West India Company. The States General agreed to examine the matter again. A committee appointed by Their High Mightinesses worked so fast that Usselinx, who had to come from Zeeland, did not arrive in The Hague until a draft for a new charter, based on the project of 1606, had already been completed. Usselinx also had prepared a draft of his ideas, but he was not in doubt for long about which plan the States liked better. A compromise committee, which included some directors of the East India Company, then prepared a third draft which was presented to the States General. Nearly a year was spent in discussing the concept. With some changes, the idea of a Dutch West India Company was finally accepted. The official date of its inception was set for June 3, 1621, a few weeks after the Truce was to end.

For Usselinx, the charter which was approved was a bitter deception. His original idea of a missionary-colonizing corporation had been transformed and mutilated into a privateering institution of a semi-dependent character. Although profit was the aim of both plans, it was not the first and exclusive motive for Usselinx. In the final draft, however, profit exclusively and profit through war were the main objectives.

Great were the expectations which surrounded the founding of the Dutch West India Company. Everyone now expected much more from the West Indies than from the East. Shrewd merchants like Reynier Pauw, Jacob de Graeff, and Andries Bicker provided the leadership for the new corporation.[53] They and other Amsterdammers pushed the project into action; the capital dominated the new organization as much as it had the Dutch East India Company.

Usselinx' ideals, missionary activity, and colonization got only secondary attention in the charter. But these ideals had been the core of his draft, the palpitating heart of it. He had certainly exaggerated, however, knowingly or not, the advantages of trade in America. In his writings, for example, he had pointed out that many Indians had reached the level of culture which made them ready customers for European textiles. But in 1633 the level of culture in the Guianas, the region that Usselinx always had in mind in terms of colonization and trade, was described in a report of the West India Company: "These nations are so barbarous and have so few needs, because they don't dress nor work for their daily bread, that all trade that is possible there can be handled by two or three ships annually."[54]

Usselinx had not been alone in his projects for colonization. In an anonymous pamphlet of 1622 entitled *Fin de la Guerre*, colonization in the West Indies was highly recommended, though for other reasons than Usselinx had in mind. The pamphlet argued instead that the United Provinces were suffering from overpopulation: "It swarms here with people and the inhabitants in every trade trample on each other's feet."[55] It went on to say that in some towns and villages from one- to two-thirds of the population lived on charity. The colonization which the author had in mind was an *asylum pauperum*. This little brochure appeared simultaneously with Usselinx' *Short Instruction and Admonition to all Patriots to invest liberally in the West India Company* and was probably almost unnoticed for that reason.[56]

If Usselinx exaggerated the cultural level of the Indians and the chance for immediate profits from trade with the American countries, he certainly was right in arguing that colonists would increase trade many times over. As did the author of *Fin de la Guerre*, he envisioned the poor as colonists and felt that not only Dutch but also German and Scandinavian people should be allowed to settle in Dutch colonies. In Usselinx' project, these settlers would busy themselves with agriculture. Industry was to be prohibited there, and this prohibition showed Usselinx to be a true mercantilist. He opposed slavery in the colonies, not on humanitarian grounds but because he believed that one colonist could do the work of three Negroes once he was acclimatized: since the sun shone directly above him as he worked, he would not be blinded by its rays. Free labor was to be the basis on which the colonies should develop and prosper. As a fervent Calvinist and a hater of Catholicism, and because he also despised anyone who was libertine and malleable, Usselinx required that all the colonists be members of the Dutch Reformed Church. He further anticipated that they would act as missionaries to the natives.[57]

But Usselinx saw more in a West India Company than a colonizing and missionary project. It was to be a tool of war designed to free the Southern Netherlands from Spanish domination. The company would provide the means to attack Spain in her *mare clausum*; it would have to send forces and fleets to protect the area. The Spanish King would thus be weakened in Europe and especially in the Southern Netherlands. The company needed warships and soldiers, therefore, as well as colonists. Usselinx knew that Spanish forts along the Wild Coast were not very significant. He also believed that the Indians there could be won over to supporting the Dutch by fair and considerate treatment, since they already nursed grievances against the Spaniards and Portuguese.

His project called for several phases to develop in the attack on Spain. At the beginning, no direct attack on Spanish-American territory was planned. Instead, the Dutch were to concentrate on intercepting imports and exports by effectively blockading Spanish ports. In the second phase of the plan, the Dutch were to attempt to seize Spanish ships on their return to Spain. Then the coast of Africa should be blockaded in order to prevent the export of slaves. Usselinx was explicit in emphasizing that the colonies were to be the property of the state and not of a private institution or a semi-private one like the West India Company. The States General should offer help and support, appoint governors and hire soldiers, and build fortresses. In general, the United Provinces was to do everything necessary for the safety of the colonies. He did not comment on what he thought the government in the colonies should be, but in reading the articles of the company's charter one realizes how many of Usselinx' ideas were incorporated in spite of many divergencies from his suggestions.

Repeatedly, after the charter of 1621 had been accepted Usselinx tried to get it amended to read the way he wanted. Although Prince Maurits recommended him to the States General several times, it did no good. The West India Company was founded without him. Jameson had rightly pointed out that the first directors opposed Usselinx precisely because they feared that this strong man would dominate them.

Disappointed and bitter, Usselinx finally turned his back on the institution for which he had sacrificed the best twenty years of his life. There were some efforts to use him in the company in some advisory position, and he was offered four thousand guilders to place his knowledge and experience at the disposal of the company. He refused the offer. Prince Maurits then admonished the States General to force the ruling board of the West India Company to acknowledge Usselinx' contributions. Although he knew that he was no longer needed, he indignantly refused the Spanish King's offers to enter his service, even though his creditors were constantly after him. He left the United Provinces and settled in Sweden to try once more to realize his plans.

He had been far ahead of his time in his ideas about colonization and free government. But his personality, his improvidence, and his inability to win supporters doomed his plans. He also seemed continuously unable to find a propitious moment to introduce his ideas. He never succeeded, even in Sweden, and at the age of 80 he could say with bitterness: "I have been treated in such a way that I do not believe anyone in history can find an example."[58]

He had had a dream that did not come true. But many men had speculated on a grandiose scale in those days and had succeeded. The Dutch colonial empire did not fall because of the narrow-mindedness and shortsightedness of its founders but because the risks that were taken proved to be too great, the burden too heavy. De Moucheron went bankrupt and left the country; le Maire lost his money; Usselinx became poor. Their money and talents had served the general interest of their new fatherland. While they had exerted every effort to make profits and become rich, they had also brought Europe and the world an unknown freedom of thought and hitherto unfamiliar rights to the common citizen.

They were merchants. Usselinx was a merchant, no more and no less. This chapter may be concluded, therefore, by quoting the Dutch historian Bakhuyzen van den Brink: "Do you find something grandiose in them, then say: he was a merchant; do you find something to blame, the excuse may be: he was only a merchant!"[59]

3

THE TARDY INTERLOPERS

Sit oneri, erit usui.

The Caribbean was the setting for what Germán Arciniegas calls the grandiose drama that was similar to the transition from the third to the fourth day in the story of Creation.[1] Space was discovered, as limitless to man of the fifteenth and sixteenth century as our own universe today is to us. The Mediterranean diminished to a lake, and European politics shrunk to local bickerings over religion and succession. The horizon widened. Men of vision saw things that no European eye had seen before.

More impressive than the gradual elaboration of a route to India along the African coast and around the Cape of Good Hope was the sudden announcement of the existence of a New World. The Spaniards, who had hammered for centuries against the vestiges of Islam in the Iberian peninsula, now extended themselves around the world. Columbus' discovery shifted the center of interest from the Mediterranean to the Caribbean.

The Sea of the New World! While the Sea of the Old World began its hibernation, the Caribbean was awakened by the cannons of the first Spanish caravels. Sailors, adventurers, and crusaders followed the Great Admiral on his route to the West, to Paradise and El Dorado. They came to plant the cross among men and women who went naked, with "not one part of their bodies covered." They came to satisfy themselves, drawn by the irresistible enchantment of the native women: "They themselves provoke and importune the men, sleeping with them in hammocks; for they hold it to be an honor to sleep with the *Xianos*."[2] They came for all reasons. It was, as Stefan Zweig has observed "a time for adventures as the world almost never has known before."[3]

A long string of Greater and Lesser Antilles, green pearls in a blue sea, hangs between North and South America and protects the central isthmus of the continent from the tides and forces of the Atlantic.

These islands enclose the Caribbean Sea. The tropical heat is tempered by a cool trade wind which can, however, become a howling gale across the islands to the North. The Indians called such winds hurricanes. But it was believed that when the Host was placed in the churches, Satan's power would collapse and the hurricanes disappear, even though the winds returned the following year.

When Columbus discovered and visited many of these islands, their population was Arawak or Carib. The former, peaceful and gentle, had been driven from many of the islands by the more bellicose Caribs, whom the Spanish accused of being cannibals. Fighting a hopeless war against a better organized and equipped enemy, the Indians still preferred death to slavery. In the end, those who escaped the Spanish sword died of illnesses brought by the new masters. Although they could escape into the hills and woods on the mainland, on the islands no escape was possible. Here, the Spanish colonial empire in America began.

The first decades of Spanish rule in the West Indies were shocking. When Columbus soon proved his inefficiency as an administrator, he was placed under arrest by the tactless Francisco de Bobadilla. The arrest provoked gossip and speculation, especially on Hispaniola. The island was not yet pacified, and the dogged resistance of the Indians in day-to-day combat was most annoying. Christian blood drenched the soil of the New World: "The coast stained with the blood of those who were among the first to go to the Indies."[4]

The Spaniards thought they were in India, and India remained the name for the heart of the New World. Because of a capricious turn of coincidence and misunderstanding, however, the whole hemisphere was named for a man whose contributions to discovery and exploration were minor: Amerigo Vespucci.

Murder and homicide followed the discovery and accompanied the conquest, but so did Western civilization and Christianity. Besides men like Pizarro and Pedrarias, who stained the Spanish name with the blood of so many innocents, there were men like Cortés and Bastidas. They all came to the Caribbean, and there the heart of an embryonic Spanish America pulsed loudly. There, in the taverns of Santo Domingo, men cursed and quarreled while the Cathedral resounded with the passionate sermons of Montesinos. There Bartolomé de las Casas, rich through the blood and sweat of his many slaves, decided to devote his life to God, the Virgin, and the Indian. The Negroes had to suffer, however, for his convictions. There the struggle for justice aroused the conscience of a few men, and there the young empire solved its critical labor shortage by importing Negro slaves from Africa.

In spite of the Treaty of Tordesillas, Spain soon had a major problem to contend with: the invasion of the Caribbean by foreign intruders. The rivalry of Charles V and Francis I found a theater in the West; the first attacks on the heart of the Spanish-American empire were made by the French who, perhaps as early as 1519, sailed through the Sea of the New World and touched some of the islands on their way back from Brazil.5 Such attacks increased when open war broke out and continued until the Peace of Cateau Cambresis in 1558. Faced with the problem of defending many little islands, the Spanish soon concentrated their defenses on the Greater Antilles and left the smaller islands almost completely unprotected.

The French efforts to open the *mare clausum* forced the Spanish to adopt a defense system that was to be the forerunner of the *armada de la carrera* of later years. The Spanish admiral appointed to rout out the pirates—as the French intruders were called—had little success, however. In the same year in which he accepted the command, the French attacked Puerto Rico. They had earlier stationed themselves at Mona Island in the passage between Hispaniola and Puerto Rico. Soon they were reconnoitering all the deserted bays, inlets, and islands, and their intrusions brought terror.6

The Treaty of Cateau Cambresis ended the Valois-Hapsburg quarrel of fifty years and brought some respite for the Spanish from French depredations in the West. This was brief, however: when the French left off, the English quickly stepped in. They seem to have visited Brazil and the Caribbean as early as 1516, and continuing, if irregular, visits followed. In the second half of the century, English visits became more regular and English pirates and smugglers concentrated on the Antilles and the Wild Coast. Hawkins set the example in 1563, and he was soon to be followed by many of his fellow countrymen, Drake, Raleigh, and Cumberland. The early attacks were largely aimed at exploring and privateering, but after Elizabeth took the throne, and hostility with Spain increased, adventures in the Caribbean resembled full-scale military operations. Those ventures had the encouragement of the queen, if not openly then covertly, since her money was invested in them. As early as 1574 she had given a patent to one such voyage "to discover and take possession of all remote and barbarous lands unoccupied by any Christian prince or people."7 This was in territory, to be sure, which Spain had already claimed as her exclusive domain.

The irregular English raids thus became more and more numerous.

The Sea-Dogs and their heirs made so many sorties on so many of the islands that Spain could not keep them out. Her defenses in the New World were hampered, moreover, by her military commitments in Europe. As Newton has already pointed out, the Caribbean was only a sideshow in the Spanish national war effort.[8] What could Spain do against them? The king regularly heard from his councils that the only hope was a proper system of security to consist primarily of police squadrons of swift, well-armed ships. In 1557 Philip had sent his finest naval expert to the West Indies, Pedro Menéndez de Avilés. He was appointed captain general of the *armada de la guarda de flotas de Indias* against the pirates.[9] Although it was an excellent choice, even Menéndez could not do the job without a sufficient naval force. The French and English continued their sacking and privateering without much interruption from Spain. The French quit, at least partly, however, after they had concluded peace with Spain. A few years later, in 1565, Menéndez was appointed *adelantado* of Florida, where he eliminated a French Huguenot colony with shocking cruelty.[10]

Meanwhile, he had sent certain proposals to Spain. In 1575 these resulted in the plan for two standing squadrons in the West Indies, one based at Cartagena, the other at Santo Domingo. About seven years later, something like a convoy system went into operation in order to protect the Tierra Firme and the Greater Antilles.[11] Menéndez, himself, seems to have been the designer of a new and faster ship, the *galeoncete*, which was built in Cuba. These two squadrons managed to curb threats against Spanish navigation, especially against that dream of every corsair: the Spanish treasure fleet, which evaded capture until 1628. Had the squadrons been consistently supplied, they might well have curtailed severely the French, English, and later Dutch intruders in the *mare clausum*.

Menéndez did more. Realizing that many of the Antilles lacked an effective defense system, he soon proposed to create a better type of fortification. Unfortunately, his plans could not be fully realized because of the huge costs which Spain had to bear in connection with her troubles in Europe. The Lesser Antilles were thus left to the mercy of the intruders. Menéndez managed, however, to have the fortresses at Havana and at other strategic places built as soon as money was available. Such precautions, it should be noted, showed that the Spanish had accepted the hard fact they were on the defensive in their own sea.

Organizing this system to secure the *mare clausum*, Menéndez soon realized that Spain was pursuing the impossible in claiming that the

Caribbean was a closed sea. He was the first who saw the essential truth that the sea is one. The vital point of defense for the West Indies, he realized, lay not in the Caribbean but in the mouth of the English Channel.[12] Consequently he offered to his king in 1573 a report worthy of a naval genius. In this document he proposed the seizure of the Scilly Islands as a base for a Spanish squadron of fifteen to twenty men-of-war which would be charged with impeding the southern and western routes of the Sea-Dogs and Sea-Beggars. The plan was never carried out.

This, then, was the situation in the Caribbean when the Dutch arrived. The Spanish were terrified by the raids of Drake and Cumberland, and by the swelling number of corsairs in the area, the sea from which "receipts of colonial remittance—gold, silver, pearls and precious stones"—were to come. The threat to Spain's finances was a real one. Despite the protection of the great galleons of the reorganized defense system, the Spanish, at times, had to bottle up the entire treasure fleet in Havana harbor for many months. The effect in Spain, as Irene Wright observes, was financial demoralization. Nor was that all: perhaps Spain was even more hurt financially by the *rescate*—the illegitimate trade—with the foreigners. This smuggling trade was conducted on a barter basis between *rescatadores*—Spanish colonists who participated—and corsairs, the foreign traders. After 1600, the latter term became synonymous with pirate. Indeed, the intruders challenged Spain's economic monopoly in the region more than they did her political exclusiveness.[13]

Comparatively speaking, the Dutch were latecomers in the Caribbean. Before 1594 Spanish governors complain only of the presence of French and English pirates; later the *flamencos* are mentioned in their reports. Before the rebellion, a growing trade had stimulated the Dutch in their navigation to the Baltic and the Mediterranean. Dutch ships were noticed as early as 1508 in the Canaries;[14] in 1528, ships from Zeeland visited the Cape Verde Islands, and trade in that westward direction seems to have been growing slowly.[15]

Although the size of Dutch trade toward the Canaries and the Cape Verde Islands is unknown, we do know that in 1562, a few years before the revolt, Holland, Zeeland, and Flanders had at least seven hundred fishing boats and kept twenty thousand men occupied in the herring industry. The merchant fleet was not small either. Around 1560, its numbers were estimated at eight hundred to one thousand ships with thirty thousand sailors—at least double the number of English ships and men involved at the same time.[16] But during this period, most Dutch attention was directed toward the Baltic and especially the port of Danzig.

The rebellion against Philip curtailed the promising development of Dutch commerce and navigation for at least twenty-five years. The Dutch resumed their upward swing, however, following the defeat of the Armada. It meant a new phase in the rebellion and a new latitude in merchant shipping. In 1590 the first Dutch ships, after an absence of many years, sailed once more past the Rock of Gibraltar and into the Mediterranean. A few years later the number had reached four hundred. Philip's arrests only briefly interrupted this rapid growth.

The general arrests of Philip II and his son Philip III, the first in 1585, and again in 1595 and 1598, were curious acts of the Spanish government which were only carried out after much debate with the king's councillors. The Spanish vainly hoped to destroy Dutch incentive, but profits were too great. Strangely, the Dutch trade in Spanish ports, in the midst of rebellion in the Low Countries, was really a matter of necessity more than choice. The Spanish needed grain, timber, naval stores, and textiles. Although France and England were not so hostile, they lacked the necessary merchantmen to supply Spanish needs. Philip's alternative was to allow the Dutch or ships from the Hanseatic League to carry the goods. But the Hanseats lacked the bottoms to take the trade away from the Dutch and moreover had to sail through the English Channel in order to reach Spain, a route too close to the Dutch coast. Philip wisely compromised with circumstances.

From time to time, the States General tried to prevent such traffic with Spain. The merchants, however, knew how to dodge the irregular placards, and they even devised an argument to serve as an excuse for their search for profits: the forbidden trade impoverishes the Spanish king while it brings great treasures to us. The Spanish money enabled them, they said, to continue the war against the hereditary enemy and to support the Dutch Reformed Church. How deeply they meant any of this is shown by the fact that they had no objection to supporting other Catholic monarchs, as, for example, France and the Doge of Venice, so long as these countries were enemies of the Spanish king.

The first arrest, in 1585, netted one hundred Dutch ships including thirty salt carriers from Hoorn.[17] The immediate result was alarm in the Low Countries and a sharp increase in the price of salt. The increase motivated the Dutch to sail past the Iberian coast to the Cape Verde Islands in the same year. As Sluiter has pointed out, this was

Fig. 1. Stuyvesant Window in Butler Library of Columbia University

Fig. 2. The Geographer by Vermeer

the first attempt of the Dutch to dispense with the Iberian peninsula as a source of supply for the commodity.[18] It was really Philip II who pushed them into the colonial world by forcing them to take that first difficult step.

In 1595 a second arrest of some four hundred to five hundred Dutch ships occurred in Spanish and Portuguese ports, but the conciliatory diplomacy of the archduke of Austria, Albert, who had just been appointed governor of the Spanish Netherlands, lifted the embargo very soon. The third arrest, which occurred immediately after the death of Philip II, was implemented by his mediocre son Philip III, who wanted to give the rebels *quelque goust de son gouvernement*. It caught some five hundred ships; half, by bribery or by fighting, managed to regain the sea. The arrests did not initiate Dutch expansion so much as accelerate it, especially in the Caribbean area.[19]

Naturally, after the first arrest, the Dutch, stimulated by so many fervent Spanish-hating refugees from the Southern Netherlands, looked for other ways to continue profitable trade without entering the dangerous Iberian ports. Rumors about the French exploring the regions between the Orinoco and the Amazon had awakened some interest. Blois van Treslong, the famous Sea-Beggar, had tried as early as 1578 to interest merchants in a company designed expressly to conquer the Spanish silver fleet. In those days, however, the war of rebellion was still in a critical stage, and every man was needed at home.[20]

It was the need for salt that brought the Dutch to unknown seas. Salt had already been found on the Cape Verde Islands by Zeelanders in 1528. Not until after the first arrest, however, when Iberian salt-pans were suddenly closed, did the Dutch really try to exploit the "Salt Islands."[21] It was a decisive step forward in shaping their colonial empire of the future.

Theodorus Velius, a well-known West-Frisian historian of that century, observes that, after 1588, when the Spanish domination of the northern seas suddenly ended, a prosperous adventure in ship-building started up. This was so especially in Hoorn, where naval architects had invented a way to make ships longer and thus able to carry larger cargoes. The invention came at a very opportune moment, just at the time when Dutch ships were once again sailing to the Mediterranean. Steven van der Haghen, one of the founders of Dutch navigation to the East Indies, was probably one of the first who dared to sail through the Strait again after 1588. At that point the new ship—called flute or *fluit*—was built at Hoorn, which made navigation in the Mediterranean and on Africa's west coast decidedly more profitable.

The Strait of Gibraltar was clearly more dangerous for the Dutch than was the Atlantic or the Caribbean. Still, these seas were also perilous because Dutch maps were poor and hurricanes sporadically ravaged the fleets. But the Atlantic was not totally unknown to the Dutch. In conjunction with Portuguese commercial houses, they had traded in Brazil.[22] Then, too, Dutch sailors, voluntarily or otherwise, had served on Spanish ships in the East and West. The Dutch had thus acquired some experience in these unknown waters. They knew that the Spanish fleets which were sailing to the Caribbean crossed the Atlantic from the Canaries, following a course before the wind until they reached the Antilles. They never returned by the same route. From Havana they went through the Florida and Bahama Channels until they reached Bermuda, and then east across the Atlantic again.

But Dutch acquaintance with Spanish routes was rudimentary and was not put to a test before 1588. The Spanish were too strong and the Dutch were too busy with their struggle for independence to voyage so far afield before then. The archives of the admiralty board of Amsterdam, the most important of the Dutch admiralty boards, rarely mention any ship or expedition to American waters before 1588. This, however, changed rapidly after 1590.

The Dutch outward thrust after this year was largely commercial in character and, because of the war, bent on profits from privateering. The Dutch sought the commodities which they had previously been able to get from the Iberian peninsula. The Canaries, Azores, Cape Verde Islands, and Madeira were soon regularly visited by the Dutch, who had only been there incidentally before their rebellion. Those islands happened to be beyond the "line of amity"; there Spain maintained a colonial monopoly. A license to trade was required.

With such a Spanish license, it was relatively easy to proceed from those islands to Brazil or to the West Indies, but without a license, there were difficulties. The Dutch, who were already running the risk of arrest in the islands mentioned, were not very apt to receive such licenses. They sailed further south, therefore, to take on badly needed supplies, and on to the African Gold Coast or as far south as Principe or São Thomé before venturing across the ocean.[23] This route was a detour, of course. Those who sailed that way took more risks and were subject to more illnesses, especially scurvy. Van Linschoten, who spoke from experience, complained of the equitorial heat and warned: "Sometimes there are calms that cause the ships to spend months there before they are able to cross the line."[24]

As noted above, because of their relations with Portuguese firms, the Dutch were actually earlier acquainted with Brazil than with the west coast of Africa. One such expedition by Barent Erikszoon of Medemblik illustrates this.[25] After having made several trips to Brazil under Portuguese auspices, Erikszoon had weather trouble on a return voyage and was forced to enter the port of Principe, a Portuguese island in the Gulf of Guinea. He was taken prisoner there and brought to the neighboring island of São Thomé where, in prison, he became acquainted with two Frenchmen who told him about the wonderful commercial possibilities of the Gold Coast. Back in Enkhuizen in 1593, he organized a company and was probably responsible for opening Dutch trade on Africa's west coast. A close second, however, was another merchant-sailor, Simon Taey.[26] The third man to visit those regions in that same year was Dirck Veldmuis, a "renowned captain" of Medemblik, who never returned from the trip. It was learned later that he was killed and that his ship was taken by the French.[27] In 1593 another sailor from Medemblik, Cornelis Freeksz Vrijer, returned safely from Angola. More Dutchmen followed.[28] Navigation to this and to other parts of the African coast increased rapidly thereafter, and well-known Hollandian and Zeelandian merchants soon became involved in the profitable trade. By 1598 there were around twenty-five to thirty Dutch merchantmen busy in these waters. In a request of 1607, which protested against the Truce negotiations, it was pointed out that, in fifteen years, more than two hundred ships had visited that coast, with more than ten thousand sailors; that great quantities of textiles had been sold there and that those ships had returned with ivory, gold, hides, and gums in excess of the country's needs. Thus, the Guinea merchants had helped support other branches of trade and industry.[29]

Company after company was founded, especially after the return of Cornelis Houtman from the first exploratory expedition to the East Indies in 1594. The list is impressive. They were called *Compagnieën van Verre*—Companies of the Far Countries: the Russian Company, the Guinea Company, several East India Companies, the North Company. Most of them were organized for very limited purposes, sometimes for only one expedition. The so-called Magellan Company, for instance, was organized solely to send an exploratory and privateering expedition through the Strait of Magellan in order to attack Spain's Pacific coast and the Malay archipelago, an imitation of the previous voyages of Drake and Cavendish.[30] A similar company was created by Olivier van Noort in the same year, and he became the first Dutchman to circumnavigate the globe.

The "Far Countries" became a contagious sickness. Well-known merchants like van der Haghen, van der Veken, Wissel, Bicker, and others sent their requests to the States General for permission to sail abroad. Many of the early companies, hurt by the mutual competition that developed, merged into a larger organization—especially those which traded in the East; thus, the Dutch East India Company was born.

Zeeland took the lead in the West, and particularly so in the enterprises of Balthazar de Moucheron. He was the outstanding organizer of expeditions in every direction. Soon other Zeelanders followed his example. Their names appear as participants or directors of the Dutch West India Company which was founded a generation later. Indeed, Houtman's expedition had given heart and nerve to the Dutch. They knew now that the world was theirs.

In 1598 at least eighty Dutch ships swarmed out of the home ports to sail in all directions: along the African coast, around the Cape of Good Hope, to Brazil, through the Strait of Magellan, and to the Caribbean. Many of them carried sloops or pinnaces which could be put together wherever it became necessary to row up rivers and to explore unknown coasts, bays, and beaches.[31] Both the provincial and federal governments understood the importance of this activity. And they supported it by giving exemptions from taxes, freedom from convoy duties, and sometimes by supplying guns and ammunition for the ships. They also set up a prize court in order to regulate privateering. This court was supervised by the admiralty boards, and it had the authority to inquire into all problems related to this special branch of trade. It guaranteed the rights of the parties involved in acts of privateering, except, of course, for the enemy, and action against him was often cruel. The days of the *buena guerra* were still far away.

Some of the intrepid and courageous enterprises of those early days deserve special attention, especially those of the expeditions fitted out by de Moucheron. The activities of this refugee from the Southern Netherlands, fervent Calvinist and protégé of Prince Maurits, seem almost incredible. His interest in the expeditions to the North, his relations in the Moscow trade, his investments in some Guinea enterprises, and his grandiose plans for the East and West Indies, make him, together with Usselinx, one of the two most important founders of the Dutch colonial empire.[32]

The projects of de Moucheron differed from those of the other merchants and companies. Since he was a man of vision, he would not limit his goals to one or two enterprises, nor even simply to profit. His great dream, it seems, was to interrelate the East and West Indies with a chain of trade through Africa and Brazil. He soon realized the importance of placing a station along the African coast for the burgeoning Dutch activity. Thus, as early as 1596 he sent two well-armed ships down the African waters to found a stronghold at São Jorge da Mina, called by the Dutch the Elmina Castle. When the Negro guides led the expedition into a trap, the plan failed, but that did not stop de Moucheron. Envisioning a marquisate for himself, and supported by the government, he soon outfitted a fleet to seize the island of Principe. The attack was successful, and his flag flew in the tropics. When reinforcements failed to show up, however, the expedition left the island after an occupation of five months.[33]

In the meantime a more regular trade with Brazil was developing. Its size is difficult to determine. Of the more than one thousand ships with chartering contracts that left the port of Amsterdam between 1587 and 1602, only a few had Brazil as their final destination. But even those few sailed first to Spain and Portugal, took on wine, grain, or other merchandise, and carried these to Brazil. They were probably licensed by Iberian authorities. In 1587 at least three Dutch vessels visited Brazilian ports; from that year to 1598, probably thirty more ships had Brazil as their destination.[34]

As the resolutions of the States General and the admiralty boards show, the beginning of the new century saw an increasing trade with Brazil. In 1600 the States General advised the boards that any one should be permitted to equip ships for trade in Brazil since that privilege was already enjoyed by Portuguese merchants who resided in the United Provinces, and it would be discriminative to Dutch businessmen to deny them rights granted to foreigners.[35] The expedition of Paulus van Caerden is further proof of a growing interest in the New World, and, even more, it indicates the intention of founding settlements on the Brazilian coast. Van Caerden was ordered to build a fort, and he carried the materials for it with him. As is pointed out before, he failed. An expedition of 1606, designed to seize Pernambuco, also failed.[36]

It was only natural that the Dutch would also enter the Caribbean Sea. Spain drew the very products she sold to the Dutch from the Caribbean islands and the northern coast of South America. The products which most attracted the Dutch were hides, sugar, tobacco, ginger, canafistula, pearls, sarsaparilla, cochineal, indigo, dyewoods, and cacao. The area also offered an abundance of white salt of excellent quality in easily accessible pans.

There were more reasons, however, for the Dutch to invade the Caribbean. In that sea intercolonial trade was considerable, a fact which had not escaped the attention of shrewd Dutch merchants with an inclination to make a profit through privateering. In addition, many of the Lesser Antilles were undefended by the Spaniards. Perhaps most important of all, the Caribbean was the area where the Spanish silver fleets would sail by—easily spied on from the *islas inútiles*, as the Spanish called the unoccupied and undefended Antilles—and easily attacked if a straggler from the fleet were spotted.[37]

As was the case in Brazil, the Dutch were already acquainted with the Caribbean. They had been recruited to serve on Spanish galleons before the arrests. Certainly as early as 1567, moreover, ships from West Friesland and Zeeland had anchored in Havana. In 1572 five ships of the Sea-Beggars appeared off the Isthmus of Panamá. Although those visits were incidental, soon the Dutch became, for the Spanish governors in the area, a very large and persistent nuisance. In 1593 the Spanish captured ten Dutch ships, loaded with dye and other merchandise, along the coast of New Andalusia,[38] which is some indication of how quickly trading activity had increased in the West Indies.

Once again, in the Caribbean trade, we meet Balthazar de Moucheron. As early as 1595 he had obtained exemption from the States of Zeeland of duties on cargo bound for the West Indies.[39] In that same year Zeeland also waived payment of export fees on a quantity of "cloth, silks, linen, velvet, and small wares" to be sent to the Indies.[40] At least two "flieboats of Middelburgh" were trading that summer at Cumaná.[41]

Once opened, Dutch trade in the West Indies grew constantly. Merchants were not always successful, however: a venture to establish trade with Santo Domingo in 1595, for example, met with a clear rebuff. But efforts continued: trading relations were established with Margarita and other places on the coast, filling those areas "with the cloth of the Netherlands and England."[42] The Dutch stationed themselves where the pearl fishing boats passed and sold their commodities on a barter basis for pearls. As a consequence the gems nearly vanished as a local medium of circulation.[43] Two other towns involved in this trade were La Guaira and Caracas.

Following the example of the Zeelanders, Pieter van der Haghen of Rotterdam planned an expedition to the West Indies at the end of 1596. In the fall of that same year ships from Guinea had brought back to Middelburg some Negroes who had probably been caught at sea. Ten Haeff, one of the burgomasters, afraid of the consequences, immediately called a meeting of the Provincial States and urged them to put the Negroes back "in their natural liberty."[44] There followed a solemn *manumissio vindicta*. Some Portuguese pilots had been captured with the slaves, and van der Haghen now asked to have the pilots aid in his proposed voyage to the West Indies. Four ships were outfitted bound for Santo Domingo, Puerto Rico, other parts in the Caribbean, and elsewhere. The shrewd merchant from Rotterdam recruited Spanish and Portuguese crews, and the vessels returned with rich cargoes.[45]

Requests from other merchants followed. Johan van der Veken got patents to go to Guinea, Peru (the Colombian and New Spain coast), and the West Indies.[46] Others followed his example. Unfortunately, the journals for almost all these expeditions are lost.

The Dutch traded in the Caribbean under very adverse conditions. They were in enemy territory, and Spain, however much in decline, was still powerful. Besides, the Dutch were not only rebels but heretics. Although the area was also infested with English and French privateers, it was the Dutch who were the most consistently ill-treated and were either hanged or sent to the galleys. But they stubbornly continued to infest the Spanish *mare clausum*. And they outcompeted their English and French rivals because they delivered the commodities for less money and were willing to extend more credit. Political events in Europe—the death of Queen Elizabeth and the murder of Henry IV—paralyzed their two rivals and, as the seventeenth century opened, assisted Dutch commercial ventures in the Caribbean.

The Dutch primarily sought hides, wood, tobacco, and sugar, and secondarily cacao and indigo. Hides were much in demand for Amsterdam's leather trade. Soon a small fleet of twenty ships began annual visits to Cuba and Hispaniola for hides, and their business transaction amounted to some eight hundred thousand guilders annually.[47] Tobacco was also important. Its main center was the North coast of Venezuela where "every Spaniard was a *rescatador* and where the Dutch openly and presistently traded."[48] Trade there, as elsewhere, was done on a barter basis: the Dutch brought cloth and hardware and exchanged it for the tobacco.

Most Dutch ships, however, were involved in the salt trade. Salt was needed for their herring industry and was transported to the Baltic as well. The presence of large salt pans in the Caribbean was probably known in the Low Countries before the turn of the century. Before long the area was flooded with Dutch salt carriers. These carriers were also illicit traders and privateers, in addition to the fact that they were invaders of Spanish territory and transporters of a product from which Spain could have made a profit. The Dutch brought home their salt cost free and tax free, and worth one million guilders a year.[49]

There is little known of the exact size of the Dutch Caribbean trade of those years. By some ingenious calculations, Sluiter estimates that around one hundred and twenty ships a year were involved.[50] Usselinx, in his *Remonstrance*, reports that the salt and hide trade kept one hundred ships at sea.[51] The same number appears in another publication, but it is limited there to the salt trade.[52]

The Wild Coast lies between the Caribbean and Brazil, its southern boundary to the mouth of the Amazon, its northern, the mouth of the Orinoco. The Dutch were early acquainted with the area because they crept along the coast to reach the salt pan of Araya—a short distance beyond the Orinoco. Southey, although not always trustworthy, maintains that the Dutch were already trading in the Guianas in the '70's; Dalton writes that the Zeelanders had a kind of trade there by 1580.[53] No evidence exists for either allegation. The States General did discuss at some length a proposal for a Captain Butz in connection with developing the Wild Coast, but nothing ever came of the project. Indeed, at that moment, the Dutch had all they could do to keep the Spanish at bay, but from that proposal perhaps stem the legends of early Dutch settlements on the banks of the Orinoco.[54]

There is no doubt, however, that the physical character of the Wild Coast attracted the foreign intruders, and neither Spain nor Portugal had any strongholds there. The geographical situation made for small native enclaves, which meant that the Indians would be easier to control by limited numbers of colonists or by the crews of ships. Whereas most European settlements in the New World soon took the characteristic form of the large plantation, the terrain of the Wild Coast, in contrast, dictated small foreign settlements, and the factories or trading posts of the area were typical.

Raleigh's description of this region, *The Discoverie of the Large and Bewtiful Empire of Guiana* (1596), stimulated the Dutch impulse to visit these regions. The inhabitants of Flushing, the *pichelingues*, especially, were attracted to this part of the New World. Perhaps as early as 1595—even before Raleigh's publication—they had developed a fortified trading post or factory called Fort Orange some twenty miles up the Amazon, and another seven miles further called Fort Nassau.

Some of these early expeditions are known to us through documents, and given the limited number of surviving records, we can be sure that many more were fitted out. Certainly from 1595 onwards the Wild Coast was systematically visited and was regularly the scene of an extended battlefield in the war between the Dutch rebels and their intolerant Spanish king. After 1597, requests for permission to go there were regular: Gerrit Bicker and his company applied to the States General for a commission to send two ships to the coasts of America and to "Peruana"—meaning the Wild Coast. Another request from two Amsterdam merchants sought permission to visit the "Kingdom of Guiana."[55]

One report of such an expedition has survived, written by A. Cabeljau, a ship's clerk. Unlike the exaggerated nature of Raleigh's description, this report gives more realistic information about the explored region. Two ships had been involved, the *Zeeridder* (Sea Knight) and the *Jonas*. They left Brielle December 3, 1597, but soon separated and did not meet again throughout the voyage. The *Zeeridder* arrived at Cape North, near the mouth of the Amazon, traded with the Indians for a while, and then visited the whole northern coast between the Amazon and the Orinoco. It also undertook a voyage up the Caroni River where the Dutch tried to find the silver mines that Raleigh described. Then the *Zeeridder* sailed home by way of Trinidad, and arrived on December 28, 1598, having discovered "more than twenty-four rivers, many islands in the rivers, and diverse other harbors which have hitherto been unknown in these provinces and not sailed to therefrom"[56] (see Appendix 1).

Cabeljau gives an account of the excellent relations between the Indians and the Dutch once the former were assured that their blue-eyed visitors were not Spanish. The same friendly treatment was accorded to the Dutch on the Brazilian coast when the Indians learned that they were not Portuguese. Raleigh's account must have been known by Cabeljau and certainly must have impressed him, but the Dutchman disagreed with the Englishman that gold digging was suitable work for merchants. Finally, the report reveals that the Dutch, although at war with Spain in Europe and intending to carry that war to the East and West Indies, were well received by the Spanish at San Tomé and Trinidad and were allowed to trade there.

At least one phlegmatic Dutchman was influenced by the legend of the Gilded Man and the possibility of easy money. He was mayor Geleyn ten Haeff of Middelburg who, in 1599, fitted out a ship of three hundred tons "to visit the river called Dorado, situated in America," and who requested exemption of duties for three voyages.

The flood of requests, often of dubious character, for government support for voyages to Brazil, the Wild Coast, and the Caribbean forced the States General to issue general instructions for captains who planned to sail to the East and West Indies. The captains were held responsible for making sure that all prizes captured at sea would be honestly administered and accounted for and that the requisite revenues would be paid. The captains learned, moreover, that only Spanish ships, or ships of Spain's allies, could be attacked. The crews were also to see to it that peaceful relations were maintained with the Indians. In a special instruction, called *artikelbrief*, rules were given for order and discipline.[57]

Unlike the Caribbean, where the Dutch were only involved in trade, smuggling, and privateering, the Wild Coast ventures were directed toward settlement. In the beginning, these enclaves had the character of factories or trading posts. The fortresses on the Amazon were also a part of this policy as was the Dutch post on the Essequibo.[58] This post, called Fort Ter Hooge, was built in 1596 on a small island at the junction of the rivers Cayuni and Mazaruni with the Essequibo River. As Spanish records reveal, it was destroyed that same year.

After 1598, the sight of Dutch ships off the Guiana coast was a regular thing. Ships from Middelburg and Flushing were sent to those regions to establish trade connections and to found factories. The trade was carried out by factors who were set up with supplies of barter goods on the various rivers and along the coast. These factors were supplied by ships on their periodic visits to different stations. The English settlements of the area, which were badly supplied by their own people, were served by the Dutch as well. The trade with the Indians was carried on by barter for products desired in the Low Countries.

The proceedings of the States General are the best source for tracing the development of Dutch power in this area. The records reveal requests for permission to trade and settle, or to find minerals. They invariably ask for exemption from import and export duties. One such request, presented in 1603, reflects the attention to detail which characterizes the memorials. It primarily concerned colonization in the Guianas but went on to say: "And as for the hope and expectation of finding a rich gold and silver mine, it is well grounded on fact and experience, for a mine has already been found, the vein of which is gold and the surrounding ore silver. There have even been tests which show sixty florins per ton of ore, while other assays gave one-half to forty-five stivers, and even florins per pound of ore."

The memorial goes on to point out that further exploration should not be undertaken until the land was well colonized and strengthened with fortresses, for otherwise "its richness might incline and induce neighboring nations, whether friend or foe, to anticipate us in this undertaking while we here were as yet busily deliberating and planning how and by what means this enterprise and scheme might most safely and conveniently be taken up and carried to the desired end." In addition to the mineral prospects in the region, the memorial also notes that the land was productive and yielded "palm and balsam oil, various kinds of gums, white incense or mastix, a fast orange dye called *annatto*, brazil wood, and other aromatic woods." There were many fine harbors, conveniently deep and navigable rivers, abundant pastures for stock, and fertile soil which was well adapted to raising wheat, wine, oil, sugar, ginger, cotton, pepper, indigo, and various other products.[59]

The treasures envisioned by the writers of the memorial could only be realized, so they argued, through colonization. The financing for such a venture could only be furnished by a group of merchants, but the project would require the favor and the protection of the government. The feasibility of colonization was enhanced by the fact that the nearest Spanish settlement was two hundred miles from the mine. The area also had some natural defenses: the sea along the coast was shallow and the entrances to the harbors were guarded by shoals, banks, and sand. No attack was anticipated from the Spanish West Indies because the area lay south of the prevailing winds and currents. Yet navigation was possible from the Low Countries at all times of the year. The memorial concludes finally that the Guianas were the most likely spot in the Americas to establish an arsenal and a *sedem belli*. The last point may not have been well received in 1603 since the States General was then considering peace negotiations with Spain. Their answer was therefore evasive: "As to the required colonization of Guiana, it was declared that the States General can not for the present take action in this matter."[60]

The flow of requests to visit the Wild Coast continued, however, in the first years of the seventeenth century. Some well-known Zeelandian merchants involved in the trade were Jan de Moor, the Lampsins brothers, and Pieter van Rhee; merchants from Haarlem and Amsterdam followed. There is even a request from Plancius for exemptions on wares "which shall be brought to this country from the north coast of Brazil and the regions of Guiana."[61]

Much trading was conducted openly; where Spanish settlements were visited, this trade was dependent on the good will of the authorities and many times deteriorated into smuggling. To find out the reaction to their arrival the Dutch followed a certain pattern. On dropping anchor in a Spanish settlement the captain would send a messenger to the local authorities requesting permission to trade after paying the required royal duties. If the governor or the *alcaldes* permitted this official recognition, they were in for trouble from the authorities in Hispaniola or Spain.[62] If they refused, however, they were in for trouble from the smuggler, who then became an enemy. Either way the Dutch trader returned home with a profit made by trade or by sacking the community. Under these conditions, the public generally preferred to trade with the smugglers, unofficially.

The problem for the Spanish authorities was compounded in most communities by the increasing number of *avecindados*—men who had taken out papers of *vecindad* and became naturalized citizens. Many of them were skilled laborers, carpenters, blacksmiths, and fishermen, and the villages could not do without them; yet sometimes they were also heretics, who distributed heretical literature and jeopardized the salvation of the rustics. Worst of all, the *avecindados* were much involved in illegal trade with the foreigners. Together with the mass of the population, they were willing to trade freely. They were certainly assets in the phenomenon of the *rescate* and Spain was unable to curb their activities.

The real root of the problem of illegal trade, however, were the *alcaldes*, a fact regularly reported to the king by his councils and governors. These town officials, creoles or mestizos, were responsible for prosecuting the *rescatadores*. Instead, however they were often the worst smugglers in their community.

Spain's attempt to eliminate smuggling and illicit trade came rather late. At last, though, she realized her blunder in leaving undefended the windward rim of the Caribbean and the Wild Coast. Yet, to do something about it would cost money she did not have. The Spanish treasury was already overburdened by her too elaborate foreign policy, and any serious attempt to keep the Caribbean closed in order to prevent access to her shores was impossible.

The unprecedented scale of Dutch invasions after 1600, especially at the salt pan of Araya, did not escape the attention of the king and his councillors. Warnings from the governors of Margarita, Cumaná, Caracas, Trinidad, Puerto Rico, Hispaniola, Jamaica, and Cuba came in steadily increasing quantities to Madrid, and they form a litany on the same sad theme. It was that of the *enemigos ynglesses, francesses y otros piratas* who infested the respective domains of the governors. After 1600, moreover, a new nation was added to the list which soon became the worst nuisance of all: *olandeses, flamencos*, or *herejes rebeldes*, as the Dutch were variously called. A large number of the complaints came from Diego Suárez de Amaya, the governor of Cumaná, since the salt pan of Araya was located in his district. Although we deal with the salt problem in another chapter, it should be pointed out here that the salt carriers far outnumbered the so-called *barcos de rescate*.[63] In 1600 Suárez was already complaining that no Spanish merchantman could provide his part of the coast because of the foreigners and that his relations with neighboring Margarita had to be conducted during the night by Indian canoes.

Antonio Osorio, the governor of Santo Domingo, voiced the same complaints. One can feel his disgust when he wrote: "It is hard to have knowledge of so many disembarkations" of the rebellious enemies.[64] The situation was similar in Cuba. Governor Juan de Maldonado had tried to arrest the *rescatadores* in 1599, but he had failed. He had then come up with a disastrous suggestion: he recommended that the old capital of Cuba, Baracoa, where the evil of the *rescate* was worst, be depopulated and its inhabitants moved to other areas,[65] a drastic action which was not taken. In 1602 Maldonado was succeeded by the vigorous Pedro de Vargas who was determined to end the illicit trade and its drain on the Spanish treasury. Although he failed to receive the necessary funds for his plan from the government, he did get them from local merchants and outfitted some *armadillas*, small squadrons which he armed to meet the pirate ships and protect the Cuban coasts.[66] But Spain did not realize its good fortune in those days: the French, English, and Dutch wanted booty and profit by trade. They did not however, desire one square foot of Spanish soil—not yet at least.

The governor's warnings became the subject of many discussions in the Council of the Indies and in the king's War Council, and serious attempts were made to deal with the problems presented. Presumably Maldonado's earlier suggestion was behind the decision to depopulate the north coast of Hispaniola where the *rescate* was much practiced.[67] This drastic plan was enacted despite the better advice of the archbishop of the island, Davila Padilla, who had suggested that Spain might send the desired supplies to that area to foil the pirates, or at least award the area those rights of free trade which were enjoyed by settlements within the line of amity.

The first *cédula* on the proposed depopulation was issued in August, 1603, and others soon followed. Three towns had to be depopulated: Yaguana, Puerto Plata, and Bayahá. The *cabildo* of Santo Domingo protested, but in vain. Osorio had to execute the order. The resultant consternation and confusion were not at all mitigated by the king's promise of amnesty to any Spanish subject guilty of smuggling. The move was made, but the dire predictions of the *cabildo* came about too. It had claimed that the inhabitants who were to be moved were the *gente común*, the poor whites, mestizos, mulattos, and Negroes and that they would not move but instead flee to the mountains beyond the reach of the law. Some of the population did move quietly, but those who fled simply waited for the king's men to leave; then they returned and continued to live in the forbidden areas and to carry on the illicit trade just as before. But some of the northern coastal ports on Hispaniola were abandoned in this action, and they were soon occupied by foreigners. Conditions were set thus for the thriving of the buccaneers, and ultimately for the emergence of the culturally and linguistically divergent republic of Haiti.[68] The strategy of depopulation had not hurt the Dutch, against whom it was directed, nearly so much as it was to ultimately hurt Spain.

The warnings from governors continued to disturb the Council of the Indies. The Dutch visited the Caribbean in ever increasing numbers, and credit should be given to Suárez de Amaya for the persistence with which he continued to write to the slow-moving Spanish court. In October, 1605, Philip III was advised by the Council of the Indies that the situation was critical. The urgency of the warning was emphasized by rumors brought from Holland about a huge project being planned against the West Indies. There was some basis for concern: such a plan had been discussed between van Oldenbarnevelt and Prince Maurits, although it had been abandoned as not sufficiently profitable. But the rumor had found its way to Spain.[69]

Discussion in the council resulted in a decision to organize a special squadron of eight galleons and four advice-boats. This *armada de barlovento*, designed to protect the Windward Islands, looked wonderful on paper, and it was to be built as quickly as possible. The initial cost, however, was figured at 130,000 ducats, and Spain, as usual, lacked funds—her elaborate European foreign policy drained every cent away. Besides this expense, she had to defend an empire on which the sun never set and which the Dutch were attacking from all directions.[70]

The equipment of a special squadron was, for the moment anyway, impossible. Spain had to find other means to stop the illegal invasions. Serious discussions continued in the Council of the Indies aimed at solving the problem in a less expensive way. An idea of 1601, to use the *flota* to attack the Dutch at Punta de Araya, was reconsidered. It had always been rejected in the past for fear that the fleet would take too much time in a military mission and arrive too late to fulfill its other duties. There were also discussions about inundating the salt pan. Of the two proposals, the former seemed most workable and was accepted. The fleet's success in 1604, when it had sunk two Dutch salt carriers and had captured two others, perhaps persuaded the council to hope for similar or better results.[71] The precious galleons were thus pressed into police duties in addition to a project to depopulate another thriving region of the *rescate*, Cumanagote.

The Spanish appointee for the mission was Luis de Fajardo, a veteran of war and a soldier of recognized ability, proven capable of energetic measures against both pirates and heretics. He left Lisbon in September, 1605, in command of a fleet of fourteen galleons and twenty-five hundred men. The Spanish, aware that outfitting such a fleet would lead to speculation about its use, planted the false rumor that the fleet was to be sent to Flanders (see Chapter vi). Walking into this trap, the Dutch made haste to prevent incursions on their home coasts. Meanwhile, Fajardo sailed to the West Indies, and surprised and captured many Dutch salt carriers at Araya. Remaining a month in the neighborhood, he managed to catch other Dutch, English, and French smugglers.[72] When word came that a fleet of foreign smugglers was assembling at Manzanillo, Cuba, Fajardo sent his vice-admiral Juan Alvares in command of five or six galleons and some smaller ships to destroy them. The outcome of this encounter was, however, not favorable for the Spanish.[73]

The Dutch reaction to Fajardo's success at Araya was a further sharpening of the war and an increase in privateering and raiding. Moreover, the blockade of the Iberian coast was intensified.[74] Haultain's expeditions and the attack on Gibraltar under Heemskerk must also be seen as results of national indignation over Fajardo's actions. Rumors now reached Spain that the Dutch were also planning a mass retaliation in the West Indies. The Spanish spies, however, confused a Dutch "design against the West Indies" with plans drawn up by the French king for a joint French-Dutch Company.[75]

The Dutch blockade of the Iberian coast forced the Spanish to send word to Diez de Armendáriz, the general of the New Spain fleet, urging him not to leave Havana until the arrival of the armada that would protect his silver galleons. These instructions said that he could sail only after a certain date. Then, after he had passed through the Bahama Channel, he was to take a prescribed route to Cape Finisterre, which was supposed to be safe. He was to remain at Cape Finisterre until he was advised about the disposition of the Dutch fleet. The Spanish had already developed, evidently, a deep fear of the Dutch threat to the treasure fleet.[76]

Early in 1606, at least 130 privateers left Dutch ports destined to roam the Spanish and Spanish American coasts. Fajardo's cruelty at Araya had precipitated this fearsome outburst of Dutch revenge, and Spain tried vainly to make the right countermove. The encounter between eight Dutch ships, probably part of the huge fleet mentioned above, and the Honduras galleons served to hasten Spanish defense measures, even though the Dutch failed to capture these richly laden ships. Their commander, Juan de Vergara, defended them with gallantry and success, and the Dutch were forced to retreat.[77]

By that time Philip III began to tighten his administrative control. A *cédula* of July, 1605, ordered that all viceroys in the Indies were to execute justice on all captured corsairs without dissimulation, dispensations, or appeal to the Crown, and without awaiting new orders. They were further ordered to impose the statutory penalties established in the kingdom of Castile.[78]

These orders were executed by Spanish authorities with thoroughness, and they were immediately countered by harsh action on the part of the Dutch. Although neither side seemed to realize it, ferocity bred only further violence. During the first year in office of Sancho de Alquiza, the governor of Venezuela, part of the crew of a Dutch trader was captured when coming ashore and all were hanged in full view of those who had remained on board. Although this Spanish efficiency did in fact curtail Dutch smuggling, it was only at the price of other less happy effects in the colony. In the first place, it stopped the supply of cloth, hardware, and other commodities brought by the Dutch. At the same time, the Spanish colonies lost the stimulating effect of an outlet for their colonial products. Sluiter gives an excellent example of this phenomenon in his account of the tobacco culture of New Andalusia and Venezuela. Early in 1606, the king ordered the depopulation of Nueva Ecija. For ten years, tobacco-growing was to be prohibited in Venezuela, New Andalusia, and the Windward Islands. The *cabildo* of Caracas and Governor Alquiza, although both in favor of stopping illegal trade, realized that the Crown was cutting the colonial nose to spite the royal face. Even though smuggling would be effectively curbed, it would only be at the expense of the economic development along the whole coast of modern Venezuela.[79]

The shortsightedness of the Duke of Lerma and his puppet king is well illustrated by the eagerness with which they tried to maintain the *mare clausum*. Neither was in the least concerned with developing the prosperity of the colonies. The *cédulas* virtually admitted that Spain could not or would not adequately supply her own colonies.

Fig. 3. William Usselinx by anonymous Dutch painter

Fig. 4. Puerto Rico in 1625

Indeed, the governors often requested that sufficient supplies be sent to eliminate the necessity for the smuggling. Alquiza, writing in 1608, for example, lamented that the shortage of supplies was so bad that he had no paper on which to write his letters of complaint.[80]

The situation was no better on Hispaniola where it was said that a Spanish ship from the mother country had anchored with supplies for the population only once in three years. The majority of the poorer classes soon went naked, and it became necessary to hold mass before dawn so that those who had no clothes could hide themselves in the darkness of the night. In many of the other Antilles and on the coast of the Tierra Firme the situation was just as bad.

In those difficult years, Spain was blessed with a number of honest and hardworking colonial officials. Indeed, the remarkable success of her unwise reaction depended entirely on the efficiency of her local administrators. An excellent example of such a functionary was the aforementioned governor of Venezuela. When he arrived at his post in 1606, the colonial society had degenerated to such an extent that virtually every free man in his province was somehow involved in smuggling. The population waited with a certain curiosity to see what the new governor would do about it. They and the captured crew of a Dutch ship learned very quickly. Although Alquiza was tolerant of what had gone on before, he was so only if his regulations were observed now. During the five and one-half years that he was the governor, smuggling on the Venezuelan coast virtually stopped, but, as a result, the population, and the governor, all suffered deprivation.

Although it is difficult to generalize, there is sufficient evidence to indicate that most Spanish officials in the Caribbean acted much as Alquiza did, albeit perhaps with somewhat less energy. The typical attitude, *obedezco mas no cumplo*, had not yet become prevalent.

The activities of the Dutch in those years did not result in any great conquest or settlement in the West Indies. Quite contrary to what was going on in the East, the Dutch confined their western activity to raiding, smuggling, and general harrassment. Henry Hudson's explorations in the North led to the foundation of New Netherland. In the South, Brazil was sometimes the target for settlement, but an expedition by van Caerden in 1603 was unsuccessful, and further ventures in 1606 also failed to establish a foothold in Brazil.

Meanwhile, negotiations had started for peace with Spain, which resulted in the Twelve Years' Truce. This meant that big plans for the foundation of a West India Company had to be postponed. And the Dutch could no longer send their privateers to the Caribbean without violating the articles of the truce. Consequently, Dutch activity decreased rapidly in the West, at least in the beginning and with the exception of the Wild Coast. The Spanish decided to discontinue the construction of the *armada de barlovento*.

The experience of twenty years in American waters, however, was to become very important for the Dutch. Their sailors received valuable experience, their merchants an incomparable schooling, and, when the Truce was over they were prepared to venture through all the seas of the world. Dutch activity in the Caribbean had not been negligible from an economic point of view either. Their smuggling had netted millions and millions of guilders. The salt carriers had saved other millions in cost and had gained huge revenues. Military efforts in those twenty years had also weakened Spain considerably: she had been forced into a defensive position in her own waters and throughout the world. Sluiter has observed, correctly, that it was precisely Dutch pressure on Spain which made possible the English and French settlement in the Guianas, in the Lesser Antilles, and in North America.[81]

In the year in which the Truce was concluded, the Dutch had captured a powerful position in the East Indies. But the situation in the West was far less favorable for them because of different circumstances. There were no permanent Dutch settlements in the West Indies before the Truce. They had, in those years, nevertheless, far outstripped their English and French rivals and could fairly claim to be the foremost smugglers and privateers in the Indies.

4

THE TRUCE

Cedant togae arma.

At the beginning of the seventeenth century, the question of whether to continue the war against Spain troubled the United Provinces. Although the financial burden of the war was great, the results in recent years had been poor. Van der Does' expedition of 1599 had been a failure from the financial point of view, even though its significance in propaganda value could hardly be underestimated. Neither the victory of Prince Maurits at Newport in 1600 nor the expeditions under Haultain in 1606 had brought any substantial gains. Heemskerk's triumph at Gibraltar had been impressive but had not resulted in any cash. Moreover, the powerful class of regents, especially in the province of Holland, viewed the growing popularity of the Prince of Orange with alarm and feared that a prolongation of the hostilities would only serve to enhance his glory. By now they had gotten a good taste of power and become enamored of a decentralized government in which the provinces were practically autonomous. Holland, of course, had the dominant position.

The complicated structure of government in the United Netherlands needs some explanation.[1] There were seven provinces: Holland, Zeeland, Utrecht, Gelderland, Overijssel, Groningen, and Friesland. Through their own efforts, these provinces had become the freest lands in the world. They were not, of course, democratic in the modern sense of the word, although in some provinces the electorate was quite broad. They were more or less autonomous republics which were ruled by provincial legislatures composed of deputies chosen by local town councils. The real power in the United Provinces thus rested in these latter institutions.

The town councils were self-appointing in some cities, and elected by a more or less wide franchise in others. Each town council sent some of its members to the Provincial States to represent it there. Although the delegation from each city varied in number, generally each town had one vote in the Provincial States. The Noble, Great and Mighty Lords of the States of Holland, for instance, was a body composed of nineteen members from eighteen towns, while one member represented the nobility. The Provincial States was assisted, moreover, by a pensionary, and the meetings took place in the provincial capital. The members were not, however, independent representatives of their towns; in important matters they were required to consult their constituents—the town councils.

The seven provinces were virtually independent; they were seven sovereign states which had joined in a loose union—that of Utrecht in 1579— and had, as their political voice, an assembly well known in European politics: Their High Mightinesses, the States General. This confederation was officially the highest executive and legislative body in the country. In composition, however, it resembled a congress of ambassadors from seven independent states. The members were deputized by the Provincial States to represent them in the deliberations in The Hague about common affairs. Each province represented in this assembly, even mighty Holland, had but a single vote. Important decisions, moreover, had to be made unanimously.

The strangest phenomenon in this governmental structure was the House of Orange. William of Orange had originally been appointed by Philip II as stadhouder over Holland, Zeeland, and Utrecht. After Philip's abjuration in 1581, the Provincial States assumed the royal prerogative yet maintained the position of stadhouder. No one, in the beginning, realized the anomaly. When William was murdered in 1584, the majority of the provinces appointed his son Maurits to the same position. To compound this curiosity, the northern provinces—Groningen and Friesland—usually appointed another member of the House of Orange to a stadhoudership as well. Thus, during the seventeenth century, there were normally two stadhouders. The most important was usually the stadhouder of Holland (and four other provinces). From 1652 to 1672, however, there was no stadhouder in the five latter provinces.

The stadhouders were appointed by the Provincial States, and their position became increasingly important during the war of independence. They were the head of the seven provincial armies and of the three provincial navies. During the successful conduct of the war in the last twelve years of the sixteenth century, respect for Prince Maurits grew. The people saw in him and in his successors symbols of the union which had no definite legal basis but which had acquired a strong historical tradition. As head of the armies and navies the stadhouder stepped in when decentralizing forces threatened the war effort or the unity of the provinces. Since the House of Orange thus symbolized a centralizing power, the provincial regent class was anti-Orangist.

At the beginning of the seventeenth century, two parties emerged in the young nation. They are usually called the "war party" and the "peace party." They were certainly not organized as their modern equivalents, but they were, however, clearly distinguished by their goals. Van Oldenbarnevelt, the landsadvocate or pensionary of the States of Holland, "unscrupulous chessplayer" as he was called,[2] became the spokesman of that part of the population that wanted peace. Sometime later, the Prince of Orange, rather reluctantly, agreed to pose as the leader of those who were in favor of a continuation of the war. Prince Maurits, like his father, was a man of few words. As a military leader, he made decisions with the sword. The war party, however, found an eloquent spokesman in William Usselinx who knew that peace would mean the end of his West Indian dreams.

The question of war or peace became a burning issue. The contest between the parties was further enlivened by the inclusion of other disputes, as mentioned before, not the least of which was that of religion. The archduke, always well informed, knew as early as 1607 that "the end of the war with Spain would probably mean the beginning of a civil war."[3] It is not exact to say that *all* the Contra-Remonstrants were for war, nor *all* Arminians for peace, although in general terms it may be true. Van Oldenbarnevelt was certainly more an orthodox Calvinist than was the Prince of Orange, but the former led the peace party. The latter supported those in favor of war because they had "helped his father to the seat."[4] There is some question about his real motives.

The intensity of the dispute is amply illustrated in the number and variety of pamphlets which were published in the period. The United Provinces enjoyed an unprecedented freedom of the press for that era, and although the States General and the Provincial States exercised some censorship, a French ambassador was correct when he wrote, "We are among people who regard as a part of their freedom the freedom of speech."[5] In the multitude of pamphlets for and against war, we can see how the free Dutch exercised their rights—we may hear the *vox populi* of the time. Often, they were inspired by fervent anti-Catholic feelings as well as by deep mistrust of the Spaniards. "Never trust your enemy because as iron always rusts again, so will his wickedness."[6]

Exceptions to the usual vulgar level of these pamphlets were those written by William Usselinx. While his writings reveal some of the same feeling and the same mistrust, they are far superior in style to the other "peace-negotiation" literature. He composed two eloquent and ingenious appeals against talks with Spain which are referred to as "among the principal documents for the history of political economy," a statement which is probably correct.[7] These eloquently written essays are called *Considerations* and *Further Considerations*. In the earlier of the two, Usselinx argued convincingly that peace with Spain would undoubtedly bring a decline in the prosperity of the free Netherlands since the refugee Flemings would then return to their southern provinces. The same warning was repeated in the second pamphlet, there buttressed by the prophesy of Nahum: "Thou hast multiplied thy merchants above the skies; now they will spread their wings like locusts and fly away."[8]

Usselinx, however, also had other objections to a treaty with Spain: he warned that the archdukes of the Southern Netherlands would not keep promises to heretics "against which the royal agreement will be of as much help as the tinkling of bells against thunder, the sprinkling of holy water against the Devil, or the bulls of the pope against hell."[9] An essential point, made repeatedly, was, "You cannot trust the Spaniard. You cannot trust Philip III. He follows very ingeniously the footsteps of his father, the anti-Christ of Rome."[10]

This last argument was energetically supported by Usselinx' Flemish countrymen, by the ministers of the Dutch Reformed Church, and by the lower classes of the population who not only resented the regent class but also feared unemployment and economic misery if peace were to be concluded. It is, however, difficult to divide the population with regard to war and peace. The regent class wanted peace; it had qualms about the growing centralizing power of the Prince of Orange, but not every regent was so inclined. Merchants involved in the Baltic or in the Mediterranean trade generally wanted peace, but those engaged in privateering or semi-commercial enterprises in the East and West Indies preferred a continuation of hostilities. Flemings, generally, wanted the war to last because it might mean the recapture of Antwerp, but not every Fleming felt that way. The Zeelanders to whom privateering was important urged war; to them, peace was a Trojan horse—"Don't trust the horse, Greeks," was Zeeland's cry.

Strong opposition to peace also came from the Dutch East India Company. In several pamphlets and in an extensive memorandum, this institution pointed out that it had made many contracts and promises to rulers in the East Indies, and that it could not consider peace without consulting those parties.[11]

The peace party had strong arguments, however, and not the least of these was financial. Van Oldenbarnevelt, the political leader of the most important province, was very much inclined to peace since the war caused a tremendous drain on the treasury. Holland had to pay the largest part of the budget—some 58 per cent—and her finances were in bad shape. Also a few pamphlets, distinctly in the minority, did appear in behalf of peace. One was written by the famous Justus Lipsius, a strong advocate of a treaty. All the pamphlets, however, bear out Laspeyres' statement, "how great the participation was in the question of war and peace and how deep the embitterment of the parties against each other."12

These pamphlets generally avoided the two main stumbling blocks in the way of a peace with Spain: navigation in the East and West Indies, and toleration of the Roman Catholics in the North. It was to Usselinx' credit that attention was drawn to the first obstacle in a third pamphlet which has already been mentioned, entitled *Remonstrance*. In this essay he voiced his fears that the Dutch with peace or truce would lose their foothold in the East, where they were extremely successful in carving out a colonial empire, and would not be able to maintain their trade with the West. As always, very convincingly he pointed to the importance of the West Indian trade, especially in salt and hides, "because it is not gold or silver that constitutes the richness of the country there, but its products."13

What was the Spanish position on peace? Spain's treasury was even more depleted, but more critical, probably, was the fact that Spain lacked the efficient leadership which the rebels seemed to have in abundance. The Duke of Lerma, although a smart courtier, was not an astute politician or an intelligent administrator. He was aware, however, that Spain could not carry on the war much longer. The mediocre king remained enthusiastic, though, especially after the general arrest in 1598 and his edict on foreign trade in 1603, which was called, because of its originator, "Gauna's placard." It promised free trade to all parts of the Iberian European empire to all subjects of the king, even to Hollanders and Zeelanders "or the other provinces which have separated and subtracted themselves from the obedience of my brother and sister."14 But it imposed a high tax of 30 per cent on all commodities. This tax, of course, was secretly designed to ruin Dutch trade and cause frictions between the Dutch and their allies. But it was much too late to accomplish such a goal. A meeting of the Royal Council in January, 1607, realized this failure, and concluded consequently that peace was Spain's only hope, by admitting that it was "hotly desired."15

Spanish and Dutch mistrust was mutual. "One doubts the ready compliance and unsteadiness of those people"[16] was a characteristic attitude of Madrid. But an empty treasury instead of wishful thinking dictated the course which politics had to take. The ruinous attacks on the Iberian empire in the East and the increasing trade and navigation of the Dutch on the African coast and in the American waters drove Spain to compromise. In addition, the Spanish entertained fears that the Dutch would arrive at an understanding with the French. Although Henry IV had converted to Catholicism, he had not become pro-Spanish at the same time.

Spanish military exploits were not successful either. Certainly Spain rejoiced at the capture of Ostend, after a three-year siege, but the infanta, realizing its emptiness, is reported to have cried at the festivities which celebrated this triumph. Another victory qualified as lamentable was Fajardo's defeat of the Dutch salt carriers at Punta de Araya. Alarming reports also reached Spain that the Prince of Orange had given letters of marque to 120 ships. Moreover, the ominous results of the Dutch blockade of the Iberian coast were clearly felt. Finally, Madrid feared that the Southern Netherlands would defect to the North if the war with the Dutch continued.[17]

About the time of Heemskerk's destruction of the Spanish fleet at Gibraltar, a temporary truce was arranged between Brussels and The Hague. This lull of eight months was reluctantly accepted by Spain, but Philip III soon realized that the agreement was the lesser of two evils. The alternative seemed to be an alliance between the Dutch and the French.[18] Although negotiations continued between the two belligerents, the issues of navigation and religion remained a plague to the negotiators. The able French ambassador Pierre Jeannin performed a difficult and delicate task in these discussions, and his only advantage was that both parties needed and desired peace.

Negotiations continued until a satisfactory compromise was finally reached. The Twelve Years' Truce arrived at was silent on the subject of religion. The Spanish king accepted this hesitantly—he had no choice—but recommended that Their High Mightinesses treat their Catholic subjects gently.

The question of navigation in the Indies had caused more difficulties. Richardot, the Spanish ambassador, declared that his master would never permit it. If he were to allow this, the French and the English would immediately claim the same privileges. The diplomatic genius of Jeannin finally found a formula which did not mention the Indies specifically, but which, using labored circumlocutions, admitted Dutch navigation in the Portuguese Indies while preventing any intrusions into regions which were in the effective possession of Philip III; of course this meant the West. It may be said that Spain thus sacrificed the Portuguese East in order to safeguard her American colonies.[19]

The Dutch accepted the diplomatic interpretation of the Truce in spite of Usselinx' eloquent *Remonstrance* and their own misgivings. Their acceptance can be explained by the fact that, aside from their small foothold on the Wild Coast, they had not yet secured any territory in the West. They did insist, however, on the right to maintain and visit their trading posts in the Guianas and in Africa.

"We must pray God our Lord and do all that we can to let the truce be to the honor of God and the prosperity of our country," wrote van Oldenbarnevelt to the Dutch ambassador in Paris.[20] Although this was the language of the century, it was also the language of a proud and independent nation. The world was aware of the shift in power which had occurred: Spain's decline was now openly manifest. A small nation of sailors, fishermen, and merchants was primarily responsible for establishing this reality. When the Truce was concluded, the Dutch had six thousand boats with sixty thousand men engaged in fishing. More than a hundred thousand seamen were sailing over all the seas of the world, although it must be admitted that the Baltic and the Mediterranean absorbed most Dutch navigation. The African and Indian trades were still in their infancy.[21]

Jealousy was soon openly aimed at the Dutch. The French and English, who had posed as friends during the Truce negotiations, and who had, indeed, even guaranteed the treaty with promises of assistance to the Dutch should Spain renew hostilities, now realized the superior position of the Dutch and were alarmed. The sheer rapidity with which the Dutch had established themselves in the East caused concern. Only Henry IV's untimely death prevented trouble with France. The English, who had supported the rebels' cause out of sheer self-interest, were now threatened by Dutch commercial competition.[22]

Both England and the United Netherlands realized in these years that their future lay on the seas and that naval domination was a *sine qua non* for their national survival. Since England had not had to fight for existence, she clearly had the advantage. Her charters to trading companies were granted as early as 1579, and these companies were in operation before the Dutch equivalents were organized. Long before the Dutch flag was seen in the Baltic or in the Levant, the English were there. The exploits of Hawkins and Drake were legends before the Dutch were even known in the West.

What really changed Anglo-Dutch relations, however, was the death of "the great queen of the sea." She was succeeded by the "weakhearted" James I,[23] and immediately a coolness in those relations appeared. The difficulties centered on what were known as the "fishery disputes" and on Anglo-Dutch competition in the East Indies. In the latter area, relations were about as unfavorable as they had been between the Dutch and the Spanish. Fortunately, perhaps, for the Dutch, the early Stuarts were not very ambitious about foreign policy, and the English thus did not provoke trouble with their Protestant neighbors until the reign of Cromwell.

The Twelve Years' Truce was characterized by a continuation of Dutch activities and hostilities against Spain in the East Indies and by repeatedly broken and renewed negotiations with England. Gone were the days when the Dutch were willing to sail under an English flag. A more independent course was deliberately adopted. Van Oldenbarnevelt precipitated such independence by his ransom of the cautionary towns for little more than a third of the sum originally asked. In June, 1616, the Dutch commonwealth was fully liberated.[24]

The redemption of the cautionary towns had a peculiar link with Anglo-Dutch activities on the Wild Coast. It added to the confusion which already existed about the character of many expeditions, since some of their colonizing enterprises were not nationally distinct. And the Spaniards could never differentiate between English and Dutch heretics. The soldiers in the cautionary towns, who were suddenly faced with unemployment, followed the call of adventure in the New World, as did so many men in those years.[25]

Dutch activities in the East during the Truce form a chain of spectacular episodes. The war there continued, but while Spain remained the enemy, Dutch hostilities were mainly launched against Portuguese settlements. The net result of these attacks was that many of these colonies were lost to the Iberians.

At the same time the English failed to maintain their position in the Malay archipelago. Their East India Company was not only utterly outcompeted by the Dutch equivalent, but very soon it was excluded from seas and ports which the Dutch considered theirs. In other words, the Dutch had become very protective over an area they had won at much expense, and they did not want the competitive company "to reap where the English had not sown."[26] The elegant Dutch defense of the *mare liberum* principle was scuttled when the opposite became more profitable.

Along Africa's western coasts, hostilities between the Dutch and Spanish continued. The Dutch had already maintained a very profitable trade here for many years, and they were determined not to give up these profits. Spain discovered this fact as early as 1611 when a fleet of seventeen Spanish sails which was operating in those waters met a Dutch fleet and lost thirteen ships in a crushing defeat. The Dutch, however, lacked strongholds in the area. Before the Truce, it is true, they had made some arrangements with the rulers of Sabou, Fetou, and Commenda, and the Dutch interpretation of Article IV of the Truce permitted them to continue trade with these kings, since they thought the Truce was obviously based on the principle of *uti possidetis*. The Spanish governor of São Jorge da Mina, quite understandably, held to another point of view. Until he was formally advised to the contrary, he felt obligated to continue hostilities against the rebels. For almost a year after the Truce was concluded, therefore, Dutch ships were captured, their crews killed, and their cargoes appropriated by Spanish and Portuguese authorities in West Africa.[27]

The consequence of this attitude was indignation in the United Provinces. The Dutch rightly feared the loss of their profitable trade. The Guinea Company, which had been organized specifically for this purpose, soon petitioned Their High Mightinesses for governmental action against the Spanish outrages. The States General accordingly outfitted an expedition whose primary mission was to establish a stronghold at Maure, close to the Elmina Castle. Before the expedition could embark, however, news arrived that the Spaniards had seized and fortified the very site which the Dutch had hoped to claim.[28]

Discussions in the States General on Article IV of the Truce resulted, however, in the decision to proceed with the plans anyway. This action was extremely successful, and by the end of 1611 the Dutch had established at that African outpost—Maure—their first governor of the Gold Coast, Jacob Adriaenszoon Clantius. Within the first few years of Dutch occupation, the terrible heat of the area claimed a thousand lives. But Fort Nassau, as it came to be called, persisted, and became strategically important for Dutch operations both on the west coast of Africa and in the American waters.[29]

Along the Wild Coast, where the Dutch had made small settlements prior to the Truce, navigation and trade continued, not only because of the Dutch interpretation of Article IV in the Truce, but also because Spain lacked fortifications in that part of the American hemisphere. Indeed, in the years of the Truce, the Dutch expanded their hold on this part of coast by setting up trading posts that sometimes developed into settlements if trade proved to be lucrative and the land fertile enough to make plantations profitable. From the outset the Dutch attempted to utilize native opposition to the Iberians to their own advantage.

In the Guianas, from the start, the Dutch were in competition with the English. The first English colony, sponsored by Charles Leigh and located on the shore of the Wiapoco River, had been founded as early as 1604. This settlement soon faced grave troubles; the competitive Dutch actually managed most of the trade there and may even have had some colonists. Soon, other English colonies in the area, such as the one established by Captain North, also found themselves dependent on the Dutch. As the colonists remarked bitterly: "The Dutch gave what they wanted and took what they liked."[30]

Ioannes de Laet, in the words of Edmundson "an unimpeachable authority," provides dependable knowledge about the earliest Dutch trading posts and settlements in the Amazon region. This has been supplemented by Edmundson's own research. Unlike the Portuguese, who used the southern channels, the Dutch and English colonists entered the Amazon delta from the north. According to de Laet, around 1600 there were two Dutch fortresses, Nassau and Orange; situated on the eastern shore of the Xingu River and commanding the maze of the islands, these had been built by colonists from Zeeland. The very existence of these fortified trading stations so far inland, and at that early date, is proof that Flushing merchants were already considering establishing permanent commercial relations with the natives in the interior.[31] There is also information available about a Dutch effort at a very early date to put to a practical test Cabeljau's statement about the strength of the Iberians at San Tomé, consisting of "about sixty horsemen and one hundred musketeers."[32] In 1602 or 1603 Dutch vessels which had been authorized by the States General attempted to sail up the Orinoco, but the Spaniards prevented them.[33] Fort Ter Hooge, a Dutch fortress some twenty miles up the Essequibo, was destroyed, as mentioned before, in 1596.

Sources reveal many enterprises in this area during the Truce. In those years these so-called obscure expeditions began to worry Spanish authorities in San Tomé and Trinidad. Since they failed to differentiate between English and Dutch colonists and settlements, however, it is not always clear in which country the expedition originated. The governor of Trinidad, for instance, reported an English settlement at the Wiapoco and the presence in that same area of *flamencos*—the term for the Zeelanders—who were engaged in the cultivation of tobacco with the help of Indian slaves sold to them by friendly Caribs.[34]

A record kept by an English prisoner at Santo Domingo, Captain

1. Map of the Amazon Delta.   From J. A. Williamson, *English Colonies in Guiana and the Amazon.*

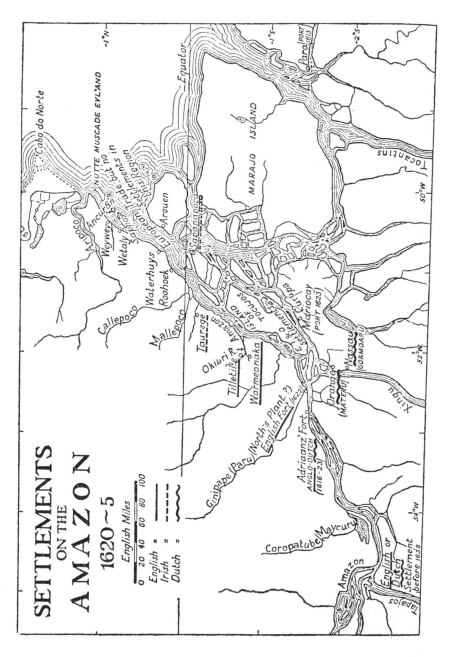

2. Map of the Guianas.   From J. A. Williamson, *English Colonies in Guiana and on the Amazon*.

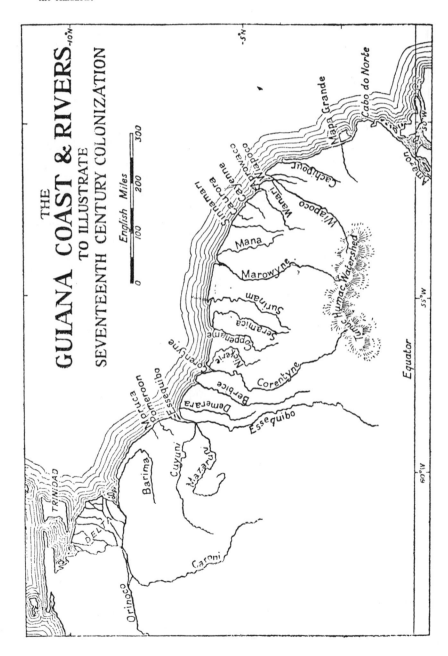

Thomas Currey, reveals that around 1610, both the English and the Dutch in the Orinoco region were carrying on a lucrative trade in tobacco. Actual settlements were not recorded. The English ventures in that area had little support from James I, since this king's matrimonial plans for his son inclined him toward peace with Spain and an unwillingness to trespass on what was admittedly Spanish territory.

In 1613 the Dutch went a step further in their efforts to control the exports of the Guianas and to colonize those areas. Their previous method had been to leave factors at various trading posts on the coast and along the various rivers, but now they started to send colonists to settle in the Guianas and provide a guaranteed cargo for the ships returning home. In the year mentioned a few enterprising Zeelandian merchants thus founded a settlement on the Essequibo and, probably later that same year, one on the Corantine. Although energetically supported by Indian allies, these colonies proved to be short-lived—destroyed by Spaniards from neighboring Trinidad.

The record of the Spanish attack on the Dutch Corantine settlement is quite dramatic. Twelve men from Trinidad, twenty from San Tomé, and a priest left Trinidad in August, 1613. Sixty days later they reached their destination. They waited until night, and then called upon the Dutch three times to surrender in the name of the king. The Dutch refused. The attackers succeeded in setting fire to the fort. Because of its palm-thatched roof it was soon ablaze, and all the Dutchmen died in the flames. The number of men in the fort is not known.

This action proves the attitude of the Spanish and Portuguese authorities in the neighborhood. They were, of course, far from sympathetic spectators of foreign intrusions in what they considered to be their domain. Thus, from the beginning they were determined to eliminate such intrusions.[35]

Despite these failures, the Dutch were back in 1615 and founded new settlements at Cayenne, on the Wiapoco, and on the Amazon. In this year a group of 280 colonists under Theodore Claessen of Amsterdam settled at Cayenne, but they seemed to have abandoned that place very soon in favor of Surinam.[36] Further to the east, Dutch colonies were again under way, while plans for a new effort on the Essequibo were seriously discussed. Here we meet the romantic and somewhat mysterious figure of Captain Groenewegen—called Cromwegle in English, and Llanes (from Adriaen) in Spanish documents.[37]

Aert Adriaenszoon Groenewegen was a Dutch Catholic from Delft who had been engaged in the service of the Courteen House, an

Anglo-Zeelandian merchant firm (see Chapter xvi). He had later
served the Spaniards as a factor on the Orinoco responsible to the
authorities of San Tomé. Learning of the failure of the Dutch settlement on the Essequibo, Groenewegen decided to desert his Spanish
masters for his countrymen. He went to Zeeland.

Here the atmosphere was quite favorable for colonizing experiments. Zeelandian burgomaster Jan de Moor was one of the deeply
interested promotors. That he, a Zeelander, went to the rival
province of Holland in order to raise funds may at first sight seem very
strange, but it is not altogether inexplicable. Flushing was a cautionary town; it was, until 1616, under an English commander and a
garrison. The town council felt the foreign presence very distinctly;
the English supervision did not make the town really independent. In
Holland the air was free; besides, this province had become an
excellent market for investments, and her merchants were also
willing to risk their capital in the kind of enterprises which Jan de
Moor was planning.

De Moor received the official support of the States of Holland, and
soon found help from two men experienced on the Wild Coast. Both
were residents of Flushing: Pieter Lodewijksz, ship captain, and his
son Jan Pietersz. Both men had just returned from the Guianas where,
on the shores of the Wiapoco, they had erected a trading post and
had cultivated tobacco.[38] The son had sailed up the Amazon for
more than one hundred miles, and had brought back dye, tobacco, and
different spices. Father and son had made a good profit and told
promising stories about much higher gains. With that prospect in
mind de Moor's company equipped a small fleet of three ships under
the command of Michiel Geleynsse. Pieter Lodewijksz and Jan
Pietersz were the captains of the two other ships. Together they
succeeded in establishing a colony on the Wiapoco.

In the meantime Landsadvocate Johan van Oldenbarnevelt, taking
advantage of the pecuniary embarrassments of James I, redeemed the
cautionary towns by a cash settlement which freed them henceforth
from foreign control. The effect was immediate. Before the end of
1616, two groups of colonists had left the Zeelandian ports for the
Wild Coast.

Our knowledge of these two expeditions rests mainly on the narrative of Major John Scott in his description of Guiana.[39] The
Gouden Haen (Golden Cocq) sailed in 1616 with 150 men who
disembarked on the shores of the Ginipape River. The commander
was Pieter Adriaenszoon Ita, perhaps an older brother of the famous
Dutch Admiral Michiel Adriaenszoon de Ruyter.[40] He was soon to

become famous himself as an admiral of the Dutch West India Company. The colonists built a fort—one of the first things they had to do—on a peninsula and established what Edmundson calls "a fair correspondence" with the Indians whose help they needed in planting tobacco. The *Gouden Haen* returned the next year with provisions and some additional colonists. On the trip home the ship carried tobacco which had been raised by the earlier colonists and some wood. The colony survived six years.[41]

The best known member of the other expedition was Groenewegen. This one was also outfitted by Jan de Moor in cooperation with William Courteen. Groenewegen left Flushing in 1616 with one small and two large ships. He founded a settlement twenty miles up the Essequibo River on a small island, taking advantage of an abandoned Portuguese fort, probably at the same spot where, more than twenty years earlier, Dutch settlers had built Fort Ter Hooge. Groenewegen called his fort *Kijkoveral*, which means "see everywhere."

Because of the excellent way he handled the Indians, they were, for as long as he lived, Dutch allies—a relationship which was strengthened by Groenewegen's marriage to the daughter of an Indian chief. The Dutch were called *parana-ghiri* by the Indians, meaning "men of the sea."[42] Groenewegen was the head of this colony for almost half a century. He died in 1664 at the age of eighty-three, an extremely wealthy man.

The founding of these settlements was very hazardous; long were the lists of those who perished in these regions and short the life span of most colonies. Inexperience and the hostile attitude of the Spanish and Portuguese were important factors in many Dutch as well as French or English failures.[43] In 1615, for instance, Philip III issued a general order that the coast of the Guianas had to be cleared of any foreign settlement. This order not only gave royal approval to former Spanish actions but also resulted in an expedition from Brazil under the command of Francisco Caldeira de Castello Branco to explore the mouth of the Amazon and to check the trading and colonizing excursions of the foreign intruders.[44] This expedition had a lasting result. Caldeira built a fort and laid the foundation for a settlement called Nossa Senhora de Belem. It meant the beginning of the Portuguese dominion on the Amazon. Caldeira also received information from a French refugee—in 1615 a French colony at the Maranhão had been destroyed—that further up the Amazon three Zeeland vessels were trading with the natives. More extensive inquiries told him that the *flamencos e olandeses*—Zeelanders and Hollanders—counted 250 to 300 men who were protected by two wooden forts. They had two sugar mills, while some 150 miles upstream, there was another settlement of Dutch who had their wives and children with them. Consequently, Caldeira immediately sent his forces to these sites. Although they succeeded in destroying a large Dutch vessel, they could not take the forts. The Dutch had a free hand for a few more years in their trade on the big river.[45]

The two forts mentioned above were probably Orange and Nassau. Many of the soldiers were English, former members of the garrisons of the cautionary towns. This explains why they are called Dutch by one author and English by another.[46] The identity of the third fort remains unknown.

Spanish expeditions sent out from Trinidad to wipe out foreign settlements were undoubtedly very successful. Mention has already been made of such action. It is not clear who bought the tobacco grown by the planters of Trinidad in those years, when Dutch *piratas* and *herejes rebeldes* did not dare to drop anchor in their ports. But although Dutch trade and smuggling decreased somewhat in the early years of the Truce, there is evidence that it still continued. A royal *cédula* of 1610 mentions this fact. The coasts and ports of Venezuela were visited, it said, "by enemies of our holy Catholic faith" who were later specified to be "English, French, Flemish, and other nations."[47] Letters from the Spanish ambassador at London to the Duke of Lerma show, in spite of all *cédulas*, that as early as 1611, ships were arriving there with tobacco from the Wild Coast and Trinidad, and the value of the smallest cargoes was 500,000 ducats. Dutch sources reveal little. During the Truce the port of Rotterdam had no record of any tobacco or sugar coming from the West.[48] The same is true for the other towns. Amsterdam regulated the sugar freights in 1610 and 1611 with some charters; they reveal the sources of the sugar to be Brazil, Santo Domingo, São Thomé, the Canaries, and Madeira.[49]

Not much is known either about Dutch activity in the Caribbean area during the first years of the Truce. Indeed, reports of *flamencos* virtually disappear from Spanish records. According to Article IV of the Truce, the Dutch, who had no settlements in the area, could not navigate there. Then, in 1613, Their High Mightinesses again handed out permits to merchants to undertake trade and privateering in the *mare clausum*. Once more the Prince of Orange signed letters of marque and commissions for captains. Spanish complaints then started all over again.

It appears, therefore, that the Truce, for the first years of its application at any rate, had the effect which the Spaniards had hoped for: it stopped Dutch activities in the West Indies. Although some have argued that the Dutch continued to harass the Spaniards in the Caribbean during the Truce, there is no proof that any Dutch sailors were commissioned to privateer or to trade in that area. While they built their colonial empire in the East with incredible speed, the Caribbean was, at least temporarily, neglected.[50]

If Spanish reports lack complaints about the *flamencos luteranos* and *herejes rebeldes* in those days, they are certainly full of another lament: an increasing shortage of commodities had begun to harass the Iberian colonies, a lack which caused much inconvenience. Then, too, the colonists found troublesome the Spanish injunction against tobacco culture, which had been instituted in order to stop the *rescate*. Negro pearl fishers of the island of Margarita, for instance, did not work as fast nor as efficiently as they had when they had been given tobacco. It was soon obvious to anyone concerned that the prohibition against tobacco-raising, which was meant to be enforced for ten years, was simply cutting the colonies' throats.[51]

Thus, although there is no evidence that the Dutch were able to continue their profitable privateering in the Caribbean during the first years of the Truce, it must be admitted that the islands and coasts close to the Guianas enjoyed some illegal trade. But in 1613 the States General, as mentioned before, changed its policy. A year later Their High Mightinesses listened to Usselinx' suggestions and volunteered, through a placard, a trading monopoly for four voyages to anyone who would discover new ports, lands, or localities.[52] In this same year the Company of New Netherland applied for a charter. Merchants from Amsterdam and Hoorn had already traded for some time in the northern regions of the American continent, Hudson's discoveries having paved the road for them. Indeed, his explorations had, if possible, aroused in the free Netherlands a still greater zeal for enterprises and explorations in the West.

During the Truce Spain was constantly informed of developments through her spies in the United Provinces. The efforts of Usselinx, although frustrated in 1609 but gaining momentum after 1614, were faithfully reported. At that time the Archduke Albert informed His Majesty about Usselinx' renewed efforts for a West India Company. This report, forwarded by the Duke of Lerma to the Council of the Indies, said:

The West India Company is likewise being pressed forward by certain merchants, reckless men and enemies of quietness; they are going about through all the towns in Holland and Zeeland to persuade the people to favor it. In no part have they received greater hopes of carrying out their object than in Zeeland, as it is a matter very consonant to the disposition of that part, and because there they will have need of sailors and employment for ships, of which they have so great a quantity that they are ruining each other. They have cast their eyes on the river Orellana, and a caravel has already been dispatched from Flushing to go up said river as far as possible and make acquaintance with the inhabitants thereof.[53]

Many rumors reached Madrid as well. One of them reported that Usselinx, presumably a general with a fleet of twelve men-of-war and six hundred soldiers, was setting out to establish colonies on the borders of three or four rivers in South America and the West Indies. According to the rumor, the colonists were authorized to cultivate rye, cotton, barley, flax, silk, crimson paint, and those things which would destroy the trade of the Canary Islands and bring the West Indies under Dutch control. A similar report advised that Dutch ships of every variety had been commissioned to carry to the new settlements cattle, horses, rabbits, doves, sheep, hogs, and herbs that did not exist in America. These rumors, obviously, envisioned a massive Dutch colonization effort.

More disturbing news followed. In November, 1614, the king was informed that the rebellious provinces were equipping a fleet of sixty sails bound for the West Indies. The main goal of this armada was to be Cuba, especially the town of Havana. Information the next year calculated the naval strength of Holland and Zeeland at seventy-one men-of-war. Another fifteen ships were being built.[54] Puerto Rico was now added as a second goal. At least two thousand pieces of artillery were allegedly being cast in Rotterdam and Amsterdam, with Swedish bronze. The disquieting news then reached Spain that a Dutch fleet was patrolling the Pacific. These rumors were not exactly calculated to reassure the Spaniards about the peaceful intentions of their former subjects.

And they continued. In 1619 it was said that the Zeelanders had been eyeing the Amazon. The Spanish king was so convinced of the truth of this rumor that he ordered the authorities in the New World to keep a special watch in that area. Since the Spaniards had seen Dutch accomplishments in the East, they knew that the United Provinces were only biding time until they could duplicate their achievement in the West. Spain also realized that, in spite of the yearly arrival of the silver fleets, her treasury was chronically empty. Indeed, the once powerful monarchy provided, from a political and economic point of view, a striking example of exploitation and corruption which had neither goals nor stimulation. Spain's intolerant fanaticism and bigoted piety, combined with her mediocre leadership, had resulted in a foreign policy strangled by "an awkward timidity in thought" inspired by fear.[55]   Rigid governmental control suffocated all initiative.

In her colonies, however, Spain continued for some time to be served by some fine governors.   But in spite of many honest and incorruptible men, her colonial system was degenerating into whole-sale exploitation of silver and gold mines, clear proof that she had lost sight of the real richness of the New World, its natural resources, as Usselinx had pointed out.   The country itself had little industry that could supply colonial needs, and its shipping facilities decreased constantly.   It is not easy to explain this "structure of the decrease"[56] satisfactorily.   Although privateering had hurt the Iberians, it was certainly not the only or most important factor that caused the decline of their peninsula.   Perhaps it was the fact that the great forces which had driven them at the outset had simply worn out.   When even Seville finally admitted that the West Indies were no longer a Spanish monopoly, Madrid was still planning to fight to maintain it.

It is doubtful whether, when the Truce was drawing to a close and Spain realized that it would not be renewed, the prospects derived from this knowledge had something to do with her decline.   What Pierre Chaunu calls "the great depression"—the years between 1622 and 1650—had begun even before the Truce had expired.   A new era opened up for Spain only at the end of the war with the Dutch, and with the conclusion of a naval treaty between the former belligerents against their common foe France.[57]

By 1620 the Spaniards realized that they could not afford a renewal of hostilities.   The country was already involved in the Thirty Years' War, the treasury was empty, and the Portuguese possessions in the Far East were gone with their rich revenues.   Out of sheer necessity and desperation Spain set out to obtain a prolongation of the Truce. The king appointed a committee under Ambrosio Spinola to study its possibilities.[58]   This committee proposed that His Majesty should insist on an amelioration of the position of Catholics in the United Provinces and—mirabile dictu—prohibit Dutch intrusion into the West Indies.

A somewhat more realistic approach, however, was provided by Philip's Scottish advisor William Semple.   As early as December, 1619, he suggested the formation of four squadrons to attack and destroy Dutch shipping in the North Sea, along the Iberian coast, at Gibraltar, and in the Pacific.   Semple also suggested that the king authorize his naval commanders to commit privateering on the Dutch, the Hanseats, and the English.[59]

Action had to be taken quickly. The English had given Raleigh permission to equip an expedition to the Orinoco, and the Dutch were said to be planning an attack on Havana. In 1620 the Council of the Indies sent a memorial to the king which declared: "Given the situation in Germany, England, and Holland . . . only a small cause will be needed for the Dutch to forget what still is left of the truce, and for the English to end the peace."[60]

Philip responded by ordering the reinforcement of the garrisons at Santiago de Cuba, Santo Domingo, and San Juan de Puerto Rico, and by equipping a fleet of twenty ships, while reorganizing Spain's military forces in the Southern Netherlands. His hope was that this show of strength would make the northern provinces more reasonable. It did not. The peace party there had lost its spokesman. Contra-Remonstrantism meant orthodoxy and war.

A last effort to bring the rebellious provinces back to their "natural princes" was undertaken in 1621 by Archduke Albert, "tottering on his last legs." But the archduke's proposals were intolerable to the North because they threw doubt on the sovereignty of Their High Mightinesses.[61]

Yet to resume the war was, for the Dutch, a courageous decision. After the death of van Oldenbarnevelt, they no longer enjoyed close relations with France, and England's jealousy was still more dependable than her aid. Then, too, the recent victories of the Catholic League in Germany had strengthened the Spanish position.

But the war was resumed. The Dutch Council of State, at the end of the Truce, sent a circular letter to the provincial governments advising them to prepare themselves for a renewal of hostilities.[62] All merchants, sailors, and companies were warned at the same time. What now occupied the Dutch was best formulated by de Laet in the introduction to his *Yearly Account*: ". . . in what way they could inflict damage on that powerful enemy . . . and take away from him the American treasuries, or make them useless to him, with which he has battered for such a long time the whole of Christianity and kept it continuously in unrest."[63] Under this religious and economic banner, the war was renewed. The man in the street was tired of the Truce, the Contra-Remonstrants were against it, and many merchants were opposed to a continuation. *Multis utile bellum.*

The Spaniards understood what the renewed war meant to their possessions in the West. Their rebellious subjects would cross the Atlantic en masse, organized under a new and powerful company. They would also have all the necessary information and the requested experience. Their goals would be clearly defined and best expressed by Usselinx: "to cut the great artery of the King of Spain" and "to enrich all the inhabitants and enlarge the State."[64]

Now there was no longer any question about the foundation of a West India Company. Frederick V, known to history as the "Winter King," hoped that the renewal of the war would distract Spain from her efforts in Germany and thus end his exile in The Hague. He advised Their High Mightinesses that "he would like to see the West India Company progress."[65] Usselinx redoubled his influential efforts. In 1620, a year before the Truce would end, the States General gave way to pressures from Zeeland. Dierick Ruyters and others, who were mainly Zeelanders, asked permission "to attack those who attacked them first, but also those who tried to put obstacles in their navigation and trade in such places in the West Indies where the King of Spain did not possess effective power."[66]

Happy with the prospects of profit, Amsterdam joined Zeeland. The West Frisian towns of Hoorn, Enkhuizen, and Medemblik, however, were not pleased. A renewed war would create a monopolistic institution that would threaten their lucrative salt trade.[67] The directors of the powerful East India Company worked also against the foundation of the new institution which they could see only as a competitor despite the difference in the areas of operation. But these opponents were in the minority. Clearly, the new company was coming.

In March, 1620, a draft for a charter was provisionally approved by the States General.[68] A final decision, however, was postponed for some time because of difficulties between Amsterdam and the towns of the Northern Quarter. While the parties argued, the representative of Morocco, Joseph Pallacho, arrived with an offer from his sultan to place at the disposal of the Dutch a harbor in his country where much salt was available—a proposition that would settle the salt disputes. But these proposals met with little enthusiasm.

The main problem which postponed the foundation of the new company was whether the salt trade was to be included in the monopoly or not. The West Frisian towns were firmly set against it, since salt was their most important revenue. In the end, the decision was placed in the hands of Prince Maurits. He offered a compromise: the salt was to be excluded from the new monopoly for the time being.

Thus the West India Company was founded. "Take up your task," said Their High Mightinesses,

with the help of God, that has never failed us. The proffered support of the High and Mighty Lords of the States General will always be at your disposal, the advice and succour of Prince Maurits you will always have at hand. Your own experience will not be of small importance. The knowledge of all kind of things was brought to you generously: yes, even the prophesies of a chronicler in Mexico, that those countries will be shortly ruled by people with yellow beards, tall of stature, who, as soon as they will be taken away from the Spaniards, will serve to your advantage.... The Lord may give you good success. [69]

The renewal of the war against Spain now saw two mighty companies in possession of such immense monopolies that they seemed to have divided the world again, as had happened before at Tordesillas. This time, however, it was not the papal authority that sanctified the partition, but instead the doctrines of John Calvin. For the glory of God and for His elect, the world was now to be divided between the Dutch East and the Dutch West India Companies.

5

THE RISE OF A BRILLIANT STAR

Herculeas ultra extulit columnas.

Ioannes de Laet, with overwhelming enthusiasm, begins his *Yearly Account* of the activities of the West India Company with the following eulogy:

Among all the miraculous virtues that have been performed in our time by the State of these United Provinces in terms of the maintenance of the true religion and the protection of our liberty, directed against the King of Spain, I thought to be very remarkable the performances of the Chartered West India Company, and too, because this company, with little power and only a small burden to the State, with money raised by a small number of subjects of this State, has performed so well that the whole world has been awed while Spain's haughtiness has had to give in.[1]

A mere perusal of the chronicle covering the first sixteen years of operation of the Dutch West India Company will reveal the outlines of an institution far removed from the dreams of William Usselinx. Indeed, what had been created had all the inherent qualities of a bellicose organization. The warlike bias of the company was frank and deliberate, because it was motivated by the exigencies of a long and hazardous struggle with Spain.

The charter had been issued only a short two months after the Truce had expired. With its issuance, Contra-Remonstrantism rose like a young David in pursuing an energetic resumption of hostilities against the foreign Goliath. The rationale which had led Their High Mightinesses to support the foundation of an East India Company—to promote unity and regularity in navigation to and trade with those far countries, to prevent quarrels and competition between the merchants, and to fight the hereditary enemy without the direct involvement of the government—prompted recognition of the West India Company as well. Among the motives for its eager acceptance was the expectation that the new company would "remove the resources which Philip IV, King of Spain and Portugal, drew from his American and African possessions."[2]

Promotors of the company called it "a beautiful shining star," and it soon became "the pride of the Contra-Remonstrant party."[3] Unlike the East India Company, the new organization did not have any predecessors in its field, nor was its existence the result of the merger of smaller competing units. It is true that two older institutions, the Guinea Company and the New Netherland Company, had worked within the limits set out by the WIC charter, but both had been liquidated well before 1621. Although many of the shareholders of these two early companies had put their savings into the new company, Dutch possessions previously held in Africa and America were turned over to the WIC as a direct result of provisions within the charter itself.

According to that document, the territory of the WIC was prescribed as the west coast of Africa from the Tropic of Cancer to the Cape of Good Hope; the east and west coasts of America from Terra Nova (Newfoundland) to the Strait of Magellan, Le Maire, or other straits and passages, the Australian or Southlands which lay between the meridians that touched the Cape of Good Hope in the east and New Guinea in the west. In other, and shorter, words it was all that part of the world which was not specifically included in the charter of the East India Company.[4]

The crucial difference between the two organizations evolved from the fact that the older company was mainly a trading institution. Although it maintained armed forces in order to defend essential strongholds and regions, the EIC had been founded for peaceful trade. The colonial empire it conquered in the course of two centuries did not contradict its main goal, namely, to secure a monopoly and a continuous delivery of raw materials.[5]

The WIC, on the other hand, was designed primarily as an instrument of war against Spain. This purpose permeated every decision and dictated every action, even when, as in 1623, the company delivered colonists and their families to New Netherland.[6] The *tâche guerrière*—task of war—always came first. That cunning diplomat and chronicler Lieuwe van Aitzema realized it, and upon the occasion of the company's foundation accurately observed that it had been created "to inflict losses on Spain."[7]

Hence, from its very inception, the WIC obeyed and duly conformed to the spirit of the times. As Andrews has pointed out already, trade and plunder in the sixteenth and seventeenth centuries were inseparable aspects of a common cause. The aims of trade were, in many cases, combined with those of privateering. They comprised together the principal occupations of the age, and attracted noblemen and beggars, rich merchants and criminals.[8] In the Low Countries commerce and plunder were gradually adjusted to meet the demands of Protestantism and patriotism to such a degree that they became indistinguishable. It was an identification particularly well suited for the Dutch. It had become evident even before the turn of the sixteenth century. Although the partnership had been briefly absolved during the Truce, it blossomed forth anew when war was resumed.

One other reason for the advent of this relationship, and likely to increase its scope, was the element of democracy which is inherent in any definition of privateering per se. The Dutch, especially, were faithful adherents of the doctrine of democracy. Calvinism promoted it in its church organization. In effect, it permitted any man before the mast to aspire—and to rise—to higher ranks. Even the most exalted posts, those of admiral or governor, were not precluded from the visions of ordinary seamen.

The Dutch West India Company was founded upon two bases: the reluctance of the national government to extend the war beyond the line, and the readiness of its merchants to accept the burden of a full-scale combat as a Protestant and patriotic duty. Of course, one should not underestimate the profit-making motive which channeled, indeed legalized, anti-Spanish sentiment, robbery, and raiding. In other words, the WIC gave every man a chance to strike at the hereditary enemy on his own account and to make profits in the process. It also alleviated a heavy burden that had reluctantly been carried by the government up until then. Thus the WIC, much more than the sister organization, became a true vehicle for national feeling.

A private person, on his own, moreover, would have been no match in a war against Spain. Intervention by the government was thought to be indispensable, not only for financial reasons but also to give the undertaking a respectable, official façade which would keep it from degenerating into sheer piracy. In this context, then, the WIC became a tool in the hands of the States General, a pliable instrument for renewing the war without running the added risk of incurring official vulnerability.

Although both the East and West India Companies saw profit as their main objects, there was a marked difference in their respective approaches to the fulfillment of this goal. Gains were sought by trade in the East, aided by force if necessary, whereas in the West profit came from privateering. The WIC's task, consequently, was the more hazardous one to carry out. In addition to presuming that privateering would net great profit, the company was also faced with the irreconcilable premise that an organization which had been founded as a war instrument could survive peace. As a matter of fact, the WIC became an anachronism as soon as peace with Spain was concluded, although this fact was not always apparent until much later.[9]

In theory, the new company was a constitutional body incorporated by, and under the auspices of, Their High Mightinesses, and it was to be financed through stocks bought and sold on the open market. The corporate structure combined some aspects of the East India Company together with the suggestions which William Usselinx had proposed at an earlier date. Its charter, or constitution, which was entirely in keeping with a still vigorous feudal tradition, carefully enumerated sovereign prerogatives in order to avoid future misunderstanding.[10] These rights were specified as privileges, licenses, and exemptions. In 1628, a memorial to the States General expressed the company's expectations that a liberal interpretation be made of the rights stipulated in the charter.

As a corporate body, the new company was divided into five chambers which were, in order of their importance, Amsterdam, Zeeland, the Maas, the Northern Quarter (the West Frisian towns), and Town and Country—*Stadt en Lande* (the provinces of Groningen and Friesland). Each chamber had its own directors who were appointed by the members of the Provincial States or by the official deputies and town councils. In addition, those provinces, districts, or towns which were not represented had a right to purchase a seat in one of the chambers for each 100,000 guilders they invested in the company. Out of the total delegates—there were seventy-four in 1621—an executive board of eighteen directors was picked, Amsterdam choosing eight, Zeeland four, and the other three chambers two each. Its nineteenth member was appointed by the States General as its personal representative. Called the Heren XIX, or simply the XIX, these nineteen directors operated under a mandate from and were directly responsible to their sovereign the States General. Besides furnishing the company with semi-official character, privateering as well as other activities were thus subjected to approval by the highest executive and legislative institution in the United Provinces.[11]

In order to discuss problems related to the central administration of the WIC, the Heren XIX were to meet alternately at Amsterdam for six years and at Middelburg (Zeeland's capital) for two. They received no fixed salary—although Usselinx had strongly recommended this—but instead earned 1 per cent on all outgoing and incoming goods except gold and silver from which they received 1/2 per cent. Usselinx had rightly feared that this system would create a fertile soil for corruption, a fact which had been demonstrated by the sad experience

of the Heren XVII in the East India Company. Instead of abrogating
the entire scheme, however, restrictions on the personal conduct of
the XIX were set forth which stipulated that neither trade with nor
within the company would be permitted to them. These restrictions
were marked improvements over the previous arrangements within
the EIC, as time was to show later on. Rather than simply being admonished to be honest, the WIC directors were fully accountable to
their respective chambers; their property and belongings, on the
other hand, could not be seized for company debts.

In the Chamber of Amsterdam, a director was required to have
invested at least six thousand guilders in the company; in the other
chambers the minimum had been set at four thousand. Although
anyone could buy WIC shares and thus become a shareholder or
participant, only those who had invested the above sums, the so-called
head-participants, were eligible to become directors.

Tenure of office on the XIX extended over six years, after which
one-third of its members were forced to resign. The turnover took
place every two years thereafter. Openings were filled from a select
list prepared by the directors and head-participants in consultation
with provincial and municipal authorities. Although this procedure
does not appear very democratic by twentieth-century standards, it
did seem to provide the adequate check on management that had been
so sadly missing in the charter of the East India Company.[12]

Loose and disjointed as this structure may seem, the organization
of the WIC to a considerable extent reflected the system of decentralized rule which was characteristic of the United Provinces, since both
were feeble unions of nearly autonomous units. Contrary to Usselinx'
original proposals, however, the control of the company was vested
in the governing body of the Heren XIX, although the wide powers
conferred on the directors by the charter ultimately depended on
maintaining the goodwill of the States General and of the five chambers. Yet Their High Mightinesses also exercised a considerable
degree of supervision through the director whom they nominated to
the XIX. He had the decisive vote in their meetings, but his association
with the official ruling party was even more important. The sovereign
still retained certain of the *regalia maiora* and commanded the subsidies
without which, in the waning years after 1630, the company might
well have floundered.

The original charter issued to the WIC had a duration of twenty-four
years, for which period the company was granted a monopoly on
navigation and trade. The European countries and waters were
excluded, as was the salt trade on Punta de Araya, mainly because of

the opposition of the West Frisian towns (see Chapter VI). The charter further authorized the company to make contracts and treaties in the name of the States General with "princes and natives" encountered abroad. The company could also build forts, supply fortifications, appoint governors and other officials, and hire soldiers. In all matters, of course, it was expressly stipulated that the States General be informed of company activities. All appointed civil authorities were required to swear their allegiance both to the company and to the States General; officers and soldiers, moreover, had to take an oath to the Prince of Orange.

To alleviate the WIC's oppressing financial burden, export and import cargoes carried aboard company ships were exempt from taxation during the first eight years of operation. In addition, the States General agreed to subsidize its tool of war with 200,000 guilders annually for the first five years, or 1,000,000 guilders. The door was left wide open for the government to intervene with even more substantial aid once the company became involved in active combat. Beyond this powerful monetary endorsement, the States General also offered to lend sixteen men-of-war of at least three hundred tons and four yachts of eighty tons, on the condition that the company would provide a matching complement of ships.[13] Even though the States General was the most important stockholder, it was willing, nevertheless, to accept only half of future dividends.

As was observed before, the charter of the WIC gave the government—at least on paper—a definite measure of influence in the management of the West India Company, a point which had been warmly advocated by Usselinx.[14] Unlike their East Indian counterpart, the Heren XIX always had to reckon with the opinion of the States General, and no decision could be made without previously consulting the governmental echelon. Independent action was vastly discouraged, and all inter-company correspondence had to be submitted to the government for official approval. The notorious financial scandals that had rocked the EIC were likewise taken into consideration in issuing the sister charter since provisions against similar abuses were already provided for. In matters of daily routine, however, the burgher-oligarchy of the XIX was, to a considerable extent, unhampered by these theoretical considerations, and it ruled almost supreme.

Although the government was thus the instigator of the new organization and delegated to it a major share of the war with Spain, the merchant community in the Low Countries was certainly less than eager to commit itself outright to such an unprecedented task and, for some time, entertained serious doubts about the advantages and possibilities of the enterprise. As a result of such considerations, it was not until late in 1623—two full years after the company shares had been put on the market for the first time—that the necessary minimum investment of seven million guilders seemed realizable. Their High Mightinesses were tireless in their efforts to reach local justices and magistrates asking them "to give the inhabitants of these Low Countries a good example by pledging themselves courageously and liberally."15 The Provincial States followed this action by sending letters to their subjects which represented the WIC as conducive "to considerable service, benefit and decency" of the United Netherlands.16 In the more important towns, campaigns promoted subscriptions; for instance, posters were displayed which urged "all princes, gentlemen and republicans, noble and private persons, without distinction of quality or condition, living within these United Netherlands or outside" to sign up. Added to this candid advertisement was the subtle inducement that the directors of the company "would be chosen from the most capable, experienced, and subscribing participants."17 In spite of these earnest endeavors, however, the subscription rate did not proceed as desired, and the period of investment, which was originally set to end in July, 1623, was necessarily extended.18

It was, perhaps, a bad time to be asking for money. In the same year in which the WIC was incorporated, the East India Company became embroiled in serious trouble because of flaming quarrels between its directors and a group of investors known as the *doleerende participanten* (complaining participants). The latter especially criticized the high-handed methods of the Heren XVII, the ruling board of the EIC, their secret resolutions, and their irregular declaration of dividends. A pamphleteering campaign was launched on these and other burning issues which everybody talked about.19 This situation invariably reverberated on the financing of the new company also. It was all very well for Usselinx, the untiring propagandist for the WIC, to say that it was the duty of every good Calvinist to bring the true religion to American shores, but the average Dutch investor saw the company as a bad risk. He based his opinion, with justification it seems, on the irresponsibility shown by the earlier corporate experience in the East. Furthermore, though there had been some trade with the West Indies and Brazil before the Truce, this kind of commerce had soon degenerated and rendered only minimum profits during the years of temporary peace with Spain. Many people doubted that trade in the West could ever be revived, especially since war was the avowed object of the WIC. In the minds of the conservative Dutch, rich profits seemed an unlikely result from privateering.

Usselinx, who had already predicted the slow process of monetary pledges, submitted several memorials and requests to the States General. Although he offered to assist in the general fund-raising, for one reason or another, his good intentions were steadfastly ignored.[20] Other people, however, did take up his cue as is demonstrated by the abundant number of pamphlets written with the special purpose of persuading people to invest, "to encourage the Patriots to a generous contribution to the chartered West India Company." One of these emphasized the obvious advantages and then described in glowing terms the inevitable profits of participation: navigation to the West Indies required only six weeks in contrast to the thirty or forty weeks for the same journey to the East. WIC ships, consequently, would be able to make many more trips than EIC ships. Another pamphlet pointed out that Spain had become a world power because of her West Indian possessions, a position which, before long, the United Provinces, in collaboration with the WIC, was destined to occupy. Such a pamphlet under the inspiring title *Vivid Discussion*, and presumably written by "a lover of the Fatherland,"[21] drew attention to the following interesting items: on an annual basis, the Guinea coast employed 20 ships and 400 men and netted a profit of 1,200,000 guilders. Punta de Araya was visited yearly by 100 ships and 1,800 men, and it produced 1,000,000 guilders in gold. The hide trade with Cuba and Hispaniola occupied 20 ships and 500 men and netted 800,000 guilders. Lastly, the Brazilian trade provided a yearly average of 40,000 to 50,000 chests of sugar, and since each chest was valued at 120 guilders, the total value was at least, therefore, 4,800,000 guilders in gold.

Vivid Discussion rightly alleged that the famed riches of the West lay not in gold and silver per se but were to be derived instead from commodities. To convince the Dutch textile manufacturer to invest in the WIC, the author of these inflammatory pages also shrewdly suggested that by converting the natives to Christianity, which was, after all, a cause close to the Calvinist's heart, the demand for cloth, to cover the former pagan's shameful nakedness, would undergo some spectacular changes.

In this and in many other ways people were sold on the idea of investing in the novel company. Actual contributors, however, continued to be few in number. Despite all these determined efforts to glorify and propagandize the advantages of overseas trade, privateering, and colonization, much more than words was needed to separate the cautious Dutchman from his guilders. Even the fact that the States General was pumping one million into the company failed to offer an inducement for investors.

This slow progress preoccupied Their High Mightinesses to a considerable degree, as the minutes of their meetings so clearly illustrate. The decision which they finally reached was to stimulate participation and increase investments by increasing the prospect of higher and surer profits. This meant the inclusion in the company's charter of the profitable salt trade of Punta de Araya. Despite much West Frisian objection, the salt trade was included in the WIC by an official decree of June, 1622.[22] The many difficulties that developed from this decision will be dealt with presently (see Chapter VI). In its initial effect, however, the move did cause a substantial boom in investment money.

Among the investing speculators were, first of all, great merchants like Balthazar Cooymans, the brothers Samuel and Daniel Godin, Laurens Reaal, and Pieter de Graeff. Second, many other people, from all classes in life, were now likewise attracted: ministers of the Dutch Reformed Church, accountants, bookkeepers, knifemakers, pharmacists, jewelers, tailors, sheriffs, housewives, and maidservants, anyone, indeed, who was eager for quick gain. Much more so than the East India Company, the WIC had suddenly become a popular investment object, especially for the little man. Foreign contributions were also substantial. The sums ranged from the 36,000 guilders put up by the Prince of Anhalt to the many small pledges of not more than 50 guilders, which were attributable to housewives and maidservants, payable in three installments.[23]

Even a partial examination of investors reveals at once that the WIC was very much a creation of popular Contra-Remonstrantism. While the EIC consisted mainly of a society of wealthy oligarchs—the so-called regent class—the WIC had more support at lower levels. Around a small group of responsible members, the head-participants, there was a large and anonymous class of shareholders. Although these investors had no voice in the management of the joint stock enterprise, they were devoted and in many cases active members of the Dutch Reformed Church, and saw the war against Roman Catholicism and Spain as a religious duty by which they could serve both God and the interests of their purses.[24]

Investments were not always on a purely voluntary basis since pressures of various kinds were occasionally exerted in order to enforce participation. The Utrecht Chapter of the Dutch Reformed Church, for instance, contributed under protest. In Rotterdam, the

chief town in the Chamber of the Maas, there was likewise a conspicuous lack of enthusiasm. The city council there found it necessary
to resort to certain devious measures in order to assure the cooperation of its own directors. A committee of subscription was specifically
designated and recruited from among its local members. The names
on the list indicate the kind of people who were willing to step
forward in the battle for WIC funds: Nicolaes Puyck, burgomaster and
merchant; Cornelis Corneliszoon Jongeneel, merchant; Dirck Pieterszoon van der Veen, merchant and sailmaker; Joost Adriaenszoon
van Coulster, brewer and former skipper in the merchant marine;
Jan Franszoon de Vries, merchant; and Jan Gilleszoon Poppe,
wine vendor.

But in spite of these tentative thrusts, only 4,300,000 guilders of
the required 7,000,000 had been received by the end of 1623, when,
in 1624, in return for a directorship whose duration was co-extensive
with the charter of the company, François Aerssen van Sommelsdijk
donated a magnificent sum on behalf of the Chamber of the Maas.
Other towns like Deventer, Arnhem, and Zwolle, without representation themselves, soon followed this stimulating example and invested—although somewhat hesitantly—their burghers' hard-earned
savings.[25] Thus the sluggish and phlegmatic attitude of potential
investors, which had prevailed until the salt trade of Punta de Araya
was incorporated in the charter, dissappeared almost completely, and
the new institution found itself finally on a solid financial basis.

In Amsterdam, the cradle of the company and the town which was
expected to benefit most from the new enterprise, subscriptions
proceeded more smoothly. The sole reasons for this exemplary
conduct were the eighty-three head-participants who gave the city
an important voice in the conduct of company affairs. From among
the latter the city-fathers appointed twenty directors, while there
were eight Amsterdammers on the Heren XIX. From the very start,
therefore, Amsterdam played a pivotal role in the company, and
unhesitatingly plunged into a venture whose outcome was shrouded
in uncertainty, by providing one-third of the initial capital needed.[26]

Because of this calculated gesture by Amsterdam to gain for itself
the upper hand in the new company, an intense rivalry between this
chamber and Zeeland was inevitable. It was not long in coming into
the open. Since Zeelanders had been the most enthusiastic pioneers
of colonization on the Wild Coast, that chamber, operating within the
company, jealously guarded its prerogatives in the area from encroachment by the vigorous contender. Fortunately for Zeeland, the
Amsterdam Chamber was more interested in North America, although

their respective interests did compete in the Caribbean. The friction between those two chambers was exactly the kind that Usselinx had feared and against which he had warned so unflaggingly. It was also the very reason why he had urged Their High Mightinesses themselves to assume supreme command of the company.

The competition between Amsterdam and Zeeland was further exacerbated by the contradictory goals which the company professed to achieve. Although it had willfully taken up the risk of war in African and American waters, it simultaneously desired peaceful settlements in those areas which were claimed by the Spanish king. Article II of the charter, for instance, authorized the company to promote "the population of fertile and uninhabited areas," yet colonization was always a secondary consideration despite Zeeland's enthusiasm. It only gained in importance after peace with Spain had been concluded.

In addition to the problems of slow subscription and West Frisian opposition to the incorporation of the salt trade into the charter (see Chapter VI), the company encountered many other obstacles. First, the town of Dordrecht clamored for its own chamber, but the charter stipulations made this desire impossible. Then there was trouble between the head-participants and the directors: the former accused the latter of committing irregularities and complained about their lack of influence in the management of the company. The States General, in an arrangement made in February, 1623, tried to straighten this situation out by granting certain rights to unsatisfied head-participants, i.e., a voice in the selection of directors. The concession was an unimportant one, and it came too late to alter—at least for five years—the terms of office for the present directors; the balance of power within the company had already been set. It was agreed, however, that the first two vacated seats in the Chambers of Amsterdam and Zeeland and the first one in the Chamber of the Maas would be occupied by an appointee of the head-participants. It was further conceded that one of the eight directors of Amsterdam, who was also a member of the XIX, had to be a head-participant nominee. Another amendment which the States General accepted forbade any individual from being a director in the WIC and the EIC at the same time; even close relatives could not serve as directors in the two companies simultaneously.[27]

Further difficulties with the Chamber of the Maas were the next item on the WIC's agenda. Because of the strong influence of Dordrecht in that Chamber, a request was submitted to allow the Maas

three representatives on the XIX, instead of the two hitherto authorized. The charter once again frustrated Dordrecht's hopes. Surviving
records of the discussions and deliberations amongst the XIX indicate
how seriously this issue was taken by both parties.

Other problems abounded. Before long, counterfeit shares were
dumped on the market, and the WIC, with the full support of the
States General, had to be protected against them. Many placards
against these forgeries were issued from time to time, which is
evidence that the evil was never effectively rooted out.[28] In 1624,
moreover, the government approached the Heren XIX with a proposal
that it merge with prospective French and English companies with
similar aims. Although the idea of combination was not altogether
foreign to Dutch experience—at the end of the Truce, for instance,
the Dutch and English East India Companies had been united for some
time—the answer of the WIC was an emphatic "No!"[29] Another
predicament which harassed the WIC was the high costs of the huge
preparations undertaken for the Brazilian expeditions in 1623 and
1624. Taken together with the equipment for two smaller expeditions, these costs forced the company to request an increase in capital
of 50 per cent. The States General consented to this increase without
question.[30]

Among the bitternesses which Usselinx had had to bear, undoubtedly the heaviest was the fact that the charter of the WIC had so
little to say either about the colonization or the Christianization of the
regions to be conquered. This omission is even more remarkable
when one reflects that the WIC was the creation of Contra-Remonstrantism, to be used specifically as a tool against Catholic Spain.
Hoorn's protest against the inclusion of the salt trade in the charter
was overruled, for instance, purportedly because of the town's
sympathies to the Arminian cause.

One finds many familiar names among the first WIC directors.[31] There
was, first of all, Ioannes de Laet, the company's first chronicler and
an eyewitness to many important events in those early years. Another
notable figure was Samuel Blommaert, who was, like de Laet, from
the Southern Netherlands. Blommaert had been in the East Indies,
and he knew Africa well. He had also participated in the New
Netherland enterprise. Other illustrious personages include the
shipowner Samuel Godijn, the merchant Albert Coenraets Burgh, the
jeweler Kiliaen van Rensselaer, and Michael Pauw, a member of the
city council of Amsterdam.

Among the Zeelandian directors, one finds Pieter Boudaen Courteen of the famous Anglo-Zeelandian Courteen firm, Jan de Moor, the Lampsins brothers, and Joost van der Hooghen, all merchants who had proven their worth many times over. The eminent van Pere family, a scion of which became the founder of a Zeelandian settlement on the Wild Coast, was also intimately involved in the company's affairs. Not to be overlooked was Geleyn ten Haeff, burgomaster of Middelburg and an ardent advocate of colonization in the Guianas.

In the Chamber of the Maas Dordrecht was represented by Cornelis van Beveren and Delft by Adriaen van der Goes. A relative of landsadvocate Johan van Oldenbarnevelt, Adriaen van der Dussen, also occupied a directorship. The West Frisian Chamber was represented by burgomasters among whom Boudewijn Hendricksz of Edam was the best known.

When the war was renewed in 1621, the WIC became a spearhead in the struggle against Spain, not only on the seas where it earned an exhilarating naval record, but also in the more prosaic field of diplomacy. For all the fighting that soon started, peace talks with Spain opened immediately at the end of the Truce. These were continued intermittently until peace was finally concluded in 1648, and were thoroughly influenced by the two great monopolistic companies. In these negotiations each success and each defeat was weighed on the scale of diplomatic arguments to see whether it contributed to or detracted from the desired goal. Any formal attempt to analyze the international position of the Dutch in the seventeenth century, therefore, cannot underestimate the major role which the Heren XVII and XIX played in the diplomatic process. For the West India Company, the obstruction of these negotiations was a matter of survival and for more than twenty years it was successful in its efforts to stimulate a continuation of the war. It should never be forgotten that the XIX rightly perceived that the end of the war was a threat to their very existence.

The WIC actually possessed very little of the enormous regions theoretically assigned to it. It controlled a small part of New Netherland, Fort Nassau, and two or three trading posts on the African coast. In the Guianas the Zeelanders had a few settlements, Essequibo being the most important one.

These then were the circumstances under which the company decided to pay more than just lip service to the nucleus of its embryonic empire. It decided to organize a system of government which would allow both a successful continuation of the war against the hereditary enemy and the pursuit of a policy of colonization. To these ends, two alternate but not necessarily mutually exclusive methods were adopted. In the first instance, the WIC decided to provide its prospective settlers with free land overseas on the condition that they conquer the area, subdue the natives, and raise the Dutch flag over the new territory. Second, the company could also choose to grant private patents to certain meritorious citizens or to corporations of citizens who would act as patrons. The patron system followed the general precedents as set by England and France, standards which, in turn, were derived from the Portuguese *donatario* system. The scheme had, in northern hands, evolved into a "proprietary patent" whose "patron" was generally a rich merchant, or a group of merchants, organized in a company.

The patent system was much like feudalism, i.e., the patron received title to a colony as if it were a fief and he had certain monopolies and political rights. In this way, a hierarchy of government was interposed between the individual subject and the company. The Heren XIX or the respective chambers thus became an intermediate source of authority as well as a court of appeal in colonial affairs. All existing and future patronships were brought under the special supervision and jurisdiction of one of the chambers.

The colonists were placed under obligation both to the company and to the patron according to a peremptory set of instructions laid down in the patent. An example of such a conditional grant is that given by the company to Abraham van Pere in 1627. He was authorized to occupy that part of the Wild Coast situated at the river Berbice.[32] The patent further stipulated that van Pere was to bring sixty colonists to the region. Transportation would be provided by the company which charged the patron a price of fifty guilders for each person over sixteen years and twenty-five for all others. Although the company furnished artillery and munitions, indeed all provisions, the patron had the right to appoint the leader of the enterprise. The appointed head was responsible for all matters of government together with the distribution of justice, after his first task—the construction of a fort—had been accomplished.

Under the leader's direction, the colonists were allowed to lay out their plantations wherever they wished within the limits of the patent, preferably near the fort. All navigation and trade between the colony and the United Provinces was to be done by the company. No other trade was permitted except with the natives, and all goods produced by the colonists had to be sold to the company at specified low prices. Lastly, the WIC enjoyed a fifth—comparable to the *quinto* in the Spanish American possessions—of the value of any and all minerals discovered in the patent territory.

For some time—usually a few years—the colonists were exempted from any taxes on food or other daily commodities that had to be imported. They were forbidden to do any weaving—this was one instance in which the company consciously sought to protect industry in the Low Countries—but ordinarily there was little insistence on curtailment of industry in the colonies. In marked contrast to their French and English counterparts, the Dutch settlers in the Guianas, for instance, were in no way prevented from building their own sugar mills. On the contrary, the company even promised to provide the necessary slaves for this industry.

As for the colonists' remaining needs, the patron was required to provide both a "visitor of the sick" and a "Bible reader," whose functions were comparable to a nurse and a teacher of religion. Although the Dutch Reformed religion was the only one originally permitted in the colony, gradually the Jews were quietly allowed to exercise their religion as is proven by several patents made out to Jewish colonists who were emigrating to the Guianas and Curaçao. Furthermore, the colonists were expressly warned not to commit adultery with the Indian women since it was "atrocious to God and most hateful to the Indians." In short, the patron was responsible for all the colonial projects that were within the limits of his patent.

In general, the advantages for the patron were many, despite the fact that the WIC had the last word. As a middleman, interpolated between the company and the colonists and backed by an exclusive monopoly on overseas trade, he was able to wring vast profits from both parties.

The van Pere patent, mentioned before, was an amended edition of the one given to Jan de Moor some time earlier (see Appendix III). Provoked by necessity, the Heren XIX had introduced changes specifically in order to promote the colonization of the Wild Coast and to make the venture more attractive to future settlers. The first expedition after 1621 was set up as a patronship under company auspices and was originally scheduled to comprise at least twenty families. The obvious intention was to bring women and children to the Guianas at this time. The article was, however, dropped in 1627. The "Conditions for Colonies adopted by the West India Company" continued to be amended several times but only in minor details.

At home, many Dutchmen put all their hopes in these patronships and were doubly assured by the fact that their investments were protected by the highest authority in the land. Although the risks were plentiful, these shrewd merchants were all too willing to have a crack at such a novel kind of profit-making. As a matter of fact, the van Pere patent soon became so popular that it served as the immediate precursor for two subsequent undertakings.

Dutch colonization in New Netherland was instigated by a patronship as were some colonizing ventures in the Antilles and on the Wild Coast. Amsterdam had been most insistent in colonizing the former area; in the latter case it was the Zeelandian Chamber that had implemented a patronship which had already existed before the foundation of the company and which now was organized under its supervision. Sometimes patrons had ideas contrary to colonization, such as establishing bases for piracy and privateering, but upon discovery, the Heren XIX quickly revoked their patents.

The weakest link in the patron system soon proved to be the paramount matter of defense. Since neither the Spanish nor the Portuguese could tolerate the presence of others in the territory they solemnly considered to be their birthright, there was bound to be trouble. The Dutch expeditions, therefore, always went accompanied by ample military power, yet, ultimately, the responsibility for defense rested solely on the leader. Although all men above the age of sixteen were compelled to do military service—in those days all colonists were likewise soldiers—nevertheless and in spite of elaborate precautions, the system did not always deter Iberian or Indian attacks.

The patron, of course expected to collect interest on his investment in short order. Hence, from the outset the colonists were made to realize that it was their duty to develop a productive colony as soon as possible. Ordinarily, the first trip by the company's ships to bring colonists and supplies overseas produced virtually nothing in return cargoes. But by the second year they could be expected to return home laden with products from the farms and fields of the colony. According to an instruction given to the Zeelander Jan van Ryen in 1626, he and his associates would receive one-third of the net profit.[33] The remainder found its way into the pockets of the company or its supervising chamber.

In the administration of the colony, the leader, who was appointed by the patron with the approval of the chamber under whose auspices the colonizing venture was attempted, received the assistance of a council that was composed of the most prominent and best educated participants. This assembly had certain legislative powers, supervised commercial legislation, and also acted as a court. In the absence of a well-groomed and seasoned system of colonial law, the maritime code in force aboard the ships which brought the colonists to their new residence was temporarily transferred to land in order to cope with the new circumstances and to preserve law and order in the new territory.

As soon as the colony became established, the West India Company applied its orders and regulations.[34]

Although representing the Dutch merchant-oligarch class, the patrons nevertheless many times lacked the prerequisite funds to finance any large-scale enterprise over a long period of time. As a result, their enterprises were customarily fitted out by the WIC on an installment plan. The XIX levied the amount of money necessary for the venture from each chamber. Not infrequently one of the chambers itself would undertake a private expedition to that region in which it had a special interest. The ties which bound Amsterdam with New Netherland and Zeeland to the Caribbean were of this private nature.

The States General supervised the activities of the company scrupulously and often summoned directors to The Hague for a personal report. When the Bay of All Saints was captured, for instance, Their High Mightinesses intervened immediately. On the spot they issued a set of regulations for the Brazilian conquest. Some years later they published an "Order of Government" which was to function as a guide for all regions already or anticipated to be under Dutch control. The right to issue such regulations was part of the *regalia maiora* which the States General had claimed as its prerogative from the outset.

The Portuguese rebellion against Spain, which was launched in 1640, ushered in an era of crisis for the WIC. The subsequent loss of Brazil followed by the English conquest of New Netherland made public the fact of the WIC's decline. These circumstances sharply curtailed its decision-making power because the States General increasingly began to interfere in company resolutions and eventually forced the Heren XIX to accept a purely subordinate and menial position. No longer did the company equip expeditions except those strictly authorized and financed by the government. After 1640 it deteriorated from a mighty war instrument into an ordinary smuggling and slave-trading organization.

Yet these first twenty years were proud years for the company. Virtually on its own, it was able to wage an offensive war against Spain in which the tremendous energy and indefatigable perseverance of its sponsors were well rewarded despite the overwhelming odds. From the outset, Spain had ample cause to fear it and to view the formidable development of its strength with suspicion and alarm. Indeed, even before the WIC had commissioned its first ship, rumors of possible attacks in Spain's enormous American domain circulated in Madrid, causing panic in the court and sleepless nights for the king's ministers. They realized only too well the vulnerability and weakness of their colonial empire, and they trembled for the safety of the treasure fleets. They were terribly aware that capture of the fleets would be a double calamity, because Spain would be deprived of her lifeblood and her European power position would be paralyzed, while at the same time an enriched West India Company would be a more dreadful opponent than ever.

The ambiguity of its goals did not keep the WIC from ambitiously aspiring to a major role in international affairs. Despite serious financial setbacks in the thirties, the company continued to expand its colonies and strongholds in Africa and America until 1640, and to maintain its initial vigorous thrust. The high point in this part of its career perhaps came when Peg-leg Jol successfully invaded São Paulo de Luanda and São Thomé. These resounding victories, however, were only a small part of the many hostilities directed against Spain on a scale hitherto unknown in history.[35] The Caribbean, which the Dutch salt carriers and smugglers had up to now visited only in a desultory way, became for twenty years the hunting ground for hundreds of Dutch ships, most of which belonged to the WIC or were commissioned by one of its chambers. Those Dutchmen who dared to interfere with its monopoly, the so-called interlopers, were threatened by the government with confiscation and other punishment.[36] During the first period of its charter, which lasted until 1647, company revenues were largely derived from privateering; a mere one-third of its profits were traceable to peaceful trade, smuggling, and salt-carrying.

In those first years, then, privateering took care of almost all company expenses. For this purpose two sets of books were kept: one accounted for legitimate or illegitimate trade, the other larger one covered the remaining more forcefully tainted entries. Article XLII of the charter carefully prescribed what was to be done when prizes were taken: the company could claim "necessary expenses," the Prince of Orange received his "righteous part" (10 per cent), and the crew of the victorious ship received another righteous part of 10 per cent of the total net value. The surplus went into the company treasury. Part of this was eventually paid to the stockholders or participants in the company as dividends; the rest was used to outfit other ships and new expeditions, to pay company officials in Africa, America, and at home, and to maintain company trading posts, forts, and garrisons. In case of such an unexpected windfall as Piet Heyn's capture of the Spanish Silver Fleet, extra dividends were paid. Because of its one-million-guilder investment, the States General was entitled, as was every other stockholder, to the full dividend paid out by the xix. In Article xxxix, however, it renounced this right in favor of accepting only half of the dividend due—another means of subsidy.

As has been pointed out various times before, the West India Company was less a commercial enterprise than its East Indian relative, and peaceful trade never really became important until after the renewal of its charter in 1647, when the company was ushered into what de Laet called "the advantageous trade in Blacks." Doubtless, the fur trade in New Netherland also offered many opportunities, as did the trade in gold and elephant teeth from the Gold Coast. These more conventional possibilities, however, were never fully appreciated. After the conquest of northern Brazil and during the governorship of Count Johan Maurits, when the company might have exploited many products from that region, it only showed interest in sugar and brazilwood and evidenced no desire whatsoever in following up the fortuitous chance to develop the new colony. This option would have involved peace and colonization plus the wherewithal to exclude every other country from dealing with the settlements. Based on its experience and that of all colonizing European nations, the wic directors were fully aware that rampant smuggling—at the expense of the Dutch this time—would be the inevitable result of such a venture. For this very reason they preferred war and privateering.

The company's experience in war and privateering suggests that it used its monopoly in quite a different manner from the eic. More than the latter, the wic showed no reluctance to license private entrepreneurs for purposes of trade, smuggling, and piracy within the physical limits of its charter. The geographical imperative forced the wic to relinquish certain rights and to loosen the rigorous maintenance of its monopoly even in the farthest corners of its extended domain. Rather than presenting opportunities for dodging its charter, it allowed private individuals—at a so-called recognition fee—to trade, smuggle, and privateer in areas not *de facto* occupied by its settlements, forts, or trading posts.[37] Many Amsterdam merchants, especially, profited from this accomodation. A regular and rewarding navigation to the Gulf of Mexico sprang up, instigated by the fact that the area proved to be an extremely valuable market for Dutch linen. The islands of St. Christopher (or St. Kitts) and Tortuga, the latter located north of Hispaniola, were indeed converted into way stations for these private entrepreneurs. After 1640, the Lesser Antilles gradually became almost exclusively dependent on this kind of licensed trader who even built warehouses on many of these islands, before English

Navigation Laws and Colbert's West India policy tried to suppress the trade. Dutertre mentions a fire on the island of Martinique in which 60 Dutch warehouses were burned with losses to these merchants of more than 200,000 *livres*. And a declaration of the governor of Barbados, Francis Lord Willoughby, issued in 1651 thanked the Dutch for their past help and assured them that "they may continue if they please, all freedom of commerce and traffic with us." This offers but another example of Dutch activities and the significance of this type of enterprise permitted by the West India Company.[38]

These licensed traders and privateers did not, of course, always respect the areas which the company reserved for itself, and many commanders of its fleets and squadrons, Jol for instance, complained bitterly about the competition. One particular problem was posed by New Holland or Dutch Brazil, an area which the company stringently claimed to hold exclusively, but which it regularly failed to provide with essentials. The inhabitants of this settlement tirelessly sent complaint after complaint to the XIX and to the States General, and serious discussions were soon heard about whether the company should or should not abrogate its monopoly there. As early as 1630, with the conquest of Pernambuco's Olinda, the States General had indicated its approval of an open policy for Brazil, retaining for the Heren XIX the right to extract a "recognition" fee from every merchant eager to encroach upon this trade. But actual free trade did not come until a few years later.

In 1632 the Caribbean was thrown open to any Dutchman who was willing to run the risk of an encounter with the Spaniards without the security of governmental endorsement. In addition to providing his ship with proper armament and ammunition, this same merchant was also expected to hand over 20 per cent of his hard-earned net profits.[39] It should likewise be mentioned that once this open trade policy came into effect, any and all merchants, Dutch, Portuguese, and Jewish, were allowed to operate under licenses issued by the WIC.

This "free" enterprise could be carried on, in addition to the payment of the "recognition" fee, under the following conditions: the captains had to pledge their word that they would respect the persons and properties of inhabitants of the United Provinces and their allies; they had to pay homage to the officials of the company; and they had to provide aid or bring themselves under the flag of the company's naval commanders when and wherever requested. Further, their cargoes had to be brought to company warehouses and sold there. In order to assure compliance in all these matters, each ship leaving the home ports carried a "super-cargo"—an official of the company.[40] He had to be treated with respect and ate his meals in the captain's cabin.

To provide additional revenue, the WIC was authorized to collect a recognition fee from any Dutch ships which sailed under a foreign flag, yet returned from the Caribbean to a Dutch harbor. After 1637 this regulation applied to all ships, Dutch or otherwise, that sailed from or entered a Dutch port. The WIC also collected convoy and license taxes levied on ships sailing within the limits of the company's charter. These taxes had once been a most important source of revenue for the admiralty boards, and their resentment at this so-called WIC usurpation was not unnatural. Yet the States General opted in favor of the company.

In 1633 trade by private entrepreneurs was expanded to include Pernambuco. Although New Netherland and the west coast of Africa never came under serious consideration for open trade, at least not during the charter of the old company which lasted until 1674, the opening of Africa became a bone of contention for the Heren XIX as early as 1642 and again later. Amsterdam was strongly in favor of open trade, and though the original proposal was first rejected, especially because of Zeelandian opposition, free trade was introduced to Brazil. The only exception was the company's fortresses, since it was tacitly understood that the whole coast included those sections still under Iberian control.[41]

Not all the chambers agreed about this free trade policy within the company's monopoly. Zeeland, for instance, stubbornly championed a strict monopolistic course, while Amsterdam, on the other hand, stood by the new trend. Both chambers had their reasons dictated, as always, by the imperative of the purse. The Zeelanders realized that once the monopoly was abrogated, they would soon be outstripped by Amsterdam in every respect. The latter city, for exactly the same reason, argued the contrary: "What has made the town of Amsterdam so splendid among so many others? Is it not the multitude of private traders, and these not Netherlanders alone, but likewise those of all nations in the world who can move and trade freely in the town according to their good liking." The argument was spiced because of strong Calvinist feelings and corresponding anti-Catholic sentiment in Zeeland. These sentiments favored continuation of the war against the hereditary enemy, and were also prevalent in the Chambers of the Maas and *Stadt en Lande*, while the capital was turning toward a less orthodox, less anti-papist, and more liberal view which favored peaceful relations with the Catholic Iberians. No free citizen, argued Amsterdam—quite unlike its position of 1621—could tolerate the stringent rules artificially imposed by the monopoly. It was "the most hideous thing in the world and the most harmful action."[42] The company, Amsterdam further contended, should be more than satisfied with the receipt of duties and fees.

While affirming free trade, Amsterdam unconsciously tread upon a dilemma which the company was never able to solve satisfactorily. The wic, it was alleged, was at one and the same time a subservient enterprise and the sovereign ruling body in the territories under its protective wing. In the former capacity, its duty demanded the maintenance of the highest possible prices; as a system of government, however, its responsibility was to keep them low. Realizing that the company was torn between such conflicting principles, Amsterdam sought to palliate the differences by encouraging plain, ordinary competition which would serve to check monetary inflation. Yet, despite many heated arguments, Zeeland was not won over to the capital's point of view, and the situation did not cease to undermine cooperative relations between the two chambers. The controversy became especially tense as the company continued to consolidate its hold over Brazil. At that point, indeed, the Amsterdam Chamber went so far as to insist guilelessly on free trade between the Lusitanians and their kinsmen in Portugal.[43]

During the conquest of New Holland (Dutch Brazil), the States General received endless complaints about the inefficiency of the wic and its shortcomings where the needs of the new colonists were concerned. These did not lessen even with the favorable course the war was taking for the Dutch, notwithstanding the fact that many merchants, with an eye on profit, had clandestinely settled at Recife, Pernambuco's stronghold. The latter were doing a thriving business in that area by exchanging Dutch and European commodities for sugar and other Brazilian products, including wood, which was supposed to be a company monopoly. Word of this illegal activity soon reached the Heren xix and acted as a powerful antidote to arguments for free trade. Only Amsterdam remained obstinate and offered her subsidies with a proviso that the limits of trade would remain undefined in Brazil. Faced with such an ultimatum, the Heren xix had no alternative but to acquiesce to the capital's wishes and to withdraw all commercial restrictions. In an attempt to offset Amsterdam's ascendancy, however, Their High Mightinesses took the precaution of recommending one of their most trusted henchmen to assume the governorship of New Holland: Johan Maurits, Count of Nassau-Siegen. Only in this way could they rest assured that their interests would not be ignored and their rights respected. Their recommendation was promptly followed by the count's appointment.

During the year 1636 deliberations on free versus closed trade continued to appear on the company agenda. The Heren XIX had appeared to agree with Amsterdam the year before, but now had second thoughts about their previous rashness and instead sided with the opposition. The States General adopted a similar stand, not only because of the notorious readiness of the Amsterdammers to trade with the enemy, but also because it was discovered that many of the *vrijluiden* or free-traders were from Amsterdam or took their orders directly from the capital. This caused alarm, especially in Zeeland, and predisposed the XIX to favor the opposite position. Hence, at the close of 1636, the XIX and Their High Mightinesses agreed on the steps to be taken. On December 27 of that same year, open trade was abolished and the company's monopoly re-established.[44]

Although this decision was much applauded in Zeeland, it was not only protested by Amsterdam, but also by the Northern Quarter, which had never forgiven the WIC for including the salt trade of Punta de Araya in its monopoly, and by the Portuguese and Brazilian merchants who were living under Dutch rule. Soon another objection came, this time from Johan Maurits. The latter's dispatch probably changed the official attitude in favor of the free-traders. In an attempt to solve this dilemma once and for all, Their High Mightinesses resolved to settle the matter by vote. It now became apparent that the Amsterdam Chamber itself was openly divided over the issue. Some of its members, for instance, abstained from voting in favor of monopoly for fear that they might meet repercussions in their trade relations from the capital's mighty town council. Eventually the city of Dordrecht declared itself opposed to free trade and sided with Zeeland; she would not concur to any increase of capital unless the matter be banned permanently. Their High Mightinesses' request for a vote brought the opposition of the Chamber of the Northern Quarter out into the open as well. The West Frisian towns, because of their interest in the salt trade, acted accordingly.[45]

Despite these contradictory attitudes, the influence for free trade because of the powerful position of the capital proved to be the stronger, and Count Johan Maurits' highly evaluated advice born out of local experience convinced those who still vacillated. The Dutch capture of Breda in 1637 led the Spaniards to renew their requests for peace or at least for truce talks, and their action ultimately tipped the scales in favor of free trade. Late in that same year, a compromise was found: the West Indies were opened subject to a license and the company's ulterior approval; the same arrangement applied to Brazil. The company, however, reserved for itself the trade in slaves, ammunition, and brazilwood. In other words, although it did not relinquish its rights entirely, it was forced to grant privileges because of circumstances beyond its control. Just as before 1636, participants in the company enjoyed certain preferential trading terms, such as 5 per cent reduction on freight rates.[46]

"With these decisions," wrote Wätjen, "the States General had created a sound basis for trade and navigation."[47] In time, the same regulations were expanded to cover the colonies in the Caribbean and along the Wild Coast. Essequibo and Berbice, however, which were both Zeelandian patronships, remained outside their scope until late in the eighteenth century.

As a self-admitted vehicle of war, the West India Company was consistently against all negotiations with Spain that might produce either a new truce or lead to an end of the war. From the outset, the directors knew that a cessation of hostilities could well mean the folding of the company.

The Spaniards, on the contrary, were eager to reach some sort of understanding with the Dutch. Yet Philip IV, ably assisted by the Count-Duke of Olivares, failed to grasp the underlying fundamentals. As an instance of their misconstruction of the facts of their position, it seems particularly well suited to note that on the eve of the great Spanish defeat at Matanzas, the king and his minister were seeking to impose truce conditions upon the United Provinces. Freedom of religion for the Dutch Catholics was demanded; the sovereignty of His Spanish Majesty in the northern Low Countries was to be recognized by an annual offering. The Spanish military commander Ambrosio Spinola knew full well that this second qualification automatically shut the door on any reasonable negotiations and hesitated to even submit these ridiculous proposals to the Dutch.[48]

In 1629 private Spanish overtures to their former subjects became common knowledge, and the influence of England and France combined to make the Dutch more amenable to peace discussions. Strong opposition, however, especially from Zeeland, prevented these mutual undertakings from bearing any fruit. Meanwhile, even the chances for a possible armistice deteriorated rapidly after the capture of the Spanish Silver Fleet by Piet Heyn.[49] That coup had not only greatly "hardened the pride of the Dutch," according to the Infanta Isabel, but had also whetted their appetite for further adventures in the West Indies.[50]

Many contemporary pamphlets are eloquent testimonials of this renewed popular interest. As an inevitable concomitance most were

Fig. 5. Eugenio Caxes: The Reconquest of San Juan de Puerto Rico

Fig. 6. Pieter Pieterszoon Heyn

frankly and manifestly in favor of continuing the war and considered a truce or peace as a "future peril." Some went so far as to repeat the old Zeelandian maxim of twenty years before, Don't trust the horse, Greeks. Most loudly they praised the WIC and were unanimous in lauding its past performances. From these general eulogies, it was only one step further to affirm that talk about peace at the time was tantamount to stifling in the bud the company's future prowess.[51] Another group not to be overlooked in this verbal skirmish was the Dutch Reformed clergy. In Zeeland, where these virtuous ministers had their largest following, a long memorial was published in defense of the war.[52]

The most vigorous resistance to talk of peace, however, came as was to be expected from the East and West India Companies. Although both foresaw more profits from a state of belligerency than could be procured if peace returned, the WIC was especially aware that its entire future was at stake. A detailed and eloquent remonstrance was presented to the States General entitled "Considerations and Reasons of the Lord Directors of the Chartered West India Company against the actual deliberations on a Truce with the King of Spain" which cleverly defined the company's official position. In this long and tedious account, the WIC argued that, since Spain's power had been so drastically depleted in the years since Philip III's reign, the WIC could not help but benefit immensely from a continuation of the war. This testimony did not fail to emphasize the many glorious achievements of the company since its inception. It had given employment to some fifteen thousand people; at sea it could count more than a hundred ships, most of which were men-of-war; the booty and riches which were brought to the Low Countries were recounted in flourishing terms, and the capture of the treasure fleet was especially given as an example which would be well worth repeating. Of course, the damage which had been inflicted upon the King of Spain was likewise alluded to in no uncertain terms, as were also the dire consequences predicted for the Dutch should they incline towards a more pacific attitude: the end of all prosperity, and a boundless opportunity for Spain to recoup her losses and to regain the initiative at will.

William Usselinx did not remain silent for very long either, and soon moved to the forefront in the clamor against a Spanish peace. Never one to hide his feelings, he wrote an ardent discourse and sent copies to the States General, the States of Holland, and the States of Zeeland. In his opening remarks, he roundly declared that the only ones interested in a truce were the Spaniards themselves in alliance with the "papist" Dutch and with other enemies of the state. He emphatically stressed the decline of trade during the first truce and concluded that if anyone could prove him in error, he would join without further ado the ranks of those proclaiming, "The truce, the truce, long live the truce!"[53]

Yet in the long run, Philip's contemptuous attitude struck a strident chord in the hearts of the Dutch, and the odds all seemed to favor a permanent situation of siege. In 1630, moreover, the possibility had come to light that France might well enter the war on the side of the United Provinces. The fortuitous capture of two important towns, 's-Hertogenbosch and Wezel, gave the Dutch another cardinal vantage point. Despite these events, the contact between the two countries was never broken off completely. Philip IV, for one, based on the report submitted to him by his spies, did not give up hope. As a concilatory gesture which was intended to promote a mutual sphere of harmony, the king tried to distract the Dutch from the West Indian salt pans by making Spanish and Portuguese salt available and by authorizing the infanta to issue fifty passports to Dutch carriers.[54] When, in 1630, the Dutch captured strategic Pernambuco, Philip became even more concerned about the need to secure a truce notwithstanding his mounting domestic difficulties, not the least of which came from the irate Portuguese. He insolently tried to put his bad luck to work for him by baiting Charles I of England with glowing accounts of Dutch strength and aggressiveness.[55]

Whenever serious peace talks seemed about to begin, however, the flurry of pamphlets increased, and the Contra-Remonstrant clergy thundered biting sermons from the pulpit. The States of Holland persuasively argued that the WIC would not perish should peace come, but the town councils stubbornly resisted the truth: "That the West India Company would be maintained does not convince us of the desirability of peace because the (Spanish) king will use all the power at his disposal to defeat us on land and at sea (and) against the Company to conquer her ... no profits can (therefore) be expected to accrue in the near future, only vast preparations and ultimate ruin."[56] In 1630 the Heren XIX also published their opinion in a "Remonstrance against a peace with Spain" which largely duplicated what they had said a year earlier.

Diplomatic parleys reached a new impasse in 1633, as a result of which the States General issued an official declaration that a truce was no longer considered appropriate. In addition, it called for general fasting and a day of prayer in behalf of the continuance of the war. The dragging negotiations were renewed a few years later, but by then, in 1635, the French had entered the Thirty Years' War and had signed a treaty with the Dutch concerning the partition of the Southern Netherlands. That agreement might well have meant the demise of these provinces except for the fact that the Dutch finally came to perceive their Belgian neighbor as a convenient buffer between them and the French.

Now the northern provinces were prompted to write a defense of the war which advocated the WIC as a pillar of the state, necessary to the salvation of the fatherland. The publication of this apology attended the current revival of an old proverb, "Il peut bien peu qui ne peut que nuire."[57] The close relationship between this saying and the activities of the West India Company did not go unnoticed and was obvious to one and all.

The loss of Breda in 1637 caused much dissatisfaction in Madrid and eliminated a valuable trump in the peace-or-truce card game. Hence Olivares' earnest and fervent prayer, "May God give us peace so that we may live untroubled and I can die."[58] In the meantime his countrymen were betraying this very purpose by simultaneously equipping a grand armada while they were talking peace in the 1638 conference at Cologne. Yet after a few more deplorable encounters with the enemy—one at The Downs, the other off the coast of Brazil—in which the Spaniards were badly beaten, Philip IV confessed, "The issue of peace with the Low Countries can no longer be avoided."[59]

But peace was still years away; in fact an agreement was not finally reached until 1648. The Portuguese rebellion at the end of 1640 changed the entire international picture and diverted the precarious course which Dutch foreign policy had hitherto pursued. Although the further vicissitudes of Dutch-Spanish relations do not concern us here, it nevertheless seems appropriate to indicate that when peace inevitably came, the flickering star of the West India Company was bound to fade. As a body whose directors could not but regard all issues primarily from the standpoint of sheer profit, this vehicle of war, at long last, had outlived its usefulness. But it still was a long time—1674—until formal liquidation.

Because of its spectacular achievements in Africa, New Netherland, Brazil, the Pacific, and the Caribbean, the West India Company had been the sparkling center of a brilliant firmament of Dutch achievements. On the other side of the ledger, however, were the continuous financial crises that drove the company deeper and deeper into bankruptcy. The sad truth came to light too late that privateering simply did not pay. Its colonizing ventures, moreover, had emerged too late and had found too little support from official and popular consensus to save it from an ignominious death.

6

THE BATTLE FOR SALT

Al is de Sallem schoon,
De Haering spant de Kroon.[1]

Through all the exitement which attended their large and small enterprises to the West, the Dutch never lost sight of an important asset, the significance of which historians have tended to overlook. The battle for salt, which lasted more than sixty years, lacked the glamour of the other activities—the glory of the conquest of Bahia and Pernambuco, the excitement at the capture of the Silver Fleet—but was no less bloody, stubborn, and cruel.

It had all started with herring. The herring fishery was, as a Dutch saying goes, "the mother of all commerce." "God had made of Holland and the herring business an example of His blessing for all the world," observed Meinert Semeyns, herring historian and lawyer of Enkhuizen, in the seventeenth century.[2] Herring brought the Dutch to the North Sea, to Dogger Bank and Spitsbergen, then on to the Catholic areas of Europe where religion provided a profitable market. Salt was needed to preserve the herring, and it was also used in the butter and cheese industry of the country, as well as for curing victuals for use on long voyages. Zeeland did little fishing, but had perfected a process for whitening salt which was in demand all over Europe.

The Dutch had found salt of excellent quality on the Iberian coast at Setúbal, often called Saint Uves in contemporary histories and chronicles. When this abundant source of supply was cut off, they were forced to feel their way beyond the old boundaries of commerce: the Sound in the North and the Strait in the South. In search of salt, the Dutch ventured south as far as the "Salt Islands" (the Cape Verde Islands) and eventually to the West Indies.[3] Any history of the Dutch in the Caribbean, therefore, cannot but emphasize the consequences of the ensuing salt trade.

Most Dutch historians of the period give an account of the size of the herring fleet: it grew from 150 ships in 1550 to more than 4,000 a century later. Already as early as 1555 there was a meeting at

Enkhuizen to discuss problems of this fleet and "to contrive plans for certain regulations and advantages or profits from this trade."[4]

Throughout the early years of the rebellion against Spain the Dutch continued to buy salt in Iberian ports. Then came the arrests; the price of salt rose drastically, and the Dutch sought new salt pans. An Enkhuizen skipper luckily hit upon an island pan which supplied him with a shipload of salt within sixteen weeks for the round trip.[5] The discovery was stimulating, and larger ships were immediately fitted out. Soon salt of good quality was procured from the Cape Verde Islands, and the provincial government of Holland permitted ships to go to these islands even though Amsterdam tried to demand a reopening of trade with the Iberian peninsula.[6] The salt trade with Spain had meant a double cargo—to and from the country—and was therefore far more profitable for the Dutch, but voices which opposed enriching the enemy through commerce and revenue did not long remain silent and could not consistently be ignored. The Cape Verde Islands thus increasingly became the main target for Dutch salt carriers. The most important suppliers—Isla de Mayo and Isla de Sal—continued to receive a vast influx of Dutch ships until 1598, the year of Philip III's first arrest. After that date they began to resort to the newly discovered salt pans in the West Indies along the Venezuelan coast and especially at Punta de Araya—or Punta del Rey—pans which provided excellent salt in nearly inexhaustible amounts.[7] As Laspeyres put it, "The purpose of this navigation was for the Dutch not to find gold or silver as it was for other nations, but in the first place to find salt."[8]

It is probable that the Zeelandian expeditions to the Guianas and Tierra Firme after 1594 furnished information about these salt pans, although the only extant account of those voyages, that of Cabeljau, does not mention it specifically (see Appendix 1). But shortages which had pushed the Dutch to the Cape Verde Islands now drove them across the Atlantic. Too late their need for salt was used by Philip III as an economic weapon to gain political ends; in a letter to Archduke Albert of the Southern Netherlands, the king pointed to the possibility that the salt shortage might drive the northern provinces to sue for peace. The archduke, on the other hand, informed by Dutch Catholics, sadly reported that the rebels had already landed at Punta de Araya and advised his sovereign of the route taken.[9]

Before the Dutch arrived on the scene, the salt of Punta de Araya had been little exploited by the Spaniards. The many accessible pans, spread all over the coast and on many of the islands, were more than sufficient to satisfy local needs. Pearls, not salt, had been the main attraction in the area for the Iberians; the beds of Margarita were already known in Columbus' time. Although salt was not of any interest at that moment—nor for some time to come—a governor of Cumaná, Diego Fernández de Serpa, had taken official possession of the salt lagoon of Araya two generations after the pearl beds had been discovered. Not long thereafter the lagoon would make its appearance in world history.[10]

It is extremely difficult to estimate the size of the Dutch salt trade before 1600. After that year the evidence is sufficient to accept an average of one hundred carriers per year.[11] Beginning in March, 1599, the resolutions of the States General are filled with requests about privateering commissions for salt ships, whose specific destination was given as Punta de Araya. That summer witnessed at least fourteen Dutch visits, and eight more Dutch ships loaded there in the fall. Soon the place swarmed with Dutch carriers; often there were fifty or more ships simultaneously, many of them from Hoorn.

Profits ran high; salt seemed to grow on the bushes, and if the heavily laden ships managed to avoid the hazards of the Atlantic and the vigilance of the Spaniards, the voyage could be completed within sixteen weeks. The Dutch ships were generally described as *grueso* (huge) in the Spanish accounts. The average carrier amounted to some three hundred tons. This means that the total annual tonnage employed by the Dutch in the salt trade was at least thirty thousand tons and probably more.

The West Frisian towns of Hoorn, Enkhuizen, and Medemblik were the most active in the salt trade, precisely because of their prosperous fishing industries. As early as 1602, when the navigation to the new pan had just been initiated, a kind of "salt congress" was called at Hoorn, attended by the representatives of West Friesland or the Northern Quarter. The meeting led to a decision to endorse the salt trade on the new lagoon. Because of the dangers involved in this intrusion into the *mare clausum*, the assembly also heard a petition from Hoorn on protective measures "for ships that would sail to the West Indies in Punto Rey for salt."[12] The provisions agreed upon included the following: that the ships would sail jointly under an admiral; that they would carry armaments, artillery, and stone throwers, and that while at the salt pan they were to choose a commander on the shore who would organize their defense. The respective vessels were levied to pay the admiral for his extra duties, and infractions of the rules brought punishment at home.

De Laet describes the salt lagoon of Punta de Araya as "a corner of the continent laying around the southern part of the west end of

Margarita; about five miles from that point a cliff runs into the sea; that is where the salt pan is."[13] The description is undeniably vague. De Laet never saw the pan and relied on the testimony of others. A far better description is provided by the Italian military engineer Juan Bautista Antoneli, who was sent by Philip III to investigate the salt pan with a view to inundating, closing, or fortifying it against Dutch intrusions. Antoneli was well acquainted with the Caribbean, for he had designed the fortifications on Puerto Rico, in Havana, and San Juan de Ulúa. Of his various reports to the king, the *Relación* on Punta de Araya is one of the most revealing.[14]

The lagoon of Araya was situated halfway between the island of Margarita and the town of Cumaná, capital of the province of the same name, on a peninsula which stretched toward the west parallel to the coast, forming the northern shore of a long bay where ships could safely anchor protected from the trade winds. The peninsula was fifty miles long and ten wide. Its western tip was called Punta de Araya; the pan lay some five miles to the southeast, less than half a mile inland from the bay. It was a natural salt lagoon and not connected with the sea in any way. Its salt, moreover, was of high quality, 30 per cent better than that of the Iberian peninsula. The pan was not a rock salt deposit, but rather a gem salt which came from the brick-colored clay of the surrounding hills.[15] The rain, separating the salt from the clay, washed it down from the slopes into the valley, where it formed a salt lake. The constant easterly trade winds, combined with the tropical sun, caused the water to evaporate quickly, leaving thick layers of salt on the lake bottom. This natural process had been going on for centuries. The size of the deposit was graphically described by Governor Diego Suárez de Amaya: "The pan is so fertile that one thousand ships can easily freight there at the same time, and it increases so fast that every twenty days another thousand ships can come and load—and this the whole year around."[16] The easy accessibility, at least from the sea, the lack of defenses in the early days, and the fact that its salt was "the finest and the best that existed in the whole world"[17] made Punta de Araya the invasion center of Dutch salt carriers.

The deleterious effects of an uninterrupted throng of hostile ships in this part of the Caribbean was soon felt by the Spaniards. The Dutch, naturally, did not limit themselves to the exclusive exploitation of the lagoon. Along with the salt carriers came the merchantmen, who carried on the *rescate* while the former went about their business. Nor were the salt ships themselves adverse to a little smuggling on the side. While the huge vessels lay at anchor in the

Bay of Refriegas—the anchor place for Araya—the sloops and pinnaces, brought along for just this purpose, proceeded to prey on
Spanish coastal shipping, to raid the pearl fishers, and to trade
generally. The results were an increase in smuggling, a serious
disruption of the pearl fishery, and a breakdown of Spanish intercolonial communications. Madrid soon received many complaints
from its administrators about a situation which was rapidly worsening.[18]

One of the first complaints came from Pedro de Fajardo, governor
of Margarita, who sent a full report to the king. He had visited the
pan, considered inundation impossible, and recommended instead
that it be fortified. His letter arrived in Spain as the first Dutch salt
carriers returned to the Low Countries with the news that Iberian salt
could be dispensed with. In Spain they had to pay duties; in Araya
they could shovel it free from the shore—and the quality was considerably better.[19]

In June, 1600, Diego Suárez de Amaya became New Andalusia's
new governor, and his eloquent pleas for help against the Dutch soon
reached Madrid. He had placed observers in the neighborhood of
the pan—on a hill named Maurica—where they could simultaneously
observe the lagoon, the islands of Margarita, Cubagua, and Coche, and
a wide stretch of the sea. When enemy sails were sighted, the town of
Cumaná was warned by signal fires to take necessary precautions.
Suárez de Amaya saw to it that the king was constantly informed of
what was going on, and his reports constitute an accurate picture of
Dutch activity in the area.

The Dutch carriers, unescorted by warships but armed, sailed in
squadrons directly from the Netherlands to the Lesser Antilles on the
east side of the Caribbean. There, usually on St. Vincent, they took
on wood and water, captured and slaughtered some goats, and proceeded to Margarita. From this island they crossed to Punta de
Araya. The average crew was fifteen or twenty men, depending on
the size of the vessel. The average armament was four to twelve
cannon, some muskets and harquebuses. As soon as the ships had
dropped anchor in the bay, the men disembarked and sentinels were
posted. Some of the crew would dig trenches, and others brought a
few cannon to defend themselves against possible Spanish attack.
They then turned to building sheds and jetties from wood brought on
the ships. These led from the shore to the salt pan. Squads of crewmen broke up the salt surface with long iron bars; the chunks of salt
were then stacked in wheelbarrows and taken to the little boats which
were to carry them to the ships. The work was impossible in the
daytime, due to heat and the glare from the salt, and thus was done in

the evening and through the night. Since the salt also ate away leather, the crews worked in wooden shoes. Spanish attacks and heavy work meant regular casualties among the men, and the dead were buried near the lagoon and their graves marked with wooden crosses.[20]

Lack of fresh water at Araya forced the salt haulers to send their small boats to nearby rivers once a week. The Spaniards often prepared an ambush at the fresh water source, yet their many ill-contrived attempts to rout the salt carriers were never effectively executed, and the Dutch continued their activities virtually unchecked. Suárez' constant vituperations, during his five years as governor, covered all phases of this activity, and regularly deplored the fact that he had so few men to stop the intrusions. By May, 1600, he requested three galleys to be stationed at the entrance to the lagoon in order to prevent access and to protect Cumaná, Margarita, and Caracas. In Madrid a similar idea was expressed in a decision which vouchsafed a squadron of eight galleys and three advice-boats for the protection of Cumaná. Later, however, the king, who was of the opinion that this force would be inadequate anyway to face the large number of Dutch ships, canceled the command. Suárez, on the other hand, did not give up and was soon requesting a force of two hundred to three hundred men to conceal themselves in the bay and catch the Dutch unawares. At the same time he suggested that the Spaniards build a fort at Ancón de Refriegas, where the Dutch usually dropped anchor.

In Madrid the problem was seriously discussed and four possible remedies emerged: to poison the lagoon, to inundate it, to dam up the lake and cut off communication with the sea, or to construct a fort manned with a permanent garrison. Inclining towards the first proposal, Suárez, in December, 1600, requested that huge quantities of poison be sent; this suggestion, however, was not accepted by Madrid. In May, 1601, Suárez made a personal inspection trip to the salt lake and wrote an extensive report of his findings. He concluded that inundation was impossible, and once again he alluded to the construction of a fort for the area. A certain hill, situated at the entrance to the bay, seemed to him of much strategic value; a fort there could block all traffic.[21] Meanwhile, the governor of Margarita suggested that the Spaniards dam the lagoon.[22]

It was difficult for Madrid to make a decision, yet a solution was increasingly necessary. Suárez' extensive and vociferous protests could no longer be summarily dismissed. Again and again the good governor pointed to the consequences of the Dutch intrusions: the loss of royal revenue, the loss of prestige, the damage done to inter-colonial traffic and to the pearl fishery. In 1601 the Dutch had kidnapped the treasurer of Margarita in broad daylight and had carried off the royal *quinto*—some thirty thousand pesos worth of pearls. A further result of the Dutch infiltration was that the *veladores* (watch-men) of Maurica had to stand watch day and night and, hence, could not cultivate their tobacco fields nor tend to their cattle in the valleys of Cariaco and Cumanacoa.[23]

According to Suárez' communications, the number of Dutch ships involved was alarming: from June, 1601, to June, 1602, his *veladores* had counted a total of 96 Dutch ships; in the next year that number rose to 172.[24] Don Diego begged the king to consider seriously this invasion of *rebeldes luteranos* (Lutheran rebels) and to send experts to the lagoon to advise on appropriate measures to impede further use of it by the *flamencos*.

In 1604, Margarita's governor, Fadrique de Carcer, had made another inspection tour of the salt pan accompanied by two engineers from Cádiz, who thought it should be possible to obstruct the entrance to the lake with stones and earth.[25] In the same year the king also sent Juan Bautista Antoneli to Cumaná to investigate the situation. Upon the latter's arrival, he was met by an ailing Suárez who, nevertheless, had himself carried to the pan on a litter. There were no Dutch carriers at Araya at the time, and Antoneli was able to go about undisturbed, drawing maps and visiting the nearby fresh water rivers where the Dutch habitually got their drinking supply. The two men next visited the governor of Margarita, who had also fallen sick. The three agreed that something must be done, and soon. Secrecy was presumed impossible because of "the accursed traffic that exists with smuggling boats." The rebels would soon be alerted to what was going on.[26]

Antoneli's report, written after his visit to Araya, included a careful examination of the possibilities of excluding the Dutch from the salt pan. He rejected damming the area because it was a much too difficult operation: it would take too many men too long and would lead to loss of life because of the heat. The dam would only act as a temporary deterrent, anyway, since the Dutch could easily shovel through the bank at another place. The construction of a fort, which was Suárez' hope, was also discussed by the Italian engineer and approved, although he did not agree with Suárez' location. That solution, as they both knew, was very expensive: it would cost thirty thousand ducats just to build it, and fifty thousand ducats a year to maintain it.[27] Because the Spanish treasury was always empty, this plan seemed hardly worth mentioning.

But in the course of his investigation Antoneli had discovered what others had denied: that the sea was at least fifteen feet higher than the salt pan. That discovery dictated the solution: inundation would be the best and most effective way to stop all intrusions by the enemy. Antoneli recommended that a canal, protected at either end by a wooden palisade, be dug from the lagoon to the sea. For his proposal he suggested that the Crown supply four galleons and six hundred men to provide a guard for the laborers. The same purpose was behind a proposal to build a platform for guards to watch the anchorage that the enemy frequently used. The Indians and Negroes, who were to be used for the digging, were to be recruited from the neighborhood; each region was to send a quota. Antoneli, who wanted the work done quickly, also proposed that the laborers be paid for their work—"as the people were poor and very needy"—and the plan executed before the Dutch learned of it and took countermeasures. To get the job done quickly would mean that more men would have to be recruited than were available, and Antoneli asked to have five hundred Moors brought from Andalucía. In case the king also chose to send Negroes, Antoneli thought it advisable if only *bozales* (men unused to hard labor) were sent, because these would die and would thus save the extra expense of their return trips.

In a letter from Suárez de Amaya to the king about the project the need for secrecy was stressed: if the Dutch found out, they could fortify the pan before the Spaniards got there.[28] In addition, the Spaniards were informed in August, 1605, that a huge fleet had left Holland and Zeeland to practice *rescate* in the West Indies. Earlier in the same year, the Spanish War Council had already heard that four other sizable Dutch ships had entered Gonaïves, on Hispaniola, and captured seventeen ships. Rumor had it that these were part of the larger fleet headed for the Caribbean.[29]

Immediate action was necessary—to inundate the lagoon would take too much time. The Dutch had already begun to supply arms to the Caribs and set up a blockade of the islands. The Spaniards countered by sending an armada to the West Indies. It sailed under Luis de Fajardo in September, 1605, supposedly headed for Flanders (see Chapter III). Unexpected in the Caribbean, it thus managed to reach its destination there without interference. Dutch carriers, in their usual anchorage off Ancón de Refriegas, were taken by surprise. The Spaniards seized eight or nine salt ships and one of the Dutch privateers. Two other privateers escaped. The Dutch crews which had escaped death in the first attack were taken to Cartagena and sent to the galleys.[30]

Dutch accounts of the capture, especially the one written by Velius of Hoorn, stressed Spanish cruelty: "They treated skippers and crews very roughly; some were hanged coldbloodedly after they had been prisoners for some time. Some were drowned, some had their legs broken." At least eight of the salt carriers were from Hoorn, and the town sustained a material loss of over 100,000 guilders.[31] Deeper than the monetary sacrifice, however, was the legacy of bitterness which the Spaniards wrought by their actions at Punta de Araya.

Fajardo remained for a month at the salt coast. Hunting was good that season; he overpowered at least twelve more Dutch ships, and some English and French ones as well. His success led to plans for a squadron of light vessels which were to be designed to guard the coast and the lagoon. That plan, like most others, floundered on the catastrophe of the Spanish treasury.[32] The king delayed, but there was no immediate hurry just then. The Dutch were thoroughly intimidated. "The salt trade," wrote Velius, "was totally lost."[33] The States General met the possibility of a sharp increase in the price of salt by refusing to grant licenses for its export to other countries.

The Dutch were frightened, but not for long. Soon they recovered and their salt carriers and smugglers returned to the Caribbean. In 1606, Suárez' successor continued the litanies about the Dutch invaders.[34] Spanish measures like the relocation of the population, taken in the meantime, had eliminated some of the menace of the *rescate*, but nothing had been done about preventing the removal of the king's salt. Once more the governor asked that the lagoon be inundated. The Crown, however, enamored of a proposal to dam up the pan, set aside six thousand ducats for the latter project. Within a year the effort came to a standstill because of lack of money. Fortunately for the Spaniards, negotiations with the Dutch for a truce were in the making, and the dam project was altogether abandoned.[35]

When the Truce was concluded in 1609, Dutch activity in the Caribbean slowed down considerably, and the salt carriers became infrequent intruders. The situation was not really due to the Dutch wholeheartedly supporting the articles of the Truce so much as it was due to the availability of salt in Iberian ports. They could now carry this commodity from Setúbal at reasonable prices, thus making excursions to the West unprofitable.[36]

Meanwhile, in the meetings of the States General and the Provincial States of Holland, serious discussions were underway concerning the launching of a Dutch West India Company. The safekeeping and development of the salt trade were pivotal factors in these conferences and determined their final outcome. The West Frisian towns, at first, offered stubborn opposition, and were quite unwilling that this trade be incorporated within the monopoly envisioned by the founders. Because of their attitude, the towns were soon accused of being pro-Spanish. The charges were, of course, groundless. The West Frisians had declared their willingness to an amicable relationship as early as 1607,[37] and only wanted to secure their ancient privileges from encroachment by the new enterprise.[38] The Truce further delayed the birth of the new company, as well as a solution to the related problem of the salt trade. Van Oldenbarnevelt was likewise opposed to a West India Company, precisely because it threatened to curtail freedom in the salt trade and thus hurt the herring industry. The West Frisian towns were ultimately appeased with a charter which specifically excluded Punta de Araya from the new company's monopoly.

Slow subscriptions to the corporation's capital, however, made the directors reconsider the decision about the salt trade. The States General was persuaded that the inclusion of West Indian salt in the company's monopoly was not against the general interest, and negotiations with the West Frisians were once again opened to amend the charter. Understandably the towns, led by Hoorn, resisted overtures from the company and sought to reason with Their High Mightinesses. The company's response was to request an exclusive monopoly in salt carrying for itself, thus, it was argued, barring the inferior salt of the Cape Verde Islands and the Iberian coasts from competition. These latter sources being eliminated, the company's directors shrewdly envisioned a rise in the price of salt, a factor of paramount importance in their calculations. Usselinx, furious with these monetary preoccupations, wrote two eloquent memorials against these proposals to the States General.[39]

Their High Mightinesses, on June 10, 1622, voted to include the salt trade of Punta de Araya in the company's charter. They did not, however, forbid the importation of salt from elsewhere. The result of their action was that noncommissioned carriers now set themselves to exploring new sources of salt outside the limits of the company's monopoly. When they found them, the monopolistic price scheme which the company had hoped for was prevented. Furthermore, ever present interlopers in their staked-out territory also upset the directors' grandiose scheme.

The West Frisian towns did not relinquish their aims without a stiff fight. The conflict between some of them, especially Hoorn and Edam, and the company was prolonged over many years. Three towns agreed to the company's monopoly so long as there was a guarantee that the price would not be forced up. Hoorn and Edam, however, because of their particular interests in the salt trade as well as their shipbuilding business, could not accept the monopoly. They refused to publish the decision of the States General conceiving the company's monopoly and continued to outfit and arm vessels for their private ventures. The tensions which resulted from this "cold war" lasted for several years. Usselinx, former foe of the company monopolies, gradually retreated from his earlier rigid viewpoint and ended up by endorsing the inclusion of the salt trade in the company's charter. His pamphlet of November, 1621, *Necessary points to have the West India Company continued*,[40] stated clearly his position in the matter. He rightly argued that the comprisal of the trade would encourage the investment necessary for the company's survival.

While the West Frisian towns were thus divided amongst themselves over the company's realm of influence, the States General, in 1625, decided to intervene and asked Amsterdam, Dordrecht, and Delft to mediate the difficulty. More than a year later the deputies of those neutral towns proposed a compromise: the belligerent towns would be allowed to exploit the Araya lagoon for four years while paying the required duties and "recognition" to the company. This solution was finally accepted, but not without rancor. It did protect the monopoly through a transition phase, and made it easier to resume at the end of the preventive period. After 1632, however, and probably as a result of continuing agitation, the company permitted free trade under certain conditions in the Caribbean.[41] No exception was made with respect to the salt trade.

Meanwhile the war against Spain had been renewed, and as early as September, 1621, the governor of Cumaná, Diego de Arroyo Daza, learned from the lookouts on the Maurica hill that at least six Dutch ships were anchored at Ancón de Refriegas.[42] The Dutch went about their business as though there had never been an interruption. Arroyo was able, however, to frustrate the Dutch attempts to get fresh water from the Bordones River, and he immediately issued a ban on the *rescate*. In his letters to the king he pointed out that the *navio de registro* which should have brought supplies to the colony had not come and that, therefore, he did not really expect the population to obey the published interdict. He also indicated that if His Majesty did not buttress the lagoon immediately, the Dutch would do so and thus threaten to reduce the entire province. Finally, the governor requested that the funds, which still remained from the abandoned dam project, be released for use in constructing a fort.[43]

A few days later, ten other Dutch salt carriers arrived. The Spaniards were able once more to prevent the Dutch from gaining fresh water, and compelled them to leave the area, forced to abandon their jetties and sheds. In the wake of Spanish destruction, more than twenty Dutchmen were claimed killed in this encounter at Bordones. In a later report to the king, the governor of Margarita corroborated the event and added that the Dutch had since taken the precaution to fortify the lagoon. This was, however, not true.

Madrid, finally, came to realize the danger of a Dutch occupation and suggested that the governors of Margarita and Cumaná get together with a local engineer to see whether the Dutch fortifications could be completed and used by the Spaniards. At the same time, the king promised to send twenty pieces of artillery, thirty harquebuses, and forty muskets, all of which were to be paid for by the governor of Cartagena. During 1622, two engineers, Cristóbal de Roda and Juan Bautista Antoneli, son of the earlier Antoneli, arrived at the pan and drew up a plan for a fort.

The governors, too, met at Araya to discuss the fortification. They agreed on a hill, the *cerro de Daniel*, on which, years before, Fajardo had hanged the Dutch he had caught at the pan together with their leader Daniel de Moucheron. Curiously, a year later, one of the governors, Andrés Rodríguez de Villegas of Margarita, wrote to the king and advised him that the Dutch threat had been greatly exaggerated and that the fortifications then being built were an unnecessary expense to the Crown.[44] In the interim between meeting and letter, however, the pan was fortified, the artillery put in place, and a garrison of a hundred men had arrived at Cumaná. The garrison was stationed at the fort of Santiago del Arroyo de Araya, a designation which, as Ojer observes, included the location, the patron saint of Spain, and the name of the governor under whose mandate it was to enter history.[45]

On November 27 of that year forty-three Dutch salt carriers made land at Punta de Araya. In spite of the Spanish fort, which must have come as a surprise to the Dutch, they dropped anchor at Ancón de Refriegas, bombarded the fortifications for two days, then disembarked more than a thousand men. Arroyo was on hand for the ensuing battle, and his men had the good fortune to kill the Dutch admiral, the ensign bearer, and four captains. Discouraged by such losses, the intruders retreated to their ships in the midst of a spirited Spanish attack which cost many Dutch lives. The Spaniards continued to fire on the departing ships, but four of the artillery pieces burst, and Spanish accuracy was notoriously absent. More thorough were their Indian archers who harassed the Dutch for a long time. With little wind and under heavy fire, the Dutch retreated across the bay, out of reach of the Spanish guns. The Spaniards boasted that they had sunk three of the salt carriers.[46]

The victory did not end Arroyo's worries, however. On the next day, a fleet of sixteen salt carriers arrived, which joined the remnants of the other fleet then in the bay, and together they sent an ultimatum to the governor: surrender our dead, the prisoners, and the fort. Arroyo declined and waited. A few days later the Dutch sent another letter which was full of dire threats if they were not allowed to take on salt. Again the governor refused, and the Dutch sailed away. They next appeared off the coast of Hispaniola where they caused much alarm but were subsequently dispersed by a heavy storm.[47]

A few weeks later, in January, 1623, another fleet of forty-one ships came to the pan. For two days these ships blasted away at the Spanish fort, but in vain—there was no surrender. Indeed, the Spaniards had gained some accuracy in their firing and drove the Dutch back out of range and eventually away from the pan. The fleet visited three other Spanish-held pans but was unable to load salt, and the Dutch returned to Holland empty-handed. By this time 106 vessels had made the trip to the West and returned without cargo. It occurred to the Dutch that Punta de Araya was lost as a source of salt unless they also seized the lagoon and fortified it. Arroyo Daza had done a great service for his king even if his claim that "I don't know if there has ever been such a great victory in the world" sounds a little exaggerated.[48]

The losses in ships and men suffered by the Dutch during these incidents were important, of course, but were not nearly so keenly felt as the decrease in profits and the shortage of salt. The fort had been a highly effective barrier despite Dutch scorn: *Kostverloren* (loss of expense), as it was nicknamed, had cost the Dutch between one million and two million guilders in cargo.[49] Encouraged by his victories, Arroyo requested funds for another, smaller fort to make the pan really impregnable. This request was met with favor. Two ships with three hundred troops and twenty pieces of artillery were dispatched to keep the pan in Spanish hands. The smaller fort, however, was never built. Indeed, in 1628, perhaps because the Dutch threat was no longer imminent, the famed Santiago del Arroyo de Araya was not even finished. This was not accomplished until twenty years after its inception and only at great cost to the Crown.[50] But Punta de Araya remained Spanish, and the Dutch never again posed a serious threat.

However, a few Dutch interlopers sometimes remained in the area

Fig. 7. Capture of the Silver fleet

Fig. 8. The Conquest of São Paulo de Luanda

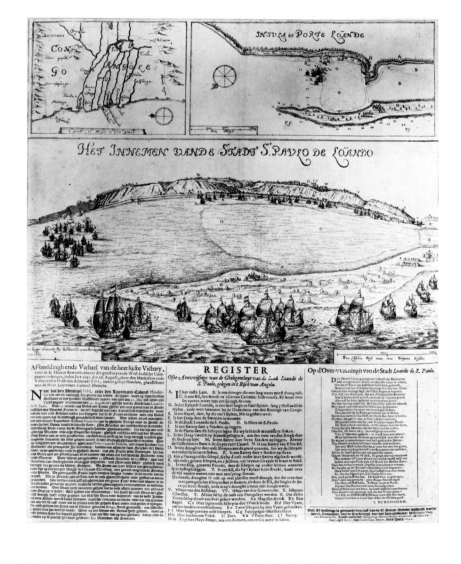

and, of course, paid an occasional visit. In 1628, after an unsuccessful attack on San Juan de Puerto Rico and Margarita, the fleet of the West India Company under Boudewijn Hendricksz sailed to the pan to see "if something could be done there."[51] The resulting skirmish was brief and inconclusive. The Dutch managed to load a small amount of salt and then departed. Some West Frisian towns tried repeatedly to renew the salt trade there, but always in vain. From a later remonstrance of the company, we know that the visits at Araya virtually ended after the fort was built (see Appendix v).

But the closing of Araya did not deter the Dutch from seeking other sources of salt in the Caribbean. At this moment Dierick Ruyters was publishing his *Torch of Navigation* and de Laet his *New World or Description of West India*. The latter included information about those Caribbean islands which were known to be rich in salt:

...the Caycos...we did not find salt there but good pans proper to make salt; Anguilla, no fresh water but there is a salt pan with enough salt for two or three ships a year and a beautiful bay; Bekia, no fresh water, on the north coast there is a salt pan; St. Christopher, at the south-east and there are a few salt pans as some say; St. Martin, no one lives on this island, there is no fresh water but there is a huge salt pan on one side and two smaller ones on the other side....[52]

De Laet's practical information was much appreciated by the sailors, who soon identified it with a profitable trade and sought out the islands he mentioned, especially St. Martin, Bonaire, Tortuga (on the Venezuelan coast), and the Unare River. As early as 1624 three ships returned to the Low Countries laden with the salt of Bonaire.[53]

The dangers inherent in the salt trade brought frequent requests to the Heren XIX for some military protection for the salt carriers. At the same time the company also hired salt carriers to carry troops, ammunition, and supplies to Brazil and allowed them to return with salt, provided that the ships were armed. Some new pans were thus discovered along the Brazilian coast, but the salt was inferior in quality. The search for salt and the pains to acquire it and get it safely home was in those years a constant theme in all contemporary accounts and reached into many phases of Dutch life.[54]

The company, whose monopoly was quickly blunted by the Spanish success at Araya, now turned its attention elsewhere. In 1627, it sent two ships to inspect the islands of Tortuga and St. Martin, the results of which were reported to the Heren XIX, proof that the Dutch were really concerned about finding substitutes for Araya. In 1629, preliminary to a planned Dutch attack on Brazil, the company conceded to some Amsterdam merchants a patronship of Tortuga and

Fernando de Noronha, but none of the patrons actually took possession of the fiefs. In 1631, Tortuga was visited by one of the directors
of the Chamber of Amsterdam.[55] This reconnaissance had not
escaped the attention of the governor of Caracas, Francisco Núñez
Melián, who immediately sent complaints to the king together with
descriptions of the ships and their armament.[56] Neither was the
governor amiss in assuming that the Dutch interest was salt; he wrote,
for instance, that the pans were large and the salt of good quality, that
their location gave easy access to both fresh water and almost inexhaustible supplies of goat and turtle meat.[57]

In 1626, the king had sent the younger Antoneli to examine the salt
pan on Tortuga and its possibilities for exploitation. The latter's
report, based upon close observation, relegated the pan to unimpor-
tance because it was inundated in the rainy season and not adequate
even in dry weather. By 1630, however, the Dutch had made improvements to the extent that Antoneli's measurement of the pan of
3,500 steps in circumference had now been increased to 7,500. They
had also constructed a pier which protruded into the sea for more than
a hundred steps, and at the end of which four trapdoors were built
through which the ships could load salt at the same time.[58] The new
pier was connected to the pan by a boardwalk.

Unlike Araya salt, the salt of Tortuga derived from the sea. The
pan was artificially made and divided into many smaller sections, all
at sea level. In the early days the pans were filled by hand; later Dutch
ingenuity had devised an irrigation system of small canals. Six pumps
propelled the sea water through the canals to the main pan, from there
five other pumps fed the smaller pans, and the sun did the rest. From
an elevated platform, three cannons stood guard over the sprawling
complex.

By 1632 this installation allowed thirty to forty ships to load salt
at the same time. While at the outset of their experiments the Dutch
had returned with thirty thousand cartloads in four ships, their improved method provided a weekly load of twelve thousand *fanegas*,[59]
or about ten times more.

In Benito Arias Montano, the governor of Caracas found the man
to stop the Dutch intrusions on Tortuga. Born in Spain in the province
of Estremadura, Arias had some of the bravado of the conquistadores.
His career had begun under Fajardo and by 1632 he could lay claim to
twenty-six honorable years in the Spanish navy. When news arrived at
Caracas of the Dutch at Tortuga, the solicitous Spaniard offered to go
and destroy the Dutch installations at his own expense. After reconnoitering the area thoroughly, moreover, he led an expedition of forty

Spanish soldiers and one hundred Indian archers against the intrepid foe. Two Dutch ships were anchored in the port close to the pans. Arias launched an attack which cost the Dutch their ships and caused the death of many of their men and the destruction of their salt works on the pan.[60]

It was a harsh blow to the Dutch, yet the effect was of short duration. The very next year the governor of Caracas had to inform the king that the Dutch rebels were once again loading salt at the island. They had not only restored their installations, but had increased their fortifications. Shortly afterward, the governor of Cumaná sent a well-equipped proa to Tortuga, and the Dutch equipment was once more destroyed.[61]

These Spanish measures, however, were not lasting and the Dutch were not intimidated for very long. A year later eighteen Dutch carriers were reported to have loaded salt on Tortuga. Arias, who had just been appointed governor of Cumaná, once again drove the Dutch from the island and, in the company of Antoneli, studied the possibility of submerging the pan. The plan, as drawn up by the engineer, called for two canals to be dug which would drown the pan in at least a yard of water. If the Dutch were able to close the duct, it would take at least six months for the water to evaporate, thus making the pan unusable for that time. The Spaniards could maintain the flooded state by sending one proa a year to check on enemy activity and to be sure that the canals stayed open. Antoneli was convinced that with the Dutch excluded from Araya, Tortuga, and St. Martin, the Caribbean would become a showplace of Spanish dexterity.[62]

With Spain determined to frustrate them, the Dutch problem in finding salt was not small in the thirties. Antoneli's hope that the rebels would leave the Caribbean was soon shattered, however. In fact, the Dutch were back at Tortuga loading salt and building their fortifications in 1638. Once again Arias Montano intervened, seizing a sloop and learning the strength of the enemy. The attack which followed was successful, the Dutch were driven off, and the pan was flooded anew. The eventual outcome of these encounters is unknown, but they probably continued until peace with Spain came in 1648.

When trouble developed at Tortuga, the Dutch had turned their attention also to St. Martin, an island of the upper Leeward group. Informed by de Laet about its salt pans, they may have been there as early as 1627, although formal Spanish complaints only began in 1631. In that year some eighty Dutch carriers arrived in two squadrons, each under the protection of three men-of-war, and commenced to load. Rock salt of pure white quality and in great abundance had been discovered by the Dutch in three small creeks. "More than four hundred ships," wrote the governor of Puerto Rico to the king in his complaint about this intrusion, "could easily have an annual cargo."[63] The source was not kept secret, and St. Martin was soon to become a center of attraction for Dutch ships, as well as for the French and English. The island lacked fresh water, but St. Christopher was well supplied with all the necessities.

The eighty ships mentioned above left thirty men with four pieces of artillery to build a fort on the site. The Dutch were, as yet, unaware that the island already had a small colony of fourteen Frenchmen. The governor of Puerto Rico, who was much alarmed at the Dutch encampment, wrote his king that "within eight months there will be more than three hundred Hollanders on the island."[64]

In Madrid, Philip IV had undertaken a policy designed to circumvent the Dutch forays in the Caribbean. He had granted fifty permits to Dutch carriers to load salt in Iberian ports. The king was certain that the quality of the Spanish and Portuguese salt would make the higher tax acceptable to the rebels. The Dutch were not disposed to agree with His Majesty and, without sincere opposition, continued their activities in the West. Philip apparently could not yet be persuaded that his former subjects constituted a permanent menace to Spanish designs in the West Indies.

An interesting witness to the Dutch development at St. Martin was William Guine, captain of an English ship who, as a prisoner of the Dutch, had been on St. Martin when the latter were consolidating their position there. He supplied the Spanish authorities in Puerto Rico with many details about the Dutch fortifications, "built," he said, "on a spot of land at the side of the bay protruding into the sea." "The fort itself was in poor condition," Guine said, "made of wooden boards and earthen ramparts, protected at the side by a ditch, with a rain water cistern and barracks for the soldiers." It had thirty-three bronze and iron cannons. With respect to the salt pan, he emphasized its proportions comparing it to Punta de Araya. In 1631 more than ninety ships were said to have loaded there, in 1632 a hundred ships on the same errand, and yet there was still enough salt left for three hundred ships a year. The observing Englishman, no fool where investment was concerned, correctly surmised that the Dutch would be forced to give up their position in Brazil only if they lost their arrangements at St. Martin. The island's salt paid for 70 per cent of the 6,000-man garrison at Recife and in Pernambuco, it was said.[65]

The governor of Puerto Rico now requested that the king outfit an armada to expel the Dutch once and for all from the area.[66] Philip IV was beset with difficulties at the time, and did not know whose suggestions to follow. He was well served by his agents in the Caribbean, yet the overwhelming corruption characteristic of his slow-moving administration constantly put good government in jeopardy and resulted in endless discussions and needless delay.

In a meeting in Madrid on March 6, 1633, which was attended by members of several councils, including the Council of Portugal, a decision was finally reached to banish the Dutch from St. Martin. To accomplish this, it was agreed that eleven ships of the Atlantic fleet would join the galleon fleet of that year. The king, however, repeatedly warned that the silver galleons must not be delayed by the activities of the Atlantic fleet because of the dangers to their cargoes. The ships embarked 1,500 to 1,600 soldiers; the expense was born by the merchants of Cádiz and Seville. The secrecy of the mission seems to have been complete: even the admirals were not allowed to open their sealed orders until they were fifty miles out to sea.[67]

The combined fleet under the command of the Marquis de Cadereyta left Spain May 12, 1633, and sailed via the Canaries to Antigua. From there it proceeded to St. Bartholomew where a dispute arose among some of the pilots, who thought they were at St. Martin. Sailing about the island the Spaniards met five foreign ships, four of which escaped. Eventually the fleet chanced upon St. Martin to the northwest. Unfortunately, upon entering the bay, they sighted no Dutch ships, all having been warned in time. The Spanish demand to surrender the fort was refused by the Dutch commander, and the battle began.[68]

During the night the Spaniards landed a thousand soldiers and three hundred crew members under the command of Lope de Hoces. The assailants took up their positions despite the dense undergrowth, which alarmed the Dutch garrison because they had not expected the enemy to be able to do so. The Spanish position was, nevertheless, gravely threatened by the lack of fresh water and the intense heat, each a more dangerous adversary than the Dutch. Lope de Hoces trusted to the advantage of speed and, as soon as his artillery was in place, opened the attack. The first day the Spaniards were driven back. On the next day, however, the Dutch requested the terms of surrender. Cadereyta had orders to be lenient and to pardon the enemy. "Conditions," the king had said in a *cédula* of April 12, 1634, "could arise in which it would be more desirable to negotiate than to fight a bloody war." These instructions were in marked contrast to those received earlier: "I bring to your attention that it is no good to fight the pirates and rebels in the Indies with honest means but they must be intimidated in a bloody war."[69]

Negotiations between the Spaniards and the Dutch—written in odd Latin by the latter—resulted in an agreement to spare the lives of the defenders and to allow them to leave the island each with a knapsack; the governor could carry off a chest and his sword. Transportation to Holland was included. Altogether the Spaniards captured, besides three Dutch ships which entered the port unaware of the situation, ninety-five soldiers, two women, thirty slaves, and one Indian. They also acquired twenty-four pieces of Dutch artillery.[70] At long last the rebels had been conclusively driven from all the main sources of salt in the Caribbean, or so the Spaniards thought.

St. Martin remained in Spanish possession for some time, and the Heren XIX, confident that their conquest of Curaçao could be successful, ruled the island out for the future.[71] As a first step the Spaniards repaired the battered defenses with materials brought from a dismantled Dutch fort on Anguilla. Although inundation of the salt pans was too big a project for the diluted Spanish forces, they did assign 230 men to the new garrison and left another 50 engineers, carpenters, and blacksmiths on the island. Also remaining were two Franciscans, a lay brother, and provisions for a year. A governor was appointed, and his letters reveal the miserable existence of these hardy souls over the next two years.[72]

The Dutch need for salt, however, was not lessened, and soon the adventurous northerners became interested in a new pan close to the river Unare, about twenty-four miles west of Cumanagoto on the mainland. At that time Arias Montano was governor of Cumaná. As noted elsewhere, he had chased the Dutch from Tortuga and had also played an important part in the conquest of St. Martin. He notified the king in April, 1634, that the Dutch had come with ten ships to the Unare, built a fort on the shore, made an alliance with the Indians, and had been informed of the location of a salt pan similar to the one at Punta de Araya. Rather than acquiesce, Arias had embarked 120 Spanish soldiers and 200 Indians into 16 proas and gone to the Unare. Within ten days Arias had attacked the Dutch, killing twenty-one of the enemy, dismantled the fort, destroyed all installations, and burned their wheelbarrows. But upon learning of a Dutch threat to Tortuga, he had left the Unare with a heavy heart,[73] and returned to Cumaná. Consequently, he wrote to the king stressing the dangers of allowing the Dutch to set themselves up in the area; in this matter he was inadvertently supported by the bishop of Puerto Rico, who also deplored the perils implicit in an alliance between the heretical rebels and the Indians.[74]

The pan at the Unare was situated close to the shore and above sea level, so that flooding was out of the question. The river provided fresh water, and there was an abundance of food and wood in the immediate area. Although outwitted in 1634, the Dutch soon returned to use the pan. They were again taught a harsh lesson in August, 1640. At that time eight Dutch carriers, en route from Pernambuco and kept at bay at Punta de Araya, cast their anchors at the mouth of the Unare, and their crews began construction of a wooden fort. They were also able to buy the loyalty of the Indians with knives, axes, and textiles. In this way they reinforced themselves by hundreds of fighting men.[75] The Spaniards, well aware of the new threat, had to act quickly. Juan Orpín, the founder and governor of Cumanagoto, a doctor of civil and cannon law, therefore assured himself of the help of the Piritu Indians by promising them exemption from the encomienda, and undertook to repulse the enemy. He approached the fort cautiously but suffered high casualties when he attacked. The Dutch also lost many men, including their commander, so that they surrendered. Their stronghold consisted of little more than a platform on a small elevation, close to the salt pan, protected by a wooden palisade and strengthened with sand. The fact that it had been prefabricated in the United Provinces aroused the frank admiration of the Spaniards.[76]

Orpín was now in a position to frustrate ensuing Dutch visits, but he knew very well that the only real protection against the Dutch lay in the destruction of the pan. Several plans to accomplish this end were put forth. The bishop of Puerto Rico desired to fill the pan with sod and faggots. Another suggestion was to conduct an arm of the sea through the pan. Orpín himself urged the digging of a canal from the river to the pan and from the pan to the sea, an undertaking which had regularly been turned down by other governors. But he had his way, and sweet water was brought into the pan, though it required three months to dig the ditches. Within two days the salt was washed away, and cattle and horses were to be seen drinking where once Dutchmen and Spaniards had bitterly contested each other's right to the area. Convinced of the project's feasibility, the Spaniards likewise destroyed all other pans there.[77]

After the Spanish victory at St. Martin, the Heren XIX realized that they were losing their battle for salt. It became an important "point of deliberation" in their meetings. Debate on the search for a profitable pan soon centered on Curaçao and its adjacent dependencies Bonaire and Aruba. These islands were taken in June, 1634, although salt was certainly not the only inducement. As a matter of fact, the Dutch were to be very disappointed with the existing supply. Not only were the natural pans not sufficient, but their attempts to create an artificial one at the entrance of St. Ann Bay resulted in an absolute failure. To remedy the situation, the Heren XIX sent an expert on salt to the island. Although records of his activity in this field are not extant, it is known that salt production on Curaçao was always negligible.[78]

The pans on Bonaire, admittedly, were far more promising. The Dutch built a small fort soon after seizing the island, and stationed a garrison of forty soldiers there to look after their salt trade. The Spaniards were not blind to this, of course, and Ruy Fernández de Fuenmayor, the governor of Venezuela—a man eager to distinguish himself—organized an expedition of 150 soldiers and as many Indians to thrust the enemy out. The allies met at night, but found themselves too far away from the port to surprise the Dutch at daybreak. The latter, however, grossly misinformed about the number of their enemies, burned their fort and set sail for Curaçao to inform Governor Stuyvesant of the attack. But the Spaniards, because of sickness among them (they later accused Stuyvesant of having poisoned the water), did not wait for Stuyvesant's attack and evacuated the island (see Chapter XI). The Dutch thus quietly resumed their former activities, although Bonaire never developed into a great center for the salt trade. The supply was probably insufficient, too, which would be substantiated by Stuyvesant's attempt to reconquer St. Martin.

The Spanish garrison at this island, as revealed in the letters of successive commanders of the fort, had been deplorably neglected and unsupplied. At one point the men had mutinied against their superior; on another occasion the fort was all but abandoned as *de navios de registro* consistently failed to show up. Under these chaotic circumstances Peter Stuyvesant and his men appeared in the harbor. The year was 1644. Presumably authorized by the Chamber of Zeeland of the West India Company which had already, in 1635, granted patents for the colonization of the island, Stuyvesant had come with twelve ships and more than one thousand men. He disembarked his troops, placed them on a hill which dominated the fort, and formally demanded surrender; when the demand was refused the attack commenced. The Dutch, in spite of a powerful fleet, were apparently unable to prevent the beleaguered garrison from receiving supplies from Puerto Rico, a factor which enabled the fort to hold out. Yet the Spaniards needed more than supplies to save them from disaster, and the way was opened by an incredible stroke of good luck. Stuyvesant was badly wounded in his leg, and the Dutch reluctantly retreated after four weeks.[79] The attack on the island had been a dismal failure.

Nonetheless, in the first months of 1648 the Spaniards bowed to the ulterior motives of European power politics and relinquished their hold over the island.[80] The Dutch immediately moved in from St. Eustatius and occupied part of it, leaving the other half to some French deserters who had stayed behind when the Spanish garrison left. The Peace of Münster or Westphalia confirmed the Dutch in the possession of half of St. Martin—the area containing the salt pans. Thus, in 1648, the Dutch possessed outright the salt of St. Martin and Bonaire.

In 1633, the West India Company opened its salt monopoly to all ships sailing between the United Provinces and the Wild Coast, the Caribbean and Brazil. The only requirement for carriers was that they pay the imposed recognition to the company. This order was reaffirmed in 1637. Salt was of such importance that its carriers were freed from all other restrictions, such as carrying a super-cargo or company agent on board.[81]

Although, at the outset, the revolt of Portugal against Spain found strong approval in the United Provinces, some misgivings soon took the place of the enthusiasm. In 1641, the Dutch and the Portuguese signed a ten years' truce, which opened Portuguese ports to Dutch ships for trade in salt and other commodities. This truce came at a propitious moment for the Dutch: almost all the salt pans of the Caribbean were now forbidden to them, except for the poorly endowed Curaçao islands. During the course of the truce, the Dutch retook St. Martin and replaced what would again be lost when the truce lapsed.

When the Peace of Münster was signed, the Spaniards, long the hereditary enemy, suddenly became a Dutch ally against the French. Negotiations with Spain included certain provisions dealing with the salt trade: Article XIII of the final draft, for instance, regulated the import of Spanish salt into Dutch ports.[82] The importance of this article becomes particularly evident in view of mounting tension between the United Provinces and Portugal. But the delicate question of Caribbean salt was not specifically handled in the treaty, although did become the subject of further discussion. The Dutch persisted the course of negotiations for the right to exploit the pan at Punta Araya.[83] The number of letters dealing with this topic suggests th t the matter was not going too well for the Dutch.

Philip IV was anxious to settle all problems between Spain and his former vassals, but the salt of the Caribbean was a ticklish one. There were frequent and serious discussions in the Council of the Indies. In a formal letter the Spaniards were reminded that the Dutch had traditionally laid claim to the Araya lagoon, and challenged "the lords, ambassadors, and plenipotentiaries of His Majesty to order that the above mentioned Company be permitted to carry salt from the mentioned Punta del Rey, just as the subjects of Their High Mightinesses had been permitted to do in the past."[84]

In the discourses before the Council of the Indies it was pointed out, and rightly, that the subjects of the States General had never been permitted, legally, to navigate in the West Indies, nor to trade there, nor to carry salt from any pan. The Dutch had invaded the Caribbean under conditions of war; their activity there had delayed the Truce of 1609, and had prevented peace in 1632 and 1633 because of the militancy of the West India Company. The council was firmly opposed to granting permission since it would open the possibility that all the other European powers would make the same request. When, two years later, a naval treaty was signed between the two parties, the question of salt was not mentioned, perhaps because Spanish gold had passed into the hands of the Dutch subscribers.

For the moment the States General did not press the matter further, but in later negotiations with the Spaniards, especially during the Portuguese-Brazilian rebellion, the salt of Araya was renewed as an object of debate. In March, 1655, Luis de Haro, cousin of Olivares, seems to have been approached by the Dutch with this offer: the United Provinces would open hostilities on the Portuguese in the East Indies if the Spaniards would agree to license one hundred salt carriers a year for Punta de Araya.[85] In the beginning, this proposal found favor with the Spaniards, for it cost them nothing and supported their plans to reincorporate Portugal into the Spanish domain. The motion was scrutinized by three Spanish councils. In the end, however, they turned it down because it gave the Dutch too much opportunity to fortify an island and to prepare a launching site for attacks on Tierra Firme. Further, since the Spanish councils ignored the exact location of Punta de Araya and unhesitatingly identified the Dutch demand with Tortuga, the plan was rejected. The silver galleons went right past Tortuga upon entering the Caribbean —too close for comfort.[86]

Two years later, with mounting resentment between the United Provinces and Portugal, the Dutch ambassador in Madrid again applied for leave to exploit Araya. His country was both willing and prepared, he argued, to submit to whatever securities Spain demanded. His Spanish colleague in The Hague reported that his country had professed her willingness to come to terms. In 1659, with war between Portugal and the United Netherlands well on its way, agents of both governments, Dutch and Spanish, were urged to forget their differences and come to an understanding, and this in spite of the strong opposition of the Council of the Indies.[87] It was tacitly recognized that only temporary licenses (given for the duration of the war) could ever hope to meet with Spanish approval. No notable progress was made, however, in the next conference, because of the strong Spanish reluctance to surrender even the smallest part of the integrity of her American domains.

Dutch success against the Portuguese in the Far East was countered by the loss of New Holland. The peace treaty, concluded with Portugal in 1661, not only included a special provision for salt from Setúbal, but also certified that the indemnification to the Dutch for New Holland would partly be paid in salt.[88] Difficulties arose, negotiations dragged on, and the Dutch were once again requesting rights on Araya from Spain—as usual without positive results. In 1670, when deteriorating relations with France led to war among the United Provinces, France, and England, the Dutch appealed to the Spanish Crown once more. The resulting agreement provided that Dutch ships could not carry salt from Araya in groups larger than ten, that the maximum size of the ships was not to exceed forty to fifty tons, that each ship had to be licensed by the Spanish ambassador in The Hague, and that the licenses were for one trip and nontransferable. In addition the ships were not permitted to anchor, nor to take in any additional cargo or provision besides salt in any other Caribbean port; they could only do so in Araya.[89]

As Ojer observes, Spain maintained with great ardor the monopolistic principle which guided her commercial relations: the small size of the admissable ships ruled out any chance of profit. In May, 1671, even these articles were uniformly condemned by the Council of the Indies.[90] Under the charter of the old West India Company, the final chapter had been written on the Dutch effort to get hold of the salt at Punta de Araya.

For almost half a century the salt lagoons of the Caribbean had been the scene of many a savage battle between the Spaniards and the Dutch. Many a time had the pure white salt been reddened by the blood of soldiers and sailors of each side. For another twenty-five years the salt pans remained as a pivotal point of controversy in the relations between the two countries. From the theater of war the contest moved to the diplomatic field, and the Dutch lost. Notwithstanding and despite their failure to win any concession from Spain, in 1674 when the old West India Company charter expired, the Dutch were in firm possession of the Curaçao islands as well as St. Martin, besides having access to Spanish and Portuguese salt ports. For a long time to come they were able to furnish their own needs as well as much of Europe's with the salt their ships carried.

7

THE FIRST GREAT DESIGNS

Force m'est trop.

As the Twelve Years' Truce drew to its close, both the Spaniards and the Dutch realized that it would neither be renewed nor converted into a peace. Spain had the greater problems: the devastating Thirty Years' War was just beginning and demanded immediate attention; France could not be trusted; and England, under James I, was threatening war also. In the Low Countries the victory of Contra-Remonstrantism meant a vigorous thrust toward renewed combat. When the West India Company was founded, it was a certain sign that war lay ahead.

Advised of Dutch belligerency and fearful of further aggression against his West Indian domain, the Spanish king had sent word that all Caribbean garrisons be reinforced and that the fortresses of San Juan de Puerto Rico, Santo Domingo, Santiago de Cuba, and Havana be strengthened.[1] Although no formal plan to harry the Caribbean had been developed by the Dutch during the final years of the Truce, hearsay had it that a raid on Havana was in the making. Already in 1619 Philip III had asked the Archduke Albert of the Southern Netherlands to examine certain rumors about imminent attacks on the West Indies and to keep him abreast of the progress in the creation of the West India Company.[2] The following year the Spanish War Council had advised that "small occasion will suffice for the Hollanders to disregard what is left of the truce, and for the English to break the peace."[3]

A year later the war between Spain and the rebels had been resumed and within a few weeks, on June 3, 1621, the West India Company received its charter. In September the Infanta Isabel sent her brother Philip III a map together with the details of the new company's designs on Havana. To forestall any inimical action by the heavily manned fortress which guarded the town from the sea, the Dutch plan first committed itself only to the seizure of Matanzas Bay. With that natural harbor securely in Dutch hands, Havana would lay stripped of its defenses, an easy prey. Needless to say, the proposed enterprise displayed an accurate acquaintance with the local situation and a keen appraisal of the fact that the Spaniards had been notoriously careless about the possibility of a landside attack.[4]

The threat of a Dutch naval base that might adjoin Havana became a major Spanish nightmare for years to come. The Dutch correctly surmised that a foothold at Matanzas would allow them to play havoc with Spanish shipping to Havana, most especially with the treasure fleets from Porto Bello, Honduras, and Vera Cruz. The Spaniards, according to all expectations, thought that navigation westward from Matanzas was an insuperable task, but the Dutch relied on their superior yardstick of experience to overcome all obstacles.

Whatever basis for truth the plan sent by Isabel may have contained (there is nothing in the Dutch archives to confirm it), the Spaniards were clearly worried. The War Council recommended an immediate survey of Matanzas and urged that a report be submitted on the feasibility of fortifying the bay. In an obscure effort to be on guard against any type of foray, the council also suggested that maps of all other indentations on the Cuban coast be forwarded.[5] The Spaniards hoped that the expenses of protecting a base in the midst of enemy territory would overtax the Dutch, as a similar English experience in Virginia and on Bermuda had demonstrated. The Spanish king also relied on the profit-seeking motive behind all Dutch enterprises. A Dutch base on Cuba would be both a needless burden, and an unjustifiable expense to the West India Company.

The alarm, which had not yet been fully allayed, rose again when Cardinal Alfonso de la Cueva reported from Brussels that three vessels were being fitted out in Zeeland for some enterprise in the West Indies.[6] The shadow of Matanzas again darkened the Spanish sky. A former governor of Havana, Gaspar Ruiz de Pereda, although once he had expressed fear of the Dutch at Matanzas, now argued that the roughness of the terrain would make a land attack extremely unlikely. He also indicated that the Spaniards were acclimatized to the area, that the enemy was not, and that sickness would fight for the Spaniards. Havana could muster six hundred men, Pereda added, and the only real danger was that the *cimarrones* (the escaped slaves) would join the Dutch, due to their desire for freedom and their hatred of their former masters.

The governor of Havana, Francisco Venegas, was alerted and replied that he was prepared. Morro Castle was virtually impregnable and the two other forts well garrisoned. He did not believe that the port would ever be attacked, since he regarded such an attempt as sheer folly. When new evidence of Dutch ambitions for Cuba was brought to the attention of the Crown in August, 1622, Venegas received a second summons.[7] Notwithstanding such royal concern, however, Venegas still felt absolutely sure that the Dutch would not risk an attack: "I have sent five ships for four months along the North coast of this island and Hispaniola. They have not met any enemy, nor received any notice of him."[8] Venegas died before he could repent of his excess of confidence and regret his presumptuous dismissal of all royal admonitions.

Rumors were persistent. The Zeelandian squadron destined for Matanzas soon grew to twenty ships and two thousand men. Spanish informants had been correct insofar as the equipment of warships was concerned, but they had inadvertently associated these with the activities of the nascent West India Company. The only Dutch ships that frequented the Caribbean at the time were salt carriers and licensed privateers.[9]

The infant West India Company could not yet assimilate the tremendous project which was thought to be forthcoming, however much it wanted to. It simply lacked the financial means to do much of anything. All that it could manage in those early years was the issue of wood and salt letters to private entrepreneurs like Jan Jaricks of Stavoren, who must have been one of the first to receive this kind of license. When Jaricks visited the salt pans of St. Martin and Bonaire, he became embroiled with the Spanish governor of the latter island. The Dutchman was put in irons, but the governor changed his mind and gave the Dutch permission to cut wood there. Jaricks returned to his homeland with tobacco, wood, and valuable information.[10] As soon as Punta de Araya was included in its charter, however, the company rigidly enforced its prerogatives on all ships that were headed for the Caribbean.

In the latter part of 1621, the States General extended a formal invitation to the West India Company to join in a proposed attack on Peru and the Pacific coast "to make big conquests and much booty."[11] The plan included a complement of 9 ships and 1,600 men under the command of Jacques l'Hermite, former official of the East India Company. A reconnoitering tour of the Spanish colonial defense system was also part of the plan. Prior to the establishment of its sister company, however, the Dutch East India Company had already made substantial investments in the project. De Laet explains why the West India Company declined to participate in this venture: lack of funds and little chance of success.[12]

This fleet, the so-called Nassau fleet, sailed in 1623, and Spain immediately assumed that it was headed for the Caribbean. Venegas was once more notified, and debates on viable targets for the Dutch fleet to attack occupied the Spanish War Council for a month. Although the Spaniards were well acquainted with many details, they were quite deluded about the objective; the Dutch had no design on the Caribbean. They sailed across the Atlantic, appropriated the island of Fernando de Noronha and, following the coast, continued south through the Le Maire Strait on to the Pacific. For some time the fleet cruised along the Pacific coast, but it failed to capture the Peruvian silver ships and proceeded on its course westward to the Malay archipelago. Only two ships completed the round trip. Although they came home with good cargoes, there was still little profit in the venture. The West India Company could congratulate itself that it had not become involved in that expedition.

When the company became solvent in 1623, it soon turned to aggressive activity in both African and American waters and took the lead against Spain in the Caribbean. Contrary to general opinion, it was the West India Company far more than the sister company in the East that bore the burden of Dutch warfare outside of European waters. The regions brought under the flag of the United Provinces in the West and in Africa far surpassed those areas captured in the East during the period of the first charter. Further, the company's activities undoubtedly exceeded English enterprises in the West Indies in that same period. Even under Charles I, who followed a more pronounced anti-Spanish policy, and despite the Treaty of Southampton which united the two Protestant nations in 1625 against Spain, the English still fought their Spanish war half-heartedly.[13]

From the outset, therefore, the company was intended to be one arm of the government for circumscribing Spain at sea. In the early years numerous schemes were put forth—elaborate plots which invariably floundered on a lack of available funds. By 1624, however, the company was well enough situated to operate three or four fleets simultaneously in American and in African waters. These fleets constantly disturbed the normal course of Spanish traffic and kept the Caribbean in a state of lasting alarm. Indeed, they enforced such a blockade on Cuba that the island was brought to the verge of economic collapse.[14]

Havana was too important and too strategic a bulwark, however, to permit Dutch activity to go unchecked. Even closer to the Spanish heart were the treasure fleets. Normally there were two fleets: the *flota* or New Spain fleet and the *galeones* to Tierra Firme and Porto

3. Map of the Caribbean with the Dutch expeditions of 1624-26. From De Laet/
   Naber, I.

Bello. The Honduras flotilla, consisting of two or three ships, is sometimes referred to casually as a third fleet.

The Tierra Firme fleet, although better protected than the *flota* and traveling a shorter distance through the enemy-infested Caribbean area, was ordered in 1623 to remain in port until further notice. The New Spain fleet, moreover, was nine months behind schedule. Financially, therefore, Spain was no longer in a position to impose either her will or her gold upon Europe.[15]

If the empire was to be spared from impending disaster, the situation demanded immediate and positive action. A fourteen-galleon fleet was thus dispatched to the West Indies to guard Havana while the treasure ships were anchored there. This fleet was under the command of Admiral Tomás de Larraspuru, who, after crossing the Atlantic, made an unexpected raid on Punta de Araya where he captured six Dutch salt carriers. Beforehand, while at anchor in Porto Bello, he sent a scouting unit consisting of four galleons to Jamaica to investigate the presence of some suspicious sails. These ships turned out to be four small Dutch reconnoitering vessels, which had earlier disembarked two hundred men at Sisal on the main coast and burnt that town.[16] The Dutch easily escaped the heavier, more cumbersome Spanish galleons. Larraspuru, in the meantime, proceeded toward Havana where he picked up the treasure fleets and escorted them to Spain. They arrived there in August, 1624, bearing thirteen million guilders in gold, silver, and other products. Despite this noteworthy achievement, the admiral had been the victim of faulty Spanish information which had led him to the wrong place. A month earlier, the terrible news had reached Spain that the rebellious provinces had successfully attacked Bahia de Todos os Santos (the Bay of All Saints); Larraspuru's actions did nothing to efface this affront. Yet the unharmed treasure lay as a potent ointment on the open wound.

A "Great Design" to attack Spain simultaneously in Europe, Africa, and America with three fleets never materialized. The sums needed for the undertaking were simply too enormous. The Heren XIX had to satisfy themselves with more realistic projects. Discussions in their meetings centered on various proposals. The West Frisian Chamber—the Northern Quarter—wanted to occupy Punta de Araya but could not gain sufficient support. A plan to attack the Peruvian silver fleet in the Pacific was also rejected, and the same outcome awaited a design to capture the Brazilian sugar fleet. The XIX were well aware that all these plans required both time and money—two luxuries that they could ill afford at this time. In order to obtain the necessary subscriptions for the company's survival, fast and easy returns were the order of the day and the most immediate exigencies.[17]

Thus the Heren XIX for a time thought of attacking the Portuguese slave trade from Africa to Brazil and the West Indies in order "to stop that spring of the king's best finances." The Dutch had long been interested in Africa and "in that profitable trade in blacks the Portuguese were carrying on there."[18] The XIX were all in favor of wresting this thriving business from the Iberians. Until this time, however, the West India Company had been reluctant to assume responsibility for Fort Nassau, the sole Dutch possession in Africa. It had surrendered it to the deft management of the admiralty board of Amsterdam, mainly because of the expenses involved in its maintenance. But the Heren XIX, when they finally realized the strategic value of this stronghold and had sufficient finances at their disposal, now moved to take over. In addition, the company well knew that an African enterprise needed little preparation and would not require expensive equipment or big fleets. It would suffice to destroy the Spanish and Portuguese ships and storehouses in order to transfer as much of the cargoes as possible. It was even conceivable that the Dutch would gain adherents among the local Negro population.

The Dutch were well briefed on the several slave-loading ports: São Tiago, São Thomé, São Jorge da Mina (Elmina), and São Paulo de Luanda.[19] Many Dutch sailors had been held prisoner by the Portuguese garrisons in these settlements and had thus acquired an intimate knowledge of their ground plans. Of the four settlements, São Jorge da Mina was the most susceptible to capture. It had a reputation, however, of being impregnable, and therefore the attention of the XIX was diverted to São Paulo de Luanda which presented the least obstacles. Its slaves were cheap and docile, the kind of working stock which would bring a good price in Brazil and the Caribbean. Profits would be assured.

For some time, discussions among the XIX centered on whether the West India Company should participate in the slave trade itself. The original plan had only called for the destruction of the Iberian trade to the particular detriment of the Spanish king. Soon the second step was taken, to monopolize it for the benefit of the company and its stockholders. To participate in this new venture opened a variety of perspectives. Profits were involved but moral issues were also. To pacify the disturbing voice of conscience, a commission was appointed to reconcile the trade in human beings with the doctrines of Calvinistic Christianity. As is not uncommon, the moral objections which were considered were no match for the tantalizing lure of profit.

While this commission worked on the theological problem, a small squadron was being fitted out by the Chamber of Amsterdam for the purpose of exploring the West African coast. Under Philip van Zuylen, this unit left for Africa in September, 1623. It carried a few selected commodities for barter, and was sanctioned by explicit privateering instructions. Its commander was specifically ordered to develop friendly relations with the Negro population. The timing of this expedition was highly propitious, since mounting tension between the Portuguese and the Negro princes in the area had already erupted into open warfare. The Portuguese governor of Luanda, João Correia de Sousa, had invaded the Congo and massacred its inhabitants. Immediately the Negro ruler of Sonho had enlisted the aid of the Dutch trading post at Mpinda and had even written Prince Maurits for support against the Portuguese. He offered to reimburse the Dutch with ivory, copper, and gold. A Dutch intervention looked profitable, and especially so since a second purge by de Sousa in this *guerra preta* (black war) caused disgust even among the Portuguese population.[20]

Van Zuylen's fleet, of course, could do little about this situation, since he was authorized only to contact the Negro princes and to pave the way for a second and larger fleet, nine ships and nine hundred soldiers, that was to follow. The combined Dutch fleet was then to conquer Luanda and to support the Negroes hostile to the Portuguese. It would effectively establish control by the West India Company over that part of the coast. Together with Fort Nassau, an excellent strategic position would be created that would allow the Dutch to hamper seriously Spanish and Portuguese slave trading.

Wandering aimlessly in African waters, van Zuylen's hands were tied until the arrival of the promised fleet. The latter ships, however, were still in the preparatory stage and the Dutch commander, meanwhile, was ordered to lay an effective blockade on São Paulo de Luanda's port. Compared to contemporary Dutch exploits in other areas of the globe, van Zuylen seemed pursued by consistent bad luck. He committed one serious blunder after another. Although he was well acquainted with Luanda's excellent port, he failed to seal it off effectively and left a less important southern entrance unguarded. The Portuguese were thus able to build up an adequate defense and to offer a stubborn fight. To make matters worse, the Dutch commander deliberately violated his instructions by lifting the blockade before the other Dutch fleet had joined him. In flagrantly disobeying orders, he sailed to the Congo in hopes of taking some prizes there. His breach of command was to have far-reaching consequences: the other Dutch expedition to Africa was to lose its purpose, and the high hopes which the XIX had entertained with regard to Africa were to be destroyed.[21]

In the meantime subscriptions had accumulated, and the company could dispose of more cash. Some of the XIX were not too impressed with the accomplishments of the summer of 1623 and were probably still reminiscing about the "Great Design" of 1621. One such was Boudewijn Hendricksz, who came forward with a new and daring proposal in the September meeting of the board. In imitation of van Zuylen's exploits, he eagerly volunteered to go to the Caribbean under the same conditions. The XIX appointed Dierick Ruyters and Frederick l'Hermite to look into Hendricksz' new proposal. Just then, an even more ostentatious project was elicited: the conquest of Brazil.[22]

The Heren XIX did not lose much time with talk. The plan to take Brazil from the Portuguese outweighed all others in its brilliant conception and was accepted with incredible speed. The XIX did not intend, however, to abandon altogether the other projects—far from it. The reconnoitering mission proposed by Boudewijn Hendricksz was to be carried out at the same time. Although the science of psychology was as yet unheard of, the Heren XIX realized only too well the psychological implications of their plan: if it were not the great design of 1621, it was certainly a "Great Design." An unexpected attack on Brazil, concluding in the capture of Bahia, would surprise the Iberians and inevitably hurt their prestige. Two Dutch fleets operating at the same time in African and Caribbean waters would add to the enemy's confusion and fill him with terror.

Although the XIX, as yet, did not know the outcome of van Zuylen's abortive attempt to impose control over the port of São Paulo de Luanda, the African enterprise had been conceived as an intrinsic part of the much larger project. Brazil, Africa, and the Caribbean were suddenly perceived in unison by the empire builders of the United Provinces. Many times classified as grocers and cheesemongers, these seventeenth-century merchants were, in fact, men of vision. The Spaniards failed to fathom this point and dismissed the raids of the *flamencos* and *olandeses* (Zeelanders and Hollanders) as mere piracy ventures.

Brazil had now become the main target of the company's activities, however, and a huge expedition was in preparation against one of the main centers of this Portuguese possession: São Salvador da Bahia de Todos os Santos. Why Bahia? "Because," writes de Laet, "that bay is so situated that every fleet could enter and leave it easily, while from there also other parts of America could unexpectedly be assaulted."[23]   A pamphlet of 1624, printed in Amsterdam, gives twenty other reasons for singling out Brazil, some of them very persuasive.[24] The Dutch certainly relied on the Lusitanians, long enemies of the Spaniards, to join them in their fight against the common foe. Besides, the Spaniards habitually regarded the Portuguese colonies as "a foreign possession for which they did not have to use their full strength."[25]

The Dutch were no strangers to Brazil. They had been conducting a profitable wood and sugar trade in the area since 1594. As Engel Sluiter has pointed out, the rebellious Low Countries had also provided a haven for many Portuguese refugees who had retained their commercial and financial connections with Lisbon, Viana, Oporto, and Brazil. After 1621, from ten to fifteen ships were built annually and assigned to the Brazilian trade; between forty thousand and fifty thousand chests of Brazilian sugar entered the Netherlands yearly.[26] Besides, Spain had never sought to inflict its own obstructive bureaucracy on the possession and had closed her eyes to an otherwise illegitimate trade. All these answers might—singly or jointly—be posed to the question of "Why Brazil?" For good measure one optimist had also calculated that the colony, in the hands of the Dutch, would yield about 8,000,000 guilders annually whereas the cost of conquest and defense did not exceed 2,500,000 guilders.[27] During the Truce it was said that from one half to two thirds of the trade between Brazil and Europe was in Dutch or Dutch-Portuguese hands. These estimates are clear proof of how the Portuguese officials in Brazil abjured Spanish monopolistic practices. They indicate, moreover, the significance of the Dutch interest in Brazil.

There were also those who favored Brazil in anticipation of the fact that it would be less well guarded by Spain with respect to her own colonies. This argument was powerfully reinforced when an Anglo-Persian fleet captured Ormuz, a Portuguese trading post in the Persian Gulf. In this case, Spain did no more than send some paper protests.[28] Yet Usselinx, for one, was not impressed with any of the arguments and insisted that "The voyage is too long, the expenses are too high." Although "the women at the wash benches and children in the alleys were talking of it lightly," Usselinx thought that Brazil was "not the kind of cat to be handled without gloves." In his judgment, the strength of the Dutch expeditionary force was totally unequal to the task, and he admonished his fellow countrymen that no matter how much the Portuguese disliked the Spaniards, it would be plain stupidity to expect them to side with heretics against Catholics. Nor, he argued, should any reliance on crypto-Jewish cooperation be counted on.[29] As was often the case, Usselinx' opinions were disregarded.

During the successive meetings of the Heren xix in the late summer and fall of 1623, enthusiasm for the planned enterprises continued to grow. The fleet of nine ships that had originally been earmarked for Africa received a new destination: Brazil. In successive meetings, this force was increased to a total of twenty-three ships and three yachts. Another Caribbean-bound squadron was set at three ships, to be commissioned by the Zeeland Chamber of the company. To mislead Spain, which had her agents everywhere, rumors were spread that a fleet of twelve sails had been equipped for peaceful ventures. In the meantime, however, the recruiting drum had enlisted 3,200 soldiers and sailors. Jacob Willekens of Amsterdam, a former herring merchant who had achieved a considerable degree of success in the service of the Dutch East India Company, was invited to be the commander of the Brazil-bound fleet. His vice-admiral was Piet Heyn. When Prince Maurits urged that a separate commander for the 1,600 soldiers be appointed, the choice fell on Colonel Jan van Dorth, lord of the manor of Horst and Perch. The artillery for the mission was supplied by the well-known Dutch-Swedish cannon caster Elias Trip.[30]

Although the difficulties of the venture were not ignored by the Heren xix, they were undoubtedly minimized and underestimated. São Salvador was known to be well protected by several forts. Yet the xix were self-assured, anxious to invest most of their funds in the project, and persistent in their requests that the government support them in accordance with Article xl of their charter. By December, 1623, the majority of the fleet's units had left Dutch ports. The ships refreshed at the Cape Verde Islands and proceeded across the Atlantic. They appeared before São Salvador on May 8, 1624—to the amazement and discomfort of the inhabitants. Since the governor, Diego de Mendonça Furtado, had not been warned until the very last moment, he had very little opportunity to organize his tactics. But then, any attempt to defend Brazil's 800-mile coastline would have been preposterous.

The Dutch attack on the Bay of All Saints ended in a resounding victory. But the cowardly behavior of many of the defenders and the panic that circulated among the civilians helped the Dutch cause. Faced by desertions and overwhelming odds, the governor abjectly capitulated. The Dutch suffered a mere fifty casualties and acquired a savory booty in sugar.[31]

The victors understood, of course, that the conquest of São Salvador only meant a beginning. The next step would be to barricade the town and to consolidate their position, followed by the submission of the surrounding regions. Obviously, immediate reinforcements would be necessary. Although news of the Dutch victory did not reach the United Provinces until August, it was already known in Spain in July. The interval gave the Spaniards a precious month in which to plan their counterattack.

The minutes of the meetings of the Heren xix in those months are eloquent testimony to the zeal of the board to sustain the initial success, to keep the town in the hands of the company, and to stabilize trade there.[32] It was well understood that Spain would do her utmost to retake the place in order to salvage her own prestige and to quiet Portuguese accusations of negligence. Dutch informers soon revealed the measures which the Spanish planned in retaliation. But even before this information had arrived, the xix had already decided to equip another fleet destined for Brazil. A yacht was sent to Willekens to advise him of this. Director Samuel Blommaert, who was mindful of the Dutch plight on the African coast, proposed a slight alteration of the yacht's course so that it could give van Zuylen the good news and inform him of the change in plans.[33] This slight modification, however, in turn caused a delay in letting the Dutch at Bahia know that help was on the way.

The decision to outfit twelve ships for reinforcing the new stronghold in Brazil was made in March, 1624. In April, the representative of Their High Mightinesses on the board of the xix suggested that this fleet first be tested in a blockade off the Iberian coast, a move which would deny Spain her access to Brazil. The same force was then to be put at the disposal of the Dutch East India fleet for safe conduct home. The Heren xix were unanimously of the opinion that they could not refuse this request by their most important stockholder, and agreed to send that part of their fleet which was ready to sail to Spain.[34] In June, 1624, a squadron of four ships and three yachts left the Low Countries. But its contradictory goals resulted in its failure to effect a blockade of the Iberian coast.

When news of the victory at Bahia was received in the United Provinces, however, the Heren xix immediately decided to dispatch a second yacht to notify the Dutch leaders in Brazil that help was coming, even though some of the rescue units had been temporarily detoured to Spain. At about the same time, the xix were informed that the traditional Iberian lethargy had been superseded by an unflinching desire to recapture Bahia. The implications of this change in Spanish response were not lost on the board of the company.

Word came that the Spanish king had appointed his finest sailor,

Fadrique de Toledo, to lead the *jornada del Brazil*. The Iberians mustered 50 ships with 1,200 cannons and 12,000 men. They arrived at Bahia by the end of March, 1625, and found the Dutch much demoralized because of inferior leadership. Van Dorth had been killed in a skirmish, and Admiral Willekens had followed his orders by withdrawing when he thought that the place was adequately fortified. With promised support for van Zuylen in mind, the Heren xix had also ordered Vice-Admiral Piet Heyn to leave Bahia for the west coast of Africa once the Dutch position in Brazil seemed secure. While the town had thus been strengthened and well provisioned for a siege of perhaps three or four months, there were no longer enough ships for a proper defense. The main reason for its forthcoming loss, however, was to be found in the incapable commanders who had succeeded van Dorth.

Don Fadrique de Toledo made a smooth entrance. Towards the end of April, after a siege of one month, the Iberians had recouped their prestige and Spain had regained *das ihr entrissene Kleinod* (the stolen jewel) in a short time and at little cost.[35] When Dutch reinforcements showed up a full month later, nothing remained of their former victory.

While the young company had worked hard to convert its "Great Design" into an unprecedented success, the Chamber of Amsterdam had, besides its cooperation in the equipment of the bigger fleet, finished the preparation of the other ships—those which were intended to come to the rescue of van Zuylen and those charged with the blockade of the Spanish coast. In the meantime, Zeeland had supplied the ships for the exploratory expedition in the Caribbean. The latter three ships were under the able command of Pieter Schouten who, on a previous excursion into American waters, had succeeded in generating a mutually harmonious relationship with the natives in the Lesser Antilles. Schouten's sailing orders included a foray into "that part of the *Sinum Mexicanum* called the Gulf of Honduras" with the stipulation that he capture the two Honduras ships which annually brought their cargo to Havana around June.[36]

The richly endowed Honduras ships had long been the object of Dutch covetousness. Efforts to capture them had already occurred prior to the Truce. In 1606, for instance, a small Dutch force had attacked the two galleons in their harbor at San Tomás de Castillo. In the succeeding scuffle, which is recorded in Spanish sources, the Dutch lost a ship and scurried off disgracefully. A few days later, they made another futile attempt to get the Spanish treasures.[37]

Schouten's expedition was the first that was organized by the West India Company to the Caribbean. His ships left port with Willekens' fleet but separated from it after refreshing at the Cape Verde Islands. He arrived at Barbados in mid-March and proceeded immediately to the various neighboring islands on exploratory and privateering ventures. Indians living on the islands were invited on board his ships and were cordially received. In return, the Dutch were rewarded with much valuable information on Spanish shipping and defenses. As soon as the circumstances permitted, the crews assembled the small sloops, transported in sections on board the ships, and rowed in close to shore to ascertain the possible location of the salt pans, fresh water, and fruit.

From the Lesser Antilles the small squadron leisurely cruised along Tierra Firme into the Gulf of Mexico. It explored that Gulf, sailed on to Haiti's southern coast, reconnoitered Jamaica, added to the consternation in Cuba, and then set course to the northern coast of Yucatán. There the Dutch plundered, raided, and looted wherever they had the opportunity. Of the two small towns on the Yucatán peninsula, Silán and Sisal, the latter was completely destroyed. At one point the squadron ran into a few Spanish ships that were engaged in plying their trade between the colonies. Without much ado, these were overpowered; their cargoes were captured and the prizes burned. After interrogation, the crews were put ashore. Schouten, then sailing north of Havana in July, caught a glimpse of a treasure fleet entering that port. He was too weak to dream of attacking it, however. One of his ships, which had been separated from the other two, met the Honduras flotilla at Cape San Antonio and was so successful that it was able to seize one of the galleons. While towing this glorious prize home, the Dutch ship was wrecked at the Dry Tortugas, and was abandoned by its crew who returned aboard the Honduras ship in September, 1624. Schouten himself sailed home to Zeeland at the end of February, 1625; he arrived in mid-April, rich in booty and information.[38]

In the interim, one week after Willekens' departure from the Bay of All Saints, Piet Heyn had left also—according to his instructions—with the intention of joining van Zuylen's squadron. Together, the two Dutchmen were to seize the Portuguese slave depot of São Paulo de Luanda. Heyn hence crossed the Atlantic with 2 ships, 2 yachts, 2 shallops, and crews totaling 250 men, not a sufficient enough force for the important assignment which he was to perform. As yet unaware of the course of events, Heyn had expected to be reinforced with van Zuylen's three ships. The Heren xix, believing the fortifications of Luanda to be flimsily guarded, had also taken it for granted that van Zuylen would meanwhile have blockaded its port successfully. He would thus have prevented the arrival of reinforcements and would have cut off the Brazilian slave supply. The move would have paralyzed the sugar mills and weakened the resistance to Dutch conquest. As a joint force, Heyn and van Zuylen were then supposed to occupy the town, to secure for the West India Company the main slave depot in Africa, and to consolidate the Dutch position in Brazil.[39] The xix were overconfident, contemplating the future with whole-some optimism and professing the utmost faith in the exhilarating destiny of their country. Absorbed by the many avenues opened to them by superior Dutch naval power and by only latent enemy op-position, they envisaged a world contracted by the sprawling arms of Dutch conquest.

No one can deny that this "Great Design" was a plan with vision. The Heren xix, whatever their other limitations, could not be accused of narrow politicking. From the outset they had concep-tualized the interrelationship between the two Atlantic coasts and had had the foresight to perceive the necessary power bases for an empire. Although the company was ultimately frustrated in this grand scheme, was it really to blame? Bahia fell because the wrong men made the wrong decisions. Although Piet Heyn failed, he was competent and courageous. When van Zuylen declined to obey orders, he thus jeopardized the whole cleverly contrived stratagem.

Heyn left Bahia in August, 1624, sallying forth along a route hitherto practically unknown to the Dutch. Accompanying him, however, was Dierick Ruyters, who had earlier described that very course in his *Torch of Navigation*. Still, it was difficult sailing, and in early October, at a fleet council called by Heyn, it was ascertained that the various captains differed by at least ninety miles in the respective estimates of their positions. The problem was one of longitude, a navigational difficulty as yet unsolved despite Plancius' improvements on the astrolabe. With scurvy and thirst threatening the crews, they sighted the African coast a few weeks later. By late October Heyn arrived at Luanda, but van Zuylen, despairing of the long delay, had left in pursuit of more tangible advantages. The "Great Design" had to be abandoned, at least its African part.

Sailing close to the shore, Piet Heyn sighted twenty-five ships anchored close to the fort. At least four of them were well armed. From a Portuguese slave trader, captured in the neighborhood, the Dutch commander found out that there were at least 1,800 soldiers in Luanda together with many thousands of Negro troops to be used as auxiliaries. Heyn could not know whether these estimates were exaggerated, and he discussed the possibility of an attack with his captains. Since the circumstances had changed for the worse, a night attack was eventually agreed upon. This plan of action inflicted only a small amount of damage on the Portuguese, and it did not accrue any positive advantages to the Dutch. Heyn consequently decided to carry through the second part of his instructions, and the Dutch fleet sailed south to the Congo River. It joined up there with van Zuylen, but the latter's squadron was badly in need of supplies, and perforce committed to a swift journey home. Heyn proceeded on his own to the Prince of Sonho who, two years before, had appealed to Prince Maurits for help. The Portuguese were not bothering that Negro ruler at the moment, however, and he denied having ever written any letter requesting help from the Dutch. Piet Heyn continued south to Luanga and the island of Annabón, where he arrived in January, 1625. He refreshed there, and then crossed the Atlantic once more to Brazil.[40]

Heyn's instructions also extended to Bahia where he was to check if his services were needed there. His landing in Brazil was too far to the south, however, at the small town of Espírito Santo, and he made an inevitable change in strategy, took some prizes, then continued north along the coast. He reached Bahia while Fadrique de Toledo had the city São Salvador under siege. Heyn's force, weakened as it was by the arduous journey, was powerless to relieve the town. Haphazardly cruising along the coast, he waited until the fall of Bahia was relayed to him. He then sailed to the island of Fernando de Noronha to refresh and give his crews a chance to unbend. Some nine days later he resumed his voyage homeward and arrived in the Low Countries at the end of July, 1625. The first "Great Design" was at an end.

Backed by the benefit of hindsight, it is no difficult task to recognize the erroneous supposition that provided the bases for the West India Company's first "Great Design." In the first place, while it was easy enough for the Heren XIX to draw up ostentatious blueprints along with appropriate instructions for their execution, once the fleets were at sea they became independent units, subject to all types of adversity, creatures of the wind, current, and other elements. Since information services were nonexistent, there was no way to amend plans once the ships had sailed.

The blockade of the Iberian coast, the expedition of Willekens against Bahia, and the two smaller ones under van Zuylen and Schouten were all part of a "Great Design." The plan aimed to paralyze Spain by depriving her of her sugar-producing colony and her slave market, while spreading terror in the Caribbean and gaining valuable information for later invasions and attacks on her treasure fleets. Two errors committed by the Dutch were obvious from the start, however sound the overall strategy may have been. The first and main error was to trust the defense of Bahia to insufficient naval support. The second mistake, as Boxer rightly points out, lay in the very dissipation of this strength. The plan to send Heyn to Africa to capture Luanda was excellent, if Willekens had held out until the arrival of the promised fleet. The separation of Heyn was undertaken, writes Boxer, because of a correct appreciation by the Dutch that to retain Brazil, they had to control the principal slave market in Africa. A vehement Iberian reaction, however, should have been a natural premise. In fact, the Heren xix were soon familiar with the vicissitudes of Spanish national pride, and knew the movements in Iberian ports down to the most intimate details. The yachts sent to Bahia which brought tidings of forthcoming help should have impressed upon Willekens, van Dorth, or their successors the need to wait for their own reinforcing fleet sent to guard the captured stronghold. Fallacious reasoning led not only to the loss of Bahia, but also to a costly and irresponsible undertaking in Africa.

Yet, the Heren xix could not have anticipated the cowardly behavior of their fellowmen at Bahia. With magazines stacked full of provisions, plenty of men at their disposal, well equipped behind a strong fortress, and advised that help was on its way, they nevertheless capitulated without a struggle. The xix could not have known, moreover, that van Zuylen, thought to be well acquainted with the local situation on the west coast, would do so poorly at Luanda and cause the expedition under Heyn to collapse altogether.

The dismal failure of their first "Great Design" was as yet ignored by the Heren xix when plans for a new project, closely related to the first, were canvassed. Emboldened by the triumphal entry into Bahia, these men of action displayed little use for self-conscious eulogies. They energetically tackled a new task. The committee of directors assigned to hatch the new scheme required only four days for the work. It proposed the outfitting of eighteen ships and seven yachts for immediate use as well as the assembly of a supplementary force of thirty-five or thirty-seven ships in which Their High Mightinesses would be offered a half interest.[41] Thus Brazil had become a powerful stimulant in whetting the appetite of the imperturbable Dutch.

Discussions by the Heren xix resulted in the resolution to prepare, first of all, a fleet of 25 ships as suggested and to man these with

1,700 sailors and some 1,400 soldiers. The choice of admiral fell to Jan Dirckszoon Lam.[42] Because of worrisome rumors of Spanish effervescence, the XIX hastened the creation of the second fleet. When the States General failed to respond immediately to their request, based on Article XL of the charter, they settled for fourteen ships and two yachts. The arrival of Willekens at the end of December, however, brought new information, which was probably influential in the decision to increase the size of this fleet. This decision was detrimental to Lam whose escort was consequently much reduced. The larger fleet, which now consisted of more than thirty ships, was placed under the command of Boudewijn Hendricksz, a burgomaster of the West Frisian town of Edam and a director of the company. Hendricksz received the rank of general, and Lam, as admiral of the smaller fleet, had to obey his orders.

Nor was that all. Lam was ordered to sail to Africa and to make amends for the van Zuylen fiasco. Once again, while aiming at Brazil, the Heren XIX did not neglect its "black mother."[43] Recognizing that Lam's flotilla was, by itself, too frail for any large scale operation, the XIX voted to equip a third fleet of twelve ships under Admiral Andries Veron who would accompany Hendricksz to Brazil. It would then be released to join Lam for a concerted attack on Africa's west coast. Hendricksz himself was instructed that, once Bahia was in safe hands, he was to sail to the Caribbean in order to raid Puerto Rico and to defy the Spanish silver fleets.

The similarities between this project and the original "Great Design" are self-evident. In addition, it might be argued that this second enterprise was really an extension of the first, a necessary and consecutive stage in a fascinating and brilliantly conceived drama. The powerful fleet of Boudewijn Hendricksz—the most ambitious Dutch fleet up to that time ever to have crossed the Atlantic—was designed to consolidate Dutch control over Bahia. Brazil was still the main center of interest as it had been a year earlier. But Africa and the Caribbean also remained as targets of concern. Lam's expedition approximated van Zuylen's enterprise. Despite its lack of political and military success, the Heren XIX did not forget that the van Zuylen venture had been highly profitable. The third auxiliary fleet under Veron had instructions which closely resembled those given the first time to Piet Heyn. Hendricksz' ordinances alluded to the surprising success of Schouten and were accordingly expanded.

The weaknesses of this second "Great Design" are also obvious. Again there would be a dissipation of forces. This serious error would far outweigh the possible advantages gained from striking Spain in several areas at once and throwing her defenses into complete disarray. As in the first instance, the goals of this second "Design" were much too ambiguous: the third fleet had to accomplish two tasks, first in Brazil and then in Africa. Hendricksz had to protect and strengthen the Dutch position at Bahia before he could proceed on the difficult mission in the Caribbean. Last but not least, the Heren xix could easily project meetings at sea, but under bad weather conditions coupled with the failure to understand longitude, such confluences were almost impossible. The actual encounter between the fleets of Lam and Veron verged on the miraculous.

Hendricksz left Texel—Amsterdam's seaport—on March 1, 1625, although some of his ships had already left earlier and others would follow. Adverse weather had kept him at home longer than predicted. In spite of the delay, however, he hoped to arrive in time at Bahia to help in its defense against the Spanish-Portuguese fleet that was expected to arrive there at any time. At the Isle of Wight he met most of the other units of the fleet. From there he sailed south and joined some of Lam's ships to his own. With thirty-three ships at this point, Hendricksz, accompanied by Veron, crossed the Atlantic and sighted the Brazilian coast on May 23.[44] Unknown to either Dutch commander, Piet Heyn was almost simultaneously leaving Fernando de Noronha to return to Holland. The Dutch fleets must have passed within a hundred miles of each other. Had they had modern communications and been able to merge forces, the Dutch would have comprised an unbeatable armada—even against Fadrique de Toledo.

As noted earlier, Hendricksz arrived too late to save Bahia. When he approached the bay and sighted the fifty or more Iberian ships, he could find no way to entice them into the open sea for battle. For two months the Dutch fleet coasted the Brazilian shore hoping for a change, waiting for the enemy to emerge. Don Fadrique, however, stayed where he was as long as he continued to receive reports on the whereabouts of the Dutch fleet.

In July the Dutch general called a meeting of his captains and reluctantly forfeited the watch on Bahia in order to undertake his other commissions. He retained eighteen ships for himself, sent twelve ships under Veron to Africa to join Lam, and dismissed the remainder to go home with the prizes he had taken. When the ships fanned out on August 4, a swift-sailing yacht went ahead to convey the news to the Heren xix.

Hendricksz arrived at St. Vincent, one of the Lesser Antilles, at the end of August, and paused there to refresh and to attend his many sick. Two weeks later anchors were lifted and the fleet sailed to the north.

It was surprised by a hurricane, not rare at that time of the year, which swept away the main mast of the general's ship, and resulted in considerable additional destruction. Altogether, four ships were lost sight of in this storm; they were reassembled, however, within a few days. The crippled fleet rested and refreshed and then sailed to San Juan de Puerto Rico.[45]

Juan de Haro, who had participated in the war against the rebellious Netherlands as an officer in the army of the archduke, was at the time governor of Puerto Rico. He had assumed command of the fort of San Juan Felipe del Morro on September 1, only to learn that the supplies of powder, weapons, fuses, and food were scarce. The news had reached him that the Dutch, now that Bahia had been recaptured, might sail back through the Caribbean. Nor had that eventuality gone unnoticed in Madrid, and the seriousness of the threat was reflected in the royal decision to warn all the governors in this area against the probability of a Dutch attack.[46]

On September 24, 1625, the Dutch fleet was sighted from the Puerto Rican fort. It sailed into the harbor the next day, firing incessantly into the very teeth of the fort's guns, but it could only inflict superficial damage and kill not more than four men. "This was a very courageous deed," wrote de Laet, inspired with awe by Hendricksz' performance.[47] The Spaniards were impressed, too. The Dutch ships dropped anchor in the port out of the reach of Haro's artillery. Intimidated by Dutch intrepidity, many Spanish soldiers and almost all the civilians deserted and fled into the woods. The governor had no choice but to retire within the fort. There he wrote two urgent letters to Santo Domingo and Havana, lamenting his predicament and clamoring for help. Because of Haro's communiqués, the Dutch attack on Puerto Rico was known in Madrid by November, and the War Council immediately resolved to send help. It arrived, of course, much too late to be effective. Aid also came from Havana but again too late.

The Dutch were unable to disembark many men on the day that they entered the harbor because of obstructive shoals. The ensuing delay acted as a reprieve for the inhabitants, and they escaped with their best possessions. The delay also allowed Haro to stock up on supplies. The next day, after an inventory, it was discovered that there were 330 men left to defend the fort, although more than 100 were old and sick. The storekeeper had done so well, moreover, that provisions would last for several weeks.

Hendricksz, in the meantime, was about to disembark the rest of his men. The Dutch general, himself, was among the first to set foot

4. "Grondt-Teeckening vande Stadt en Kasteel Porto Rico ende Gelegenheyt vande Haven" (map of the town, castle, and port of Puerto Rico). From De Laet/Naber, I

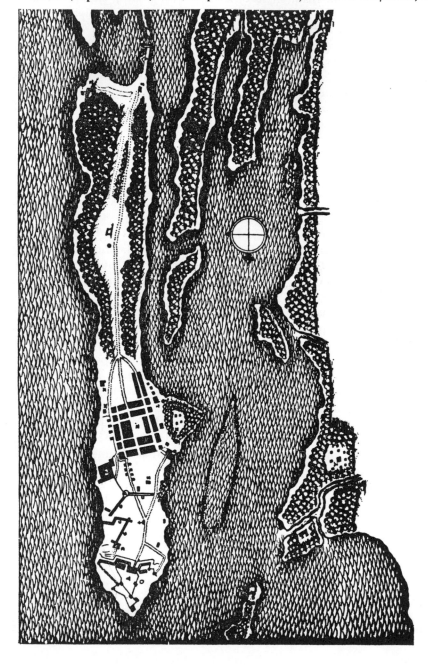

on Puerto Rico's soil, followed by seven hundred to eight hundred soldiers. The abandoned town was soon occupied, and the flag of the Prince of Orange was flown from the platform of the governor's mansion. Very likely, this was the first time a Dutch banner waved over a Caribbean island. From there the Dutch advanced toward the cathedral and smashed the images. A reconnaissance was made of the fort, and a day later trenches were dug on the landside of the castle. Hendricksz relied on his fleet to impede provisioning of the fort by sea. He learned from prisoners that supplies in the castle were dangerously low.

The Dutch had soon set up a battery with six pieces of artillery which began firing that same day. The fort answered the fire, and there were casualties on both sides. The shooting continued for several days. At the end of September Hendricksz summoned the garrison to surrender. Haro refused rather tartly: "I have seen in Flanders," he wrote, "the boasts of those people."[48] The siege continued, and the Dutch dug in, hoping to starve out the enemy. Small boats from the neighboring regions were sneaking through the Dutch guard, however, and were able to make all kinds of deliveries to the Spaniards. The only positive advantage accruing to the Dutch in this stage was a small deserted fort, called Cañuela, situated at the entrance of the bay. Hendricksz posted a ship in the Caño San Antonio to stop infiltrations from the plantations, farms, and cattle ranches east of that area, while his sloops kept the shores of the big harbor under constant vigilance. He could not cut off Haro's supply lines, however.

Since the Spanish governor realized very well the strategic location of Cañuela, he tried desperately to retake the fort. Occasional sorties followed, and, after three weeks, the Spaniards succeeded. Hendricksz was never able to recoup this loss. The point had been driven home, and the Dutch general finally realized that the only way to force the main fort to fall was with the help of siege engineers. The situation was far from auspicious for the Dutch: they were in possession of the town, but that was all. An expected supply ship did not arrive. They sent a second letter to Haro requesting surrender and threatening the town with fire. Once again the answer was defiantly negative. "Go ahead," was Haro's proud reaction, "we have plenty of wood and other materials in the hills to rebuild it."[49] Hendricksz began to withdraw from the island that same day.

Yet, other problems now rose to the surface which required the general's full attention. He still had to leave the harbor, a difficult maneuver because, in the interim, Haro had ordered his artillery to be rearranged to cause the most harm to the Dutch fleet. The town was set afire on October 22; some Spanish ships in the harbor were also burned. The Dutch fleet then began edging out of the port. Haro opened fire immediately and the deadly aim of the Spanish cannon spread fear and havoc among the Dutch. Contrary winds added to Hendricksz' bad luck. Finally, after a week of evasions, trying to stay out of the reach of Haro's guns, Hendricksz could give the final signal for departure. Fate, however, continued to persecute the Dutch. The ship of their vice-admiral ran aground. On November 2, at last, the Dutch said goodbye to Puerto Rico, towing many disabled ships as a reminder of their encounter. Another ship ran aground, and in the end, had to be abandoned. Spanish sources report it to have been a new ship of five hundred tons with forty pieces of artillery. Had they known, the Dutch would have been partly consoled by the fact that in the battle of their departure, the brave governor of the island had been severely wounded.

The Dutch occupation of San Juan de Puerto Rico had lasted five weeks. As soon as the successful beginning of Boudewijn Hendricksz' daring exploits had become known in the United Provinces, strong action had been taken by the Heren xix to keep the island. These efforts had very soon been stranded by the gloomy tidings of the outcome.[50] It could not be denied that the Dutch had inflicted substantial damage: the town had been virtually destroyed and Haro had died shortly after the Dutch withdrawal, but Dutch ambitions had sustained a definite loss.

Hendricksz retired his fleet to the Bay of San Francisco, on the northern coast of the island, to survey the destruction wrought by the Spanish holocaust. He had lost many men, perhaps as many as two hundred; one ship had been sunk, while others had either run leaks or lost their masts. Little solace was derived from the possession of the library of San Juan's bishop Bernardo de Balbuena, of whom Lope de Vega says:

> You had the crozier of Puerto Rico
> When the fierce Hendrick,
>   Rebel Dutchman,
> Stole your library....[51]

For almost a month Hendricksz licked his wounds at San Francisco. Meanwhile, five ships were sent to Santo Domingo on a privateering mission and two others, loaded with booty, returned home. The remaining ships set sail to the west at the end of November. Along the way, the fleet was rejoined by the five privateering ships, which had returned with little profit. Adverse winds drove the Dutch backward toward Puerto Rico, however, and at the beginning of January, 1626, Boudewijn Hendricksz once again found himself in the Bay of San Francisco.

Governor Haro had learned from captured Dutch prisoners that Hendricksz' intentions were to go to Margarita to try to take that island.[52] Warnings were sent to its governor and to Tierra Firme. The Dutch general, in the meantime, had set out for the Lesser Antilles in the face of terrible weather, although no ships were lost. When the fleet soon sailed in tranquil water again, it hopped from island to island, trying to find something worthwhile to attack. On February 22, the Dutch entered the port of Pampatar on the island of Margarita.[53]

The Spanish authorities on that island had been warned, however, and had called up all the colonists and Indians from their *ranchos* to defend the settlement. As soon as the Dutch fleet was sighted, the governor deployed his men over all the points he considered important. He left twenty men at a watchtower which overlooked the harbor, flanked by two small bastions. It was the only fortification, if this construction merited the name, which defended the port of Pampatar.[54]

Hendricksz divided his fleet into two squadrons. One sailed into the harbor firing at the citadel, whose garrison defended itself stoutly for more than an hour and a half. Then the Dutch had a stroke of fortune: one of their shots happened to explode in the mouth of the fort's bronze cannon, which caused headlong flight among the Spanish defenders. Hendricksz, in the meantime, had sailed with the other half of the fleet towards Lance de los Burros, a small inlet used by the Guaiquerí Indians to bring their proas onto the beach for caulking. The site was found to be undefended; the Spanish governor had thought it unworthy of attack, even by the heretic Dutch. Hendricksz landed about five hundred men here. In spite of Spanish resistance, they managed to make their way towards Pampatar. Under the personal command of the general they attacked the stronghold, surprised the fleeing Spaniards, and planted their flag on the tower. The cannons were brought on board the Dutch ships, the fort was razed to the ground, and the little town was burned.[55]

It may have been Hendricksz' intention to launch a similar raid against the capital Asunción, two miles distant. Informed by a Negro deserter, however, that the Spaniards had fortified themselves along the main road, the Dutch general decided upon a change of tactics. The fleet parted and the individual ships set sail for distinct ports on the island. Most of them, nevertheless, converged upon Pueblo del

Mar (Porlamar), two miles south of Asunción. But the Dutch ships had too much draught to come in close to the shore, and the Spaniards lay in wait. Their governor was well prepared for any such emergency and had evacuated his soldiers and some Indian archers to hastily constructed trenches and fortifications. Soon aware of these circumstances, Hendricksz recalled his men and scurried off. In an age in which manifest destiny and personal bravado characterized the Dutch, Puerto Rico and Margarita were humiliating depressions.

From Margarita the Dutch fleet sailed to Coche and Cubagua, two small islands south of Margarita, where the dead were buried and a small village was burned. The fleet afterwards coasted Tierra Firme, visiting little ports like Mochima and Santa Fe where soldiers disembarked to loot and set fire to the neighboring settlements. It also visited the lagoon of Araya and, paying the price of a few men lost, took in a small amount of salt. A yacht was dispatched for home to report what had been accomplished thus far—certainly not much. On Easter, April 10, when the fleet arrived at Bonaire, its crews captured many sheep and cut some wood. The exploratory voyage continued for three more weeks toward the north.

It is clear what Hendricksz had in mind. His instructions had been threefold: to relieve and provision Bahia (yet he had arrived too late); to take Puerto Rico (but that mission had also failed); and to catch a treasure fleet. It may be well to emphasize the point here that neither France, England, nor the United Provinces had, at the time, any designs on the treasure galleons of the Tierra Firme fleet. Hendricksz was, therefore, admonished to avoid any such encounter. The Spaniards, on the other hand, had variously ascribed this policy to cowardice. Again it will be recalled that profit and not glory was the all-powerful motive behind persistent Dutch probes into the West Indies. The Tierra Firme fleet, which was guarded by impressive Spanish sea-power, was considered unassailable. The Honduras flotilla and the New Spain fleet were comparatively less protected, and hence became the main targets of Dutch cupidity.

The New Spain fleet was not due in Havana until July, as Hendricksz knew, and he could thus count on at least a month to cruise in the Caribbean and seize whatever came into his hands. Although at times he split the fleet into units of three or four vessels, they frequently all sailed together. The Dutch were everywhere: south of Hispaniola, around Île à Vache and Cape Tiburón, on the coast of Jamaica, south and north of Puerto Rico, and in the Mona Passage. In the latter place two ships coming from the Amazon—under the command of Hendrick Jacobszoon Lucifer who had provisioned a

Zeelandian colony—joined Hendricksz' fleet. Reinforced, the Dutch sailed about, encountered and sunk more Spanish ships, and generally spread terror and fear in the Caribbean.[56]

As early as the spring of 1625, Madrid had counseled its governors in this part of the New World to take every precaution against the redoubtable menace of a Dutch invasion.[57] It was suggested that the governor of Havana patrol the north coast of Cuba, from Cape San Antonio to the island of Tortuga, and alert the New Spain fleet to any suspicious sails in these waters. At about the same time the viceroy of Peru, convinced that the Dutch were out in force on the Pacific, postponed the conveyance of Peruvian silver to Panama.[58]

In November, 1625, Cuba became really alarmed when news of the attack on Puerto Rico spread like wildfire over the island. Governor Venegas had died, and no successor had as yet been appointed. Cuba was leaderless. Under pressure of popular fright, though, the provisional government hastened to act by sending two ships to Puerto Rico's governor for information and support. Haro could not assuage their fever since he suspected that the Dutch were somewhere close by. Up to April, 1626, no further report on the activities of the Dutch fleet disturbed Havana. Still, the Spaniards could not altogether suppress their premonitions and had kept up a constant state of vigilance. Then the news arrived that Hendricksz had sacked Margarita. A month later more was learned about Dutch privateering. Indeed, the enemy fleet was now reported to be in the vicinity of the Isle of Pines.

Having rounded Cape San Antonio, Cuba's extreme western cape, the Dutch fell upon a small Spanish vessel and were told that while neither the Honduras ships nor the New Spain fleet had yet arrived at Havana, they were expected any day. On June 14, the Dutch entered the Bay of Cabañas at 8 o'clock in the morning, if we are to believe the Spanish slave who communicated these tidings to Havana. Within three days Hendricksz left again, after having loaded his ships with oranges, lemons, bananas, pigs, and calves—an impressive booty, according to de Laet. His powerful fleet of at least twenty-three units now set sail for Havana, a move which posed an ominous challenge to Spanish prerogatives. For more than a month the Dutch occupied themselves by keeping a sharp watch over the area hoping to intercept the New Spain treasure fleet.[59]

Then, without warning, Hendricksz died, "leaving posterity with the name of a gallant, bold, and intrepid naval hero," writes de Laet.[60] His successor, a Fleming named Adriaen Claesz, proved unable to maintain the required discipline and failed to keep his men in line.

Only Hendricksz himself had known how to handle the crews and soldiers on the long and tiring voyage. His demise removed the last bar between discontent and mutiny. Sensing the mounting tide of anger, Claesz tried to appease the men by fanning the fires of greed and by dangling the prospect of Spanish booty constantly before their eyes. But the dream of the treasure fleet could not keep the men quiet. The fleet was then sailing close to Cuban shores. The Morro Castle could be seen from the ships, and its impregnability struck the men. Claesz called a meeting of the ship captains. Faced with the prospect of continuous hardship and heavy losses, they decided to go home. There was no alternative.[61]

The fleet sailed to Matanzas to take in the necessary provisions and to disembark the prisoners. Some of the captured ships were no longer presumed to be seaworthy and were burned. The Dutch next set their course toward the Bahama Channel. They had accomplished almost nothing. Reports from captives mention the Dutch returning home after having lost half of their men. De Laet's account states: "Because of this untimely return of the fleet of General Boudewijn Hendricksz from the regions around Havana, it not only happened that the Company was presented with a beautiful but virtually empty fleet and little compensation, yet had also lost the finest opportunity to inflict losses on the enemy."[62] The full significance of these words is revealed when, ironically, within a month after the Dutch departure the object of their covetousness, the New Spain fleet, sailed safely into Havana.

Early in 1626, the Heren xix had decided to outfit another fleet, composed of nine ships and five yachts, to join Hendricksz in the Caribbean.[63] Although this was not an impressive power by itself, if it were joined to Hendricksz' ships, a mighty battery would be formed capable of tackling the whole New Spain fleet. The admiral of this potent aggregation was Piet Heyn, by whom the Heren xix had already been served well.[64] Heyn was now ordered to place himself under Hendricksz' command. A yacht was sent in April to advise the latter of Heyn's coming.

Meanwhile, the xix had lost track of Hendricksz' exact whereabouts and doings. They had received reports of the events at Bahia, Puerto Rico, and probably also Margarita. His fleet was presumed to be somewhere in the Caribbean, north of Cuba, waiting for a chance to strike at the Spanish treasure. To reassure Hendricksz of their full-fledged support, the xix dispatched 14 ships, 1,700 men, and their finest admiral.

But the Heren xix, masters in the delivery of instructions with a twofold or threefold goal, also had something else in mind for Piet Heyn as he sailed. Once the New Spain fleet had been captured, Heyn was ordered to sail on to Brazil. From the viewpoint of the Heren XIX it is difficult to perceive how Heyn, accompanied by a mere fourteen sails, could even hope to accomplish anything in Brazil except to plague the small coastal towns and to harass Iberian shipping in the area.

Heyn left Holland in mid-May, 1626. He crossed the Atlantic in less than eight weeks and on July 6 touched at Barbados. He next proceeded to the Mona Passage for a prearranged meeting with the yacht that had been sent earlier to advice Hendricksz of the coming reinforcements. Its mission had been unsuccessful, and nothing was learned of Hendricksz' whereabouts. Following instructions and weakening his fleet, Heyn sent two yachts on an exploratory errand to a mysterious "Green Island." He sailed on to Cape San Antonio himself. Although the Dutch ships kept out of sight of the Spanish lookouts, they nevertheless managed to stay close to the Cuban coast. From a captured Spanish vessel taken at the end of August, Heyn learned about Hendricksz' death and the subsequent departure of the latter's fleet.[65]

Confronted with the unforeseeable, Heyn hesitated until he received positive information from a Spanish captive that the New Spain fleet had left Vera Cruz a month before and was undoubtedly safe and sound in Havana. He now sailed to the Dry Tortugas, west of Florida, to wait for Spanish stragglers. While there, the entire treasure fleet, consisting of about forty ships, among them thirteen galleons, passed by his gaze. In a hastily called meeting of the fleet's council, Heyn and his captains weighed the chances for a successful attack. This idea was reluctantly thrown overboard, however, because of the small numbers of the Dutch. Thus de Laet's bitterness: if Hendricksz' ships had been present, the Dutch might easily have overpowered all the Spanish ships. Heyn recorded, "If I had found the beforementioned Hendricksz there...I would, with the help of God, have taken the whole fleet. It grieves me that I had to let so beautiful an opportunity slip through my hands only because of a lack of assistance."[66]

The forty Spanish ships which the Dutch had counted were indeed the fleets of Tierra Firme, New Spain, and the Honduras flotilla, led by Tomás de Larraspuru. Although Heyn's force did include some large ships, it was simply no match. Contemplating the Dutch presence from afar, the Spaniards regarded the latter's weakness as a godsend. The governor of Havana, Lorenzo de Cabrera, however, was not so jubilant since he judged rightly that the reprieve was of temporary nature. He was apprehensive lest the Dutch hibernate in some West Indian port, only to redouble their energies in the next summer for "some undertaking with which to offset the many misfortunes which had befallen them and the thin picking they had found."[67]

For the moment his fears were groundless. After realizing the foolhardiness of further deliberation, Piet Heyn devoted all his attention to the second part of his instructions—Brazil. Except for water, he was still well provisioned. His other supplies were more than sufficient and were augmented with those originally laid out for Hendricksz' fleet. His first concern, consequently, was to fill the water barrels. He set forth for the nearest accessible land. In the neighborhood of Cape Canaveral (Cape Kennedy), he succeeded in obtaining much-needed fresh water by having his men dig wells.[68]

This problem solved, Heyn was now confronted with the difficult task of leading his men through perilous waters to Brazil. The passage was further complicated by the prevailing northeastern trade winds. The only course open to the Dutch was to sail north and to trust in their luck until, at the prescribed latitude, the west winds would carry the fleet to the Azores. The ships could set sail from there for the west coast of Africa and then across the Atlantic to Brazil. It turned out to be a long and troublesome voyage. Arriving at the Azores, a yacht was detached with orders to report home. The rest of the fleet continued the voyage south. At one of the Cape Verde Islands the Dutch refreshed. Many of the men were suffering from scurvy, but they recovered slightly during the respite. Pausing once more at Sierra Leone, the fleet crossed the Atlantic and touched the Brazilian coast early in March, 1627, a month later than was expected.

Piet Heyn decided almost immediately to attack Bahia, and, in a way this venture was reminiscent of Hendricksz' raid on Puerto Rico. The Dutch fleet sailed into the bay, sank or captured twenty-six Iberian ships, and sustained only minor setbacks. According to de Laet: "This had been one of the bravest acts done by Admiral Pieter Pietersz Heyn for the West India Company—by which happy result this company—by so many proceeding disasters and damages so much weakened—began to recover her breath and bounced back on her feet."[69] In July, four richly laden ships were dispatched to the United Provinces. Heyn replaced his own losses with captured Spanish vessels and thus amplified his fleet. After undertaking a very profitable privateering expedition along the Brazilian coast, he again turned to Bahia and seized more Iberian ships. He sailed home in October,

1627, and was received with honor: the Heren XIX awarded him a heavy gold chain and a medal.[70]

Thus the second "Great Design" had failed, not only in its Brazilian project, but also in the Caribbean even though the Dutch admirals had sown terror far and wide. The third goal of this design, which concerned the African coast, was not achieved, and it too succumbed to catastrophe.

Lam, the commander of this third wing, must have had some influential friends among the XIX since his military record was far from promising.[71] Although he found part of his fleet usurped by Hendricksz' expedition, he nevertheless enjoyed the full confidence and corroboration of the XIX in the execution of his part of their grand scheme. On January 4, 1625, while some of his ships were already under way, Lam himself set forth. He briefly joined Hendricksz before the latter crossed the Atlantic. Perhaps he commanded only as few as four ships when he approached the Guinea coast. His activities there have not been consistently recorded. At least not much is known before October, 1625. In that month he aligned himself with Admiral Veron who had crossed the Atlantic from Brazil for a corporate attack on the Portuguese castle of Elmina. Additional help was forthcoming from Arent Jacobsz of Amersfoort, the Dutch governor on that part of the coast. Together, they considered their forces adequate: at least 16 ships and 1,200 men.

Although the Portuguese at the castle were weak, the governor had placed a number of allied Negro troops in ambush. He promised them a reward for each Dutch head they could bring him. The carelessness of the Dutch leaders, in spite of Jacobsz' protests, led to four hundred deaths, including Admiral Veron's. Jacobsz was saved by his own slaves. Lam also escaped and arrived in the United Provinces in June, 1626. The Dutch would have sustained greater losses if the Negroes had not hankered after European clothes. They forced their captives to strip before beheading them so that the shirts would not be stained with blood. The time involved in selecting their prospective outfits allowed many Dutch to save their hides.[72]

This was the end of the second "Great Design." Notwithstanding heroic efforts and enormous expenses, the Dutch had not succeeded in depriving the Spanish king of one square foot of his African or American realms. Nor had they been very effective in depleting Spain's treasury. They had interfered with intercolonial trade and caused it to decline drastically, and they had also spread terror and nightmares throughout the Caribbean; but they had only implemented minor goals and fallen short in all their major designs.

Concern for the large-scale operations of the West India Company during the first years of its existence is too often excessive. This obliterates, almost without a trace, the various smaller expeditions fitted out during this same period. In addition to the parties of van Zuylen and Schouten, which were both intrinsic parts of a "Great Design," several other missions were executed in 1625 and 1626. In terms of information and finances, the results of these smaller expeditions not uncommonly benefited the larger, more famous enterprises.

Late in 1625, for instance, the Amsterdam Chamber fitted out two ships for a privateering venture to Brazil. These ships left Texel in December, 1625. The little squadron was joined by three Zeelandian ships near the Canary Islands. On the Brazilian coast near Pernambuco, another squadron of five sails was encountered which had also been commissioned by the West India Company. In unison, at times sailing under one command and at others separately, the combined Dutchmen constituted a chafing irritant to Portuguese navigation. After congregating at Fernando de Noronha, most of them proceeded to the Caribbean, where they subsequently refreshed at Grenada, set their prisoners ashore at Margarita, and policed the southern coasts of Puerto Rico and Hispaniola. The privateers returned home in October, 1626, after a very propitious voyage.[73] A remainder of this group, led by Commander Thomas Sickes, had an inopportune meeting with a Portuguese fleet of twenty-two sails but was able to elude the persuers, and arrived in the Low Countries in March, 1627. Others, operating on their own, like the yacht "Otter" under Cornelis Corneliszoon Jol, embarked upon a profitable career in privateering along the coast of Brazil and in the Caribbean area.[74]

The accomplishments of the Dutch West India Company in those early years were truly exceptional. If the number of miscarried enterprises were large in the West Indies, Africa, and along the Brazilian coast, still Piet Heyn's adventure in Brazil was a huge financial success, as were those of Schouten and van Zuylen. The positive aspects of a markedly pecuniary nature more than compensated for the suspension and abrogation of the all-encompassing but idealistic greater schemes. Spurred by these results, small expeditions were once more outfitted in 1627 by the Chambers of Zeeland and Amsterdam.

The Zeeland ships of 1627, under the command of Lucifer, transmitted colonists to their new home on the Wild Coast. They afterwards turned their bowsprits towards the Caribbean area and were soon employed in privateering pursuits and exploratory missions.

Near Coquibocoa, this squadron of three ships chanced a meeting with two yachts, which had been endorsed by the Chamber of Amsterdam and which had, in the course of things, lost contact with their admiral. This little fleet roamed the Caribbean together.

The maintenance of contact between ships or fleets was a weak link in all Dutch operations. Contact was often made by letters left at a certain prearranged rendezvous. The Amsterdam yachts, for instance, found letters from the Zeelanders at St. Vincent which announced that the latter were anchored at Grenada. The Zeelanders had just left, however, when their compatriots arrived. Both squadrons roamed the Caribbean in search of each other, ransacking Spanish settlements and taking Spanish prizes wherever they could. When they finally met at Coquibocoa, they sailed on together to the southern coast of Cuba. Three of the vessels almost collided there with the two treasure ships from Honduras which were en route to Havana. One of them was captured; the other escaped and limped into Havana port a few days later. The captured ship fetched the handsome gain of 1,200,000 guilders for the company's stockholders; the Dutch admiral Lucifer, however, died of wounds received in the encounter.[75]

Dirck Simonszoon van Uytgeest's commission of 1627, despite the presumed loss of two of his ships, also evolved into an extremely rewarding undertaking. Along the Brazilian coast and without serious impairment to themselves, the Dutch were responsible for the spoliation of at least eight Spanish or Portuguese ships. Van Uytgeest met Heyn's fleet at Fernando de Noronha, but after a few days the two leaders parted company. All in all, after the Spanish trophies had been carried home, the efficacy of this last mandate had been well assured.[76]

The failures of the "Great Designs" were thus to some extent offset by the successes of the smaller enterprises. Van Zuylen had stripped, destroyed, or made useless at least twenty-nine Iberian ships and had brought most of their cargo home. In Bahia the Dutch had overtaken eleven ships when they subjugated the town. Schouten had captured at least six, and Piet Heyn the same number. The total number of Dutch spoils in 1624 is impressive: sixty-nine ships, with almost no losses for the Dutch. In 1625 eighteen ships were seized, in 1626 another twenty-nine. The year 1627 was especially profitable for the company: no less than fifty-five Spanish or Portuguese ships, most with rich cargoes, fell into Dutch hands. Of these Piet Heyn could claim thirty-eight in Brazil.[77]

As Andrews rightly observes, the amount of Dutch booty fetched here and there was not too important when compared with the amount of bullion which ultimately reached Spain.[78] But it is equally true that the cumulative effect on the Spanish economy of recurring and severe shipping losses warranted disaster. Spanish bankers correctly interpreted the problem as they staggered from one crisis to the next.[79] They became increasingly aware of the pernicious anemia which drained both the government and the commercial system. In the Low Countries bankers and merchants, backed by their government, were just then experimenting with the joint-stock company. The surplus, derived from the worthwhile results of 1627, enabled the Heren XIX to equip four new fleets destined for the West Indies in the following year. One of these fleets captured the long desired treasure fleet—the dream of every pirate in that unscrupulous century.

8

THE SILVER FLEET

Piet Heyn, zijn naam is klein,
Zijn daden benne groot,
Hij heeft gewonnen de zilvervloot...[1]

The West India Company, encouraged by the success of its small ventures in 1627, results which Piet Heyn, that "worthy successor of Heemskerck,"[2] had largely provided, continued to plan expansively. Even before Piet Heyn had returned from Brazil, the Heren XIX had outlined some additional projects and submitted them to the States General for support. These projects involved three fleets. The first one, composed of twelve ships, was destined for Brazil. It sailed from the home ports early in 1628 to privateer along the enormous Brazilian coastline. Because of the strong winds encountered crossing the Atlantic, this fleet arrived north of Brazil and was forced to cross the ocean twice more before arriving in the neighborhood of Pernambuco. But the success of this venture was notable: it captured at least eleven or twelve Spanish and Portuguese ships, transferred their cargoes into their own, and sailed back home by April of the following year. This very profitable enterprise has been so overshadowed by Piet Heyn's exploit at Matanzas that the story has been almost completely forgotten by the chroniclers of that period except, of course, by de Laet.[3]

The other projects involved two fleets: one of thirty-six units which was to leave in the spring of 1628 and the other of forty-five ships to leave port in the fall of that same year. The States General was requested to provide the money for supplies for these ventures which were designed specifically to attack the Spanish treasure fleets.

The Provincial States of Holland which favored these plans soon passed a resolution to promote them. The States General, however, hesitated, and in the end offered only part of the requested sum for supplies. The Heren XIX, modifying their huge plans, accepted the government offer because the situation had changed; privateering, after three or four years of continuous losses, seemed finally to be swinging to the company's advantage.[4]

Together with the fleet destined for Brazil, the West India Company soon had a second fleet of twelve ships operating. It left the Low Countries about the same time—early in 1628—and began operations in the Caribbean after March 15. The expedition was commanded by Pieter Adriaenszoon Ita and soon yielded substantial prizes: within a few weeks it had captured four enemy ships, one with a rich cargo of ginger. Another ship, carrying a cargo of Negro slaves, had been sunk by an unfortunate shot.[5] Plans were laid to sail into the port of Santiago de Cuba, as Boudewijn Hendricksz had once done at San Juan de Puerto Rico, to capture a ship loaded with copper bound for Havana. This did not materialize because Ita felt that the port lying beneath the fort was too narrow for maneuvers.

The ships of this fleet, spread all over the Caribbean, gathered on the orders of the admiral at a rendezvous situated at Cape Tiburón, the extreme western tip of the island of Hispaniola. Thus united, the Dutch embarked to Cape San Antonio and proceeded from there to the Dry Tortugas, Florida's most western outpost, the legendary lookout for all privateers watching for the Spanish treasure fleets. Ita's force, much too small to attack the Tierra Firme fleet from Cartagena or the New Spain fleet from Vera Cruz, cruised in the area, hoping to capture the two Honduras galleons which were then expected at Havana.

The Dutch, as shall be seen in the course of this chapter, were well advised about the movements of the Spanish fleets in the Caribbean. Their invasion of the *mare clausum* with regular fleets produced, as mentioned in the previous chapter, much concern in Havana and throughout the West Indies; it disturbed the Spaniards considerably more than the amateur efforts of earlier years. The invasions had, moreover, lost their incidental character; they now consisted of professionally organized pillagers acting under the auspices of a powerful organization and backed by the High and Mighty Lords of the States General of the United Netherlands.[6]

The appearance of Ita's fleet, soon known to Spanish authorities, prompted the governor of Havana to dispatch *navios de aviso* to Vera Cruz, Cartagena, and Porto Bello with a warning not to sail. The brave commander of the Honduras ships, Alvaro de la Cerda, therefore requested and received arms and ammunition from Havana to assist in the defense of his ships. Perhaps the reinforcements convinced Cerda that his strength was now sufficient to risk the crossing by way of the Yucatán Channel, proceeding thus to Havana.

The Dutch were waiting for him. Sometime earlier they had captured a ship laden with hides and sarsaparilla from Honduras; they were advised that the treasure galleons were following. Indeed, the sails of the two huge ships were seen almost as soon as the smaller ship was taken. The galleons were formidable; they had crews of two hundred to three hundred men and were armed with twenty cannons. Within two miles of Havana and in sight of the port, the Dutch attacked. Cerda, in panic, tried to escape along the coast into the port, but the faster Dutch ships—they were smaller, had less draught, and could sail closer to the shore—prevented this maneuver. A terrible fight ensued. The Spaniards enjoyed a preponderance in firepower, but the Dutch had more ships and these were more maneuverable. The brave Spanish defense, carried on in full view of Havana, lasted all through the morning of August 1, 1628.

In the afternoon of that day, Cerda and his vice-admiral beached their ships and began to disembark their crews. The Dutch continued to fire on the ships, wounding the admiral and nearly causing him to drown. The vice-admiral, still fighting, almost managed to capture one Dutch ship, but Ita came to its rescue and the *almiranta* was forced to surrender. De Laet reports that half of the Spanish crewmen were killed, not a few by drowning in an attempt to escape from the ships.[7]

Governor Lorenzo de Cabrera of Havana had not been idle while all this was going on. He had dispatched two well-armed frigates to Cerda's support, but Ita countered with one or two of his ships and the governor's frigates retreated back into the harbor. Thus the Dutch had seized the richly laden Honduras galleons for the third time since the end of the Truce. The captured cargoes consisted of indigo, ginger, silver, hides, and other products of the Honduras region.[8] This particular victory, however, was partially unsuccessful because of the inability of the Dutch to free one of the captured ships from the shore and the consequent necessity of burning it.

Rumors reached Ita that the Tierra Firme fleet would soon arrive. Since the Dutch admiral knew full well that his twelve ships were no match for this fleet, he decided to evacuate the area north of Havana. Ita's fleet, towing the captured Spanish *capitana*, left the area, passing so near the fortress at Havana that they were fired on. In the Bahama Channel the Spanish galleon was set afire, presumably because it was too badly damaged to survive the Atlantic crossing. After a thanksgiving service on board the ships, the Dutch sailed home, arriving in September, 1628.

The departure of Ita's fleet, which was soon known to the Spaniards, led them to make a grave mistake.[9] They did not know that another Dutch fleet, this one commanded by the celebrated Pieter

Pieterszoon Heyn, had already entered the Caribbean. Heyn's secretive approach to the West Indies, combined with his superb leadership and able seamanship, permitted him to capture the Spanish Silver Fleet—the one and only time that feat was ever accomplished.

"The Chartered West India Company," related de Laet, "having kept her eyes constantly on the fleets of the King of Spain from Tierra Firme and New Spain, now having received the means to do something more than before, and wanting to satisfy the good inhabitants of these countries completely, has thought it expedient to outfit still another powerful fleet, in addition to the two before mentioned fleets, and to send the former to the West Indies under the command of Pieter Pieterszoon Heyn as general." The reason for the choice of Heyn was the fact that he had "rendered so many useful services before."[10]

This very powerful fleet, "fitted out more first-rate than ever before, both in officers and crews," according to the historian van Wassenaer, was composed of thirty-one ships, most of them more than three hundred tons. The *Amsterdam*, Heyn's flagship, was a thousand tons; the *Hollandtsche Tuyn* ("Dutch Garden") of his aide was eight hundred tons. Perhaps as a counterbalance to Heyn's widely known intrepidity, the Heren XIX had appointed as his second in command the "prudent" Hendrick Corneliszoon Loncq.[11]

Pieter Pieterszoon Heyn—Piet Heyn as he was called—was born in Delfshaven, near Rotterdam, in 1577. Almost nothing is known of his parents except that they belonged to the lower class: "He emerged from his parents' modest background because of his courage and the glory of his actions," says the epitaph of Heyn's mausoleum in the Old Church in Delft. In the democratic Netherlands, humble parentage did not necessarily mean that a man must remain poor. And indeed, it is known that Pieter Corneliszoon, alias Heyn, the sea hero's father, was the proprietor of a house in Delft. From the widow's inventory of her husband's possessions we know that in addition to the Bible, the elder Heyn possessed some books on navigation and a Dutch translation of Grotius' *Mare Liberum*. The father was thus probably an intellectually inclined man who, at least shortly before his death, had been a captain of a ship convoy which protected the herring fleet.[12]

Aitzema, the well-known chronicler of this period, was curiously hostile to the great general, calling him a "sailor of fortune, though risen to the rank of general of a mighty fleet."[13] We prefer the accolade accorded to Heyn by his own local historian: "the never-enough praised sea hero Pieter Pieterszoon Heyn."[14]

Heyn probably began his naval career when he was sixteen in 1593.

5. Map of the Caribbean with the routes of the treasure fleets.

At the time, the Dutch were just beginning their adventure to the East and the West. Young Pieter soon realized the dangers of that perilous drive—he was taken prisoner by the Spaniards and was forced to serve in the galleys. The experience was not entirely negative, however, for Pieter gained a masterful command of the Spanish language. Minister van Spranckhuysen, a personal friend of Heyn's, reports that Pieter had more than once fallen into the enemy's hands "who often pointed their pikes and rapiers at his chest and throat, but did not do worse because his time had not yet come."[15] At one time he was also taken prisoner in the West Indies, held at Havana, and served in the galleys of Santa Marta. This is confirmed by some of the Spanish prisoners captured in Heyn's adventure with the Silver Fleet.[16] His epitaph was later to read: "He has had India, Spain, and Flanders as witnesses, first of his slavery, then of his freedom and victories." Once Heyn was released in a general exchange of prisoners which took place before or in 1598; another acquittal might have taken place in 1602.

In 1607, the thirty-year-old Heyn sailed in the fleet of Admiral Verhoeff to the East Indies. During this voyage he rose to the rank of skipper, leaving the East in that capacity in 1611. He married soon thereafter. In 1617 he probably made another voyage to the East Indies, returning in 1622. In that year he was made a magistrate of Rotterdam; some opposed his appointment because he was not a burgher of the town, but the opposition was overruled because Heyn "had married a burgher's daughter and had lived at least ten or twelve years in that town."[17]

In 1623 Piet Heyn was appointed vice-admiral under Jacob Willekens with the fleet which was destined to take Bahia. His operations in that area against the Portuguese during 1624 and 1625 merited his promotion, upon his return to the Low Countries, to admiral of the West India Company. This commission placed all other officers except Boudewijn Hendricksz under his command.

Hendricksz had died by the time Heyn arrived in the West Indies late in the summer of 1626. The latter, following instructions, proceeded to Brazil. This was the voyage on which he distinguished himself by sending home some four prizes and by his formidable attack on Bahia where he took twenty-two ships from the Iberians. He returned to the Low Countries from that mission in October, 1627.

By this time Heyn's reputation was such that the Heren XIX found him the most qualified candidate to entrust with the mission of capturing one of the Spanish silver fleets in the Caribbean   The

Dutch had the advantage of knowing the movements of these fleets. As early as 1561, the Spanish government had attempted to control the annual crossings; from 1596 onwards, subject to small changes, the sailings had become more regularized.[18] In addition, since 1623 the Heren XIX had made a systematic study of the movements, composition, strength, armament, crews, and cargoes of the annual silver fleets. This knowledge was passed on to Piet Heyn.[19]

The information, when it reached Heyn, consisted of two parts: a general memorial on the ships which sailed annually from Spain to the New World, including the Tierra Firme fleet, and a second more specific report on those destined for New Spain and Honduras.

From San Lúcar, the port of Seville, and from Cádiz, both fleets, at different times of the year, sailed to the Canary Islands and from there across the Atlantic to the Lesser Antilles. The Tierra Firme fleet was to sail from the Canaries to the Galleon's Passage between the islands of Tobago and Trinidad and enter the Caribbean in that way. This fleet—called the *galeones*—ordinarily left Spain in April escorted by eight galleons, six of which belonged to the finest and biggest of the Spanish war navy and were known as the "silver-galleons." They measured more than 600 tons, were armed with 24 to 28 pieces of artillery, had crews of 250 to 300 men and, in addition, often had around 100 soldiers. These eight galleons convoyed twenty or more merchantmen to Tierra Firme. The fleet also dispatched boats to notify officials in Margarita, Puerto Cabello, Río Hacha, and Santa Marta of its forthcoming.

Sailing along Tierra Firme it paused at Cartagena to disembark passengers and cargo to be sold in the area. Then it proceeded to Porto Bello, eighty miles west of Cartagena, where it arrived early in June. The remaining passengers—Spanish officials, merchants, and colonists—disembarked there. The fleet next took on the precious metals and other products brought from Lima to Panama by ship and to Porto Bello by mules. It then returned to Cartagena to load more goods. Toward the middle of July, the fleet, now worth an estimated ten million guilders in cargo, sailed through the Yucatán Channel to Havana. It passed Cape San Antonio about August 10, though sometimes as much as eight days sooner or later than that date.

The second fleet, called the *flota* or the *flota de San Juan*, consisted of four galleons. Two of these were destined for Honduras, two for New Spain. They were part of a convoy of fifteen or more merchantmen destined for the Greater Antilles, Honduras, and Mexico. This fleet sailed later in the year and entered the Caribbean between Guadeloupe and Dominica, usually in August. In that neighborhood it anchored and refreshed. From the Lesser Antilles the *flota* set course to Cape San Antonio, sending off dispatch boats to San Juan de Puerto Rico, Santo Domingo, Jamaica, Santiago de Cuba, and Campeche. Two of its four galleons sailed then to Trujillo. After the *flota* had passed Cuba's west point, it changed course more to the west and proceeded to the fortress of San Juan de Ulúa. Once the fleet was in that harbor, it was moored to the iron rings embedded in the fort walls; it would be protected in this way from the northern winds known to sink those vessels not properly anchored. The fleet ordinarily reached San Juan de Ulúa in early September. It unloaded its cargo, valued at eight million guilders, and remained there during the winter, not leaving until the following June. During the winter it was laden with gold, silver, cochineal, indigo, hides, tobacco, campechewood, and many other products with an estimated value of fourteen million to fifteen million guilders.

In June the *flota*, now sailing without the two of its escort galleons that had been sent to Honduras, proceeded to its next destination, Havana, passing Cape San Antonio for the second time in the first half of July.

The two Honduras galleons ordinarily passed Cape San Antonio shortly afterwards. In its wake the Tierra Firme fleet would also pass this strategic outpost. All the ships usually arrived at Havana in this order, although irregularities in this schedule were not uncommon. From here, under the protection of the twelve galleons, they proceeded at the end of August through the Bahama Channel to the Azores—the route which Columbus had once followed. From the Azores the combined fleet sailed to the port of San Lúcar, then up the Guadalquivir River to the *Puerto de las Mulas* where the officials of the *Casa de Contratación* took charge.

The instructions of the Heren xix to Piet Heyn included some significant touches. The Heren xix had specifically added:

You must take care that you maintain strict discipline. You must incite all who have sailed out for the defense of our so brave Provinces, against the common enemy. This is the fleet which brings to Europe the golden rod which chastizes the whole of Christianity and discourages it, a rod the force of which can be subdued by twenty-four well-armed men-of-war and twelve well-provided dispatch boats armed with guns and ammunition and manned with courageous soldiers whose only wish is to fight the enemy.[20]

They pointed out that the size of the fleets often differed, that while the port schedule was fairly regular, no time schedule was reliable because of weather conditions. Another fact which could delay sailings, though it was not specifically pointed out, was the presence of privateers. The activities of these foreign intruders were closely watched by the Spanish. If a foreign fleet of any size was hovering in the area, officials immediately sent out warnings.

In 1626, while operating in the Caribbean, Heyn had experienced the frustration of witnessing the passage of the combined silver fleet without having the means to attack it. At that time he had written a report of the affair which confirmed the fact that Heyn was well aware of the system of Spanish navigation and vigilance. According to his calculations, the more vulnerable of the two treasure fleets was the one from New Spain, and the most logical place to launch an attack was San Juan de Ulúa, despite its fortress. Another possible choice, Havana, was much too impregnable for the Dutch purposes. A third choice was the area between Havana and Cape San Antonio. Heyn had accordingly asked the Heren XIX for twenty-eight ships, six yachts, and twelve heavy sloops, which he felt was a sufficient force. In all probability, when the Heren XIX appointed him as their general over a fleet of more than thirty sails, they had this projected attack in mind.

Heyn also had an alternative plan for his venture in the Caribbean. During his previous trip to join Hendricksz' fleet, he had captured a small Spanish yacht and had learned about the Honduras galleons from its crew. These galleons, he had been told, wintered in the virtually undefended Bay of Amatique, west of Trujillo, and sailed from there in June or July to Havana. Heyn was confident that it would be easy enough to capture these two ships if the moment were correctly chosen.[21]

Heyn's report also mentioned the *sine qua non* for any attack on a Spanish fleet in the Caribbean: the commander who wishes to succeed must, at all cost, avoid discovery by Spanish officials while he awaits his chance. It is to Heyn's credit that he followed his own advice, and it is undoubtedly due partly to this strategic technique that he prospered in his own attempt at Matanzas.

In April, 1628, Piet Heyn received his commission as admiral and captain-general in the service of the West India Company. His formal title was general.[22] Second in command was Hendrick Corneliszoon Loncq who, strangely enough, had refused the upper command twice before, in the Bahia expedition of 1624 and as well in the one of Boudewijn Hendricksz of 1626, but now accepted a secondary position under Heyn. The fleet, described heretofore, was equipped with 129 bronze and 550 iron cannon, 2,300 sailors, and 1,000 soldiers. Its extraordinary component was the size of some of the ships: eight hundred and a thousand tons. Vessels of five hundred to six hundred tons were in those days generally the largest used.[23]

The fleet left Texel during May, although some ships did not sail before June or July. Some, indeed, barely arrived in time to take part in the capture of the Spanish fleet in September. East of Portland, Heyn paused to impart to his men the provisions of the "ship regulations," as well as to give the stragglers a chance to catch up. Van Spranckhuysen reports that Heyn ordered the Bible read morning and evening, a psalm sung, and did not allow cursing or quarreling aboard. The minister's conclusion reads, a mission which begins that way simply cannot fail for "the righteous man is courageous as a young lion."[24]

As Heyn's fleet lay in wait, five ships drifted away due to a heavy fog. These returned, however, bearing news from an English privateer that the Spaniards were preparing more than a hundred ships in La Coruña. This rumor had probably been spread by the Spaniards themselves in the hope of deferring Dutch fleets from American waters. Heyn did not believe it. He narrowed down the number of ships in the area by sending off those which were not under his command. His hope was to keep his presence unknown to the Spaniards.[25]

Late in June, Heyn's fleet was sighted sailing south of the Canaries, but it was not known there whether it would sail to Brazil or to the West Indies. After opening his instructions Heyn crossed the Atlantic, refreshing on July 12 at St. Vincent, one of the Windward Islands. He rigidly prevented communication between his crews and the native population. A second stop at Blanquilla supplied the fleet with fresh goat meat. Its departure from the island was postponed for one day because of the disappearance of one young crew member. When the boy was not found, Heyn left but ordered one yacht to remain an extra day in case the boy returned. He did not. The disappearance of this boy, apparently an unimportant loss, proved to have consequences Heyn may well have anticipated.

Proceeding with care toward the Greater Antilles, Heyn sailed to the Isle of Pines, south of Cuba, and from there around Cape San Antonio. The Dutch general believed himself to be unobserved. By the beginning of August, he had placed his ships in the best strategic position to await the treasure fleets: the open sea between Havana and Cape San Antonio to the south, the Tortugas Cays—or Dry Tortugas— to the north (see map). His fleet was not yet complete; two additional ships joined him on August 3, and Vice-Admiral Joost van Trappen, alias Banckert, arrived five weeks later with another six or seven ships.[26]

Despite his caution, however, Heyn's presence had been known for some time to the Spanish authorities. Twenty-seven of the Dutch ships had already been sighted from Morant Point, the extreme southeastern point of Jamaica, and in a letter from Francisco Terril, the island's governor, to Admiral Tomás de Larraspuru, this fact was not only mentioned but details about the size of the ships had also been added. The letter mentioned, moreover, the fact that the fleet was sailing westward and was not the Tierra Firme fleet, which was usually sighted south of Jamaica at this time.[27]

In another letter to the admiral, written by Domingo Vásquez, governor of Caracas, news came that a Spanish vessel, which had been repeatedly plundered by foreigners, had sighted a fleet of 150 sails stationed in the Caribbean with the obvious purpose of attacking the *flota* and the *galeones*. Some of the information in this letter had come from a young stranded Dutchman at Blanquilla—the young crew member Heyn had lost previously—and who now communicated the disturbing news that more ships were coming.[28]

Warned by this information, the Tierra Firme fleet did not leave Cartagena, and it thus escaped capture by the Dutch. Meanwhile, other evidence of impending danger reached the Spaniards. The two ships which joined Heyn on August 3 had violated his strict orders about caution and had refreshed at Grenada and St. Christopher. Their crews had been attacked there, and thirty-eight or thirty-nine men had been lost. This incident also gave ill-needed publicity to the Dutch presence in the Caribbean. In addition, Vice-Admiral Banckert had anchored at Tobago where fifty-four of his men, sent to obtain provisions, had been killed by the natives. The presence of the Dutch was thus revealed in that area.

Piet Heyn was completely unaware of these instances. In addition, he probably did not know that he had been seen off Cuba's southern coast on July 28. But as luck would have it, the Spaniards presumably ignored the fact that there were two Dutch fleets operating in their sea, one under Ita and the other under Heyn. When Ita's fleet was reported leaving the area and sailing home, the Spaniards made the disastrous mistake of concluding that all Dutch ships had left the region.

Thus, for almost a month, the Dutch fleet under Heyn sailed undetected in the narrow sea of the Florida Straits, wrestling against the wind and current which were driving the fleet deeper into the Straits. Heyn's problem was to remain relatively in the same spot in order to maintain reconnaissance. For this purpose the fleet council agreed to move the fleet more to the east of Cape San Antonio. This maneuver brought the ships so close to Havana that on August 22 the crew could see the Morro Castle and, of course, the fleet could likewise be seen from the castle.

Governor Lorenzo de Cabreza, realizing by now that this was an entirely different enemy fleet, immediately dispatched fifteen boats to various ports with warnings. How many of these reached their destination is not known. Nine warnings were sent to the New Spain fleet, supposed to be close to the Dry Tortugas. Not one of the nine boats arrived. Meanwhile, on August 21 Heyn had captured two Spanish dispatch boats which were posing as innocent fishermen and from them he learned that neither the New Spain nor the Tierra Firme fleet had as yet come to Havana. A week later he captured another dispatch boat. He now gathered that his presence was no longer a secret to Spanish officials, but he suspected that neither treasure fleet had as yet been warned and that it was his duty to watch and wait.[29]

The Dutch general was a born organizer. Immediately after arriving with his fleet in the open sea between Cape San Antonio, Havana, and the Dry Tortugas, he had developed his plan of attack. Dividing his fleet into three lines, one to sail behind the next, he had carefully composed each division into two squadrons. Each squadron consisted of one large ship, one smaller ship, and one or two yachts. The squadrons formed units with defined instructions and a definite goal. As soon as the enemy was sighted, each Dutch officer was to attack his Spanish counterpart. However if a treasure fleet was sighted too late in the evening for such a maneuver, the general was to attack the first galleon, the others were to attack those following in order. A system of signals was developed to warn or inform the other ships; a system of flags was also drawn up. Finally, leaving nothing to chance, Heyn devised a list of punishments in the case of cowardly or treasonable neglect of duty, together with a list of remunerations for bravery. A special award, moreover, went to the man who first sighted the treasure fleet.

From port to starboard the order of ships was as follows:[30]

FIRST LINE

Second Squadron	*First Squadron*
2 yachts, Adm. Loncq, 1 ship	1 ship, Gen. Heyn, 1 ship

SECOND LINE

Fourth Squadron	*Third Squadron*
1 yacht, Comm. Root, 1 ship	1 yacht, Vice-Adm. Claesz, 1 ship

THIRD LINE

Sixth Squadron	*Fifth Squadron*
1 ship, 1 ship, 1 ship	1 yacht, Rear-Adm., 1 ship

When, on August 3, the two additional ships had increased the strength of the fleet, Piet Heyn added a fourth line to this order, consisting of one squadron. A few yachts were not included in these lines but performed tasks of information and communication.

Trying to keep abreast of the strong current, now east, now west of Havana, the Dutch fleet cruised closer to Havana and tried to keep its ground. The wind continued to be strong, a factor which would become essential to the capture of the Spanish fleet. On September 1, the Dutch fleet was three to four miles west of Morro Castle, four miles from the coast, and struggling to come in closer. It managed to come as near as a swivel-gun's shot and carefully scrutinized the port from that distance. The treasure fleets, Heyn learned with pleasure, had not yet arrived.

On September 2, Heyn ordered a yacht to intercept some warning boats leaving Havana and sent a ship to look for Vice-Admiral Banckert who had not yet joined the fleet.[31] On September 3, the wind again blew from the west, and, although the Dutch tried desperately to stay close to Havana, they were driven back into the Florida Straits. By September 4, Havana was seen in the southeast; on the next day the ships were pushed eight miles east of that city.

The wind blew more from the south on September 6, and the Dutch saw Pan de Matanzas—a high mountain having the form of a loaf of bread—eight or nine miles to the west. The wind, blowing more and more from the south, caused the Dutch—but also the approaching Spanish fleet—to drift away from the coast. On September 7 the wind shifted again and came once more from the west.

On that same day Vice-Admiral Banckert joined the fleet with his squadron of six or seven ships. The strong wind then drove the entire Dutch fleet almost to Matanzas, fifty miles east of Havana.

Early in the morning of September 8, Piet Heyn heard shots and sent out a yacht to investigate. This yacht learned that a ship of the sixth squadron had captured a vessel of the Spanish fleet, whose captain had mistaken the Dutch ship for one of his own. From the Spaniards, Heyn learned that the main body of the Spanish fleet was on its way.

On July 22, 1627, the day of St. Mary Magdalene, the *flota* of St. John, under the command of Juan de Benavides, knight of the Order of Santiago and general of the fleet, left Cádiz to convoy a number of merchantmen to Honduras and New Spain. He was a veteran sailor, having served his king for eighteen years, and had made a fortune on various voyages to the West Indies. His admiral on this expedition was Juan de Leoz, also an experienced sailor. As scheduled, part of the fleet took off by itself and sailed for Honduras; the remaining ships proceeded to Vera Cruz and arrived there September 16, 1627.[32]

While Benavides' fleet wintered at Vera Cruz, excitement ran high in the Spanish Court when it became known that the Dutch West India Company had sent Heyn with a huge fleet to the West Indies. Although the Spanish government knew precisely how many ships were involved, curiously, it did not seem to have grasped what Heyn's objective was. It thus delayed warning its Caribbean governors until it was too late.

Benavides' fleet left Vera Cruz toward the end of July, 1628. It then consisted of twenty-one or twenty-two ships. Of these ships, only four were of real importance: the flagship, the *Santa Gertrudis*, the *San Juan Bautista*, and the *Nuestra Señora de la Antigua*. They carried treasure, while the other ships carried cargoes and provisions: hides, brazilwood and other products of New Spain. Of the named vessels, only the first two were men-of-war, and all of them were heavily laden with merchandise. All carried passengers; the four or five larger ships, probably because of their size and more comfortable arrangements, were actually crammed with people. The disastrous result was that the pieces of artillery on deck were completely surrounded by temporary cabins, luggage, and merchandise and proved useless when the attack came.

During the fleet's stay in Vera Cruz, many of the crew had deserted in order to try their luck in the New World. They had been replaced by persons who were actually passengers bound for Spain. Reports reveal that the muster and the distribution of arms could only have been superficial. Signals and passwords had not been agreed on, and there was a conspicuous lack of discipline. Witnesses testified, however, that conditions on this particular voyage were neither better nor worse than on other occasions.

Benavides left San Juan de Ulúa on July 21, 1628. Unfortunately, even as it was leaving port, the fleet ran into trouble. The general's flagship ran aground and had to be unloaded in order to refloat her. The *Santa Ana María* was now made the flagship, and it took some eighteen days to put the cargo of the stranded ship in the new *capitana*. The fleet left Vera Cruz for the second time on August 9. Before the end of the month it was broken up by storm. The *Santa Ana María*, the *San Juan*, the *Santa Gertrudis*, the *Antigua*, and a few other merchantmen stayed together. The remainder of the fleet, however, was scattered and out of view when those ships approached the Florida

Straits.[33] Most of them, however, sailed together, at not too great a distance west and northwest of the galleons. This was the situation on the morning of September 8.

It is not too difficult to reconstruct what happened on that September morning because Spanish and Dutch sources substantially agree. Piet Heyn, in his report to the XIX, mentioned the wind as blowing from the southeast.[34] Stated another way, this meant that Dutch sources concur in that a land wind was blowing from the direction of the Cuban coast. In view of the maneuver of the Spanish fleet in its first moment of distress, trying to escape the Dutch, a sea breeze must have blown, at least in the late afternoon. This is confirmed by Spanish witnesses who declare that on the night of September 8 the usual land wind did not rise. Whatever may be true, both sources agree that in the evening there was little or no wind at all.

Advised that the Silver Fleet was on its way, Piet Heyn proceeded northeast of Havana and sighted twelve Spanish sails, nine of them at lee, the remainder at windward. This Spanish vanguard had unknowingly been guided all night by the lights of the Dutch fleet. Indeed, one Dutch ship had even sailed among the Spanish reconnoitering their strength. Heyn immediately seized the nine ships at leeward, although it took him all morning. Since Heyn knew the bigger prey to be somewhere in the vicinity, he did not waste any effort in pursuit of the others, and, consequently, the other ships managed to escape.

About noon the Dutch spotted another nine or ten ships. Six of the ships lay to the east at windward. Their size made them easily identifiable: Piet Heyn knew he had found what he had been waiting for. The Dutch and Spanish fleets had apparently crossed each others' lines during the night. Benavides had not paid enough attention to the discovery of a Dutch ship among his own. More important, from his point of view, was the fact that at daybreak he found himself east of Havana and north of Matanzas. His pilots had been following the lights of their vanguard during the night, but the vanguard had sailed in the wake of the Dutch. Benavides now found himself far offshore and at Heyn's mercy.

On board two of the galleons, the *Antigua* and the *almiranta*—and perhaps also on board the *capitana*—orders were given to clear the decks of all the passengers, sleeping accommodations, and luggage so that the artillery could be used. A huge Dutch fleet was bearing down on the Spanish from the northwest, but Benavides failed to call a fleet council while he might still have done so.[35] Instead he called for a meeting of the staff of his own ship, including two members of the *audiencia* of New Spain who were his passengers aboard. There were

6. Map of the Dutch attack on the New Spain fleet.

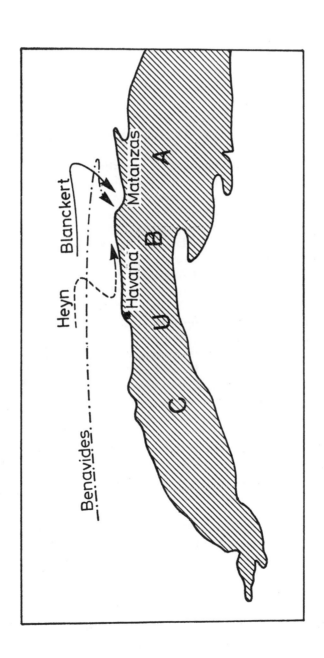

serious discussions on what to do. In the meantime orders were given to sail back in the direction of Havana.

The Spaniards had two alternatives: to strike for Havana, which meant a certain fight with the Dutch, or to attempt to reach the nearer Bay of Matanzas southwest of the fleet. Benavides' pilots assured their general that they knew that bay. The plan finally agreed on favored the second choice; in addition it was decided to close off the bay by stationing one or more ships at the entrance. An immediate attack would thus be impeded. The next step called for the men to unload the treasures and either carry them off into the hills, or drop them overboard into the bay. The last measure was to set the galleons on fire.[36]

Between the several sessions of the meeting Benavides decided to call a general fleet council. At the same time, however, his *capitana* increased sail so that the *almiranta* and the others lagged behind and could not send any representatives over.

Piet Heyn realized that his primary mission was to prevent the Spanish ships from reaching Havana. The enemy fleet had already turned south and was heading for shore. The Dutch sails were faster, however, than the heavily laden Spanish, in spite of the fact that the latter, trapped, had the advantage of the wind. Piet Heyn also knew that short of Havana, the Spanish could escape into the Bay of Matanzas—or at least make an attempt. He made his decisions quickly. He immediately dispatched nine ships under Banckert—probably the sixth, seventh, and the Banckert squadron—to sail southeast, thus getting in front of the Spanish and obstructing their escape to the east. Together with his remaining squadrons, Heyn sailed southwest to prevent a Spanish effort to escape toward Havana. Thus the Dutch fleet held the Spanish in a vise, or as Benavides was later to testify, "The enemy fleet had divided itself into two squadrons, the one which came behind our fleet, while it tried to take the wind out of our sails—the wind was blowing east or southeast—while the other sailed in front of our fleet in such a way that we were closed in."[37] Thus the Spanish were driven to take refuge in the Bay of Matanzas—a cul-de-sac.

Benavides might still have saved his treasure, even then, had not panic broken out among the men. Because of their anxiety to get out of reach of the enemy's guns, the men refused to obey orders, and the ships ran ashore. As Benavides later complained, everything seemed to lead to his ruin.[38] Worse yet was the fact that the Spanish ships now found themselves unable to direct their artillery toward the entrance of the bay; only the smaller pieces of the stern-posts could be brought into action, but these could not be fired without endangering their crews. Even darkness did not aid the Spaniards since it was a clear tropical night with an eleven-day-old moon.

Benavides tried to execute an orderly plan. A small group of soldiers disembarked, taking the treasures ashore to protect them. By the beat of the drum, it was forbidden for anyone else to leave the ships. But confusion soon broke out. The first Dutch ships appeared at the entrance of the bay, and although they dropped anchor, their presence nevertheless upset the Spaniards to a considerable degree. Night was quickly falling, and the Dutch were awaiting orders. After some time Vice-Admiral Banckert arrived, sailed with his nine ships into the bay, and ordered the others to follow him.

With the Dutch so close, Benavides now countermanded his orders and sent word to his captains to disembark their passengers and to set fire to their ships. Explosives were brought out and fires started, while Spanish sloops ran back and forth unloading the terrified passengers. Mass confusion soon reigned everywhere.

A huge white sail spread out by the Spaniards to protect their munitions and other supplies formed a clearly visible target for the Dutch, who soon directed their heavy guns toward it. They also fired on the sloops, probably in the belief that the Spaniards were unloading their treasures. The Dutch firing was deadly enough and contributed to the general havoc on board the Spanish ships. The latter ventured seven or eight shots and were then quiet. On the beach, the terrified Spaniards ran for cover. The crews refused to return to the galleons even when the general, sword in hand, intervened personally, loudly declaring that salvation lay in obedience. No one listened.

Now Piet Heyn reached the bay. Night had fallen. Heyn ordered a shot fired to halt the ships ahead of him. He then had two fires lighted as seamarks, since he wanted to wait at the bay entrance until his entire fleet had been reassembled.

It was probably the Dutch firing that completed the confusion among the Spaniards. Because of the danger, the sailors were unwilling to return to their ships which they now expected to explode at any minute. Many still on board tried to reach shore but drowned in the process. Hundreds waited on the ships in despair, watching the Dutch disembark their men, and asked quarter: "*Amigos, amigos, buena guerra.*" Now Benavides panicked himself and ordered someone to bring him to the governor of Havana.

No slaughter took place. It seems that the Dutch hesitated before boarding the Spanish vessels because they expected resistance. Heyn had to use threats before his men were willing to climb up the ropes hanging from the galleons.[39] Even then they held back until a young Dutch boy boarded one of the Spanish ships and whistled a tune which all the Dutch recognized. No one on board the Spanish ships was killed. "Piet Heyn," wrote van Spranckhuysen, "behaved like a Christian captain, mixing the sterness of his fists with the sweetness of his words and promises."[40]

The Spaniards surrendered without a fight. The many prisoners taken by the Dutch were immediately put ashore. Among them was Admiral Leoz who, having had a chance to change uniform, had not been immediately recognized by the Dutch. Actually he fared far better than his superior, having tried in vain to organize some sort of resistance.[41] The Spaniards, in general, had behaved in a most cowardly way in this situation.[42]

While one would not disagree with the designation of Piet Heyn as a "Christian captain," it is certainly clear that he was inspired by more than humane considerations. Although even his enemies the Spaniards praised him for the charitable and kind treatment of his prisoners—priests and Jesuits joining in the accolades—the Dutch general understood perfectly well that his masters at home were interested in profit, not in glory and blood. Therefore Heyn soon boarded the Spanish ships and investigated each of them for cargo. All Spaniards were escorted ashore—in one ship the general found 150 men—so as to prevent any mishap which might rob him of the precious treasures he had captured. Some of the Spaniards tried to leave with gold and silver hidden on their persons, but it was all largely recovered.[43]

Once the Spanish ships were in his hands, and the Spaniards removed to the shores, Heyn had to prevent looting by his own men. He thus ordered the Dutch to return to their own ships and left only guards aboard the captured Spanish vessels. Soon thereafter a thanksgiving service was held by the Dutch.[44] After all, they had won this victory with virtually no casualties, although the enemy had lost three hundred men and at least the same number had been wounded.[45]

The Dutch general had achieved the dream of the century: the capture of a Spanish treasure fleet. Four huge galleons and two smaller vessels were captured in the Bay of Matanzas; nine Spanish ships had been taken earlier that day. Later a Spanish wine ship was also seized. Of the three ships that had successfully escaped earlier that day, two were later driven ashore where they burst. Only one ship reached Havana, and two or three stragglers of the fleet managed to arrive there also. It was a great victory.

The Dutch fleet did not linger in the Bay of Matanzas; Heyn well knew that the silver galleons of the Tierra Firme fleet would soon come by and could capture him in his moment of triumph if he delayed. So he made all possible haste in unloading the captured ships and taking over their cargoes. Chests, cases, and bags marked *por el Rey* (for the King) or *por su Majestad* (for His Majesty), or directed to the Jesuit College in Rome, passed from the Spanish ships into those of the Dutch.[46] The transfer required eight days. In spite of all precautions, however, some of the silver and gold was stolen. Heyn called an inspection and recovered part of this "improper booty." A few of his men had acquired at least fourteen pounds of gold. Most of it was returned by the offer of rewards. Nevertheless, when the fleet, on its return journey dropped anchor in Plymouth, some English members of the crews deserted, giving up their pay and promised prizes, a sure indictation that they had already compensated themselves with Spanish gold.

Except for the four galleons and one other smaller ship, all the captured ships were then burned. Heyn divided his crews to man the salvaged ships. With a few exceptions, the Spanish prisoners were set free and given provisions to survive for three or four days until help could get to them from Havana.[47]

On September 17, the Dutch general ordered sails hoisted, and the Dutch left Matanzas. In addition to his own ships Heyn now commanded the four Spanish galleons which represented some ninety to a hundred pieces of additional artillery. He wrote his report and dispatched two fast-sailing yachts to the Low Countries to inform the Prince of Orange, the States General, and the Heren XIX of the wonderful news. Simultaneously he requested their advice with respect to the situation at Dunkirk where privateers in Spanish service were constantly harassing Dutch merchantmen. The two yachts left Heyn's fleet on September 26. They arrived home with the good tidings around mid-November. Amidst all the rejoicing, however, the Heren XIX and the States General did not overlook Heyn's request; indeed, the States General decided to send a squadron to convoy Heyn's fleet through the English Channel.

The voyage home was an exciting but tiring experience for the brave and successful general. In a letter written from Falmouth, December 8, 1628, Piet Heyn gave a substantial account of the happenings during this long crossing of the Atlantic. During the first seven or eight weeks, heavy storms blew continuously. One of the Spanish galleons, the *San Juan*, ran a leak and could not be kept above water. During the next three days of improved weather it was unloaded. The cargo—hides and campeche wood—was transferred onto some of the other ships, along with its artillery. Then the empty hulk was burned.

Another Spanish ship, the *Santa Gertrudis*, damaged its bow, its bowsprit, and its foremast. These were replaced as efficiently as possible under the circumstances. This same ship then became separated from the main fleet because of bad weather, but was fortunately able to join Heyn after almost a week. Once again the ill-fated ship was lost, and it was not to be seen again until it reached Falmouth, leaking but safe. Others also were dispersed on the journey home, not always because of bad weather, but simply because they sailed faster. The *Santa Ana* lost her topmast. One of the Dutch yachts was forced to cut his own mast to create an emergency rig for the damaged Spanish vessel.

Nevertheless, and in spite of all adversity, the main body of the fleet reached the Isle of Wight on December 4.[48] Now Heyn learned that some of his ships had already arrived home, but he was also told that many "pirates" were lying in wait for his fleet at Dunkirk. Since contrary winds prevented Heyn from anchoring at Wight, the general, after some hesitation, decided to sail on to Falmouth. He arrived there four days later with eight of his ships. He immediately sent letters to the English ports of Wight and Plymouth to reestablish contact with the lost units of his fleet. While he waited at Falmouth, the *Santa Gertrudis*, so long lost, limped in, leaking like a sieve. The cargo she carried had to be transferred into the other ships. This meant, however, that some of the Dutch ships were now overladen, which caused more headaches for the general. In addition, the *Santa Gertrudis* had unloaded three hundred spoiled hides, and the English port officials insisted on collecting the corresponding duties. This demand proved to be the source of some friction. As a result, Heyn mistrusted the English and took steps to have his ships guarded at all times.[49]

In 1625, the Dutch and the English had concluded the Treaty of Southampton which guaranteed free access and departure to and from the ports of each country. Just at the moment when Heyn needed the friendly cooperation of his hosts, however, the English were riled over certain actions taken by the Dutch East India Company, in particular the so-called Ambon atrocities. It was perhaps fortuitous that, although the English fleet arrived home while Heyn was at Falmouth, its ships were badly in need of repair and quite unable to launch an attack. Had they been able to join the Dunkirkers just then—and considering the English and Spanish desire for peace this was not an unreasonable possibility—Heyn could certainly not have escaped. Prior to his arrival, there had been rumors that London might delay any Dutch ship which came to an English port.[50]

The States General, aware of Heyn's precarious position, had already sent a squadron to Heyn "for his best security against the Dunkirk 'pirates' as well as *otherwise.*"[51] The Prince of Orange, as admiral-general of the United Provinces, was authorized to order the squadrons of the various admiralties to watch for the expected fleet. News also came that the Dunkirkers were preparing an attack. Rumor had it that the Spaniards were outfitting sixty ships for the same purpose. Finally, the situation was compounded by the fact that Dutch harbors were filling up with many of their own men-of-war which should have been at sea protecting the fleet of Heyn.

This was partly the result of Lieutenant-Admiral van Dorp's incompetence, and partly because of the fact that the five admiralty boards simply could not agree upon any concentrated action. Thus Holland's Provincial States met with the Prince of Orange to demand a new lieutenant-admiral. The prince delayed in the matter, claiming he did not know of one capable of filling the position—the plan to nominate Piet Heyn may already have been forming in his mind.

In the impasse created in spite of the Treaty of Southampton, the States General not only sent the aforementioned squadron to assist Heyn against the English, Spanish, or Dunkirk attacks, but, urged by the Heren XIX, secured from Charles I a declaration which confirmed the said treaty. Heyn, as yet unaware of the royal pledge, wrote to the Dutch ambassador complaining of his circumstances and defending his actions regarding the aforementioned three hundred hides which he had managed to sell in England. The affair was soon settled to the satisfaction of everybody, and the English made no further trouble for the Dutch.[52]

On January 2, Heyn ordered the units of his fleet at Wight and Plymouth to sail; he left Falmouth on January 3. Four days later the Dutch had passed the danger zone near Dunkirk. In another two days the general was home. Since the fleet had been sailing in three or more units, these arrived home at different times. The galleon *Santa Ana* had managed to run aground off the Irish coast, but the cargo and the crew had been saved. The rest of the fleet also arrived home safely. Losses had been negligible: only 150 men had been killed, although many were ill when the ships finally docked in the Low Countries. Of the four captured galleons, only one reached the Netherlands; the cargoes of the other three, which had been wrecked or so badly damaged that they had had to be abandoned, had been saved.[53]

Having dropped anchor in the port of Hellevoetsluis, Piet Heyn and his admiral, Loncq, traveled to The Hague. On January 14, 1629, together with four members of the Heren XIX, they appeared in a meeting of the States General. Heyn reported on his voyage and chronicled its fantastic success. Both he and Loncq were treated magnificently: fifty cannons were fired, there were fireworks, and the church bells tolled "all to express joy and give honor to the present persons and thanking the Lord in the churches."[54] Indeed, the whole country was proud of the man who had made true the inscription on his pedestal erected some 250 years later: *Argentum auro utrumque virtuti cedit.*[55]

From The Hague, Piet Heyn and his admiral proceeded to Leyden, the well-known university town, home of director-historian de Laet. The tumultous welcome there provoked these words from Piet Heyn: "See how the people now rave because I have brought home such a huge treasure, for which I did not do much; but before, when I had fought and did many things much greater than this one, they really did not care and did not notice it."[56]

From Leyden, the triumphal procession moved on to Haarlem, from there to Amsterdam, where both men were received by the directors of the WIC in the West India House. A huge celebration was held in the evening and another one the next day. The Prince of Orange honored the general with a gold chain and a medal, while all over the United Provinces manifestations of joy were given publicly, especially in the border towns so that the enemy would know about the great victory.[57]

Nor was that all. After Heyn and Loncq had appeared in the States General, Their High Mightinesses presented the general with another gold chain and a medal worth 1,500 guilders, and gave the admiral a smaller set worth 750 guilders. Each carried this glorious inscription:

INDICA CLASSE INTERCEPTA,
PARTISQUE SINE SANGUINE OPULENTISSIMIS SPOLIIS
AD CUBAE PORTEM,
HISPANORUM NUNC DAMNIS QUAM OLIM CAEDE NOBILIORUM,
FOEDERATAE BELGICO-GERMANIAE PROCERES,
E GAZA CAPTIVA MONUMENTUM,
CUDI FECERUNT. CIƆDCXXIX
CUM PRIVILEGIO.

The other side read: HEINIADES NUPER SENSIT SPOLIATA MATANCA.[58]

More medals were struck, all exalting the incredible feat, the
courage of the Dutch, and the humiliation of the Spaniards. But they
were not the only medium through which popular feeling manifested
itself. It also found eloquent expression in the pamphlets or "blue
books" which were now published. Van Spranckhuysen wrote a little
book under the long title *Triumph of the Happy and Over-Rich Victory
which the Lord our God September 8 of the Year 1628 has brought to the
Fleet of the West India Company under the Command of General Pieter
Pieterszoon Heyn against the Silver Fleet of our Enemy coming from Nova
Hispania at the Bay of Matanzas.*[59] With the Bible and the classics as
his reference, the good minister further rejoiced: "Saul has slain his
thousands, but David his ten thousands" and "Let ancient times show
off their heroes: those of Troy their Aeneas, those of Macedonia their
Alexander, those of Carthage their Hannibal, those of Rome their Julius
Caesar." The Dutch now had a hero to rival these ancient giants.

Van Spranckhuysen, who called himself "not a merchant, not a
soldier, but an ambassador in the Name of Jesus Christ," offered also
the following advice to the Heren XIX about the disposition of the
treasure: "May a good college be built for the education of the alert
minds and God-fearing souls in order to propagate through them the
true religion in the countries of the West Indies."

Another eulogy of the time praised God and welcomed Piet Heyn
as "the wise, resolute and brave Sea-hero."[60] In still another, the
King of Spain was brought onto the scene protesting:

> What? Must a Monarch, head of the Castilians,
> Who signs "Yo el Rey," be put on the spot
> By those Lutherans who are my Rebels?[61]

Most of the pamphlets, however, confined themselves to the simple
voicing of popular mirth: "Welcome, welcome, brave hero, with
your treasures, with your silver...."[62] A more pious and learned touch
was added in the Latin verse that closed: "You, eternal God, our
Victor and Ruler, the Guard and Protector of this Republic, the only
one whose help we acknowledge, adore and venerate in this victory."[63]
Perhaps this feeling was really at the bottom of popular sentiment.

The value of the gold, silver, and merchandise brought home by
Piet Heyn was estimated at 11,500,000 guilders (see Appendix IV).
Another estimate, this one by Witte Corneliszoon de With, captain
of Piet Heyn's flagship, placed the value at 13,000,000 to 14,000,000
guilders. Net profit, after deduction of expenses, must have
been around 7,000,000 guilders; the Prince of Orange as admiral
received 10 per cent or 700,000 guilders. The officers, crews, and

soldiers, received a liberal 10 per cent of the total or 17 months of full pay. Piet Heyn himself thus wound up with 7,000 guilders. The total for the entire fleet, including the men who had been killed and whose heirs received the payments, amounted to almost 950,000 guilders.[64]

According to Article xxviii of the charter, the directors themselves together received 70,000 guilders. Many discussions by the Heren xix took place concerning the amount of dividend to be paid to the shareholders. The latter, referred to by Aitzema as the happiest people in the country, immediately requested huge payments. There were many voices urging a modest dividend since they wanted the wic to keep most of the money in the company treasury, on the model of the eic which had always paid low dividends and which had, consequently, "risen to the power it still has."[65] The Heren xix finally decided to please the participants and pay 50 per cent of the net profit or more than 3,500,000 guilders. Together, total payments amounted to almost 5,500,000 guilders, leaving only 1,500,000 guilders in the treasury of the company.[66] In addition to this capital, Heyn's success made possible an increase of capital by one-third through new investments.

Although His Excellency the stadhouder was quite content, the directors pleased, and the participants overjoyed, not everyone was satisfied. The crews which had accomplished the feat were not happy. Riots broke out in Amsterdam, and if we can believe the Dutch poet Joost van den Vondel, the crew members even acquired a cannon to blast their way into the West India House. They asserted that the Heren xix pretended that the booty was smaller than it really was, which cost them three or four months pay. Troops were summoned quickly, the rioters dispersed, and the leaders taken into custody.[67]

Perhaps Piet Heyn was not entirely satisfied with his share either. It might be true that in those days 7,000 guilders represented a huge sum of money, but it was not much when compared to the 31,000 guilders that had been paid to Heemskerk after he had taken a Portuguese *carráca* in the East.[68] However, there is no proof for the assertion that Heyn, unhappy about his reward, left the West India Company to become lieutenant-admiral in the service of Their High Mightinesses—the first admiral to serve them who did not belong to the Dutch nobility.

The impression which the capture of the Silver Fleet left on the hearts and minds of the Dutch was deep and lasting. Mention has already been made of the many manifestations of noisy but well-meant joy and cordiality with which the general was welcomed everywhere.

Men of letters were also excited. Historians like Barlaeus, Pontanus, and van Wassenaer, as well as many others, composed Latin poems in honor of Heyn. Their themes were taken over by the vernacular. It was, as was stated before, the great century of the Word of God. De Laet thanked Providence for the great victory; the sceptical diplomat Aitzema called it a "singular guidance of God." There was an abundant flow of poetry, most often bombastic, sometimes in stately hexameters, sometimes with little or no rhythm at all. Proof of the effect of Heyn's triumph is that while it produced a flourish of praise immediately afterwards, it also remained one of the sources of inspiration for nineteenth-century popular songs.

Heyn's fame soon spread beyond the borders of the United Provinces. Some in Europe may have felt a slight tinge of sadness for the Spaniards, who, deprived of their Mexican revenues at the same time that they had allied themselves with the Catholic League, would not be able to consummate their warlike plans against France nor stamp out the heresy of the German countries.[69] But many could not hide their joy. The French ambassador in The Hague congratulated Their High Mightinesses, as did the "Winter King" (then residing in the Netherlands), the Ambassador of Venice, and the envoys of England, Denmark, and Sweden. The States General also ordered its ambassadors to communicate the glad tidings to the kings of France and England.

In Paris, where the news was received with the greatest interest, even French adherents to the Spanish party at court paid their respects and complimented the Dutch envoy. Richelieu, of course, was strengthened in his anti-Spanish intentions to send his armies into Italy.

In London the Dutch ambassador used the Spanish humiliation of Matanzas as a counterweight to the pressure being exerted upon England to sign a peace treaty with Spain. To this possibility the Dutch now were able to add that under no circumstance would they accept conditions for a truce or peace from Spain. Charles I, pro-Spanish by nature and envious of the Dutch, behaved courteously, making *bonne mine à mauvais jeu*—showing them a happy smile—and congratulating them, but as to what went on in his mind, one can only guess.

The most curious reaction came from the Vatican. It seems logical that the Church would express deep sorrow and much compassion in this crushing defeat of a Catholic king by heretics and rebels. However, the tensions and bad relations between the pope, the Italian Urban VIII, and the Spanish king at that time led the pope to comment that the news of Piet Heyn's victory was to him as appetizing as the Gospel itself.[70] All of Rome rejoiced and was happy with him.

The United Provinces, enriched with a booty of millions, could now open an offensive war against Spain. It laid siege to 's-Hertogenbosch, an important bishopric in Brabant. This extremely difficult military operation was carried out successfully by the young Stadhouder Frederik Hendrik. But soon the delighted country had bad news to consider. Rumors ran that Piet Heyn, who had performed so brilliantly for the West India Company for the previous four or five years, had resigned. This soon proved to be true.[71] Certain conditions set by Heyn which concerned improvements in the fleet had not been accepted by the Heren xix. The good relations between Heyn and the stadhouder resulted in his appointment as lieutenant-admiral of the official war-navy of the United Provinces. The wic replaced Heyn with Loncq.

Piet Heyn served but a few months in his new capacity. In June, 1629, in an engagement with the Dunkirk pirates, he was killed. Aitzema wrote: *Mori nos est turpe, sed turpiter mori.*[72] Heyn's body was taken to Delft and buried with great ceremony in the Old Church. There lie the mortal remains of the man who was the most dangerous and successful adversary of the Portuguese and Spaniards since the death of Drake. Heyn was, at the same time, one of the most able commanders in the Dutch West India Company, and certainly the most popular.

When news of the Dutch victory reached Spain—via the Low Countries—"it tortured the Court, made the merchants tremble and bewildered everyone."[73] The loss of the treasure was bad enough, but worse was the fact that the Spaniards now had to deal with an insult to His Majesty. For the first time in history, in spite of many attacks, an entire fleet had been lost.

As soon as Benavides and his admiral reached Spain, they were arrested and put in prison. They had arrived with the Tierra Firme fleet under the command of Tomás de Larraspuru, who, warned by the governor of Havana, had stayed in Cartagena until he was certain the enemy had left the Caribbean. Benavides and Leoz were held incommunicado. So blameworthy did the behavior of his general seem to the king—especially the fact that he had left his ship without putting up a fight—that His Majesty at first refused to allow him to defend himself.[74] Philip's early indignation seemed to mean that nothing less than Benavides' head upon a pike would satisfy him. Unfortunately for Benavides, the affair was not to be handled with such dispatch.

After the king's primary reaction, the prisoners were put into the hands of the proper authorities. Juan de Solórzano Pereira of the Council of the Indies was appointed as public prosecutor. He had been a member of the Audiencia in Lima and was considered an excellent jurist. His address to the court on the guilt of Benavides, liberally spiced with numerous Latin and Greek quotations, certainly illustrated his fine erudition if not his objectivity.

It took five years to bring Benavides to the scaffold and his admiral to lifelong exile. Many witnesses appeared for the prosecution, few for the defense. When the first main point of the trial came to public attention—the circumstances in which the catastrophe had taken place—Benavides was already revealed as a man who had followed neither general rules nor specific instructions. The amount of deck cargo which he had permitted and which prevented the effective use of his artillery counted heavily against him. Another point brought up by the prosecution was the accusation that both Benavides and Leoz had been the first to desert their ships. This certainly was not true of the admiral, while in the general's case, his presence ashore was probably more necessary than his presence aboard. What weighed, however, most heavily against Benavides was the fact that he had not called for a fleet council until it was too late. Instead, without consulting anyone, he had given the order to retreat to Matanzas. Had he called this council at noon, when the Dutch fleet was first discovered, resistance might have been organized, or so it was claimed, and it would have been possible to reach Havana. The prosecution argued that since Benavides' fleet was nearer to the coast, it would have been dark before the enemy could have met it in battle, thus making good its escape. Not only the testimony of Captain Hernando Guerra, "one of the most experienced men," but that of all others was unanimous in this respect.[75]

Benavides' reputation was further damaged by the testimony that he had panicked when he saw the Dutch so near, and that he had not done much to control the confusion. It should have been possible, it was said, to save the treasure, since there had been enough time to throw it into the water, which was only four fathoms deep at that point. The Dutch, it was claimed, had no divers. Benavides himself was charged with an obvious lack of discipline and with the virtual absence of any attempt to save the king's gold.

The trial revealed that the Spaniards believed that all would not have been lost had there been adequate leadership. Witnesses testified that the Dutch had hesitated to board the Spanish ships. The Dutch, so it was alleged, were "cowards" and had not dared to climb aboard even after the ships had been abandoned until Heyn himself had arrived on the scene and threatened them if they did not obey. Spain, it was said, was deeply hurt about losing her beautiful ships and marvelous treasure to "those men in rags, without personality, without dash."[76]

Her greatest calamity, as a nation, was that her reputation as a strong power was decisively undermined by Heyn's venture. "Who can hear of this and not seize high heaven itself in angry hands? Who, at the risk of a thousand lives, if he had them, would not avenge so agrievous an affront?" asked an angry Spaniard who advocated an immense armada to recover this lost repute. "The Hollander has so degraded us that commonly, in adjacent kingdoms, where formerly they called the Spaniards 'unchained lions' they now call us 'embroidered Marias' with braided hair and padded legs."[77]

The trial dragged on, but it was clear from the outset that Benavides was a doomed man. He could not provide any satisfactory answers, and the written testimonials which had been received from Havana long before the trial were discredited because it was suggested that they were unduly influenced by Benavides and his friend the governor of Havana.

Leoz shared the ill fate of his commander, though to a lesser degree. The most serious accusation against him amounted to negligence and failure to set his ships afire.

Solórzano y Pereira summed up his accusation in two tremendous points: first, that even if the accused had not been guilty they should be punished as an example and, second, that such crimes permitted no pardon and had to be dealt with harshly. Benavides was sentenced to death; Leoz was exiled to Africa where he died. *Vae victis.*

On May 18, 1634, Benavides, attired in black with the cross of Santiago in his hand and sitting on a mule also draped in black, covered the last mile to the scaffold. He passed through the most important streets of Seville where the population saw the once so arrogant general humiliated as he proceeded toward the square of San Francisco. He was accompanied by 250 monks carrying burning candles. Passing the door of the Royal Audiencia building the public crier announced, "This is the justice that the King our Lord and his Royal Councils ask to carry out on this man for his negligence in the loss of the fleet of New Spain, which the enemy took in the year 1628. Whoever did this, let him pay for it."[78]

At the square Benavides was led to the chair in the middle of the scaffold while some officials and priests accompanied him. The general knelt at its side, received absolution, then sat down holding in his right hand the cross given to him by the bishop of Santiago. Then Benavides asked the executioner to do his duty. The latter tied the general's arms, legs, and body to the chair, and bandaged his eyes. Then, according to custom, he buried a knife three times in Benavides' throat.

Once again the public crier repeated the proclamation which he had called out before the Royal Audiencia, warning the people not to touch the body. After a few hours the monks of San Francisco took the body and dressed it in a Franciscan robe. Benavides, says the narrator of one moving account, looked like a Saint Paul with his grey beard. The nobility of Seville gave the general a magnificent funeral as an expression of public sentiment, and as a silent protest against the tyrannical cruelty of Olivares who had punished as a crime what had only been, in the public eye, an unfortunate occurrence.

The capture of the Silver Fleet was the result of a combination of excellent planning, preparation, order, and strong leadership by the Dutch. The total absence of leadership on the part of the Spaniards combined with a conspicuous lack of discipline and an amazing negligence contributed to their crushing defeat. The testimony of many eyewitnesses proves that during this whole expedition, and especially in the confused period while both fleets were in the Bay of Matanzas, Piet Heyn conducted himself as an efficient commander. The same cannot be said of Benavides.

Heyn had failed to reach Cape San Antonio unobserved, although he had tried hard to do so. He may not have known about the excellent spy service maintained by Spain at Brussels and Antwerp and her system of lookouts along the Caribbean islands. He had arrived at the right time—during July and August—and at the right place—north of Havana—where the Spanish fleets, once they had left their ports, could not escape him. He had taken excellent care to intercept all warning boats. Even so, Benavides might have avoided him because of his long delay at San Juan de Ulúa. In addition, the fact that no news reached him from Havana should have aroused his suspicion.

There is some evidence that Heyn had made up his mind to go home when, on September 8, his patience was rewarded. The rapidity and exactitude of the maneuver which he executed to enclose the Spanish fleet reflect the determination and perspicacity of a great leader and the fine control he had over his fleet and his men. Spanish and Dutch sources agree that, at Matanzas, Heyn maintained good discipline among his men under circumstances which were both confusing and difficult. He was kind to the prisoners and sent most of them to Havana as soon as possible to prevent disorder. The remaining prisoners were well treated.

Pressed for time, he had nevertheless managed to compile a substantial inventory of the captured cargo. The governor of Havana, for unknown reasons, had not dared to intervene, and everything had proceeded in order. The fact that he was able to bring his fleet home under the most adverse climatological conditions as well as dangers threatening him from Dunkirk is yet further testimony to his ability. Indeed, in this whole venture the best man had won.

It may be well to conclude this chapter with a quote from a letter written by the English ambassador in The Hague to his Home Office:

It is the greatest prize that was ever taken from the Spaniards, and being added to the fleet of the Honduras taken in the beginning of August in sight of Havana, and verie many other prizes taken most by the shippes of the West India Company and much by particular Freebooters of Zeland, will amount to above twenty hundred thousand pounds of sterling, all taken within the space of a year. Soe that the losses suffered by the Dunkerkers are well repaired, and the Spaniard of certaine soe impoverished that he was not in worse condition when he begged peace of our late King and of this State. The consequences hereof are many and great....[79]

Meanwhile, even before Heyn's successful mission was known in the Netherlands, the energetic Heren XIX had fitted out another fleet with the West Indies as its destination. This fleet was under the command of Admiral Adriaen Janszoon Pater, and it left the Low Countries on August 15, 1628.

9

THE KING'S VEINS

In fervore belli.

Piet Heyn's spectacular tour de force may have temporarily paralyzed the government in Spain, but His Spanish Majesty could not afford to abstain very long from further activity in the Caribbean. Demands from his governors in that area, requesting reinforcements "for the love of God," were simply too urgent to ignore. Havana needed immediate help; its garrison of some 250 men represented only one-fourth of its requisite strength. Furthermore, the Cuban governor requested that the *situado* for that year, which had been lost to the Dutch with the New Spain fleet that had conveyed it, be reimbursed from Crown revenues "for otherwise it will not be possible to maintain the garrison."[1]

Were the king and his councils now alerted to the fact that the West Indies, and indeed their entire American domain, had suddenly been converted into a front in the war between Spain and the rebellious Low Countries? Certainly Madrid was well informed about future propensities of the Dutch West India Company which had been bolstered in that most fortunate year 1628 to the same degree that Spain had been weakened. Espionage revealed that the Dutch intended to secure a permanent base in the Caribbean, perhaps Jamaica, from which they might wage a continual campaign to thwart Spain's colonial traffic. Rumors regarding the preparation of several powerful fleets poured into Spain; one of these was described as a great armada which was to be unlike any ever built.

The Spanish War Council determined to send a fleet, headed by an expert, to the Caribbean. In this connection Antonio de Oquendo's name figured pre-eminently. The Council of the Indies concurred in this idea, but found itself face to face with an empty treasury, a persuasive deterrent. At this juncture the king abandoned his habitual lethargy and encouraged his councils: "This is no time to yield. If the Indies are well cared for this coming year it will compensate for all the damage and bring our enemies to sue for peace."[2] Although Philip IV did not care to admit his own diminishing power nor the corresponding ascendancy of the Dutch—a fact well attested by the treaty negotiations of that year—he certainly roused the councils and inspired his people with new determination at a crucial moment.

Rallying to Philip's behest, his ministers sent word to Cabrera, Havana's governor, to lay in supplies of food and water, and if necessary, to call on New Spain for assistance. Admiral de Larraspuru was instructed to leave the equivalent of the lost *situado* in Havana, deducting it from the Crown revenues aboard the New Spain treasure fleet which he commanded that year. The Duke of Medina-Sidonia was ordered to recruit an additional two hundred men for Havana's depleted garrison. Finally, firearms, powder, fuses, and lead were soon dispatched to the Caribbean.

Persistent references to the opponent's growing strength incited the Spaniards to attempt even more vigorous measures, notwithstanding a severe financial crisis and a precarious international situation. With the West Indies as its destination, a mighty fleet was assembled at San Lúcar. It was to be commanded by one of Spain's finest *hidalgos*, Don Fadrique de Toledo. In a deliberate attempt to mislead the enemy, the news was unobtrusively circulated that the impressive array of force would soon be leaving for Brazil and that it would restrict its activities to policing that area.

The Dutch were not Spain's only contenders in the Caribbean. English and French privateering enterprises and colonizing ventures— the difference was not always entirely clear—were also abusing the *mare clausum*. The Lesser Antilles, long neglected by Spain, had become the intruders' main targets for colonies and naval bases, which were essential way stations for fleets operating so many thousands of miles from home ports. Curiously, the Dutch had not yet expressed much concern or interest in overseas settlements and, except for those located near the salt pans, had only desired to establish colonies and bases after colonizing possibilities had considerably declined. For this reason they had to be content with only a few and these by far the least suitable islands in the Caribbean.

In 1625 the French under Pierre Bélain d'Esnambuc and the English under Sir Thomas Warner came to settle St. Christopher—or St. Kitts—almost simultaneously, an occurrence described by Dutertre as "an admirable act of Providence."[3] The problem of the two nations living side by side on the same island was solved only after both leaders had returned to their respective countries. D'Esnambuc received the support of the "Company of St. Christopher" in 1627; Warner's colony, which originally had been undertaken without royal patent, was soon incorporated into the Carlisle grant. In 1629 Richelieu moved against the English, partly in response to the realistic complaints of d'Esnambuc about English aggression and in spite of the *traité de partage* concluded by the two leaders on their return to the island. Undoubtedly intimidated by the threat of a Spanish fleet which had been delegated to expel all foreign intruders from the Caribbean, he decided to lend his official support to the French colony by sending a fleet of nine ships under François de Rotondy, Sieur de Cahuzac.

De Cahuzac left France in June, 1629, and arrived at St. Christopher near the end of August, to the delight and encouragement of the French colonists. The English were immediately cautioned to retreat to their own quarters. Apparently the latter had chosen to take up residence where, according to the partition treaty, French rights had been reaffirmed. Warner sought to buy time by requesting a three-day pause in order to consider the French demand—and to solicit the aid of ten neighboring English ships. But the French granted him only fifteen minutes. De Cahuzac went on to capture six of these vessels, and he thus had the English settlers completely at his mercy. The English had no choice but to retire to their own territory, and the two nationalities once again lived *en bonne intelligence*—on good terms.[4]

War of a totally different kind, however, was hovering over the two little colonies, although neither realized it until it was too late. De Cahuzac, having arranged matters on St. Christopher, and after establishing a colony on St. Eustatius[5]—or Statius—protected by a fort, concluded that since he had received no confirmation about the expected Spanish fleet, his presence on St. Christopher was no longer utterly necessary. Disastrously, therefore, he allowed his captains to roam the Caribbean, and he himself was soon bound for the Gulf of Mexico to try his luck at privateering. This uncalled-for dissipation of the French fleet precipitated the downfall of both the French and English scttlements on St. Christopher and Nevis.

The Spanish fleet had left the Iberian Peninsula in August, 1629. The strength of the fleet is variously reported by contemporary authors as between seventeen galleons to thirty-eight men-of-war and three provision ships. Its goals: to punish the enemy, French, English, or Dutch, to protect the mainland galleons, and to restore Spanish dominance in the Caribbean. Its destination—presumed secret, although Richelieu knew where it was bound—led observers to believe that Spain, in using such a potent force for such a limited goal, was trying to kill a sparrow with a cannon. To Spain, on the other hand, this display of power was amply justified if only to regain some of her lost prestige.

Near the Canary Islands, the Spanish fleet sighted some units of a Dutch fleet which were en route to Brazil. Without chancing an encounter, the Spaniards proceeded to Nevis where they landed on September 16. Eight English ships were taken by complete surprise, and the next day the English colony on the island surrendered. On September 18, Don Fadrique disembarked his troops on the island of St. Christopher. The Spaniards missed de Cahuzac by at most a few days. As often happened, the indentured servants of the colonists, who were regularly mistreated, deserted their masters, swam out to the Spanish ships, and betrayed all that they knew. For a brief time the English and French settlers fought side by side to resist the Spanish effort to subjugate them. In time, some of them escaped, while the rest tried to negotiate with Don Fadrique. The result was the surrender of the island's occupants, the dismantling of their fort, and the destruction of their tobacco warehouses. The labor of four years was thus totally lost.[6]

Of the colonists whom the Spaniards had managed to capture alive, some two thousand were placed aboard six ships and forcibly returned to England. Others, over eight hundred of them, all Catholics, transferred their allegiance to Spain.[7] The former group reached England "all naked and many sick."[8] Those who joined the Spaniards wintered at Cartagena and sailed on to Havana the following spring.

Needless to say, the results of this Spanish action were not lasting. The English and French colonists on St. Christopher, those who had fled at the coming of the Spaniards, disregarded the capitulations of their leaders, awaited the departure of the Spanish fleet, and then returned to their properties. Furthermore, some of them emigrated to the nearby islands of Antigua, St. Bartholomew, and Montserrat. As a bizarre coincidence, the Spanish actions had occurred while a substantial French force under de Cahuzac was diverging around the area, and, indeed, under the very nose of a Dutch fleet. A most interesting sequence of events, promoted by the aggressive intrusions in the Caribbean of the Dutch West India Company, unfurled itself before Don Fadrique's eyes while he leisurely hibernated in Cartagena.[9]

While Spain possessed neither lucid nor explicit knowledge about Dutch ambitions, she believed, correctly, that the West India Company had many projects in the planning stage. Even before Piet Heyn

had captured the New Spain fleet, the Heren xix had equipped a fleet
of eight ships and four yachts, most of which had already left the dock
by August 15, 1628. This fleet was under the command of Adriaen
Janszoon Pater of Edam, a worthy successor of his townsman Hendricksz.[10] Instructions first called for him to cross in the neighborhood
of the so-called Flemish Islands[11] in order to follow up Heyn's mission
in the event the latter had no opportunity to ensnare his prey, and to
be on the alert for stragglers from the 1628 treasure fleet. Pater
patrolled the area in vain for several weeks, unaware of events which
were then occurring in the Caribbean.

Tiring of his futile delay, Pater sailed to the Cape Verde Islands,
then crossed the Atlantic to Brazil. He was exhorted to reconnoiter the
Bay of All Saints and Pernambuco and to relay his observations to the xix
who were then formulating a second attack in that region. After another fruitless search for prizes in the area, the Dutch admiral decided to
try his luck in the Caribbean. His instructions were to divide his
fleet prior to its entry into the West Indian archipelago. One part
was to sail along Tierra Firme, the other north of Puerto Rico, south
of Hispaniola, and north of Jamaica. The two squadrons were then
to reassemble at Cape San Antonio, to sail together toward Havana,
and to bide their time until the passage of the treasure fleets which
they were ordered to keep under close surveillance and, if needed,
follow to Spain. The entire venture may have been instigated purely as
an evasive device to keep Spanish governors unaware of the real nature
of Dutch intentions.[12]

The Heren xix wanted Pater, quite simply, to imitate Piet Heyn and
surprise one of the treasure fleets. His original force, of course, was
far too small to accomplish such an exalted mission; he was, therefore,
constantly receiving reinforcements. The xix's long-range plan was
equally guileless: should Pater prove unable to capture one of the
Spanish fleets en route to Havana, nevertheless by his very presence
in the area, he might still compel the Spaniards to remain in port. Two
consecutive years of unremitting hardship, as a result of the failure of
the treasure fleets to deliver their precious cargoes, would draw Spain
deeper and deeper into a dizzy vortex of financial catastrophe.

Approaching Grenada on April 1, Pater opened his secret directive,
divided his fleet into two parts, and did as he had been ordered. For
more than two months both Dutch squadrons roamed the Caribbean,
foraging, sacking, and pillaging the poorly defended enemy towns
along the coasts.[13] Not only did Pater's presence thus inflict severe
hardship upon the Spaniards, but the Dutchmen had also acquired a

group of pirates and smugglers who followed in their wake and consummated the "work" begun by the official representatives of the West India Company.[14]

About mid-June Pater arrived at Cape San Antonio and joined up with the other squadron.[15] Prior to this meeting the Dutch ranks had been swelled by two Zeelandian ships which had brought the glad tidings of Heyn's marvelous feat. Heyn's return to the United Provinces had prompted the Heren XIX to implement with haste their previous decision to reinforce Pater's fleet. At least thirteen additional ships were equipped; three were larger than five hundred tons. Some had already been sent out in April of 1629; most of these units, however, joined Pater in June and July of that year.[16] They were placed under the command of Jan Janszoon van Hoorn who encountered many problems locating Pater—a case which illustrates the almost unsurmountable handicaps in seventeenth-century communications.[17] The Dutch ships converged as a unit upon the historic site where Piet Heyn had lain in wait the previous year. From some captured Spaniards, it was learned that a large Spanish fleet was due to arrive in the Caribbean at any time, but this information was much too vague to have caused Pater any particular concern.

Pater's presence in the Caribbean was soon well known to Spanish authorities, although they were not always fully cognizant of his strength. The Dutch admiral, himself no fool, surmised as much, and assumed that his movements were being vigilantly watched. Spanish prisoners from Santiago de Cuba supplied the information that not a few ships loaded with copper were crowding the harbor, dissuaded from their scheduled departure by the Dutch menace. Other sources told Pater that his presence had been officially reported to Cabrera and that the governor had broadcast a warning to all important Caribbean ports.[18] It had thus come about that Fadrique de Toledo had stayed the entire winter at Cartagena.

His fleet strengthened to twenty-six or more sails, Pater persisted in traversing the area in which Piet Heyn had met with such incredible luck. The stubborn Dutchman resolutely stood his ground until late in the dreaded hurricane season. His ships did not survive the ordeal unscathed. Yet Pater waited for the evasive enemy in spite of the frightful risk. The Spaniards, meantime, sojourned in safety at Cartagena, Porto Bello, and San Juan de Ulúa. They were in no hurry and felt themselves and their treasures well protected underneath the thick walls of these time-honored fortresses. The only tangible gain the Dutch achieved at the time was that their presence thoroughly disrupted Spanish intercolonial navigation and trade.

Admiral Pater, disheartened as his fleet lay immobilized and fast running short of provisions, finally sent nine of his ships home. They carried with them tobacco, sugar, hides, and other products in small quantities. As de Laet commented, however, "This did not mean much against the great expenses of this fleet."[19]

The Dutch admiral was certain that his quarry was wintering in the Caribbean and that it would not sail until the following spring. He informed the Heren xix of his opinion in a letter dated September 13, 1629. In conformity with the spirit of those times, the Heren xix replied, "The Lord has decided the times and places where and when it shall please Him to bless us. We have seen that in spite of all your good work and vigilance you could achieve nothing advantageous for us."[20] They instructed him to remain in the area and promised more reinforcements. For the moment they recommended that he alternate his course between Cartagena and Porto Bello and keep a sharp lookout for the Tierra Firme fleet.

The purpose behind their ordering Pater to stay in the Caribbean was fairly transparent and has already been pointed out: his presence would probably terrorize the Spaniards, cut off their navigation, and disrupt completely their trade in the area. Even more, Pater's fleet had come to be considered an integral part in the latest "Great Design." The company's treasury, filled to the brim after the extremely profitable year 1628, also led the Heren xix to entertain high hopes for accomplishing now what they had failed to do earlier. Once again they were planning to capture one of the Iberian colonies in the New World, while "cutting the king's veins"—referring to the treasure fleets—in the Caribbean. They had not entirely relinquished the idea that Pater could still catch one of these fleets, and once again they focused their attention on Brazil.[21]

Pernambuco instead of Bahia was indicated as the proper target, since it had many unsurpassable advantages. With its capital Olinda and the excellent port of Recife, this site was, as Wätjen rightly observed, "a magnificent stronghold for the domination of the southern Atlantic."[22] The area was also noted for its fertility: sugarcane sprouted everywhere, and there were many choice and magnificent plantations where all types of fine wood were to be had for the picking. Once a plan for the conquest of this Brazilian province had been developed and voted on, the Heren xix appointed such illustrious figures as Hendrick Corneliszoon Loncq,[23] Pieter Adriaenszoon Ita, Joost van Trappen, alias Banckert,[24] and Dierick Ruyters as their representatives. Although the story of this second Brazilian adventure would carry us far beyond the original scope of this text, it would be a gross mistake to overlook certain relevant facts that are significant in the Dutch war against Spain in the Caribbean.

In the first place, there is the curious circumstance that the West India Company undertook this fourth "Great Design" at a time when truce negotiations between the free Netherlands and Spain had reached a very active stage. The WIC's position on the subject of peace with Spain has already been remarked: its remonstrance of November 16, 1629, was explicit. In this protest entitled "Considerations and Reasons of the Lord Directors of the Chartered West India Company against the actual deliberations on a Truce with the King of Spain" the Heren XIX claimed to have confidence that the States General would not countenance the company's ruin by allowing Spain a breathing spell.[25] The company was persistent in reminding Their High Mightinesses that its efforts had been largely war-directed for the benefit of the country and that it had, for the most part, avoided strictly commercial enterprises.

Another interesting aspect of the plan for Brazil was the advice given by the old champion William Usselinx, who had returned to Holland in March, 1629, just as the company was dividing up Heyn's spoils. Usselinx petitioned the States General to be paid for his past endeavors. His letter received nothing more than a recommendation to the Heren XIX. Shortly afterwards, Usselinx presented the company with the following assessment of its project for Brazil: if the company wanted to avoid defeat, it would be well advised to invite the Portuguese pretender to accompany and collaborate with the Dutch expedition. If Emanuel was recognized as king in Brazil, the colonists would surrender more easily to him than to the heretical Dutch. Perhaps unwisely, Usselinx' counsel went unheeded. Once again he was frustrated and ignored.

The fourth "Great Design" soon approached maturity. It was hoped that Loncq could set sail in the autumn of 1629, but at that moment the war with Spain took a decisive turn for the worse. The stadhouder Frederik Hendrik, who had succeeded his brother Maurits in 1625, had laid siege to 's-Hertogenbosch south of the Maas River. In order to relieve the beleaguered town, the Spaniards invaded the province of Gelderland and penetrated as far west as Amersfoort. The stadhouder, however, clung tenaciously to his siege.[26]

The States General, in this moment of distress, appealed to the West India Company to lend the government the soldiers which it had already recruited for the second Brazilian enterprise. The company yielded and willingly postponed its expedition in order to save the fatherland. It even went so far as to advance Their High Mightinesses a loan of 600,000 guilders from its abundant savings. As a consequence, the Spanish invasion failed miserably, 's-Hertogen-bosch surrendered to the Dutch, and the West India Company became a public idol. Not incidentally, of course, the States General now found it rather more difficult to continue the peace negotiations that would destroy this patriotic institution.[27]

When this alarm had passed, the company was free to pursue its new "Great Design." The number of ships which it employed remains a secret and can only be presumed. This ignorance is explained by the fact that ships left at different times and from different ports in order "to mislead the enemy."[28] De Laet lists twenty ships and six yachts, but these were probably already underway when the crisis of the Spanish invasion was instigated. They remained, in the interim, at St. Vincent, one of the Cape Verde Islands. During September and October, many other ships and yachts arrived there to join Loncq, the general of the new fleet. When he finally left the island in December, he probably commanded a total of 52 ships and 13 sailing sloops, which were manned with 3,780 sailors and 3,500 soldiers. "Thus," wrote de Laet, "went a fine and powerful fleet, the like of which has probably never sailed from these countries."[29]

Pernambuco offered no effective resistance, and the enterprise was a resounding victory. The situation resembled the Dutch attempt at a similar raid on Bahia which occurred six years earlier. Now, however, Spain was in no position to raise a spirited offensive and could only muster a weak protest. Notwithstanding, the Heren xix did not forget the lesson learned in the earlier venture and in November, 1629, commissioned some of the directors to draw up the necessary plans to bolster Loncq's force. Nor were they unmindful of Pater's plight. He was also in dire need of reinforcements if his mission was to be effective and fruitful.[30]

Once Loncq had raised his country's flag over Pernambuco, therefore, he was ordered to return home via the Caribbean. The similarity to their prior directive to Boudewijn Hendricksz is obvious. Loncq was to find Pater and to join forces with him. Some minor tasks had to be performed also. He was to try to capture some Grenada natives who posed a powerful threat since they regularly killed members of Dutch crews sent to that island for water and wood. He was to leave all Negro slaves abducted from Spanish prizes on Tobago where the Dutch, since 1628, had been settled. To round off these diversionary tactics, he was next to proceed to Cape Tiburón on the west coast of Haiti and wait for news of Pater. Should the latter be found, the two fleets were to merge, under Loncq's flag, and, after offering "a fiery penetrating prayer to God Almighty" for His blessing, were to sail boldly into the Bay of Santiago de Cuba, eliminating its defenses and taking the town by storm.

Nor was that all that was demanded. If Loncq and Pater defeated their Spanish opponent, they were then reminded to investigate the copper mines in the area, offer the laborers better wages, and undertake to exploit the mines themselves. Loncq was cautioned not to mistreat the Indians nor to chafe the Spaniards, although the latter, of course, had to be disarmed. As soon as Santiago was in Dutch hands, he was admonished to entrench himself to withstand a Spanish reprisal.

The proposed outcome of this latest grandiose scheme rested upon the supposed reality of an encounter between Loncq and Pater. In the event such a meeting did not transpire, Loncq was left with the option of proceeding to Cartagena and abiding in the area between that port and Porto Bello as Pater had done. He was enjoined not to disembark any men, however, nor to provoke the enemy in any other way until July, when, as the Heren XIX reckoned, the silver from Peru would arrive. After he had once again offered a prayer, Loncq might then attack Porto Bello, take as many ships as he could, and destroy the fortress. The XIX did not leave much to chance; in case this first attack did not materialize, Loncq was ordered to make his way to the Dry Tortugas in order to ambush the New Spain fleet. Finally, if he learned that the fleet he awaited had not yet left Vera Cruz, and instead had retreated behind the relative safety of San Juan de Ulúa, he was authorized to attempt to escalade the fortress, to subdue the town of Vera Cruz, and to make off with whatever else he could lay his hands on.[31]

The above summary clearly reveals the aims of the Heren XIX with respect to Brazil as well as the Cuban copper and the Spanish treasure fleets—cutting the king's veins in the Caribbean. Once a foothold in Brazil had been secured, moreover, Spanish ports in the West Indies would be highly vulnerable to further encroachments by Dutch trespassers. Then, too, from such a vantage point in South America, the Dutch fleets were in a far better position to watch the movements of the treasure fleets. From Pernambuco it was a mere two weeks' sailing to the Lesser Antilles and the copper mines of Cuba. Intercolonial trade would also be at the mercy of the Dutch. The depredations of Piet Heyn and other Dutch commanders in the South Atlantic had already drastically reduced the amount of Iberian shipping; in two years the port of Viana do Castelo alone lost twenty-six out of a total of twenty-nine ships engaged in the Brazilian trade. The situation in the Caribbean was similar; coastal communication virtually ceased in 1629 and 1630, and Spanish defensive naval power in the area was reduced to zero. With the capture of Pernambuco, the United Netherlands, with its West India Company, was considered the mistress of American waters. The Dutch really believed that they were on the threshold of a Golden Age and depicted their Prince of Orange as the embodiment of their God-speed: *Aurea condet saecula*.[32]

The Dutch were soon to learn, however, that the future still held some bitter disappointment. The fourth "Great Design," having achieved its first goal in Brazil—which was now called New Holland—collapsed in the Caribbean. In vain did the Heren XIX plan "Great Designs" and hand out excellent instructions to their generals and admirals while remitting during this and the coming year small squadrons of three or four ships—perhaps a total of more than thirty—to join Pater. But most of these reinforcements could not locate him. And to no purpose did Pater abide north of Havana; he roamed the area but took only small prey. The one remaining spark of hope was that Spain would be driven to her knees by dire poverty because she received no treasure from the New World.

At this juncture it is necessary to follow the movements of each fleet in order to apprehend the reasons behind Pater's ill-fated attempts to meet with other Dutch forces. The admiral, according to his instructions and after having sent part of his fleet home because of the lack of provisions, left the Dry Tortugas region in late September just as Don Fadrique was sailing for Cartagena from St. Christopher and Nevis. The Dutch set their course for Barbados through the Florida Straits to the north, then south of the Bahama Islands to the Lesser Antilles, where they arrived some six weeks later. At that time Barbados was already a prosperous English colony, a settlement enriched by tobacco and other crops. In 1628 it had been invigorated by more pioneers sent out by the Courteen House and now, with 1,600 people, was too strong for the Spaniards to challenge.

Pater again divided his fleet investing Commander Jan Janszoon van Hoorn with the task of visiting some of the Leeward Islands—especially St. Christopher and Nevis—where he was to inquire about the alleged presence of a sizable Spanish fleet in the area. Van Hoorn, indeed, confirmed this rumor and sent the Heren XIX a written account of Spanish depredations supplied with all the gory details.[33] Until the end of the year, he continued to dally between St. Christopher and the Mona Passage.

With their twenty sails, Pater and his Vice-Admiral Marten Thijsz had, in the meantime, set course to the south before skirting the coast eastward and up the Orinoco.[34] For three weeks, the strong current and the lack of wind prevented the Dutch from dropping anchor at San Tomé. Once they had managed to do so, when the first Dutchman arrived ashore, the native population immediately set fire to its own town. But the settlement was soon surrounded on all sides, the fire extinguished, and everything of value carried off to the ships. En route to Trinidad, Pater sailed westward along the coast. His plan to overrun Punta Galeota had to be relinquished, since the strong current in the Dragon's Mouth—the northern exit of the passage between Trinidad and the continental coast—would have impeded a fast getaway.

Pater continued his course along the coast and dropped anchor at Blanquilla and Bonaire. On the latter island an entire village was razed to the ground in retaliation against those Spaniards and Indians who had killed one of his men and wounded another. Leaving the scene of their devastation, the Dutch sailed north to Puerto Rico and then to the Mona Passage in order to rendezvous with van Hoorn. Since provisions were not low, Pater determined—in accordance with certain sly hints in his instructions—to raid Santa Marta. The Dutch had found aboard a captured Spanish ship letters from the governor of this town, Gerónimo de Quero, to the king in 1626; these contained complaints about the poor defenses of Santa Marta, the lack of war material and the unwillingness of his neighbor the governor of Cartagena to give the necessary assistance.[35]

Thus it was that on February 16, 1630, the Dutch fleet sailed within sight of the seemingly impregnable walls of Santa Marta, dropped anchor, and launched a slashing attack on the fortress. Soldiers were disembarked and their steady advance sent the enemy reeling in retreat. Within a few hours the fortress surrendered, and the Dutch occupied the virtually deserted town.[36] They remained here for a week, sowing utter devastation and wanton vandalism, according to the testimony of Spanish officials.[37] Dutch sources, incidentally, claim that Pater spared the town in return for a ransom of 5,500 *reales* which were raised by members of the clergy.

Although Pater was shrewd enough to grasp the strategic importance of the area, he was certainly in no position to effect a permanent conquest. Since he had few men, no specific instructions, and was too near mighty Cartagena, he was deterred from undertaking such a risky occupation. One unanticipated advantage for the town which accrued from the Dutch attack, however, was the final realization by the Crown of the urgent need to improve Santa Marta's flagging defenses.

While Pater was directing the rape of Santa Marta, Fadrique de Toledo and his fleet had left Cartagena for Havana. Quero's letter to his colleague in this city, warning him about the impending Dutch attack, arrived two days after the departure of the Spanish admiral.

Don Fadrique remained in Havana until mid-June, 1630. Governor Cabrera, honored by the presence of such an exalted countryman, organized receptions and banquets and expressed his thanks many times over for the arms and ammunitions which the king had awarded freely. The Spanish governor now thought that he would be able to reallocate Havana's defenses and thereby transform the city into an unassailable Spanish bulwark in the Caribbean. Don Fadrique left Havana convoying the Tierra Firme and New Spain fleets, the first time in two years that American treasures were once again hailed in Spain. Needless to say, great sighs of relief were heaved throughout the country when the treasure fleets were escorted to San Lúcar without serious mishap. The Spanish title to fame in the Caribbean had been reinstated to some extent, although the results of Fadrique's clearing action in the Lesser Antilles proved to be inconclusive and of short duration.[38]

As mentioned before, the Heren XIX had resolved late in 1629 to send reinforcements to the Caribbean. Small squadrons left the Low Countries bound to join Pater, but separated in order to confuse the enemy.[39] At the same time, the XIX undertook to keep Loncq well posted regarding their future intentions. There are indications that he was instructed to consider attacks on Rio de Janeiro, Bahia, and Buenos Aires; his secret instructions are extant, though affirming only the fact that he was to join Pater in the Caribbean and together they were to make a new attempt on the silver fleet.[40] Although similar orders were dispatched to Pater, it is doubtful if they ever reached their destination. In any case, when, because of a lack of provisions, Pater left the Caribbean after the sacking of Santa Marta, he apparently knew neither that Loncq nor any other reinforcements were en route.

There is some irony in the fact that the Spanish invasion of Gelderland in the attempt to relieve 's-Hertogenbosch, while it did not achieve that goal, nevertheless appears to have shielded the treasure fleets from a second seizure in 1630. It provided the reason for the several months' postponement of the Dutch attack on Pernambuco. This, in turn, upset all prior arrangements and caused the Dutch to sail from Brazil to the Caribbean months behind schedule. A union of the Brazilian squadron with Pater's fleet was thus prevented.

Consequently, Pater decided to abandon the area where, for almost two years, his name had been a byword for holy terror, since he felt too weak to risk a confrontation with the Spaniards alone. About the same time that he left the Caribbean, Loncq ordered Dierick Ruyters to sail to the West Indies. The Dutch squadron under the latter's command left Pernambuco on May 5, 1630. Although it reached the Caribbean two weeks later, the arrival was too late. This mistiming inadvertently brought to a head the Dutch inability to capture one of the silver fleets that year. Ruyters' venture from Brazil, as a preliminary to Loncq's visit, was one of the many attempts to locate Pater that year in order to aid him in "cutting the king's veins."[41]

Pater sailed for home at the end of April. He arrived in the United Provinces in June and was joyously received by the Heren xix, who had sailed out to meet him and to welcome him "magnificently." They accompanied him to Amsterdam and held a reception in the West India House. The crews received a thaler bonus with their pay. The celebrations, however, did not succeed in raising Pater's spirit, since the admiral could not forget that, in spite of all his efforts, he had bungled his primary mission. In two years he had only managed to fill the coffers of his patrons with the barest hint of treasure. The Heren xix, however, realized that circumstances and not inability or bad leadership had caused this failure, and they soon appointed Pater general in a far more ambitious mission than the one from which he had just returned.[42]

In July, 1630, a month after Pater, General Loncq arrived in the United Provinces with part of the fleet that had waged the successful campaign at Pernambuco. His victory there had been followed by a violation of his instructions; he had been ordered to sail to the Caribbean to seek out Pater for a combined attack on a treasure fleet. If the meeting did not occur, he was to head for home by the shortest possible route. His arrival, therefore, did not bring out the xix *in plano*; only four members were commissioned to escort him to Amsterdam. Although he was well treated at the West India House, it was only, perhaps, that the Heren xix dared not indulge in the public abuse of a popular hero.[43] There are certain clear indications, however, that the xix were not completely satisfied with the performance of their general.

It had not been Loncq's fault, of course, that the Brazilian expedition had been three months overdue. The Heren xix, though, were distressed to hear that Loncq had sent Ruyters to the Caribbean instead of going himself, and even that show of force was too little and came too late. Only six ships and 655 men had left Olinda in Pernambuco in the beginning of May, while Loncq had been instructed to reinforce Pater at Grenada by mid-April.

Loncq seems to have been a stubborn man, disinclined to follow orders, especially those which came from so far and so long ago. Under the circumstances, he undoubtedly felt free to undertake what he thought expedient, frequently in open defiance of his masters' will. Whatever his personal feelings, however, and assuming that his own presence in Pernambuco had been indispensable, Pater and Ruyters still should have been allowed to meet and join forces. Loncq's mysterious and lackadaisical attitude had not only prevented the capture of another Spanish treasure fleet but had also destroyed the plans to keep this fleet in American waters. Although the public adored Loncq for his role in the capture of Olinda, the Heren xix, with their regularly ambitious goals, looked beyond the immediate and were disappointed.

Thus the crucial aspect of the fourth "Great Design" had been frustrated. Spain now again had the financial wherewithal to proceed with her expansive European wars. Even though the Dutch conquest of Brazil was a major tangible gain achieved by this "Great Design," it proffered small consolation for what might have been generated.

This setback, however, did not deliver the Caribbean from the plague of Dutch intruders. On the contrary, more than ever this sea was to be infested with Dutch ships, especially in the neighborhood of Havana. In the weeks before he left this port Don Fadrique, tired beyond measure of the activities of the Dutch *piratas*, had sent some of his ships out to seize an enemy vessel and thus frighten the others away. The captured ship's crew revealed that they had left Holland five months earlier and that they had been in the Caribbean two months hoping to get a signal from Admiral Pater's fleet.[44] From other sources Don Fadrique learned that there had been seven or eight Dutch ships at St. Vincent which were preparing themselves to sail to Cape San Antonio. He was also informed that there were eight more Dutch vessels on the coast of Hispaniola.

Overcoming their vexation, the Heren xix were meanwhile soon engrossed in their fifth "Great Design." This project had already been conceived while Pater was still in American waters in dire need of support. Accordingly, as mentioned before, ships were sent to reinforce his fleet, and he was advised to stand fast. Unfortunately, this message never reached Pater who, unaware of the changed circumstances, was on his way home. The fleet which was dispatched from the Low Countries to join him, under the command of Jan

Gijsbertszoon Booneter, reached the Caribbean just as Pater returned. Booneter was carrying further instructions to Pater, which, as before, closely testify to the intentions of the Heren XIX.

In the first place, reference was made to the possible seizure of the Honduras ships at Trujillo.[45] If this plan did not seem feasible, it was suggested that Pater execute the "former design," to wait for the treasure fleets at the Dry Tortugas and, at the same time, keep an eye on Santiago because of the copper mines. A campaign against San Juan de Ulúa was part of this plan of action, as well as an attack on the Spanish fort at Punta de Araya.[46]

Booneter left home port on May 1, 1630, together with eight ships loaded with provisions for Pater. Fortunately, before he entered the Caribbean, he somehow picked up the information that the latter had already left the area. He expected to meet Ruyters, however, for he must have known that the instructions of the XIX could hardly apply to himself and his miniature fleet.

Undeniably, the year 1630 was a remarkable year in the history of the Caribbean. In the course of that year no less than three fleets equipped by the West India Company appeared in the area. All three soon joined to form a powerful threat to Spanish shipping and to navigation in general, but particularly to the treasure fleets. Ruyters' squadron was operating in the Caribbean when Booneter arrived. Shortly after Ruyters had left Olinda, its Political Council had decided to assist him. Fearing that his fleet was too weak, the council had dispatched Admiral Ita to the West Indies with eight ships and 545 men.[47] At Pernambuco seventeen men-of-war remained behind, and this number was soon increased.

Ita sent a yacht to advise Ruyters that he was on his way. He managed, as Ruyters had, to reach St. Vincent within fifteen days. He received word there from Ruyters that the latter would wait for him at Ile à Vache, south of Hispaniola. It is possible that Ruyters, who was finally operating independently after years of sub-commands, was not too anxious to place himself under Ita's command, and for some time played a cat-and-mouse game with his superior officer. Finally, however, Ita found Ruyters at Cape Tiburón and placed him and his ships under one flag.[48]

For some time thereafter Ita with his combined fleet and Booneter with his squadron operated separately, unable to locate one another, although each was soon aware of the other's presence. Booneter was under specific orders to find Ruyters, if he did not meet Pater, to place him under his command, and then to undertake the fifth "Great Design." The Heren XIX, of course, and Booneter, too, in the beginning, did not know of Ita's appearance on the scene. As usual the obstacles of communication were a constantly harassing factor for each side in these encounters.

Booneter continued to linger north of Havana, hoping for Ruyters to heave into sight before the treasure fleets could drop anchor in Havana port. His orders provided the possibility of intercepting the *situado* ship en route to Havana from San Juan de Puerto Rico. He might also, according to instructions, station himself somewhere between Santa Marta and the Río Magdalena in order to capture Spanish ships sailing from Santo Domingo to Cartagena. These ships usually brought hides and tobacco to the Tierra Firme fleet harbored in Cartagena and would be rich prizes if they could be caught.[49]

Booneter and Ita thus roamed the Caribbean, each following the traditional procedure of dividing their fleets into several units in order to operate more effectively. They left a trail of plunder in their wake. The prizes which they took were substantial if unspectacular. Late in June, Ita guided his ships to the traditional hunting grounds for the Spanish treasure fleets, north of Cape San Antonio and Havana, while Booneter assumed responsibility for the Spanish watchboats at this cape. From the crew of a small captured Spanish ship, the admiral learned that Don Fadrique had left Havana for Spain with eighty ships two weeks earlier in mid-June, although he had sent eight ships back to Cartagena to await further orders.

Notified of Don Fadrique's uneventful journey and safe arrival in Spain, the Heren XIX forthwith sent out a yacht to inform Booneter, who was the presumed commander of their fleet in the Caribbean while Ita's whereabouts were still unknown. Admiral de Larraspuru had stayed behind in the Caribbean, and the XIX had ascertained that it was his duty to convey the Tierra Firme silver of 1630 safely into Havana. The board dutifully expressed the hope that Booneter reinforced with Ruyters' units would have no difficulty in capturing the eight rich Spanish galleons en route from Cartagena to Havana.[50]

Some ships belonging to Booneter's small force had already joined the ranks of Ita's fleet, when, finally, on August 17, the commander himself arrived and placed himself under the admiral's command. The combined fleet may then have been as strong as twenty-four sails or even more. It was manned by at least 1,900 sailors and 240 soldiers.[51] Together these ships patrolled the area around Havana, and occasionally ventured within shooting distance of the Spaniards who, angered by their impudence, retaliated with vehement volleys of fire.

Ita cruised north and west of Havana until September 25, deep into the hurricane season, when, after discussing the state of provisions with the fleet council, he was urged to return home. He acquiesced and took seventeen ships with him; Booneter, with eight or ten others, remained in the Caribbean. Strictly speaking, another of the company's "Great Designs" had met with visible failure.

It is plausible that Ita's decision to yield was also based upon certain knowledge that his quarry had evaded him by returning to Spain along a different, rarely used route. Although de Larraspuru, safe in Cartagena, had been waiting impatiently for the information that the Dutch enemy had evacuated the area, when this news was not forthcoming, the generally level-headed Spaniard decided, against his better judgment, to set sail in August, 1630. While Ita lay in ambush at the Dry Tortugas, Larraspuru left Cartagena behind, promising the "Blessed Souls" an offering of a thousand ducats to preserve his safety, a small amount in light of the fact that his fleet bore some seven million pesos in cargo, much of it in specie and bullion.[52]

Certain that the Dutch were keeping a close vigil over the normal route to Havana, however, Larraspuru directed his fleet east between Cuba and Hispaniola, leaving the Caribbean area through the Windward Channel and the Caicos Passage, Pater's itinerary of a few months earlier. He thus utterly out-maneuvered his enemies.[53] Although the silver galleons were brought home safely, Spanish general navigation was yet to pay a high price: Dutch privateers, not connected with either Ita's or Booneter's fleet, seized or sunk twenty-three miscellaneous Spanish vessels. The treasure had stolen away unscathed, but Havana had no ships to export its products that year.

After Ita had been thus outwitted by the Spaniards, he dejectedly prepared to go home at the end of September, 1630, leaving Booneter to make any possible seizures. Since the latter had carried provisions destined for Pater, he was well supplied and could hold out for some time. Following instructions Booneter penetrated deep into the Florida Straits and the Bahama archipelago.[54] It took him forty-eight days, however, to regain the Leeward Islands (see map).

During the ensuing months Booneter's fleet infected the Caribbean, looting and pillaging according to established procedure. In May, 1631, his ships congregated at Ile à Vache or, somewhat later, at Cape Tiburón in order to execute a joint offensive against the Honduras galleons that were supposed to arrive in Havana at any time.[55] In a letter from the Heren xix dated February 15, 1631, but not received by Booneter until May, the latter was told that, at the time, the West India Company could not reinforce him because of the rumors that Spain had equipped an armada to recapture Pernambuco. However, contradictory to this statement, they did send orders to Brazil to send a fleet to his support. Because of the threat of an Iberian attack, this fleet was reduced to the size of a squadron, one ship and two yachts under the command of Jonathan de Neckere. One of the sub-commanders was Cornelis Corneliszoon Jol who would one day make himself a name as *Pie de Palo*, Peg-leg Jol.[56]

De Neckere never joined Booneter because of some quirk of fate. On April 26 he left Olinda, early enough to be able to meet Booneter at the place agreed on, and is known to have arrived at Barbados on May 12, 1631. He lost a precious week at St. Vincent, taking his time to refresh, then went on to arrive at Ile à Vache early in June. He missed Booneter by at least three days. Apparently the latter ignored his coming, since an order would have been posted to relay his whereabouts.

It will always remain a mystery why the Brazilian squadron under de Neckere, having missed Booneter so narrowly, did not sail on to the Dry Tortugas, the usual site for watching and waiting. Instead, its commander set sail from Ile à Vache to Santa Marta. From a purely economic point of view this expedition was quite successful; Captain Jol distinguished himself by capturing several prizes and had the small satisfaction of watching the Tierra Firme galleons pass right under his nose.[57] From a strategic point of view, however, de Neckere's failure to join Booneter had a paralyzing effect on the latter's undertaking. De Neckere returned to the Low Countries in mid-September, followed by Captain Jol who, with his yacht *Otter*, arrived in the United Provinces more than half a year later.

In Booneter's new instructions from February 15, 1631, the Heren XIX alluded to Larraspuru's effusive welcome in Spain with the Tierra Firme fleet, but without the ships from New Spain—information that might already have been gleaned from local sources.[58] The board no doubt believed that Booneter's forces had been considerably augmented with the few Brazilian ships it had ordered to be sent. He was now instructed to watch for the new treasure fleets; the possibility that the commander might not be strong enough to attack was completely ignored. If the season passed without success, Booneter was admonished to sail home, taking care, however, not to drop anchor in any English port "because of the peace made between the crowns of Spain and England."[59]

Although the Spaniards knew that the Dutch fleet under Ita was gone, they were also aware that other Dutch units were still in the area. In March, 1631, the new governor of Havana, Juan Bitrián, had already been informed of eight Dutch ships skulking along the island's coast, and a month later the same ships were detected near

Havana. They might have been the reinforcements from Holland which Booneter had so urgently demanded but which had failed to locate or join him during all this time.

Booneter circled just outside Havana for a month and then moved to Matanzas in order to release some Spanish prisioners. These advised the Cuban authorities that Dutch strength consisted of twenty-six well-armed ships carrying eight hundred men, a flagrant exaggeration. On May 20 the ships reappeared on the Havana horizon and by June 4 a tight net had been drawn around the port. Nevertheless, more than twenty Spanish ships managed to slip through to find sanctuary inside Havana harbor, one indication that the effectiveness of the blockade was limited by the number of available Dutch ships. More prisoners were set free at the end of June, and they repeated the previous hearsay that the enemy was expecting at least eighty ships from home at any time.[60]

Booneter, meanwhile, lingered north of Havana as summer approached. He may or may not have been strong enough to attempt an attack on one of the treasure fleets, but no such fleet appeared; meanwhile his provisions were being depleted and mutiny was threatening. Despairing of any success, he finally returned to the United Provinces and arrived in August, "bringing home for his masters too little to compensate for the expenses lavished on this fleet."[61] The Tierra Firme fleet of that year was once again convoyed across the Atlantic by Larraspuru, although at a very unusual time—in February, 1632. The New Spain fleet, which was held up at San Juan de Ulúa far beyond its scheduled departure, finally set out for Spain only to meet with terrible weather and to be all but destroyed by a hurricane. Even though these mishaps could ultimately all be blamed on the Dutch, the latter received little palpable comfort from these Spanish misfortunes.

The Dutch presence in the Caribbean caused constant alarm among the Spaniards and resulted in definitive military measures being undertaken by the new governor of Cuba. Since his concern was to defend the island at all costs, he created a civilian militia in all Cuban towns. The larger cities, Havana and Santiago, were given companies of nonprofessional soldiers for their local defenses; professional soldiers—the *capitanes a guerra* or war captains—were commissioned as officers to command these local encampments.[62]

Steps were also required to restore intercolonial trade in the Caribbean. The new sugar mills that were still in operation were threatened by the lack of available markets for their surplus. Ships which might have carried sugar and tobacco were blockaded in port by the Dutch dragnet. Exports were not the only exigency, however; imports had also fallen off to virtually nothing, and all kinds of commodities were in urgent demand. Since money was becoming increasingly scarce, a barter system gradually developed which was quick in spreading to neighboring Spanish colonies. This revival of primitive times sharply encouraged illicit trade—especially with the Dutch, who had themselves instigated the dilemma. *Rescate* and the *rescatador* once again returned to badger not only Spanish authorities but rich merchants as well. The latter, who wanted to protect their monopolies from further encroachments by the detested foreigners, organized private armed ships to seek out and seize enemy ships. Hispaniola followed the example of Cuba and took similar precautions.

At the time of Booneter's plight, the Heren XIX were ready to put into effect a project which had been close to their hearts since its inception. Well aware of the mistakes they had made in the conquest of Bahia six years earlier, they now commissioned the dependable Adriaen Janszoon Pater as general of a fleet bound for the new acquisition and the Caribbean. This fleet left the United Provinces in small units which united in Olinda between January and April, 1631. Sixteen ships, more than half of which were over 300 tons, joined the 900-ton flagship under Pater. His admiral, Marten Thijsz, had arrived in Olinda in December of the previous year in command of some ships, among them an 800-ton man-of-war.

Pater's renewed double mission incited the Iberians to act. The Dutch, it was believed, meant to strengthen their garrison in Brazil and consolidate their hold over the northern part of the country. But then they were also destined to try once again to intercept a treasure fleet. In order to thwart these Dutch plans, a strong armada under Antonio de Oquendo left the Iberian Peninsula in May, 1631. It arrived near Pernambuco in September to be met by Pater in an heroic battle that cost the lives of five hundred Dutchmen and many more Spaniards. After Spain's initial advantage of surprise, the encounter quickly degenerated into a duel, albeit a Homeric one, between the two flagships, this despite the fact that Oquendo commanded fifty-six ships and Pater had only sixteen sails. In the end, Pater's ship the *Prins Willem* ("Prince William") caught fire and had to be abandoned. The general himself, who could not swim, hung from a rope on the prow of his ship until he fell exhausted into the sea and was drowned. Few of his ships survived the encounter, but the human cost was even higher. De Laet admits that it was a Spanish victory and berates the other Dutch captains who did not dare to relieve their commander.[63] "Pater lost his life, but not the battle," wrote Wätjen.[64]

The Spaniards claimed the victory, despite their high casualties, and the Dutch fleet was forced to withdraw in order to make way for Oquendo to disembark his men. In Madrid jubilant voices were raised to honor this feat; it was one of the few exciting events to color the otherwise dull reign of Philip IV, and a medal was struck which pictured Samson defying the Dutch lion.[65]

If it was a victory, it was a pyrrhic one, "A barren victory," wrote Edmundson, "in which the victors lost far more than the vanquished, and in which they entirely failed to loosen the hold of the Netherlanders upon Recife or to prevent their keeping the command of the sea."[66] And, perhaps even more telling, Oquendo was unable to prevent Pater's Admiral Marten Thijsz from sailing into the Caribbean to make another attempt at "cutting the king's veins," the sixth "Great Design." Thijsz, however, was to first take an active part in the hostilities against the Iberians, most importantly consolidating Recife–Olinda and disembarking troops north of the capital in a determined attempt to rout Matthias de Albuquerque who, from Pernambuco, continued to put up a stubborn resistance against the Dutch invaders.

In April, 1632, after the stabilization of Pernambuco, Thijsz, following instructions, left New Holland with a strong force and arrived in the West Indies during the right season.[67] He was accompanied by twenty-two ships; the remainder were left behind under the command of Jan Mast who had earned his laurels in the battle against Oquendo.

Between Booneter's departure in June, 1631, and the arrival of Thijsz almost a year later, the Dutch blockade of Cuba had gradually been eased, until the threat to the treasure fleets had all but disappeared. There were still some small Dutch units that patrolled the Caribbean, the de Neckere squadron, for example, and the two yachts left behind by Booneter under the command of Jan van Stapels, but the very smallness of their number made them an unlikely menace to Spanish shipping.[68]

By the time of Thijsz' arrival at Barbados on May 15, the Tierra Firme fleet had long since reached safety. But the staunch Dutch admiral tried to pursue his ambitious goal despite this bad luck. His fleet of some twenty ships, however, was not even strong enough to risk an encounter with the New Spain fleet. Here again, the ambiguity of the company's goals—colonizing in Brazil and raiding in the Caribbean—led to utter frustration. The Heren XIX had not dared to weaken further the defense of Pernambuco and had retained a considerable naval force in New Holland.[69] This necessary precaution as well as the fact that the treasure fleets had not followed their routine time schedule doomed the success of the entire scheme.

Thijsz' presence in the Caribbean was soon known to the Spaniards, partly because some of his ships, while refreshing in a bay on the southern shores of Hispaniola facing the Ile à Vache, had lost more than twenty men in skirmishes with the natives. Many of the Dutch vessels, including the admiral's own, had also been spotted by coastal watchers who had been posted by the Spaniards throughout their domain. The carelessness about security which seemed to characterize all Thijsz' movements stands in marked contrast to the caution exercised by Heyn just four years earlier. All in all, the latest Dutch operation did not add luster to their fame.

Thijsz cruised north of Havana during most of August, vainly hoping for the opportunity to cover himself with glory.[70] Early in September he was finally forced to admit that his provisions were too low to risk waiting any longer. The Heren XIX did not send him much help. Thus, on September 4, the admiral met with the captains of his ships and reluctantly agreed to return to the Low Countries. The scourge of bad weather was already upon them, and many unexpected hardships further delayed the fleet, yet in November of the same year, most units dropped anchor in the home ports. Thus ended the sixth "Great Design."

During each of the four consecutive years after Heyn's triumph, then, all of the West India Company's attempts to repeat his coup were abortive. The consequent drain on its treasury, which was compounded by heavy expenses in Brazil, forced the Heren XIX to consider an alternate plan that Heyn had suggested to them some years earlier: a daring raid on Trujillo, the point of departure for the Honduras galleons. Although this goal was obviously more modest than those of previous years, the company could no longer afford to equip the powerful fleets which it normally sent to American waters. The States General had indeed promised to commit itself further with substantial subsidies to the company. The money was slow in coming, however, and was largely absorbed by the Brazilian venture.

As early as 1632, the Heren XIX, who anticipated the possibility for profit offered by the raid on Trujillo, had instructed Galeyn van Stapels, an able seaman who had an illustrious naval record, to survey the Honduras coast. He was sent to Thijsz as the commander of a small reinforcement squadron. Van Stapels, who met Thijsz at Bonaire in July, undertook the reconnoitering mission with two yachts. He entered the little-known Gulf of Campeche, sailed along the Yucatán coast, and sacked the small town of Sisal, a prior victim of Schouten. He returned to search in vain for Thijsz. Eventually, surmising the latter's departure, van Stapels also returned home with his valuable information.[71]

The decision to outfit a small fleet to realize the Trujillo plan had been made, however, before van Stapels dropped anchor in his home port. The Heren XIX, in their meeting of November 3, 1632, had already agreed, at the instigation of the Amsterdam Chamber, to divert a small fleet from Brazil to the West Indies. This squadron, which was originally comprised of only two yachts and three sailing sloops,[72] grew in size after van Stapels had reported the results of his investigation. It now included four ships, three yachts, three sloops, five hundred sailors, and four hundred soldiers. The command of the Honduras expedition fell to Jan Janszoon van Hoorn, a boon companion of Pater's and a man thoroughly familiar with the area.[73]

Van Hoorn left Pernambuco on April 26, 1633, to attack the Portuguese fortress of Ceará, and to advise the commander of St. Martin, at that time the only Dutch possession in the Caribbean, of the results of this foray. He was then to proceed to Trujillo. In flagrant contravention of his official orders, van Hoorn instead chose to adhere to the version as interpreted by the Dutch representatives in Brazil. Consequently, he conducted a tour of inspection of the port of Maranhão and then went directly to Barbados.

Although van Hoorn's mission was no outstanding financial success for the West India Company, it did bring about definite military and monetary advantages. He arrived unnoticed at Trujillo on July 15 and battered the town mercilessly. It surrendered within two hours. Seven Dutch lives were lost. Regrettably, there were no galleons at Trujillo. The port had not been used for two years, and no trace of prosperity thus remained to taunt the Dutch. The colonists had apparently set fire to their own homes, and the invaders had to satisfy themselves with what was left: a few bronze and iron cannons, some hides, and the beggarly ransom of twenty pounds of silver.[74]

After six days, van Hoorn forsook the area of Trujillo and sailed to the village of San Francisco on the Bay of Campeche, a well-known depot for exporting wood. Once again taking the Spanish by surprise, the Dutch doggedly advanced against considerable resistance since the governor enticed his garrison of 350 men and an additional 1,000 Indians with subtle promises of rewards. Van Hoorn's superior guidance prompted de Laet to comment: "For a long time this has been one of the most courageous acts committed by so few people."[75] Spanish tenacity also extended, however, to the payment of ransom for the town. Royal orders, the governor said, proscribed the defrayment of one *real*. The Dutch, however, did not leave empty-handed, since there were twenty-two ships in the harbor. Although most of their holds were empty, some were laden with substantial quantities of wood and cacao. Van Hoorn took possession of nine of the best ships and sold four of them back to the Spaniards. The remainder were burnt. After having inflicted negligible damage on the town, since most of the buildings were of stone or brick, the Dutch left San Francisco on August 24.

Van Hoorn appeared north of Matanzas three weeks later, but he was unable to explore the area because of contrary winds and currents. Nothing exciting was ascertained about the contents of the Havana harbor, and an attack on the city was naturally out of the question. In the end, it was decided to return home. As a last measure, he sent one of his captains, Cornelis Corneliszoon Jol, to inquire about the disturbing rumors that Spain had retaken St. Martin. Van Hoorn arrived home in November, covered with glory, and displayed at least five captured if half-empty trophies.[76]

The Spanish treasure fleets of that year left Havana in December, some four months behind their normal time schedule. Jol, sailing west from Matanzas to Cape San Antonio, had to content himself again with the role of an impotent bystander, when he unexpectedly came upon the galleons en route to Havana. Proceeding to Tortuga via the Windward Passage between Cuba and Hispaniola, he learned that the Spanish recapture of St. Martin was indeed an accomplished fact. When he returned on the same route—passing Cape San Antonio on December 3—he once more sighted the treasure galleons, now on their way to Spain. A disappointed captain docked in Texel early in June, 1634, even after what was generally considered a not unprofitable raiding voyage around the Caribbean.[77]

The years from 1629 to 1633 were five years of tremendous activity and vigorous output for the West India Company. The most important consequence of the Dutch invasion of the Caribbean was undoubtedly the crucial destruction of Spanish naval power. A second result which developed from this war of attrition was Spanish inability to stop the occupation of the Lesser Antilles by foreign—non-Spanish—nations. The loss of Spanish naval power was to have a tremendous effect on the status of the Dutch war for independence, as might have been anticipated. The legacy from foreign colonization would radically and permanently alter the balance of power in the Caribbean. Thus, the Dutch "Great Designs" of this period, even if they did not accomplish their primary missions, assuredly germinated long-range goals of great significance. Besides, there was the capture of Pernambuco, which was the culmination of years of patient expectation. But the Dutch never considered Brazil isolated from other areas, West Africa and the Caribbean, where they were increasingly mobile. If no one were able to duplicate Piet Heyn's achievement, they did manage at least to terrorize the West Indies, dislocate intercolonial relations, and drastically alter the carefully maintained routine of the treasure fleets' departures.

Pater, Ita, Booneter, Thijsz, van Hoorn, van Stapels, and Jol had undoubtedly, as a memorial to the States General in 1633 very pointedly stressed, caused the Spanish king great deprivations. It was also admitted, however, that their expeditions had not contributed much to the treasury of the company. The various commanders had together captured almost seventy ships in the Caribbean alone; along the Brazilian coast, the booty was twice as large.[78] While this privateering represented a substantial loss to Spain, the truth of the matter was that in the Caribbean, as in Brazil, the company was still operating in the red.

Pernambuco—this fortuitous gift of Providence—provided the Dutch with a much-needed base from which to launch successive attacks on Africa's west coast and the Caribbean. However, the odds which should have thus been tipped in their favor were to some extent equalized by the fact that the journey to the Caribbean was strictly a one-way affair. From there it was simply easier to sail straight back to the United Provinces than it was to attempt the hazardous detour twice across the Atlantic in order to land back in Brazil. The Heren XIX, fully aware of this dilemma, were plotting solutions. They concluded that they needed a secure port in the Caribbean, and although Hendricksz' attack on Puerto Rico had failed, it had opened their eyes to such an alternative possibility. The possibilities narrowed to a good port, which was not too strongly defended by the Spaniards, yet still centrally located. Before long a site was fancied, one of the most delectable in Spain's *mare clausum*.

10

PIE DE PALO

Het klotsen van zijn stelt
Dreunt Aragon in d'ooren
Gelyk een donderslagh....[1]

The major role in the continuing pursuits of the West India Company in the Caribbean was played by the man whose nickname serves as a title for this chapter. The dynamic Peg-leg Jol—*Pie de Palo* to his Spanish contemporaries—was invariably at the center of Dutch action from 1634 until his death in 1641. Born on the coast of the North Sea in the little village of Scheveningen, he became a sailor at an early age and devoted his life to the sea. His last sixteen years were spent largely in the Caribbean or on the Brazilian and African coasts. At the latter site, he met his death on the island of São Thomé, where his remains were buried in the captured cathedral. When the island was retaken by the Portuguese one year later, Jol's bones were disinterred. The furious Portuguese could not bear to have such an enemy and such a heretic resting within the walls of their main church.

Although Piet Heyn, the man who had committed one of the truly great piracies of all time, was frequently called *el almirante* by his Iberian enemies, Jol, whose actions never matched those of Heyn, was regularly called *el pirata*. He was certainly a privateer, as were all the Dutch seamen in that era. But Jol lacked some of the qualities which set Heyn apart. Jol was a man of little culture and few—most of them raw—words, although his bravery was legendary. Barlaeus, the Dutch diplomat-historian of that period, who wrote a well-known account of the Dutch conquest of Brazil, described Jol, whom he did not like, in the following words: "...from his early years educated by the sea and the waves, indomitable as the elements which he knew so well, fearless beyond comparison, never holding back, exulting in enterprises at sea, brave without expending many words, courageous in attack, inexhaustible of energy and perfectly trustworthy—but tough."[2]

De Laet also knew Jol personally and called him the *manhafte*, an old Dutch term meaning "courageous" which the chronicler often applied to brave men. Samuel Blommaert, another director of the West India Company, had a more dynamic personality than the philosophical de Laet and thus was more appreciative of Jol's rough character. He called him "an experienced man in the West Indies."[3] The often more reserved Aitzema, whose account of Dutch performances in the Caribbean is very sketchy, described Jol as "a famous captain who has caused incredible damage to the Spaniards at sea."[4] Aitzema, however, never specifically mentions Jol's ten expeditions to Brazil, the Caribbean, and the African waters. De Laet describes the first seven; Barlaeus has preserved an account of the other two as well as of the expedition to the west coast of Africa.

The crews under Jol's command, his friends, and his enemies knew him as *Houtebeen*, *Pie de Palo*, or Peg-leg. While very young he had lost a leg in some unknown battle or accident, probably even before he entered the service of the West India Company. But he never allowed it to become a handicap to him. He walked so well on his wooden leg that many did not suspect the cause of his limp and on board his ships he moved about as nimbly as most of the men of his crew.[5] In spite of his quick temper, his roughness, and his lack of tact, he was the company's great champion in the thirties and the primary cause of its brief renaissance after the frustrating five years related in the previous chapter. Yet, no historian has ever written his biography; no painting or engraving of him is known to exist.[6] In Scheveningen, his native town, there is still a street which bears his name, but no statue adorns the streets or the squares of this famous spa. The average man in the street has never heard of Jol or of his deeds.

But far from Scheveningen's beaches and the gray waves of the North Sea, Cornelis Corneliszoon Jol defended his country's honor— off Puerto Rico, Hispaniola, Cuba, Tierra Firme, Yucatán, on the Magdalena, on the Brazilian coast, and on the west coast of Africa. For his exploits, he became a legend in his own time. The barest hint of his arrival, if but with a single ship, created panic in all Spanish coastal cities. Apparently, he inflicted more damage on Spanish shipping than any other Dutch captain except Piet Heyn. He was involved in the capture of several prizes off the Brazilian coast in 1626; he seized at least three and perhaps four ships in 1628, and in 1629, several more. Sailing under Ita in 1630, he took at least one ship; the following year he captured four, and in 1632 he returned with five more. It is difficult to trace his record in 1633, because in that year he joined a larger fleet, but in 1634 he again operated alone and collected three prizes. In 1635, near the peak of his career, he captured eleven Spanish and Portuguese ships and in the following year not less than fourteen. He was, indeed, a valuable servant of the West India Company.

Jol's first visit to the American hemisphere occurred in 1626. As captain of the *Otter*—a ship whose name was to become as famous and as dreaded as its master's—he left Texel in January of that year. His orders were to join three other yachts at St. Vincent and to proceed to Brazil by way of the Cape Verde Islands. The small squadron remained there until May, ambushing several valuable prizes. After six months Jol returned via the Caribbean to Texel.

The following year Jol sailed with a fleet of twelve sails under the command of Dirck Symonszoon van Uytgeest. Once more the destination was Brazil. Jol again took an important part in the capture of the first three caravels which carried some 1,100 chests of sugar, tobacco, and brazilwood. A fourth ship was seized soon after, and van Uytgeest decided to transfer the captured cargoes to his own ships at the island Fernando de Noronha, which was northeast of Pernambuco. Because wind and current prevented this action, van Uytgeest sent Jol to the Caribbean with four of the Dutch ships and the four captured Iberians. It was the latter's second visit to the West Indies. At some unknown port Jol completed the transfer of cargo, burned the captured vessels, and sailed for home. He arrived at Texel on October 23, 1628.[7] A few weeks later he learned of Heyn's spectacular capture of the Spanish treasure fleet. Indeed, he had, unknowingly, nearly been a witness to the coup. It no doubt made a great impression on the young sailor and stimulated his ambition to follow in the footsteps of his fellow countryman from Delft.

It was again on the *Otter* and under van Uytgeest that Jol hoisted anchor on October 20, 1629, to meet with General Loncq at St. Vincent and execute the fourth "Great Design." Jol was the first to notify Loncq that the Spanish invasion of Gelderland had failed and that more Dutch ships were forthcoming. These indeed arrived in December. Loncq then dispatched Jol and another captain to Brazil "to take some ships and prisoners" in order to get more information about the proposed attack.[8]

As stated elsewhere, Loncq chose to ignore the Heren XIX's suggestion that he proceed to the Caribbean to assist in the capture of a treasure fleet. Instead of going himself, he had delegated Dierick Ruyters in his place. Ruyter's squadron included the *Otter* under the command of Jol. This expedition, led by one who knew the Caribbean as no other, became for Jol an enviable experience and the finest possible introduction to the *Kraal*.[9]

Ruyters' instructions for this mission emphasized that he and his men were not to mistreat the Indian population, a warning which was to be repeated time and time again in the company's directives. He was explicitly ordered to find Admiral Pater and to assist him in an attack on Santiago de Cuba. Although the Heren XIX, as mentioned before, were primarily interested in the copper mines, they were also possibly considering the merits of the town as a naval base in the Caribbean. With extraordinary ambiguity, Pater was ordered to destroy Santiago, while Ruyters was instructed to leave the town intact and to avoid inflicting injury on the Indian population. Because of Ruyters' failure to locate Pater who had already left the Caribbean, the combined attack did not get off the ground at this time. Somewhat later, a ship under Commander Booneter scouted Santiago, but it took no action.

After a series of prolonged delays, Ruyters' squadron finally joined Ita's fleet, and Peg-leg Jol was summoned by Ita to sail near him in the *avant-garde* of the fleet. This was clear evidence that Jol was beginning to acquire recognition for his courage and seamanship. However, after cruising for a month near Havana without sighting anything of importance, Ita departed for Cape San Antonio and sent small units of his fleet in search of the Spanish treasure fleets. Jol led one of these scouting trips. During this mission he intercepted a Spanish ship laden with cacao but, since he did not realize the value of the cargo, he allowed the ship to continue on.[10] Although Ita returned home with seven prizes, Jol's part in their capture is not known.

On his next excursion, this time under Jonathan de Neckere, Jol was promoted to vice-commander. His destination was Brazil. The small squadron of one ship and two yachts carried orders for the Dutch authorities there to organize a fleet of twenty-five ships to proceed to the Caribbean.[11] But lack of provisions and rumors of an approaching Iberian armada drastically altered the original plans. De Neckere accordingly sailed with the same squadron from Brazil to the Caribbean, where Jol was able to capture a Spanish slave ship from Guinea. Jol, slightly embarrassed by the tainted cargo he had acquired, let his prey escape.[12] Although de Neckere returned home, having lost his chance to find Booneter's fleet, Jol remained in the area and on two occasions caught a glimpse of the Tierra Firme fleet between Cartagena and Porto Bello. His hands were, of course, effectively tied by the enemy's superior force. Trying to escape detection and possible onslaught, Jol slipped furtively into the Magdalena River. This maneuver was a great risk to his yacht, not only because of the many reefs and imbedded rocks but also because of hostile shore settlements.

Fortunately no danger was encountered, and after the Spaniards had passed, Jol was able to return to the Caribbean to continue his exploits.

Peg-leg realized that the ships he had just seen were not bearing any treasures but had just arrived from Spain. He learned from some prisoners that eleven of them, under Larraspuru, were on their way to Porto Bello to load silver from Peru. In spite of this disappointing information he remained in the neighborhood, and took what prizes he could, standing watch. In October, 1631, an attempt to sail to Porto Bello was frustrated by lack of wind. It was not until late in that same year, that Jol left the area and put in at Ile à Vache for repair. Reinforced by two additional yachts, he soon set out again and sailed west along Hispaniola. He sacked a small town at the island's western tip, and then sailed on to the Windward Passage and Tortuga. He turned south again to Santa Marta and the Colombian coast, and from there he passed through the Yucatán and Florida Straits home to the Low Countries (see map). His ships arrived in June, 1632, carrying the profits seized from five prizes. In addition to the monetary value of his captures—a sum not to be sneezed at—Jol had gained considerable experience. His year in the Caribbean had enabled him to learn the enemy's tactics, and he now knew thoroughly the territory of his future exploits.

In the fall of 1632, after a respite of four months, the *Otter* under Jol left the Netherlands once more bound for Brazil. He dropped anchor there in December after having captured in passing a Portuguese prize which carried Madeira wine. From Pernambuco he briefly sailed under van Hoorn to the south, but reached Rio de Janeiro on his own. While in those surroundings he seized a slave ship, but, once again, unable to decide what to do with the black cargo, he allowed it to pursue its course. Jol returned to Olinda in March, 1633, after a largely unprofitable voyage.

On April 26 he left Brazil for the Caribbean as a part of van Hoorn's fleet. Although his role in this expedition is not precisely known, the intrepid attacks on Trujillo and San Francisco betray his spirit. Afterwards, he was dispatched to investigate certain rumors about the Spanish recapture of St. Martin. While returning to Cape San Antonio he witnessed the passage of the treasure fleet en route from Havana to Spain. Jol followed the fleet for five or six days, hoping to catch a straggler. Quite abruptly he came upon a Spanish frigate bound for Puerto Rico. He captured the ship, but, as luck would have it, the frigate was empty. Jol then sailed to the Dry Tortugas, harassed or destroyed several other ships, and returned home, setting foot on

Dutch soil on June 6, 1634. Together with van Hoorn's squadron, Jol had actively participated in the capture or destruction of at least thirty Spanish or Portuguese ships.[13]

While Jol was at home, the West India Company inaugurated an ambitious plan for the conquest of Curaçao and the adjacent islands. This expedition, led by Jan van Walbeeck and Pierre le Grand, was eminently successful, although problems of occupation and maintenance almost led to the evacuation of the captured islands. When the Dutch decided to remain, Jol once again set sail on Christmas Day, 1634, and his destination was Curaçao. He arrived there on February 22, 1635, with specific orders that the island was not to be abandoned. Although the Heren XIX regarded Curaçao as "a place well-fitted for obtaining salt, wood, and other products, and for infesting, from this base, the enemy in the West Indies,"[14] they had also concluded that Curaçao was strategically important, since "ships of the company could refresh there." Its possession by the Dutch would make "insecure for the King of Spain the returns of his fleets from the West Indies because ships from Angola, and other places to New Spain had to pass there."[15] Plans had already been made by the XIX to send a fleet from Pernambuco to the Caribbean that year. Curaçao was included as a naval base.

Jol was not the man to stay longer than strictly necessary. On March 3 the *Otter* left Curaçao together with another yacht, the *Brack*, captained by Cornelis Janszoon van Uytgeest. Despite the weakness of his unit, Peg-leg nourished some bold plans. He wished to realize one of the fondest dreams of the West India Company, namely, the conquest of Santiago de Cuba. Jol's audacity is well attested by this adventure. The two yachts, which were adorned with Spanish flags, sailed unmolested into the port. Jol had disguised his crew, which had to be on deck, in the traditional robes of the orders of Christ and Santiago.[16] They met no resistance and anchored close to the Spanish fort. Unsuspecting, the governor sent a sloop to greet them, but the officer in charge soon perceived that his "guests" were Dutch and belatedly ordered his men to turn around and make a fast getaway. In the resulting skirmish, the Spanish officer was killed, and his crew surrendered.

Now, however, the governor recovered from his error and rallied his men. Jol, sensing the game to be over, opened fire on the fort to give cover to the men sent to plunder the five or six ships which were anchored in the harbor. Unfortunately, they were nearly empty. The copper had already been turned over to the New Spain fleet. The fort, in the meantime, had begun to retaliate with a hail of missiles.

Jol, learning that his objective was barren, ceased fire "because it did not give any advantage any longer."[17] Instead, he undertook to negotiate with the Spaniards concerning his captives and a ransom for the empty frigates. The governor, although he commanded a mere fourteen men, indignantly refused to discuss the matter and sent the Dutch commander a contemptuous reply. Infuriated, the Dutch next attempted to set fire to the Spanish ships, but they were impeded by continuous enemy fire. Jol thereupon resumed his attack on the fort and the town, which caused panic. As evening fell, the Dutch departed from the port. At the entrance of the bay they were more fortunate, for they met an in-bound frigate carrying provisions for the town. Without much ado, the vessel changed hands, its cargo was transferred, and the empty hull burnt. Two days later Jol released his prisoners.

From Santiago the two Dutch yachts made for Havana. Their exploits at Cuba's former capital were soon common knowledge across the island and the news quickly spread all over the Caribbean. The garrisons at the Isle of Pines and Cape Corrientes were promptly ordered to warn all Spanish ships in the area to be on the lookout.[18] The crew of a Spanish barque, which had been lucky to escape the wrath of the irate Dutchman, subsequently gave the alarm that the fearsome *Pie de Palo* had sworn an oath not to abandon the Caribbean unless he was compensated by a handsome booty in silver, cochineal, and silk.[19]

But Jol did leave the Havana area in order to try his luck off Tierra Firme. There, near the port of Cartagena, he encountered his former colleague Pieter Janszoon van Domburgh commanding a ship and a yacht on a similar mission, but each continued on his own way. Jol sailed with his two yachts and a recently acquired prize so near to Cartagena that "he saw the town clearly." A few days later, in hot pursuit of two Spanish ships, Jol found himself at the mercy of four enemy frigates which had been dispatched by the governor of Cartagena. Peg-leg, not daring combat, beat a hasty retreat until, by chance, he again caught sight of van Domburgh. Now, with four ships at his command, Jol turned on the Spanish frigates and gave them their hard-earned battle. Although the Spanish vice-admiral's ship was captured, the other three escaped. Jol released his 150 prisoners, and sent a priest to the governor of Cartagena with a pre-emptory demand to reciprocate. The priest returned accompanied by two Dutchmen, a few hens, and some fruit. Jol, not quite appeased by this exchange, burnt the Spanish ship.[20]

Peg-leg's presence in Spanish waters caused unabated alarm and created a state of permanent siege. A letter written by the governor of Havana, Francisco Riaño y Gamboa, reveals some telltale details of the conditions in the area during the summer of 1635. On June 3, a frigate sailed into the port of Santiago after having survived an encounter with the fearsome Hollander in which the Spanish ship had been driven on the beach. On June 26, according to the personal testimony of Bartolomé Jaramelo, who had been a witness to the incident, an English hulk was attacked by two Dutch yachts in the waters between Curaçao and Santo Domingo. On July 2, Jerónimo Hernández declared that a Dutch yacht had seized a Spanish frigate, then turned it loose to return to Havana. Baltasar Venegas, a veteran Havana pilot, described one of Jol's recent encounters that had sent an *almiranta* to the bottom of the sea off Cartagena. Reports came from the Isle of Pines that the *Otter* had captured two ships. On September 10, Manuel Núñez stated that his ship had been overpowered by two enemy ships. Eight days later a "dispatch boat" limped into Havana port after having been plundered by Peg-leg Jol. The only bright spot in this dreary record of Dutch activities is the notice, which was conveyed to Havana on September 23, that the Honduras ships would spend the winter in the comparative safety of a friendly port. One other happy note occurred: the Tierra Firme fleet had arrived at Havana safely on September 13.[21]

It is difficult to determine to what extent the Spanish governor's letter corresponds to de Laet's account of Jol's exploits. De Laet records the *Otter*'s meeting with a yacht from Maracaibo laden with silver and hides. This encounter was followed, a few days later, by a battle between Jol's two yachts and two Spanish ones in which the smaller Spanish vessel, carrying hides, sarsaparilla, and tobacco, was captured. A frigate bearing sugar and salt was the next victim in de Laet's catalog. On the Havana coast in September, while Jol was probably watching for some straggler from the Tierra Firme fleet, he captured a large ship from Cartagena. In the latter encounter, after a contest which had lasted many hours, the Spanish ship was forced to surrender its cargo of tobacco, copper, indigo, and seven thousand *reales*. The ship, leaking and sinking, was allowed to make good its escape.[22]

Jol, having fulfilled his boast not to go home without booty, now decided to return. He had amassed more than two thousand hides, five thousand pounds of tobacco, four thousand pounds of sarsaparilla, much silver and other products, and had burned or otherwise destroyed at least eleven Spanish ships.

In sight of home, however, Jol had the misfortune to run into a band of privateers from Dunkirk led by that group's most notorious captain Jacques Colaert. Although Jol was not a man to give up without a stiff fight, the ensuing battle was, too much of course, hopelessly lopsided. On November 2, the *Otter* was towed into the privateers' den. "Thus," complains de Laet, "this valuable yacht, which had done so much damage to the Spaniards, and which had come safely home through so many perils, was taken within sight of the Fatherland."[23] Peg-leg Jol and his crew, promised quarter, were imprisoned in Bourbourg and St. Winoxbergen in the Spanish Netherlands.

Jol repeatedly wrote to the directors of the Amsterdam Chamber and the Heren XIX of "his sad prison, and that the conditions, promised by the enemy, were not regarded."[24] The wives of the imprisoned men beseeched the XIX if "their husbands might be freed, or something done, because the mortality rate was high." They also requested the XIX to pay their travel expenses to Dunkirk and to send additional food to their husbands.[25] For more than six months, from the beginning of November, 1635, until May, 1636, Jol waited impatiently for help. Although rumors abounded that he would be remanded to Spanish custody on orders of the king,[26] he finally gained his freedom in a general exchange of prisoners arranged by the States General.

On August 19 of that same year, Peg-leg Jol reported to the Amsterdam Chamber and was given leave to pursue his seventh expedition.[27] The *Otter* was gone. Instead, Jol now commanded the 260-ton *Swol* and sailed accompanied by two yachts, the *Kat*, commanded by his brother, and the *Jong Otter*. His former flagship still lay in Dunkirk and would probably sail again under another name.

In charge of this small squadron, Jol headed for Curaçao. Van Walbeeck, governor of this youngest possession of the company, had specifically asked the Heren XIX for Jol "so that I, having him here and having a very high regard for him, might be assisted with advice and action."[28] The Heren XIX, who also held the stouthearted mariner in high esteem, had previously counseled him about the composition of his squadron. Jol had replied that since it was winter and no treasure fleets would be about, one ship and two yachts should suffice to discomfit the enemy and take some prizes.[29] Peg-leg, however, did suggest that the XIX reinforce him with some well-equipped ships in May of the following year. He pledged that if the promised ships arrived in time in the Caribbean, the summer would be extremely rewarding.

Jol's secret instructions, opened en route, advised him to bring all his booty to Curaçao, including slave ships.[30] As previously noted, the absence of a Dutch port in the Caribbean had regularly paralyzed any profitable use of human cargo. The XIX, anticipating Jol's usual luck, had now provided a depot for his prizes. This decision of the XIX initiated the role which Curaçao was to play as a slave market, a function which it developed in scope and in importance after Peter Stuyvesant became governor of the island.

Jol left Texel on August 30, 1636, and, after a very fortunate passage, sighted the island of St. Bartholomew on October 19. Six days later he dropped anchor at Ile à Vache, as instructed, to refresh. Within two weeks the Sierra del Cobre of Cuba appeared on the horizon, and Jol was back in his familiar hunting grounds. He cruised here until mid-December but acquired only one small prize. Realizing that "because of that time of the year there was nothing to do at Havana,"[31] he decided to sail, through the Bahama Channel and along the north coast of Cuba and Hispaniola to the Lesser Antilles, thus re-entering the Caribbean. This maneuver was completed in twenty days, a feat which left de Laet breathless with admiration.[32]

Again Jol sailed to Ile à Vache to take on wood and water. While there he met the Dutch yacht *Brack*. This ship was under the command of Captain Abraham Michielszoon Roosendael, who had been commissioned by the Heren XIX to find Jol in order to join him as second-in-command of the squadron and to patrol the area together. Not incidentally, Roosendael's instructions included a reminder to Jol to transfer his prizes to Curaçao. The squadron sailed to the Havana area and hovered about for some time. The *Brack* was soon dispatched to Curaçao with one captured ship. The Jol squadron then returned to the Lesser Antilles along the route used previously, and now completed the journey in only seventeen days. On April 18, 1637, Jol dropped anchor for the third time off Ile à Vache to scrape his ships and to refresh.

He was occupied there for more than a month, finally departing on June 2. Three weeks later he spotted the Spanish treasure fleet as it left Cartagena en route to load silver at Porto Bello. He remained in the area, hoping, no doubt, to light upon a straggler. Not infrequently he managed to catch the Spaniards unaware, but the effort was seldom justified. On August 3, the Tierra Firme treasure fleet, now twenty-six sails strong, was again flaunted in his face as it set off for Havana.[33] Jol's presence was detected on this occasion, and the Spaniards, relying on their superior numbers, decided to crush the Dutch nuisance once and for all. Hampered neither by weight nor by cumbersome sailing tactics, however, Jol sounded the order for a swift retreat and easily outmaneuvered his opponents. Once out of reach of the enemy's massive armament, the Dutch executed a streamlined *volte-face*, and within a few hours, joined by seven nearby privateers also hankering after the majestic game, Jol returned to the attack with augmented strength. As one of the Spanish ships fell back, the birds of prey swooped down for the kill, intent upon devouring their victim. But in the ensuing confusion created by the greedy competition between the seven voracious pursuers, each begrudging the others a part of the booty, the Spanish vessel made good its escape. Furthermore, other privateers soon arrived on the scene demanding a share in the booty. Some were armed with commission letters from the Dutch West India Company. No wonder Jol was to complain bitterly of the folly of this senseless competition.[34]

Despite his inability to get the better of his fellow-countrymen and colleagues, Jol persisted in standing fast off Havana. He knew that the New Spain fleet was bound to arrive soon, and he probably hoped to intercept a straggler from that entourage. His persistence was rewarded. On September 6 the *flota* sailed into view, sixteen merchantmen escorted by a bare four men-of-war, leaving Havana. Then, according to de Laet, Jol suffered a remarkable stroke of bad luck. As he surreptitiously approached, weighing his chances, the Tierra Firme fleet, thirty-three sails strong, suddenly struck out brazenly from Havana port also on its way to Spain. Jol was caught between the two fleets, utterly at the mercy of the enemy's guns and beside himself with anger and pent-up frustration. Typically, he maintained his nerve and boldly attacked one of the smaller merchantmen of the windward Tierra Firme fleet. It was a ship from Dunkirk, and its capture— despite the ominous threat of the two Spanish galleons which rallied to its support—gave Jol more than usual satisfaction. The ship carried goods from Puerto Rico: ginger, hides, coffee, silk, and wood. But it was small consolation to Jol who, had Director Blommaert's advice been followed, should have already been reinforced and in a condition to do much more with this remarkable opportunity. The captain returned home carrying the cargoes of seventeen ships and nourishing the memories of a great encounter. Before the Heren XIX he claimed the treasure fleet had been his for the taking on five different occasions, had he had six good ships with him.[35] At least one member of the board took special note of these words.

Samuel Blommaert, a merchant from Amsterdam, was a bold planner and a man of vision. He had been a director of the West India Company at its inception, and had resigned in 1629 in conformity with the charter. When he returned to the directorship in 1636, he believed that the company had found, in Cornelis Corneliszoon Jol, a true successor to Piet Heyn. He thought Jol would be the agent for the company's second capture of a treasure fleet. In the midst of his struggle to acquire Swedish participation in the WIC and to create a sixth chamber for Gotenburg, ideas which failed to materialize because of a lack of capital in Sweden, Blommaert was busily engaged in mapping out strategy for a renewed effort to ambush one of the treasure fleets.

It had been several years since the West India Company had sent a large fleet to the West Indies. The last major attempt to seize Spain's silver ships had been the expedition of Marten Thijsz in 1632. Van Hoorn's contingent in 1633 had been exclusively aimed at the Honduras ships. With matters in Brazil now apparently under control and the company's position on Curaçao relatively secure, the Heren XIX, inspired by the enthusiasm radiated by Blommaert, determined to have one more fling at the biggest prize of them all.

In letters dated September 4 and November 13, 1638, Director Blommaert boasted of the new "Great Design," the expedition of 1638, as his brainchild.[36] Its preparation and organization, however, proved a difficult task which consumed more than two years. For some time previously there had been open friction in the company between the Amsterdam and Zeeland Chambers on the issue of free or open trade.[37] The official decision to accept Amsterdam's position on free trade infuriated the Zeelanders. The problem was complicated during Blommaert's planning stage by the fact that the meetings were being held in Middelburg, Zeeland's capital. The Chamber of Zeeland, despite the ban of Their High Mightinesses, wanted to reopen the issue and place the question once again on the agenda. All concerted action on the part of the XIX, therefore, was virtually paralyzed. The States General, in despair, appointed a commission to begin preparations for the West Indian expedition, a policy which circumvented the melée of petty deliberations. Although Zeeland was invited to send a deputy, she refused, a position which did not prevent her from becoming increasingly irate that company decisions were being made in her absence.

Blommaert, of course, was part of the commission to plan the new venture, and he unfolded his project to the delegates. During the previous December, 1637, the Political Council in Brazil and Count Johan Maurits had been approached about the expedition. Blommaert had also consulted with the Prince of Orange. As was usually the case, the Heren XIX again combined two ends by endorsing the final proposal: first, the conquest of the Bay of All Saints; second, the capture of a treasure fleet. The leader of the expeditionary force was to be Peg-leg Jol.

Blommaert's strong influence convinced the XIX that Jol was their man. The latter was thereupon appointed admiral of the expedition and later given approval by the States General.[38] It was the fulfillment of Peg-leg's lifelong ambition. All his life he had sought to equal Piet Heyn, and now he was finally offered his chance. Barlaeus condemns the sailor from Scheveningen as a man who would try "to become famous by some memorable action and acquire for himself an immortal fame."[39] Even this learned historian, however, had to admit that Jol's crews would follow their leader anywhere. Like them, he was a simple sailor, a man of few pretensions, even though he had climbed to the highest ranks. Because of his alertness and unsurpassed courage, they held him in the highest regard and were prepared to obey his every order unquestioningly. No greater praise can be lavished on a leader of men.

The Heren XIX's original intention to use Jol in an attack on Bahia was never carried off. Count Johan Maurits, governor of New Holland, recovered from a serious illness, and, in anticipation of the outcome of promised reinforcements from the United Provinces, had launched an attack in April, 1638, against São Salvador. Leading some 3,600 Dutch and 1,000 Brazilian troops, he had nearly succeeded, only to have to face defeat in the end. The count effected a masterfully conceived withdrawal and returned to Olinda. Had he accomplished his aim, Blommaert's claim "by which conquest the situation of the company in this country would have been sufficiently consolidated" would have been completely realized.

The failure to capture the Bay of All Saints had been the count's first real setback in his rule over New Holland. In spite of seemingly insurmountable difficulties, he had hitherto performed excellently. For instance, he had successfully attacked the Portuguese fortress São Jorge da Mina, called by the Dutch the Elmina Castle, "although the strength of the old castle São Jorge was still regarded as formidable."[40] The foray had achieved its object with remarkable ease, and a regular supply of slaves had been secured for Pernambuco.

Rumors hinting of the anticipated arrival of Jol's expedition soon reached Madrid and touched off a new flurry of excitement. Affairs in Spain at the time had reached a disturbing low. In October, 1637, she had lost the town of Breda, at whose surrender in 1625 Velásquez had painted the masterful *Las Lanzas*. In earlier years, Breda had magnanimously been offered to the Dutch in exchange for Pernambuco. Olivares, for one, had been determined to wrest Brazil from Dutch control and had sought this means to pacify both his countrymen and the Portuguese. Now, of course, it was too late. At the same time the Spaniards narrowly missed losing Fuenterrabía. Impressed by their near brush with disaster, Spain as well as Portugal resolved to close their ranks against the insolent heretic invaders. Before long an Iberian fleet set sail from the Tagus to Brazil.

Although Dutch counterespionage agents soon knew of the Spanish attitude, the Heren XIX made a serious miscalculation by assuming that Spain was too busy on the European front to be actively concerned about Brazil. The Dutch discovered from intercepted letters, however, that Spanish plans for the colony were slow in taking form and that the situation was fast deteriorating in the Portuguese-controlled areas, especially in Bahia. These same letters had already led to Johan Maurits' precipitous attempt on São Salvador with the results mentioned earlier. The count advised the XIX that he would have succeeded if the promised troops had arrived in time. It was little comfort to him to find, on his return to Olinda, that Peg-leg Jol was safely anchored in the bay.[41]

Jol had left Texel on April 14, 1638, with a fleet of ten ships and appeared off Olinda on June 8.[42] His instructions, which had been altered to the extent that he was not to become involved in further Bahia projects, disappointed Maurits. He had repeatedly begged for more men and ships, and now he had to be content with promises that a large fleet was being prepared for his needs.[43] Nevertheless, he complied with the orders relayed to him by Jol and supplied the latter's force with some additional ships, six hundred men, and provisions. He must have acted with a heavy heart knowing that the gesture was certain to weaken his own delicate position. On June 22, Jol departed at the head of fourteen or fifteen ships, with supplies for seven months. He commanded nine hundred sailors and six hundred soldiers.[44] On this, his eighth voyage, his high-rising aspirations were finally to be consummated.

Peg-leg definitely understood that fourteen or fifteen ships were simply no match for the silver galleons. Blommaert, however, had vowed that he would send additional recruits from Holland under the command of Roosendael. In hope of establishing contact with these reinforcements as soon as possible, Jol dispatched a yacht to seek out Roosendael, who was presumed to be somewhere in the Caribbean. Jol also wanted to collect information from Spanish captives. No prisoners could be freed.[45] The admiral had learned a lesson from Piet Heyn and was trying to keep his movements within the Caribbean strictly secret.

The expedition weighed anchor under a bad omen. Jol, while setting out aboard a sloop to take command of his flagship the

Salamander, injured his one good leg when he was caught between the sloop and the projecting edge of a cannon. Count Johan Maurits reported the misfortune to the Heren XIX: "Some say the hip bone is broken, but he, Jol, told us that he could still manage."[46]

"The noise of his stump sounds in the ears of Aragon as a thunder," wrote a Dutch poet,[47] alluding to the great expectations that accompanied Jol as he departed for the Caribbean. Both the Heren XIX and the Dutch in Brazil were equally enthusiastic. And indeed, Spain was deeply concerned and weary of the great uproar in the North. The king, when he received news of Jol's departure, immediately sent four yachts to the West Indies to caution the coastal towns against *Pie de Palo* and his fleet.[48] But his warning ships failed to impress Don Carlos de Ibarra, the Spanish general, nor did it deter the Tierra Firme fleet. Almost foundering under their heavy load, the treasure ships left Cartagena for Havana in spite of the rumors about the presence of an enemy fleet nearby, probably Roosendael's squadron. The Spanish general considered the danger to be largely illusory and refused to be intimidated by this *poca ropa*.

After entering the Caribbean, Jol cruised directly west. Roosendael joined him, although the exact site of their rendezvous is not known. Without hailing any passing ships, Jol cautiously proceeded to the traditional arena, the Dry Tortugas, north of Havana. He ordered his captains to use every precaution to remain out of sight of the Spanish coastal watches on the Isle of Pines and Cape Corrientes. No one, not even privateers from Holland and Zeeland encountered in the area, had knowledge of the true goal of this enterprise.[49] During this voyage, Jol sent various dispatch boats to reconnoiter different areas and to locate the Tierra Firme and New Spain fleets. One of these missions ventured close enough to Havana to conclude that the Tierra Firme fleet was approaching. It consisted of seven galleons and a royal yacht from Margarita convoying six merchantmen.

Don Carlos de Ibarra, Viscount of Centenara, the commander of the Spanish fleet, was a veteran and intrepid navigator. His character was quite unlike that of his unfortunate predecessor Juan de Benavides. Ibarra had commanded squadrons and fleets in the Caribbean since 1618. Now, at the close of his career, he would live through the most glamorous episode in his entire naval life. He had cast off from Cádiz on April 28, 1638, and can only have missed Jol's crossing to New Holland by a few days. By June 12, Ibarra had landed at Cartagena. He made a swift voyage to Porto Bello to load the king's silver and returned to Cartagena on August 1. There he learned from Madrid of

Jol's fleet and the latter's bold intentions. He was further notified that *Pie de Palo* was to be reinforced in the Caribbean. The Spanish authorities expected their general to do his utmost to avoid Jol, but if an encounter came about, Ibarra was to make certain that Jol was defeated. The Spanish commander was forcibly reminded of the state of the treasury, and he was assured that an auxiliary force was underway to join him.[50]

The Spanish general quickly decided upon a course of action. On August 7, knowing full well that he would undoubtedly meet the Dutch en route, he deliberately set out for Havana. He was not too certain of the strength of the enemy until, at Cape Corrientes, he received word from the governor of Havana that the Dutch fleet which had been sighted off Cuba amounted to no more than seven or eight ships.[51]

Acting upon suggestions by Blommaert, Jol had meanwhile deployed his ships so that he prevented the Spaniards from ascertaining his precise strength. The Dutch admiral, with six of his ships, lay in wait off Cape Apalache; five more of his ships were near Matanzas. The other seventeen ships in his fleet were patrolling the area with specific orders to report to Jol at once if the Spaniards were sighted.

On August 30, Ibarra's fleet of eight galleons and seven smaller vessels made its first contact with the Dutch.[52] The Spaniards discerned not seven or eight but seventeen or eighteen enemy sails that first evening. By the next morning several more had come into view —the Caribbean indeed was literally swarming with Dutch privateers. Many were not under Jol's command. All had been commissioned by the West India Company, however, and some of them may have placed themselves voluntarily under Jol's orders at this time.[53]

While converging upon the enemy, Jol held a fleet council to discuss the inevitable clash and to arouse the spirit of his captains. The strategy was thus: Jol, leading two ships, would distract the Spanish *capitana*; Roosendael and some other ships were to engage the *almiranta*; Jan Mast, Jol's rear-admiral, was to occupy his Spanish counterpart. The remaining Dutchmen were to choose their respective victims and board them. When a precise order of attack was drawn up, each captain was admonished to post a lookout to watch for damaged Dutch ships that might require their assistance.

At the fleet council Jol inspired his men with valiant words. He impressed upon them that they were fighting notorious cowards, that Spanish ships carried more loot than arms, and that the treasure could neither protect the Spaniards nor wound the Dutch. He further encouraged them by claiming that the Spanish galleons, although they were huge, carried only gleaming sand and not warriors.[54] After he had the captains properly aroused and in high spirits, Jol ordered a prayer said for Dutch victory. The battle was on.

As the opponents veered closer, Carlos de Ibarra hoisted the royal banner and fired a volley. This was the prearranged signal for his captains to assume their specific stations in a battle line. The Spaniards sailed in good order toward the enemy, in accordance with Ibarra's express commands. The same cannot be said for the Dutch. Jol, Roosendael, and Mast and a dozen other captains attacked as had been prearranged. Jol himself opened fire on the *capitana* and attempted to board the Spanish galleon. Somehow, despite the great disparity in size, Jol maneuvered his *Salamander* so that he plowed into the side of the Spanish vessel and threw a hook into her. His men gathered on the quarterdeck and climbed on board their prize. The Spaniards hardly expected such enthusiasm nor were they prepared for the ensuing vigorous onslaught. Jol had offered a reward of one thousand guilders to the first men to bring him the banner flying from the enemy's flagship. Ibarra's decks were soon bombarded with a deluge of Dutch grenades clearing the way to the rear. However, at the height of the battle Ibarra resumed his fire on the *Salamander*, and his admiral, who had managed to elude Roosendael, came to his assistance. It was only after Jol had been forced to beat a hasty retreat that he learned that many of his captains had refused to join in the attack; they "stayed above the wind, looking at the game."[55]

Hostilities raged on unabatedly for eight hours before the two fleets consented to a brief respite to lick their wounds. Jol was boiling with rage, simply beside himself with frenzy; he had missed taking the silver fleet only because his orders had not been obeyed. He cursed and bitterly reproached his captains for their cowardice and reminded them that on the very same spot Piet Heyn had won immortal fame with no greater odds and no more danger. He very pointedly resuscitated their solemn pledge "that in this affair they even had to sacrifice their lives; that it was a matter of the glory and salvation of them all." He concluded his sermon with "Let us, with combined power, start the battle again."[56]

When Barlaeus described the event, he provided his reader with the various excuses submitted by Jol's captains. Yet no explicit mention is made of the most obvious one: that the Dutch captains simply stood in awe of the huge Spanish ships and were afraid to tackle them. Many complained that the odds were overwhelmingly against them and that Jol was leading them to certain doom. Others excused themselves by alleging that they had only been authorized

to attack the New Spain fleet. While no conspiracy was ever uncovered to explain the Dutch calamity, most of the captains seemed
to have agreed that the encounter could only end disastrously. The
privateers not under Jol's command, understandably, had stood idly
by as the tide of the battle heaved before their very eyes. During
Jol's second attack, which resumed an hour later, some captains
remained just as reluctant to engage the enemy. The attempt was
therefore abandoned.

A temporary lull was declared for two days, although the two fleets
were careful not to lose sight of each other. Jol used this time to
summon his subordinates, exhort them once again, and entreat them
to sign a new oath which would force them to fight to the death at
the next opportunity. A new strategy was devised. On September 3,
assured of support, the Dutch admiral hoisted his battle flag anew.
Now, however, since the Spanish had secured the windward side of
the Dutch, approaching them was much more difficult. Jol's
captains, despite their new oaths, did no better than they had before.
This third attack was likewise abortive.

For the next two weeks, while Jol, through dispatch boats, kept
informed of the movements of the Spanish fleet, no acts of belligerency
flared up. He accidentally overheard the not ungratifying news that
many sailors in his fleet were outraged at the cowardice shown by
their captains. At a next fleet council, he was able to effect the
replacement of five of his subordinates. Now, although it was already
September 17, he stubbornly undertook one last attempt at Ibarra's
fleet, which had been reported laying off Cuba at Los Organos. But
when he reached that site, it was only to learn that the Spanish fleet
had already departed.

Despite Dutch cowardice during these encounters, the Spaniards
had been damaged considerably. There were many casualties. Two
of their merchantmen had been abducted by privateers. One of the
Spanish galleons, the *Carmen*, was so heavily damaged that its brave
captain Sancho de Urdanivia believed that it would be an almost
impossible task to save it. It had been in the thick of the fray in a
dramatic rear-guard action. In even the more prosaic accounts of
this battle in the official documents, it was described as a highly
colorful sea fight. Urdanivia's cargo was transferred from the *Carmen*
to some other galleons, and he was allowed to take his ship to the
port of Cabañas.[57]

While Jol was reorganizing his fleet, however, Ibarra was also
holding a fleet council. At that meeting it was suggested that the
Spaniards should make for Vera Cruz instead of Havana. Although

they had so far been able to resist the Dutch attacks, their cargo was too precious to place it in jeopardy. The Spanish general had as a passenger aboard one of his vessels the important *visitador* of the Audiencias of Lima and Charcas. He sought the latter's advice, and, after learning that half the munitions supply was gone and that the Dutch had been reinforced, he hesitated. Should the fleet arrive safely in Havana, the harbor would almost inevitably be blockaded until late that winter. The arguments were thus made to retreat to the comparative safety of Vera Cruz and the protection of the fortress of San Juan de Ulúa.

But Ibarra was a man of inflexible character; indeed, his tenacity and perseverance were simply attributes of the willful obstinacy of the Spanish *hidalgo*. He and his admiral, Pedro de Ursua, still firmly believed that they should try to reach Havana at all costs. When Ibarra made his determination known, the fleet council adjourned. But in the meantime Jol had, indeed, received his long overdue reinforcements. He now commanded twenty-four or twenty-five ships. When he learned of this, Ursua recognized that the situation had become too adverse for the Spaniards to gamble. He admonished his superior to return to New Spain. Ibarra bowed to the inevitable, therefore, and prepared to reverse his course. When he arrived at Vera Cruz on September 24, he found the New Spain fleet safely at anchor at San Juan de Ulúa. Both fleets participated wholeheartedly in the general celebration; the crews rejoiced at having served the king so well by so severely punishing and ridiculing the enemy.[58]

Spanish casualties had been heavy: 108 men dead, 84 wounded. Ibarra, himself, had also sustained a serious injury. He had grabbed a grenade which had been thrown at his feet, and it had exploded before he could throw it overboard. The Dutch had not escaped the encounter unscathed either: 50 dead and 150 wounded.[59] Among those killed were the brave Jan Mast and the courageous Abraham Roosendael, two of the best exponents of seventeenth-century Dutch maritime expansion.

This abortive attempt, called the battle of Los Organos, then, constitutes the final outcome of Jol's major endeavor to capture the Spanish treasure fleet. It had not failed because of a lack of organization; Blommaert and his commission had done their work well. It had not faltered through lack of leadership either; the West India Company had placed the task in the most proficient hands at its disposal. It had been a fiasco because of the treachery and cowardice of a handful of incompetent Dutch captains combined with the firm determination of Carlos de Ibarra to fight. Blommaert, when he learned how nearly Jol had come to bringing off the coup, was utterly dejected and wrote:

It would not only have strengthened the company to fight the next year against the King of Spain with more power in the West Indies and elsewhere, but the King of Spain would have been brought to his knees because the war that is fought here in Europe he fights with the huge treasures from the West Indies, and if that root is cut off from him so that he cannot grow any longer, then some peace would come to the whole Christian world and his so-called monarchy would receive a heavy blow.[60]

Jol resolved to delay no longer in the Caribbean and thus add further to his masters' expenses. He sent part of the fleet back to Brazil and divided the remainder so that one squadron would stay in the area while the rest would accompany him to the Low Countries. When the ships set out for home, they encountered such bad weather that rumors soon abounded both in Spain and in the Netherlands that the entire fleet had been destroyed. Nevertheless, Jol arrived safely home in November and reported at once to the Heren XIX and to the States General, where he vehemently denounced the conduct of seven of his captains. Their High Mightinesses thanked their admiral "for his courage and ability in the meeting with the Spanish silver fleet," but these words and the golden medal and chain given to him must have been small comfort to a man of his temper and ambition.[61]

As admiral, Jol could have court-martialed his cowardly captains while still in the Caribbean. He had deferred prosecution, however, since he had lost Roosendael and Mast, two important members of the fleet court. When the accused captains were arrested in the Low Countries, they, of course, retaliated with countercomplaints about Jol. But Peg-leg enjoyed the confidence of the Heren XIX and the States General, and the accusations against him went unheeded. The impeached captains were severely condemned to exile, to confiscation of goods and salaries, or, for the lesser offenders, simply the payment of expenses incurred by the trial. Aitzema, vindicating the relatively light sentences, explains, "They had ships of twenty-three or twenty-four pieces, manned with one hundred or one hundred and ten men, while the Spaniards had galleons."[62]

Although Ibarra wintered in Vera Cruz, he sent word to Spain so as to relieve the king of worry. Madrid was placated but the court contemplated the future with apprehension. Since the silver had failed to arrive, the treasury would once again be forced to borrow money at high interest rates in order to administer the state; this would burden its already weak credit to its limits. Eight galleons were dispatched to reinforce Ibarra, and all the ships returned to

Spain the following summer without having touched Havana en route. Once again Cuba would experience dire economic problems. Ibarra was received ceremoniously in Spain and given the title Marquis de Caracena.[63] Shortly after he was sent with a fleet of fourteen sails to crush the rebellion in Catalonia, after which he died in Barcelona.

The unfortunate outcome of Jol's adventure in the Caribbean might easily have turned into a personal debacle, but he continued to be honored and respected by the XIX and by the States General. He enjoyed a good reputation until his death, a fact that is borne out by his participation as commander of the fifth Dutch squadron in the celebrated Battle of The Downs in October, 1639. This battle, led by the famous Dutch Lieutenant-Admiral Maarten Harpertszoon Tromp, resulted in the total defeat of the Spanish armada and ended for all time Spanish naval power in the North Atlantic.

Another catastrophe soon overtook the Spaniards across the ocean. A huge Spanish fleet under the command of Fernando de Mascarenhas left the Iberian peninsula approximately ten weeks after the disaster at The Downs. Near Itamaracá this fleet unfortunately encountered a Dutch fleet of twenty sails under the command of Willem Corneliszoon Loos. Although Loos was killed the first day of the ensuing four-day engagement, his second in command, Jacob Huygens, so effectively broke the resistance of the Spanish fleet that the Dutch claimed to have defeated the enemy. Boxer admits that, strategically speaking and in spite of heavy losses on both sides, the advantage in this engagement was wholly on the side of the Dutch.[64] The battle did far more than bring the Dutch a strategic advantage in their Brazilian venture. It radically ended the last Spanish effort to take the offensive in the Caribbean. From 1639 onward the proud Spanish navy of the days of Lepanto was no longer a protagonist in the ensuing dramatic struggles among England, France, and the United Provinces in the *mare clausum*.

Jol missed being present at the Battle of Itamaracá. He sailed from Texel on January 17, the final day of the four-day encounter. Count Johan Maurits had repeatedly asked the Heren XIX to arm a fleet against the rumored Spanish armada then en route to the Brazilian and Caribbean Dutch colonies. Finally, at the very end of 1639, the XIX readied some ships and placed them under the double command of Peg-leg Jol and Jan Corneliszoon Lichthardt. The latter was an accomplished sailor, a man who knew Portuguese fluently since he had lived in Lisbon for many years. He was also thoroughly familiar with the situation in Brazil because he had fought there for his country.[65] As usual, Jol's instructions ordered him first to Brazil and then to the Caribbean for another try at the treasure fleet. The West India

Company was in dire need of success—and cash. Lichthardt would be the first in command in Brazilian waters, Jol in the Caribbean.

The expedition was well planned, and the selection of Lichthardt and Jol suggests that Blommaert once again masterminded the project. Spanish rumors, however, had exaggerated the size of the Dutch forces; Madrid believed that Jol commanded sixty vessels and that once in the Caribbean he would take command of all the Dutch vessels already in the area. Although not nearly that strong, Count Johan Maurits must have felt greatly relieved when this fleet arrived at Pernambuco on March 26: "Above all we are very pleased and we have to thank Your Graces very particularly for the heads of the fleet sent to us, Admirals Lichthardt and Cornelis Corneliszoon Jol, men whom we always have kept in the highest regard because of their great talents."[66]

Jol's raids and exploits on the Brazilian coast fall outside the scope of this study, but would fill interesting pages in the history of New Holland. In all certainty, he was back in Olinda in June preparing for the execution of his second mission, the capture of the treasure fleet.

On July 14, 1640, Jol left Pernambuco accompanied by a fleet of 24 sails, 2,000 sailors, and 1,700 soldiers. Just before this date, Jorge de Mascarenhas, the new viceroy of Portuguese-Spanish Brazil, arrived at the Bay of All Saints. Count Johan Maurits, well aware of Mascarenhas' escort, could only hope that Dutch raids would stifle any Portuguese initiative for the time being. Jol's orders from the Heren XIX, together with his own insatiable drive, could simply not be circumvented. The count, irritated by the meddling and constant interference of the Heren XIX, had already asked to be relieved of his post. Yet, when the XIX refused his request, he amended Jol's orders to the extent that Peg-leg had to return to Pernambuco after his exploits in the Caribbean.[67]

Early in August Jol refreshed at Ile à Vache. He reached Havana about September 1. Here he was joined by two yachts from Curaçao and ten privateers, the latter having been relayed to his command by the Prince of Orange. Jol dispatched some ships to Cape San Antonio and the Dry Tortugas to reconnoiter, and in the meantime he drafted his plan of attack. He divided his fleet into three squadrons of seven ships and four yachts each under himself, Vice-Admiral Lichthardt, and Rear-Admiral Bartel Wouters.[68]

On September 2, the Dutch captured a small Spanish barque with forty-five persons aboard; these captives were dispersed throughout the fleet. Jol moved about the area stealthily, aiming to keep his presence a secret. He was unaware of the fact that he had long since been discovered and that the new governor of Havana, Alvaro de Luna Sarmiento, not only knew of his arrival but had taken vigorous steps to cope with the situation. Warnings were speedily sent to Cartagena and Vera Cruz, and coastal guards were doubled everywhere, especially at Cape Corrientes. Meanwhile, he did all he could do to strengthen the defenses of Havana and sent a request to the viceroy of New Spain for more money and ammunition. His financial problems were enormous; more than anything else he needed to break the pernicious Dutch blockade off Havana so that the island could return to trade and prosperity.[69]

On September 3, Sarmiento was notified that a Dutch ship had come in dangerously close to the Morro Castle and had inspected the empty harbor. A day later the entire Dutch fleet of thirty-six sails could be seen from Havana. Sarmiento once again dispatched warning ships to New Spain and Cartagena. The *veladores* at Cape Corrientes were admonished that the Tierra Firme fleet might already be at sea and should be carefully watched for and cautioned.

Jol cruised in the area, absorbed in his watch-and-wait policy. As yet, he was unaware of the mission of the Spanish warning boats and had failed to intercept any of them. Then, on September 11, a hurricane struck the Dutch fleet. The tempest continued for three days, and the Dutch were terror-stricken. So frightened, indeed, was Lichthardt that he is reported to have considered a retreat into Havana, and asked a captive priest aboard his vessels, "Father, if I enter Havana, will they treat me well and save my life?"[70]

On the fourth day the storm passed. Jol learned, to his dismay, that seven of his ships had disappeared. Four of them had been thrown up on the Cuban coast which provided Sarmiento with at least sixty-five pieces of artillery. Almost 230 of his men were taken captive by the Spaniards on that particular occasion.[71] One of the lost ships was later found so badly damaged that Jol permitted it to sail home, where it communicated the sad tidings of natural disaster to the Heren XIX.[72] The other three wanderers made it safely into Pernambuco. With his depleted force Jol stubbornly remained near Havana.

About one week later Peg-leg Jol sent a sloop with a white flag into Havana to solicit an exchange of prisoners. While he could only boast about forty-five prisoners, he himself readily admitted that the Spanish governor had at least five times more. Although this messenger did not report the exact numbers of Jol's prisoners, Sarmiento politely declined the offer of the exchange and sent his condolences to the Dutch for their losses. He advised the Dutch admiral that Spanish concern for the captives had been so great that the floundered crews had been quickly brought to Havana in order that they might be more adequately taken care of. With undisguised irony he also assured Jol that he hoped that the Dutch would fare well until the Spanish fleets arrived since the Spanish victory "which we expect from God's hand" would then be all the sweeter.[73] The Dutch prisoners, all of whom had indeed been treated well, were eventually returned to Pernambuco. Jol released his Spaniards at the first opportunity.

Sarmiento's wish was not fulfilled. Jol hovered about the area until the end of September. Then he withdrew to Matanzas to refresh; he presumed that the treasure fleets had taken cover in other ports for the winter. Once at Matanzas, his men, venting their pent-up anger, plundered the farms in the area for supplies. On October 7, Jol left the Caribbean through the Florida Straits and headed for Pernambuco.[74] The last Dutch attempt to capture the treasure fleets was definitely concluded. The Spaniards, learning of his departure, sailed at once for Havana and from there to Spain in the following spring.

This was, as observed, the Heren XIX's last grand effort to tackle the treasure fleets. Although it had begun auspiciously and enjoyed several spectacular early successes, the West India Company thereafter devoted itself to the same problem that troubled the Spanish monarchy: an empty treasury. Money came in slowly; privateering, after all, was not such a profitable business, and subsidies from the government, repeatedly promised, trickled in even more slowly.

The venture was also Jol's last visit to the Caribbean. He arrived in Pernambuco with but sixteen ships and considerable losses in men to learn that the Portuguese had at last severed all ties binding them to their Spanish masters and had proclaimed the Duke of Braganza their king. Although the political consequence of this event will be dealt with in a subsequent chapter, it is significant to note here that—in the very beginning—the Dutch were enthusiastic and sympathetic adherents to the Portuguese cause because they expected the latter to become their natural allies against the hereditary enemy.

At Pernambuco Count Johan Maurits held a celebration to commemorate the news of the revolt and the accession of João IV. The Portuguese planters of the area were cordially invited to attend. These convivialities, however, masked the count's steadfast intentions to continue the war against the new king's vassals in Brazil and Africa. He politely rejected a Portuguese-Brazilian request for a temporary local truce pending the negotiation of a definitive treaty. For a change the count found his proposals endorsed by the Heren XIX and the States General. He was authorized to seize whatever territory he could until the official proclamation of a truce between Portugal and the United Provinces brought an end to further hostilities. Although the directors expressed their fond desire for the prompt capture of Bahia, Count Johan Maurits, tuned to more strictly local needs, was more in favor of the conquest of a great Portuguese slave depot on Africa's west coast.[75] Since slaves were in such urgent demand, slave trading had become extremely profitable. Pernambuco could not long survive without the blacks, and circumstances directed the attention of the Heren XIX once again toward São Paulo de Luanda, the same site where van Zuylen had once notoriously blundered and where Piet Heyn had been foiled in a frustrated night attack. Capturing this town would give the Dutch access to the most fertile slave area in Africa and would drastically cut the Spanish and Portuguese export of labor for their American mines and plantations.[76] Fortunately for the Dutch, the Portuguese delayed ratification of the treaty which they had already concluded.

Angola was the prize which the Dutch now wanted. On May 30, 1641, Jol sailed from Pernambuco with 20 ships, 850 sailors, and more than 2,000 soldiers.[77] Among the latter were some 240 Brazilian Indians. His instructions were simple and concise: he was to seize both São Paulo de Luanda and the fortress on the island of São Thomé. Neither Jol nor his subalterns had any previous experience in Africa and were all aware that the company had failed dismally on three previous adventures in that area.

Peg-leg was also informed that the garrison at Luanda amounted to 2,500 men. This figure could be considerably augmented by the adult males of the community and by auxiliary Negro troops.[78] Virtually everything else transmitted to Jol turned out to be useless information once he neared his destination. Although he was, for instance, ordered to drop anchor in St. Bras which was described as the only bay in the area, in fact the coastline was dotted with more suitable inlets. The Dutch admiral understood full well that the success of his mission hinged upon whether he could hire able pilots, alive to local pitfalls, to guide him along the coast.

The Dutch fleet crossed the Atlantic under adverse circumstances. In normal weather the journey required about four weeks, but wind and current delayed Jol for twice that length of time. The entire fleet, already severely rationed and almost out of water, must have sighed with relief when land was sighted. On the evening of August 9, the fleet dropped anchor in the Bay of Mossamedes, where Jol refreshed and rested his men.[79] He dispatched Vice-Admiral Jacob Huygens to Cape St. Bras in search of a reliable guide.[80]

Luanda, meanwhile, had been informed that treaty negotiations were underway between the United Provinces and Portugal. Its citizens were overjoyed since they had lived for years in dread of attack. In the past Dutch ships had appeared menacingly within sight of the harbor. The news from Brazil and Portugal seemed to indicate that peace between the two countries was simply a matter of formalities. Perhaps the Portuguese, except for their governor, were already anticipating a period of harmonious collaboration with the Dutch, despite the fact that the latter were regarded as heretics and the clergy was firmly opposed to fraternization with enemies of the faith.[81] It was the highly lucrative slave trade that was at stake.

As hope rode high in Luanda just then, news was circulated that a powerful Dutch fleet was approaching the area. It was August 23, 1641. Although Jol had not managed to locate a pilot, the lack was no deterrent for the Dutch. Preparations were made to disembark the troops, and Jol admonished them, "Every captain will be required, without exception, to do his utmost duty."[82] Soon afterward and quite unexpectedly, Jol had an amazing stroke of luck. One of his ships had captured a small caravel which had an experienced pilot aboard who, for gold, agreed to act as Jol's guide. Luckily this man knew of a path that would bring the Dutch behind the undefended rear of the town.[83]

Jol took his cue accordingly, and he moved stealthily, on August 25, to the northern entrance of the port. His ships blocked the entrance of the harbor containing fifteen ships. Luanda was in a furor: were the Dutch allies or enemies? The Portuguese governor, who had had some personal experience with the Dutch in Brazil, Flanders, and Angola, summoned his troops. He placed them along the shore and ordered his batteries to fire at any Dutch attempt to land. Two of the ships in the harbor were sunk near the town to barricade the inner harbor, and reinforcements were sent to assist the ships which were nearest the Dutch blockade. Things looked black for the attacker.

But the Portuguese expected the Dutch to concentrate their forces against the two forts at the entrance of the harbor; they were wrong. Jol lowered sloops, manned them, and had them rowed toward the beach between the two forts just beyond the reach of their guns. As soon as the governor realized what the Dutch were aiming at, he knew that Luanda was lost. From the Dutch landing site, a path led through the hills north and from there into the town. Wisely, Jol had decided on the plan that had been suggested to him by his captive pilot.

As a final effort the governor of Luanda sent troops to the Dutch disembarkation point, but they arrived too late. The Portuguese, caught in merciless fire from the Dutch sloops and the ships blockading the harbor, fled helter-skelter behind the safety of the town walls. The fort's guns were effectively silenced in the afternoon, and in the course of the night the Dutch entered the town from both east and west.

To their amazement they found the place completely deserted. The ships in the harbor surrendered meekly and troops entering the city encountered little resistance in the streets. The inhabitants and the soldiers had all slipped away on the presumption that the enemy had come only to plunder.[84] It had been a comparatively easy victory, one obtained at the cost of few casualties. Exuberantly, Jol wrote to Count Johan Maurits that the mission had been accomplished.[85]

The governor of Luanda, who soon realized that the Dutch nourished intentions of a more permanent nature, wrote a letter to Jol admonishing the latter that Portugal and the United Provinces were allies and that his military action had been outrageous. Jol, denying all formal knowledge of the existence of a treaty alliance, nevertheless couched his rejoinder in cautious and unprovocative terms.[86] Not knowing what party, Spanish or Portuguese, the governor sided with, he had judged it wise not to commit himself irrevocably on the subject. Not his arguments, therefore, but the power of his guns decided the final outcome in this verbal fencing.

Jol's victory made the West India Company the proprietor of one of the busiest and most profitable slave ports in Africa. The average annual trade from Luanda amounted to some 15,000 slaves and 6,600,000 guilders.[87] Not long thereafter, this highly profitable source of revenue was adroitly monopolized under a new company regulation. The loss to the Catholic king could be calculated as close to one million guilders annually. It can be argued that Spain would probably have been deprived of these profits in any event after the successful Portuguese revolt. For the time being, however, both parties lost out and felt aggrieved. Feeling against the Dutch ran high in Lisbon.

Jol, on the other hand, had only half completed his task. Just three weeks after his victory, he left Luanda on September 17, with nine ships and five yachts manned by four hundred sailors and six hundred soldiers. His instructions now directed him to the island of São Thomé. Many years before, the Dutch, under van der Does, had embarked on a similar mission which had ended disastrously (see Chapter 1). Flushed with his recent victory Jol now undertook the project. His main goal was the capture of the fort of São Sebastião, which was situated on a narrow peninsula at the northeast side of the island, close to the capital. With its four bastions and with walls twenty-four feet high, armed with thirty cannons, the fort was considered one of the strongest outposts on Portuguese Africa's west coast.

When the Dutch arrived at the island on October 2, they landed their men two miles south of the peninsula. Peg-leg himself assumed command of the troops; his vice-admiral Matheus Jansen was ordered to drop anchor as close as possible to the castle and not to open fire unless the enemy provoked him. The Portuguese acquiesced and soon the battle was raging. After an hour of heavy shooting and fearsome losses on both sides, the initial attack was repulsed. This event signaled the beginning of a two-week period of continuous Dutch assaults and equally stubborn Portuguese resistance. Jol, at last recognizing the futility of this approach, changed tactics and ordered his men to blast the castle with heavy mortar fire. This seemed to produce vastly better results. On October 16, the Portuguese governor requested a parley and surrendered São Sebastião. The Portuguese, officers and soldiers alike, were allowed to keep their personal property and were sent home. In the meantime the Dutch had occupied the abandoned town of São Thomé. Complete annihilation was prevented by the payment of 300,000 pounds of sugar and 5,500 cruzados, which represented a total value of 100,000 guilders.[88]

The main foe in that continent, however, had not yet been beaten. Within a few days after the Dutch had taken possession of the castle, the first men fell sick, and soon hundreds of soldiers and sailors succumbed to the terrible heat. Barlaeus commented: *Non in Martis sed Mortis triumphum servata fuisse viderentur*.[89] Jol, who had been active day and night without rest, took to his bed on October 25. He continued to give orders for the benefit of the West India Company up to the very last moment, naming Matheus Jansen as his successor and appointing a new vice-admiral. He died on October 31, 1641, and was buried with great pomp in the cathedral of the town, Nossa Senhora da Conceição.[90] He left posterity no personalized account of his exploits; as his secretary shortly thereafter followed him in the grave, no accurate Dutch record of Jol's last deeds survived.

One year later the Portuguese recaptured the town, though not the fort. They unceremoniously opened Jol's grave and removed his body. The Dutch were shocked and clamored for restitution; Portugal arrogantly refused to repudiate the offense: "It is ridiculous that you accuse us of unburying the dead. If you knew correctly the basis of our religion you certainly would not have done so, because this is a question of the clergy and not of secular power."[91] Somewhere, in a forgotten corner of the island, Jol found his final resting place in an unmarked grave.

With Cornelis Corneliszoon Jol's death the last of the great admirals of the West India Company departed from the scene, and with his demise the company lost its redoutable aggressive potentiality. Although Jol never captured a Spanish treasure fleet, he had earned a reputation as a highly successful privateer. The specter of his presence haunted Spanish officials in the Caribbean for years. A courageous man, an inveterate gambler who risked the very fortune of his country, he persevered in the face of danger and misfortune. Never losing confidence, a stranger to fear and doubt, and impervious to weariness or boredom, "he continuously verged on the abyss of death."[92] Throughout his life he was faithful to his country and to the company which employed and honored him. His crews knew that he was a rough leader and his temper tantrums were legendary, but they followed him willingly. He had been one of them before he rose through sheer talent to the highest rank that the company could bestow, and he remained one of them to the end, avoiding the airs which often undertake rising men of destiny. His passing was deeply mourned. Indeed even Barlaeus, the cultured Latinist who disliked the tough ill-mannered sailor, conceded him the highest praise: "He was not a man to boast nor to habituate elegant courts, but he persisted in what he started, especially in the destruction of Spain."[93]

11

THE DUTCH PEARLS

Nos tera ta baranca.[1]

Although the Dutch had already established themselves on the Wild Coast and in New Netherland early in the seventeenth century, their expansion into the Caribbean required more time. The Greater Antilles, of course, had been firmly in Spanish hands for more than a century, but the Lesser Antilles had been regarded as *islas inútiles* —useless islands—and had been left to their Indian populations. Soon they were to become tempting bait for the intruders in the *mare clausum*, and Spain was simply too weak to successfully drive her hardy rivals from their outposts in the West Indies. Too late she realized her error in neglecting these little Caribbean pearls and in ignoring their *de facto* occupation by foreign powers.

The early inducements to overseas settlements have already been demonstrated. The significant difference between the Dutch and other European interlopers, however, was that the latter seemed determined to occupy and to colonize the Caribbean. On the contrary, the Dutch, who were not plagued by problems of religious intolerance or economic unrest at home, were more interested in salt and in trade.

Although there are rumors of earlier colonization attempts around 1604, foreign occupation of the Caribbean effectively began in 1625 with the simultaneous settlements of the French and the English on St. Christopher—or St. Kitts, as the latter called the island. In 1625 also, English and Dutch colonists appear to have occupied the island of St. Croix, one of the Virgin Islands. Barbados was examined and claimed by Captain John Powell. Nevis, St. Eustatius, St. Martin, and many others of the Lesser Antilles were soon occupied, but it is impossible to trace always which country settled which island and when because so many of these early pioneers were of dubious nationality or of mixed blood.

The confusion surrounding colonization in the Lesser Antilles is also compounded by the fact that the first Stuart, James I, made his grants orally. Although these were later confirmed by his son in written documents, Charles I was obviously confused in his designations to the Earl of Carlisle and the Earl of Pembroke. The Dutch firm of the Courteens also appears to have played a part in the general intrigue that renders inscrutable this entire episode. Whatever the legal implications of all this confusion may have been, it is certain that the archipelago between Trinidad and Puerto Rico was very soon occupied by either English or French or both.

Dutch privateers had indeed visited the Caribbean before the Truce, but the systematic invasion of the area was the work of the Dutch salt carriers. During the Truce these incursions had stopped for the most part, but after 1621 they were vigorously renewed, and the salt carriers were quickly joined by increased numbers of Dutch privateers in search of profits. More than three years were to pass, however, before an official fleet—actually only a squadron—bearing the flag of the Dutch West India Company showed itself in the Caribbean. The fleet of Pieter Schouten dropped anchor at St. Martin on October 5, 1624.

This island, a barren rock, probably discovered by Columbus on his second voyage together with the islands of Saba and St. Eustatius and some others of the Lesser Antilles, was among the Spanish *islas inútiles*. Even the Dutch found no solace in its scowling hostility, and after Schouten's search for wood and water had turned out to be futile, he was forced to go on to Dominica to satisfy his needs.

The visit of Boudewijn Hendricksz to Bonaire in 1626 has been recounted in an earlier chapter. While anchored there, his crews had captured two hundred sheep. A welcome variation in the sailor's monotonous menu, it was booty enough to cheer the men over the Easter holidays. But Hendricksz left the island after a week, using it only as a depository for some Spanish prisoners he had acquired on his raids.

Again in 1626, Piet Heyn sailed within sight of Saba and St. Eustatius, but he did not stop at either island. In the spring of the following year, a squadron under Lucifer passed near Curaçao and Aruba after having brought some Zeelanders to settle on the Wild Coast—one of the first Dutch colonizing efforts after the termination of the Truce. When van Uytgeest visited St. Martin in April, 1627, he reported to the XIX that there was a huge salt pan on the island. He could find no fresh water, however, and left after two days. He later cruised along the coast of Aruba but would not risk a landing there.

Piet Heyn's Rear-Admiral Banckert, in the expedition of 1628, dropped anchor at Tobago and lost several men in skirmishes with the

Indian natives of the island. He next proceeded to Bonaire where he spent three weeks cutting brazilwood. Admirals Pater and Thijsz both visited the Curaçao area the following year, and Admiral Ita is known to have also been to a deserted Indian village on Bonaire.

This cursory review[2] shows only the official visits of the Dutch to some of the Lesser Antilles. Unofficially, of course, their privateers and salt carriers had investigated most of the unoccupied islands in the area. Although some of their colonists were among the heterogeneous populations of English and French settlements in the Caribbean, Dutch interest was basically focused on monetary gain instead of colonization. Profit was the goal, profit by privateering against Spain or through trade with English and French colonists. The only exceptions to this general rule were some Amsterdam and Zeeland investments in settlements on the Wild Coast.

Although it is possible that a Dutch colony existed on St. Martin as early as 1627 or 1628, the lack of fresh water on the island would seem to have been an insurmountable handicap to settlement. Colonization, therefore, could only indicate the desire to control the salt pans. The Zeeland Chamber, while primarily interested in establishing trade arrangements with the English and French on St. Kitts, may also have sent some pioneers to the island around 1630. The first formal request for settlement dates from that year. Yet as early as 1627 the Heren xix had all available information about the island and its relative distance from Tierra Firme and from the other Lesser Antilles.[3] The Zeelandian settlement on Tobago might well have been the result of this information.

The punitive expedition of Fadrique de Toledo in 1629 to evict all "trespassers" from Nevis and St. Christopher was only temporarily successful. Within a year a French captain, Giron, had gathered up the scattered colonists—among them some Dutch—and had returned them to their former abodes "as happy as the Jews upon leaving Egypt."[4] In 1629 the Zeelanders also managed to resume their commercial relations with the inhabitants of these islands. Hamelberg is probably correct in asserting that this trade was sufficiently important to lure the Dutch into establishing trading posts nearby. Before the English and French had settled there, Zeeland had previously considered St. Christopher as a prospect. She was now interested in St. Martin, despite its ominous disadvantages. Consequently, in 1630, the Heren xix decided to establish a colony on this island and charged the Chamber of Amsterdam with executing the plan. In turn, Amsterdam asked Samuel Blommaert to serve as patron of the settlement.

Since Blommaert was disinterested and did not accept the invitation, the Amsterdam Chamber was forced to assume the role itself and appointed Jan Claeszoon van Campen as its local representative. Van Campen subsequently became the first Dutch commander of the island. So far as is known there was no actual opposition to Dutch occupation, which makes credible the allegation that the island was deserted.

Legal objections, however, were not long in appearing. Founding their case on the Carlisle grant, the English complained to the Dutch ambassador in London who responded that the island had been found "uninhabited and desolate."[5] Their High Mightinesses, who were never ones to be very much impressed by Stuart grants, chose to regard the Carlisle grant as an illusory pretension and ignored it. Van Campen, meanwhile, organized some sort of government and began the construction of a fort to guarantee Dutch permanence on the island. In November, 1632, this fort was completed and equipped to hold a garrison of 100 men and 34 pieces of artillery.[6]

St. Martin was soon a bustling port. The salt carriers especially —including many English and French ships—became regular and important visitors to this hospitable little haven. Some ships laden with products badly needed in the Caribbean favored the island as a general depot for commercial ends; others, especially those Dutch plying their trade between Brazil and Europe, frequented St. Martin to load salt. Indeed, salt was by far the most important single item determining the fate of the island. The truth of this assertion is amply demonstrated by the fact mentioned before that salt revenues paid for some two-thirds of the company's expenses in maintaining its 6,000-man garrison at New Holland. When carriers disembarked their crews to lend a helping hand in preparing crude salt for shipment, they spent the intervening time in search of more lucrative gains, i.e., smuggling and taking Spanish prizes. St. Martin had thus rapidly become an important center both for salt and privateering activities. As reported before, the Spanish under Cadereyta captured the fort in 1633, destroyed the colony, and ended Dutch control of the salt pans.

St. Eustatius, too, witnessed a Dutch attempt at settlement. If Dutertre is correct, the French under de Cahusac had already established themselves on this island in 1627 and had built a fort which the Dutch were to use later for their own defense. In December, 1635, however, Jan Snouck, an enterprising mariner from Flushing and a man destined to play an important role in the history of the Dutch Leeward Islands, received permission from the Zeeland Chamber of the WIC to found a colony on some uninhabited island in the West Indies.[7]

The Snouck expedition started for St. Croix, but for some reason—probably because the English were already in residence there—found it unacceptable. After dropping anchor off several other islands, fifty colonists led by Pieter van Corselles, the founder of a Dutch colony on Tobago, chose to stay on St. Eustatius. Like St. Martin, this island had also been included in the Carlisle grant, but it was as yet unclaimed when the Dutch went ashore. A fort was soon erected from the ruins of an old French one, and the island was rechristened New Zeeland. Snouck informed his patrons, the well-known Zeelandian merchants Abraham van Pere and Pieter van Rhee, of his actions and the latter requested approval from the Zeeland Chamber of the WIC. Recognition was granted and confirmed by the Heren XIX. Snouck tried to promote his island by loudly proclaiming the fact that "good tobacco could be planted and vast profits could be reaped."[8]

Settlement stipulations for the colonists were probably much like those earlier prescribed for similar ventures. In addition to these general territorial provisions, however, it was further stated that the colonists would be exempt for ten years from duties, except on salt, wood, and other "products delivered by nature itself."[9] With the acquiescence of the Zeeland Chamber and the endorsement of the States General, the Heren XIX named van Corselles commander of the island. Not long afterward the latter formed a government that was to set a pattern for future Dutch patronships in the Leeward Islands. Elsewhere in the Caribbean, Dutch settlements had a prevailing form of government which largely excluded private citizens—military leaders and employees of the company were more acceptable candidates. In the Leeward group, however, thanks to van Corselles, a system evolved which allowed some of the colony's wealthier citizens to attain high positions. This oligarchic structure was soon to become prey to nepotism and feuds since some appointments, notably to the governing council, were for life. In contrast, at Curaçao and on the Wild Coast, the governors or commanders of the respective settlements managed to retain a much greater degree of independent power.[10]

As might be expected, the English soon accused the Dutch of illegal occupation, but their complaints were ignored and were summarily dismissed. Dutch designs had not escaped notice by the Spaniards, either: the Spanish commander of St. Martin, for instance, advised Madrid that increasing numbers of foreign ships were infesting the *mare clausum*. The king's War Council was likewise informed that the Lesser Antilles were "sown with French, English, and Dutch who could levy thirteen thousand armed men,"[11] but no official reprisal was taken against them.

The Dutch colonists on St. Eustatius knew what was expected of them. As soon as their fort was built, they began to cultivate tobacco; within two years their crop could thus be sent home to Flushing. Indian labor was imported to work on the tobacco plantations since the Dutch did not yet possess an African slave port. Indians were in short supply, however, and St. Eustatius was soon notoriously a party to ignominious raids to procure red slaves. These were hunted down from the other islands and from the Guianas where, in 1645, Aert Adriaenszoon Groenewegen was to protest sharply the loss of eighty Indians who had been taken to St. Eustatius by trickery.[12]

In ensuing years the population of St. Eustatius grew to the dimensions required for recognition as a patronship—sixty members. In October, 1639, its patrons received a renewal of Snouck's original patent.[13] During the next twenty years, the colony did not change much except that its main crop became sugar instead of tobacco. This transformation, in turn, was to lead to a great increase in slaves.

Of Saba, the other Dutch outpost, little is known before 1630. Although the island had been claimed by d'Esnambuc for France in 1635, no French had ventured forth to settle there. In 1640, the island was colonized from St. Eustatius, and planters from the parent island occupied the southern coast, built a small fort, and cultivated their habitual crops of cotton, coffee, indigo, and tobacco. Hamelberg also says that Saba soon developed into a shoe storehouse for the West Indies. This should explain why the small village on its eastern coast was called Crispien, in honor of the cobbler's patron saint.[14]

Spain's strengthening of her defense system in the northern part of the Lesser Antilles—as a result of Toledo's and Cadereyta's actions— was instrumental in increasing Dutch activity in behalf of a Caribbean port. Eventually, the Curaçao group was chosen because of the excellent harbor on the main island, its strategic location off the Venezuelan coast, and the presence of salt pans on Curaçao as well as on Bonaire. Dutch relations with these islands dated, as shown elsewhere, from the twenties. Having been discovered, originally, in 1498 by Alonso de Ojeda, it had probably been the latter's first pilot Amerigo Vespucci who first sighted Bonaire and Curaçao, calling the latter *Isla de los Gigantes*—Island of the Giants—although no real proof exists to support this supposition. The main island eventually came to be called Curaçao, perhaps after the first cartographers had mistakenly sketched its form as a heart or a *corazón*. More probable, however, is that all three islands have hispanized Indian names, in which case the Spaniards induced the word Bonaire because of its healthy climate, while Aruba, the third and smallest island, derived its name perhaps from the Indian *oruba*, or "well located."[15]

The discovery of these islands in 1498 resulted in their being incorporated in the Spanish colonial imperium which, although still embryonic, was nevertheless growing rapidly. The consolidation of the continental coastline, moreover, converted the Caribbean into a real *mare nostrum*—our sea. The waters between the Curaçao islands and the mainland came to be called in those first years the Sea of Venezuela, and the rest of the Caribbean, the Sea of Our Lady. The Dutch called the entire area the *Kraal*.

But Spanish interests in these islands was never overwhelming. In 1502, Ojeda was sent to colonize the area, including portions of the mainland, but the venture became a general fiasco. Diego Columbus finally declared them to be *islas inútiles* because of their lack of pearls and gold. They eventually became favorite hunting grounds for *indieros*—hunters of Indians; for example, a slave raid in 1515 sent two thousand Indians from these islands to Hispaniola. As a result the islands became practically deserted within a relatively short span. This destructive raiding policy was stopped after 1526, and Juan de Ampués was sent with orders to repopulate the islands. He had some success, primarily because he handled the Indians with consideration, christianized them, and introduced European cattle. In 1528, Ampués also effected an amicable relationship with the mainland *cacique* Manaure, an alliance which could only be mutually beneficial. Ampués' work was supplemented by the Church's appointment of Rodrigo de Bastidas, son of the conqueror by the same name, who, as Bishop of Coro and Venezuela, organized the Church in the area.[16]

Although the Curaçao islands remained part of the ecclesiastical province of Venezuela for 135 years, they were not included in the grant given by Charles V in 1528 to the German commercial house of Welser. A Spanish official remained on Curaçao to supervise the government and oversee activities of the local *cacique*. This representative, who held the title of *factor*, was formally appointed by the Audiencia of Santo Domingo. At this time there were some four hundred Indians on the island; although reliable figures for Aruba and Bonaire do not exist, their populations can safely be said to have been much smaller.

The Dutch first landed on the islands around 1625, after their defeat at Punta de Araya led them to seek other salt pans. On Bonaire, as well as on Curaçao, they did manage to gather some salt and to cut brazilwood, but in small quantities. When they lost St. Martin in 1633, however, a new salt lagoon became necessary, and the colonizing prospects in Curaçao assumed new impetus. Yet the first choice of this island was motivated by more than sheer economics. The Dutch wanted and desperately looked for a port in the Caribbean. Since their position in Pernambuco strengthened daily, they needed a base from which they might perennially infest the West Indies.[17]

Although de Laet includes some detailed information on Curaçao in his *New World* of 1625, the Heren XIX relied largely on the information which was provided them by Jan Janszoon Otzen. Otzen had been taken prisoner by the Spaniards at Tortuga. While en route to Santo Domingo, his escort had stopped at Bonaire, where eighteen Spanish ships were anchored, a fleet which he presumed destined for the deliverance of Pernambuco. Along with his fellow captives, he was sent ashore to cut wood, but had tried to escape. He had been caught and transported to Curaçao to resume the cutting of wood.[18] He was eventually sent to Spain, released, and arrived back in the United Provinces in the spring of 1634.[19]

Soon thereafter Otzen got in touch with the Heren XIX. Pretending to know all about the islands, he undertook to describe them, and took great pains to sketch out the great bay of Curaçao which he claimed was immune to enemy attacks. Once Curaçao was in Dutch hands, Otzen alleged, it could never be retaken by the Spaniards. Hitherto unheard of benefits would naturally accrue from its possession. The pecuniary greed of the directors was further incited by the reminder of the salt pans to be found on the island. Otzen's testimony was substantiated by Cornelis Rijmelandt who had for some time been a prisoner at Cartagena.[20]

It thus came about that the Amsterdam Chamber introduced the conquest of Curaçao as a point of deliberation in the meetings of the Heren XIX. The plan was seriously discussed in the meeting of April 16, 1634, and was unanimously approved. Instructions were next written out, and six ships duly readied for immediate departure: the *Groot Hoorn*, the *Eenhoorn* ("Unicorn"), the *Brack*, the *Engel Gabriel* ("Angel Gabriel"), and two Biscayan sloops. Although this squadron was being equipped by Amsterdam, Zeeland, and the Northern Quarter, all five chambers shared in providing the contingent of 225 soldiers. Together with the crews, the expedition could thus count on around four hundred men. Provisions for nine months were also gathered and construction material for a fort. Unaccountably, the quality of arms turned out to be inferior, and the quantity was insufficient for the number of men involved, but these facts were, woefully, discovered too late. Officers were named: Joannes van Walbeeck, a man of varied background in his early thirties, became head of the enterprise; Pierre le Grand, a professional soldier who had distinguished himself in Brazil, was placed in charge of the military division.[21]

The official instructions for this expedition, written on April 6, 1634, ordered the small fleet to embark for St. Vincent in the Lesser Antilles, and to wait there for all the ships to assemble. At this point, van Walbeeck was authorized to open the first of his secret orders. He was to make for Bonaire in all haste and to decoy this action by sending one disguised ship on a raid on the Venezuelan coast and especially on La Guaira, the port of Caracas, choosing "a Sunday or the day of a saint" by way of catching the enemy off guard.[22]

At Bonaire, a second secret missive was to be opened. It ordered van Walbeeck to sail directly to Curaçao, to enter the harbor, and to disembark his men. Detailed instructions for this phase of the plan were included. If the general attack were accomplished "with God's help," van Walbeeck was ordered to hold the island against any force that might be launched against him. In addition, he was explicitly forbidden to maltreat the native population in any way. One or more of the ships were then to be laden with salt and wood and sent home; the yachts were to patrol the waters along Tierra Firme and seek out ships engaged in coastal navigation and intercolonial trade.

The expedition left the United Provinces on May 4, 1634. On June 23, the Dutch were already at Barbados; the next day they arrived at St. Vincent where, in accordance with the itinerary, the yacht *Brack* was dispatched to La Guaira. The other ships surreptitiously headed for Bonaire where the second part of the secret instructions was disclosed. The time had now come for the attack on Curaçao. At this juncture the *Brack* rejoined the fleet with the news that it had sighted many ships along the Venezuelan coast, but had not had an opportunity to seize one. Van Walbeeck now conceived his general strategy and, if we may believe the statement of a Dutch deserter, he offered rewards to those men who captured both the governor and the priest of Curaçao.[23]

The fleet left Bonaire totally dependent on Otzen's pretended familiarity with existing affairs. Backed by wind and current, it arrived near Curaçao on July 6, in sight of a big cross at a bay's entrance. Otzen presumed it was to mark the main harbor, but his habitual assurance failed him now and in those moments of hesitation, the ships were driven west making it impossible for them to regain their former position. Van Walbeeck then proceeded west, following the coast, in search of a bay, but after many disappointments a fleet council was held in which the captains agreed to change their tactics and cruise along the northern coast of Curaçao. This maneuver also met with bad luck, and the fleet was ultimately forced to sail for Hispaniola, thence to Bonaire where it anchored on July 26.

Excluding the incompetent and overly confident Otzen, the Dutch leaders laid up at this island for three days in order to prepare a new line of attack. Their small force had, meanwhile, been augmented by the capture of a Spanish barque, taken in passing, and by accidentally meeting a Dutch merchantman.[24] On July 28, the second assault on Curaçao was executed without mishap. One by one the Dutch ships slipped unopposed through the narrow St. Ann Bay into the spacious Schottegat.[25]

Until 1634 Curaçao and its adjacent islands Bonaire and Aruba were part of the province of Venezuela from which they had only been separated during the time of the Welser grant. Spanish authority on the island was represented by Governor Lope López de Morla. The total Spanish population at the time of the Dutch conquest, however, was a mere thirty-two persons including the priest and the governor's twelve children. There were almost five hundred Indians.[26]

No resistance was offered to the Dutch ships when they gained the harbor. After they had all entered, López de Morla appeared with a flag "to fight or to convene," but he had also taken the extra precaution to station some fifty-two Indians in a trench nearby with orders to wait until the Dutch had made their intentions clear. No actual fighting occurred, however, even though the Spaniards claimed that the Dutch *almiranta* kept up a continuous fire while entering St. Ann Bay. The standoff was broken on the second day when van Walbeeck disembarked his soldiers in seven sloops. Four of these were unwittingly sent directly toward the entrenched Indians, yet they realized the danger in time and retreated to land elsewhere.[27]

At this juncture one comes upon a singular and outlandish episode preserved for posterity in Morla's personal account. From the bow of one of the Dutch sloops, a man named Diego de los Reyes, a well-known privateer, rose and loudly called toward the shore that he wished to speak to a Spaniard. Morla, accompanied by seven of his men, cautiously advanced and asked Reyes what he wanted. The reply was an invitation to the governor to come aboard the Dutch admiral's ship, while two Dutchmen would be put ashore as hostages. Morla declined, feeling that he could not abandon his post right then. At this point it can be supposed the Spaniards fully believed that the

Dutch aim was to defend their share of the *rescate*. Fear of the Audiencia of Santo Domingo persuaded the Spanish leader to refuse flatly any terms.

But talks continued. Morla was slow to realize what was happening; he temporized and delayed, however, hoping to prevent the Dutch from cutting wood or from taking away any that had already been cut by his Indians. Only after van Walbeeck had put ashore his entire military contingent did the Spanish governor understand that the game was over. He had been beaten without even a proper chance to defend himself. In an orgy of frustration, his subjects set fire to their homes and to their wood while Morla ordered the main wells to be polluted with dirt and rotting hides.[28] Several miserable days passed before the Dutch discovered the excellent wells on the other side of the bay, around the Schottegat, near which they built their first fortified camp. In the meantime, some men were sent to reconnoiter the eastern side of the island. Occasional skirmishes between these Dutch patrols and native Indians vividly illustrated the disastrously few guns among the Dutch.

But there was no real conquest of Curaçao. Spanish forces were simply too weak to resist the victorious Dutch push, and they knew it. After only a few days of nerveless opposition, they slowly withdrew toward the west with the enemy close upon their heels. Villages encountered by the advancing Dutch or located by separate contingents searching the island had been destroyed by retreating Spaniards and Indians. Before long, the Dutch concluded that the capture of the island was a *fait accompli* and that they would be better off to concentrate on the second part of their task, the defense of their acquisition.

As a first step, their camp at the Schottegat was fortified. Van Walbeeck next turned to building a fort at the southeast corner of St. Ann Bay;[29] he soon realized that, despite Otzen's glowing account, Curaçao would be difficult to defend because of the many unprotected bays on its southern coast.

At the location indicated, called *Punda*—the Point—the Dutch constructed a fort from the material which they had brought, using with it the abundant rocks in the area. Pressed into this work, the soldiers protested, and mutiny was twice only narrowly avoided. The exploration of the island meanwhile continued; Spaniards and Indians were relentlessly hunted down as the Dutch reached into the farthest nooks of the island. Morla's report, for instance, claimed that three Dutch companies—120 men—hotly pursued him without a moment's rest. Letters to invite surrender were pinned to trees, but to no avail. As the Dutch gradually came to control more and more of the island's water supply, however, the Spanish governor finally realized his increasingly untenable position. The Dutch cornered him near Ascension, in the western part of the island, and, deserted by his Indians, the humiliated Spaniard was forced to bow to the inevitable negotiations. Van Walbeeck, thereupon, magnanimously agreed to transport all the Spaniards and most of the Indians to Venezuela. Indeed, he did not trust the natives and, except for a few families of laborers, wanted all of them evacuated from the island.

Three ships were used to move all the Spaniards and some four hundred Indians; only some seventy-five of the latter were left behind. The forced emigrants were all set ashore about fifteen miles from Coro where an undaunted Morla, who had been dispossessed without so much as a change of clothes, full of chagrin, offered his services to Coro's governor. Expressing a strong desire to take part in any effort designed to recapture his island, even if he had to impersonate the lowliest soldier, Morla pleaded for a chance to participate in a reconquest that never took place. Four weeks after the Dutch had first sailed into the Schottegat, the island was theirs.

Van Walbeeck, immediately after the Spanish surrender, had written a detailed account for the Heren xix about his mission and the events thereafter. In this document he painstakingly described the military developments after his arrival on the island and the pact which he had concluded with López de Morla. He also enclosed a geographical report that drew attention not only to Otzen's errors about the island's easy defense and the impoverished salt lagoons that the company had built its hopes on, but also to the 750 horses, some cattle, abundant goats, and sheep. In order to provide the island with an adequate garrison, he next requested the xix to send an additional three hundred soldiers to the bays of St. Ann and St. Barbara in order to man the forts which had to be built and to guard the wells.[30] Le Grand noted solemnly that there were at least seven inlets on the southern coast that would accommodate the enemy without danger. Both leaders requested that provisions, ammunition, and victuals be sent promptly and abundantly.[31]

These vivid descriptions did not pass unnoticed at home, even though the Heren xix scarcely needed to be prodded into action. Although the constant threat of an Iberian effort to repossess Pernambuco limited the scope of the xix's effort, the narrow profits in recent years made some aggressive activity mandatory. Late in August, therefore, the Heren xix advised the Political Council in New Holland to equip a squadron of three ships and three yachts for a foray into the Caribbean. Part of this force was to stop at Curaçao to advise van Walbeeck to prepare salt and wood cargoes for later shipment. The remainder was to be dispersed in the area with the obvious purpose of seeking prizes. All were ordered to bring whatever they captured back to Curaçao. Finally, the yachts were to be sent to patrol the waters between St. Vincent and Guadeloupe in order to watch for the St. John's fleet—the New Spain treasure fleet—and to report its arrival to Curaçao. Ships from that island were to take care of the rest.[32]

Even though this privateering project was never to be implemented, it cannot be doubted that the Heren xix wanted very much to preserve their recent conquest in the Caribbean. Their determination was further encouraged when the Provincial States of Holland made it conspicuously clear that it likewise strongly favored the retention of the island.[33] Curaçao, it was maintained, promised a good salt supply, had productive agricultural areas with established herds of sheep and horses, and had two excellent harbors. The special committee appointed by the States to study the problem argued, moreover, that the Dutch should not humbly relinquish a perfect launching site for attacks on the Tierra Firme fleet and the Spanish main as well as a safe retreat from Spanish vengeance. About one month later the States General unanimously requested an extraordinary subsidy to sustain the occupation of the island. The amount of 264,000 guilders was subsequently granted for this purpose.[34]

Only ten days after this request had been submitted, Peg-leg Jol was dispatched forthwith to the Caribbean with specific orders to van Walbeeck to hold Curaçao at all costs and with the news that help was on its way. Van Walbeeck had already been informed that the Spaniards were planning to take the offensive against Curaçao. Six Spanish ships and two frigates were soon to leave Cumaná for La Guaira in order to join twenty-four *piraguas* which had been assembled there, under Benito Arias Montano, governor of Cumaná, to reconquer the island. Providing adequate defenses for the island before the Spaniards could mount a counteroffensive had become an urgent necessity and a matter of prime concern. The Amsterdam Chamber volunteered to send men-of-war and to provision ships at once. In the spring of 1635, the *Swol* and the *Bontekoe* did indeed leave for the Caribbean. Prince Frederik Hendrik, meanwhile, after he had cautiously contemplated the matter, eventually concurred in the formal decision of the xix that was presented to the States General for its final approval.

Having come to a decision at last, the stadhouder now quickly took the initiative in asserting that van Walbeeck be rescued from an uncertain fate and that reinforcements be sent to assist him without delay. On April 20, 1635, the Heren xix, convinced of the seriousness of their countrymen's plight, took definite measures to remedy the situation. As a first step, they delegated their authority over the island to the Amsterdam Chamber, which had formerly been a fervent promotor of the conquest and was now an enthusiastic advocate of its defense.[35] This meant, of course, that all the expenses for the venture had to be borne by Amsterdam, but all profits would accrue only to this same sponsoring group.

The Spaniards soon learned of this new and portentous turn of events since the Curaçao islands were too near the Venezuelan coast for anything to pass unnoticed for very long. Even before Morla's official report had been written, the bad news of Dutch occupation had already reached Francisco Núñez Melián, the governor of Coro. A few days later, when Morla's communication arrived, it confirmed the worst. The unfortunate governor's account was later authenticated and supplemented by Juan Mateo, former *justicia mayor* and *mayor domo*—judge and mayor—of Curaçao, a very influential man in the small island community. Mateo estimated that six hundred Dutchmen were on the island and commented that construction of a fort was well advanced.[36] Núñez, meanwhile, had already sent a ship in order to follow up the first rumors of the Dutch landing. It returned with little more to report than that the Dutch were determinedly on guard. Hopes to capture a stray Dutchman for questioning came to nothing, however, until a former Curaçao *cacique*, Pedro Ortiz, was able to take a prisoner who divulged much of value to the Spaniards.[37] This information was relayed immediately to the Spanish War Council.

The council had already met in January, 1635, when the first reports of the loss of Curaçao had reached Madrid. The august body was highly aroused by the emergence of this Dutch dragon's mouth so close to the Tierra Firme fleet routes. The possibilities of reconquest were endlessly discussed. Deliberations ultimately resulted in the advice to the king to send a considerable armada to Curaçao as soon as possible. The importance of this matter to the Spanish court is well demonstrated by the creation of a special "Curaçao Council" whose highly illustrious membership included the Count-Duke Olivares, the Archbishop-Inquisitor-General-Cardinal Zapata, and important members of other councils, including that of the Indies.[38]

In a meeting of this "Curaçao Council" held in Madrid on March 8, 1635, a proposal was made to convoy the silver galleons that were then ready for embarkation to Tierra Firme. This contingent of six or more ships and three thousand men was also intended to reconquer the

9. "Korte Beschrijvinge van het Eylandt Curaçao" (Short Description of the Island of Curaçao). From M. D. Ozinga, *De monumenten van Curaçao in woord en beeld.*

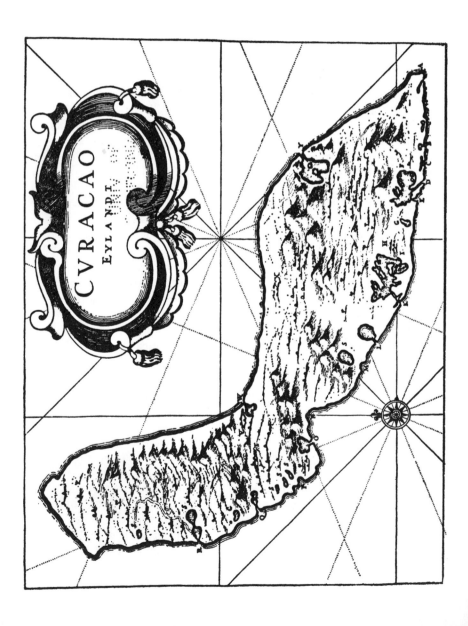

island. This plan was largely, although not exclusively, abandoned for financial reasons. The Council instead agreed to divert the fleet that was destined to retrieve Pernambuco to the more immediate purpose of subjugating Curaçao. Its general Jerónimo de Sandoval was now authorized to depart with whatever ships were ready, to gather help from various governors in the Caribbean, and to attack the Dutch on Curaçao as soon as possible. But the "Curaçao Council," dependent as it was on various governmental departments, realized that Spain's beleaguered colonial officials would have little help to spare for the fleet, and the expedition was thus augmented with four hundred veteran soldiers and an additional five or six ships. Finally, the council recommended to the king that Sandoval be ordered to conduct a *buena guerra*—a war in which the lives of prisoners were to be saved. The subtle motive behind this bid for leniency was, of course, that even if the enemy were rebellious and heretic, he could still be expected to respond in future situations according to the way in which he was now to be treated. So long as the king did not send overwhelming forces to the Caribbean in order to protect his coasts, he must necessarily practice moderation.[39]

The Spanish reconquest of Curaçao never got off the ground, although Núñez did his best to bring the plan to fruition. Carefully gearing his plans to prevailing needs, he cleverly used Indians to spy on the enemy and also enticed some Dutch deserters into betraying needed details about progress on the construction of the forts.[40] While scrupulously forwarding such information as he was able to obtain, he was nevertheless forced to sit by helplessly as Dutch ships came and went freely, and Dutch entrenchment proceeded apace. He knew that he could not expect any help from either Cartagena or Santo Domingo, his neighbors, and as the months slowly passed, he even despaired of the king's promise to put a strong military and naval contingent at his disposal.

Early in 1636, however, Sandoval arrived in Brazil with a powerful fleet meant to sustain the flagging spirits of the brave governor of Coro whose hopes now soared to an all-time high. According to his orders, Sandoval abstained from any attack on Pernambuco, and he did send north Lope de Hoces y Córdoba, an experienced and valiant sailor, but with a squadron of only three ships instead of the sixteen or eighteen planned. After an unavoidable delay caused by an accidental encounter with a Dutch squadron, a crushed and humiliated Hoces arrived at Cumaná much later than was expected, short of food, men, and able pilots.[41] But at least a gesture to regain Curaçao had been mounted, even though misfortune continued to check every Spanish move.

At the end of May, news arrived in Coro that Sancho de Urdanivia, the future hero of a naval battle against Peg-leg Jol in 1638, was in charge of a small fleet carrying additional reinforcements and provisions. But he had met with bad weather and had lost his ships, even though the men had been rescued. In spite of these unpropitious beginnings, however, the leaders of the various Spanish contingents gathered at Cumaná late in May, after the arrival of Urdanivia, in order to discuss the prospects of a Curaçao offensive. Núñez submitted his reports to this council together with various reconnaissance files. From all these sources, information about the strength of available Spanish soldiers was collected and, if possible, substantiated. But everything pointed to the same obvious conclusion, that Curaçao was irrevocably lost. The lack of men and material ruined any chance of successfully defeating the superior forces of the Dutch. Henceforth, the three pearls along the Venezuelan coast were regretfully abandoned to their conquerors.

Some Spaniards, nevertheless, did not quite give up hope so easily. These descendants of a proud race were sure that the Dutch would eventually be expelled, and they regularly petitioned the Council of the Indies to take remedial action against this "pernicious ambush."[42] Soon their plight was compounded by rumors that the Dutch now planned to attack and occupy Dominica, Marie Galante, Guadeloupe, Matalino, and other islands in the Lesser Antilles as well.

The Spaniards were quite correct in their estimates of the extent of the calamity, although the rumors never materialized. Their War Council continued to be concerned about developments in the Caribbean and regularly admonished the king on this subject. Not only the Dutch, but the English and French as well were considered dangerous adversaries who had no other aim but to bring Spain to her knees.

Yet the protests and warnings with which the council belatedly sought to guard its prerogatives were to no avail, since Spanish power in the Caribbean was slowly evaporating into thin air. In May, 1637, for instance, the council was forced to notify His Majesty that Guadeloupe and Martinique had fallen to the French. Not long afterwards, deliberations centered on the English settlement on St. Kitts (St. Christopher) which was fast becoming a point of embarkation for further English encroachments on neighboring islands. The Earl of Warwick, a prominent advocate of English colonization in the Caribbean, was reported to have bought the Pembroke patent. His perspicacity was amply rewarded by the number of additional colonists who now flocked to Tobago and Trinidad. English Puritans had taken over the island of Providence.

Even more alarming for the Spaniards, however, were the activities of the Dutch.[43] As early as 1628, the latter had established a colony on Tobago but had to abandon it around 1630 because of persistent attacks by the Caribs from nearby St. Vincent. They returned, however, in 1633 and lasted three years before the governor of Trinidad effected their removal. The Dutch had, meanwhile, also grown roots on Trinidad's northern coast but were driven off in 1636 or 1637. They retaliated by raiding San Tomé, on the Orinoco, and other Spanish settlements and by offering to buy Providence from the English for seventy thousand pounds.[44]

Zeelanders had, in 1636, also settled themselves permanently on St. Eustatius. In addition, in 1638 an Anglo-Dutch expedition from Providence under Nathanael Butler raided Trujillo in Honduras and extorted from its inhabitants a ransom of sixteen thousand pesos. From Curaçao came the disturbing news that the Dutch were completing the construction of a strong fortress as the defense center of a growing town soon proudly called Willemstad after the son of Frederik Hendrik, the later Stadhouder William II.

Although these trials and severe hardships were not without repercussions at home, the existence per se of foreign colonies in their midst was not a primary worry of Spanish authorities in the Caribbean or at home; most of these establishments were too weak to gain much importance as such. In contrast to other foreign settlements, however, the Dutch used theirs in the first place as bases for highly rewarding and extremely damaging privateering. Colonizing aims in the Curaçao conquest, for instance, were of secondary importance. Furthermore, Dutch occupation usually went hand in hand with an increasing volume of trade, not only with other foreign colonies but also with Spanish settlements. Indeed, in all these places, the arrival of the Dutch merchant was eagerly anticipated since the latter sold his commodities—slaves included—for less money and with better credit. By force where necessary and by connivance when possible, the Dutch were thus able to expand their illicit traffic and to break Spanish monopolistic aspirations in the Caribbean. By itself, this was what made them such formidable adversaries.

Rumors also reached Madrid that the Dutch were laying the groundwork for an attack on Havana, just as this city had recovered its breath after a few years of comparative rest. The new governor of Venezuela, Ruy Fernández de Fuenmayor, wrote to the king in 1638 with enough particulars to cause widespread alarm and consternation.[45] Reports from the governor of Puerto Rico about Dutch and French infiltrations in that area also compounded the concern.[46] In every instance the news showed that the Dutch were cooperating with the English and French; the English seizure of Tortuga (north of Hispaniola), for instance, was a case in point.[47]

Some action was mandatory if Spain were not to lose the very core of her empire in the New World. Some measures had to be taken, and, dispensing with their characteristic apathy, the Spaniards took the bull by its horns, aided by the rumor that Tortuga was alleged to be in danger from an attack by Peg-leg Jol. This information came from none other than an *oidor* of the Audiencia of Santo Domingo.[48] Without delay the Spaniards hurried to protect Tortuga, and the island was reclaimed at the cost of forty thousand *reales*.[49] One hundred and ninety-five foreigners, most of them Dutch and French, were killed, and thirty-nine were captured.

Shortly thereafter, Fuenmayor, the Spanish commander in this action, began to flood Madrid with reports on Dutch activities on Curaçao together with his ideas about how to dislodge the enemy. Energetic and dedicated, he also took it upon himself to provide for adequate defenses before he sought to engage the Dutch in open conflict. His experience with the Tortuga buccaneers now proved to be of invaluable assistance. The Dutch were first prevented from taking salt off the Venezuelan island of Tortuga and then were driven from the salt lagoon at the Unare River where they had begun to build a fort (see Chapter VI). Fuenmayor eventually proposed that with help from Puerto Rico, Cumaná, and Margarita, he would be able to evict the Dutch from Curaçao once and for all.[50] His plan found sympathetic adherents in the Spanish War Council, and the active governor was authorized to carry it out. The order was reiterated in royal letter of April 9, 1639.[51]

Yet Venezuela's spirited leader soon learned, to his chagrin, that none of the other governors in the area could spare a single man for the venture. Imagine his joy upon hearing of the arrival at Cumaná of a few units from an armada under Juan de Vega Bazán, which had escaped the onslaught of the battle of Itamaracá where the Dutch had clearly emerged as victors. Bazán promptly offered aid if his ships were first reconditioned. Virtually without food and ammunition, Bazán, however, delayed at Cumaná only long enough to complete critical repairs, and then departed. Although he left some ships behind to be used for a possible attack on Curaçao, they were in such poor shape that to use them would only risk the success of the venture. Vice-Admiral Francisco Díaz Pimienta was also not inclined to be much more cooperative, and in March, 1640, the sad remainder of the Spanish fleet set sail for home.[52]

From other parts in the Caribbean the tidings were even less reassuring. Four forts had been built at St. Christopher, one fort had been erected on Matalino, and another built on Guadeloupe. On St. Eustatius, where the Dutch had built Fort Orange, sixteen pieces of artillery had been assembled. On Curaçao, Aruba, and Bonaire, the Dutch availed themselves of all possible means to improve their military position. It was now considered impossible to enter the Schottegat without their leave because of the guns which overlooked St. Ann Bay and the chain stretched across the narrow entrance to the harbor. Although van Walbeeck had been forced to work with recalcitrant and reluctant soldiers, he had quickly completed the defense system of the main port on Curaçao.[53]

Although Spanish threats to reconquer the islands never did materialize, they nevertheless had to be reckoned with and especially during the first months—and even years—of Dutch occupation. Van Walbeeck certainly took them seriously, and he was therefore forced to disperse his troops in various parts of Curaçao in order to guard against a possible invasion. During and even after his difficulties with the near-mutinous soldiers, he continued to have internal problems. A few months after his takeover, for instance, a conspiracy among the Indians was uncovered, and the Dutch governor found himself in something of a predicament. He dared not punish all the Indians involved and consequently incur their hostility for fear that they would assist the Spaniards in driving him away. He had to content himself, therefore, with punishing only the main leaders of the plot.[54]

However, as the months slowly passed without any sign of Spanish retaliation, the Dutch governor soon felt secure enough to reclaim some men from his outposts on the island and to consolidate his strength. Rumors persisted, of course, and the Indians were never to be trusted, but everything proceeded satisfactorily, and Dutch ships brought colonists and supplies in ever increasing numbers.

The island was successfully retained, therefore, primarily because of the influence of the Amsterdam Chamber. The directors of this institution, who were convinced of the colony's potential usefulness, flagrantly overruled Zeeland's objections.[55] Both le Grand and van Walbeeck were eventually replaced in their respective functions, but others followed their policies. Communication with the mother country was soon established on a regular basis. In due course, the neighboring islands of Aruba and Bonaire also fell into Dutch hands. The first became a ranch for horse-breeding, and Bonaire supplied the main island with maize and the United Provinces with salt. Although in 1642 it was restored to Spanish rule, it was not for long.

Van Walbeeck's successor, Jacob Pieterszoon Tolck—Petertolos to the Spaniards[56]—continued the policies established by his predecessor. The Heren XIX were not satisfied with the two-headed form of government under van Walbeeck and le Grand that had resulted in some friction between the two. The military and political leadership were combined and Tolck, consequently, was simultaneously governor of the Curaçao islands and head of their military forces.[57] Fresh from Brazil, he was, according to the testimony of Jonas Aertsz, the first Dutch Reformed minister on the island, a man of edifying life who kept order and discipline and maintained justice honorably.[58]

Merging the offices during Tolck's administration belies the enduring significance of Curaçao as a naval base. In this respect, the Heren XIX soon ordered a number of men-of-war for use throughout the Caribbean, these to be permanently stationed in the main harbor of the island. They thus emphasized the authority at their governor's disposal and made him relatively more influential in the administration of his island than, for instance, Count Johan Maurits in New Holland who, at every turn, found himself at odds with the powerful Political Council there.

With his enlarged executive powers and backed by a strong fleet, Tolck was anxious to counter Spanish offensive efforts with an offensive of his own. Since the defenses at Punda were in good condition to guard the entrance of the main harbor, he now ordered two new forts built, one to protect the other large bay of the island, St. Barbara Bay, with the so-called Tolcksburg and another, smaller construction to be erected east of the Schottegat. He reassured himself that these forts would guarantee Dutch possession of the island against any Spanish attempt to retake it. Once this construction had been accomplished, Tolck zealously brought the Spaniards to bay, and the lessons he taught them were not soon forgotten. His men-of-war raided the Venezuelan and Colombian coasts with virtually no opposition except for the ineffectual groups that Fuenmayor had organized.[59] It was also under Tolck that the first steps were taken to make Curaçao a center for the slave trade.[60]

In 1641, Jan Claeszoon van Campen, a six-year resident of the island, succeeded Tolck as governor. He had formerly been in charge of the government of St. Martin until the Spaniards seized the island in 1633, and he had been sent by the XIX to Curaçao as a salt expert. His tenure as governor was exceedingly brief, cut short by his unexpected death that same year or early in 1642. In his short reign, however, van Campen continued to pursue Tolck's policy of aggression against the Spaniards.[61] An earthquake along the Venezuelan coast that had done considerable damage to the forts of La Guaira prompted the belief that an attack in that area could not help but be successful. Accordingly, in October, 1641, four Dutch men-of-war together with two sloops advanced along the Venezuelan coast, entered Lake Maracaibo, and laid siege to the fort. After a brief delay the squadron moved on to the village of Gibraltar, and this site, along with two other villages, was raided. The Dutch were primarily interested in tobacco and cacao, and they pretended not to have any hostile intentions. In a letter to the officials of Maracaibo, for example, they asked to open negotiations. The Spanish authorities, of course, politely refused. The Dutch then disembarked four companies at Trujillo—at the entrance of the lake—and seized eight thousand *arrobas* of Barinas tobacco, the best in the area, a very valuable prize. On this same voyage several other villages were also bombarded, sacked, and pillaged.[62]

But Fuenmayor was not a man to let such matters go unanswered. He immediately advised the king about the current state of events. He tacitly reminded His Majesty that the profits reaped by the Dutch in these ventures would only serve to encourage them to redouble their piratical efforts. Although he was pleading for reinforcements in men as well as in provisions, he did not neglect to voice his request through the proper local channels, these being his fellow governors in the area and the Audiencia of Santo Domingo. The Dutch successes, which were graphically described and epically illustrated by Fuenmayor, indeed shamed the Spaniards into action. Before long the governor received all that he had asked for and could move to the offensive. With two companies of soldiers, Fuenmayor embarked for the Curaçao islands to challenge the enemy on his newly conquered ground.

The Spanish forces arrived at Bonaire in October, 1642, about a year after the Dutch raid at Lake Maracaibo.[63] Although it was late at night and the sea was rough and boisterous, Fuenmayor decided to disembark the three hundred men, partly Spanish, partly Indian, without delay. He was later to have ample cause to regret this rash decision since many of his men, including himself, very narrowly escaped death by drowning. But the weak Dutch garrison was intimidated by the superior enemy forces and set fire to the fort. They retreated in all haste for Curaçao. Bonaire was in the hands of the Spaniards. Unworthy of the responsibility entrusted to him, however, Fuenmayor, during the first week of his stay on the island, permitted a wantonness among his men for which the Dutch revenge was not long forthcoming (see Chapter VI).

A war council held on Bonaire discussed the pros and cons of an attack on Curaçao, but there was not much enthusiasm for the plan. The leading Spanish officers reported that their ships were leaking, their provisions low, and their men in no condition to fight. Fuenmayor was highly skeptical of these statements and suspected that his subordinates were not above drilling holes in his flagship in order to prevent him from enforcing his will. But the Spanish commander was eventually brought to his senses by the sobering fact that with less than three hundred men at his disposal, the rest ill or feigning sickness, there was little to do but to abandon all hope of a quick victory. Blaming the high incidence of casualties among his men on the existence of poisoned wells, he did send one man to Curaçao not only to protest such an unethical procedure but also to spy on the enemy. Subsequently, the Spanish fleet left Bonaire on October 17. En route to La Guaira, Fuenmayor had the bitter satisfaction of lobbing a few shells at the Dutch fort at the entrance of St. Ann Bay.

Meanwhile, on Curaçao, a new head of government had been appointed, a man who was soon to make his mark in history. This was Peter Stuyvesant whose later career as governor (or director) of New Netherland is well known.[64] Born in Friesland in 1611 or 1612, Stuyvesant had come into this world as the son of a Dutch Reformed minister. In his youth he had received a strict education, including some training at Franeker's university. While attending classes at this institution, however, he had become involved in a scandal with his landlord's daughter and had been forced to relinquish his studies. While overcoming this blot on the beginning of his career, Peter developed his notorious steadfastness and singlemindedness of purpose, character traits which sometimes degenerated into obstinacy and sheer stubbornness.

Peter Stuyvesant was, to be sure, never a very tactful diplomat, but the Heren xix, for reasons of their own, chose to ignore this aspect of his reputation. He had the obvious leadership qualities they wanted. He was intensely loyal to the company, moreover, and absolutely honest and incorruptible. He was also one of the company's better and proven servants. Like van Walbeeck he had served the wic well in Brazil, and was rewarded, in 1638, with the post of clerk of victuals on Curaçao. At the time of his appointment to this office, he was twenty-seven years old.

After van Campen's death, four years later, Stuyvesant rose to the top as governor. During his tenure in this office on Curaçao, another chapter in Dutch-Spanish relations was unfolded, a story which follows presently. At the battle of St. Martin (see Chapter vi), Stuyvesant was severely wounded and was forced to return to Holland in order to have his leg amputated. While at home the Heren XIX, with the consent of the States General, decided on a reorganization of their American possessions; New Netherland and the Curaçao islands were to be united under a single governor. Peter Stuyvesant was chosen for this august post.[65]

As governor of New Netherland, Stuyvesant has become a controversial figure among historians. The judgments vary from "a brutal tyrant" and "a narrow minded bigot" to "a man of great decisiveness and strength of character, with no inclination to conventional refinements...thoroughly interested in the welfare of the community about to be entrusted to his care."[66] Yet he curiously shared a certain intolerance with many of his contemporaries. Perhaps Washington Irving comes closest to the truth in describing him as "a tough, valiant, weatherbeaten, mettlesome, obstinate, leathernsided, lion-hearted, generous spirited old governor."[67]

Stuyvesant had just become governor of Curaçao when Fuenmayor's spy arrived under the pretext of protesting the Dutch poisoning of the wells on Bonaire. This agent, a certain Andrés Rodríguez, on orders from Fuenmayor, had sailed into St. Ann Bay under cover of a white flag. When the Dutch had indicated their acknowledgment, Rodríguez had proceeded slowly—taking his time to look around to reconnoiter the fort. He found soldiers placed at the main entrance to the bay and directed his attention to one man standing slightly aloof, whom the Spaniard took to be an officer. He asked that the "general"—the governor—be informed of his arrival. The man replied, "Come ashore, Spaniard," and after the spy had done so, added, "I am the general."

Rodríguez next handed Stuyvesant Fuenmayor's message, after which he was compelled to wait aboard his sloop. Later that day, he was invited to the governor's home in the fort overlooking the bay to take part in a cordial tête-à-tête. At the time Stuyvesant showed himself a genial host, ordering beer and toasting the King of Spain and the Prince of Orange while Rodríguez duly answered each salute. Conversation followed about the allegations of the poisoned wells, and Stuyvesant's wry allusions to the failure of the Spaniards to mount a serious attack against the Dutch. That evening a bewildered Rodríguez dined with the Dutch governor and his aides-de-camp. Stuyvesant soothed his confusion with, "Don't worry, Spaniard. The Prince of Orange is also a soldier and so am I, as all these captains are too." Thus the spy sat at Stuyvesant's side, ate the roasted goat and the Dutch bacon, and finally joined in the toast to his host. At the point of leaving, his curiosity was satisfied with a versatile rejoinder in Latin to the *Generoso ac nobilissimo generali Rooijs Fernandez* which denied the charge as "against all war custom."[68] As a token of his appreciation, Rodríguez now decided to reveal what he considered to be possibly secret information, that as he had arrived at the island a huge ship had simultaneously left an eastern bay in his pursuit. This he swore to be true.[69] Upon hearing this confession, Stuyvesant turned to his staff and smiled benignly. It is the only Stuyvesant smile ever to be recorded.[70]

Rodríguez returned to his master with the lowdown on everything worth knowing about Curaçao. But Fuenmayor was no longer in a position to take advantage of it since his pet expedition had already cost the king some eighty thousand ducats, not including the losses which had been suffered by the inhabitants of his province amounting to another eighty thousand. Then, too, many of the Indian draftees had died, and many of his ships had been irremediably damaged. At that precise moment, moreover, the governor was in a heated dispute with the bishop of Caracas, a controversy which had already resulted in the excommunication of one of Fuenmayor's relatives. The bishop now chose this inopportune moment to write a disparaging and insinuating letter to the king about the governor.

After this Spanish rebuff and under the dynamic and vigorous leadership of Peter Stuyvesant, the Dutch resumed their lead in the feud for Curaçao, although originally the stout governor might have had nothing more in mind than to retaliate for Spanish action on Bonaire. The Spaniards, to wit, had been especially wanton with regard to the destruction of cattle the Dutch had been forced to leave behind. And Curaçao was dependent to a large extent upon the Bonaire herds for its meat supply. Subsequently, Stuyvesant sent a raiding party to the Venezuelan coast. At the end of November, 1642, the Dutch attacked Puerto Cabello and sunk four ships in the harbor "to revenge the outrageous tyranny" which their enemy had shown on Bonaire.[71]

The Spaniards, however, under the chivalrous guidance of Joaquín de Belgarra, *maestro de campo* of Coro, were able to repulse this attack. Stuyvesant sent him a personal message explaining and justifying his raid, adding, for instance, such telltale examples as the fact that the Spaniards had killed seventy horses on Bonaire. He offered to release any prisoners-of-war if Belgarra would only allow the Dutch two days of freedom on the Venezuelan coast in order to load goats. The Spanish leader, for reasons that are no longer clear, offered no objections to this affable offer of exchange. Although the Dutch left the area with 2,500 cattle, sheep, and goats, they did not bother to confiscate the valuable Barinas tobacco. As suddenly as they had come, they were gone again.

Yet Fuenmayor had not heard the last of Stuyvesant, nor was he saved the crucifying experiences of having to cope with many other Dutchmen who flocked to the tiny pearls of the Lesser Antilles. It was not until 1644, the year in which he was replaced, that his ordeal was over at last. Stuyvesant was soon to leave the area also, headed for other greener pastures. For almost twenty years to come, he was to play an important role as the leader of the Dutch settlement in North America, until its capture by the English in 1664. Meanwhile, the Curaçao islands had become a permanent Dutch possession and a festering wound in what was no longer a healthy Spanish body.

12

THE YEARS OF CRISIS

Qui trop embrasse, mal étreint.

As an instrument of war the West India Company had rendered inestimable services to the United Provinces. Far more than the sister company, the WIC had reduced the enemy's trade to a mere trickle, had deprived him of important possessions in Africa and in South America, and had cut some veins through privateering and looting. In the first sixteen years of its existence the company had bought or commissioned the construction of 219 ships: of these 118 cost on the average 25,000 guilders, and 101 ships cost approximately 10,000 guilders. All these ships had been suitably armed with bronze and iron cannon. In the same amount of time, within the limits of its charter, the company had dispatched 806 ships and 67,000 men at a total investment of almost 5,000,000 guilders. Total expenses for the company during these first 16 years had been more than 45,000,000 guilders, including 18,000,000 in salaries and wages. Since most of this money had been spent within the United Provinces, it was an important economic asset for the struggling young country.

With an initial capital of 7,000,000 guilders, then, the WIC had not fared badly. In 1629 and 1630 it had returned 75 per cent of this capital to investors as dividends; 50 per cent was paid from the net revenue of the Silver Fleet and 25 per cent a year later from income of trade and smuggling. From 1621 through 1636 the total damage to the enemy, as reckoned by de Laet, amounted to 547 ships valued at well over 5,000,000 guilders. Additionally, 62 Spanish ships taken by the Dutch had been utterly destroyed. A detailed scrutiny of losses to His Spanish Majesty, including cargo and supplies liquidated by the Spaniards themselves to prevent their falling into Dutch hands, came to more than 83,000,000 guilders. Other expenditures and barren projects, including a reduction in revenue as well as expenses for outfitting special expeditions, totaled another 28,500,000 guilders. In summary, according to de Laet's estimate, by 1637 Spain's treasury had been depleted in the amount of 118,000,000 guilders![1]

For the first two decades of its existence, the company's record had been unexcelled in the history of the country. It had inflicted vast losses upon the Spanish-Portuguese empire in America and in Africa. It had conquered a huge segment of Brazil, had extended the New Netherland territory, and had captured a stronghold in the Caribbean. Its privateering successes had reached a hitherto unprecedented scale. As everyone fully realized, the tacit fact behind all this exhilaration was that Spain and the United Provinces were at war with each other. Peace would mean the end of the company's main source of revenue. Not so well realized, perhaps, was the fact that the company's goals, defined in its charter as warfare and colonization, were incompatible. The company's founders had simply ignored Usselinx' advice and had failed to realize "the enormous burden that bore down on the shoulders of the Company."[2]

The first twenty years had brought much fame to the company, but some stockholders, interested in profit and not in glory, now refused ambitious proposals for further undertakings. They had begun to sell their shares shortly after the capture of the Silver Fleet when it had become obvious that the Brazil adventure would drain the company's resources without yielding commensurable profits.[3] For various reasons the conquest of New Holland revealed one of the important causes for the decline of the company. When peace with Spain occurred in 1648, it was another contributing factor in the decline. The company had survived the constant peace overtures of the thirties by persistently memorializing the States General. Public awareness of the consequences of peace may be abundantly illustrated by the large number of extant pamphlets on the subject.[4] When it became clear, however, that the Brazilian adventure could only be maintained by government subsidies, the company's protests against peace with Spain were less and less acceptable. It was an undeniable fact, which was evident in the Portuguese rebellion of 1640, that the company had developed into an overt instrument of war, an instrument which *qualitate qua* had to oppose any rapprochement with Spain in order to suppress a devastating crisis within its own ranks.

The Dutch historian Johan Huizinga posed a challenging question when he asked how it was possible for a small nation like the United Provinces to have aspired to the status of a leading world power. It was certainly not due to advanced economic ideas, because these were essentially the old medieval principles of municipal liberty which had continued to dominate seventeenth century Dutch life. Neither can it be explained as an extraordinary development of a young nation wholly dependent upon the internal vigor of the community, for this vigor was limited indeed. It was rather the European political muddle which enabled the Netherlanders to make full use of their newly acquired freedom and to develop their inherent capacities. In other words, the strength of the United Provinces in the seventeenth century was inversely proportional to the weakness of other European powers during the same period.[5]

The West India Company could thrust its way forward during its adolescent years notwithstanding the disunity of government and its own decentralized organization. The constellation of Europe allowed it to thrive: Spain was a "broken rod," Portugal a satellite, France had internal troubles with her Huguenots and her restless nobility, England under the first two vainglorious Stuarts was absorbed in problems of Crown and Parliament, and the German nations were engaged in their disastrous Thirty Years' War. All these external political factors worked to the advantage of the Dutch West India Company in spite of the fact that from the economic point of view, it had drawn its first breaths as "a weak vessel, much under the influence of ancient provincial and municipal particularism."[6]

European power politics favored the company. There were, of course, certain capable men who saw opportunities whether they existed or not and grasped them. For many years Usselinx and other Flemish refugees were particularly important factors in the founding and management of the company. The city of Amsterdam was another crucial determinant in its rise and fall; this does not, however, necessarily imply that the city shared in the company's ups and downs.[7] The decline of the company was intimately related to an alteration in the European political situation outlined above. Amsterdam sensed this political change, and her subsequent withdrawal from the company was to have momentous consequences.

Soon after the foundation of the West India Company, Amsterdam's city council had taken great pride in noting that a majority of the directors of the new institution were natives of the city. One should bear in mind, of course, that in the early seventeenth century, Amsterdam was vigorously Contra-Remonstrant and the refuge of most Flemish exiles. Some sixty-six of the earliest company directors had been from Amsterdam. Forty-six of these had been appointed by the regents of the capital or by the Flemish newcomers. Of the remaining twenty, some may well have been Flemings. The refugees, of course, were rabidly Contra-Remonstrant.

It became evident in the 1630's that the political predominance of the Contra-Remonstrants, to whom the company owed its existence, was declining. A libertine party, which was noted for its conciliatory attitude towards other than orthodox Calvinists and which was markedly anti-Orangist, was steadily growing in importance. The leaders of this new faction, the brothers Andries and Cornelis Bicker, eventually came to dictate the policies of the capital in the 1640's and 1650's and thereby controlled the international tendencies in the United Netherlands.

The extent to which the West India Company was regarded as a stronghold of Calvinism and of Contra-Remonstrantism is illustrated by Dutch poet Joost van den Vondel's ode of 1629 entitled "On the rescue of Piet Heyn's booty." This poem described an unsuccessful assault by Heyn's discontented crews on the West India House in Amsterdam. Vondel, who was not a friend of orthodox Calvinism and who later became a pious Catholic, took advantage of this opportunity to lampoon the Contra-Remonstrant directors of the company and to identify it with their cause.[8]

Times were changing, however, in the Town Hall of Amsterdam. Members of the city government, charged with appointing new officers for the Amsterdam chamber of the company in 1626, did not select a single Hollander. The incident passed quietly, but three years later the Amsterdam city council openly complained that northerners were being victimized in favor of the Brabanders, i.e., the refugees from the South. How this internal problem was ultimately resolved is not known. Indeed, the situation persisted, which clearly indicates that the company was still a stronghold of orthodoxy, although this fact had by now become an aggravation to the libertine party. The situation also suggests that there was a growing antithesis between indigenous and immigrant Amsterdammers.

The Bicker brothers were natives of the city and were also avid libertines. Whether they dissociated themselves from the WIC because of its Contra-Remonstrant identity is difficult to determine. Each was a tough and determined businessman who cared not a whit about the source of his profits. Cornelis Bicker had been a director of the Amsterdam chamber of the company until 1629 when his financial acumen—permitting him to look "a little further than the tip of his nose"[9]—persuaded him to sell his shares and resign his directorship. He turned at once to open competition with the company in its Brazil trade, and took full advantage of his experience as a director in the past. Typically, he was a champion of free trade and a consistent Amsterdam supporter of this doctrine against Zeeland's monopolistic programs.

Amsterdam's influence in behalf of free or open trade implied specifically that the West India Company could not maintain its monopoly to the fullest extent. At the same time the company was not able to bear the full expense of its venture in Brazil. Indeed, the Dutch goals in New Holland were incompatible: "the highest law in terms of Brazil has to be the glory of God and the well-being of the participants."[10] The hard realities of life made such a combination almost impossible to achieve. If money were required for the exaltation of God, even more was needed to insure the welfare of the humble authors of that glory, the shareholders of the Dutch West India Company. Whenever capital was involved, moreover, the logical focus for further activity was the richest city in the United Provinces, perhaps in the world—Amsterdam. It was a merchant town, and it knew the basic principles of its trade: to make money and to drive a hard bargain.

Amsterdam hedged its contribution to the WIC with the important provision that all the provinces should also contribute their requisite share. Unfortunately for the company, the other provinces proved to be less well endowed, and their contributions always lagged behind. The WIC had to satisfy itself, therefore, with promises of a less substantial nature. The reluctance of Amsterdam to continue to bear the entire financial burden became even more apparent after 1632. In that year, it became obvious to everybody that Brazil was an expensive and noncompensatory gesture, and the town refused to support the project at every turn.[11]

Nonetheless, aside from a stupendous indebtedness of eighteen million guilders, the West India Company was outwardly at the height of its greatness in 1640. It had conquered an empire which encircled the Atlantic: New Netherland, the Caribbean pearls, New Holland, and the west coast of Africa. Only insiders, such as the Bicker brothers, recognized the feeble basis behind the company's exploits, and chose to withdraw their patronage. Under their influence, Amsterdam was ultimately responsible for the loss of Brazil and for the eventual decline of the company.[12]

A debate in 1649, which was recorded in a pamphlet, shows that burgomaster Bicker took this opportunity to announce that he regarded the company as a lost cause. The question at issue was whether or not to advance further funds. "The money," Bicker dourly observed, "might as well be thrown to the birds." This opinion was evidently shared by one of his colleagues in a rather bizarre way: "I used to sell seven hundred to eight hundred oxen to the company; now it cannot even afford to buy one." Bicker's obvious prejudice against non-native Amsterdam members of the chamber was reflected in his exclamation, "Let the Brabanders and Walloons see what they can make of their baronies now."[13]

The company's decline was assured within a very few years after Piet Heyn's great exploit at the Bay of Matanzas. If one compares a memorial dispatched to the States General in 1633 (see Appendix v) with one sent just four years prior, it can no longer be denied that the company, at least financially, was over the hill.[14] In each of the two years mentioned, peace negotiations with Spain had reached a fever pitch. In 1633, after Frederik Hendrik's resounding victory at Maastricht, the Spaniards were surprisingly willing to initiate mutual talks. The States General, desirous of a reciprocal détente, approached the subject, however, under the pretense of dealing with the recalcitrant southern provinces rather than with Spain herself. Contacts were made in Maastricht and carried through in The Hague. Although the North had to relinquish the fiction of concluding a truce *exclusis Hispanis*, things were moving along at a promising pace. At this juncture, the wic, which was fully cognizant of the dangers inherent in these negotiations, sent the memorial mentioned above to the States General. The memorial documented its many accomplishments where the hereditary enemy was concerned. The gesture was fervently acclaimed by the Provincial States of Friesland which on this occasion referred to the West India Company as "a pillar of this State" and "a thorn in the foot of the King of Spain" which should not be liquidated since it was *in medio victoriarum cursu*.[15]

Indirectly, the States General had already agreed to consult both the East and West India Companies in the ticklish matter of peace with Spain. For the latter more so than for the former organization, it had developed into a desperate struggle for life.[16] Four or five of the provinces were inclined towards peace overtures to Spain. Only Friesland and Zeeland remained faithful to the company. The stadhouder, although he was gravitating towards peace, publicly endorsed the wic "because it could do great damage to the Spanish king in foreign parts of the world."[17] His statement betrayed the exact crux of the prevailing controversy: the position of the East and West India Companies and their activities beyond the line.

The official Dutch proposal of twenty-one elaborate articles, later reduced to eighteen, affirmed Article iv of the Truce of 1609 with regard to the East Indies and required the maintenance of the status quo in the West Indies. The recent death of Gustavus Adolphus had somewhat relieved Spain in Germany. Therefore Philip IV's counterproposal imperiously demanded an exchange of Spanish-held Breda for Dutch-controlled Pernambuco. At this point, the States General requested the advice of the stadhouder. The latter's reply was unequivocal: that the West India Company should be maintained by war or by other expedients with the consent of and in agreement with the company, and that in any case the forts of Recife should never be returned to the Spaniards, not for money nor for other means of exchange.[18]

The company memorial of 1633 repeated in many instances its claims for consideration which were first made in 1629. It had served the country to the best of its ability and had inflicted great damage upon Spain and the Spanish overseas empire. A difference in tone between the two documents is perceptible, however. In 1629 the company could boast of its capture of the Silver Fleet. In 1633, after five years of bitter frustration with Brazil devouring every profit, its record was not so captivating. The memorial of 1629 stated that the company had equipped one hundred ships annually and employed ten thousand to fifteen thousand men per year. In 1633, it was revealed, this number had declined to only fifty ships and a mere six thousand men. In the latter year it might boast of having captured 204 ships since 1629, while in the five years prior to 1629 it had seized 220, but the difference was in the cargoes. There was, indeed, nothing in 1633 to compare with the proud claim of 1629 that the company had robbed Spain of "a miraculously high number of raw hides—twenty-six thousand in that year—such an excellent quantity of cochineal as ever had been seen in this country, a huge quantity of tobacco and . . . a great number of all kinds of precious stones."[19] When compared to the magnificent booty of the WIC's conquest of Bahia, the victory of Pernambuco only produced two hundred puny chests of sugar which had been saved from destruction. Although the Spanish king may well have estimated his losses at two million ducats, the company gained little in material advantage and had nothing to show for its efforts.

Matters had not improved during the last few years. Pater's expedition accrued negligible benefits to the company. Ita's fleet of twenty-five ships returned with only six or seven prizes whose largest cargo contained 323 chests of sugar, 523 hides, and 27 chests of tobacco. In 1631 the one profitable venture had been de Neckere's capture of six prizes and seven thousand hides. In 1632 only a few Spanish ships were taken; Jol's five captives had disappointing cargoes, and Marten Thijsz did not take one prize. Although Van Hoorn's expedition in 1633 netted twenty-seven ships, the four or five he brought home had meager cargoes. Fleets destined to Brazil had encountered better luck but also had larger expenses.

The memorial of 1633 did not neglect to remind the States General of the West India Company's magnanimous gesture when the Spanish invaded Gelderland, and, indeed, the point was a strong one in its favor. Certain other claims might have been put forward at this time but were not. WIC activity in the Caribbean, for instance, had been a powerful motive behind Spain's belated attempt to provide more ships which further taxed her treasury. WIC vigilance against the treasure fleets had also been instrumental in delaying and rerouting these fleets, a tactic which led to substantial Spanish losses due to weather. Even if these actions had not enriched the company by one cent, though, they had brought about certain political advantages for the United Provinces which could not be dismissed lightly. It was unquestionably true and relevant that the very fact of Spain's acquiescence to negotiations with her former subjects constituted a tribute to the efforts of the Dutch West India Company.

The memorial of 1633 may not have been as illustrious as that of 1629, but it was, nevertheless, to have serious repercussions on the issue of war and peace. The States General were reminded succinctly that peace or truce with Spain would be a tacit approval of an opportunity for the enemy to repair his fleets and restore his credit in order to resume the contest with the Low Countries. The company knew that Spain was anxious to recover Pernambuco and was not adverse to paying a sizeable indemnity. Although the WIC would thus be rescued from financial difficulty, its patriotic duty was to advocate continuing the war. Its survival depended on prolonging hostilities; without war there would be no future for the company.

Yet subsidies were sorely needed. Without these "the government of this State cannot expect any service," its memorial stated. If, the Heren XIX maintained, the States General could subsidize foreign rulers for the war against the hereditary enemy, why could Their High Mightinesses not honor their obligations to the company? The money would be spent at home, moreover, and would thus provide double profits.

In this respect, a most remarkable argument emerges from the memorial of 1633. For ten years, said the company spokesman, the WIC had been "too involved" with the war and neglectful of a colonization policy that would have provided it with a profitable trade. The government, so it was asserted, was responsible for this emphasis on war in the company and had so delayed this possible alternative to continuing the war that no remedy could be expected. The Caribbean in 1633 was declared to be closed to colonization.[20]

The decline inadvertently detailed in these pages was largely due to the record-breaking expenses which were entailed by the Brazilian conquest. This adventure rapaciously devoured funds by the hundreds of thousands of guilders. The company had exhausted itself, and the government, because of Amsterdam's recalcitrance, was as blind as the capital was to the portentous chances and the boundless opportunities offered by an empire around the Atlantic—particularly in Brazil. Thus, its lucky star, at zenith in 1628, rapidly declined: shares fell from 134 per cent in 1640 to 76 per cent in 1643 and 36 per cent in 1646. This was far below the value of shares in the East India Company. In its year of triumph, when the WIC had been so bountifully endowed by Piet Heyn's great victory that it could advance a dejected government 600,000 guilders in cash, it had said to Their High Mightinesses: "We need money, and money can only be recruited in an unremitting war against Spain."21 Eighteen years later, however, the situation was desperate. The Brazilian investment alone averaged around 300,000 guilders a month. Every year the company debt had continued to accumulate, and its capital of Spanish silver was dwindling away rapidly. The folly of high dividends was soon painfully apparent.

Incredible as it may seem, many of the current and former directors of the company were realizing enormous profits in spite of the general atmosphere of despair. Bicker himself, after his resignation, actually pocketed a profit of more than 100,000 guilders from Brazil alone. His example stimulated other directors within the company to follow in his footsteps. Discussions about monopolistic or free trade soon came to involve the very private interests of many directors. When sugar became a profitable crop, the Heren XIX seriously considered closing many American ports to free enterprise because this would inevitably increase company as well as personal benefits. They received 1 per cent of all incoming and outgoing merchandise without risking any capital investment except their initial share. The decision to close trade between 1636 and 1638 had thus much to do with sheer private greed and personal cupidity. Their connection with the company made many of the directors privy to special information which guided their selfish investments. Only a few men resisted using this knowledge to their own advantage.

Perhaps more serious in the long run, as far as company stability was concerned, was its long-term adherence to unprofitable privateering. Undoubtedly, some years had not been without result. The company's fleets, squadrons, and single units had, indeed, inflicted vast losses upon Spain, but without always garnering much in the way of profit. On the other hand, its expenses in this field had been exorbitant, namely as mentioned, 45,000,000 guilders. Netscher, very correctly, writes: "These enormous outlays and the considerable distributions with which the company yearly regaled its shareholders, made it, in the eyes of the enemy, more awesome than it really was."22 Indeed, to the archfoe the WIC may have appeared indestructible in the thirties, but the façade of glory covered a weak structure. Years of crisis would soon reveal its true identity: a colossus on feet of clay.

The company's most crucial problem was raising the vast sums required to meet everyday expenses. In 1629, immediately after the news of Heyn's victory and with the fabulous 50 per cent dividend still fresh in everyone's memory, the Heren XIX nevertheless requested and received permission to raise its capital by one-third.23 The demands of the Brazilian conquest as well as the huge fleets sent to the Caribbean soon depleted this additional source of revenue, however, and the company had no other choice but to ask the States General for a subsidy. The basis for this request was provided by Article XLI of the company's charter which promised official aid "in case the company should succumb under the heavy burdens of war."

The first petition reached the States General in 1632.24 It asked for an immediate grant of 500,000 and an annual continuing grant of 700,000 guilders. The company assured Their High Mightinesses that the support would allow it to persist in its war effort to the continuing distress of the enemy and considerable relief of the United Provinces. The Heren XIX included a detailed budget which had as its foremost item, incidentally, the maintenance of thirty-six companies of soldiers in New Holland.

The States General, which was evidently seriously concerned about the affairs of the company, wrote to the Provincial States asking for their endorsement. It was not, therefore, the federal so much as the local governments of the United Provinces which ultimately sealed the doom of the flagging company. Each year the several provinces subscribed to their respective subsidies, but these were frequently granted with certain stringent restrictions and almost always with delays. For reasons to be examined later, Friesland refused to contribute after some time, although the other provinces, at least on paper, continued to be interested and sympathetic. Unfortunately, however, the company could not survive on promises alone. Actual receipts after 1632 can no longer be traced, though some money must have been received during the next few years. Thereafter, from perhaps 1636 until 1648, the provinces found themselves confronted with an ever increasing debt to the company which amounted, in the latter year, to 6,500,000 guilders.25 The situation was further compounded by the fact that the Heren XIX, who had acted in good faith, could not hope to repay the money borrowed against the delinquent subsidies.[26]

After 1629 the company repeatedly ventured, moreover, to increase its operational capital. The consent of the head-participants had to be ensured to accomplish this objective. The permission had to be granted also by the States General, which represented, after all, the major single investor in the company. It took the XIX seven or eight years to negotiate an increase of 50 per cent.[27] Although Their High Mightinesses were willing, most Provincial States and town councils were not. The latter groups delayed compromising on this urgent matter for many years. It was finally decided to effect the increase by a loan at 6 per cent. This transaction netted the company a sum of almost six million guilders.[28] It used this money to sustain a renewed offensive in Brazil as well as pay for Jol's expeditions to the Caribbean and West Africa.

The Heren XIX and the States General, at long last, had concluded that privateering was no longer desirable and that they needed to embark on colonization. Coincidentally, old Willem Usselinx, a lifetime advocate of colonization, lived to witness this radical change in policy. Brazil, the foremost preoccupation of the Dutch, did not seem to produce much tangible benefit. Interpreted in this light, the appointment of Count Johan Maurits was good business from a purely practical point of view. His primary responsibility was to develop the nascent productive capacity of the territory, a course which, if successful, would lift the company out of the depths of bankruptcy into which it had been cast by the Brazilian undertaking.

The Heren XIX could hardly have made a better choice, yet from the start the count was given little palpable encouragement and assistance. His inescapable failure, therefore, can be attributed to this and to the Portuguese rebellion which culminated in the fall of New Holland. The loss was exacerbated by the XIX because of their complete lack of understanding of the situation. The latter, of course, were not altogether at fault. Their existence, in the final analysis, hinged on the suffrage of the niggardly provinces, on whose budgets the West India Company appeared to be the most dispensable item. Pleas by the company at regular short intervals, which attested to the urgency of its plight, all floundered in a sea of provincial indifference. The crux of the matter, however, was misunderstanding rather than aloofness. It simply was not recognized at the time that the conquest of New Holland signified much more than a mere crossing of the Atlantic, and that the project was worthy of and entitled to

full-fledged support. *Verzuimd Brazil* was a subsequent Dutch interpretation of this attitude: neglected Brazil.

The advantage of hindsight simplifies matters by putting the blame
squarely on the men who had converted the United Provinces into a
great and powerful nation. Yet, is it completely fair to expect these
merchants to see all the inherent possibilities and to have insight into
all the intricacies which accompanied their emergence and expansion?
It is sometimes alleged that a successful general is one who makes the
least mistakes. The same can be said for a merchant. And the men
who composed the xix were, in any sense, just that. Although they
worked for the glory of their country, they combined it in a rather
subtle way with their own profit. But they were handicapped in
many ways. Their most salient adversary was the unavoidable need
to view everything from a profit angle. This profit motive hampered
their communication with overseas agents, and obscured the relevance
of the implications of communication, particularly when dealing
with sea captains and spies. Finally, profit prejudiced the development of a truly free and objective press which might have played a
constructive role in offering criticism and advice.

In 1640 the Portuguese, who had been under Spanish rule for sixty
years, suddenly and unexpectedly rebelled to shake off the obnoxious
yoke. At first, the reaction in the United Provinces was entirely
sympathetic to their cause.[29] The two countries now found themselves
bound by their hatred for the common foe. King João IV, for instance, issued a manifesto which might have been written by a Dutchman.[30] The Prince of Orange made no secret of his glee, and
immediate measures were taken to support the Portuguese. In
January, 1641, private Dutch merchants were expressly authorized
to export ammunition to the new allies.[31]

The Dutch, however, soon had causes for misgivings. In the words
of Handelmann, "The Portuguese declaration of independence had
drastically altered the relationship between the two nations which,
until then, had bitterly contested each other's right to be in Brazil."[32]
The Dutch East and West India Companies were not oblivious to the
fact that an independent and vigorous Portugal might well reclaim her
former colonies in the East and in the West.[33] These misgivings were
soon confirmed when, in April, 1641, barely four months after the
revolt, a Portuguese ambassador, Tristão de Mendonça Furtado, arrived in The Hague. The Dutch delayed his formal reception until
assured that Portuguese envoys had likewise been welcomed at the
French and English courts. Upon the occasion, Furtado offered the

States General five proposals, one of which referred to the return of Brazil. At that moment, all enthusiasm for Portugal and ebullience over the revolt dramatically ended, especially among the two great chartered companies. On the popular level, nevertheless, there was continued support for an alliance between the Dutch and the Portuguese—a coercive necessity for the latter.[34]

For the next few years the West India Company was an almost impotent but deeply interested bystander in the negotiations which gradually defined the affinity between the Dutch and the Portuguese. The company would raise its voice every so often, but the reverberations were lost on Their High Mightinesses. Nothing so well illustrates the imminent fall from power as this utter failure to make itself heard. Its position failed to be adopted as a fundamental cornerstone of the Dutch-Portuguese talks. True, the States General did refuse to consider the restitution of New Holland, but only when it became known that Portugal wanted a truce rather than peace. It might be persuasively argued that this factor, in conjunction with never slackening Portuguese ambitions in Brazil, furnished the justification for the sometimes aggressive, sometimes tortuous policy employed by the Dutch in their treaty talks.[35]

Once Furtado had withdrawn his restitution proposal, however, the States General agreed to a compromise, in spite of the reluctance of Holland and Zeeland.[36] The intervention of the stadhouder on behalf of a Portuguese truce prevailed over all the provincial and company resistance. His intervention rendered impertinent the widespread concern which developed when Portuguese Brazil chose the side of the new king and sent the WIC's shares plummeting from 128 per cent to 114 per cent.[37] A treaty finally emerged on June 12, 1641, which guaranteed a "solid, faithful, and unbreakable truce" and which not only defined the Spaniards as common enemies but also affirmed that the Portuguese and the Dutch would wage a "common war against the Castilian Indies."[38] The treaty was to take effect in the East Indies one year, and in the West Indies some eight months, after ratification. The Portuguese explicitly recognized the possession of New Holland—Dutch Brazil—under the West India Company. A cessation of all hostilities between the signators would extend for ten years after the date of ratification. The States General also committed itself to second any Portuguese naval action with twenty Dutch men-of-war.

The most striking element in this arrangement consisted of the fact that it embodied both a military alliance and a cessation of hostilities. These mutually incompatible aspects are ordinarily difficult to incorporate in one agreement. The most prominent surviving problems were still the boundary between Portuguese and Dutch Brazil and the enforcement of the truce outside Europe. Furtado's reticence was fully responsible for these major defects. He consistently refused to heed the WIC's proposals to settle Dutch-Portuguese differences once and for all in an all-encompassing treaty before proceeding to an alliance.[39] The converging influences of France and of the Prince of Orange combined to foster this untenable compact.

Troubles between the two new confederates were never far off. Notwithstanding the fervent protestations of friendship which were espoused by the States General and by the stadhouder, and despite all the pro-Portuguese demonstrations in Amsterdam which envisaged a highly profitable liaison with the new rebels, Peg-leg Jol was at the very moment crossing the Atlantic for an assault upon Portuguese West Africa at São Paulo de Luanda and the island of São Thomé. Technically, of course, this surprise attack could not be rigidly defined as a breach of the truce which was as yet unratified. It was, nevertheless, hardly conducive to healthy and stable Dutch-Portuguese relations.[40] Within a year after the Portuguese uprising, the Dutch had considerably strengthened their position on both sides of the Atlantic and had posed an undisguised threat to their allies in Brazil, although this position was not, as Boxer observes, without its grave weaknesses.[41] That the Portuguese realized their own precarious footing is evidenced by Father António Vieira's sermon in which he bitterly denounced the Deity for favoring the heretic Dutch at the expense of the Catholic Portuguese and urged God to change His mind before it would be too late.[42] The exposure of their military and naval vulnerability forced the Portuguese to rely on the diplomatic probabilities at The Hague as their only alternative.

As soon as Count Johan Maurits had been advised that the truce with Portugal promised the new ally twenty ships, he asked to be relieved of his duties. The Heren XIX delayed action on his request temporarily, but soon they perceived the inherent advantages of this highly opportune petition. A spirit of vindictiveness based on misinformation attended the company's replacement of the one man who might have saved Brazil for the Dutch and thus retained their status as a world power. In his absence the company soon learned that, in the cat-and-mouse game with Portugal, it was the dupe.

A smug Furtado left the United Provinces for Lisbon on a Dutch man-of-war enriched with a tea set valued at six thousand guilders, a present from his grateful hosts the States General. Shortly thereafter the count of Auersperg, an envoy of the Austrian Hapsburgs but also a

Spanish agent, departed from the Low Countries. It had been his mission to foil the Dutch-Portuguese alliance. He had, for the moment at least, been frustrated, and Spain had temporarily abandoned hope of inducing Their High Mightinesses to discuss peace or a truce. The Spaniards did not need to peruse the document to know that all its clauses had been aimed directly at them.[43]

Suddenly, however, news arrived in Lisbon and Amsterdam that Jol on August 26, 1641, had captured Luanda; next came the word that he had also occupied the fortified island of São Thomé. Needless to say, the new Portuguese ambassador in The Hague complained, in "a somewhat barbaric Latin" wrote Aitzema.[44] The Dutch primly pointed out that the truce had not yet been ratified at the time that Jol had made his conquests, and they emphasized the fact that the official government position backed the West India Company all the way. Restitution was out of the question, said the Dutch, and added that they could adduce some complaints against Portuguese violations of the truce as well. A riot in The Hague, which culminated in the ransacking of the Portuguese embassy, embarrassed the Dutch government but gave a clear picture of the widening gap between Dutch and Portuguese loyalties.[45]

At that time, Francisco de Andrade Leitão, Furtado's successor, became a frequent caller at Their High Mightinesses' official residence in The Hague. He persistently badgered them with vague accusations and demanded the immediate restitution of the new Dutch-held African territories. The States General referred these awkward jeremiads to the Heren XVII of the East India Company and the Heren XIX who, in turn, were not too eager to accommodate the ally.[46] The two companies supposed, as Boxer observes, that they held a whip hand over the Portuguese, and they were not hesitant to crack that whip whenever the States General wanted to curb them.[47] The XIX even threatened that if the Portuguese did not withdraw their outrageous demands, the company would proceed to make further conquests at the expense of the Portuguese Crown.

King João IV was in no position to force the issue.[48] He was, at the time, submerged in mortal combat with Spain and thoroughly alarmed when tentative discussions between the United Provinces and that country were once again initiated—in Westphalia. The appointment of a new Portuguese ambassador to The Hague confirmed Portuguese uneasiness. The man who would now shoulder the burden of diplomatic representation was Francisco de Sousa Coutinho, a faithful supporter of the House of Braganza and an adroit emissary.[49] His instructions were to gain for Portugal a place at the peace table in

Westphalia and to effect the restoration of the terrain invaded by the Dutch after the conclusion, although before the ratification, of the truce. Should he be unable to find agreement on this second issue, he was authorized to go even further and to offer the West India Company two million *cruzados* for Dutch Brazil.[50]

Coutinho never really understood that the checks which balked his every step were not Dutch ploys to torment him but were simply the result of government in what the English diplomat William Temple called the "Disunited Provinces." For all his ability, the Portuguese ambassador never managed to inspire confidence and friendship. His only satisfaction, if he but knew it, was that the shares of the WIC continued to decline.[51]

The company's hold over Brazil had notoriously deteriorated after Count Johan Maurits had left the territory in 1644. It soon became common knowledge that the WIC was moving downhill, that it had lost its striking power, and that it was playing a steadily decreasing role as an instrument of war. Peace negotiations with Spain hardly boosted company stock. The Heren XIX did not surrender quietly and sent request after request to Their High Mightinesses, but scant response was forthcoming. Even Holland and Zeeland, the two provinces with most to lose as the position held by the WIC gradually worsened, were internally divided concerning its support. Although Asher's pen is biased in favor of the West India Company—"the province of Holland always excusing itself on the flimsy pretext that the other provinces were still more behind..."[52]—it cannot be denied that Amsterdam's increasing pacifism was becoming more and more detrimental to the company's welfare.

Added to these sorrows the WIC was forced, in 1645, to submit its charter for renewal consideration. Certain of the provinces had been highly critical of the alleged corruption in the company's management and had recommended prolongation only if restrictions were designed to curb abuses by company officials. The problems attendent upon the issuance of new charters—for the East India Company's was also bound to expire—came under discussion as early as 1642. These problems were closely related to the Portuguese question and the decision about continuing the war against Spain. Late in 1643 a suggestion was made to merge the two monopolies, and this proposal provoked a flurry of debate throughout the country. The Heren XIX were solidly in favor of a union; the XVII were diametrically opposed.[53]

The question soon became a popular issue. Pamphlets appeared, and one of these, strongly sympathetic to combining the two companies, provides an even more detailed summary of the WIC's con-

tributions to the country than that of de Laet mentioned before.[54]
It reports that from 1621 to 1643 the company had sunk or captured
more than six hundred Spanish ships and their cargoes. Many people
had gained employment as a result of the company's activities: 1,250
ships and yachts had been built in those 23 years, 3,653 bronze and
17,485 iron pieces of artillery had been cast, and nearly 100,000
soldiers and sailors had been engaged to fight Spain. The company had
expended 54,000,000 guilders within the country and had provided
prosperity for all. The pamphlet went on to note that the burden of
war had been carried by the company; since 1637 it had had to support
eight thousand men in Brazil alone. The conclusion was obvious:
the merger was highly recommended not only because the two companies would be in a better position to maintain the Dutch effort in
Brazil but also since, without great risk to either of them, the King of
Spain could be prevented from receiving his treasures from the West
Indies.

The West India Company believed, with some reason, that union
was its only hope. The XVII, however, deliberately delayed sending
representatives to The Hague to discuss a combination, although they
were not unfamiliar with the dens of despair inhabited by their
colleagues.[55] The WIC had more debts than assets and its credit rating
had been, for some time, abominable. When it did offer to contribute
3,600,000 guilders to the partnership, the XVII scoffed at the idea and
deprecatingly added that the WIC had 5,000,000 less than nothing to
call its own.[56] Government subsidies, all that stood between the WIC
and total disaster, came in slowly. In March, 1642, for instance,
the province of Holland alone was delinquent in its promised subsidies
to the company to the extent of almost 900,000 guilders.[57] Provincial
concern, perhaps to encourage the merger, determined to pay 466,000
guilders to the company, but only 200,000 were actually forthcoming.[58] Persistent requests from the Heren XIX drove the States General
to intervene, albeit reluctantly, in behalf of combining the companies.
The Heren XVII, closing their eyes to the massive corruption which
marked their own institution, harped endlessly on discrepancies
within the sister organization. Demands were voiced for a general
audit.

The East India Company spokesman finally arrived in The Hague to
discuss the affair and to weigh the reciprocal advantages. After careful
consideration, he based his objections entirely on the alleged inability
of the EIC to endorse the sister company's vast and pretentious overseas
conquests. The Heren XIX fought valiantly against the overwhelming
refusal. They incessantly argued the merits of the merger; they

pointed out that the nation had sprouted from just union, that the East India Company had begun as a combination of smaller units, and that superior strength would inevitably result. The prosperity of the EIC, as the delegate of its rival pointed out, was in part due to the WIC's acceptance of the burden of the war in the major theater of the engagement. This action had left the EIC free to conquer and trade. Finally, the WIC argued, the expansion to the West Indies was properly a national enterprise to which end its directors had been merely the servants and executors.[59] Could not the representative of the EIC see that the combination of powers could only create more power and thus insure Dutch hegemony and international status?[60]

Count Johan Maurits, just returned from New Holland, strongly favored the merger, but the now old although tireless Willem Usselinx vehemently protested against it.[61] For the man whose efforts had virtually created the WIC out of nothing, a union with the sister company could only mean ruin. He who had seen the folly of a war policy at the outset now roundly condemned the WIC for its concentration on military ventures, although he enthusiastically praised the company for its part in the humbling of Spain. Usselinx wanted no part in furthering the pretensions and postures of the EIC and would submit to a merger only if accompanied by a radical alteration in both charters.

The final objection of the EIC now came as a meek plea for peace. It claimed to have spent forty years in a unrelentless effort to secure a base in the Malay archipelago. It had no intention now of jeopardizing that situation by being drawn both into an unpopular war and an unjustifiable financial encumbrance of maintaining Brazil: "We are tired of the war and we are tired of its heavy costs."[62] The company lawyer claimed that the EIC would prefer dissolution to an association with the pernicious drain represented by the group "which everyone knew was almost bankrupt."[63]

The States General were divided on the issue. Although Holland and Zeeland were ready to favor the XVII and their individualistic standpoint, the other provinces inclined toward combination. Frederik Hendrik's contribution to the dilemma was that a joint merger of the two companies could only work if both parties were to acquiesce. The WIC-sponsored expedition of Hendrik Brouwer to Chile and to other regions of South America was advanced by the Heren XIX as evidence of their vigor and as visible proof that "God Almighty had granted...apparent advantages."[64] Fearful to see the merger project shatter before their very eyes, they were willing to grasp at any straw. Discussions continued for so long that the States General ultimately had no choice but to prolong each of the charters provisionally for a limited time.

The only area of agreement between the two companies lay in their relations with or toward Portugal. A similar course was pursued here, although neither was free of a certain ambiguity. Officially the United Provinces and Portugal were allies in a common war against Spain. In practice, however, in the East as well as in the West Indies, each of the monopolistic institutions regarded Portugal as no different from Spain and both as enemies. The Portuguese were soon aware of this indiscriminate treatment and were quick in voicing their dismay. Simultaneously, however, they also sharpened their swords. In 1642 they regained the island of São Thomé, leaving only the fort in Dutch hands. Unknown to the victors, however, the Heren XIX had been discussing a withdrawal from São Thomé for some time, and the Portuguese attack was thus relegated to futility.[65]

In the summer of 1644, envoys from Spain and from the United Provinces met once more to take up the lingering question of peace. The States General requested that both the Heren XVII and XIX send their considerations. The EIC's position did not favor a continuation of the war but would agree to accept peace if the government would assist the company in restraining the Spanish and Portuguese from the Malay archipelago, soon a Dutch *mare clausum*. The XIX opined that if a merger of the two companies was to be realized, a prolongation of the war would be desirable. If, however, no such combination could be achieved, they felt they could continue, with government support, to function at a profit through trade. In the communiqué no mention was made of the fact that the Portuguese would assuredly take firm steps to relieve their Brazilian subjects from the cursed yoke of the Dutch.

In the meantime, the expired charters were, whenever necessary, extended for short periods. This policy was favored by those who still adhered to a merger and also by others who wanted the EIC to pay a heavy sum for the renewal of its patent. The uncertainty surrounding the entire matter led some merchants to offer Their High Mightinesses 15,000,000 guilders for the renewal of the EIC charter in 1645, to be payable in yearly terms of 600,000 guilders.[66] It seems, however, that this proposal was never seriously considered by the States General, although it may have been the catalyst which moved the States of Zeeland to declare their dissatisfaction with the provisionally prolonged charters. Some other provinces arbitrarily pronounced the charters expired. The States of Holland directed themselves to the stadhouder. In the legalistic ballyhoo which followed, where the provincial hostility to Holland was clearly demonstrated, the only decision made was that merger of the companies was for the time being unfeasible. In July, 1645, Holland again opened deliberations on the prolongation of both charters. The EIC, meanwhile, remained firm in its determination not to be sacrificed to its languishing sister. To buttress this position, moreover, it now came out unreservedly for peace.

At the same time the rebellion against the Dutch in New Holland became known in the Low Countries. In November, 1645, an oral report confirmed the perilousness of further encroachments in Brazil. The complicity of the Portuguese government was accepted as a fact, and urgent messages began to arrive daily in The Hague demanding that sacrifices be made to save the situation. The Provincial States of Holland appealed to the States General: "Without Brazil all other conquests of the company will be worthless."[67] The Heren XIX sent an urgent remonstrance to request immediate support. Holland agreed to pay its share of a suggested 700,000-guilder subsidy, but the other provinces withheld their approval pending the putative possibility of forcing the EIC to accept the burden.

In this critical moment, the cumbersome governmental structure of the United Provinces proved its inability to make a necessarily quick decision. In the fall of 1645, when the Brazilian crisis required urgent attention, unanimity was beyond reach. A proposal from the States of Holland to loan 500,000 guilders to the WIC, to be obtained from the EIC as payment for a renewal of its charter, was doomed because Amsterdam would not acquiesce. When that hurdle was overcome, the other provinces withheld consent until the matter of the WIC charter was settled.[68] No Dutch orator appeared to remind his fellows of the fate of Saguntum.

In November, 1645, when the eyewitness testimony of Balthazar van Voorde was still fresh in everyone's mind, some directors of the WIC appeared in a meeting of the States of Holland to make an impassioned plea for men and ships for Brazil.[69] No decision was made, although the majority of the states' members were sympathetic and fully aware of the danger. Opposition to assistance was raised by one member who represented the nobility. When this individual was at last won over by the Prince of Orange himself, the States of Holland concurred with the other provinces to provide the WIC with a subsidy and to send immediate relief to Brazil in the form of twenty ships and six thousand men to be paid for by the States General.

Admiral Witte Corneliszoon de With—Double With—and his fleet happened to be available, but his departure was unavoidably

delayed by a coincidence of adverse circumstances. Dunkirk privateers
and a severe winter were two of the factors which influenced the size
as well as the exact date of departure of this expedition. Only a few
men-of-war with some transportation ships carrying two thousand
soldiers sailed out in the beginning of 1646.[70]

The circumlocutions of diplomatic intrigue had contrived to render
all questions—negotiations with Portugal, peace with Spain, prolongation of the charters, the question of a merger, even the equipment
of a huge *secours*—inseparable. Money provided the solution to at least
one issue: the charter of the EIC was continued for 21 years upon
payment to the WIC of 1,500,000 guilders.[71]

The renewal of the EIC charter was complicated by Holland's
reluctance to consent until Zeeland had agreed to peace with Spain.
Zeelandian opposition had always been vociferous on this point.
Amsterdam, speaking for the merchants of Holland, now contrived
to buy off Zeeland at the price of supplying aid for Brazil and prolonging the WIC charter. The extension of the EIC thus implied that
that company underwrite the future of the WIC. At the same time, the
WIC was granted a prolongation of its charter for twenty-four years.
The consummation of this protracted operation was accelerated by the
fact that, in 1647, peace with Spain loomed certain and imminent.
The money and the extended charter, together with a long-overdue
secours sent to Brazil, relieved the crisis of the Dutch West India
Company.[72] It did not, however, solve its main problems.

Peace with Spain meant that the days of privateering were nearly
over. In order to survive, the WIC had to convert its emphasis to
trade—including smuggling—and to colonization. Although colonists
and natives in America had little money to buy, they had valuable
commodities to exchange: hides, sugar, wood, tobacco, cacao, and
red dye. If New Holland could be retained, eventually her sugar would
pay for all the expenses of conquest and settlement. The Dutch
colonization effort in the Americas—in New Netherland and New
Holland—miscarried, but not, as is sometimes suggested, because the
Dutch lacked colonizing abilities; the prosperous Cape colony was
soon eloquent proof to the contrary. The American colonies failed
because the large-scale settlements of the West had been and had
remained a second or third choice after privateering and trade.

Profit had always been the life spring of the WIC under its first
charter. It had hoped to achieve this through intermittent privateering
and smuggling. After the fallacy of this policy had been reluctantly
accepted, every Dutchman gradually became convinced that the
company, with its huge debt, should have been dissolved long before

or at the end of its first charter. Its survival was an illogical phenomenon, and can only be explained by Zeeland's stubborn refusal to
agree to peace with Spain unless the WIC charter was renewed.

Zeeland, the cradle of sailors and privateers, restless within her
tiny islands torn from the North Sea and deeply involved in the
Guianas and the Antilles, remained staunchly committed to the
survival of the WIC. The art of privateering had lost none of its almost
allegorical attractiveness. It was, perhaps, still hoped that under more
auspicious circumstances, this occupation could be reinstalled in all
its former magnitude. Piracy or its milder alternative privateering,
rather than colonization, appeared to the Zeelandians as the only
option for restoring part of the company's credit.

The Dutch citizen, easily provided with a good life at home, was
never a likely candidate for overseas settlement. Religious toleration,
the pride of Dutch life, meant that there was no persecution to
escape from—a common motivation for emigrants from England and
France. No Dutch company was ever so distracted from profit as to
seek glory or freedom abroad. No Dutch company had any desire to
create a new Jerusalem.

The WIC discovered too late that smuggling paid poorly and
privateering hardly at all. Illegal slave trading, which was to become
highly lucrative in the future, had only just begun during those
critical years of the mid-seventeenth century and would only reach
its apogee in later years. The Dutch had managed to provide all the
American colonies—Spanish, French, or English—with better products at lower prices. This had even won them a begrudged official
toleration from many Spanish, French, and English authorities in
America. But this monopoly could not and did not last forever. Once
the mother countries themselves were in a position to supply their
own colonists' needs, rigorous laws against foreign, i.e., Dutch,
trade were passed and enforced. This mercantilistic process was
already under way in the crucial years of the WIC. The Dutch merchant was soon to learn that he had smuggled and traded himself
right out of the market. Only a few islands, conquered at the last
moment, remained to him.

Then, too, the United Netherlands in 1650 numbered a mere
1,500,000 inhabitants who, during this same period, found themselves
completely surrounded and outnumbered by the English at New
Netherland, by the English and French in the Caribbean, and by
the Portuguese in Brazil. The Dutch, unlike the other European
powers involved in the Western hemisphere, had no excess population
from which to draw the requisite pioneering families nor did they

have the human reservoirs needed to replenish their depleted human forces. While it is true that the Portuguese had limited manpower as well, they were much more familiar with the intricacies of overseas settlement. For one thing, the Iberians always enjoyed better race relations with the subject peoples, as well as a far superior record of adaptation to climate and ethnological differences. The Dutch, as the Anglo-Saxons, had a perfect horror of miscegenation and never produced mixed offspring in huge quantities, a fact which put them at one other marked numerical disadvantage vis-à-vis the Portuguese and their swarm of Lusitanian halfbreeds. In Brazil, at least, the Dutch were never viewed as "liberators" from the Iberian yoke, if—one hesitates to state— the Portuguese were ever considered oppressors.

Dutch participation in European affairs was another important cause which prevented the concentration on colonizing projects and, specifically, the Brazilian conquest. Peace with Spain in 1648 brought temporary respite, but the Dutch were soon embroiled in the first Anglo-Dutch war, which severely hampered communications. This exhausting involvement made it possible for the Portuguese to re-occupy vast stretches of New Holland territory since Dutch interests were too expansive and too thinly spread to maintain uninterrupted control. There were just not enough people to go around; insufficient military strength at the disposal of the WIC was henceforth a primary reason for failure to materialize its grandiose designs.

It must also be admitted that the WIC was administered by merchants, not politicians or soldiers, and that a "grocery mentality" is not conducive to successful enterprises which depend on military backing. Wätjen comments, "This hard judgment hits the nail."[73] Although true in its more general aspects, this statement lacks something of the essential truth. The Dutch colonial empire in the West collapsed not only because of political miscalculations, but also because its designs proved too immense for its available potential in human and economic resources. In the seventeenth century the Dutch undoubtedly witnessed a remarkable growth, numerically as well as economically, but France and England did so at an even more accelerated pace.

Contributing influences to the crisis and to the ultimate decline of the West India Company have to be weighed also. Internal quarrels between Holland and Zeeland, which were intensified by financial worries, did increasing damage to the prestige of the WIC. The two provinces were at odds about New Netherland, New Holland, free trade, the abandonment of Curaçao, and many other problems. The controversy between Amsterdam and Zeeland, for instance, became almost a religious dogma. Add to this the flagrant disloyalty of some of the directors, who traded in open competition with the company, and some idea is gained of what the company had to face internally. One example of the latter abuse is instructive: Samuel Blommaert, noted above for his active role in the Jol expeditions, occupied a directorship in the company and, at the same time, was a prominent agent of the Swedish African Company and an advisor to Oxenstierna. The Swedish African Company, of course, was in open competition with the WIC on the African coast, and was kept informed on all the latter's activities by one of the WIC's most trusted men.

Another contributing factor to the crisis of the WIC was the studied and deliberate opposition of the East India Company. The EIC feared that a prosperous New Holland would detract from its Asiatic trade and would be to its ultimate disadvantage. Politically, in its own interests, therefore, the EIC allied itself with the radical anti-Orangist party which, in the coming two decades, was to dominate the United Provinces thoroughly. The East India Company, which from the outset had kept aloof and detached from the States General and had enshrined this policy in its charter, managed by this political maneuver to retain for itself a certain freedom of action in the political realm. The telling influence of the EIC hinged upon its intimate connections with Amsterdam.

The Dutch West India Company had witnessed the passage of a number of opportunities for greatness: New Holland, under the eminent leadership of Count Johan Maurits; Curaçao with her excellent harbor and strategic location; New Netherland, a prosperous settlement which could have been used as an arm to fend off English expansion and keep it at a minimum; Africa with its unlimited slave reservoirs, all provide even the most casual observer with an adequate understanding of the company's potential as a global force. Why was it then that the many illustrious projects so brilliantly conceived by the company's spokesmen never progressed beyond the initially successful stages? Insufficient funds, compounded by the folly which followed Heyn's seizure of the silver fleet, condemned the WIC to crisis and to the ultimate failure from which it was never to recover. Lately, it had not even been able to finance its privateering satisfactorily. What real hope was there for colonization? The two tasks that the company had set itself, privateering and colonization, far surpassed its financial capacity. Ultimately, Zeeland secured the much sought-after renewal of the WIC charter and the EIC made a substantial, although enforced, donation to its treasury, but this only prolonged the company's tottering existence until 1674, when it was faced with even more insurmountable difficulties.

The six years of crisis, dating from the Portuguese rebellion to the renewal of the charter, actually had little effect on the company's Caribbean interests, although, of course, there was no longer any effort to seize a Spanish treasure fleet. The only strong man who played a role there in the forties, Peter Stuyvesant, after the disastrous episode at St. Martin in 1644, was soon appointed governor of New Netherland, to which the Curaçao islands were added, and departed with his bride, via Curaçao, for New Amsterdam. His historical importance is to be sought in connection with this new office.

Except for a brief respite en route to his new governorship, Stuyvesant never saw Curaçao again. A vice-governor was appointed for the island as well as for the adjacent ones. During the next seventeen years—from 1647 to 1664—Stuyvesant governed the Caribbean territory along the Venezuelan coast from New Amsterdam. Under his guidance, a change in governmental organization was inaugurated which was followed for many years. The revisions, which applied specifically to the Curaçao islands, marked the realization of the eventual loss of New Holland in the policy of the Heren XIX.

After the conquest of the Bay of All Saints in 1624, the States General had drawn up certain elaborate governmental regulations regarding the intricacies of colonial administration. Even before the victory at Pernambuco, these official rules had been amended and expanded into a general policy for all of Netherlands America under the title "Order of Government in Police as well as in Justice in the Places conquered or to be conquered in West India."[74] These regulations were consistently adhered to by the WIC wherever this institution was organizing a government in conquered territory. Prior to the capture of Curaçao the States General had added a "Rule for Colonization" to the 1629 policy. This code, together with a prescription for the newly established government of New Holland, became the leading principle or rule to be meticulously adhered to in any territory.

The regulations of 1629 made a clear distinction between the so-called low and high governments. The latter, functioning in New Holland, was composed of a Board of Councils for the West Indies, in the service of the XIX but required to take an oath of loyalty to the States General and the Prince of Orange. This Board of Councils served to unite under its jurisdiction the highest authority in the fields of justice, police, war, trade, religion, internal affairs, and finances. The Curaçao islands were to be administered by a governor who, aided by several subordinate councils, constituted the mainstay of a "low" government. This system, initiated with the administration of van Walbeeck, was ultimately dependent on the government of New Holland. The close relationship between Curaçao and Dutch Brazil was continued all through the rule of van Walbeeck's successors, Tolck and van Campen. After the appointment of Stuyvesant, the latter advised the Heren XIX to abandon the Curaçao islands as unprofitable and suggested that, in case the XIX were not inclined to do so, the islands be politically united with New Netherland. The XIX concurred with the second suggestion, although the ties between Curaçao and New Holland were not immediately broken.

Thus Stuyvesant's memorial to the XIX on a reorganization of government was, in many aspects, well received. It did not provide, however, a solution to the ticklish problem compounded by a Dutch naval base in the midst of the Caribbean, the existence of which might very well prove detrimental to the gradually evolving peace talks with Spain. One obvious alternative to this dilemma was accepted when Curaçao became a slave dump, a locally well-known marketplace for the black merchandise.

Apparently the plan to unite Curaçao with New Netherland was well conceived and one based on complementary needs. The North American colony supplied the islands with food; the latter responded with horses, salt, and blacks. These slaves were known as *mancarrons*, only useful as domestics and therefore not of prime quality.

Upon his departure for New Amsterdam, Stuyvesant had appointed in his place as vice-governor Lucas Rodenburch, who was soon to be succeeded by Matthias Beck. Stuyvesant's instructions to Beck became the basic guide for governors of the Curaçao islands until the end of the eighteenth century.[75] Beck was the highest company authority on the islands, but he ruled together with a Board of Councils composed of the commander of the armed forces and chosen members of the civil and military employees of the company who were active on the islands. All executive, legislative, and judicial powers were vested in the vice-governor and the board. An important sub-official was the clerk of victuals, provisions, and trade, an office which had once been held by Peter Stuyvesant.

The position of vice-governor was characterized, however, by certain inherent peculiarities. It was nominally under the control of the governors of New Netherland, but the authorities of New Holland also had their say in the matter. Beck, for instance, had copies made of all his correspondence, one to be sent to New Amsterdam, the other to New Holland. This situation persisted until Dutch Brazil was lost in 1654. At that time the Curaçao islands reverted to the control of New Netherland until that colony fell to the English in

1664. Thereafter, the Curaçao islands were governed by their own separate governor under the immediate supervision of the Chamber of Amsterdam.[76]

The development of Curaçao as a slave depot received its main impetus under the governorship of Stuyvesant and was both reinforced and accentuated with the demise of New Holland, when the traffic in "black ebony" became the most important means of exchange between the Dutch and the colonies of Spain, France, and England. It may well be that the character and extent of the slave trade, by which Curaçao was soon identified, became instrumental in her retention by the Dutch. Elsewhere in the Caribbean on those islands held or claimed by the Dutch, one encounters a history of repeated flag-changing, from which Curaçao was saved.

In this respect the history of St. Martin is illustrative. The Dutch, driven from the island in 1633, never really relinquished their claims. After the Spanish left, early in 1648, the Dutch commander of St. Eustatius, assuming that the island was uninhabited, organized several migrating ventures under the auspices of his patrons the de Moors of Flushing. The French were likewise interested and may have sent some colonists at the same time. They established a claim to the island based on the notion that after the Spanish action of 1629, French settlers had moved to and occupied that area of the island which today is still French. Although these notions were dropped during the Spanish reconquest, the governor-general of the French Antilles, Philippe de Lonvilliers de Poincy, steadfastedly duplicated the efforts of the Dutch commander of St. Eustatius.

The two parties met on the island and ultimately decided to co-operate. Thus its territory was divided between them. The mere fact that there would be two different nationalities on one island was not a *unicum*; the same had precariously occurred on St. Christopher, while later a similar situation developed on Tobago. On St. Martin the French and Dutch agreed to the following arrangement: the representative of each group would set off from a designated point on the island and walk along the coast until both met again. This procedure allotted the French the biggest part of the island, while the Dutch acquired the smaller but more profitable segment.[77]

Dutertre gives a different but more plausible story of the island's division. According to his version, four or five Frenchmen escaped the Spanish abandonment of 1648 and hid in the woods. So did five Dutchmen after the Spanish had left. Both parties informed their respective leaders on the neighboring islands. This motivated the commander of St. Eustatius to action. He dispatched some men to prevent de Poincy's thirty men from disembarking. But the French soon returned with three hundred men "to take possession of the said island in order to protect the king's interest."[78] The Dutch realized the French strength and expressed a desire to negotiate. The bargaining took place on a small hill located between the Dutch and French camps, and a formal agreement was reached in March, 1648. It confirmed the division of the island into a Dutch and a French section. Until 1672 the colonists of both nations lived in peaceful harmony.

The Dutch colonization of the Lesser Antilles forms only a small and relatively insignificant part of the history of the Caribbean. As pointed out before on several occasions, the Hollanders and Zeelanders were primarily interested in trade; they were more anxious to secure markets than to establish colonies. In those years commerce was steadily rising in importance and large numbers of Dutch vessels called regularly at French, English, and Spanish settlements in order to sell provisions and manufactured articles while loading themselves at the same time with indigenous products. Early attempts to exclude them from this trade were totally unsuccessful. English tariff laws as proclaimed as early as 1634 were aimed at separating the Dutch from profit, but these and other measures pressed heavily on the colonists and were, consequently, circumvented.

Unfortunately for the Dutch West India Company this extralegal situation could not last forever. Eventually French and English colonies, yielding to strong legislation of the mother countries, did refuse to buy or sell, and the Dutch were left without markets. Much too late they came to the conclusion that they had been negligent in providing themselves with enough colonies abroad to keep themselves in business, and that this very negligence in setting up stable overseas settlements forced them, ultimately, to rely upon a foreign market, a market which at any time might turn its back upon the erstwhile suppliers and transform them overnight into clandestine interlopers or, worse, salesmen without buyers.[79]

THE DECLINE OF A BRILLIANT STAR

*C'est ainsi que par la faiblesse, l'incapacité & la lâcheté de
deux ou trois hommes et par le peu de soin et de moyens que
l'on avoit en Hollande de les secourir, l'Estat & la Compagnie
des Indes Occidentales perdirent ce gran & beau Pays.*[1]

Following the years of crisis, which ended with the renewal of its
charter, it became obvious that the semi-bankrupt West India Company was incapable of coping with the Portuguese-Brazilian rebellion.
Only massive financial aid could save it from disaster. That the States
General was aware of the situation is demonstrated by its resolutions.
In the spring of 1647, Zeeland, after having won the extension of the
company's charter, pushed for immediate and effective support in
the Brazilian problem. At Munster in Westphalia, meanwhile, peace
negotiations between most of Europe's nations were drawing to a close.

Fearful of what peace with Spain would bring to their institution,
the Heren XIX continued to plague the States General with memorials.
Yet their efforts were to no avail. Zeeland, although reluctantly
agreeing to peace, continued to plead for a continuation of the war.
Amsterdam, however, was more interested in trade and thus supported
a cessation of hostilities. Its merchants were deeply involved in the
gold trade on the Guinea coast, in the slave trade from Guinea and
Angola (fifteen thousand to twenty thousand blacks a year), and in
general commerce with the Iberian peninsula. In the end its influence
outweighed that of the *pichelingues*, the Zeelandian privateers. Indeed,
it was to Amsterdam's advantage to ruin the company, since an end
of the charter would have made the city the chief recipient of the
company's monopolies.

As noted earlier, the Arminian, anti-Orangist, libertine party was
at that time steadily gaining power in Amsterdam. It was a slow
process, of course, to undermine the position of the stadhouder
whose status, because of the long war, had gradually and imperceptibly
been transformed into a near-monarchy. A clash was inevitable, and
matters took a turn for the worse under Frederik Hendrik's talented
but restless son William II. With an army, he marched to Amsterdam
and forcibly removed from the city council those members of the

Bicker clique who then dominated city affairs. Nevertheless, the sudden death of the young stadhouder that same year (1650) enabled Amsterdam to revert to its former anti-company position.

Amsterdam had to compromise, however, with Zeeland on the issue of peace by agreeing to equip a huge *secours* for Brazil. Fortunately, both the East and West India Companies had directed their attacks against Portuguese possessions, and this circumstance facilitated the conciliatory negotiations between Spain and the United Provinces. As a result, peace with Philip IV could be concluded without disturbing any of the influential circles in the United Provinces. The treaty, which was signed on January 30, 1648, ended the eighty-year struggle for Dutch independence.

From the standpoint of the EIC and the WIC, the most important provisions of the treaty were Articles v and vi. The former stated that, in conformity with charters already given to both companies, navigation and commerce could continue in the East and West Indies to all places actually possessed by the United Provinces. Traffic with Spain would be open to the inhabitants of the independent Netherlands, although it was explicitly stated that Spanish possessions in the East Indies were closed to Dutch traders. Curiously enough, the West Indies were not specifically mentioned in this respect, but Article vi further stipulated:

...the subjects and inhabitants of the kingdoms, provinces and countries of the foresaid King and States General respectively, shall restrain themselves from navigation and trade in all the ports and places occupied and possessed by the other party with forts, trading-posts or fortresses: i.e. the subjects of the foresaid King will not navigate and trade in the ports and places that are kept by the foresaid States General, while the subjects of the latter will not do so in places kept by the foresaid King. And among the places that the foresaid States General will possess are included those places taken from the Portuguese, excluding those places taken by the Portuguese since 1641 and still in Portuguese possession.

These two articles formed the extremes that limited Dutch trade and navigation to both Indies. Twenty years earlier, Spain had offered peace on terms which excluded the Caribbean and which had demanded restitution of all territory gained by the Dutch in the American hemisphere. In 1648, she relinquished a great deal to her former subjects. Despite the concessions, however, the WIC was left with the problem of how to provide for the defense of New Holland. It was unable to solve this dilemma alone, because, as Wicquefort surmised, the situation there was "in such poor shape" as it had never been before.[2] The Portuguese were united; ambition and avarice devoured and ruined the Dutch. Nor could the company turn the tide of decline into one of renaissance. Gone were the days when its influence could tip the scales of war and peace. Conclusions were now reached and decisions made without and in spite of the company.

The renewed charter, dated March 22, 1647, committed the West India Company to a protracted death struggle. The first charter period had witnessed the capture and the loss of the Bay of All Saints, Piet Heyn's venture, the conquest of Pernambuco, the exploits of Pater, Ita, Thijsz, and the exciting career of Peg-leg Jol. On the other hand, the second charter reveals only decline and defeat: the loss of New Holland, of New Netherland, and of some of the West African acquisitions. Such highlights as there were under the new extension were rendered under official orders of the States General or of the Provincial States of Holland or Zeeland: the raids of Michiel Adriaenszoon de Ruyter, of Abraham Crijnssen, of Cornelis Evertsen, and the heroic adventures of Jacob Binckes. All the offensive power of the second quarter-century of the company's history was, therefore, the work of the federal or provincial governments of the United Provinces. These governments now became deeply involved in all overseas action, and they endorsed this involvement by sending powerful fleets to Brazil, the Caribbean, and New Netherland. The company itself received no credit for these victories, and reaped profits only from the slave trade. At the end of the second charter, in 1674, although the West India Company controlled the slave market, it no longer had any offensive power nor a trade monopoly in the Caribbean. There, England had become a dangerous competitor.

The true heart of the problem for the WIC was always financial. Provincial subsidies continued to remain delinquent. Friesland, once a fervent supporter, was frustrated in its attempt to establish a Frisian East India Company. This province, therefore, with only one or two exceptions throughout the entire second term of the charter, abstained from supporting the WIC. The Frisians also refused to take part in any venture which was undertaken by the company. They even declined to attend meetings of the XIX or their own chamber. The period of the second charter continued the debacle of the years of crisis, and the official archives of this period are full of requests, petitions, and anguished cries for assistance.

The States General took the position in 1647 that it was obligated to come to the support of the company in Brazil. Allegations concerning the motives of the gentlemen in government render their support something less than disinterested. Even with this consideration, however, the federal assembly could reach no agreement on how help was to be supplied.[3]

The Brazilian adventure had reached its zenith with Jol's conquests of the newly independent Portuguese in Africa. These acquisitions were particularly valuable with respect to the slave trade. A year later the Dutch lost the island, although not the fort, of São Thomé. In 1647, Salvador de Sá left Lisbon for Rio de Janeiro, and, in 1648, accompanied by thirty ships, made his way back across the Atlantic with specific instructions to conquer Luanda. A smiling Portuguese ambassador communicated this fact to Their High Mightinesses with visible satisfaction.⁴ The Portuguese, at this juncture, offered to exchange for Luanda such territory as they had reclaimed from the Dutch in Brazil. This seemed to the Dutch positive proof that the Portuguese king had been instrumental in the overseas activity of his subjects in Brazil. It was a further breach of the truce, and the maneuver seemed to be a delaying tactic to provide the Portuguese with an opportunity to regain all their former West African and Brazilian possessions. The XIX's response to the restitution offer was a demand for the indemnification of damages which had been sustained by the Dutch in Brazil. The resulting deadlock doomed the success of an agreement.

The Portuguese had initiated the discussion with the expectation that mighty Amsterdam wanted an understanding. The States General, however, strongly influenced by the new Stadhouder William II, had already committed itself to assist the WIC in Brazil. The Dutch government thus replied to the Portuguese ambassador that restitution of all parts of Dutch Brazil now under control of the Portuguese together with what was lost by the Dutch on Africa's west coast had to be the basis for any rapprochement. Coutinho, despite lavish bribes, failed to dispossess the WIC even after offering to buy these territories for eight million *cruzados*, a sum equal to sixteen million guilders. But even this huge sum would not have been sufficient to pay the company's debts. Although ignored at Westphalia, the Portuguese found the Dutch determined to assist the WIC in Brazil.⁵

The departure of Count Johan Maurits had left New Holland in incompetent hands. Delinquent contributions to the WIC treasury had delayed help which might have saved its precious jewel. The Heren XIX were in no position, however, to enforce payment. Tired of waiting and postponing, they declared their treasury empty. A balance sheet, which had been made up some time earlier, showed some alarming figures: the expenditures for New Holland had alone exceeded 3,000,000 guilders a year.⁶ Although in open accord that aid should be sent Brazil, the States General had bogged down in discussions about which provinces should pay.

In November, 1646, it was agreed to send seventeen ships and six thousand men, partially paid for by the company, under the command of Admiral Witte Corneliszoon de With, one of the outstanding members of the group of Dutch fighting admirals.[7] This expedition was intended to follow up any accomplishments by the smaller *secours* mentioned in the previous chapter.

Although Coutinho did his utmost to delay the departure of this huge fleet, the usual governmental inefficiency plus a very severe winter were what ultimately detained the fleet until the beginning of 1648. Admiral de With was to spend the next two years cruising along the Brazilian coast. He was unable, however, to restrain the inspired and wisely led Portuguese from their reconquest of Brazil.[8]

Negotiations with Portugal, meanwhile, proceeded at home. It was clearly to Portugal's advantage to keep them dragging. She succeeded. When news reached the United Provinces in January, 1649, that Luanda had fallen, war sentiment increased. Pamphlets appeared in quantity, and they indicated that all the Dutch, except the Amsterdammers, favored an open break with Portugal. Just at this time, Spain proposed to join the Dutch against the Portuguese. The Spaniards offered to bear two-thirds of the financial burden of war and to be content with one-third of the collective gains. When the issue was turned over to the Provincial States, it was hotly contended. Zeeland wanted war, as usual; Amsterdam remained predictably conciliatory.

At this juncture the Dutch were thus irrevocably divided. The loss of Luanda caused five provinces to court war. Friesland abstained while Holland tried to moderate. In the course of January, 1649, the Heren XVII and XIX were both authorized by the States General to disburse letters of marque and reprisal. A list of redresses for the West India Company was drawn up, and shareholders were forced to make contributions to the company.[9] All these signs pointed to an immediate outbreak of hostilities.

But it was destined to be a cold war. Mighty Amsterdam, playing directly into Portuguese hands, paralyzed efforts to effectuate war measures. Zeeland continued to demand more preparations, Friesland refused to become involved, and all the other provinces vacillated. Although some historians credit this inability to get organized to the wiles and intrigues of Coutinho, it was probably more attributable to the normal inefficiency and rivalry of the Dutch provincial governments with their peculiar intransigent local automatons.

In the end New Holland was neglected, and the Dutch suffered defeat after defeat. Even at sea their traditional stronghold was crumbling. In 1649 the once so powerful West India Company did not have one capital ship at its disposal. De With's fleet, ineffectual at best, was a government fleet, and it was the only one available at that particular moment. The admiral's quarrels with the Political Council at Pernambuco, moreover, were compounding the tragedy being enacted there. Privateering was also thoroughly frustrated by the fact that the Portuguese had established a *Companhia geral do Estado do Brasil*. They now sailed only in heavily armed convoys.

When word reached The Hague that Portugal was preparing a vast armada, the States General stirred from indecision and approved a new *secours* for New Holland. Since the West India Company was now totally insolvent, any attempt to save Dutch Brazil was entirely up to the government. A blockade of the Portuguese coast was also decided upon, although no war had as yet been declared. But talk of an alliance between the United Provinces and Spain filled the air, and pamphleteers from both sides bombarded the public with "blue books." Once again, Amsterdam's opposition crippled decisive action; nothing came of the decisions. Aitzema could indeed write truthfully, "The affairs of the company again plummeted downhill."[10] Nothing was accomplished. At the end of 1649, de With returned from Brazil without authorization and claimed rightly that the Dutch position there was beyond hope.

While battles raged fiercely in Brazil, a strange "cold war" immobilized the combatants in Europe. As negotiations dragged on, both parties were swept up in the vicious circle of unrealistic demands. Coutinho's position was certainly not to be envied. At one point he was recalled for his failure to achieve all of Portugal's demands. When this punitive action was reversed, Coutinho advised his king that there were only two choices: either accept the Dutch conditions or embark upon war against the Hollanders in Brazil, the Far East, and Europe. Popular feeling in the United Netherlands again expressed itself rather rashly when the riff-raff of The Hague attacked the Portuguese embassy. This attack signaled the end of Coutinho's political fortunes there. As Wicquefort observes, "the way he acted," on account of which "l'on avoit traitté de ridicule en elle mesme"[11] in The Hague resulted in his departure without the usual pomp meriting his rank.[12]

A slight reprieve for the Dutch position in Brazil was gained when a fleet of modest size, six ships and six yachts carrying 2,800 men, left the Low Countries at the end of 1649. But the situation in Brazil had become even more desperate with de With's "French leave." Only massive measures could effectively hope to alter the obvious collapse of the colony. Portuguese inability to strike a final and telling blow was due to an adverse international situation. Portugal was still at war with Spain and unable to find allies against her peninsular foe. The element of chance—and time—now seemed to be on the side of the Dutch.

In an era when, to all appearances, the Dutch should have been able to bring the tiny Iberian nation to her knees, nothing of the kind occurred. Some explanation of this phenomenon is required. It must be sought in connection with internal and international problems with which the United Provinces had to cope. The war party had lost its major advocate when the Stadhouder William II died suddenly of smallpox in 1650 at the age of twenty-four. Playing upon Dutch fears of losing the Setúbal salt trade, the resurgent libertines were able to postpone an open break with Portugal. This delaying tactic lost its force, however, as the WIC regained control of St. Martin. Coutinho had definitely been correct in his estimation that the Dutch were more interested in salt for their herring industry than in possible profits from the slave trade. This policy, however, was changing rapidly now that St. Martin salt had become again available, and the trade in "black ebony" was gaining in momentum.

Discussions in the Low Countries proceeded about further help to Dutch Brazil, and encouragement was given to both the East and the West India Companies in their privateering against Portugal. The new Portuguese ambassador Antonio de Sousa Macedo arrived at this same time to resume negotiations. The States General, still enraged at the tactics of his predecessor, took a firmer stand now that the opportunity seemed to offer itself. Their High Mightinesses ignored the new ambassador for half a year. Not before March, 1651—when difficulties with England clouded the Dutch political sky—was he received by this august body. But his eloquent opening address: *Tandem aliquando*... "At last, Your High Mightinesses, the right of nations triumphs, reason is heard and justice sits on her throne" failed to command respect from the levelheaded Dutch. His offers of vast concessions in exchange for the return of Dutch Brazil were inspired by Portugal's feeling of isolation. The offers were met with silence or with polite rejections. A memorial from the Heren XIX at this time may be partly responsible for the government's intractable attitude: the company's losses in Brazil because of the Portuguese-Brazilian rebellion impressed the Dutch politicians far more than the dramatic rhetoric of the new Portuguese ambassador.[13]

Eventually and in spite of the offers of the Swedish queen to mediate, all relations between the United Provinces and Portugal were severed.

Open war with the late ally now seemed only to be a matter of time. Despite Macedo's initial jubilance—*Sum parvus homo sed habeo magnum cor*[14]—he had failed. Soon afterwards he left the country. Negotiations with Spain were renewed, and the WIC magnanimously offered to surrender the southern part of Brazil—those regions never conquered by the Dutch—to the Spaniards. The Dutch were to keep the northern portion after the territory had been taken from the Portuguese. Panic hit Lisbon when the nature of these procedures became known, and the grand inquisitor, long opposed to restitution to heretics, now claimed that the king "would sin if he did not conclude peace, even on such terms as the Dutch desired."[15]

The Portuguese were spared humiliation by none other than Oliver Cromwell. The United Provinces now refused to enter into an alliance with the English, one which had been designed to strengthen the Protestant cause as well as Cromwell's own position. Faced with Dutch obstinacy, his compliant parliament had vented its anger and procured a set of Navigation Laws calculated to end Dutch trading competition. Increasing tensions with England thus led the Dutch to tread gently with Portugal. This was especially so while King João seemed inclined to remain accomodating. Adapting itself to the realities of the situation and listening to new offers from the Portuguese, over the vigorous disapproval of the Heren XIX, the States General agreed to settle the Brazilian problem on the condition that the Dutch retain Pernambuco and receive an indemnity.

Negotiations on this basis were interrupted by the startling news that Cromwell had dispatched a powerful fleet against royalist Barbados. The mission had miscarried, but the English had overpowered twenty-four Dutch traders in one of the island's ports.[16] They justified this action on the pretext of carrying letters of reprisal, an excuse which allowed them to seize outright all ships trading on British islands in violation of the new Navigation Laws. This instance was the test case for the new laws in the Caribbean.

The Dutch were well aware that war with England was imminent and unavoidable. "We know the nature of that 'superb' nation, so help us God, only too well," wrote the Heren XIX to the States General,[17] and they were no doubt voicing popular sentiment. Disturbing news from the East Indies and renewed English complaints —*ad nauseam*—about the alleged "Ambon atrocities" contrived to distract attention from Portugal altogether. In the States General, emergency measures were legislated for 50 ships and long-range plans for a fleet of 150 ships "to make the seas safe and to preserve the navigation and the commerce of these United Provinces."[18]

The ensuing first Anglo-Dutch war, which was lost by the Dutch, took place almost exclusively in that area arrogantly referred to by the English as the "British Seas." Except for some unauthorized privateering, New Holland, the Caribbean, and New Netherland remained outside the scope of hostilities. The Dutch were chiefly concerned about New Netherland which was surrounded by the English. Zeeland, though, at one time, insisted that help for Dutch possessions in the Caribbean and the Guianas be delegated at once.[19]

In the meantime, the Brazilian situation continued to deteriorate rapidly and was soon beyond repair. The States General knew that the position there was critical and made various desperate attempts to win Frisian approval of concerted aid to the area. A unanimous vote was required for action. But that province persisted in its refusal and announced that the resolutions of Their High Mightinesses were not binding unless its own provincial assembly concurred.[20]

The one acceptable alternative was to send envoys to Lisbon. These diplomats were dispatched in the course of 1653 and carried new offers having to do with Brazil. By now, however, positions on the political chessboard had dramatically shifted. The future had considerably brightened for the Portuguese while the Dutch were now pressed by adverse circumstances. Thus, the Portuguese looked on as interested spectators in the Anglo-Dutch conflict, since they realized that they could only benefit from the situation. Besides, the States General's demands were totally unrealistic since Dutch power in Brazil had by now been reduced to a defense of their capital. No help was apt to be forthcoming, moreover, from the Low Countries while the nation was at war with England. The Portuguese did concede their willingness to surrender some part of Dutch Brazil in return for the unconditional restitution of their East Indian possessions. But the Heren XVII were entirely unsympathetic to that idea, and the Dutch envoys returned home with nothing to show for their efforts.[21]

The Anglo-Dutch war provided King João with what he considered to be his golden opportunity to end the stalemate in Brazil. He had prevented, heretofore, a direct attack on Recife, the fortified outpost of the last Dutch stronghold in Pernambuco. At last he ordered an all-out siege on the city by land as well as by sea. On December 20, 1653, 63 well-armed Portuguese ships dropped anchor in that harbor, while troops simultaneously advanced toward the Dutch positions from the opposite side. Although the Dutch had provisions for a year, they lacked the will to fight. On January 25, 1654, negotiations began, and twelve days later Portuguese-Brazilian troops occupied the area. New Holland belonged to the past.[22]

A deep stir of emotion over the loss of Dutch Brazil swept through the United Provinces, but it was soon lost among the other pressing problems facing the country. Although a stream of refugees continued for some time to pour into the humiliated Netherlands, they could occasion little more than a display of superficial sympathy. The days of a dynamic West India Company were gone forever. There were desultory discussions about reconquest which were followed by the sober realization that this was impossible.[23] The States General undertook to compensate for the financial loss that had been suffered by the company under the guise of official demands for restitution from the Portuguese.

The end of the Anglo-Dutch war and the death of King João in 1656 eventually furnished the Dutch with a chance to take the offensive against Portugal, and a fleet of fourteen sails was speedily equipped to blockade the Portuguese coast. It was well known that the rich sugar fleet from Brazil was expected in May or June, and the purpose of the expedition was to intercept this valuable prey. Amsterdam had at long last stopped its opposition and seemed willing to cooperate. Only Friesland continued to abstain.

This meant, of course, that war had become only a matter of formal declaration. France sought to mediate, but her motives were immediately suspected by the Dutch. The latter, although defeated in Brazil, had achieved considerable gains in the East Indies, and thought they held the trump cards in the bargaining game. The Portuguese, moreover, were in a conciliatory mood since they were still at war with Spain and threatened by the Dutch in India. But the proposals submitted to the Portuguese queen by the Dutch envoys who arrived at Lisbon with the blockading fleet were too high-handed. They were too bitter a pill for the Portuguese to swallow unprotestingly. In summary, the proposals demanded restitution of all territory conquered by the Portuguese since 1641. The impossible position taken by the Dutch resulted in a new stalemate. The Dutch representatives left Lisbon after a proclamation of war had been officially handed to the Portuguese.[24]

Actual fighting, however, did not take place since England and France brought pressure to bear on both parties. Despite the fact that a state of war had been formally declared, Amsterdam continued handing out passports and permits for trade with Portugal. Negotiations were once more resumed, and a new Portuguese ambassador appeared before Their High Mightinesses in July, 1658, accompanied by offers of indemnification. No specific mention was made of restitution, and the Dutch remained cool to the ambassador's proposals despite the fact that Portugal by now could count on both French and English support. News that French and other privateers were operating with Portuguese commissions intensified Dutch suspicions of these "good neighbors,"[25] and the increasingly tempting offers of the Portuguese ambassador continued to be ignored.

Portugal benefited this time from Dutch involvement in the Baltic war. Her ambassador now published a manifesto damning the Dutch in general and the WIC in particular for faithlessness and for atrocities. The Netherlanders retaliated by again issuing letters of reprisal against the Portuguese as a warning. When the Baltic war had reached the stage where it was obvious to all that the Dutch were clearly winning, the Portuguese ambassador thought it opportune to initiate conciliatory talks once again.

It was 1661, however, before real provisions for a treaty were written down and submitted to the Provincial States for approval. Five provinces were in favor of peace; only Zeeland and Gelderland were opposed. Disregarding the provisions of the Union of Utrecht— which had stipulated that every province was to concur in such matters—Holland, led by the Grand Pensionary Johan de Witt, pushed the treaty through. The final draft did not mention restitution for any territory taken by the Portuguese from the West India Company. It did provide, however, for an indemnity of eight million guilders to be paid partly in gold, partly in sugar, salt, and other commodities.[26] For many years to come, recurrent quarrels about the prices and delivery of these products were not infrequent, yet both sides were too desirous of peace to consider them seriously. Although the money put the treasury of the company back on its feet for a short while, it was small compensation for the sacrifices which had been made in *verzuimd* (neglected) Brazil.

The treaty sealed the fate of the company. Amsterdam and the triumphant East India Company had safeguarded their interests in the Malay Archipelago and in India and had used the West India Company's precious jewel New Holland as bait to protect the colonies the EIC had seized from Portugal in the Far East. The Heren XIX realized that this peace meant the end. Portugal had not defeated them, but their own capital together with its mighty monopolistic institution had. On the agenda of their meeting shortly afterward, the statement was made that the company had been rendered "weak and powerless."[27] It was a moderate statement. Its impotence was now no secret to anyone and its implications were soon realized by another seapower fast growing in importance, England. The English, consequently, suddenly became very much interested in relieving the Dutch of their possessions in the African and American hemisphere. It was precisely this rivalry that precipitated the second Anglo-Dutch war, the first colonial war in the Caribbean. Unable to take care of its own defense, the West India Company desperately needed government assistance. But the States General, although not opposed to help, could no longer provide it under the auspices of the company. The Dutch fleets which crossed the Atlantic in this and in the third Anglo-Dutch conflict sailed under the red-white-blue banner of the United Provinces.

The rise of the Dutch West India Company had been brief but glorious. Its decline, almost imperceptible in the thirties, more obvious in the forties, and manifest in the fifties, spans a period of thirty years. This extended death struggle was protracted unnecessarily by the company's lengthy fight to regain New Holland and by its unrealistic approach to the problem. Deeply involved in the matter, the States General was constantly faced with the question of how best to reconcile the company or, as it was euphemistically phrased at the time, how to "redress" the company. It appears that it continued to cling tenaciously to the idea that the WIC could survive in spite of the loss of Brazil. In this connection, the surrender of New Netherland a brief ten years after the fall of Pernambuco should have provided conclusive evidence to the contrary.

The Portuguese victory in Brazil, although counterweighted by great losses in the Far East, thoroughly alarmed the Dutch people, since it was executed by a European state which was widely held to be impotent. Nothing "did more damage to the honor and reputation of the Republic" than this defeat by a nation known to be one of the weakest of all Europe.[28] Although the United Provinces' commitments in European affairs suffice to explain the defeat, they do not justify it. An objective analysis would reveal that the West India Company paid the price of Dutch existence as a world power in the seventeenth century.

New Holland's loss marks the real beginning of the bankruptcy of the company. From a "Summary Report"[29] of 1648 it appears that in the previous year the company's Brazilian expenses had been 1,100,000 to 1,200,000 guilders; on the other hand its income was estimated at only 400,000 guilders "from which," the report concluded, "the total ruin and decline of the company is to be expected." In the years which followed Count Johan Maurits' departure, a marked decline in revenue became noticeable. The incompetent management which succeeded him was unable to reverse this trend. Quite literally the company bled itself to death in order to defend and maintain its pretentious colony. As was often the case, Usselinx' prediction was proven correct: the conquest and defense of Brazil would cost ten million guilders and would require ten thousand men. At no time in the company's history were such funds and such manpower freely available.

Although the WIC's financial problem was undeniably complicated by mismanagement within the directorate, the real source of difficulty must be sought in connection with undisguised provincial rivalry concerning the company, especially between Holland and Zeeland. This jealousy is particularly well reflected in the voluminous and vituperative pamphlets of the era. On the other hand, the XVII virtually escaped criticism of this type for a century and a half after 1623.

In the early thirties, the company tried to retrieve the 600,000 guilders that it had loaned to the government during the Gelderland crisis. Its difficulties in this respect should have warned its administrators against trusting the provinces. Although perhaps without too much choice, the Heren XIX instead borrowed in good faith against the promised 700,000-guilder annual subsidy which had been voted by the States General in 1632. They were soon to learn that these commitments made by the federal government were not too assiduously honored at the provincial level. Evidence of this local deferment is apparent in the following account dated 1649.[30]

General account of what the respective provinces owe to the WIC in the matter of subsidies for the period since 1635:

The Province of Gelderland:

Debit	ƒ 589,617 : 3 : 10¼	
Paid	ƒ 142,999 : 12 : 8	
Remains in debt for		ƒ 446,617 : 11 : 2¼

The Province of Holland:

Debit	ƒ 5,818,536 : 11 : 8¾	
Paid	ƒ 2,348,238 : 16 : 12	
Remains in debt for		ƒ 3,470,297 : 14 : 12¾

The Province of Zeeland:

Debit	ƒ 915,153 : 8 : 5½	
Paid	ƒ 336,541 : 13 : 8	
Remains in debt for		ƒ 578,611 : 14 : 13½

The Province of Utrecht

Debit	ƒ 615,308 : 13 : 2¾	
Paid	ƒ 208,605 : 16 : 8	
Remains in debt for		ƒ 406,702 : 16 : 10¾

The Province of Friesland:

Debit	f 1,357,113 : 6 : 4
Paid	f 230,098 : 2 : 12

Remains in debt for f 1,127,015 : 3 : 8

The Province of Overijssel:

Debit	f 397,538 : 8 : $10\frac{3}{4}$
Paid	f 94,243 : 4 : 8

Remains in debt for f 303,295 : 4 : $2\frac{3}{4}$

The Province of Groningen:

Debit	f 334,449 : 11 : $15\frac{3}{4}$
Paid	f 27,452 : 8 : 0

Remains in debt for f 306,997 : 3 : $15\frac{3}{4}$

The collector Doublet debit on the remaining
since the closed account, 1635: f 5,753 : 16 : 7
Landscape Drente paid: f 2,000

f 7,753 : 16 : 7

TOTAL DUE WIC: f 6,647,291 : 5 : $8\frac{3}{4}$

Financial adversities continued to be a deliberative item on the agenda—the so-called *poincten van beschrijvinghe*—of the Heren XIX. The resolutions of the States General, however, provide eloquent testimony of the persistence and optimism of the XIX. Ample evidence of the cumbersome system of administration of the United Provinces, the resolutions show the virtual impotence of the federal government when confronted by provincial autonomy.

Before the continuation of the charter had been granted, the Province of Gelderland—the first in rank, although not in importance, since it had been a duchy while all the others were counties—had proposed to ask the East India Company how its sister company might be compensated for its losses.[31] This proposal implied that prolongation of the WIC charter would require a program of restoration for the company. The Heren XIX, who met in Middelburg in 1646, inspired by this request, drew up and submitted a balance sheet that was accompanied by suggestions for their own survival. Included also, of course, was a request for assistance. This fervent plea, dated February 6, 1647, or prior to the renewal of the charter, admitted that "with a longer delay of the final and effective resolution of Your High Mightinesses we have no means nor do we know how to get the means to defend our conquests in the future or keep our affairs at home out of confusion."[32] Other petitions followed, regularly pleading with the

States General to urge, cajole, or force the provinces to meet their obligations.

The EIC charter was renewed on the condition that this company should pay 1,500,000 guilders into the WIC treasury. The latter institution then requested permission to borrow 100,000 guilders against the promised subsidy. The States General offered no objection, inundated as it was at that moment by reports from West Africa that testified to the fact that the company's position there was deteriorating almost as quickly as it was in Brazil.[33] Desperate men are reduced to desperate means. The XIX were soon to learn, however, that stopgap measures provided no adequate solution to their dilemma.

Once the charter had been renewed, the Heren XIX immediately requested 600,000 guilders for Brazil.[34] This plea differed from preceding ones because of its urgency. Thereafter, during all of 1647, attention was increasingly concentrated on Brazil which left little time to consider a redress for the company. A special committee was selected from members of the States General, however, to work on this problem with the Heren XIX.[35] It released the Summary Report already mentioned on the general issue of reparations which examined the condition of the company and offered the opinions of the five chambers upon the matter.[36]

The statistics of this document made it clear that total collapse of the company was imminent unless prompt provisions were made for its restoration. In the Brazil matter alone the company's 1647 budget showed a deficit of two-thirds. The report presumed, rather whimsically, that funds would be forthcoming and that New Holland would be saved. The committee thus considered seriously such illusory problems as the future defense and maintenance of the colony. Diverse responsible ideas for a reduction of expenses were also included: the elimination of the annual allowances to the eighty-eight directors and their attendants, the discharge of many useless servants in New Holland, and a special clause which made company employees at all levels accountable for their respective offices to the company's Chamber of Accounts.

Improvement in the company's financial situation was confidently predicted as a result of a recently passed regulation that was designed to promote trade to the Caribbean islands. A special fund for redress, which had been suggested in a 1637 resolution of the States General, was urged also. Finally, the report solemnly recommended federal and provincial support for the company's ventures in Angola, the Guinea coast, New Holland, New Netherland, and the Caribbean for the furtherance of national pride and for sheer profit.[37] Specific financial remedies were also mentioned. The company ought to be allowed to raise a 500,000-guilder installment from its stockholders against debts in arrears. It was argued elsewhere that the Dutch envoys at Munster be empowered to negotiate, on behalf of the company, a guarantee for the salt trade on Punta de Araya. Spain drew no salt from this deposit, and great profits were expected for the company through this monopoly. Almost as an afterthought, the committee for the restoration and redress of the company advised that cultivation in the company's territorial acquisitions ought to be advanced. Immigration was to be encouraged.

After Their High Mightinesses had solemnly thanked all those who had participated in this special report, they submitted copies to the provincial assemblies and urged their prompt response. In an "Address on the present distress of the West India Company" in the Chamber of the Northern Quarter, the comment was made that a thousand suggestions for rehabiliation were possible. But if the Provincial States persisted in their delinquencies, the only conceivable outcome for the wic was a slow and certain death.[38] The Heren xix supplemented the record with an attractive proposition to their stockholders that money henceforward invested in the company would only be used for purposes of trade in Guinea, São Thomé, and elsewhere in Africa. Nothing ever came of the grandiose promises that were made by this official proclamation.

Some time later, just as news of the fall of Luanda trickled home, Gelderland again submitted a declaration to the States General for the sustenance and maintenance of the wic.[39] This appears to have been the first of the "quick responses" asked for by Their High Mightinesses. The "Declaration of Gelderland" vigorously endorsed the position that the provinces should support the company in Brazil and in other ways. Such assistance, it claimed, should be forthcoming as soon as possible. Four or five of the other provinces acquiesced in this statement.

After a few weeks, the States General reopened the general question of redress. An account was made of overdue indebtedness, and proposals were made to have these debts paid off in installments.[40] Participants were requested to subscribe for 12 per cent of their shares. As the largest investor, the States General was to furnish an example. But, some months later, discussions about the installment proposal failed to achieve concrete results. The return of de With renewed the debate which led to making *in casu* accomodations for free trade in New Holland and in the Caribbean, severe salary cuts for directors and Brazilian employees, as well as the dispatch of an actual *secours*

—although smaller than originally planned—to New Holland. That any decision was reached, at this stage and after so long a time, bordered on the miraculous.

The market quotations from 1628 to 1674 further clarify the company's desperate straits. In November, 1628, before Heyn's capture of the Silver Fleet, the stocks of the company were steady at a modest 115 per cent. When Heyn arrived home two months later, they had jumped to 206 per cent. The collapse to 61 per cent in Feburary, 1633, was occasionally relieved by temporary "ups" as good news reached home. But no expedition really altered the decline in the percentage. Jol's exploits in 1638 and 1640 must explain the resurgence of the price of shares to 134 per cent in May of the latter year. Thereafter the decline was slow but steady. Stocks hit 16 per cent in 1650. In 1655 they were down to 10 per cent. From 1660 to the end of 1673 they stood around 3 per cent with an "up" to 9 or 10 per cent in 1664 because of the expectations raised by de Ruyter's mission. Without lengthy and superfluous details, the chart succinctly reveals the decline of the Dutch West India Company.[41]

In 1650, a new petition was received by the States General from some of the head-participants of the company,[42] proposing complete reorganization. This document is remarkable because the company's decline was not blamed on the success of the Portuguese nor on the failure of provincial support. Instead, the directors were openly accused of bad management in financial affairs, in military matters, and in trade regulations. This vituperative denunciation was soon followed by other pamphlets bitterly attacking the company's directors. It was demanded that all their salaries should cease immediately and that offenders be excluded from the advantages, bonuses, freedoms, and privileges which they had enjoyed since the founding of the wic.

The 1650 proposal also included certain positive steps for the rejuvenation of the company. The States General was asked to appoint a new Board of Directors to be called the "Council of the Indies." This council was to have seventeen members: four from Holland, three from Zeeland, and two from each of the other provinces. Acting under the immediate supervision of the States General, the council would be in charge of general management but would not have the accompanying duties of administering capital, revenues, expenditures, equipping fleets, or purchasing supplies. It was also suggested that the government in New Holland be reorganized to make its governor directly responsible to the company when he returned—a process comparable to the Spanish *residencia*. Three ideas were advanced to bring about the political change: peace with

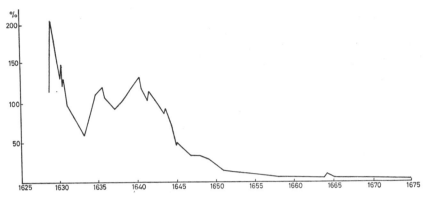

Market quotations of the West India Company, 1628–1674

Portugal based on restitution, exemption from taxes for New Holland for a stipulated period, and simplification of the navigation regulation for the Caribbean.

This documentary evidence may well have been the cause of the vehement criticism of company management which soon flourished. A pamphlet entitled "The Amsterdam ferry-man to Middelburgh" argued against the directors, using the device of a conversation among travelers.[43] Aitzema and van der Capellen report that some attempts were made to correct the bad management and administration,[44] but there is no proof that more than minor reforms were actually undertaken, despite the articulate and hostile reviews of the time.

The directors unflinchingly sent their usual request for aid to the States General in 1651.[45] Groningen, in particular, was deeply moved by "the desolate condition of the West India Company," as revealed in this request.[46] Notwithstanding this support, in January, 1652, the States General again came to the reluctant conclusion that New Holland was a hopeless cause.[47] This did not, however, prevent its members from voting a subsidy to the company. An immediate sum of 310,000 guilders was proposed lest the company go bankrupt and the prestige of the United Provinces be damaged.

Discussions on this latter proposal had just begun when the first Anglo-Dutch war broke out. Although the Dutch lost this encounter, they remained dangerous competitors to the English. The war was brief—less than two years—and ended in the Caribbean with a situation that was roughly the *status quo ante bellum*. Each combatant had suffered undeniable losses in trade. The enforcement of the Navigation Laws of 1651, however, contributed directly to the decline of Dutch commerce in the Caribbean. Consequently, the

States General appealed to the "Caribbean navigators" for ways to protect their trade in the area. The response from these commercial agents contained some remarkable suggestions for a redress of the WIC. They may be considered the last real program for rehabilitating the company.[48]

The merchants who traded in the Caribbean concluded that the WIC could no longer protect Dutch interests in that area. The States General, therefore, was advised to take such matters into its own hands, to outfit a fleet for the capture of Barbados, and to anticipate future problems by expanding quickly to other English-held islands. They also suggested that a mission be sent to capture the rich tobacco land of Virginia. Furthermore, in order to maintain and protect trade under the auspices of the company, whose charter and rights were fully recognized, they proposed the creation within the company of a Caribbean corporation which would be placed under the direction of the Chambers of Amsterdam and Zeeland. This "Caribbean Company" would direct all trade in the area and enlist colonists for inhabited islands.[49] The recommendations closed with the insistence that the first requisite for the Caribbean was a new government-sponsored fleet. As might be expected, nothing ever came of these admonitions. When the war with England ended, much of the threat was removed. The project had proved to be purely academic.

The West India Company did manage to survive both the first Anglo-Dutch war and the loss of Brazil. Immediately after the war, in 1655, certain creditors attempted to seize company property. After all, the shares were down to 10 per cent. But the States General stepped in and prevented that action. Thereafter, all discussions for the redress and restoration of the company disappear from the minutes of the States General, the Provincial States of Holland, and even from the meetings of the Heren XIX. Since everyone seemed to have accepted the fact that the company was beyond repair, it was simply allowed to sink into limbo without comment. In 1667, some debates were held about the sale of the company's charter to the highest bidder in order to pay the debts.[50] Financial support from the States General, however, and some advantages granted by the treaty with Portugal in 1669—i.e., the aforementioned eight million guilders— enabled the company to limp through the next few years. In the seventies, the company was generally assumed to have reached its lowest point.

The effects of the second and third Anglo-Dutch wars on the Caribbean area were much more dramatic than those of the first conflict. The prolongation of the last war into a bitter Franco-Dutch conflict caused especially severe losses from which the Dutch never recovered. As a war instrument the West India Company had vanished. The States General—or more correctly the provinces of Holland and Zeeland—had taken over the company's role and had waged the wars in the Caribbean. One of the consequences of this situation was to revive somewhat the lethargic Heren XIX and to make them appraise their current predicament. English depradations in Africa were troublesome, of course, but there was also friction with Sweden. Most important of all, as the 1660's were drawing to a close, the company was faced once more with the problem of renewing its charter.

Anticipating the apathy which would meet any request to prolong the charter, the XIX had submitted a "concept for redress" to the States General in 1668, three years before the second term of the charter was to expire.[51] Their High Mightinesses appointed a special committee to investigate and study the concept.[52] This committee, however, had already worked out answers to any charter renewal petition before really studying the company's projects. Its memorial to the States General was negative. The company countered with a new proposal which requested an extension, the payment of promised subsidies that were in arrears, and help in the matter of collecting from the Portuguese the monies awarded to the company by the treaty between the two countries.[53]

Difficulties between the directors of the company and the head-participants added to the problems which the company had to contemplate in those years. Even after the "amplification" of June, 1622, the latter had never had much voice in the management or in the direction of the company. Yet the head-participants increasingly became the directors' most vocal critics in these years of decline. The program for redress which they now submitted to the States General reviewed changes and offered alterations in the company's charter, while it proposed a "trade fund" that was designed to promote commerce.[54]

Although little was done about the various draft proposals handed to Their High Mightinesses, the charter of the company was provisionally renewed on the condition that the head-participants would supply a capital of one million guilders.[55] Since, quite naturally, the latter were loath to invest money in an institution whose books were closed to them, they complained to the government. A new "memorial of grievances" was drawn up. The company's financial records, they claimed, were so hopelessly behind that no audit would make a fair accounting of the WIC available in time for the scheduled renewal.[56]

Discussions on prolonging the charter were resumed in December,

1671. They resulted in a decision to grant the WIC another year to give the Heren XIX time to realize some of the hints and recommendations about the company and to bring their books up to date. No account of revenues, profits, and losses had been made since 1665. No wonder that the memorial stated, "There is no hope in the world that at the end of this charter an account or financial statement will be ready."

But early the following year when the United Provinces became embroiled in war with France and England, company problems were relegated to the background. For some months the international situation looked very black indeed for the Dutch. But victories at sea by de Ruyter and a good defense on land by the young and vigorous William III, who was called to the post formerly held by his father, soon swung the pendulum of war to the advantage of the United Provinces. The States General now felt assured enough to renew provisionally the WIC charter for eight months starting in August, 1672.

In February, 1673, the problem of the WIC charter once again appeared on the official agenda. The heavy financial burden of the war had moved the Dutch to enforce a "capital loan" on all those whose annual incomes exceeded four hundred guilders. By the same legislation, all corporation and business had been compelled to submit a complete statement of their stocks and bonds. The West India Company's exemption from this obligation is eloquent testimony of its desolate condition.

Deputies from the five chambers of the company met in The Hague in March, 1673, to consider the future of their institution. They agreed that the provision for prolongation, mentioned above, could not be met. It was decided, nevertheless, to request a new continuation. On March 30—mirabile dictu—it was granted until the end of the year. In December, the States General authorized an additional extension until April, 1674.[57] Before the initiation of this reprieve the company had submitted a request for renewal together with a proposal to provide the necessary one million guilders.[58] The ingenuity of the plan suggested at this time may have been the deciding factor in a new prolongation of three months.

The company's actual plight was no secret to anyone—least of all to the States General. In April, 1674, Their High Mightinesses determined to dissolve the West India Company. Although they believed that a monopolistic organization was still the best way to handle navigation and trade in American waters, their project now was to create a new and different institution in order to accomplish these ends. The new charter drawn up by the government differed in so many ways from the charter of 1621 that it entailed the creation of an entirely new company.

The novel organization—called the New West India Company to distinguish it from its predecessor—was provided with capital through incorporating the participants of the old company and by recognizing their earlier investment if they would invest in the new institution. The old debts were brought back to 30 per cent and converted into stocks, while creditors were required to pay an extra 8 per cent if they wished their claims to be heeded. These manipulations furnished the new company with an initial capital of 120,000 guilders.[59]

The end of the old WIC had come. Started fifty-three years earlier with excellent prospects and with inspired leadership, the company had performed excellently for one decade and reasonably well for the second. In its declining years, its only notable activity occurred in the development of Curaçao as a slave depot, and even then it had encountered determined competition from the English at Jamaica. The demise of the WIC, moreover, also signaled the close of the Dutch "Golden Age." The West India Company had been a manifestation of that age, both an outgrowth and a contributor to the brief period of Dutch grandeur. Indeed, the passing of the old WIC was the end of an era.

There was much popular feeling about why the company had failed. One pamphlet, Glorified Netherland by the Restored Navigation, criticized such defects in the company as its unwillingness to colonize, its unbearable tax system, and its curious inability to govern efficiently abroad.[60] It urged that colonists be allowed to name their own officials, even their own governors. All such ideas and suggestions, of course, came too late to save the company. Long before 1674 it had been forced to admit that it had attempted a task beyond its strength. It had also been compelled to face the fact that the other countries of Europe, notably France and England, were determined to prevent a Dutch monopolistic position in Africa and America. Hannay rightly observes that the magnificent dream of the Dutch West India Company was dispelled in the melée of international rivalry.[61]

During the years of the company's decline, great changes had occurred in the Caribbean area. Sugarcane, which had been introduced in the West Indies by Columbus a century and a half earlier, was under cultivation on most of the islands prior to 1650. The English and French, however, had not known how to convert the cane into sugar, molasses, and rum. Dutch refugees from Brazil, who poured into the area after 1654, brought with them the techniques of sugar cultivation and manufacture. Furthermore, Dutch capital helped the French and English planters purchase the necessary equipment on a credit basis. Dutch control of the slave markets in Africa secured the necessary labor. Dutch ships bought up the sugar crops and provided the colonies with food, hardware, and other needed commodities throughout that period of English civil strife when the London government could do little to help them. The Dutch did the same for the French.

Burns observes that the Dutch would not have had this opportunity to trade with foreign colonies under normal circumstances, since contemporary mercantile policies reserved colonial commerce for the mother country.[62] France, with the rebellion of the Fronde on her hands, and England, engaged in a bitter civil war, were simply unable to enforce their mercantile authority and prevent this new form of *rescate*. The colonists, needless to say, entirely supported the Dutch trade that was so absolutely essential to their survival.

The English—and to a considerable extent the French—colonies had thus come to depend on Dutch shipping and on the Dutch slave supply. The passage of the first of the Navigation Laws, "for the increase of the shipping and the encouragement of the navigation of this nation which, under good providence and the protection of God, is so great a means of the welfare and safety of this Commonwealth,"[63] was, in the English Antilles, viewed as a mortal blow to their very existence. More than any other consideration these regulations drove the English colonists to take a stand against the mother country. Francis Lord Willoughby of Barbados, together with his legislature, issued a "spirited declaration" which denounced the Parliament "in which we have no representative" and assured the Dutch that "they might continue, if they please, all freedom of commerce and traffic with us."[64]

It was not long, however, before Parliament had re-established complete control over the English settlements in the Caribbean, in spite of a royalist attempt under Prince Rupert to reach the islands before they had surrendered to Commonwealth forces under Ayscue. Although Cromwell's "Western design" did fail, he managed to bring Jamaica under the English flag. The result was a strict enforcement of the Navigation Laws which brought about the utter collapse of Dutch trade with English bases. Nor did the Restoration of Charles II bring a revocation of the restrictive laws, much to the dismay of both the colonists and the Dutch. Indeed, soon after Charles regained his father's throne, he added to the laws of 1651 the well-known "enumeration clause," a provision which made cotton, sugar, tobacco, and other named products from the colonies exportable only to England or to another English colony.

Dissatisfaction continued to mount in the English overseas territories. Soon smuggling developed to circumvent the most unfavorable aspects of the legislation. Yet with a few minor changes, the spirit of the Navigation Laws dominated English colonial trade for almost two centuries. Backed by close policing, the English eventually ended all Dutch trade in their settlements. The Dutch were left to face the bitter irony that their skill, enterprise, and money had created the sugar islands and had made them successful enough to produce a closed market against their former benefactors.

A similar situation evolved in the French Antilles, although of a less disruptive nature. Richelieu's Compagnie des Isles de l'Amérique, charged with responsibility for the French islands in the Caribbean, never achieved a very powerful position against the Dutch because of a habitual lack of capital. In 1650 this company sold its colonies to *seigneurs*, thus creating a French equivalent to the English and Dutch patronships.[65]

In this same year Martinique and its dependent islands became such a *seigneurie*. A year later Philippe de Lonvilliers, Sieur de Poincy, one of the influential members of the Maltese Order, brought St. Christopher and some other islands—including the French part of St. Martin—under his order. De Poincy himself furnished 120,000 francs, and it was agreed that he should act as governor until his death. At that date the French Antilles were reorganized by Colbert under the Compagnie des Indes Occidentales, and stricter laws to exclude foreign trade were more rigidly applied.

The Dutch islands in the Leeward group, as noted before, were patronships. After the death of Jan de Moor, the patron of St. Martin, his heirs sold their rights to the Lampsins brothers. The patent in question, which was identical to that of Tobago, was similar to all WIC patents for colonization in the American hemisphere. It was granted in 1648 for six years and was renewed in 1655. The Dutch colony on St. Martin probably contained some three hundred men. The patent specifically excluded the colonists from the profitable salt trade, a business which the company reserved for itself. De Rochefort, practically the only source for this period, adds that the emigrants, while trying to cultivate tobacco, were forced to build great cisterns because of the lack of fresh water. He also reports that they employed many slaves and that the island provided an attractive hunting ground for sea turtles, wild boars, doves, and parakeets.

On St. Eustatius the Dutch colonists initially concentrated upon

the cultivation of tobacco and cotton. Somewhat later they changed
to sugar and anil. In the fifties the colony was thriving. Nearby
Saba, as mentioned earlier, became the shoe supplier of the
Caribbean islands—at least for the Dutch. Other settlers on this
small island made their living by fishing. In all these places, the
earliest slave labor consisted of Indians who were supplied clandestinely by *indieros* or Indian hunters. After 1650, however, Negro
slaves replaced the Indians almost entirely.

Throughout the Caribbean the changes of flag which accompanied
the furious European rivalry of England, France, and the United
Provinces during the second half of the seventeenth century provides
a bewildering spectacle. With the exception of the Curaçao islands,
which always remained firmly in Dutch hands, all the others changed
masters rapidly in a wild display of international power politics. The
island of St. Martin, Spanish from 1633 to 1648, remained Dutch
until 1672 when the French settlers of the island seized control. The
next year Commander Jacob Binckes reconquered the island briefly,
but it was soon in French hands again. In 1676, Binckes occupied the
island once more, but it became French again for the next fourteen
years after he left.

The developments on St. Eustatius were even more hectic. It
became English in 1665, French in 1666, and was returned to the
Dutch in 1667. During the third Anglo-Dutch war, the island was
again captured by the English in June, 1672; the Dutch reconquered
it a year later, but could only hold it for ten days, after which it
became English again. The second Peace of Westminster, in 1674,
returned the island to Dutch control. The Dutch did not take possession of it, however, for fear that the French would seize it before
peace was established between France and the United Provinces.

The fate of Saba followed a similar course. It remained in Dutch
hands until lost to the English. Although the Dutch regained the
island with the Peace of Breda in 1667, the English recaptured it
during the third Anglo-Dutch conflict. Once again the Dutch retook
it through peace negotiations with England, but as with St. Eustatius,
they actually took possession only after peace with France had been
concluded in 1678. The history of the three Dutch Leeward islands
occupies only a minor phase in the history of the Dutch in the
Caribbean. But today, with the Curaçao islands and Surinam, these
outposts are the last remnants of the great Dutch empire which was
built around the Atlantic in the seventeenth century.

The brief history outlined above reveals that from the Peace of
Munster in 1648 until the outbreak of the second Anglo-Dutch

Fig. 9. Governor Peter Stuyvesant (1592-1672) by anonymous master

Fig. 10. Cornelis Lampsins

conflict in 1665, the islands enjoyed a long era of peace and its consequent prosperity.[66] This ended abruptly with the new war, which was not limited to European waters but carried over to Africa, the Caribbean, and New Netherland. In spite of British assertions to the contrary, there is no doubt that the so-called Dutch provocations were exaggerated by Albion, and that England initiated the hostilities in West Africa as well as in the West Indies and New Netherland.

The response of Their High Mightinesses to English raids is told in another chapter (see Chapter xvi). The Curaçao islands, however, escaped most of the commotion of the conflict, and Willemstad continued to develop as a slave-trading center. Although after 1678 Jamaica gradually became a more important slave depot, Curaçao had more advantages as a strategic staging area against enemy navigation. The proximity of Tierra Firme made smuggling highly profitable, and Curaçao enjoyed a brisk and active illegal trade. Ships which sailed from the island were engaged in privateering and in the recovery of other Dutch territory in the Caribbean. Several French efforts against Curaçao—in 1673 and 1678—met with complete failure (see Chapter xviii).

As mentioned earlier, Curaçao was, politically speaking, united to New Netherland. After the fall of the latter colony in 1664, however, the Curaçao group became a colonial unit supervised directly by the Amsterdam Chamber of the wic. It received a governor with headquarters in the capital Willemstad, while the two adjacent islands were governed by commanders. The governorship of Curaçao was coveted by some of the more important personages of the company. After 1674, Curaçao and the other islands were all incorporated into the charter of the new company.

At Curaçao the governor and his Raad (council) formed the main government of the islands. The military was also represented in this ruling body, because some of its members held their seats ex officio. During the seventeenth century, the merchants and planters of the island also gained admission to this body. Members of this council were appointed by the governor with the approval of the xix.

In 1673, Jan Doncker was named governor of the Curaçao islands. A merchant with connections in New Holland and in the Leeward Islands as well as a member of the council, he had earned the governorship when the French, under Jean Charles de Baas, disembarked their troops on the island. The Dutch were virtually leaderless because of the death of Doncker's predecessor Dirck Otterinck, but the French attempt to conquer the island was nevertheless ill-fated. Doncker was provisionally appointed by the council as Otterinck's successor—an appointment which was later confirmed by the Chamber of Amsterdam and by the Heren xix. He inspired his men with confidence, and the defense of Curaçao was well provided for. Doncker remained in command for the next six years and was highly instrumental in promoting agricultural pursuits in his domain. During the troubled years of this period, Dutch supply ships had not been able to keep the island provided, and Doncker was undoubtedly moved to his agricultural program by necessity.[67] He also completed the fortifications of the island.

In 1675, partly because of recurring trouble with Spain over the *asiento*, the States General declared the harbor at Curaçao to be a free port, open to all nations. Slaves and other commodities could be sold without restrictions at Willemstad. Although no consequent prosperity on the island is recorded from the period, this unprecedented step did serve as a break with the generally mercantilistic climate of the seventeenth century.

In addition to the slave trade, Curaçao and Bonaire also supplied the Dutch with much-needed salt. A record from 1672 reveals that the amount of Curaçao salt (from Bonaire) which was in storage at the West India House in Amsterdam was worth 100,000 guilders. It is certainly true that the directors used every means at their disposal in order to encourage this salt trade.

Although the Dutch reformed religion was the official creed of the Dutch settlements, its adherence was never rigorously enforced, and, in fact, there was much tolerance. Priests could say mass but could not wear their frocks in public, and Jews were soon numerous and among the most highly assessed families on the island's tax rolls.

The Dutch Antilles, six small islands, were of little actual value during the seventeenth century. Even their strategic importance declined after the peace with Spain in 1648 and as England and France began to dominate the Caribbean. Curaçao remained an important slave market for some decades to come, but the other islands were too small to be of any significance. They were all that remained of the Dutch-American colonial empire, a tiny remnant of the domain of the once haughty West India Company. Ironically, perhaps, they became, with Surinam, the only permanent part of the far-flung Dutch possessions which had been acquired and maintained during the Dutch Golden Age.

14

BLACK EBONY

Onmenschelyck gebruyck! Godloose schelmerij,
Dat men de menschen vent tot paertsche slavernij.
Bredero
The slave trade is a benefit to be encouraged by public premiums.
Bolingbroke[1]

Slavery became an evident necessity in the New World within ten years of its discovery. The instructions given to Nicolás de Ovando, the first administrator of the Spanish American empire, permitted the introduction of Negroes into the Western hemisphere.[2] From the outset Spain tried to organize the importation of Negro slaves through official channels; such intentions are obvious in the first *asientos* granted by Charles V to Lorenzo de Gomenot, the governor of Bresa.[3] De Gomenot was licensed to import four thousand Negroes—a fact which reflects the influence of Las Casas—yet these were far too few to solve the labor problem.

After 1580, when Spain controlled the main sources of black merchandise within her realm, her government concluded these *asientos* on a much more regular basis. As a majority of the slave centers were located in West Africa, the Portuguese *asentistas* were the only people of that nation who willingly accepted Spanish domination.

One of the best known *asientos* given by Philip II and concerned with the Caribbean was granted to the Portuguese Pedro Gomez Reynal in 1595. This agreement called for an annual delivery of 4,250 slaves over a period of nine years; these were destined for the Antilles, New Spain, Honduras, Río Hacha, Margarita, and Venezuela,[4] perhaps also for Brazil, Gomez paid the Crown 900,000 ducats for this concession. But the Caribbean proved to be such an insatiable market for Negro slaves that many other *asientos* soon followed. Edward G. Bourne estimates that the legal importation of slaves in 1550 was three thousand per year, plus five hundred illegal imports. Another contemporary estimate suggests an annual importation of two thousand: two-thirds was believed to be illicit traffic.[5]

The value of slaves continued to rise with their numbers. In 1555 the price of a healthy Negro in the Antilles was approximately 100 ducats; the same Negro would bring 140 ducats in Tierra Firme.

Ten years later such a slave would bring up to 178 ducats in Venezuela. The ratio of Negro slaves to the total population continued to increase as well: in Venezuela alone there were approximately 5,000 slaves in 1550, less than 2 per cent of the population; 100 years later their numbers had risen to 30,000 or 8 per cent, and in 1787 they amounted to 53,000 or 15½ per cent.[6] Although numerous historians have pointed out that colonial slavery grew with the developing sugar economy, it is also true that it increased in other areas of the economy as well.

The regularly quoted numbers of imported slaves does not include the many blacks clandestinely introduced into the area by English, French, and Dutch slave traders. That this illicit trafficking was increasing and perhaps assuming even vaster proportions than was the legal trade is tentatively suggested by the fact that in 1678 the governor of Puerto Rico appointed a special official to put a stop to the contraband in slaves between Jamaica, Curaçao, and his own island. His plan was frustrated, however, by the failure to find anyone willing and able to accept the post. The popular consensus was strictly in favor of a continuation of the illegal commerce.[7]

The limited statistics about the actual importations of slaves are supplemented by the letters to the Crown from Spanish officials in the Caribbean area. These invariably ask for more black laborers. On occasion such letters reveal a new and significant dimension in this all-compelling need for slaves; in 1600, for instance, the governor of Cumaná appealed to the king for more slaves since his Spanish *rancheros* were abandoning the area in large numbers and the province would soon be totally undefended.[8] The Dutch had recently made their appearance in this area, and the governor was properly concerned about maintaining his colony.

The earliest Dutch involvement in the slave trade has yet to be investigated. The contract between the Spanish government and the commercial Welser House in 1528 has caused some confusion because Donnan referred to the Germans as "Flemings." The Dutch certainly had no connection with the black trade at this early date. Fort Nassau, the first Dutch fortress in Africa, was built in 1611, according to official documents, to protect only the trade in gold, elephant tusks, and camlet.[9]

One well-known Dutch story concerns the arrival of some Africans in Middelburg in 1596. An enterprising Dutch privateer had acquired them together with the crew of a Portuguese ship and had brought them to Zeeland. Soon afterwards, Burgomaster ten Haeff appeared in a meeting of the Provincial States of Zeeland and argued "that [those Negroes] could not be kept by anyone as slaves and sold as such, but had to be put in their natural freedom without anyone pretending [to have] rights to them as his property."[10] The assembly completely agreed and the hundred Negroes were given their liberty. This decision established an important precedent, however, since it spared the United Provinces from creating a slave market such as seems to have developed in Antwerp in the sixteenth century.[11] An expedition in 1597, which was designed to thwart Zeeland's determination on this matter, failed when its commander Melchior van den Kerckhove was imprisoned in Angola.[12]

Eight years later, however, Dutch merchants are known to have accepted an order from Spanish planters on Trinidad for five hundred slaves to be delivered in the following year. The illegality of this agreement is evident; only the Spanish government through official *asientos* could provide their colonies with black laborers. The stipulations of the contract were met with captives from Angola, probably taken at sea, and possibly the first Negroes from that part of Africa to reach the Caribbean. The whole transaction was exceptional; in the future, whenever the Dutch succeeded in capturing a slave ship, they were regularly faced with the dilemma over disposing of the human cargo. The point made here is also illustrated by de Laet's repeated statements that when his countrymen took a Spanish slave ship, the ship was turned over to the Negroes.[13] That these Negroes, who were, of course, ignorant of navigating, were helpless, and in all probability were soon recaptured by Spaniards might not have occurred to the Dutch. If it had, it did not make the slightest difference.[14] If the Dutch took a ship that they wished to keep, they released the Negroes on the nearest land.

It is unlikely, however, that the Dutch were long unaware of the value of slaves. The actions reported above were, of course, due to their lack of markets for Negroes. Prior to the founding of the West India Company, the Dutch had only a few settlements along the Wild Coast. Their inhabitants did not require slaves at that time, since their needs were supplied, probably, by Indian slaves or by free laborers. The same can be said for the new and tiny English and French colonial establishments in the Caribbean. Since all intercourse with Spanish colonies was regarded as smuggling—the *rescate*—there are no figures available concerning potential markets for slaves.

It is also true and relevant that until the founding of the wic, public sentiment in the United Provinces was decisively opposed to slave trade. Ten Haeff's ideas were not singular. Popular views are also reflected in the following lines from a comedy written by the Dutch poet Bredero in 1615:

> Inhuman practice, godless rascality,
> That human beings are peddled like animals... !

It may be fair, then, to conclude that, until the third decade of the seventeenth century, the Dutch were not involved in the slave trade. The Dutch "man of warre" which sold slaves in Virginia in 1619 undoubtedly represented a quirk of fate and certainly must have captured the Negroes at sea.[15] Ruyters' *Torch of Navigation*, published in 1623, mentions the Spanish trade in blacks but does not refer to Dutch participation in the business. Ruyters, however, does note that Indians seemed to have been found quite useful as slaves.

Karl Marx observed, correctly, that with the progress of capitalistic production, the public consciences of Europeans rapidly lost such idealism as ten Haeff and Bredero had expressed earlier. Indeed, the Dutch were possibly the most profit-conscious nation in all Europe. Since profit was the vital artery of the WIC, even in the earliest discussions of the Heren XIX the pros and cons of the slave trade were aired. Only the lack of markets detained the directors from pursuing that objective. When the capture of the Bay of All Saints in 1624 provided a market, Lam's and Veron's attack on the Elmina Castle and Van Zuylen's and Heyn's expeditions against Luanda must all be interpreted as parts of a deliberate plan of the WIC to capture Portuguese slave stations on the West African coast. But since both of these missions failed and Bahia was soon lost, the slave market was once again closed.

Even before the Dutch conquered Pernambuco and thereby established a new outlet for slaves, there had already been official mention of the slave trade under the auspices of the WIC. In 1626 the Zeeland Chamber decided to provide a ship for the express purpose of transporting slaves from Angola to its colonies on the Amazon and the Wild Coast.[16] The plan was soon copied by others, and licenses were given to various patrons of the Zeelandian settlements at Berbice and Tobago. In 1629, the same chamber also took upon itself the obligation to provide New Netherland with slaves. After the capture of Pernambuco, Zeeland concentrated on the new Brazilian demand, and it was ultimately this area, rather than the Caribbean islands, which captured the major interest of Dutch slave traders.

In 1634 the Dutch took possession of Curaçao. The first director, Johan van Walbeeck, who was acquainted with Negro slavery because of his long years of experience in Brazil, wrote to the Heren XIX and emphasized the urgent need for "a good prize with Negroes, to use them for all kinds of labor on the land."[17] Captured slave ships, however, were not plentiful, and the XIX became increasingly aware that the only way to guarantee a continuous supply of slaves to their Antilles was to take steps to secure some portion of Africa's west coast. Van Walbeeck was not yet envisioning Curaçao as a slave depot; his only concern was with labor for the islands. Since he was very distrustful of the Indians, and not without reason, he wanted them replaced as soon as possible.

After van Zuylen's, Lam's, and Heyn's abortive landings in Africa, the Dutch had abandoned for some years all further notions of occupying that region. But in 1633, Abraham van Pere, the merchant-patron of Berbice, hoping to meet the demands of his colonists for slaves, again proposed to the Heren XIX a joint mission to conquer the island of Arguin in Senegal. Although van Pere was to have a seven-year monopoly at first, the WIC would enjoy all rights on the island after that. One year later, van Pere's son did capture the fort and became the first Dutch commander of Arguin.[18] Some time afterwards, the island duly reverted to the company's custody and was placed under the control of the Chamber of Zeeland. There is no information about the actual number of slaves that van Pere was able to acquire there and bring to his colony on the Wild Coast.

In addition to the comparatively lower demand for slaves in the Caribbean and in the Guianas, the need for slaves in New Holland, after the consolidation and expansion of the Dutch position there, continued to grow at a dazzling pace. Meeting records of the Heren XIX for October, 1635, report that since New Holland was continuously clamoring for black labor the Heren XIX were determined "to lay hands on a great number of slaves as soon as possible."[19] For that express purpose, a ship was fitted out for Angola in July, 1636. Soon thereafter the most influential members of the Zeeland Chamber petitioned their directors to urge the XIX to initiate and sponsor the trade in blacks since the plantations in the Guianas and the Antilles could no longer function "because of a lack of slaves."[20]

In January, 1637, an employee of the company was appointed to take charge of the slave trade in Angola. This official, in turn, hired two assistants; one could "write Portuguese and Dutch" and the other "had traded in blacks." Additional evidence of a growing interest in the slave trade was the equipment of a Zeeland ship with iron bars and beads to barter for slaves in Africa.[21] Nevertheless, none of these measures managed to bolster sufficiently the slave supply to the Dutch colonies in the New World. Other and more permanent means were obviously required in order to satisfy the demand.

In 1635 the Heren xix had already received a report from the Dutch official stationed on the Gold Coast; it surveyed extensively the existing situation and contained special information about the Portuguese stronghold at Elmina.[22] This communication got oral confirmation from the official's predecessor who happened to be in the Low Countries at that time. On the basis of this knowledge the Heren xix determined to attack the fort. The Dutch official on the Gold Coast and Count Johan Maurits in New Holland received certain specific instructions regarding the nature of the planned attack which was to proceed from Pernambuco. Although the count was straining for action, he had to temper his enthusiasm when an unforseen delay occurred following the death of the official in Africa. But the latter's successor soon let it be known that everything was ready and, at the same time, described some of the major weaknesses of the Portuguese garrison. He advocated prompt action. Although the initiative for the military move was provided by the xix, the execution of the operation was in the capable hands of Count Johan Maurits.

On June 25, 1637, a fleet of nine ships, with four hundred sailors and eight hundred soldiers, crossed the Atlantic headed for the Elmina Castle. Anchor was dropped close to the fort two months later, and hostilities began immediately. The Dutch expedition, which involved some Brazilian Indians, achieved its goal quite easily. Although an attack by pro-Portuguese Negroes against their vanguard temporarily threatened the Dutch with a repeat of the catastrophe which struck Lam and Veron twelve years earlier, they soon recovered and repelled their assailants with heavy losses. Arriving at their immediate destination, they took the Portuguese by surprise with their new weapon, the mortar. This recent invention was able to launch grenades into the castle and thoroughly demoralized its defenders. The unexpected happened: the Portuguese, with thirty bronze cannons and many provisions at their disposal, surrendered abjectly after only a brief show of force. The current Dutch official from the Gold Coast, van Yperen, moved his seat of government from Fort Nassau to the Elmina Castle. There he opened strategic negotiations with the Negroes whose collaboration was necessary for the success of the company's new undertaking. Van Yperen's successors managed to bring other Portuguese settlements along the coast under the control of the wic, and the fort itself remained in Dutch hands until 1872.

Dutch status and prestige in Africa was noticeably heightened by this victory. In the first instance, the slave trade was perceptibly stimulated, although not in the expected degree. The number of slaves imported from Elmina into New Holland in 1636 was about 1,000; in 1637, after the capture of the castle, the annual number rose to 1,580. But Count Johan Maurits' optimism in calling Elmina the "key to the Gold Coast" was never really justified. It was soon discovered that slaves acquired in that particular district were not very strong, so "that most of them were used for domestic services and to serve at the table."[23] In contrast, praise for the Negroes from Angola and Cape Verde was virtually unanimous; these were indeed "the best and strongest of them all."[24]

Although the Dutch continued for some time to purchase the majority of their black labor from Guinea—and Elmina was ideally located to facilitate that trade—the newly conquered castle never did become the headquarters for their slave trade. In the second quarter of the seventeenth century, the main slave center shifted from Guinea to Angola and the Congo, regions farther south. Slaves from these territories soon commanded much higher prices in the international market for they were found to be more tractable and more easily domesticated than other blacks. In addition, slave shipments from Africa's southern regions were vastly more dependable because they missed the calms that delayed the Guinea ships.[25]

The Dutch were quickly aware that they had been taken in by a second-class slave market in the Guinea enterprise. A contemporary WIC memorial points out that better slaves were to be acquired elsewhere and successively evaluates the various stations: "the Gulf of Guinea provides twenty-five hundred to three thousand slaves per year; the Rio Benin delivers Negroes for the textile industry; at Rio Calvary the Negroes are cross and stubborn and prone to suicide, and none of the potential buyers in the Caribbean are very eager to buy this particular group of slaves; Angola can supply three thousand slaves annually."[26] Although this document dates from 1670, the information can be assumed to have been common knowledge for some time. The Dutch laid their plans accordingly.

Prior to 1640, the slave trade had not yet become the company's main source of profit, although the Heren XIX clearly kept a close watch over its potential advantages. The Portuguese rebellion drove them to new action, and Peg-leg Jol's capture of Luanda and São Thomé was the result. These moves secured for the Dutch the main centers for the trade in black ebony. Soon all the Portuguese holdings along the western coast of Africa were controlled by the Dutch: Luanga, Mpinda, and Calumbo.[27] These conquests solidified the

short-lived but important Atlantic empire which the Dutch put together in the middle years of the seventeenth century. The conglom-
eration was largely financed by revenues from the slave labor which
kept the New Holland and Caribbean sugar mills in operation.

Winning from the Portuguese was one thing, but competing with
the English was quite another. In this respect, the company resorted
to a practice called *claddinghe*, a term that can be compared to our
"dumping." When an English ship arrived off the African coast, the
Dutch would make every attempt to discover its contents. Good
relations with the Negroes of the area helped secure much information
when other sources failed. Once advised of the nature of the cargo,
the Dutch would immediately cut prices on all products carried by
the English. The result was that the latter, finding no buyers for their
goods, realized no profit and were forced to return home without the
usual purchases of gold, ivory, or camlet. English settlements or
trading posts in the area made desperate attempts to get hold of this
trade by imitating textiles and other products of Dutch industry.
They even hired former WIC employees in efforts to discover the
secrets of the Dutch success in Africa. None of these measures were
effective. The Dutch secured themselves by stationing ships and
yachts at strategic points of the coast and added to their good reputation by offering Negro rulers advantageous treaties. As Donnan
observes, these tactics gave the Negroes some sort of assurance against
attack, something they did not get from either the Portuguese or the
English. Such guaranteed continuous and harmonious trade relations accomplished the ends of the West India Company in West
Africa.[28]

The empire created by the Dutch on both sides of the Atlantic
had its economic basis—as the Heren XIX had hoped—in the profits
from the slave trade as well as in the products obtained with slave
labor in the American dependencies of the company. In 1641, Jol's
capture of Luanda and São Thomé had helped such a profitable arrangement, although the great toll illness took of the victors led the
Dutch to refer to similar ventures in the future as *santome* enterprises.
By adopting the Portuguese slave-acquisition procedures, which have
been vividly described by Boxer, the Dutch came to depend on loyal
Negroes to hunt down and enslave the blacks of the interior. The
captured slaves were then marched to the coast in flying columns to
be guarded in large buildings pending their embarkation. They would
usually arrive in poor physical condition because of the hundreds of
miles that they had been forced to travel with little food or rest. This
state of affairs did not alter when the Dutch supplanted the Portuguese

in one fort or trading post after another: the Elmina Castle, Axem, Luanda, Benguela, São Thomé, and Anstrom.

Life in these coastal settlements was difficult for everyone. Dutch journals from the period reveal how WIC employees struggled against tropical diseases, the unaccustomed heat, and unfriendly competitors. The never-satiated greed of the Negro chiefs was a constant complaint, along with the need to undercut English, Swedish, and Danish companies. Other problems arose from the blackmail practices directed against the Portuguese planters of São Thomé, the troubles with Negro tribes, the cruel disciplinary punishments meted out to their own soldiers, plus the usual drunkeness, prostitution, and consequently outraged sermons of Dutch Reformed preachers.[29]

However uncomfortable it may have been for the Dutch, their complaints fade into nothingness when compared to the situation of the blacks awaiting shipment to colonies in the New World. Although well fed, because they brought better prices if they looked healthy, they were confused and afraid and often victims of suicide on board the ships. Soon the "midpassage" had become notorious, since the ships were without exception overcrowded, and the average death rate by suicide and sickness was extremely high. A few authors have outdone each other in describing the wretched journey, with its cramped quarters—less than the space in a coffin for each slave—and heartless treatment. The fact that agents of the Royal African Company were permitted to purchase slaves on their own account, transport them in their own ships, and then market them privately abroad further aggravated the already apallingly high mortality rate at sea.[30] The Dutch West India Company, which charged captains according to the size of their ships—not the number of slaves each carried—did nothing to relieve the plight of the transported Negro either.

Dutch trade on the West African coast was conducted with ships of three hundred to four hundred tons, which were especially fitted out for these kinds of transactions.[31] Various types were used—frigates, flyboats, snows, barks, and others—and all were provided with guns as were merchantmen. Indeed, guns were essential equipment aboard the slave ships since there was always a chance of rebellion. Many such ships made triangle voyages. They brought trinkets, the so-called *cargazoenen*, from the United Provinces to Africa's slave markets and traded for Negroes. The slave cargoes, the so-called *armazoenen*, were then carried across the Atlantic and sold in Brazil or in the Caribbean for local products on a barter basis: sugar, tobacco, hides, coffee, cacao, and wood. In turn, they sailed back to Europe, where these cargoes were sold for hard cash.

The first stop on such a voyage from the Low Countries was usually the Elmina Castle. Ships spent some eight to ten weeks in the vicinity, cruising along the neighboring coast where they unloaded cargoes, disembarked soldiers and other personnel destined for the settlements and trading posts, and refreshed. They then took aboard slaves, soldiers whose tour of duty had expired, and passengers en route to the New World or to Europe. Dropping anchor at the second African stop, São Thomé or São Paulo de Luanda, the ship would receive another precious load of living cargo, sometimes together with sugar or cotton. At other times, the ship would wait for slaves at several trading posts on the Angola coast.

If the ship's captain did not have specific instructions, he was free to proceed to New Holland or to the Caribbean. Besides buying slaves, the colony at Pernambuco provided a valuable return cargo of sugar or wood. The route back from Brazil was generally made in convoy with other ships which thus afforded some opportunity to avoid attacks by the Dunkirk privateers. The same was true for the Caribbean. Needless to say, the ships engaged in smuggling—the *rescate*—whenever and wherever possible.

Generally, vessels of the size used to transport slaves were too large to come in very close to shore. For this purpose, the Dutch used canoes, sloops, and yachts which were especially built to accomodate their cargoes and could carry up to two hundred Negroes. Sailing up the coast until signaled from shore, these small vessels would anchor and wait for the native canoes to reach them. If the Dutch liked the proffered articles—slaves, elephant tusks, and sometimes gold—the haggling started. Brandy and tobacco rendered good service in this stage of the game. The Negro chiefs who conducted this trade were the so-called *acanists* and *pombeiros*. The former were independent traders and shrewd merchants. They tried to play off the Dutch against the English, although they usually preferred to deal with the former. The *pombeiros* were contemptuously referred to as servants of the Portuguese.

The slaves all had to be bartered for, since prices were subject to great fluctuations. Other merchandise was usually traded for gold; at São Thomé the coin of the realm was sugar. Gradually, the Dutch familiarized themselves with those products the chiefs wanted most. The following list of commodities—*formulieren van cargazoenen*—offers some interesting illustrations.[32] Bars of copper were preferred exchange items in every instance. In addition, slaves were sold at São Thomé for 1,250 to 1,500 pounds of sugar the price of which in the United Provinces was 380 to 450 guilders.[33] The items shipped to

Ardra in 1638 to barter for slaves reveal the variety of goods that tempted the Negro chiefs:

80 rolls of Indian damask of different colors at 40 gld. a roll
50 rolls of colored textiles at 10 gld.
50 rolls of striped textiles at 10 gld.
30 rolls of *slechte sloers** at 10 gld.
12 rolls of colored satin at 60 gld.
100 ells of *sloers* intertwined with gold
100 ells of *sloers* intertwined with silver
50 rolls of checkered cotton, fine quality, at 10 gld.
2000 ells of fine Dutch linen at 1 gld.
800 pieces of white *cloth* at 4½ gld. apiece
150 ells of napkin clothes at 12 nickels
400 pieces of Cyprian cloth at 4 gld.
10,000 pieces of copper bracelets at 5 nickels
150 ells of gold leather on a red and green front at 4 gld.
250 pounds of fine beads at 20 gld.
60 ounces of round, fine beads of finest quality at 6 gld. an ounce
200 pounds of cornelian, ground, at 10 gld.
600 pounds of burned beads at 15 nickels a pound
80,000 pieces of Portuguese bracelets at 4 nickels apiece
2500 pounds of red copper bars at 65 cents a pound

---

* *slechte sloers*: coarse Dutch linen.

In the thirties and forties of the seventeenth century, slave prices in Guinea varied from twelve to seventy-five guilders. In Angola the amount fluctuated between thirty-eight and fifty-five guilders. Of course, since barter was the mode of trade, the Negro agent was paid for his merchandise with articles that equaled this money value. For a male slave the following was an average price:

100 bracelets	20-40 pounds of beads
9 iron bars	4 pairs of multi-colored socks
75 knives	24 cans of oil
150 ells of linen	25 pounds of copper
1 pipe of Spanish wine	6 pieces of coarse sheeting[34]

Differences in prices were common. On the Gold Coast, around 1645, an average male slave brought twenty-three copper bars, a female eighteen, boys sixteen, and girls fourteen. At other places prices for a healthy young Negress might variously be four iron bars, ninety bracelets, or twenty-three copper bars; for a boy four iron bars, eighty bracelets, or twenty pounds of copper. A popular item in this trade was the iron bar of thirty to thirty-one pounds. An adult male slave was worth up to ten such bars, a female up to eight.

Gains must have been considerable. Since records of Dutch trade on the African coast have been lost, however, it has become almost impossible now to allocate profits. From a balance sheet of seven Dutch ships trading on the coast in 1640 and 1641, the Amsterdam Chamber calculated a loss of 165,000 guilders, but the Zeeland Chamber estimated a profit of more than 800,000 guilders. This descrepancy cannot be explained since both accounts failed to depreciate ships and buildings, or to deduct the costs of provisions and salaries. The Dutch historian Ratelband, thoroughly familiar with the slave trade, concludes that the slave traffic on the African coast provided benefits but that all of them disappeared into the bottomless pit of Brazil.[35]

It is to the WIC's credit that, once involved in the slave trade, it meticulously insisted upon good treatment for the Negroes, although it is equally true that healthy, robust slaves were worth good money. The "good treatment" began as soon as slaves came on board the ships, three hundred to four hundred at a time, and is described for posterity in the "Instruction for the Skippers in the Service of the West India Company sailing in the Slave Trade."[36] Typically, Article IV of this guide orders the captain to provide religious exercises for his human cargo. In this respect it is observed caustically that all participating in the slave trade always valued a good footing in heaven. The company also prescribed that the slaves be well fed: the regular diet of rice, bananas, and coconuts was supplemented with beans and groats, and scurvy was curbed by a daily ration of lemon juice. Meat and bacon were also daily additions to the menu. The "Instruction" even contained prohibitions against using dirty copper kettles. Article XV regulated hygiene for the slave quarters: the sprinkling of vinegar in the area, fumigating, or cleaning with juniper berries and incense. After the slaves were disembarked, their quarters were washed down with sea water. Every precaution was taken to isolate sick Negroes and to doctor them: "In terms of the sick he [the captain] shall do whatever the illness requires him to do in a proper way, showing them all love and compassion; he shall immediately separate them from the healthy ones, to prevent all kinds of discomfort." Article XXXIII strictly forbade the crew "to mix with the Negro women."[37]

In addition to requiring compulsory physical exercise at regular intervals, the company was also concerned with the mental health of the slaves. Wooden drums were carried aboard in order to keep the slaves in buoyant spirits and to de-emphasize the sorrowful nature of their bondage. Father Rinchon reports that Negroes danced and sang after their meals "in order to prevent them from giving way to melancholy."[38] The slaves were also encouraged or forced to perform certain tasks aboard ship.

The need for slaves in the Dutch settlements in the Caribbean was never as great as the demand in New Holland before 1645. In the Caribbean, the demand did increase rapidly, however, following the change from a tobacco to a sugar economy, especially because of the many needs of the French, English, and Spanish colonies in the area. But Brazil was the main market for slaves in the years of Dutch occupation. After the conquest of the Angola ports, Count Johan Maurits reported to Their High Mightinesses that Brazil alone could absorb fifteen thousand slaves annually, at a profit to the company of more than two million guilders. The Dutch directors on the West Coast estimated unrealistically, however, that the benefits would be even higher at six million guilders. A proposed account of what the company was expected to net in the slave trade after the capture of Luanda is provided in the following example:

Purchase of 15,000 Negroes at ƒ 50 each	ƒ 750,000
Victuals for 6 months at ƒ 5 per month	ƒ 405,000
30 ships for transportation at ƒ 10,000	ƒ 300,000
Possible losses: 1000 blacks at ƒ 300 ea.	ƒ 300,000
	ƒ 1,755,000
1500 men, soldiers, ammunition, etc.	ƒ 582,000
	ƒ 2,337,000
Sold at ƒ 300 apiece	ƒ 4,500,000
Net gain for the company	ƒ 2,163,000[39]

Although many figures for the slave trade from Angola are no longer extant, Wätjen mentions that from 1636 to 1645 some 23,163 slaves were sold at Pernambuco for a total of 6,715,000 guilders.[40] As Boxer observes, these amounts represent an enormous windfall on paper, since these slaves were purchased for trifling goods worth only twelve to seventy-five guilders per man. Yet these same slaves were later sold for two hundred to eight hundred guilders each.[41] They were needed on the sugar plantations, and planters paid for them—on credit—with pledges against the next sugar harvest. Unfortunately, however, the figures fail to account for the large number of creditor defaults and consequent losses to the company. An estimate from 1644 claims that the company realized 840,000 guilders annually in the slave trade, but Boxer, correctly, doubts the reliability of the figure.

Meanwhile, the cry for slave labor swelled even more mightily in the Caribbean. Van Walbeeck encouraged the importation of Negroes to Curaçao. A request of 1639 to allow some slaves who had been delivered to this island to be transferred to St. Christopher may be regarded as the first attempt to supply slaves to the Caribbean from Curaçao.[42] By this time, too, the agenda of the Heren xix begins to be marked by frequent references to the slave trade—*de slaeffsche handel*—as an item of discussion. The deliberations concerned "how this trade could be maintained for the best service of the company and to the exclusion of all foreign nations."[43]

Tolck, van Walbeeck's successor, continued to encourage the delivery of Negroes to Curaçao. Perhaps his suggestions led the Chamber of Zeeland to its decision in 1641 "concerning the capture of blacks in the West Indies which had to be brought to Curaçao."[44] Its resolution provided that each company-commissioned Dutch captain in the Caribbean was required to deposit all his captured slaves on Curaçao and to sell them to the government for sixty-five guilders. Under no circumstances could a sale be made to anyone else. Payment was made in Amsterdam two months after the Zeeland Chamber received confirmation of purchases from the Curaçao director.

The idea of making Curaçao into a slave depot was also evident in a memorial to the xix in 1642 that discussed "how and in what way the trade of Negroes from Luanda to Curaçao should be directed."[45] Considerable interest was expressed in making Curaçao the chief provider of black laborers for the entire Caribbean. This suggestion was acted on by Peter Stuyvesant despite the xix's reluctance and Zeeland's curt remark that Brazil was the place for Angola's slaves and that "the island of Curaçao was totally unsuited."[46] A request to the xix at that time for the delivery of two hundred to three hundred slaves to St. Eustatius and St. Croix was given to the commissioners for the slave trade, but its results are not known.

A remarkable report from a virtual unknown, Arnout van Liebergen, had much to do with enhancing Curaçao's importance in this respect. Van Liebergen, with or without having lived on Africa's west coast, claimed after a visit to New Netherland in 1642 that Curaçao was the natural site for the sale of slaves to all the countries which operated in the Caribbean.[47] Resistance to this plan arose from the satisfaction with the triangle trade that provided sugar and brazil-wood as return cargoes from Brazil. Making Curaçao a slave depot, some argued, was also tantamount to asking Spain to mount a concerted effort to recapture the island. Van Liebergen, however, predicted the correct outcome of the matter; because the Spaniards needed slaves, they made overtures to the Dutch at Curaçao to supply this black ebony. Furthermore, the soon-to-be-critical situation in Brazil only contributed to the reality of van Liebergen's suggestions.

Fig. 11. Arms of Cornelis Lampsins

Fig. 12. Jacob Binckes by Nicolaes Maes

The Dutch had wrestled the West African coast from the Portuguese precisely for slaves. And they maintained a successful competition against the English in the trade, and continued to resist the infringements of Englishmen, Danes, and Swedes. When the situation turned critical in Brazil, moreover, the WIC possessions in Africa became correspondingly more important. And, if peace with Spain were a foreseeable certainty, the slave trade stood out as the one secure source of revenue still at the disposal of the WIC. A "point of deliberation" from a meeting of the Heren XIX in 1645 regarded the slave trade as "the soul of the Company" and its decline would cause "the ruin of the Company." This statement was made five years after the WIC's last effort to capture a Spanish treasure fleet. The realization had finally come that privateering did not pay. Since slave trading did, however, a transition in emphasis soon took place within the company.

But before this change was complete, the slave trade became an issue in discussions over free trade and monopoly which racked the company in the late 1630's. In October, 1639, Zeeland professed herself aghast at the possibility of removing the slave trade monopoly. Four years later, two directors of the Amsterdam Chamber—one of whom was Ioannes de Laet—alluded to a possible expansion of the trade in blacks. But Dutch officials in Africa steadfastedly opposed breaking their monopoly and were ardent supporters of Zeeland's unflinching stand in this matter.[48] In March, 1644, when rumors circulated that the Amsterdam Chamber had permitted private merchants in Angola to deal in slaves, the Zeelanders carried a motion that such trade should not be allowed to take root outside the company.[49]

The issue, however, was far from settled, and it continued to plague the meetings of the XIX for years to come. Even as late as 1662, just prior to the granting of an *asiento* to Grillo and Lomelino, the opening or closing of the *slaeffsche handel* appeared on the agenda.[50] The large profits which were secured under the mentioned *asiento* decided the company once again in favor of maintaining the monopoly.

The fall of Luanda to the Portuguese in 1648, and the loss of New Holland in 1654, led the XIX to delay no longer in establishing Curaçao as a slave depot. A proposal to use this colony "for the pursuance of the slave trade" met with quick approval.[51] The island's brisk business in slaves now increased as Dutch refugees from Brazil settled in the Caribbean and transformed the Lesser Antilles into sugar-producing islands. The major result was that for the last two decades of its existence, the WIC was almost exclusively a slave-trading operation.

Very soon, however, the company had to face determined competition from British Jamaica. For some time, despite this rivalry, the Dutch had been able to meet the demand for slaves at better prices. Difficulties were intensified, however, as some English governors attempted to enforce the Navigation Laws. Stuyvesant tried, in vain, to effect the release of eight captured Dutch ships and even paid a personal visit to the governor of Barbados. But all the while, the Dutch were busily engaged in supplying slaves to all the English colonies. In 1640 Barbados only had a few hundred slaves; by 1651 when the Navigation Laws were issued, these had grown to twenty thousand. The eleven-year increase must be attributed mainly to the Dutch. By 1666 there were more than fifty thousand Negro slaves on the island, but by then the Dutch were no longer the sole and probably not even the chief supplier.[52] The same developments, although on a smaller scale, occurred in the other English Antilles and also in the French islands.

At this point it should not be forgotten that slavery was never limited to the Negro race. There were also white slaves on English islands, the so-called indentured servants and many transported Irish after Cromwell's drastic purges. Burns cites an instance in which the Dutch sold as slaves in Barbados fifty Portuguese who had been captured in Brazil. These men were released, however, by the governor who was shocked by the sale of white, Christian men. About that same time, 1643, Count Johan Maurits ordered the arrest of Jan Maxvelt who had "brought...a few Brazilians from the Maranhâo and sold them as slaves on the islands."[53] Maxvelt was shipped to the Low Countries, bound over the Zeeland Chamber, and held for prosecution.

In the early years of their involvement in the slave trade, moreover, the Dutch lured Indians from the Greater and Lesser Antilles aboard their boats for the express purpose of selling them as slaves. When word of this practice spread, the Dutch soon found their Indian allies alarmed and suspicious. Peter Stuyvesant, not long after he was appointed governor of the Curaçao islands, complained to the Zeeland Chamber of the company "that some tradesmen had made the Wild Coast very unfree and were making the Indians—by force and molestation which they inflict—very adverse from sympathizing with us."[54] It may have been this charge that prompted the Zeeland Chamber to adopt a resolution which forbade the unauthorized seizure of Indians and requested that the XIX take measures to prevent such actions as "not only unchristian but also to the great disadvantage of the company."[55] Similar decisions followed in 1645 when the commander of St. Eustatius was reported to be commissioning ships in order to capture Indians on the Wild Coast for his personal gain. Allowing such action to be repeated would, it was stated, "make the aforesaid coast so unfree that no one would dare to come aboard any more."[56] In addition, coastal trade with the Indians had also suffered.

It also appears that the English governor of St. Christopher, Sir Thomas Warner, was not altogether innocent of Indian hunting. A resolution of the Zeeland Chamber of February 2, 1645, mentions a commission to a Dutch captain written in English that authorized the bearer to seize Indians for sale as slaves. This permit stipulated that such captives were to be taken under the Dutch flag.[57] The position taken by the XIX against Indian slavery, however, seems to have been sufficiently severe to discourage any such further activity.

Although Spain and the United Provinces remained at war until 1648, trade between the combatants continued to be conducted through the usual channels. With Curaçao as a base, the Dutch soon became the major suppliers of slaves to Tierra Firme; indeed, after 1640, slaves were the most important item of the *rescate*. The Dutch exchanged them for hides, tobacco, cacao, and wood. Figures on this illicit trade are, of course, not available, but it is well known that after 1648 there was a noteworthy increase. The Spanish colonists cooperated fully in the illicit traffic, as is illustrated by a letter written by the Spanish ambassador in The Hague to the Council of the Indies; it included a copy of an agreement between a named Spaniard and four Dutchmen for the delivery of eight hundred Negro slaves. This Dutch instrusion into Spanish exclusivism, which was hardly a novelty, was not allowed to pass unnoticed, and the governors of Tierra Firme were soon alerted.[58]

But the Crown's impotence against the *rescate* is evident in the very plethora of prescriptions against it. On the whole, Spanish policy continued to be unrealistic. After the Portuguese had won their political independence—and lost their *asientos*—the Spanish colonists in the Caribbean had either to rely on foreign traders or else witness the decline and subsequent ruin of their sugar industry. Spain could not provide them with slaves. Her officials, high and low, recognized this fact, and it made them more willing to accept foreign bribes. They were thus steadily corrupted by the "winepots" of the Dutch when each new royal cedula against the *rescate* met with a new rain of Dutch gold. These were the circumstances that explain how Matthias Beck could so openly discuss with Stuyvesant his dealings for the regulation of trade between Curaçao and Venezuela. Although the governor of the Spanish colony lacked the courage to make a formal treaty, he did agree to an unofficial arrangement. The only future problem was that Curaçao could never quite meet Venezuela's demands for provisions and slaves.

As negotiations for peace with Spain reached the final stages in Westphalia, the XIX sent a "Short Remonstrance"[59] to the States General asking that they stipulate a free slave trade to the Spanish Indies. They also suggested that the diplomats at Munster require Spain to turn over Puerto Rico to the Dutch as a second depot for the slave trade. Puerto Rico, the company claimed, was of little value to the Spanish, but an "inestimable treasure" to the Dutch; its fertility exceeded that of Surinam, and it would be easy to colonize. The island could also supply slaves to all the Greater as well as the Lesser Antilles. Surely Boudewijn Hendricksz rejoiced in his Edam grave at this outrageous request. So far as is known, however, the question was never posed at Munster since the Dutch diplomats there had more sense than the Heren XIX.

The traffic between Curaçao and the Tierra Firme was conducted mostly in ships under the Spanish flag. Partly, of course, this was done to save appearances, but it was largely due to the fact that the sailing was done by Spaniards, albeit under Dutch sponsors. During the 1660's, when the English represented the greatest danger and the Spaniards had already acquiesced in their dependence on the Dutch for slaves, Spanish authorities in the area requested that the WIC conduct the trade under the Dutch flag.[60]

Generally speaking, the Dutch and the Spaniards cooperated very closely in these ventures. But again no figures exist on the extent of this trade nor on the precise amount of Dutch profit. Nevertheless, in this period in which no official *asiento* was granted, no Spanish colonists are known to have complained about a lack of slaves until Grillo and Lomelino took over. After that, the outcries are easily understood since these two Genoese intended to purchase slaves only from English and Dutch sources, which added a link in the trade chain, increased prices, and complicated the entire matter.

The Dutch-Portuguese war of the 1650's was actually more of a contest between each country's commissioned privateers than one fought by the respective parties' armed forces. As a patriotic gesture, the XIX agreed to open Curaçao to Dutch privateers who had captured Portuguese prizes with slaves aboard. The captured Negroes were to be sold on the island at a price of 150 guilders for each man or woman between the ages of fifteen and thirty-five. Those who were younger and older than the desired ages would be gotten rid of at the bargain rate of three for the price of two. The attractive part of this concession for the privateer was that the governor of Curaçao was authorized to pay hard cash for the slaves so long as his funds lasted. Otherwise, the privateers could always present their bills, as usual, in Amsterdam.[61]

The prices which were offered at Curaçao under this emergency measure were, incidentally, much lower than the actual market value of slaves. In 1659 a WIC ship that was carrying slaves to Curaçao was stranded on one of the Roque reefs. An English frigate, cruising in the neighborhood, was able to capture the cargo of forty-eight Negroes, and swiftly made for the home colonies. Dutch merchants claimed a loss of 84,000 guilders, or 175 guilders for each of the lost slaves.[62] On the other hand a letter from Peter Stuyvesant to the XIX reveals that New Netherland buyers were only spending 140 to 150 guilders for each slave, but that these were deficient Negroes, the so-called *mancarrons*.[63] Although Beck continued to send Stuyvesant these inferior slaves in order that the fortifications of New Amsterdam might be completed, the *mancarrons* did not save the town. It surrendered to the English in 1664.

In its arrangements with colonial patrons, the WIC ordinarily undertook to furnish the necessary slaves for agricultural cultivation. In the patent of Abraham van Pere, for instance, the following statement occurs: "The Company shall take pains to provide the colonists with as many Negroes as shall be possible, on condition that it receive therefore as above, namely, two and one-half fares [?] without its being required to clothe them after having delivered them over."[64] Although the company could not always meet these obligations, it continued to contract for them. In another grant, to David Nassy and partners dated September 12, 1659, the stipulation appears that "They [the colonists] shall also be given by the Company such number of slaves as may be required from time to time, in accordance with the orders and regulations made or to be made by the XIX."[65]

While not much is known about the actual delivery of slaves to colonists, we do have access to the text of an original contract that was, no doubt, repeated again and again between different parties with only minor changes. This "Rule in What Manner and Condition the Negroes shall Bee Delivered in the Wilde Coast" is sufficiently curious to be reproduced here:

1. That there shall be delivered in the said cust soe many negroes as each shall have occasion for, The which shall be paide heere, shewing the Receipt, in ready money at one hundred and fifty guilders for each man or woman.

2. Children from eight to twelve years thei shall counte two for one piece, under the eight years three for one the breeding goeth with the mother.

3. Hee that shall advance the Paiment beefore the Receipt comes shall enjoy the discounte of Tenn £cent.

4. To all them that shall Paye and buy for Ready mony if thei will thei shall have sutch number of negroes Trusted to Pay wichin five years and after them shall Pay for each man, whoman or child as above the sume of two hundred and fifty and he that shall advance the Payment shall have discount of Tenn Per Cent a yeare and them shall buy for ready money shall bee ingaged for the Paiment of the others.[66]

In such contracts, it is not always clear who was supposed to deliver the slaves to whom. An agreement of January 25, 1658, with David Nassy, for instance, "in pursuance of which he was to transport to Nova Zeelandia several hundred slaves"[67] would seem to suggest that some party other than the company was involved. The documents in the archives, however, also provide evidence that the company was so charged. One thing is certainly clear: Nassy never delivered a single slave to the colonists.

The excellent terms of the above and similar contracts induced such men as Otto Keye, an ardent colonist, to advertise the Wild Coast widely. After some calculations that are difficult to follow in his publication of 1659, Keye advises prospective colonists that emigrating to New Netherland will cost them 1,850 guilders. Surinam, however, would be available to those who wish to go for only 611 guilders. Nor does the blandishment end there: for those colonists who start out with five thousand guilders, Keye estimates their net gain for the first few years after their departure. The rosy prospect for making a fortune in Surinam is as follows:

Said colonist must begin by purchasing 30 slaves at 125 guilders each. This means an initial investment of 3750 guilders. Each slave can make fifteen nickels per day for his master, but taking into account other factors the average may be safely set at ten nickels a day—five days a week—and at the end of the first year said colonist has gained a profit of 3900 guilders in tobacco, indigo and cotton.

The master next invests the profit in the purchase of twenty additional slaves. With fifty slaves, at the beginning of the third year he has a profit of 5850 guilders. He now uses this to buy thirty-two more slaves and the equipment with which he can convert to sugar cane.

At the beginning of the fourth year said colonist has netted a profit of 8450 guilders. He uses this to buy an additional forty slaves and to build a sugar mill. At the beginning of the fifth year, with 122 slaves, his profit has risen to 13,910 guilders. The next year will net 21,190 guilders, and the potential continues to rise as each year passes.[68]

Unfortunately for all concerned, the realities of life on the Wild Coast were never so good.

About the middle of the seventeenth century, slavery gained momentum in the Caribbean as the area was transformed from tobacco to sugar production. Although this was true for all colonies, the Dutch first realized the importance of slavery to the new economy, and were prepared to deliver slaves on demand and at better prices. There are simply no extant figures on the number of slaves transported and sold. What does remain, however, are some ideas and facts about Dutch commercial practice. In the 1650's they supplied slaves and other commodities on credit and were willing to wait for payment until harvest time. In the sixties and seventies they discovered to their dismay that they had sown for others to reap.

In the Caribbean, the Dutch had English competition to face, of course, but they also encountered rivalry from companies that had been founded in other countries but operated with Dutch capital, ships, sailors, and experience. One remarkable case in point was the Swedish company, one of the WIC's greatest trials on the Guinea coast. The creation of this institution had been inspired by William Usselinx during his voluntary exile. Although the Netherlands had ignored him and denied him a seat on the XIX, the court of Gustavus Adolphus honored and heeded him. The Dutch were in the unenviable position of wishing, on the one hand, to maintain good relations with the nation which had been at one point the foremost defender of Protestantism in the seventeenth century. On the other hand they also wanted to forestall Swedish activity in Africa. An endless correspondence between the officials of the Dutch and Swedish companies is testimony to the WIC's dilemma.

Danes also appeared on the African coast where, in 1642, they established themselves by force. They were soon to be joined by the French. Richelieu and Mazarin had revived Henry IV's colonial policy while compromising French strength in their titanic struggle with the House of Hapsburg. There was also the English Guinea or African Company, which had been organized in 1630. All of these competitors were sources of consternation for the Dutch, although none of them was really a particular danger except for the Royal African Company in the sixties. By that time, however, the WIC was in such financial straits that it could no longer adequately defend itself, let alone drive off competitors.

Far more harmful to the company, indeed, even in its years of power, were the so-called *lorredraaiers*—the Dutch interlopers on the company's monopoly. These men sailed and traded from Africa to

America with impunity—i.e., in slaves—and they never, of course, paid the WIC its "recognitions," the fees which had been granted to the company in its charter. Violations of these provisions were reported to the XIX—and through them to the States General—as early as 1624. In the ensuing fifty years this illicit traffic never abated. The company repeatedly indicated that piracy against Spain was one thing, piracy against the WIC was something altogether different. Yet such dodging was difficult to prove and thus went largely unchecked.

Dutch participation in the slave trade presented Spain with a curious dilemma. Slaves were urgently necessary in Spanish America, yet slaves could be had in satisfactory quantities only through the cooperation of the WIC—back of which stood the government of the United Provinces. Spain's problem was to prevent squabbles between *asentistas* and the West India Company from becoming questions of state between Spain and the United Provinces, the latter a country which was now too powerful to be safely irritated. The Council of the Indies undertook to solve the dilemma.[69]

In 1662 an *asiento* was concluded with the Genoese commercial house of Domingo Grillo and Ambrosio Lomelino. The agreement caused considerable dissatisfaction in Spanish America when it became known that the new concessionaires had no intentions of getting slaves from Africa. They fully intended to buy slaves from Dutch and English sources and simply resell them. For this purpose an agent was soon established in Curaçao. In this instance, contrary to normal Spanish practice, the firm of Grillo and Lomelino had won for itself the exclusive right to procure and sell slaves in the Spanish colonies in America. The Council of the Indies had hoped to limit smuggling in this way, but, of course, nothing of the sort happened. In fact, the *asiento* limited the number of ships that could be used, and thus curtailed the transport of other commodities to the Spanish colonists. Fewer ships also meant that the slaves were crowded even more than they had been heretofore.

As anticipated, the delivery of the slaves was actually undertaken by the WIC and the Royal African Company. The latter had been reorganized to supply slaves to the English colonies, but its regular financial crises drove it to consort with Grillo and Lomelino. Charles II, who was a shareholder, in order to make an agreement easier for the Spaniards, permitted a dispensation of the Navigation Laws for Spanish ships in the Caribbean whose purpose was to purchase slaves. This measure met with no success. Spain needed neither Jamaica nor the English to supply her colonies with black laborers "being so plentifully and cheaply supplied with Negroes by the Genoese who had contracted to supply them with twenty-four thousand Negroes in seven years."[70] These 24,000 slaves were first delivered by the Dutch to Curaçao "on which cursed little barren island they have now 1500 or 2000."[71]

The Dutch were blessed with the lion's share of the slave business in Spanish America. The Spanish government, however, which was deluged with protests over the prices charged for slaves by Grillo and Lomelino, tried in vain to force the *asentista* to procure his slaves directly from Africa. Such insistence was understandably ignored, and Curaçao remained for many years to come the main source of supply for the Caribbean area. In 1667 Charles II again vainly attempted to get a share of the business for himself.

In 1668 Grillo and Lomelino contracted to supply 3,500 slaves annually to the Caribbean. At the same time, they subcontracted with the WIC for the delivery of two thousand slaves at Curaçao. This arrangement guaranteed the WIC a secure position in the slave trade with the Spanish colonies. The following year the contract was renewed, and the number raised to four thousand slaves. The Spanish government continued to protest against the *asentista*'s purchase of slaves from the island and created difficulties—although the documents do not reveal of what character—that seemed to have jeopardized the slave trade via Curaçao.

In 1670, because of the gradual insolvency of Grillo and Lomelino, the *asiento* was awarded to a Portuguese, Antonio Garcia, whose contract called for the delivery of four thousand slaves per year for five years. He was, of course, fully expected to procure slaves from the Portuguese colonies in Africa. But Garcia, contrary to all expectations, bought them instead at Curaçao from the WIC.[72] Although he lost his concession temporarily to Grillo and Lomelino, two years later it was renewed, and the wily Portuguese resumed his purchases from the Dutch. Indeed, so dependent was he upon Curaçao and the WIC that his new *asiento* stipulated relief by half of his obligation should Spain go to war with the United Provinces. Despite the complex war situation in those years, the WIC promised and fulfilled its annual slave quota.

Dutch influence is particularly apparent during the Garcia *asiento*. While throughout the Genoese tenure, a Portuguese agent had been residing in Amsterdam, under the Garcia concession two Amsterdam merchants, Balthasar and Joseph Cooymans, acted as bankers and representatives of the *asiento* for the Portuguese principal. Because of the fact that Balthasar Cooymans was later able to overcome Spanish reluctance and win the *asiento* for himself, there is even reason to believe that the Garcia concession of 1675 was financed by Dutch capital and that the *asiento* actually came into Dutch hands this same year—Garcia simply posing as the concessionaire. The acquisition of the *asiento* placed the Dutch first in the slave trade, and from that time on, both the Portuguese and the English shrank in importance as competitors.[73]

Curaçao thus became the most important slave depot and the principal market for slaves throughout the Caribbean. A warehouse for the black ebony was built there which, by 1668, housed three thousand Negroes for immediate delivery. After that the wic was virtually reduced to a slave trade organization, "by curtailment and reduction of which [the slave trade] the ruin of the company was caused."[74]

Some evidence for the development of this trade, and its importance to the company, appears in the 1669 and 1670 agreements to provide 9,000 slaves for a promised 2,400,000 guilders.[75] It was, of course, not purely profit. Besides, the slaves had to be fed during their stay at Curaçao, which required considerable sums. To care for these expenses, the *asentista*, Grillo and Lomelino at that time, placed several thousand guilders in trust at Willemstad.

The continuing importance of the trade is also illustrated by a contract of 1683; in this case, the wic guaranteed the provision of eighteen thousand slaves over the ensuing six years. At Curaçao only 600 slaves were employed in agriculture, and 1,800 in domestic services. The bulk of those arriving at the island were for sale to non-Dutch markets in the Caribbean.

At Willemstad on Curaçao, an "agent-general" of the *asiento*, as he styled himself, soon became a well-known figure. His main task was to function as a middle-man between the *asentista* and the xix. Balthasar Beck, the lieutenant-governor of the island under Stuyvesant, was such an agent, as were many directors of the colony in later years. No better evidence is needed to prove that there was no official opposition to the slave trade nor any attempt to discredit such an enterprise as beneath the company's dignity.

Any ship involved in the slave trade, however, had to have a license. Under no circumstance was the company going to abridge its monopoly on black ebony, and even after the loss of Luanda, there was no change in policy. Its officials there simply moved their headquarters to the island of Annabón. Slave traders filled out and signed the following form in order to qualify for a license:

In the way and on the conditions explained hereafter, the commissioned Directors of the Chartered West India Company on one side and .... on the other side have agreed and pacted that the said Directors accept to have ready the ship named .... on which is Skipper .... to send this, with the first favorable weather and wind to the coast of Africa; with special promise and agreement that if it arrives safely there, to permit the Skipper, the Clerk or other officials of the WIC to purchase and embark in said ship the quantity of .... Negroes from Ardra, Boche or Angola, men and women, young or as old as can be purchased; with which quantity of Negroes said ship will sail away (but will be allowed to touch and drop anchor at any place as might be judged necessary and expedient for refreshment) to Curaçao where, having arrived, the Skipper or Clerk will acknowledge his arrival to ....[76] who have agreed to said contract to have them (the Negroes) received or taken over from said Skipper or Clerk of the said ship within a period of 15 days after their arrival, under penalty of laying each day thereafter one piece of eight daily for every deliverable Negro brought with the aforesaid ship.[77]

A slave ship was authorized by this form to transport commodities to Africa and trade them for slaves. In an account given by the director-general at Ardra similar to the one given before, it is possible to extract the main kinds of commodities used in this exchange, largely those which have been mentioned earlier. Also evident is the amount the WIC paid in the sixties for its slaves, an average of thirty-seven guilders and eighteen cents. A contract made by the Zeeland Chamber calls for a price per slave of forty-four to forty-eight guilders. There is some evidence, moreover, that on occasion, the rate dropped to thirty guilders.[78]

The contracts between the WIC and the *asentistas* stipulated a price of $107\frac{1}{2}$ pieces of eight for a mentally and physically healthy slave between the ages of fifteen and thirty-six. By estimating a piece of eight at 50 nickels and a guilder at 20, the price per slave becomes approximately 270 guilders. When compared with the purchase costs just mentioned, an enormous profit seems certain, even if one takes into account that the slaves had to be fed, that crews had to be paid, and that ships had to be purchased. From the expense account of a particular vessel destined for Ardra with a crew of twenty-seven men one can obtain the following figures:[79]

Purchase of 450 slaves		ƒ 14,500
Supplies for 27 men for 15 months	ƒ 2971,16	
Expenses for barrels, casks, etc.	ƒ 185, 4	
	ƒ	3157
Supplies for 450 Negroes for 3 months	ƒ 2640	
Expenses for barrels, casks, etc.	ƒ 2308, 4	
Labor	ƒ 101,16	

Various expenses, medicine, fire wood,
   etc.   ƒ 1300
Two months pay in advance for crews ƒ 1070
                       ƒ   7420

                                           ƒ 10,577
                                           ƒ 25,077

If this trip from the United Provinces via Ardra to Curaçao and back occupied all of 15 months, additional pay for the crew of 6,955 guilders would have to be included. Total expenses for buying and delivering of 450 slaves, then, would come to around 32,000 guilders, or less than 73 guilders per slave. To this one would have to add such overhead and fixed costs as ships, buildings, and fortresses with their garrisons. This would raise the cost per slave to at least one hundred guilders. On paper, this figure still would leave the company a net gain of 170 or more guilders per slave, although loss of life in "midpassage" regularly reduced the profit by 25 per cent. By considering the company's expenditures in Africa and Curaçao, the amount per slave is further reduced to such an extent that one might well question whether any profit was realized.

Company shares in 1650—at the low level of 15 per cent—speak more eloquently to this question than do any other statistics. Moreover, slave ships occasionally became floating coffins. On one shipment in 1664, 471 slaves were originally purchased; of these, 419 never reached Curaçao because of illness during the Atlantic crossing.[80] Although such drastic figures are not common, they cannot be disregarded.

Before the second Anglo-Dutch war, it appears that some English slave traders also brought their black cargo to Curaçao. The XIX, however, had some misgivings about this kind of cooperation with a probable enemy, and as tensions mounted between the two countries, the directors advised Beck to disallow English slave ships in the port. This instruction was presumably also directed against some others; in 1657, on behalf of the Swedish Africa Company, Laurens de Geer had contracted with three Amsterdam merchants to transport five hundred to six hundred slaves from Guinea to Curaçao. This kind of arrangement may also have been ended by the letter to Beck, but on the other hand, it may have been tolerated by the monopolistic WIC since so large a part of Swedish trade was in Dutch hands and was financed by Dutch capital.

The island of Curaçao, as noted earlier, was under the special direction of the Amsterdam Chamber. It was this chamber, therefore, that concluded contracts with the *asentistas*. Africa, however, which provided the slaves, was under the executive control of the XIX who thus had to be consulted on all matters concerning the slave trade. But evidence of mutual concord is provided by the first contract with Grillo and Lomelino which stipulated, "The Directors who signed acted not only as members of the Chamber of Amsterdam but mentioned at the same time that this Chamber was authorized by the XIX to conclude said contract."[81]

Contracts which were made before 1674, when the old company ended its existence, reveal many important changes over the years. The first of these, concluded in 1662, shows the directors' emphatic pledge to deliver one thousand slaves. In later contracts, however, the promises become more circumspect; they only mention the release of a sufficient number of ships to purchase and transport the four thousand slaves of the contract. If there were no Negroes available for purchase on the African coast, therefore, the company was protected. In the earlier contract, it was obligated to pay compensation in every instance.

All slaves to be put on the market had to be *leverbaar*—deliverable— which meant that they had to be physically and mentally fit. In 1662, when the Dutch were ignorant of many details of the trade, *leverbaar* had simply implied that the slave could not be blind or mutilated and had to be able to walk on board without help. In later contracts, this *leverbaar* concept was narrowed to exclude any "considerable defect" and there were specific proscriptions against slaves from Rio Calabary, Rio del Rey, and Rio Cameronis because of their poor quality. Health stipulations continued to grow even more strict; Willem Bosman in his *Accurate Description of the Gold, Ivory and Slave coasts of Guinea* observes "that slaves that had grey hair, missed a tooth or suffered from chronic diseases were 'non-deliverable.'"[82] One agreement with the *asentistas* provided that all slaves "older than forty years, sick, blind, lame or paralyzed, or that have another considerable deficiency" would be considered *mancarrons* and thus purchasable at a lower rate.[83]

Over the years, the ratio between male and female changed also. In the seventeenth century, it was usually stipulated that a delivery of slaves should be composed of 75 per cent males. Frequently, an extra premium for additional males was included in the contract. Women slaves were paid for at the same or at a slightly lower rate than men, since Negro fertility was generally thought to be high. The infant was always included with the mother at no extra price, no real bargain since the mortality rate for children below three was too high to risk money on them (see Appendix x).

At Curaçao the slaves were interned on two plantations until such time as they could be examined and removed by the agents of the *asentistas*. This procedure sometimes took several days or weeks, during which interval the company would put the Negroes to work. If the *asentista* delayed too long, the company reserved the right to sell the slaves to other buyers, although this provision, which violated the monopoly of the *asiento*, was rarely exercised. To further discourage infringements on the *asiento*, ship captains were not allowed to drop anchor in the Caribbean except in case of emergency. Yet none of these comprehensive regulations could stop the illicit traffic in slaves. Ultimately, the company resorted to branding Negroes in the possession of the inhabitants of Curaçao.[84] All slaves without a branded mark were to be confiscated and turned over to wic officials. Punishments in the form of flogging were meted out to those who attempted to counterfeit a brand. In 1668 bills of lading were introduced; these made the captains responsible for delivery under penalty of their wages, ships, and a percentage of the cargo.[85]

All these rules and precepts, unknown in 1662 but widely accepted in 1668, illustrate the difficulties experienced by the *asentistas* in implementing the monopoly which they had supposedly achieved on paper. The company, too, had its share of problems; in 1672, however, these were somewhat alleviated when the *asentista* was forced to declare the number of ships which he would have available to transport slaves from Curaçao to his markets in the Caribbean, and to promise that a said number of ships would constantly be available. Ships of the wic were often needed to fulfill his agreements.

Zeelandian ships were permitted to land slaves on Curaçao despite the rivalry at home between the Chambers of Zeeland and Amsterdam. Although the capital administered the island, the slave trade was financed until 1671 by a special fund, which was provided by the company shareholders. The profits from the trade made through these reserves were divided one-third for the participants and two-thirds for the company. Apparently a one-third profit margin was a sufficient enough lure to entice shareholders to investment. The two-thirds share, however, was not enough to save the old company from bankruptcy.

The terms of payment in the contract of 1662 stipulated that the *asentista* had to pay fifty thousand pieces of eight upon signing. The pre-payment arrangement betrays the probable need of the company for cash to execute the provisions of the contract. The *asentista* also had to guarantee the restitution of any company ship lost en route to and from Africa. In the early days the WIC's credit rating was so poor that its director's personal signatures were required in order to formalize a contract. By 1668, with the slave trade booming and a special slave fund operating, no such advances on signatures were required.

Much can be said about the treatment of slaves in Dutch colonies. Slaves were important and valuable property, and their general state of health and mental attitude were consequently matters of some concern. A slave, however, was also a possession, a *res*, not a person. A special tax, the poll tax, was soon levied on all those who owned a slave, which pertained also to import and export duties. It even became possible to mortgage slaves. Furthermore, the master was required to provide food, clothing, and shelter for his slaves. His financial position, of course, determined how well he did this and how well his slaves lived. Indeed, many times the latter's needs were the last item on the master's budget. In times of war, moreover, when food was scarce for all, the poor slave suffered first, and he was relieved last when the company's ships arrived with fresh supplies.

The Dutch almost never had equivalents to the English "indentured servants" or to the French *engagés*; color, therefore, remained the major status item in Dutch Caribbean society. A mulatto group certainly appeared, however, even in color-conscious Dutch colonies. Although there is a variety of Dutch names for such offspring,[86] a child who was born of a slave remained a slave notwithstanding the father's position. On the other hand, it is true that mulatto children received preferential treatment from their masters and were almost never used for heavy labor in the fields.

From the moment of his arrival on Dutch soil, the slave also enjoyed some rights. Primitive as it may seem today, certain legislation did exist for the slave's protection. Although few of its provisions reflect a modern social conscience, the *code pénal* for whites was not much milder. The essentially pragmatic Dutch mentality is nowhere better illustrated than in a letter from the Chamber of Amsterdam to the Director of Curaçao concerning the punishment of four Negroes who had been condemned to hanging, the loss of a hand, and internment in the gallows. The Amsterdam Chamber stoically observed in its reply: "That it would have been more convenient to inflict another punishment, not because the penalty was not in proportion to the committed offense, but because a slave, by this chastisement [of losing his right hand] was totally disabled for any service, for which purpose he is held captive and it thus becomes a burden to support him."[87]

In case circumstances demanded action that was not specifically foreseen in national legislation, company officials reverted to Roman law. This usually meant that a delinquent slave was turned over to the whims of his master. Because of the absence of any legal personality or status, moreover, a slave was always wrong vis-à-vis a white. In seventeenth-century courts, a slave could not be called upon to testify against a white even though he may have been a witness to a crime. His word had weight only against another slave. In the early days of slavery, a master could kill his slave and not fear the law. Although this discriminatory situation did change in due course, it nevertheless remains a fact that the master, when he infringed the rules, was never more than lightly punished, usually with a fine. Bodily chastisement of slaves, ordinarily in the form of a beating with a bull's pizzle, was legally unrestricted, although it was usually reserved for crimes only. A further refinement on this measure was to have the slave appear naked for his punishment and to endure the whip from his fellow slaves' hands. No real horror stories have come down to us about the Dutch colonies; no instruments of torture like the Spanish stool are documented for this area, but the fact cannot be overlooked that, even according to the yardstick of the age, the future for an erring slave looked pretty grim.

From a purely expedient standpoint, the company strove to control excesses in the treatment of slaves. It undertook although never full-heartedly to have slaves converted to Protestantism, supplied medical help, and founded hospitals. The humanity of the slaves, however, was always ignored, if not denied altogether. To complete the parallel of treating Negroes like cattle, the slaves who were branded at Curaçao carried lifelong monograms, adding letters or numbers in the case of a company slave, and a cloverleaf for others.

Dutch occupation in the Caribbean and the Guianas inevitably brought in its train the Dutch Reformed religion. In 1635, a year after Curaçao's conquest, a candidate for the ministry arrived. By 1638 an instruction for ministers was drawn up which admonished "that all pains will be taken by them to instruct the Portuguese, Spaniards, and their children in the fundamentals of the Christian religion, and also the blacks and Indians." In fact, little Negro conversion occurs in the documents of the company, as though it is repeatedly urged "that the poor and blind pagans on Curaçao should be led to the knowledge of God and their salvation." Formal counsel aside, however, the laziness and inefficiency of the clergy, combined with the prejudice of the masters at having their slaves conversant with their religion, resulted in minimal religious training for slaves.

Hamelberg writes, "The prevailing opinions on slaves were totally contrary to the idea of considering them as brothers in the Lord." What the company slurred over, few of its servants bothered themselves about. The Dutch all-consuming desire for profit left no room for any other concern. In this very respect Thomas Lynch, governor of Jamaica, concluded the case when he wrote that on Curaçao "Jesus Christ was good, but trade was better."[88]

In the Spanish colonies the Roman Catholic faith had always been an inseparable arm of the secular government. After the conquest of the Antilles and in the Guianas, the WIC disavowed this religion for the Indian populations. When increasing numbers of black slaves came to the area, however, the directors of the company, who were concerned about the fact that a huge anti-white and religiously ignorant mass was being formed, put a program of conversion into operation. The only actual religious training in this effort, though, was provided by Catholic priests. The Dutch, who generally considered the public exercise of Catholicism to be "an offense to the glory of God," were yet extremely negligent in enforcing those rules of the XIX that might have curtailed the priesthood. It is certainly true that, especially on Curaçao, there was more tolerance of Catholics than Protestants experienced in Spanish and French colonies. Commercial interest, undoubtedly, had something to do with this attitude.

The permissive atmosphere placed the Dutch colonies in an exceptional position. There were many rich Catholic merchants on the the islands as well as in the Netherlands. So long as the priests could be safely ignored, however, Dutch officials were satisfied to leave them in peace. The company and Their High Mightinesses even allowed the Roman Catholic clergy to work among the slaves and to baptize their children. Priests, however, could not solemnize marriage vows between slaves, a practice which stood in sharp contrast to Spanish tradition and legislation. Clandestine marriages were soon introduced, but, although performed in the presence of a priest, they still had no legal validity before civil authorities.

A kind of labor code was soon in existence also. A briefing from the States General to the high and low governments of the WIC contained a clause insisting "that the Negroes and slaves must be well-treated and sent at proper times, when it was the hour for church, to be admitted to the public exercise of religion and not burdened with labor on the holidays."[89] This provision was never enforced except by the Jews. Living, at the time, very closely to the letter of the law, they did not allow their slaves to work on the Sabbath in accordance with the third commandment.[90]

The real flowering of the Dutch slave trade occurred in the decades following the Peace of Nijmegen when Balthasar Cooymans obtained the *asiento* from Seville. Spanish squeamishness about the heretical Cooymans faltered and fell before the fact that the latter paid more in cash. This blustering Dutchman went so far as to agree to carry Roman Catholic missionaries to Africa to provide religious training to the slaves before they were transported to the Americas. The story of this *asiento*, however, colorful as it is, properly falls outside the scope of the present work.

15

"THAT 'SUPERB' NATION"

*The English always stay English and a change
in government does not change their mood.*
Johan de Witt[1]

The relations between the United Provinces and England, which had
been far from cordial since the Stuarts had mounted the Tudor throne,
deteriorated rapidly after Oliver Cromwell became the leader of the
island republic. Sincere or otherwise, the Protector's attempts to
effect closer political and economic ties with the Dutch, his "shortcut
to prosperity," failed miserably.[2] The Navigation Laws that were born
out of his miscalculation were the proximate cause of the first Anglo-
Dutch war, an encounter which the Dutch lost. At the same time
Cromwell initiated his great "Western Design" which was a grandiose
scheme to attack Spain in the Caribbean, but which collapsed with
the capture of Jamaica. In 1655, this island became the chief English
stronghold in the Caribbean. Although the loss was a heavy, albeit
not fatal, blow to Spain, it was also detrimental to the Dutch position
in the West Indies.

In the United Provinces it was generally feared that the long-standing Dutch trade with English colonies in the Lesser Antilles, and
especially with Barbados, could now be more effectively checked. On
the other hand, Dutch hopes rested on the fact that some of these
English islands remained royalist and thus deeply dependent on Dutch
good will and support. The faithful governors of those territories
made public pronouncements about their gratitude for Dutch help,
and the Dutch provided them with arms and ammunition in exchange
for sugar. The English planters gave assurance that the trade would
continue and claimed not to believe "our number so contemptible nor
our resolution so weak to be forced or persuaded to so ignoble a
submission" which meant, of course, acquiescence in Cromwell's
Commonwealth.[3]

For a long time, Francis Lord Willoughby, ardent royalist governor
of Barbados, resisted Cromwell's attempt on his island. He had five
thousand men to use against the one thousand sent from England on

seven men-of-war under Sir George Ayscue. One coup, however, turned the course of events against the Barbadians: a Commonwealth mission comprised of three ships succeeded in surprising and appropriating twelve Dutch ships at Carlisle Bay; the English claimed that they were violating the Navigation Laws. The Commonwealth's capture of these vessels cut off supplies to the island and, within a few months, Willoughby was forced to discuss surrender terms. His capitulation led the other royalist islands to surrender also. It should, however, be conceded that this Commonwealth victory did not exclude Dutch trade from the islands. On the contrary, the new laws were disregarded as much as possible, and this general attitude made their enforcement extremely difficult. Admiral William Penn's fleet, which arrived at Barbados in 1655 just after the first Anglo-Dutch conflict, found several Dutch ships conducting trade there.[4]

The conquest and consolidation of Jamaica, although it fell short of Cromwell's pretentious plans, did eventually result in England's determination to control commerce to and from English colonies. Jamaica was to become the spearhead of competition with the Dutch in the Caribbean. Although this fierce mercantile process took more than half a century, it did succeed in the end. English intentions were already clear in Cromwell's instructions to Penn. The admiral was authorized to seize any and all foreign ships that arrived to trade with the English colonies.[5] What Cromwell failed to understand was that the islands, in the throes of transforming themselves from tobacco to sugar production, desperately needed Dutch machinery and African slaves in order to survive. Further attempts to curtail Dutch trade resulted in the latter gaining surreptitious commissions as "English ships" from colonial sympathizers in the British Isles.[6]

Cromwell's shortcut to prosperity was an engaging project that required Dutch cooperation. But it floundered on the States General's reluctance to make the United Provinces a sloop behind the English man-of-war. Although the Protector's successors, the restored Stuarts, tried once more to effect the same goal, their efforts were quite different from Cromwell's. The primary authors in this new bid to dislodge the Dutch from their advantageous and strategic positions on Africa's west coast, in the Caribbean, and in New Netherland were Charles II, his crypto-Catholic brother James, Duke of York, and their cousin Rupert, son of the "Winter King." All three had every reason to be grateful to the government of the United Netherlands for their long and comfortable exile in that country. None of them, however, once he had risen to power in England, deigned to cooperate with his former benefactor.[7] Years of experience had merely confirmed the belief that the United Provinces would endure a great deal politically so long as their profitable trade was not encroached upon.

As early as 1630 a British Guinea Company had been granted certain rights by the English government in the principle slave area of Africa. This company failed, however, largely through Dutch "dumping" practices combined with the latter's strong position on Africa's west coast. In the 1650's, when the English Antilles converted to sugar production and the need for slaves grew by leaps and bounds, the English Navigation Laws closed the islands in the Caribbean to Dutch slave traders. This maneuver satisfied no one except Cromwell, since it deprived the Dutch of profits and the English colonists of an adequate supply of labor. Consequently soon after the Restoration, the three royal adventurers, Charles II, James, and Rupert, founded the Royal African Company to supply English colonies with slaves at the modest rate of one black for one ton of sugar.[8] Unfortunately for the English, the tenacious Dutch caused—through their policy—the Royal African Company to raise its price to two tons of sugar per slave.[9] In addition, the company had to put up with heavy losses since its monopoly made it prey to precisely the same risks as the WIC—interlopers, corruption, and collusion among its own agents. Finally, the RAC was specifically interdicted by the Spanish because the latter preferred the Dutch. The English were thus restricted in their slave trade to their own limited market.

At the command of the three royal *brasseurs d'affaires*, however, were the inestimable services of George Downing, the British minister in The Hague. There is little disagreement about this man; Boxer calls him "unscrupulous," and a contemporary French ambassador referred to him as "a very disagreeable person."[10] Downing combined in his person a high degree of perfidy with a conspicuous lack of conscience. It is not difficult to imagine what this Royal African Company agent was charged with in his sensitive position in the United Provinces.

The exalted trio were very interested in New Netherland and the West African coast. Both of these areas were under the control of the Dutch West India Company, a joint stock company chartered by Their High Mightinesses. The WIC was hence, as pointed out before, a semi-official institution—not exactly identical with the government of the United Provinces though closely identified with it. This dualism offered unlimited prospects to the unscrupulous. Here was a perfect way to impede the prosperity of the free Netherlands through attacking a private institution without risking the kind of official action which might lead to war between nations. It would simply be one private company, the Royal African Company, against another, the WIC. The English assumed that the States General would vigorously protest action taken against the WIC yet could be counted upon to stop short of war.

The contest—or as the directors of the West India Company called it in a letter to Their High Mightinesses, the "frivolous practices"[11]— of the three English adventurers began in 1661 with an attack on the Dutch position at Cape Verde. The Dutch clerk in charge of that settlement, a man named Cop, was summarily advised by the commander of an English squadron, Sir Robert Holmes, that England held a trade monopoly on the African coast from Cape Verde to the Cape of Good Hope. All Dutchmen were to evacuate that territory at once. Needless to say, Cop refused even to discuss such a proposal. The English then occupied the Dutch fort at Gambia.[12]

Notice of this outright breach of international relations reached the United Provinces and aroused great indignation and ill-feeling. The Heren XIX immediately presented a memorial to the States General. Their High Mightinesses responded by dispatching a letter to His British Majesty which asked Charles to prohibit his subjects from encroaching on the prerogatives of the WIC in Africa. Charles, through his envoy at The Hague, apologized profusely and assured the Dutch that henceforth their rights would be respected and that future offenders would be severly punished. Holmes was, in fact, brought to trial when he returned home, in a noisy public display of deference to Dutch claims. Meanwhile, the English moved swiftly in a counter-complaint against the WIC and Johan van Valckenburg. They charged that the latter called himself "Director-General of the Coast of North Africa" and that, in the name of the States General and of the Dutch West India Company, he had published a "remonstrance" or "memorial" in which "he pretends for said company the whole coast of Guinea, called the Gold Coast, and the places appurtenant to it with all their trade . . . to the entire exclusion of all other nations."[13] This, said the English, was a provocation of their rights and an insult to their national pride. They began systematically moving against Dutch trade and fisheries; at The Hague, Downing, in the meantime, explained away the actions of Holmes in Africa.

As the English probably hoped, the complexity of all this led to an impasse. At that point, with no admission of Dutch claims, the two governments entered into a treaty. It stipulated that earlier grievances would be forgotten and that isolated incidents between their respective subjects would not constitute cause for hostilities in Europe. The

Dutch leader of international relations during this period, the Grand Pensionary Johan de Witt, fully realized the English game, but he assumed that the alternative to such a treaty would be war. As a result of their experiences in the turbulent fifties in which successively England, Sweden, and Portugal had been the national enemy, the government officials realized that a growing Orangist party would be enhanced by a new war. Reluctantly and dejectedly, de Witt danced to George Downing's tune.

The theme of the English composition was to keep the Dutch occupied with talking and other diplomatic subterfuges. The British public, meanwhile, was entertained with horror stories about Dutch aggression against English territories and people.[14] In these instances, both the great Dutch monopolistic companies were charged with insolence and treachery against the innocent English. The propaganda worked very well indeed; after a short time the English public was thoroughly incited and wanted action. The Dutch, meanwhile, were busy explaining and protesting as the English adventurers simultaneously moved to the offensive in Africa, the East and West Indies, and North America.

In the case of New Netherland, its immediate future was roughly similar to what had happened in Africa. A royal charter of 1662 permitted New England to extend itself to the Delaware River, which was interpreted to mean, incidently, that it could annex the Dutch region in between. The Dutch considered this charter a violation of their prerogatives, which had been established in 1614 but which now were conveniently ignored by Charles II. False rumors were spread to the effect that the Dutch were planning to move against New England and Virginia. In a generous mood, Charles II donated the disputed area between the two English colonies to his brother James, together with four thousand pounds to be used in its occupation and defense. James did not delay, and on September 8, 1664, before any war had been declared between the two countries, New Amsterdam was taken and renamed New York. As Commander Richard Nicolls, who had been instructed by Charles as early as April, 1664, put it to Peter Stuyvesant, "The right and title of His Majesty to these parts of America is indisputable."[15]

But in order to have a better understanding of such events, it will be necessary to take a step or two backwards. Another unmistakably anti-Dutch action had already been perpetrated by the English in 1663 when, under the guise of a mission of the Royal African Company, Commander Holmes was dispatched once again to the West African coast. This time the pretext involved some highly dubious English claims of interference in their trade. A "protest" from the RAC charged that the Dutch had endeavored to drive the English company from the coast, had followed her ships from port to port and hindered her coming nigh the shore to trade; they had persuaded the Negroes to destroy her agents and to capture her forts; they had seized her boats and goods, violently taken possession of Cape Coast, and aimed to shoot at His Majesty's royal flag.[16] Holmes, who might or might not have been ordered to assume the offensive, reported that he had found the Dutch so hostile and their influence over the Negro chiefs so inimical to English interests that he had no choice but to take action. A year before war was officially declared early in 1664, he forcibly occupied Dutch trading posts at Goree, Cape Verde, Cape Coast, and elsewhere and ambushed the WIC slave ships visiting the area.[17]

From the Caribbean came similar news. English activity there made it plain that the Dutch were to be driven from the West Indies. English ships in the vicinity of Curaçao announced that they had been commissioned by James to stop and overpower ships with Spanish goods aboard. A look at past events reveals how odd this assertion was. The English were no more at war with Spain than they were with the United Provinces. The ruse was probably designed to provide a legal basis for attacking the Dutch and to establish a pretext for confiscating both their ships and cargo. In short, Charles, James, and Rupert—assisted by the ever intriguing Downing whose patriotism may have been boosted by his ownership of RAC shares—were everywhere courting aggression without actually going to war.

Johan de Witt's policy finds its justification in this English display. Indeed, from the Dutch point of view, de Witt acted adroitly as well as honestly, notwithstanding loud English cries of "foul play." Downing continued to press simultaneously claims of Dutch bellicosity along with protestations of the undying fellowship Albion felt for the Dutch. But the government of the United Provinces, spurred on by continuing reports of English militancy and Zeelandian determination, now agreed to use armed forces to redress and repair the WIC's losses in Africa.[18] The boards of admiralty were ordered to equip a fleet with all haste and unobstrusiveness so as not to alert the opponents. It was to be sent to Vice-Admiral de Ruyter in the Mediterranean. This bold decision was made a few days after Downing had boasted to Their High Mightinesses that force would be met with force.[19]

French offers to mediate the imminent conflagration were rebuffed by the Dutch. In spite of a treaty of alliance with the United Provinces, Louis XIV had not only closed the French Antilles to Dutch trade but had also dispatched a fleet to Cayenne. The subsequent fall of that fort and settlement both upset and angered the Dutch. A caustic memorial was forthwith dispatched to Louis advising him that Cayenne had been Dutch since 1656 and harbored not a single French subject.[20] But in spite of the Dutch-French treaty of 1662, which forfended all hostilities between the two countries, Louis XIV would neither call his men back nor condemn their actions.

The Dutch soon realized that their newly authorized fleet would take too long to prepare. Forewarned by their informer Downing, the English would have ample time to make even deeper inroads into what were hitherto Dutch spheres of influence. Acceleration was mandatory. De Witt, who was to all appearances counseled by Hiob de Wildt, then secretary to the Amsterdam admiralty board, secretly manipulated an influential committee of members of the States General known as the *Secreete Besogne*. This committee ordered de Ruyter from the Mediterranean to the west coast of Africa to consult with van Valckenburg and to reconquer all forts, trading posts, and other possessions lost by the West India Company.[21] A special rider to this effect on the general resolution was read, passed by vote, and signed by Their High Mightinesses as though it were a routine matter, yet it was well understood by the few who were informed that de Ruyter's mission was synonymous with war.

No one knew what had transpired at this meeting of the States General except, of course, for de Witt and his *Secreete Besogne*. By some adroit maneuvering, the entire project even escaped detection by Downing's intricate spy network. Yet rumor of some secret mission did reach Downing not long afterward, inducing him to seek out the grand pensionary at once in order to inquire whether "the States of Holland had ordered any official action on Africa's West coast." The phrasing of Downing's question allowed de Witt to reply, "I can assure you that the States of Holland has not given de Ruyter any order about which your Master the King, needs to worry; and as far as the States General is concerned, I do not have to tell you anything; is it not true that nothing there happens without your immediate knowledge?"[22]

Fully satisfied with this official retort, Downing wrote his king that de Ruyter had not been sent to Guinea. Despite his intimate acquaintance with the complex government of the United Provinces, the Englishman had been deceived. It was precisely Downing who had written his king, "You have infinite advantages upon the account of the form of government of this country [the United Provinces], which is such a shattered and divided thing."[23] It is ironic that this otherwise astute observer could so have stated his question to de Witt as to narrow the implementive body to the States of Holland. It was not the latter but the States General that had the final say in a measure of such far-reaching national consequences.

The extremely competent and worthy de Ruyter had, in the meantime, however, received his orders on September 1, 1664, while at Malaga. The courier's arrival had aroused a notable flurry of excitement, but de Ruyter had been forced to pacify his staff with the news that the instructions he had received contained no official war orders. It was to be hoped, de Ruyter had added, that the existing differences with England and the United Provinces could eventually be settled peacefully.

The expedition de Ruyter was ordered to undertake involved only the possessions of the WIC on the Guinea coast. At the same time, the admiral was explicitly advised to avoid all English ships. After a brief delay to take on stores, his fleet left the Mediterranean only to be met off Malaga by an English fleet of eleven ships. The meeting of the two fleets was friendly. The Dutch saluted with a gun shot and lowered their flag; the English returned this first greeting but kept their flags up because the encounter had taken place in an area haughtily referred to as "British waters." Both fleets were to meet occasionally again, but always on a cordial basis. By the time of the third meeting, however, the element of chance had disappeared since Sir Thomas Allin, the new English commander, was under specific orders to keep track of de Ruyter's fleet. Yet responses continued to be marked by an imperturbable air of politeness as both leaders literally outdid each other in amicability. Allin wrote in his diary, "He [de Ruyter] came under our sterne and asked me how I did, and saluted me with seven guns and drank to me."[24] Each man fully realized the other's role in the drama that was unfolding.

Three days after the Dutch fleet left Cádiz, sailing westward in order to mislead the English and Spanish in the area, de Ruyter called a council of war. Only at this time did he reveal to his staff the full contents of his secret instructions, i.e., to repair the losses suffered by the WIC at the hands of the English on the African coast. The men were aware that war was the probable outcome of their venture, but all were satisfied and were particularly pleased at the prospect of booty to be gained at the expense of the Royal African Company.

The fleet proceeded cautiously toward the Canary Islands, and near Gran Canaria all flags were lowered to avoid recognition. Meanwhile, preparations were being made for future action. The first goal was to be Goree, a small island close to Cape Verde. The Dutch arrived there on October 22. A spark of fire set off hostilities on both sides, an encounter which was described by a contemporary British horror propagandist as "De Ruyter's barbarities in Guinea in 1664."[25]

When the Dutch appeared in the offing there were eight English merchantmen and one man-of-war in the port basking in the protection offered by the flag of the Royal African Company which hovered over the two fortresses. De Ruyter ordered his fleet to attack, and his ships formed a semicircle around the English ships. The English governor Sir George Abercrombie thereupon sent two deputies to ask what was going on. Were not England and the United Provinces still at peace? De Ruyter answered drily that this was true; the United Provinces were at peace with England, but not with the Royal African Company.

At this point, the captain of the English man-of-war, excusing himself with all delicacy from the fray, tried to leave the port, but a shot across his bow encouraged him to remain. De Ruyter now demanded surrender and gave the governor twenty-four hours to consider his terms instead of the ten days the latter had requested. On October 24 the English yielded, and the Dutch flag once more flew over Forts Nassau and Orange. The English ships were temporarily detained, their cargoes expropriated, and their captains taken into custody. The smallest ship was dispatched with a load of hides to Holland. Sometime later the English man-of-war was allowed to go free on condition that it would leave the area (de Ruyter would meet it again in the West Indies). The merchantmen also received permission to go after promising never again to visit the African coast. The Dutch admiral, with Goree newly under the auspices of the WIC, left behind a garrison of 130 men and proceeded south along the coast.

Sierra Leone, the next station, surrendered without a struggle. Its warehouses were emptied of the merchandise belonging to the WIC. The fleet next moved on to Tacorary. The English commander there refused to negotiate, but after a brief fight he capitulated. Following the suggestions of van Valckenburg, who had been informed by de Ruyter, the Dutch dismantled and destroyed the fort.

On January 7, 1665, de Ruyter set foot at Elmina, which was the official residence of Director-General Johan van Valckenburg, and one of the few points along the African coast that the Dutch had managed to retain during Holmes' raids. Here the admiral received new instructions from home which authorized him to seize all English men-of-war and merchantmen so long as the king delayed satisfaction for English hostilities in Africa and elsewhere. The States

General let it be known that although an English fleet of eight ships and ten armed merchantmen was en route to Africa, twelve Dutch ships under Jan van Campen were also on their way to reinforce de Ruyter.

Following his orders to the letter, the admiral now set out to attack the fort of Cormantine. On February 7, 1665, he disembarked nine hundred to one thousand Dutch and as many Negroes. He was, however, forestalled in this project by the loyalty of John Cabessa, a Negro chief who was more devoted to Charles II than many of that sovereign's own subjects. De Ruyter, instead, had to satisfy himself with taking the small island of Annabón, where he blew up the fort, and secured the help of the anti-English Fantine Negroes. On his way back he attacked Cormantine again and defeated its garrison without great difficulty. The Dutch gave quarter to the English; Cabessa cut his own throat, and the Fantines were turned loose to commit atrocities among the pro-English Negroes. The Dutch left a few men behind and returned to Elmina.[26]

At the castle, the Dutch admiral received further instructions from the States General. Since the English fleet under Prince Rupert had not sailed to Africa after all, Their High Mightinesses had temporarily decided to keep van Campen at home. A second letter, twenty days later, informed de Ruyter and van Valckenburg that English ships were now indiscriminately seizing Dutch vessels in the so-called British waters—which meant all around Europe. De Ruyter was instructed to capture all the English forts he could, anywhere he wished, as a means of retaliation. His new mission was "to cause all possible damage and injury, be it at Barbados, New Netherland, Terreneuf [New-foundland] or other islands and places,"[27] culminating in the fleet's returning to the United Provinces. The letter was also probably the first news de Ruyter had received about the English conquest of New Amsterdam. The English government, which pretended not to know anything about Nicolls' deed, referred all claims to the Royal African Company. It denied its responsibility for the actions of a private institution.

De Ruyter's new orders brought him face to face with the problem of pacifying his men whose home voyage would now have to be postponed for many long months. The admiral determined to keep silent and not tell them at this time what lay ahead. Together with van Valckenburg, he discussed an attack on the English base at Cape Corso, but both men agreed that since Negro allies in that area were not entirely dependable, de Ruyter would be better off to cross the Atlantic and try his luck in the West Indies. He would have the element of surprise to his advantage, moreover, and any action taken there would have a better chance of success. Consequently, the fleet, now fourteen ships strong, left Africa on February 27, 1665.

De Ruyter's departure from the Mediterranean did not remain a secret very long.[28] The English reaction to the Dutch admiral's mission is mirrored in the diary of Samuel Pepys: "For newes, all say de Ruyter is gone to Guinny before us," wrote Pepys in October, 1664. About two weeks later he added, "All the talke is that de Ruyter is come over-land home with six or eight of his captaines to command here at home, and their ships kept abroad in the Straights [of Gibraltar]; which sounds as if they had a mind to do something with us." In December, Pepys knew war could no longer be avoided; eighteen or twenty merchantmen from the Dutch Bordeaux fleet had been brought into English ports. Many more soon followed and all were to be confiscated once war was declared. At this juncture Pepys laconically remarked: "...so that the war is begun; God give a good end to it."[29] At the same time, the States General concluded that "the main issue at stake will be disputed with arms."[30]

Pepys' diary, of course, provides us with a personal insight into current events, an advantage almost totally missing in the dehumanized, more formal minutes of the meetings of the States General. London's most popular street rumors found their way into the diary: "I hear fully the news of our being beaten to dirt at Guinny by de Ruyter with his fleete...it being most wholly to the utter ruine of our Royall Company, and reproach and shame to the whole nation, as well as justification to them [the Dutch] in their doing wrong to no man as to his private [property], only taking whatever is found to belong to the [West Indian] Company and nothing else." Pepys was also much concerned about the great cost of a new war, for the last one had cost England 1,623,000 pounds a year.

As time went on, however, Pepys' commendable impartiality was badly shattered by the terror propaganda that labeled Dutch actions "atrocities" and "barbarities." In February, 1665, the Englishman wrote, "I hear the most horrid and astonishing newes that ever was yet told in my memory, that de Ruyter, with his fleete in Guinny...taking forts, goods, and ships...tied our men back to back and thrown them all into the sea, even women and children also." Four days later he entered, "The late newes of the Dutch, their drowning our men at Guinny." To these comments he later added in justification: "What I fear is that he [de Ruyter] was informed (which he was not before) of some of Holmes' dealings with his countrymen, and so his anger was mitigated."[31] The truth about the situation in Africa, which the celebrated English diarist may have gleaned afterwards, was too complex and so entangled in the foils of international politics as to confuse the noblest mind. As an example of diplomatic duplicity, the English Governor of Cormantine himself assisted at the farewell dinner for de Ruyter's fleet at Elmina.

The gap between the known and the expected was filled in those days, as it is today, with rumors. In those days, however, it was much wider. The ships that brought the sad tidings of the conquest of New Netherland to Amsterdam also circulated the controversial news that two English ships had departed for Curaçao. Since there was general concern for the Caribbean possessions, this sort of hearsay easily became current "news." The English were undeniably considering the entire Caribbean area a new theater of war, even though they were more interested in Tobago than in Curaçao. The Dutch were not ignorant of their preference. In August, 1664, the Lampsins brothers, who were the patrons of Tobago, had informed the States General that Charles II had signed a secret compact "to start, under some pretext, an unprovoked action on a certain island of the Caribbean, earlier named Tobago and now New Walcheren."[32] A month later the States of Zeeland warned the federal government that an attack on Tobago seemed imminent. Not until then, however, did the States General authorize Zeeland to send her contingent of van Campen's fleet—three men-of-war—to the aid of New Walcheren.

Unknown to any of the Dutch at the time was a secret arrangement that had been concluded between Charles II and Duke Jakob of Courland. In November, 1664, with utter disregard for the Dutch title to the island, the Stuart king had granted to the duke and his heirs—because he saw Jakob as a possible ally against the Dutch—the island of Tobago, which had already been granted by his father and grandfather to the Courland dukes, on the condition that settlement of that island be confined to colonists from the two countries. Although denial of Dutch claims everywhere was, at the time, a general policy of the royal adventurers, the Dutch also, it must be admitted, shared this peculiarly convenient point of view and were quite willing to ignore English pretensions.

Although the exact story may never be known, since English designs on Tobago were artfully concealed beneath the flag of the Duke of Courland, the Dutch historian Japikse is undoubtedly correct in his belief that the second Anglo-Dutch war had its prelude in Africa, New Netherland, and the Caribbean. Protected by a treaty which foreswore hostilities in Europe over antagonism abroad, England felt particularly advantaged and refused to negotiate on Africa and New

Amsterdam. De Ruyter's success merely confirmed her intransigence. Indeed, as Clarendon addressed Downing after the English humiliation in Africa, the States General had provoked the king and "fighting was thought the better husbandry."[33] Downing's task, to continue his insistence on the right of his king to retain the regions conquered by the English, was seriously compromised by Dutch victories: "Guinea is lost, what can we do now more with the Dutch?"[34] He charged that the Dutch had pretensions to a *mare clausum* in African and East Indian waters, while he managed to forget English conceit in regard to the so-called British waters.[35] The royal trio, severely chastised in Africa, now muttered darkly about the perfidious Dutch and imminent retaliation.

Aware that war was not far off, the Dutch were peculiarly exhilarated. WIC shares rose from 5 to almost 10 per cent. Groningen and Utrecht, besides Holland and Zeeland, immediately agreed on the subsidy which financed de Ruyter's expedition, and even Friesland did not stand apart.

Talks concerning the colonial claims of the two antagonists continued, but to little avail. Dutch claims were said to be insufficient; England's claims were held to be extravagant. Each country could and did pretend that accusations against the nation were misdirected because only private companies were actually involved. Charges and countercharges were filed, and each believed that the other had begun the violations.

A new offer of France to mediate an exchange of possessions was refused, since it came too late and was clearly disadvantageous to the Dutch. The English had agreed to cede the not insignificant island of Pulau Run in the Malay Archipelago in return for all it had or would conquer of Dutch possessions in Africa and America. The XIX declined this curiously impertinent offer.[36] Mistrust of France, of course, grew deeper with this episode.

Backed by strong popular feeling, the Dutch were ready to accept the English challenge. On the other hand, were they familiar with Charles II's efforts to maintain a friendly co-existence situation with the French king?[37] Louis' hesitation to enter into such an alliance was all that delayed Charles' declaration of war on the United Provinces. But hostilities were sure to break loose officially, and soon de Ruyter's mission could hardly be regarded in England as less than a national insult. In November, 1664, Dutch ships were seized in English ports, an open act of aggression. Although de Ruyter had been authorized to capture English ships, too, he seized only those of the Royal African Company. But war was not yet declared by either side.

Shares in the East India Company rose 13 per cent as a result of this official restraint.

England's hesitation continued during the first two months of 1665, attributable, perhaps, to the rivalry between English hawks led by Clarendon and the doves under the leadership of the Duke of Albemarle.

The situation finally erupted with an English attack on the Dutch "Smyrna fleet" near Cádiz. Downing was probably responsible for urging this sudden act of war on such an important Dutch fleet of thirty merchantmen and three men-of-war. The Dutch fought and resisted the assault, however, and disabled two English men-of-war. Furthermore, the States General now felt justified in passing a resolution which permitted the Dutch to prey upon all English shipping in European waters. The EIC and WIC were fully authorized to inflict as much damage as possible. Pepys wrote, "The Dutch have, by consent of all Provinces...applyed themselves wholly to the warr."[38] *Kaperbrieven* were issued, largely at the insistence of the ever piratical Zeelanders. The war, although not officially proclaimed, was in fact underway.

Contrary to English charges, the Dutch did not actually appropriate enemy ships until a state of war was indeed affirmed in March, 1665. For some time, however, they had been busily engaged in equipping their fleet and bringing it up to fighting condition, a fact which might have led the English to believe that the worst had already taken place. "The Dutch...without doubt, will have a great fleete in the Straights," wrote Pepys on January 15. Once England did issue her war manifesto, which the Dutch did not deign to answer, it was woe unto King Charles II. Pepys cried out barely one month after the war had begun, "God, send us peace, I cry."[39] Albion suffered the most humiliating experience in her entire history—the "Medway disaster"—in which de Ruyter sailed up the Thames, drove London into panic, burned, destroyed, or captured many of the best English vessels, and absconded with the flagship the "Royal Charles." The main focus of this chapter, though, is the development of the war in the Caribbean.

After consulting with van Valckenburg concerning Cape Corso, de Ruyter decided to attempt a surprise attack in the West Indies. It was not the admiral's first trip to the area, since he had been in Brazil in the service of the Lampsins, and during the 1640's he had visited many islands in the Caribbean archipelago. In 1651 he had concluded an agreement with George Ayscue—called Joris Haskus in Dutch documents—to meet the latter at St. Vincent for some business transaction, an encounter which never materialized.[40] During the

Fig. 13. Attack on Tobago, March 3, 1677

Fig. 14. Cornelis Evertsen the Younger by Nicolaes Maes

troubles with Portugal, de Ruyter had also blockaded the Portuguese coast; later he had even protected the Spanish treasure fleets from Portuguese attacks. Although in the service of the government of the United Provinces in those later years, de Ruyter had actually supported the interests of the West India Company.

His current mission may well be regarded as one of the most remarkable of his exploits outside Europe. Although he did not duplicate his African successes, for he did not achieve the initial advantage of surprise he had hoped for, his actions caused his name to be on everyone's lips and raised the fame of Dutch aggressive power to a higher level.

De Ruyter's fleet left Africa late in February, 1665. It crossed the equator within a week, passed São Thomé and Annabon, and, finding favorable winds, traversed the Atlantic in six weeks. On the morning of April 29, the admiral unfurled the "Prince flag" from his great mast as a sign that Barbados had been sighted, and the fleet council decided to sail into Carlisle Bay the next morning. That evening de Ruyter wrote in his journal, "May it please God to be with us with His peaceful blessing. Amen."[41]

Within Carlisle Bay lay thirty English ships; twenty-seven were laden with sugar, but only one belonged to the Royal African Company, and one was the man-of-war that de Ruyter had released at Goree.[42] News of de Ruyter's forthcoming arrival had thus already been received by the inhabitants; they sighted the Dutch in the morning of April 30. A little later, de Ruyter boldly made for the bay in absolute silence, without firing one shot. The fort broke the stillness and opened fire, followed by many English ships which acquitted themselves gallantly. Undismayed, de Ruyter and his fleet moved forward into the harbor until the flagship was only a few fathoms from the enemy ships. At this point the admiral ordered a full volley, turned about, and fired another. The remaining units of his fleet attacked either the fort or the English ships within range.

De Ruyter then turned his full attention to the English king's ship, and as he sailed past it he saw its commander fall. Heavy artillery continued to do its damage for a few hours, but one after another English ship cannons were successfully silenced. In the midst of the confusion, their crews tried to run their disabled ships aground rather than surrender. De Ruyter's own ship *De Spiegel* ("The Mirror") had lost its foresail and its main yard. His vice-admiral's ship sustained similar injuries and neither could catch the wind. Meanwhile, the town had hardly suffered at all. An eyewitness to the battle, in which approximately five hundred shots were ex-

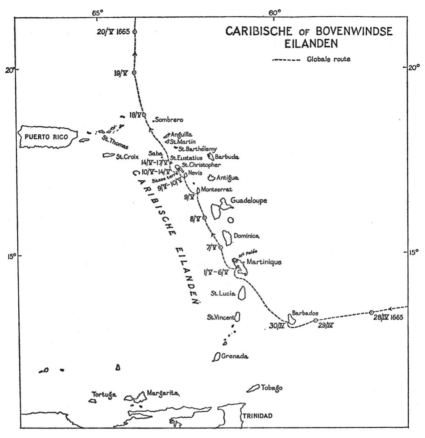

10. Map of de Ruyter's route through the Caribbean in 1665. From P. Verhoog and L. Koelmans, *De reis van M. A. de Ruyter in 1664-1665.*

changed, reports that the Dutch "killed only one negroe, one christian & a dogge."[43]

After two or three hours of unrelenting warfare, de Ruyter conceded the futility of his efforts. He was unaware that the English, after having accidentally spilled thirty-three barrels of gunpowder, had almost exhausted their supplies. Subsequently, the Dutch fleet left the bay and retreated to the French island of Martinique to lick its wounds. The Dutch did not know how near they had been to victory. They realized, however, that the king's ship had warned Barbados and that surprise had been an illusion. The narrow Carlisle Bay, moreover, was no proper arena for combat. Their decision to leave was, therefore, sound.

The Dutch were well received at Martinique because of improvements in Franco-Dutch relations that would, some time later, result in French entry into the war on the Dutch side. Visits were exchanged between de Ruyter and French officials, and the governor even presented his guests with six hundred pounds of gunpowder.[44] The Dutch remained at the island until May 5, repairing the damage caused by the English guns, refreshing, and burying their dead. The unharmed ships had already been dispatched to reconnoiter passing English vessels, and the entire fleet was ordered to rendezvous at St. Christopher on May 12 and 13.

De Ruyter was soon informed that a dozen English merchantmen were taking on cargoes at Nevis and Montserrat. En route to the latter island, the Dutch admiral also learned that war had finally been proclaimed. At Montserrat, in full range of the fort's guns, he seized four or five English ships. Yet their cargo was disappointing and not worth the very considerable peril in capturing them. The fort had not fired, perhaps because of the dire threat of the Dutch "to disembark with all our men and kill everything we should find."[45] At Nevis the Dutch sank the only valuable ship which was anchored in the harbor, and captured the others in spite of the vigorous fire raining down upon them from the forts. These prizes were taken to St. Christopher and sold to the French for twelve thousand pounds of sugar each. From there the fleet sailed to St. Eustatius.

De Ruyter sold some of his remaining prizes at this island for cotton and sugar. He supplied the commander with some seven hundred pounds of gunpowder which the latter badly needed and which would come in handy during the coming months. Then, still not rid of all their captives, the Dutch sailed by way of St. Martin to the Bermudas. They left the Caribbean on May 17, 1665. The admiral's instructions permitted him to proceed to New Amsterdam—New York at the time—but various reasons compelled him to make for Newfoundland instead.

De Ruyter's "daring raid" in the Caribbean had completely destroyed the season's export cargo for the English and restored Dutch confidence, but it had not realized any other practical result. Although Dutch exploits in Africa were certainly used as a pretext for the English declaration of war, those in the Caribbean came too late. The outbreak of war, therefore, cannot be attributed to these latter "provocations."

Once the Dutch admiral had left the Caribbean, the immediate danger for the English colonies was over. At home, in European waters, de Ruyter would continue to render his country immeasurable

services in the war against England. In addition, after some months
of hesitation, France joined the Dutch, a move which caused the
English much trouble and added to their desire to sue for peace in
1667. The war in the Caribbean which had been initiated by de
Ruyter's raid also played an important role in the conflict between the
United Provinces and France on one side and England on the other.

Even before de Ruyter had arrived in the Caribbean, Governor Willoughby of Barbados had requested help for his island against what he
thought were aggressive policies that had been adopted by the Dutch
and the French in the West Indies. At about this time, moreover,
Governor Thomas Modyford of Jamaica was suggesting that the
English employ the Caribbean buccaneers before they sided with the
French at Tortuga or with the Dutch at Curaçao. The English colonists knew that in the event of war they would be left with only local
resources. The idea of using buccaneers for "the great occasion His
Majesty might have for them" and thus supplementing their meager
manpower was very attractive. Modyford soon became more expansive with his plans. The Dutch, he claimed, could be easily
rooted out of their settlements in the Caribbean and on the Wild
Coast, both areas within range of an attack from Barbados and the
English colonies in Surinam. His suggestion was to employ these
outlaws for this design; such a step would drive the Dutch out of
the West Indies and keep those same buccaneers too busy to prey
upon English shipping.[46]

In addition to these proposals, another plan was also forwarded to
the king by a Captain Abraham Langford which suggested the reduction of Curaçao, parts of Hispaniola, and Tortuga. Langford was
appointed to go to Jamaica with two ships and join Modyford.[47] The
exact outcome of his tentative ideas is not known. It is probable,
however, that Langford's plans were eventually incorporated in the
projects of the governor of Jamaica.

Meanwhile, on the day before the official outbreak of the second
Anglo-Dutch war, an examination of Holmes' actions in Africa was
conducted in London. The latter's defense was based on a decree,
signed by the king himself, that ordered him to protect the goods,
ships, forts, and factories of the Royal African Company and to
preserve "freedom of trade" by force if necessary. The English
apparently never realized that this concept was diametrically opposed
to their own policy as represented by the Navigation Laws. Holmes'
activities against the Dutch in Africa were just the contrary of the
English practice wherever they had control. Like the Dutch they

defended freedom wherever they lacked power. A disciple in this ambiguous school of thought, Holmes defended his actions by raising the usual complaints which English factors made against the Dutch as excuses for his violations of Dutch title and navigation. Perhapy Holmes' examination and trial, full as they were of Dutch atrocits stories, pushed the war party of Clarendon to the fore and precipitated the almost instantaneous declaration of war.[48]

By that time, Lieutenant-Colonel Edward Morgan had been commissioned to carry out Governor Modyford's design. Morgan organized a fleet of ten ships and five hundred men from "chiefly reformed privateers... being resolute fellows and well armed with fusils and pistols." The idea was, first of all, to fall upon the Dutch who were trading at St. Christopher. The fleet was then to take away the islands of St. Eustatius, Saba, and Curaçao. Success in such ventures was guaranteed to ruin or to seriously impair the Dutch position in the Caribbean. The expedition was to be financed by plunder; the king's treasury provided only gunpowder and mortar. "God sending good success," wrote Modyford, "the Dutch will have no considerable place left them in the West Indies." Luckily for the Dutch the governor's project was too grandiose to be accomplished by such an undisciplined force, and it soon came to naught.[49]

The offensive by Colonel Edward Morgan's buccaneers initiated an interisland encounter of hitherto unknown dimensions. The fleet departed for St. Christopher, but somewhere en route the plans were altered and Morgan directed his ships to St. Eustatius. He hit the island in July, 1665, two months after de Ruyter had left. While disembarking his 320 men there, Morgan, a very corpulent fellow, leaped forward from his ship and pursued the enemy so earnestly that he died from overly zealous activity in the tropical heat. Colonel Theodore Cary took command and succeeded in forcing the surrender of the Dutch fort. It had certainly not yet used the seven hundred pounds of gunpowder received from de Ruyter shortly before. Dutch planters who refused to take an oath of allegiance to the English king —some 250 men, women, and children—were soon removed from the island and sold into slavery on Barbados. The booty, guns and ammunition, 840 slaves, 300 cattle, and 50 horses, caused much dissension among the privateers and was a primary factor leading to their breaking up.[50] The name of the island was changed to New Dunkirk.

Some three weeks later Colonel Cary sent Major Richard Stevens and seventy men to occupy the nearby island of Saba, disposing of the non-juring population in the same manner. The best spoils from this small island were represented by the capture of seventy slaves. As at St. Eustatius, sugar and cotton plantations were destroyed. All the slaves were either sold on St. Kitts (the English part) or were taken to Jamaica. On the orders of Governor Willoughby of Barbados, the Dutch colonists were auctioned off as "white slaves" to planters in the English Antilles.

The English, for whom things were going very well, now hoped to proceed to Curaçao. Without wasting any time, Cary raised an additional two hundred men for an intrepid raid on this "strongest Dutch fort in the Indies."[51] At the same time Willoughby was avidly making plans to campaign against the Dutch at Tobago and on the Wild Coast. Notwithstanding all this heady planning, however, Cary found that his ruthless followers, all of whom had agreed to "no purchase, no pay" terms, now refused to budge for anything less than the customary arrangements. The colonel concluded that he was doomed to fail with a crew near mutiny and reluctantly abandoned the project. Appointing Thomas Morgan as governor of St. Eustatius and Saba, he departed for Jamaica. Although his fleet met storms en route to this island, the majority of the ships arrived eventually with most of the men and some four hundred Negroes.

Some time later, in January, 1666, another fleet of privateers led by Edward Mansvelt and Henry Morgan, famous names in the Caribbean, and including many Dutch and French pirates, now left Jamaica with designs on Curaçao. As it sailed south, however, it occurred to Mansvelt that his haul would be larger if he were to direct his attack at the Spaniards. Consequently the fleet altered its course and headed toward the Spanish island of Providence off the Nicaraguan coast. The garrison there offered only nominal resistance and was easily driven off. After the privateers had given free reign to their lust for loot and pillage, they continued their exploits among the Spanish colonies of Honduras and the Mexican Gulf and spread terror wherever they set foot ashore. Curaçao, however, was saved from their onslaught, for these hardheaded realists knew only too well that the island was impregnable without the backing of a substantial fleet and disciplined troops.

Meanwhile, the war continued. English buccaneers had gained a few islands for their king, but little else of value. Dutch ships, on the other hand, were so successfully harassing English shipping that a royal order was issued that all English vessels were to return in fleets at given times—on the last days of March, June, and September. An identical decree was dispatched to Governor Modyford at Jamaica. In the interim, Governor Willoughby of Barbados had not been idle. Late in 1665, he had equipped six ships and 350 men for an assault on the prosperous Dutch colony on Tobago.

Since 1662 Tobago had been under the patronship of Cornelis Lampsins, who had received in that year the title of Baron of Tobago from Louis XIV. In November, 1664, just a few months before the outbreak of the second Anglo-Dutch war, Charles II, whose notoriety in granting countries and islands he did not possess rivaled that of his father and grandfather, had given Tobago to his relative Duke Jakob of Courland. Although Francis Lord Willoughby was soon notified of this grant, Modyford of Jamaica had already taken things into his own hands by capturing the island with two small frigates. Arriving a few days later, Willoughby's forces surprised Modyford's privateers in the act of dismantling the sugar mills. An agreement was made in which Willoughby was to assume official control over the island, and a fifty-man garrison of official English troops was left behind. Some time later, Willoughby proposed to the king that he would undertake to settle the island if it were granted to him for a period of thirty-one years together with the privilege of free trade.[52]

Thus, during their first year of the war in the Caribbean, the Dutch lost Tobago and two of their Leeward Antilles. But retaining Curaçao amply compensated for these minor setbacks, and the Dutch position in general remained strong. Their possession of Curaçao, particularly because of its growing importance in the slave trade, could only mean further detriment to the Royal African Company and the English. As Commander Nicolls, the victor of New Amsterdam in 1664, wrote to Arlington, this Dutch island remained "a thorn in the foot of the Leeward Islands."[53]

Dutch stature was considerably heightened in January, 1666, by France's entry into the war against England. Although Louis XIV had been a nominal ally of the United Provinces since 1662, the French king could hardly be called pro-Dutch. In the poetic version of his views as given by de la Roncière, Louis dreams: "If I execute the treaty of 1662 to the letter I will greatly prejudice my principal interests, and for people that will never give me any help."[54] The Sun King dallied, but eventually he stepped into the war, although not "obligated by his commitments,"[55] but rather motivated by Dutch losses in the Caribbean which he had every intention of converting into French gains. Someone had to stop the English: they were now refusing to renew neutrality agreements with the French Antilles and had occupied St. Lucia without paying any attention to French claims.[56]

The Franco-Dutch alliance was very strong and represented a real threat to the English in the Caribbean.[57] Indeed, a new dimension was introduced to the war with the French entry. Although the English dreaded the Dutch as dangerous competitors, they actually shared many traits with them, not the least of which was religion. Feeling between the English and French ran on a different level, however; the latter had gained for themselves the reputation of being merciless to the vanquished. Many English garrison commanders, therefore, such as Colonel William Byam of Surinam, preferred to surrender to the Dutch.[58] Generally speaking, and in spite of much propaganda to the contrary, the Dutch and English would treat each other honorably, in a way quite different from French behavior with either.

An immediate result of French involvement in the war was the English loss of St. Christopher. Colonel William Watts, governor of the English segment of that island, supported by the privateering rubble of St. Eustatius and Saba, took the initiative and gave the French residents three days' notice to leave. The French, however, did not need this respite to pounce upon the unsuspecting English. In the ensuing confusion, they managed to kill or mortally wound the English leaders Watts and Thomas Morgan, the chief of the buccaneers. These pirates, infuriated by the loss of their chief, accused the English militia of treachery. English resistance subsequently collapsed, and a humiliating defeat followed. Many English colonists who refused to take an oath of allegiance to the French king were forced to leave St. Christopher. Considerable damage was done to their property.

The French at home were ecstatic, and a medal was struck to commemorate the happy event. It was indeed a far-reaching victory, for it initiated a series of English defeats that caused alarm in London. Although Antigua and Nevis were still in English hands the French had gained the initiative in this part of the Caribbean and the Dutch were pleased bystanders. For the other English islands, the immediate result was their subjection to daily incursions of the French naval forces, many times combined with the Dutch. The latter, especially, expanded the range of their raiding activities and were literally everywhere. The English fleet that was intended for an attack on Curaçao had dispersed,[59] for the buccaneers had proved to be unreliable allies. Led by Willoughby of Barbados, the English governors barraged the home government with requests for help: "Barbados and the other Caribbee Islands are in great danger from the attempts of Dutch, French, and other enemies, and the insurrection of slaves.... The Dutch are sending privateers that way and the French have landed 3000 firearms in one of their colonies."[60]

From their unassailable position in the Caribbean in 1665 and the beginning of 1666, the English were now deteriorating rapidly. By the summer of 1666 they were on the defensive. Using buccaneers to further national goals had been a dismal failure. Taking advantage of English impotence, the French continued the offensive and consolidated their hold over the area. Colbert developed a new colonial policy for the French Antilles and organized another French West India Company. A representative of the changed order, Alexandre de Prouville, Marquis de Tracy, was sent forth to confirm royal authority in the French islands by appointing new governors selected at home. Before long, however, the new French appointees, who had not always been chosen for their ability in colonial administration, soon had French planters aroused and indignant. Before long the islands seethed with unrest as the new governors, who were following Colbert's orders, imposed strict restrictions on trade with all foreigners.[61] French planters had long enjoyed an amicable commercial relationship with the Dutch and had established a useful credit arrangement with them. Agents of the Dutch West India Company lived among them. Dutertre claims that de Tracy found all the French Antilles "burdened by excessive debts to the Dutch" and that Dutch heretics and Jews were even permitted to practice their religion openly.[62] De Tracy's crackdown seems to have been undertaken without any real understanding of the reciprocal need which was evident between French planters and Dutch merchants. The band that tied the two together was mutual benefit, and when one partner was forcibly withdrawn, an *extrême misère* of the other was the noticeable result.

Two exceptions to the generally incompetent French administrators were to be found on Martinique and Tortuga. Martinique's Governor de Cloderé will be met later in connection with a combined French-Dutch attack on the English fleet at Nevis. Bertrand d'Ogeron, governor of Tortuga since 1665, soon proved to be one of the ablest French officials in the Caribbean. Having started out as a planter on Martinique, he became, through circumstance, a highly respected man among the buccaneers who visited Fort Royal. When Colbert sought an effective leader to consolidate French power in the islands, d'Ogeron was suggested as the one candidate who commanded the respect of both the French buccaneers and the malcontent planters.

D'Ogeron's task was to make Tortuga a center of French authority and to extend this influence to nearby Hispaniola, a complex assignment which he accomplished with consummate skill. He not only succeeded in overcoming the opposition of the buccaneers and their insistence on fraternizing with the Dutch, but he was also able, in a very short time, to settle seven hundred or more Frenchmen on the northern coast of Hispaniola. Some of these settlers were reformed buccaneers, and some were French emigrants who were brought to the Caribbean at d'Ogeron's expense. Within a few years, their number had grown to two thousand and an ever increasing quantity of slaves. Taking his cue from the English, d'Ogeron enlisted some of the recalcitrant buccaneers in order to further national ends; a war had begun and France was in desperate need of men in the Caribbean.

England felt so threatened by France's entry into the war that Charles' ministers were driven to seek a rapprochement with Spain. To this end a special envoy was dispatched to Madrid in order to bargain for the recognition of England's prerogatives in the Indies as well as for a share in the slave trade. The Spaniards were naturally not forthcoming, since Charles Stuart was married to a Portuguese princess and was thereby committed to that country's defense. All was not entirely lost, however. In 1665, Philip IV had died and had been succeeded by the dim-witted Charles II of Hapsburg. In the same year the Spaniards had suffered a crushing defeat at the hands of the Portuguese which ended all hopes of reconquest. Only the long arms of Louis XIV kept the frustrated Spaniards from reaching an understanding with the English, for this monarch sought to preserve a balance of power that best suited his own interests. Indeed, if not for this political factor, France and England would have fought side by side against the Dutch.

The second Anglo-Dutch war had thus far resulted in unmistakable advantages for the French, and their allies the Dutch expected to reap also some sweet fruits of victory. The English, of course, wanted desperately to regain the initiative, and Governor Willoughby was ordered to recapture St. Christopher. Heading a fleet of eight ships and one thousand men, he left Barbados on July 18, 1666, for this purpose. Aware of the fact that his forces were too weak to take on both the French and the Dutch, Willoughby must also have known that the hurricane season was due. After capturing a few prizes en route, the English arrived at Guadeloupe, where Willoughby probably intended to join his brother William and the latter's five hundred or six hundred men. His fleet, however, was severely battered by a violent hurricane which followed on the heels of a battle with two French ships. Only a few ships reached the safety of the Leeward Antilles. Willoughby's own ship was lost in the storm, and the governor was never seen again. The English crewmen who survived were immediately taken prisoner by the French population of the islands. The English were, understandably, morose. Pepys was hysterical, and in his own words "mighty troubled at ill newes from Barbados." The Dutch and the French, on the other hand, rejoiced at this stroke of fate which seemed to be God's own intervention. The Caribbean now lay entirely at their mercy, and far-reaching consequences were not long in making an appearance.

Tobago was one of the first islands to be recaptured by the French when its tiny English garrison surrendered to French planters from Grenada in August, 1666. In November the French attacked Antigua but were repulsed by an English garrison that had just been reinforced by three hundred men. In December, however, they returned with seven hundred men, and successfully occupied the island. Early in 1667 the island of Montserrat was forced to surrender to a French fleet under Admiral Antoine le Febvre de la Barre. Of the Leeward Islands, only Nevis now remained in English hands, yet the island was flooded with starving refugees from St. Christopher and elsewhere, all suffering the effects of the French-employed buccaneers' blockade. In the west Jamaica was still English, as was Barbados in the southeast.63

Meanwhile the Dutch, inspired by the example of the victorious French and unwilling to allow the French to reap what they had sown, moved to offensives of their own. One was initiated from Curaçao, the other more important one by the States of Zeeland. Although the main sources describing the reconquest of St. Eustatius differ in details, the story seems to be that the Dutch, operating from Curaçao and led by Gerart Bogaert, came to the island in November, 1666. According to Bogaert's report the English garrison, consisting of around 200 men, soon asked to discuss peace terms with the 120 Dutch assailants. Only a few days were needed to agree upon the necessary conditions, and during that period the Dutch were reinforced by fifty Frenchmen from St. Christopher.

In the meantime, though, the Lieutenant-General of the French Antilles, de la Barre, dispatched two men-of-war to St. Eustatius with 150 men. The French captain of this mission asked the Dutch for permission to be the first to march into the surrendered fortress because, after all, the French were their allies, and as the subject of a king he should have priority over the republican Dutch. Once they were in the fortress, however, the French secured the English surrender and treacherously drove the Dutch from the island. They seized everything of value and so thoroughly looted the place that it thereafter altogether lost its attraction as a colony. Leaving a garrison of eighty men behind, the French departed. In August 1667, after months of tortured negotiations, Louis XIV ordered his countrymen to evacuate the island, and, together with Saba, it was returned to Dutch control.[64]

This miscarried effort to reconquer one of their lost possessions was soon followed by an offensive of a much stronger character. The war situation in Europe throughout the year 1666 still demanded the full attention of the States General, since the federal government had been engaged in equipping and supporting Dutch fleets in European waters. Too busy to divert their time to minor scenes of conflict, Their High Mightinesses had condescended to leave these problems to the care of the provincial governments. Their acquiescence had moved the States of Zeeland to attempt to wrest away the English settlements on the Wild Coast and in the Caribbean. The former Dutch colonies in the Guianas, with the exception of Berbice, had all been conquered by order of Willoughby, and virtually the whole coast was under English control. The United Provinces, and particularly Zeeland, had long regarded this area as a valuable possession. Some of the settlements had been under the direct supervision of the Chamber of Zeeland, others under patrons. All had been governed under the nominal authority of the West India Company. Zeeland now sought help for her project from Holland.

The original plan for such a Zeelandian expedition was drawn up by Pieter de Huybert, who since 1664 had been pensionary and secretary of the States of Zeeland. He proposed the following: twelve ships with thirty to forty guns were to sail to St. Helena in an attempt to intercept the English East India merchant fleet. Achieving this, not only would Dutch honor have been avenged and lacerated national feelings assuaged, but also, once and for all, England would be made to "feel deeply the sorrows of war."[65] Afterwards, six of the ships would proceed to the Caribbean to prey upon enemy trade and disrupt English communications.

De Huybert's plan, however, required the unflinching support of Holland. Yet Amsterdam was intent upon controlling such an expedition in order to promote its own special interests in the Mediterranean. De Huybert and Grand Pensionary de Witt continued to squabble over the issue. At a meeting of the admiralty board of Amsterdam, the Zeelandian proposals were discussed and rejected, although an invitation was extended to incorporate her contingent into a powerful Amsterdam fleet which would operate in European waters.

Zeeland had no interests in European waters, and her unwavering leaders determined to undertake the project in spite of Amsterdam's refusal. De Huybert, nevertheless, maintained contact with de Witt, and since he was not easily discouraged, he constantly accosted the grand pensionary with new ideas. His latest proposals were designed to inflict damage on the English in the Caribbean "not only to incommodate their trade and navigation, but also to lash out at their naval power and to reconquer, with God's help, the territory they have taken away from us." Zeeland's ambitious representative also harped on the patriotic value of this mission which not only would render "a considerable service and reputation to the State but would also be of great detriment of the enemy."[66] Advantages would also accrue to Dutch trade if such a venture were undertaken. He further pointed out that the enterprise could not but please Louis XIV, and the Dutch might be able to count on French help. With some luck, they might even become eligible for "free and open trade" in the French Antilles.

De Huybert's persuasive arguments were not lost on deaf ears and de Witt became openly sympathetic while displaying an avid interest in detail. Since French successes in the Caribbean were not yet known in the United Provinces at this time—around May, 1666—and because the Dutch national fleets were committed to European waters, where they had won a decisive although pyrrhic victory in June, no real effort was spent in realizing de Huybert's dream.

The vast damage suffered by the Dutch in June and August of that same year in the battles on the North Sea seriously interfered with any plans for the Caribbean. Zeeland's foray was once more postponed as the States General saw its first responsibility to restore its fleets for operation in Europe. Still not yet resigned, de Huybert, late in the year, made another appeal to the admiralty boards to join Zeeland in an attack on the common enemy in the West Indies. But again the Zeelandian pensionary received no support and was left with the understanding that such a venture must be undertaken by the individual province or not at all. Thus, after a year of discussions, negotiations, and correspondence, the Provincial States of Zeeland decided to take matters into its own hands and ordered the secret equipping of five ships, later increased to seven, to be sent to the Wild Coast, the Caribbean islands, Virginia, and Newfoundland.

Abraham Crijnssen, scion of a highly reputable seafaring family and a fellow countryman of de Ruyter with whom he shared many qualities, was appointed to command this squadron. Famous for his courage against the Dunkirk privateers, when he had earned himself an enviable reputation as a "new Beggar," Crijnssen had also behaved admirably during the first Anglo-Dutch war. The Dutch eighteenth-century historian van Kampen qualifies him as "a valiant commander" and "a Zeelander."[67]

Crijnssen left Zeeland on December 30, 1666, with a commission which Warnsinck, a Dutch naval historian, has called "one of the most remarkable documents in Dutch maritime history."[68] So comprehensive were the tasks which the States of Zeeland had laid upon Crijnssen's shoulders, so unlimited its confidence in his fearlessness, so sanguine its expectations, that the tiny force it put at his disposal now seems ludicrous.[69] The Dutch squadron was authorized to reconquer Surinam, which had been seized by Captain (later Major) John Scott on orders from Willoughby in 1665; to evict the English from Berbice, Essequibo, and Pomeroon; to re-establish Zeelandian authority on the island of Tobago; and, despite the severe setback experienced by de Ruyter's larger fleet the year before, to attack Barbados. Whatever the results of these ventures, Crijnssen was ordered to take as many islands as possible from the English without French help, and afterward expected to contact the French at Guadeloupe and invite them to join him for a series of raids on those islands then supposedly still in English hands.[70]

Nor was this all. Crijnssen was then supposed to make sail for Virginia in all haste and to arrive no later than April, 1667, to inflict damage on the enemy and, believe it or not, establish the authority of the Zeelandian Chamber of the WIC there also. All this was to be done without bloodshed, if possible. Furthermore, since Zeeland did not quite trust the French allies, if Crijnssen were to come upon the French anywhere in control of former Dutch possessions, he was to thank them profusely for saving him the problem of recapturing these colonies and politely ask for their surrender. Should the French, against all reasonable expectation, refuse to turn over these regions, Crijnssen was to inform them of his obligation to take them by force. The commander carried with him a letter from the States of Zeeland that was directed to French Admiral de la Barre expressing the hope "that you will not neglect to heed [the advice]."

To all appearances the Zeelandian States were sincerely of the opinion, as evidenced by Crijnssen's supplementary instruction, that their representative could implement these orders, and that with able leadership and good luck, even more might be accomplished. The future would justify the surmise that if the voyage out had been blessed by favorable winds and if Crijnssen had not assumed responsibility for the reorganization of the colonial governments on the Wild Coast, the expedition might well have progressed along the lines that were set out for him by the masters in Middelburg.

Three frigates and four other small vessels with 750 sailors and 225 soldiers made up the entire force. The squadron's first stop was made at the Canary Islands in order to harass English shipping in this area. After the fruitlessness of this task had been proven, however, Crijnssen altered his course and set sail for Cayenne, then in French hands. He abandoned any hope of taking this settlement from the French, since he did not wish to antagonize these questionable allies so soon. The relations with the French governor of Cayenne, although not overly warm, remained officially correct. Crijnssen now proceeded to Paramaribo, capital of Surinam, and arrived below the fortress on the afternoon of February 26, 1667.

The following command for surrender was sent to the English governor of this area, William Byam: "Your self, & all ye Inhabitants of ye Country shall absolutely retaine ye Entire property & possession of what they have wthout loss of ye last thing," if they surrendered, but adding: "In case you refuse it I am resolved to attaque you by Sea & Land, wth ye designe of killing all that shall oppose, not giving Quarter to any one."[71] Exactly fifteen minutes were given to the English to make up their minds.

In due time, Byam informed Crijnssen that his honor obliged him to resist. The very next day, the Dutch closed in on the fort, a maneuver not expected by Byam. The raiders disembarked. Fighting was intense and the Dutch gunners from aboard the ships were doing their job with deadly accuracy. With his gunpowder supplies nearly exhausted and many of his men killed or wounded, Byam was forced to surrender before long. Crijnssen gave quarter to the garrison and permitted Byam and his soldiers "to march forthwith out of ye said Fort wth all his Officers & Soldiers wth flying colours, light Matches, Drums beating." He then announced that all private property would be respected for those who took an oath of allegiance to the States General of the United Provinces. A great number of English soldiers went over to the Dutch, "some for gain, others for Fear" and "swore Fidelity to ye States."[72] Yet their capitulation was in the main stimulated by rumors about the imminent arrival of a French fleet at Cayenne coupled with the Dutch promise to defend them. Crijnssen's victory was gilded by the capture of an English merchantman which was unaware of the situation and entered unsuspectingly. Fort Willoughby, as it was called by the English, not only changed hands; its name was erased to make way for a reborn Fort Zeelandia.

Although many of the colonists were happy enough to be free of the regal government imposed on them by Francis Lord Willoughby and his brother William, Byam still influenced a significant part of the population with whom he was busily plotting a counterattack from the interior. Crijnssen's position, however, was aided by a feared invasion of Arawak Indians "which will effect such mischiefe, as will consequently produce yᵉ inevitable ruine of us all."[73] Still at large, Byam soon realized that his defeat was only a matter of time and that he would be able to get better conditions from the Dutch than he would from the French or the Indians. He thus entered into new negotiations with Crijnssen. Their sharpest dispute arose over the oath of allegiance. The problem was ultimately resolved with an agreement to change the wording to allow the colonists to remain neutral in the event of an English attack on Surinam. Subjects of His English Majesty could now take the oath in all honor and conscience.

Further disputes, which were aggravated by a lack of interpreters, concerned a ransom of 500,000 pounds of sugar to be paid to the Dutch. Wrangling brought the figure down to 100,000 pounds with the added guarantee that English subjects would be given equal rights and the permission to sell their property and depart.[74] The treaty was signed on March 6 aboard Crijnssen's ship *Zeeland*.

In Barbados and England Byam was loudly accused of treason and cowardice. William Lord Willoughby, who had succeeded his brother Francis as governor of Barbados, considered the surrender an infamous act. He wrote to Clarendon, "upon articles to one Crynsen...He received it in the name of the Noble & Mighty States of Zeeland— Brewers & Cheesemongers I presume most of them to be...I thought that Byam would have defended it to the last, but he yielded without a stroke, & still remains there."[75] But Byam was later vindicated by a court-martial.

Crijnssen's reduction of Surinam had been very fortuitous, but now he neglected the most emphasized aspect of his instruction, namely speed. It is true that much remained to be done: the fortress needed repair, and the Zeelandian commander wanted particularly to post the officers of the neighboring Dutch settlements. Thus it was that instead of sailing to Virginia in late March, Crijnssen was still in Surinam on March 27, where he was surprised by the arrival of a frigate under the command of his fellow countryman Boudewijn Keuvelaer, who had been sent to his assistance in January. Crijnssen used this reinforcement to establish more firmly Dutch rule in the western part of Guiana. When he finally did leave Paramaribo, three weeks behind schedule, he still did not head for Tobago or Virginia. Instead, after two English prizes fell into his lap, he sailed to Berbice.

Keuvelaer had already preceded his commander to this Dutch colony which was governed under the private patronship of the heirs of Abraham van Pere. Two other settlements, Essequibo and Pome-

Fig. 15. Admiral Michiel Adriaenszoon de Ruyter

roon, had previously been lost to Willoughby's forces under John Scott. They were, however, technically restored to Dutch authority by Matthijs Bergenaer, who was himself commander of Berbice. Crijnssen's problem was to persuade Bergenaer actually to submit Essequibo and Pomeroon to the provincial control of the Zeelandian States. In a letter to Bergenaer, Crijnssen advised that he was sending Keuvelaer to assume command and that the latter was authorized to use force if necessary. The commander of Berbice received Keuvelaer cordially, however, and relinquished all claims to the two colonies in return for compensation for any expenses he had incurred in their recapture.[76]

Having lived for many years without any formal religious observance, the colonists were especially happy to learn that Keuvelaer had a minister among his crew. While the two leaders worked out the details of the colonial transfer, this representative of the Dutch Reformed Church busied himself baptizing the many young ones who had flocked in at the news of his availibility. Two weeks later when Crijnssen himself arrived, he endorsed the agreement that had been worked out, and appointed commanders for Essequibo and Pomeroon. The booty taken from the English, including 400,000 guilders worth of sugar, was sent to Zeeland.[77] At long last Crijnssen felt free to pursue his other objectives and subsequently he departed with most of his ships for Tobago, where he arrived in April of the same year.

Unaware that the site had been deserted for quite a while, Crijnssen worked out several alternative plans of approach to the island. If it were held by the French, he would have to try to persuade them as allies to turn the island over to him. If, on the other hand, the English were there, arms would decide the outcome of the contest. But the Zeelander was delighted when he learned that Tobago was uninhabited by Europeans and that the natives were inclined to be friendly. Although the fort and all other buildings were found in an advanced stage of ruin, a grim reminder of French occupation and havoc, the soil of the island had retained its fertility, and there was an abundance of vegetation. In the cane fields, for instance, some 500,000 pounds of sugar was ripening and labor was plentiful. Crijnssen decided to restore the fort and station a garrison of twenty-nine men before leaving for Guadeloupe.

Meanwhile, news of Francis Lord Willoughby's abortive mission and his presumed death at sea had reached England and stirred the government to an unwonted display of energy. William Willoughby, Francis' interim successor, in England at the time, urged the government to equip a powerful fleet to re-establish British prestige in the Caribbean. The situation in early 1667 was very serious indeed. In addition to losing the islands, England had also been expelled from the Wild Coast. In February of that year a powerful French fleet of fifteen sails had taken possession of Antigua after a previous conquest of some months earlier. The French had imposed the oath of allegiance to Louis XIV, and once again plundered the inhabitants. Contrary to the articles of surrender, they then left the colonists at the mercy of the natives. Another French fleet of sixteen or eighteen sails was reported heading for Cayenne to invade the Caribbean from there, and the threat of Dutch interlopers was never far from the English.[78] His Majesty's government was, therefore, not long in acting.

As a first step a fleet was fitted out. The decision was made to place at Willoughby's disposal a regiment of well-disciplined and experienced soldiers under Sir Thomas Bridge who, as Newton says, "had seen much war service."[79] In lieu of a large fleet, which would take up too much time to equip, some reinforcements were forthwith dispatched to Barbados. These stood under the command of Sir John Berry. The remainder, under Sir John Harman, would follow as soon as possible.

Meanwhile, Spain was conspicuously absent during these events in the Caribbean, which is certain evidence of her decline as a great naval power. Curiously, until the last quarter of the seventeenth century, the Spanish government had consistently refused to issue letters of reprisal against English and French privateers. Such a recourse might not only have proved efficacious against the pirates, but it would have also saved the king a pretty penny, for it would have filled American seas with armed vessels without a single royal expenditure. This reprisal measure, then, can only have been frustrated by the Casa de Contratación and the rich merchant guild of Seville, either of whom would have been concerned lest such commissions should lead to infringements on its commercial monopolies.

In the 1660's, therefore, one of the councillors of the *Almirantazgo* —mercantile guild—of Flanders sought permission to send privateers from Flemish ports to the West Indies to punish the Caribbean pirates and to defend the coasts of the Spanish colonial empire. This request was denied. Three years later, analogous proposals were made by certain *armadores*—shipowners—of Biscay. These offers promised to send six to eight ships to America for defensive purposes in return for the privilege of sending free of duty two additional ships full of merchandise. The ulterior motive behind this scheme was too transparent to escape the suspicious eyes of the Casa, and it too was turned down. Not until 1674 did Spain choose to fight evil with evil and to employ privateers against privateers.[80]

When news reached Crijnssen that an English squadron had overpowered four merchantmen at Guadeloupe—two of them Dutch ships from Amsterdam and Zeeland—and had sought refuge at the Leeward Islands, the Zeelandian commander decided to set sail for Martinique to discuss counterattack plans with the French governor. A proposal to join forces was reluctantly accepted by Crijnssen after he had received permission to inspect the French ships. "We know the power the English can acquire with so many ships," he wrote, "but have never seen any proof of French valor at sea." The combined fleet—five ships from the French West India Company and the five Crijnssen had then at his disposal—was supposed to pursue and give battle to the English. After the Dutch had acquiesced to the terms of the agreement, the French captains expressed some hesitancy about the limited nature of allied power, and the whole project might have been called off except for the arrival of de la Barre and his nine ships.

De la Barre had become famous as a result of having taken Cayenne from the Dutch in 1664 without much bloodshed, but he was soon to prove himself unworthy in the present situation. "An informant of the French States General, suddenly transformed into a man of war" is de la Roncière's appropriate judgment.[81] In spite of this limitation, it was de la Barre who realized from the start that the island of Nevis represented one of the main keys to English hegemony in the Caribbean. When he had proposed its conquest, a French war council had summarily turned his plan down.

Discussions about a combined French-Dutch action were again revitalized. Although Crijnssen's instruction did not authorize him to involve the Zeelandian squadron in a joint enterprise, the situation in the Caribbean, where pirates, privateers, buccaneers, and filibusters —four different names for only slightly different professions—were disturbing all the European nations, required some unforseen decisions; preventing the English foe from trying to regain the initiative was the main point. Crijnssen, therefore, presumed a merger with de la Barre against the English fleet to be the best solution.[82] Unfortunately for the Dutch, however, the French were in the best position to exploit this situation.

The English squadron appeared off Barbados in March, the forerunner of a bigger fleet that would bring William Lord Willoughby and Sir

Tobias Bridge's soldiers to this island, just after de la Barre had recaptured Montserrat and while Crijnssen was losing precious time in Surinam. Its commander Sir John Berry knew the Caribbean well. His courage in many encounters against buccaneers had earned him an excellent reputation among English colonists, and they quickly agreed to increase his squadron with eight additional ships. By the beginning of April, Berry commanded twelve ships, including his own four frigates, and he departed at once for Guadeloupe to undertake the highly successful venture to which we have alluded.

News that Berry's fleet was blockading St. Christopher intensified the discussions that were going on between the governors of Martinique and Guadeloupe, de la Barre and Crijnssen. The Dutch commander now made his cooperation and aid contingent upon dividing the combined French-Dutch fleet into two squadrons, one of which was to be under his command. When this was agreed to, the project, at least on paper, seemed to have everything to guarantee a quick victory. The two squadrons together counted eighteen ships, including Crijnssen's five Zeelandian sails—the others were still on the Wild Coast—and six hundred troops; five hundred more were enlisted at Guadeloupe.[83]

On May 17, the fleet sailed toward Nevis in anticipation of catching Berry unaware at St. Christopher. The surprise attack failed, however, because of poor timing. Although the two squadrons were scheduled to reach Nevis at dawn on May 20, they were still many miles south of the island at that time, and, as bad luck would have it, the French and Dutch sails were sighted by some English frigates that were cruising between Nevis and Redonda. De la Barre did order his ships to pursue the frigates and fire on them, but the English sailed faster—they were probably better sailors—and made safe escape to Charlestown. The incident alerted Berry and gave him time to put his fleet to sea.

The so-called Battle of Nevis ensued, the only sea battle of the second Anglo-Dutch war in which French and Dutch ships took joint action against the English. Since the two sides were well matched in numbers, armament, and crews, the victory would presumably go to the force with the better leadership.[84]

De la Barre immediately gave evidence that he lacked this essential completely by scrapping the combat plan (see Appendix IX) and sending his Vice-Admiral de Cloderé to fight in the vanguard. Although de Cloderé apparently understood the sudden change in rotation, the same cannot be said of the rear-guard units. These latter presumed that they were still following the original instructions and stayed close to the admiral. They thus remained some distance from the core of the encounter. Crijnssen, who headed the other squadron, was confused by these consecutive bad maneuvers, but nevertheless pursued the attack and headed straight for the English flagship *Coronation*. He opened such a heavy fire "that her courage soon disappeared," and her musketeers and gunners fled to the stern.[85] Two English fireships came to the admiral's rescue and forced Crijnssen to relinquish his quarry. But in this maneuver the Dutch were unable to prevent the enemy from sailing windward, which kept the Zeelander safely at bay.

Meanwhile, the Dutch vessels had followed their leader and launched out at the other ships in Berry's fleet. The French ships under Crijnssen's command hung back, however, and followed their admiral who, for unknown reasons, sailed away toward St. Christopher, leaving his allies to an uncertain fate. His Vice-Admiral de Cloderé, in fury, shouted as the admiral passed by "that it was a shame to run away from the enemy in such a way and that he should again attack him."[86] But he and the Dutch ships were left at the mercy of Berry. The Englishman, for reasons not quite clear, did not pursue his easy victory, although he had lost only one ship, probably blown up by its own powder. French and Dutch losses were likewise minimal.

A sorrowful Crijnssen was forced to retire and followed the treacherous de la Barre to St. Christopher where he engaged him in a heated discussion of the battle. The Frenchman was scathingly attacked by the Dutch commander, and support from his fellow naval leaders went to Crijnssen. In response to de la Barre's shallow pretexts and flimsy reasons, Crijnssen reported to the Zeelandian admiralty board, "He made many excuses because his captains did not fight well and his ships were not very sailable."[87]

At St. Christopher Crijnssen's squadron was joined by the rest of his ships from the Wild Coast. On May 25, the Zeelanders, again seven sails strong and glad to be rid of such questionable allies as the French, set course to Virginia and there caused heavy losses to English shipping.

When Crijnssen finally returned home to Flushing, peace negotiations between the Dutch and the English had already been concluded at Breda. Crijnssen's report on the "Battle of Nevis," sent by de Huybert to Johan de Witt, caused the grand pensionary to remark that "the French have conducted themselves so womanly and disloyally that I would like to hear how Commander de la Barre reported this affair to his king."[88]

There is no question but that, after the "Battle of Nevis," control of the Caribbean shifted again to the English. Berry had begun an offensive prior to this engagement and was now free to pursue his former objective. Antigua and Montserrat were soon recaptured, and nothing prevented him from returning once more to St. Christopher. Somewhat later, perhaps pushed by Henry Willoughby, William's son, and reinforced with some ships from Barbados and a landing force of 3,500 men, he tried an attack on this island, only to be decisively beaten off. The setback, however, was easily assimilated as the English position continued to improve.

When the larger fleet under Sir John Harman arrived a few days after this rebuff, the Dutch had already left the Caribbean. Ensuing battles were, therefore, fought only between the English and the French. The first of these encounters, undertaken when Harman refused to endorse another attempt on St. Christopher, aimed instead at the capture of Martinique. De la Barre's fleet, as could be anticipated, lay at anchor in the harbor of St. Pierre, and the French admiral resolutely refused to leave his safety to meet the English in combat. Harman and Berry were reduced to cruising up and down the coast of Martinique sniping at French ships and fortifications. Harman finally decided on a general attack. He boldly sailed into the harbor sowing destruction and utter confusion. The French fleet was either disabled or destroyed. This "long-drawn-out action," as Newton calls it, represented the end of French naval power in the Caribbean and effectively restored English supremacy.[89]

The English were now free to consolidate their hold over the area and to take whatever they chose from the French and the Dutch. Harman did not care to occupy St. Christopher, however. Instead, Berry was left to continue the blockade of that island while Harman and Henry Willoughby set sail to wrest Cayenne from the French and Surinam from the Dutch, in that order. By August the English fleet, which had been reinforced with seven sails and 850 troops, was ready to set sail. Although a lull in trade winds much delayed the crossing, the fleet finally made Cayenne late in September. The French vainly attempted to obstruct the disembarkation of English troops, but they were quickly driven to surrender while their governor Lefebvre de Lézy fled to Surinam. The English had no intention of keeping the colony for themselves, however; they did remove the biggest guns and all the gunpowder, loaded many provisions and 250 slaves, and left abruptly on October 9.

Unmolested, the English fleet proceeded to Paramaribo on October 13, anchored in full view of Fort Zeelandia, and dispatched an ultimatum to the Dutch commander Maurits de Rame "the which if you refuse to doe, you are to expect noe favour but such as is customary in stormed places."[90] Troops were landed half a mile below the fort, and before dark the entire area was surrounded by the English.

A lull in the wind delayed Harman's attack for four days, until October 17 to be precise. A blistering fire was then opened against the fort from the ships which had been brought in as close to the shore as possible. The Dutch garrison suffered heavy losses, and de Rame, whose men refused to man the cannons, was forced to raise a flag of truce. As he wrote his conditions for surrender, the fort was forcibly entered by some English soldiers who had swum ashore and who decided to act without Harman's leave. De Rame protested vehemently against this unorthodox procedure, but the fort was in English hands and there was not much he could do. Of his original garrison of 250 men, about 200 had survived the grueling attack. Losses by the assailants were heavy, too. Among the prisoners taken by the English was William Byam, the former governor. Harman and Henry Willoughby now returned to Barbados where they learned that peace had been concluded on July 31, 1667. According to Articles III and VI of the treaty, Cayenne and Surinam had to be accorded to their former owners. Three weeks after the English departed, therefore, a Dutch fleet arrived and demanded the return of Surinam (see Chapter XVI).

"England," observed a member of the English delegation to Breda, "had been beaten into peace" by the Dutch.[91] Growing dissatisfaction about the course of events brought the English to the little town that had been Charles' choice and where he had lived for many years in exile. But still England came away with substantial gains: New Netherland remained New York, and although Surinam was lost, British commercial enterprises continued to thrive in that area to such an extent that part of the region eventually became a permanent part of the British empire. The Dutch did manage, after suitable delays by Louis XIV, to reclaim St. Eustatius and Saba from France.

The net effect of two years of war in the Caribbean was tragic as well as costly. Most of the non-Spanish colonies had lost such prosperity as they had known during the previous forty years. Peace had not come a moment too soon since the situation on many islands verged on the desperate. A few had escaped attack, but they had nevertheless paid a crushing and excruciating price in taxes in order to finance their safety. England had probably suffered the most: St. Christopher's English half had to be colonized all over again, Nevis had suffered from overcrowding and starvation, and Antigua had been devastated from one end to the other. Most of the Lesser Antilles had also been pillaged and victimized by the continuous onslaught of buccaneers.

The war proved a mortal blow to the WIC. Although the company had never laid claims to any exclusive rights in the Caribbean, it had built up excellent trade relations with French and English colonists, and its ties with the Spanish settlements continued to be close. The Peace of Breda put an end to Dutch supremacy in the commercial field since the Navigation Laws were thereafter rigidly enforced, and French policy similarly restricted the Dutch from trade with the French Antilles. It is true that Dutch ships were still sufficiently numerous to drive the English and French together in an anti-Dutch effort five years later, and that struggle was to be the final fatal blow to the moribund Dutch West India Company. But with Breda the Dutch were already over the hill.

One other consequence of the Peace of 1667 should be noticed here. The settlement among England, France, and the United Provinces marked the final distribution of colonial possessions in the Caribbean. The exchange of colonies game which had plagued the area for forty years now came to an end and for the next hundred years there was virtually no alteration in colonial holdings. After 1667, therefore, the islands returned to prosperity and peace, only slightly disturbed by the third Anglo-Dutch war of 1672, and when buccaneering ended in the 1680's, true political stability of a highly durable variety was the enviable result.

16

THE WILD COAST

...toon mij eerst dat gij besit goeden moet,
En dat gij vooraf de rijs naer Suriname doet,
Zoals van outs ieder opregt Zeeuws joncman past
Dien eene Zeeuwische maeght door haer schoonheyt verrast.[1]

Dutch interest in the Wild Coast, or Guiana—that area of the South American continent between the Orinoco and the Amazon rivers—dated, as shown previously, from the era which preceded the Truce. Unlike their purely privateering and smuggling activities in the Caribbean, the Dutch created fortified trading posts in this region. During the Truce, and persistently later, in spite of many frustrations, they tried to establish colonies there; one, Surinam, still survives as an autonomous part of the Netherlands. The colonial rivals of the seventeenth century on the Wild Coast find their modern counterparts in British, French, and Dutch Guiana. The British and French probably settled in the area after the Dutch.[2]

Some information about the Dutch trading posts survives. They were frequently situated in very remote parts of the territory because their customers, the Indians, lived there. Trade was conducted on a barter basis; knives, other hardware, or cloth were exchanged for tobacco, red dye, cacao, and other products of the country. One typical commodity was slaves; the ferocious Caribs enslaved other Indian tribes for the purpose of selling them to the Dutch.[3]

The trading posts were wooden shanties which were surrounded by an earthen wall or palisade as a precaution against surprise attacks by unfriendly Indians. A "postholder," two or three Dutchmen of inferior rank, some twenty soldiers, and a varying number of Indian slaves were the usual inhabitants. Gradually some of these posts developed into small settlements, dependent for their livelihood upon a highly profitable trade with both the neighboring settlers and Indian tribes. The Dutch regularly sold cheaper and bought at better prices. In addition, before and during the Truce, separate colonizing attempts had been made in the area.

Soon after the foundation of the West India Company, the Heren XIX turned their attention to the Wild Coast. Prior to 1621, the Dutch settlements in that area had been independent patronships; in others, founded after 1621, the patron stood under the immediate supervision of the company. In the early years friction between the patron and the company was not an infrequent occurrence. Although the charter of the WIC specifically forbade private trading within its monopoly, it was, according to Edmundson, never entirely suppressed especially in the patronships.[4] A collision of this sort is revealed in the following interesting example.

In the proceedings of the XIX for November 4, 1623, we find a request from burgomaster Jan de Moor of Flushing for permission to send seventy colonists to the Amazon.[5] It will be remembered that during the Truce this type of expedition was a favorite among Zeelanders. However, the XIX considered de Moor's request an infringement of their charter and refused his petition. But de Moor, having expected approval, had already sent his two ships. Faced with this situation, the XIX ordered their admiral, Willekens, who was about to depart for the conquest of the Bay of All Saints, to bring back the seventy colonists at his first opportunity. They were returned with a rich cargo totaling some sixty thousand pounds sterling in value.[6]

Jan de Moor and his company were now moved to the following step. Realizing that private enterprises were doomed because of such opposition from the WIC, he opened negotiations with the XIX and the Chamber of Zeeland for trade in the Amazon at a valuation. He and his partners saw that they were in no position to oppose company policy.

The attitude of Spanish and Portuguese authorities toward foreign invasions on the Wild Coast has also been noted. Madrid bestirred itself to warn the Portuguese that the nuisance should be stopped before it increased. In 1623 through special orders to Luis Aranha de Vasconcellos, governor of the area, Lisbon roused itself to authorize the removal of the Dutch and all other foreign settlers. Aranha found an energetic and brave ally in the *Capitão Mor* of Grao Pará, Bento Maciel Parente. Together, they levied 100 Portuguese and 1,000 to 1,500 Indians for the mission. After destroying some settlements (probably English and French) in the Amazon Delta, the two leaders proposed to sweep away the Dutch who were further upriver. Aranha set out first late in May of 1623. Near a Dutch settlement at the Curupá River he halted and waited for Maciel since he believed the Dutch to be too strong for his forces alone. Maciel, accompanied by one Pedro Teixeira, a *flamenco* hater, soon to be famous in those regions, joined Aranha in late June or early July. With little effort the Portuguese first destroyed a "joint" settlement at the mouth of the

Ginipape which was held by French, English, and Dutch colonists. This may have been Fort Adriaensz.[7]

Maciel next attacked and burned several other settlements, including the Dutch post at the Curupá. He and his men then moved up the Xingu River, attacked and captured Forts Orange and Nassau, and killed or captured all their occupants. A large Dutch vessel with reinforcements for these colonists under the command of Pieter Adriaenszoon Ita was attacked by Maciel's Indians and forced to drop anchor at the mouth of the Okiari River. The ship's captain and crew escaped, however, and presumably made their way safely up the river to an English settlement. The Dutch colonies on the Amazon were thus eliminated, if only temporarily. At the Curupá River Maciel founded a Portuguese fort, called Mariocay, to serve as an outpost against future invaders; he left a garrison there and returned to Pará covered with military glory.

Meanwhile, before news of the Portuguese success had reached the United Provinces, another venture to the Wild Coast was well under-way. The Duifken ("Pigeon") sailed from Texel in July, 1623, pre-sumably without the permission of the Heren xix. Aboard were ten families who bore, like their leader Jesse de Forest, French names and who were, no doubt, French Huguenots who had fled to the Low Countries.[8] At the Amazon the Duifken met another Dutch vessel under Pieter Janszoon of Flushing, and learned of the Portuguese attack as well as of the burning of Ita's ship. Because they were afraid to settle too close to the Portuguese, the colonists sailed for the Wiapoco River. Pieter Janszoon, before joining them, successfully attacked and destroyed Fort Mariocay. After the Franco-Dutch colonists had been settled, both ships left.

Zeelanders had already established a colony under the patronship of Jan de Moor on the Wiapoco in 1615—the Jan Pieterszoon colony. It is not known whether these settlers still occupied the site when the Duifken group made its appearance. The new colonists suffered many hardships before the next Dutch ship, the Vliegende Draeck ("Flying Dragon"), arrived under orders from the wic to take them home. This ship had come out with a squadron under Admiral Lucifer who brought a group of colonists to establish themselves on the Amazon.

The Heren xix, stimulated by the Chamber of Zeeland, had decided to found a new colony on the Curupá River as a key base for trade on the Amazon. Zeeland dispatched the above-mentioned squadron under Lucifer; it brought two hundred Dutch-Irish colonists under Nicolaes Oudaen and Philip Purcell, who were both acquainted with the area. This group settled on the island of Tocujos in the Curupá.

Many more colonists, largely English and Irish, soon joined them. The Portuguese, alarmed by this new influx, sent Pedro Teixeira to eliminate the settlement, which he accomplished at the end of May, 1625. After a fierce struggle, Oudaen and his followers fled to a nearby English trading post, only to have Teixeira follow and destroy this site, too. Leading the forty-six sole survivors, Oudaen tried to escape by going upriver, but the dissension among them allowed the Indians to attack and kill all but three. These three were later discovered, and two more were killed. The lone survivor, who had almost forgotten his mother tongue when found, was able to tell the new settlers his story two years later.[9] A number of prisoners had been taken at Tocujos and brought back to Pará.[10]

Teixeira's decisive actions meant the end of Dutch efforts to settle colonies on the Amazon. Meanwhile, however, the Heren xix and the patrons had come together amicably and agreed to allow the colonizing of the area at the discretion of the respective chambers. This far-reaching decision must have been directly influenced by the fact that important patrons like Jan de Moor and Abraham van Pere had recently become directors of the Chamber of Zeeland. Only Zeeland and Amsterdam showed interest, however; Amsterdam concentrated on settling New Netherland and some of the Caribbean islands, while Zeeland, with some occasional spurts from Holland, began to think of the Wild Coast as her private domain and to send expeditions there regularly.

Of all the fortified trading posts founded before or during the Truce, only one, Fort Kijkoveral on the Essequibo, developed into a permanent settlement. The Zeelanders, however, were not easily discouraged. This race of stubborn merchants and brave sailors, inured by many years of fighting against the Spaniards, found in Jan de Moor, Pieter van Rhee, and Abraham van Pere magnificent representatives of its finest qualities. Zeelandian efforts to expand in Guiana were soon underway; two missions, one bound for the Wiapoco, the other for Cayenne, were sent forth in December, 1626.

These expeditions, which seem to have been initiated by the Chamber of Zeeland, were soon left in the hands of Jan de Moor and Abraham van Pere. Both were from Flushing and were directors of the chamber; both had been sent as Zeeland's agents to the meetings of the Heren xix within three days after their installation. There they had proposed to finance a colony according to a plan submitted by van Pere.[11] With some amendments and corrections this colonization project, patterned after the patronships in existence before the founding of the wic, became the model for all future patron-colonizing expeditions. Its main feature was that of a colony composed of families.

The outcome of these two enterprises was not very encouraging. The Cayenne project, under Claude Prevost, disappeared as had that earlier attempt under Claessen; after 1632, this Zeelandian effort can no longer be traced.[12] More is known about the Wiapoco venture under Jan van Ryen: the three ships dropped anchor at the Wacogenive River and found the sole survivor of the Oudaen massacre, but Indian hostility drove the colonists away. They escaped the area in homemade sloops; only four of them ultimately succeeded in reaching the Lesser Antilles, two at St. Vincent and two at Tobago.[13]

The settlement which was sponsored by Abraham van Pere at Berbice had a more permanent character. Van Pere read his proposal to the head-participants of the Chamber of Zeeland in March, 1627, after the two previous expeditions had already left. He offered his own money and undoubtedly sought additional support from his audience. One month later the chamber adopted his "Conditions for Colonies" and allowed him to transport forty men and twenty boys—"sixty eaters"—to the Wild Coast. The attempt to send families had apparently been relinquished because of the difficulty in recruiting them. The group left in July, 1627. The colonists arrived at Berbice in late fall, and evidently prospered for some time. Details of the early history of this settlement, however, are barely known because of the paucity of documentary information.

Much more information is available about the Dutch settlement on the Essequibo River, although certain baffling circumstances need to be explained in this case. The Zeelanders had founded a trading post there as early as 1616, successfully resettling the area after the debacle of 1613. According to John Scott, our most reliable source, Aert Adriaenszoon Groenewegen headed the colony around 1626. We know, however, from the minutes of the Chamber of Zeeland, that Jacob Canijn had been appointed commander at Essequibo in that year, and until 1644 the appointments of three other commanders can be traced, but none of these was Groenewegen.[14]

Nor is this the only puzzling contradiction. A dispatch from Trinidad to Madrid in 1637 reported, "The Dutch threaten the island of Trinidad with a powerful fleet and are in league with the numerous Indian tribes...the Dutch being so mixed with the Indians that they marry with the Carib women, as well as with those of other tribes."[15] From other Spanish sources it is shown that the Dutch were quite strong in Essequibo. A further letter from the *cabildo* of San Tomé stated, for example, "The forces of the enemy have increased in this government [Guiana] on the mainland, with new settlements among the Carib and Aruac nations, who are allied with them, and they are settled on the river Essequibo...." And the governor of Trinidad wrote, "In those three settlements of Amacuro, Essequibo and Berbis the enemy have many people...all the Aruacs and Caribs are allied with him."16

More alarming letters followed. In May the governor of Trinidad again wrote, "Essequibo, a fort lying in this province of Guiana, where the Dutch are carrying on a great trade with the Indians, keeps the inhabitants of the Orinoco in constant alarm." Later he advised Madrid, "The enemy is strongly fortified in an islet formed by the river Essequibo; they have a quantity of artillery and a number of people, and the constant assistance of four or six ships from Holland... and the Indians frequent them very willingly for the sake of the considerable articles of barter they give them."17

All these statements point to the strength and prosperity of the Dutch colonists on the Essequibo. They also coincide with reports of Dutch retaliation against a Spanish massacre of forty colonists from Tobago, who had surrendered on condition of preservation of life (see Chapter XVII). Groenewegen had attacked the Spanish settlements at San Tomé and Trinidad in 1637, and ransacked and looted these areas with the help of Indian allies. The assaults prompted requests for help and warnings of future Dutch raids. Letters included the disturbing news that the Dutch were building forts from Cape North to the mouth of the Orinoco, with help from the Indians, and variously report Dutch strength at "40 Dutchmen with 25 Negroes" and "120 Dutchmen and many Negroes." Santa Fé de Bogotá, which received the majority of these appeals for help, refused aid but notified the king.18

All these reports, however, stand in marked contrast with the minutes of the Chamber of Zeeland. The proceedings of August, 1637, read: "In as much as Jan van der Goes had written from Essequibo that he, with the folk that were with him, were minded to come home by the first ship, it was some time resolved to send thither in the place of said van der Goes, by the ship *De Jager* Cornelis Pietersz Hose; and on account of the great demoralization of the folk and their wish to come home it is resolved that they be allowed to return, and the colony provided anew with twenty-five other respectable persons, from whom the Company may receive more service and more edifyingly withal."19

Edmundson, the recognized authority on the early history of the Guianas, offers the following solution. He distinguishes between an earlier settlement run by Groenwegen under the patronship of the De Moor–Courteen House since 1616, and a later colony begun through the initiative of the Zeelandian Chamber of the West India Company. The latter was administered directly under the Zeeland Chamber and received its commanders by Zeeland's appointments. It languished, as the minutes quoted above illustrate. The other settlement, under Groenewegen, flourished under the auspices of a private patronship.

Groenewegen's colony survived as well as it did because its commander knew how to handle the Indians. Captain Llanes, as the Spaniards called him, spoke Carib and Arawak fluently. Two years after his attack on San Tomé a Spanish officer, in a sworn disposition, reported, "Captain Llanes commanded in Essequibo, and besides his own forces they [the Dutch] were further protected by 10,000 to 12,000 Caribs in the vicinity of which they frequent, and who are their allies."[20]

The De Moor–Courteen House was an Anglo-Dutch company begun by William Courteen, a Fleming, who had lived in Zeeland before going to live in England. In London he had developed a thriving trade which maintained connections in Zeeland. He became a great merchant, and his company soon enjoyed a remarkable position in the commercial world of the early seventeenth century. His two sons followed in his footsteps; his only daughter married a Zeelander and bore a son, Pieter Boudaen, who soon played an important role in the business also. The Dutch were the preponderant partners in the company, and the books were kept at Middelburg.

Despite its association with the Groenewegen settlement, the De Moor–Courteen House was to become far better known as the sponsor of the 1625 expedition to Barbados under a Captain John Powell. Upon his arrival, Powell, a personal friend of Groenewegen, immediately got the latter's help: not only supplies of roots and seeds for planting, but also thirty-two Arawaks to teach the settlers how to grow maize, cassava, tobacco, and other crops. The understanding was that the Indians would be returned to Guiana after two years. This enterprise was financed jointly by English and Dutch money, though the latter far exceeded the former.

Groenewegen apparently continued in his semi-official function as factor of the De Moor–Courteen House until the death of Jan de Moor in 1644. Then the two colonizing entities on the Essequibo merged, and Groenewegen became a servant of the West India Company. This explanation would reconcile the conflict between Spanish and Zeelandian records. It was Groenewegen, the capable agent of private enterprise, who kept the Spanish and Portuguese inhabitants of the Orinoco region in constant alarm and who extended Dutch activity to Western Guiana. Of Groenewegen, John Scott says that he "was the first man that took firme foteing on Guiana by the good likeing of the natives...whose humours the gent perfectly understood."[21]

The fact that most early WIC colonies on the Wild Coast did not flourish, added to the disappointing returns from Marten Thijsz' fleet, impelled the Heren XIX to drop the Guianas in favor of Brazil. The formal decision was taken in 1632. Zeeland, always obstinate, demurred and chose "not to abandon the colony of Isekepe";[22] with the approval of the XIX the chamber of this province now took the Guianas under its special protection. This measure did not exclude other chambers from ventures into that area, but Zeeland thereafter definitely considered the Wild Coast as a private enterprise, and tried to maintain a monopoly of trade and navigation in that area.[23] The Heren XIX, who had not intended any such consequence, pushed the States General to pronounce a "free trade" policy for the Wild Coast, limiting, of course, such "free trade" to special permits and the payment of recognition. The government's regulations in this matter, which were repeated several times, never mentioned Guiana explicitly, but were designed to open trade in all those areas where the WIC could not possibly maintain shipping. All of the "free-traders" had to pay recognition to the company.

Zeeland, of course, was irritated by successive incursions on her pretended "monopoly." The minutes of the Zeeland Chamber are replete with angry outbursts: "Because the company is suffering great damage, several inhabitants of these countries having the insolence to navigate in West India on the Wild Coast under different pretexts, and have a profitable trade, the members should please take into consideration what measures have to be taken to prevent disaster."[24] The Zeelanders appealed many times to the Heren XIX "to determine that no colonists nor other persons would be allowed to sail to the Wild Coast than by this chamber, and confrère van Pere alone."[25] Although the XIX refused to acknowledge the pretensions of Zeeland, the chamber of this province expressly wrote to its commanders in Essequibo and in other settlements to obey only its orders.

It is little wonder that the Wild Coast settlements were close to every Zeelander's heart. Except for one abortive expedition which may have been inspired from Amsterdam—the Claessen enterprise— all of the tiny Dutch outposts in Guiana had been founded, nourished, and protected by Zeelandian money and blood. Groenewegen, although a Catholic, was a Zeelander, as were all the others involved in the colonies. There was, therefore, real alarm in Zeeland when Amsterdam threatened to repeat the effort of Theodore Claessen and to send its own colonists to Cayenne again in 1634. The Heren XIX were immediately petitioned to recognize Zeeland's "rights."[26] This request was denied. Zeeland now issued a statement which prohibited all navigation to Guiana except for the chamber itself and for patron Abraham van Pere.

The expedition to Cayenne was financed by Holland merchants and led by David Pieterszoon de Vries of Hoorn.[27] It consisted of one ship, the *Koning David*, ("King David"), which set out with thirty colonists aboard. This venture had the express approval of the Amsterdam Chamber of the WIC.[28] It left in July, 1634, less than three weeks before Zeeland had adopted the resolution that forbade settlements in her "private domain."

The *Koning David* reached Cayenne early in September, 1634, and disembarked the colonists on a small island, Mecoria, "to plant tobacco, annatto and cotton."[29] Somewhere near here, Prevost had founded a colony seven years earlier. De Vries came upon seven or eight Zeelanders, presumably the sad remnant of that colony, sponsored by Jan de Moor.[30] The new colonists did discover also the ruins of a small castle which had probably been built by French colonists in 1613 and which was soon destroyed by the Indians. At the river Sinamari, the Dutch encountered twelve French settlers under their captain Chambon, and at the Surinam River a bigger English colony of sixty people.[31]

Having restored the old fort, the first requisite for survival, the new colonists of Mecoria turned to cultivation. The soil was very fertile. Hartsinck gives some interesting details: cane grew in abundance, the stems as thick as a man's arm; there were soon 80,000 oriane trees, 100,000 cotton plants, and 100,000 tobacco plants, all thriving and promising abundant profits.[32] De Vries departed carrying 150 Indian fugitives from the Caribs. At Demerary, where he paused to settle these Indians (except for the son of a former Carib chief who wanted to see the United Provinces), he encountered the newly appointed commander of Essequibo, Jan van der Goes.[33] He then returned home via Curaçao, Virginia, and New Netherland.

The colony de Vries left behind quickly collapsed. The lack of leadership led to faulty discipline, and a few English members of the settlement incited the Dutch to seize some Spanish barques which had come to the area in pursuit of slaves. The colonists killed the Spaniards, took the loot, and made for the English Antilles. The colony's failure may well have been joyously received in Zeeland.

Jan van der Goes, while he was commander of the official colony at the Essequibo, had made some trips to the interior and had sent the directors of the Zeeland Chamber a "Project for the Discovery of Silver Mines at the Orinoco." Although he was soon replaced, he did manage to stir the chamber to take interest in his plan. Consequently, a ship was prepared, and van der Goes was dispatched with fifty men to search for silver in what was then Spanish-Portuguese territory. He returned in the following year, empty-handed. Furthermore, he neglected to build a fort on the Orinoco, which would have given the Dutch a stronghold on that river; this resulted in his fall from Zeeland's favor.[34]

With the death of Jan de Moor in 1644, Zeeland saw her opportunity to take over the patronship of Essequibo. In the minutes of her chamber for May, 1645, we find the following: "The commissioners are of the opinion that the river Essequibo has now, for some time, been navigated with small profit for the Company, for the reason that private colonists are permitted to trade there as well as the Company, so that the goods coming from there cannot fetch their proper price on account of competition; they are, moreover, of the opinion that at the expiration of the charter either the trade ought to be reserved exclusively for the Company, or it were better that aforesaid place should be thrown open under payment of proper dues."[35]

It is safe to presume that this resolution was designed to curtail rival chamber trade as well as the activities of the de Moor heirs. It is now difficult to reconstruct just how Zeeland manipulated the Essequibo settlement into her grasp, and, indeed, to what extent she succeeded, for it is apparent that her patron was appointing factors there as late as 1665. The minutes of the chamber do reveal, however, that Groenewegen remained as leader under the chamber, a position which he held until his death in 1664.

While the Dutch were stationed at the Essequibo and at the Berbice, French and English colonizing expeditions were continuously pouring into the area. All had come to the Guianas to trade and settle; the English expedition under Charles Leigh in 1604 may well have had as its contemporary the voyage of the Huguenot la Ravardière. One hundred and sixty French families appear to have settled near the Wiapoco River in 1613. The French character of the expedition under de Forest in 1623 has likewise already been noted. Evidence also exists concerning further French settlements at Cayenne in 1625, but a supply vessel which was sent out during the same year found no survivors. In 1627, more than five hundred people from La Rochelle showed up in the same area; within three years, however, the site was abandoned for another one on St. Christopher.

Other French expeditions followed. In 1628, a colony was established at the Conomana River, reinforced by new colonists two years later. In those days Richelieu founded his Cape North Company, and sent 370 colonists to the Saramacca River. This settlement managed to hang on for a few years until the inhabitants grew careless, quarreled with the Indians, and were wiped out in a single day. The French returned to Cayenne in 1643 and again in 1652. After a few tumultuous years of mismanagement, illness, and discord, the survivors of the last expedition deserted to Surinam and Barbados.

English efforts on the Wild Coast are reported by John Scott. The expedition under Captain Marshall in 1643 seems to have been significant. This group started out from Barbados for Tobago and ended up at the Surinam River. Soon branch colonies were begun at the Saramacca and at the Corantine. In 1645, however, the settlers became involved in a dispute with a neighboring French colony and gave the Indians the opportunity to eliminate all "intruders" at the same time.

Prior to Marshall's settlement at the Surinam, the Dutch had established a trading post there in 1633.[36] The report of Jacques Onsiel, public advocate and secretary of Tobago, confirms the fact that the Dutch had founded in 1635 and 1637 seven colonies on the Wild Coast, one of which was at Surinam.[37] This colony was increased with Jews from New Holland after the departure of Count Johan Maurits from that territory. At mid-century there must have also been some Dutch sugar plantations at the Marowine and Commowine, twenty-five miles upstream. Whatever happened to these trading posts and settlements after Willoughby came to Guiana is not known; they were probably incorporated under the English flag in the territory then known as "Willoughby-land."

The West India Company was not founded for the sake of Guiana. Indeed, the area always remained of little significance to the architects of the "Great Designs." Peace with Spain in 1648, as mentioned, stripped the company of its main source of revenue—privateering—and threatened its very existence. The Treaty of Westphalia, however, conferred upon the Dutch title to two former Spanish territories, the settlements at the Essequibo and Berbice. It also confined Dutch trade to Guiana very specifically: "...the subjects of the said Lords and States shall not sail or trade in those areas held and possessed by the said Lord the King."[38]

In spite of the fact that Zeeland had acquired the excellent services of Groenewegen, the colony at the Essequibo never did very well. Only the scantiest material is available, however, for evaluating the condition of Dutch colonists, both there and at Berbice, at the close of the long war with Spain. So far as it is plausible to infer, the two settlements consisted of two or three dozen men, mostly unmarried, employees of the WIC, housed in a fort and engaged in trade with the Indians, especially in dyes.[39] There is little reason for supposing agriculture existed save for the necessary food supply. Of tobacco and sugar nothing is heard following the mention of the specimens received in the time of van der Goes. Such results are very curious for settlements which had been established for the express and avowed purposes of cultivating tobacco, cacao, and sugar.

With the conclusion of a lasting peace with Spain and the renewal of the WIC charter for an additional twenty-four years, one might have expected a rapid colonial development at the Berbice and the Essequibo rivers. The company, however, was now curtailed in its privateering and bankrupted by the long and fruitless struggle for Brazil. It was not until 1654, or later, that the West India Company finally realized the hopelessness of its Brazilian undertaking. Only then did the Zeelandian Chamber once again venture to colonize Guiana, and only on the express condition that colonists buy all their supplies from and ship all their products to Zeeland. The Heren XIX were apparently, at the same time, promoting the colonization of Surinam. Some sort of cooperation between these two entities—the XIX and the Chamber of Zeeland—might very well have been instigated to make the project feasible. A Zeeland memorial, for instance, quotes from the now lost minutes of the WIC a body of "liberties and exemptions, for patrons."[40] This document also reveals how very little had been accomplished in the development of the Guiana colonies and the company's consequent disappointment:

Whereas the Directors of the Zeeland Chamber of the West India Company, for many years, by all conceivable means and ways, both by its, the Chamber's, own means, and by contracting with private persons, have tried, not only to increase its trade and commerce from here to the coasts and islands situated under the charter, but also and especially have made it their aim to further the colonization and agriculture of the aforesaid lands, and yet without such success, results, and fruits as they could have hoped.

Therefore, inasmuch as they have found by careful observation and long experience, that not only the islands lying in their district but also the mainland coasts, and especially the Wild Coast...are of such situation and soil that one can there cultivate, plant, raise, and gather everything which it has been possible to cultivate and gather in the famous regions of Brazil...they are disposed to offer, and do hereby offer, with the knowledge and approval of the States General of the United Netherlands and of the General Chartered West India Company, in order thereby to encourage each and everyone, these following conditions.[41]

The resolution was confirmed by the States General on special request of the xix in November, 1658.[42] The Amsterdam Chamber soon moved into action and approved a request by Jan Claessen Langendyck to settle on the Wild Coast. Accompanied by thirty or forty colonists, Langendyck forthwith took possession of Cayenne and established a successful Dutch colony there. After a few years, however, the small settlement ran into difficulties and in 1659 Langendyck transfered his patronship to the Chamber of Amsterdam and complained of the lack of financial support. He remained as commander of the colony until he was replaced in 1663 by Quirijn Spranger. This colony, protected by the original fort, survived until, shortly after Spranger's arrival, it was forced to surrender to the French.[43]

Similar terms were offered to the enterprise sponsored by a Zeelander raised to the French peerage, Balthasar Gerbier, baron d'Ouvily. This adventurer claimed to know the exact location of a gold mine on the Wild Coast and contracted with a number of credulous Zeelanders for an expedition in 1655. The ensuing colony was located at the Aprowaco River, but disintegrated after some time because of internal discord. The gold mine, of course, was never found.[44]

Early in the fifties, Zeeland undertook a serious effort to colonize in another part of Guiana. Scott reveals that the colonists in this venture were drawn from Tobago. West of the Essequibo, they established themselves between the Pomeroon and the Moruca rivers closer to the mouth of the Orinoco. When Dutch affairs at Pernambuco took a critical turn this settlement enjoyed a population boom because of an influx of Brazilian refugees, many of them Jewish. Since all these Dutch Brazilians were experienced planters, the new colony at the Pomeroon soon began to flourish.[45]

In 1651 Governor Francis Willoughby of Barbados sent three hundred men from this island to found an English colony on the Surinam River. Their leader, Anthony Rowse, made a treaty with the Indians, providing for this settlement in that area. Willoughby financed this venture himself and saw to its sustenance. In 1652 he made a personal tour of the new colony and organized its defenses. By 1654, when Rowse departed, the prevailing atmosphere was one of evident success. Like Willoughby, the next governor William Byam was an ardent royalist; he was also an energetic and devoted administrator as the settlement continued to prosper. After the Restoration Charles II was easily persuaded to grant to Willoughby "all that part of the mainland of Guiana called Surinam to be held in free and common socage and to pay two thousand pounds of tobacco and one-fifth of all ore or gold and silver mined, into the Custom House of London yearly."[46]

The impact of the first Anglo-Dutch war on the Wild Coast is not well known. An interruption of communications with the mother country and a lack of supplies can be presumed. At the end of the war the political situation in Guiana was as it had been at the outset. There were three permanent Dutch settlements (Essequibo, Berbice, and Pomeroon), the English colony at the Surinam, and many trading posts. No French settlements existed in 1655. The war had not been fought in the Caribbean, and no apparent encounters occurred among the colonists of the various European nations.

Zeeland's colonies at the Essequibo and Pomeroon continued to have difficulties. Although more is known about the former, the same problems probably applied to both settlements. Despite the capable leadership of Groenewegen and the free colonization policy, results had been meager. The Chamber of Zeeland soon shrank from assuming sole management of such a venture. In June, 1657, it petitioned the States of Zeeland to take over the direction of the enterprise. The provincial government was inclined to, but negotiations floundered on the reluctance of some of its noncommercial members. Late in that same year, however, the three great trading towns of Middelburg, Flushing, and Vere offered to undertake the matter on their own. It thus came about that the colonization and management of the entire coast, subject to the supreme jurisdiction of the company and of the Provincial States, was transfered to the "Walcheren cities."[47]

"The aforesaid cities," ran their contract with the company, "shall establish and plant colonies on the continental Wild Coast between the first and tenth degrees."[48] The agreement between the cities themselves (December 16, 1657) was content to speak of the enterprise as "the business regarding the peopling and cultivation of the Wild Coast in America under the charter of the West India Company."[49] The direction was settled upon eight men: four members of the Chamber of Zeeland, two burgomasters of Middelburg, and one each from Flushing and Vere. Their headquarters was the West India House in Middelburg, and they rechristened the Wild Coast "Nova Zeelandia."[50]

The new management, in which the Chamber of Zeeland retained an important voice, set about its task with great zeal. Inter-city meetings, between November, 1657, and March, 1658, lead to a budget figure of 24,000 guilders. This soon proved to be insufficient; the amount was trebled, but it was still not enough. They recruited Groenewegen to stay in the colony as governor and sent an engineer, Cornelis Goliat, to his aid as "Commissary over the stores of the aforesaid place and commander over the twenty-five soldiers to be sent thither, and furthermore engineer for the parceling out of lands, the making of maps, and the laying-out of sundry strong places or forts for the protection of the colonists."[51]

The cities dispatched a ship to Nova Zeelandia with colonists and a second ship to Africa to get slaves. Goliat, burdened by his many functions, arrived on the first ship, and by August, 1658, he submitted a description of the Demerary, Essequibo, Pomeroon, and Moruca rivers. The new colony, according to Goliat's instructions, situated itself at the confluence of the Pomeroon and Moruca.[52]

The site to which Goliat directed the settlers had already been subject to a previous colonizing venture by the Dutch. After enjoying a brief period of growth and prosperity, it had subsequently suffered a series of setbacks, although its probable demise is still shrouded in mystery. The orginal Essequibo settlement around Fort Kijkoveral had not been abandoned, and this remained Groenewegen's headquarters.

The new site on the Pomeroon, or rather the old abandoned one which was to be named New Middelburg and which was to be protected by an imposing fort, Nova Zeelandia, never really got off the ground. Although both Groenewegen and Goliat did their utmost to promote the development of the new settlement, by encouraging the migration of Dutch-Jewish planters from Brazil, for example, their dreams did not materialize. Even they finally became disillusioned. Only bare foundations stand where forts and buildings were once planned. As a final note, a minister sent to inspire the colonists had to be recalled for misconduct in 1661.[53]

At the outset, however, everything seemed auspicious. Although sugar became an important crop, its production during this early period was confined to older Indian methods of mashing the cane between two wooden rolls; but by 1664 a sugar mill was operating in the Essequibo colony. It is not known when the first sugar mill was built at the Pomeroon. But the colonists decided before long that the Walcheren cities were not looking after their affairs too well. In September, 1660, some Jewish planters asked "Whether the Commissioners propose to attend to the colony, since, if otherwise, they intend to depart and abandon it."[54] The cities, apparently, were also negligent about procuring slaves for the colonists.

In January, 1658, a Jew, David Nassy, received a patent as patron of a colony to be established at Cayenne.[55] His settlement was populated by Jews from Brazil and from Livorno as well as by some other Portuguese or Dutch Jews. The colony established itself at a certain distance from the older Langendyck-Spranger settlement, but, in the end it suffered a similar fate: the French captured it in 1664. A third settlement which was undertaken by Gerbier's "Guyana Company" at the Aprowaco was also untenable, as previously mentioned. It fell to the English in 1665.

The name of David Nassy inspires some investigation about the role which Dutch Jews played in settling the Wild Coast. Although Jewish participation was not important in the founding of the West India Company, Jewish interest continued to grow and increased in significance as the old company drew to a close. Dutch-Portuguese-Brazilian Jews traded wherever the Dutch traded. Many Jews were driven to the Wild Coast because of the situation in New Holland, and their knowledge of sugar production was an asset wherever they settled. Nassy and some of his co-religionists may well have settled at the Commewine in 1644.[56] Eight years later he similarly received a patent from the Chamber of Amsterdam to found a Jewish colony on Curaçao.

John Scott tells us of another Jewish colony on the Essequibo in 1650: "The twelfth Collonie was of Dutch setled by the Zealanders in the rivers Borowma (Pomeroon), Wacopon and Moroca, having been draue of from Tobago anno 1650. And ye yeare following a great Collonie of Dutch and Jewes, draue of from Brazile, by the Portugaize, setled there, and, being Experienced Planters, that soone grew a flourishing Collonie."[57] It is, however, generally understood that the year given, 1650, is an error and should read 1658.[58] Jews were, as previously mentioned, found in the Pomeroon settlement, and when the French took Cayenne they "carried the Jews and Christians, bereft of their property, and in deep poverty, to La Rochelle whence they were permitted to go afoot to their Fatherland."[59]

The wording of grants or patents issued to Jewish colonists followed the original Nassy document of September 12, 1659, and was similar to all other patents issued by the West India Company. Of the highest significance was Article VII which guaranteed freedom of religion and education to the settlers: "It shall be permitted to the Jews to have freedom of conscience with public worship, and a synagogue and school, in the same manner as is allowed in the City of Amsterdam, in accordance with the doctrines of their elders, without hindrance as well in the district of this Colony, as in other places of our Dominions...."[60] This liberality and tolerance, infrequent in the seventeenth century, made Dutch colonies a haven for this so often persecuted people.

In spite of the new start afforded by the Walcheren cities, colonization was far from a success in Western Guiana, even after new "liberties and exemptions" were offered. Notwithstanding vast efforts by the Chamber of Zeeland, only a few colonists could be persuaded to participate in this uncertain undertaking and not more than twelve reached the Essequibo.[61] Soon all of the colonies were languishing, despite an advance of 500,000 guilders made by the States of Zeeland.[62] Goliat died in 1661, Groenewegen in 1664. A few months after the latter's death the colony was destroyed by the English.

A very sharp contrast to these Dutch efforts is the prosperous English colony at Surinam under Byam. English Jews, known to have accompanied Francis Lord Willoughby in 1652, participated in this settlement. It expanded in 1662, and again in 1664, when, after the fall of Cayenne, many Dutch-Portuguese-Brazilian Jews under David Nassy took refuge there.[63] In 1663, this settlement boasted a population of four thousand, slaves included, and numbered five hundred plantations. When David Nassy and his followers arrived in 1664, bringing their experience in the cultivation of sugarcane, a marked increase in prosperity could be noticed. After the outbreak of the second Anglo-Dutch war, Byam's colony was used as a basis for Scott's attacks on the Dutch settlements along the coast. These were eminently successful and, as Byam writes about the major, "In few months his great Fortune and gallantry prudent and Industrious Conduct made him master of all the great province new Zealand and Dessecueb settled a peace with the Arwayes left both Collonys in a Flourishing Condition and well garrison'd for the King of England."[64]

Shortly after Scott's return to Barbados, however, with Indian help and under pressure caused by French aggravation, Fort Kijkoveral's English garrison "through want of ammunition and irresistible hunger" surrendered to the Dutch under their commander Bergenaer from Berbice. About the same time, the starving English garrison of Fort Nova Zeelandia on the Pomeroon was destroyed by the French. As both of these colonies were considered Dutch—at least by the Dutch— the States of Zeeland commented tersely, "Essequibo and Pomeroon, first taken by the English, then plundered by the French, have now been abandoned by the whole world."[65]

The conquest of Surinam and the restoration of this and the Essequibo and Pomeroon settlements by Abraham Crijnssen to Zeelandian control are told in the preceding chapter. The Peace of Breda restored to the United Provinces all their colonies on the Wild Coast, and Zeeland once again took "possession" by appointing Willem Hendricksen to take over the administration. The latter arrived there in November, 1667, with three ships and orders for the English governor to surrender the fort and the colony according to the articles of the treaty. Governor James Bannister declined until bid by his king, a message which was not received until a fortnight later. Just as Hendricksen's possession seemed imminent, however, Henry Willoughby arrived, and by delaying the takeover on the pretext that Bannister must wait confirmation of his orders from Barbados, he generally proved himself a menace. Willoughby spent his time burning sugar mills, inducing colonists to leave, and seizing slaves and cattle in a general effort to make the colony useless to the Dutch. Not endowed with any evident gifts of diplomatic talent or artful subtlety, Hendricksen's impotence as a mediator was soon revealed. A stern letter of protest to the States of Zeeland remains today as testimony of frustrated endeavors.[66]

The matter was finally referred to the Dutch ambassador in London, and Crijnssen was sent to assist Hendricksen.[67] He arrived on April 15, 1668, with letters from Charles II authorizing the contested restitution. Negotiations began, and Henry Willoughby was persuaded that orders from his king ought to have prompt obedience. Crijnssen, who was rather more impatient than Hendricksen and had the advantage of more guns, announced that he was prepared to attack if any more delay was offered. This language was clearly understood by the English, and the governor handed over the fort at once. The Dutch imposed an oath of fidelity on all the colonists and published a declaration concerning the new government. Bannister was taken prisoner and sent to Zeeland. William Lord Willoughby had to pay for all damages perpetrated by himself and his son Henry in Surinam. English colonists were allowed to leave, and a great many—some 1,200 people (slaves included)—took the opportunity.[68]

With the exception of Cayenne, Crijnssen's first expedition had reclaimed the whole Wild Coast for the Dutch, and the States of Zeeland took possession of most of it as its patrons. Official Zeelandian actions, however, were limited to sending garrisons to Essequibo and Surinam. Pomeroon was abandoned. Three years passed without any volunteers to take over the management of the colonies, since the Walcheren cities, dismayed at the expense of a fresh beginning,[69] declined to receive the settlements and even suggested selling them. Finally, in 1670, the Zeeland Chamber of the West India Company was persuaded to take control and to agree to supply necessary slaves for the plantations. The colonies were thrown open to any and all prospective colonists from Zeeland; free trade, with the exception of the very profitable red dye, was permitted under the usual regulations. The States General approved the agreement, and Zeeland had won, at long last, virtual acceptance of her rights in trade and in colonization on the Wild Coast.[70]

The new entente provided more stability in the government in Guiana and more confidence among the colonists. Whereas the Pomeroon and Moruca settlements had been reduced to little more than isolated outposts,[71] Essequibo had suffered little, and cultivation and trade were quickly booming in those surroundings. New plantations, in allotments of five hundred acres, were laid out, and soon their produce were to be found in Middelburg. In 1669, for instance, a ship reached Zeeland from the colony bearing six thousand pounds of sugar and twenty thousand pounds of letterwood.[72]

This renewal of confidence and productivity may well have been responsible for the grant of territory on the Guiana coast to the German Count of Hanau. This strip, thirty Dutch miles wide, was ceded by the West India Company with the concurrence of the States General and the stipulation that "His Excellency will be entitled to select, provided he keeps at least six Dutch miles from other colonies there established or founded by the said West India Company or with her consent."[73] Nothing ever came of this gesture.

In that same year, the States of Zeeland had assigned the active and energetic Hendrik Rol to the Essequibo settlement to foster its interest. When, in 1670, the Chamber of Zeeland assumed authority over the colony, it affirmed Rol as commander.[74] At that point, there seems to have been no private planters in the colony, but with better conditions, two or three Zeelanders came to Essequibo and began to clear land. When a fresh supply of slaves reached the colony, new sugar plantations were laid out.

Rol's concern from the start, however, was not with cultivation, but with trade. This preference, of course, was in keeping with what had brought the Dutch to Guiana in the first place. It was at the outset, and for more than a quarter of a century, their chief function. Even after plantations had been established and the colony thrown open to private planters, trade primarily motivated the Chamber of Zeeland, trade which remained the main source of income and the object of jealous care. Commerce drove the colony to build forts, plant outposts, and maintain garrisons. Rol's ability to act accordingly needs no emphasis.

A Spanish Jesuit, Father Joseph Gumilla, reveals some interesting details about Dutch trade in Guiana. He could speak from personal knowledge, since he had been in the Guianas for a considerable time. He reports that before the Dutch founded their colonies, the Indians of the area fought each other for badly needed women and children. With the coming of the Dutch, the object of wars changed; commerce became the chief concern of the Indians, too. As the Dutch purchased all prisoners of war from the Caribs—even paying in advance—the latter now regularly went upstream to buy captives from other tribes. Each slave was worth two choppers, two axes, some beads, or other trifles. Some of these exchanges were conducted six hundred miles in the interior, and it was no uncommon occurrence for the Caribs to leave part of the superfluous hardware behind as a down payment on the next human cargo. In that case, some of the men remained to keep guard on the merchandise they called *rescate*.[75]

Of still greater significance, perhaps, was trade in the products of the country. The natural supplies of dyes, woods, oil, and balsam were inexhaustible. Growing demand, however, sent the search for them ever farther afield. Colonial authorities employed various means for procuring these commodities. First, there were *uitlopers* (outrunners) who scoured the country and stirred the Indians to bring their wares to the Dutch trading posts. These agents also carried trinkets with them to buy products. As regular employees of the West India Company, they corresponded to the French *coureurs de bois* in Canada. In the beginning these *uitlopers* had been predominantly white men—Groenewegen was a white *uitloper*—but later they were usually half-breeds like Groenewegen's sons, or Negroes familiar with the Indian tongues.

There were also *uitleggers* (outlyers). These men came later some fifty years after the Dutch began to trade on the Wild Coast. The *uitleggers* dwelt in small groups deep in the interior to trade with distant Indian tribes. In 1671, when the Demerary River passed into the control of the Essequibo settlement, the Berbice authorities had knowledge of a group of fifteen or sixteen *uitleggers* in that area who had been there for years.[76]

Rol's efforts to build up trade took several forms. Fort Kijkoveral was maintained as a trading post, but it was gradually transformed into a central market as Rol established more and more stations for the *uitleggers* in the interior. In 1673 these outposts reached as far as the Barima River. In a letter to the Chamber of Zeeland Rol pointed to his achievements: peace had been made with the Caribs and the Arawaks and trade between them encouraged. In addition, he intended to send a boat after carap oil and to make a trail of linseed oil. He had even dispatched his *uitleggers* to the Orinoco for purposes of trade. These men were mistakenly brought to Trinidad as prisoners, but Rol soon commissioned others with the same goal.[77]

Rol's services were very satisfactory to his Zeelandian masters. In 1672 he was promised, at his request, a considerable reinforcement of personnel and war materials against "the threatening and apparent surprise attack of our dreadful enemies" the English and French. His salary was likewise increased from thirty to fifty guilders a month and an assistant was assigned to him—all this "in consideration of his faithful service and extraordinary vigilance."[78]

Up to now the development of Berbice has been ignored since, before 1670, little is known of this patronship of the van Peres. A rare source of information is the description of this colony by Adriaen van Berckel, the patron's appointee as merchant and secretary in that year. In his *American Voyage, containing a voyage to the Rio de Berbice, with another one to the Surinam colony*, van Berckel presents a detailed and lively picture of life in a seventeenth-century Dutch colony on the Wild Coast.[79] In 1672, there were said to be five sugar plantations and some trading posts; there was a regular trade with Zeeland, most of which was done by private entrepreneurs who paid a recognition to the chamber of this province.[80] Little else about this community can now be discovered.[81]

More important than Essequibo and Berbice was Surinam. In spite of Henry Willoughby's destruction, this colony was soon prospering again, most importantly because a steady supply of slaves made possible a revival and expansion of the sugar industry. In due time it was destined to become the center of Dutch power on the Wild Coast. When a New West India Company was chartered in 1674, Surinam kept its status as a Zeelandian prize of the second Anglo-Dutch War and was not incorporated in the new mandate.[82] The colony was spared from attack during the Anglo-French controversy with the Dutch in 1672. The expedition of 1676, which recaptured Cayenne for the Dutch, did not touch at Surinam first. Since that territory was so firmly in Dutch hands, a delay was deemed unnecessary.

Under the New West India Company, the States of Holland drew up conditions for a new colony on the Wild Coast. The Chamber of Amsterdam was much impressed with this project and urged the States General to approve plans for a settlement on the Wiapoco or the Aprowaco. Since either of these rivers was easy to defend and neither was then occupied, Amsterdam's enthusiasm is understandable. In addition, the Indians of the area were peaceable, and slave-trading to these regions was easier than to Tobago. Unfortunately for the chamber two of the colony's officials, the governor and the minister, the latter a former English preacher from The Hague, quarreled just as this project was being established on the Wiapoco. Hence, the French from Cayenne—retaken from the Dutch by Vice-Admiral d'Estrées—found it very easy to destroy the settlement and take its members prisoner. Thus ended the last Dutch effort to claim the Wiapoco.[83]

To summarize the results of sixty-five years of colonizing efforts —from 1613 to 1678—in the Guianas: the Dutch, from the beginning of this period, had a trading post at Kijkoveral on the Essequibo and two or three others in the Amazon delta. The latter were obliterated by the Portuguese in the twenties. Fort Kijkoveral remained in Dutch hands, with a short exception during the second Anglo-Dutch controversy, but had not been expanded much beyond a trading and agricultural center of small importance. Its territorial growth had been slow and frequently interrupted. Until well into the eighteenth century, the plantations on the Essequibo clustered themselves around the fort for safety. The settlement on the Pomeroon, after an initial good start, met with gradual decline. Berbice, unquestionably the most successful of all Dutch colonies, was able to resist an English attack in 1666, and had enough power left to reconquer the other two settlements.

The colony at Cayenne, after several frustrated Dutch efforts, passed finally into French control with the conquest of d'Estrées in 1676 and the conditions of the Peace of Nijmegen. The Dutch secured Surinam during the second Anglo-Dutch war and retained it through the Peace of Breda, notwithstanding the English reconquest of 1667.

In addition to Surinam, Essequibo, and Berbice, the Dutch had established a network of stations, forms of occupation defined by the Treaty of Munster and often called *loges* or warehouses. These posts were located on the main rivers and on important branches, such as the Cuyuni and the Barima. The policy of distant trading, initiated by Hendrik Rol, was pursued by the Chamber of Zeeland for many years. However, the actual political significance of these depots, if any, is difficult to determine.

The Wild Coast, during these sixty-five years, witnessed vast bloodshed between the chief contenders for its possession. All the settlements except Berbice changed hands during this period, many of them more than once. Merchants such as Jan de Moor and Abraham van Pere invested fortunes in these localities, and hundreds of colonists gambled their lives. The impact of the sacrifice is mirrored in a pamphlet of 1676, which records a conversation between a country dweller, an urbanite, and a sailor.[84] The questions and answers in this dialogue reveal that little was known in the United Provinces of the Wild Coast and its opportunities, even after the many expeditions and ever recurring wars.

Nor was much information for popular consumption forthcoming from the sundry body of inducements publicized by the West India Company in those years. In these, it is repeatedly assumed that the entire Wild Coast was open to Dutch colonization. The territory is variously described as stretching from the Amazon to the Orinoco or "from the Amazon to the Wild or Caribbean Islands."[85] This scanty description is about all the information future Dutch colonists could acquire about the region which had been purchased with so much of their blood and money, and which was to become a permanent part of their colonial empire built in the seventeenth century.

Those who were really interested could have gleaned some idea of conditions from the contracts between the patrons and the Heren XIX. They would have learned, for example, that they would receive land on the understanding that they would cultivate it within three years. The traditional Dutch principle of local autonomy was also preserved by a prescription for regional and provincial councils.[86] But even a prospective patron would not have found real information, little of which was attractive, concerning the Wild Coast in such official sources as a "General Order for the Colonies on the Coast of Guiana." A typical Zeelandian charter—of 1631—briefed the patron that his settlement could not be within a radius of seven or eight miles from any other colony, and left the governing of the community to him with the ultimate approval of the Chamber of Zeeland. The patron enjoyed certain exemptions and immunities, all specified, and some sub-soil rights after payment of a recognition to the WIC. But none of these sources revealed the real situation in Guiana, or gave any information on climate, soil, and agricultural possibilities.

When Brazil was lost, the Chamber of Zeeland concluded that Guiana would be just as valuable, if populated. Consequently, a plan of colonization was drawn up to stimulate emigration to the Wild Coast. In this plan, under the sovereignty of Their High Mightinesses and the supervision of the Heren XIX, any inhabitant of the United Provinces was free to sail to the Wild Coast, "to take into possession such stretches of land as they shall need of for their purposes and cultivation, to administer, populate, till, and plant it, on condition that they provide themselves with proper shoulder and side-arms with their appurtenances."[87] When the population had grown to two hundred families, a local government would be selected from among them. The settlers were to possess the land in fee simple, although after five years they would have to pay a poll tax; the sub-soil clause was abolished. Colonists were allowed to carry on trade free of all dues, and they could even arrange for slaves. The only restrictions, aside from general approval by the company, were limited to the trade in dye.

The Chamber of Amsterdam, already interested in the Wiapoco and Cayenne regions during the Truce, renewed its interest through the resolution of the Heren XIX of August 30, 1655, and gave support to various colonizing expeditions which, for several reasons, all failed. The charters drawn up for these enterprises were all similar to the one issued to van Pere in 1627 and to other charters which regulated colonization in New Netherland. They were liberal enough, as is proven by the one granted to David Nassy on September 12, 1659, the "Colonization Regulations" of January 18, 1663, for the Cayenne colony under Quiryn Spranger, and the one for the Wiapoco settlement of 1677.[88]

An examination of the failure of so many colonial undertakings on the Wild Coast does not substantiate Laspeyres' assertion that the Dutch were incapable of founding colonies, not at least for the Guianas.[89] There are certainly as many examples of lost labor among French and English efforts in these regions. The same causes may be found for virtually all the losses: lack of knowledge, supplies, discipline, and cooperation, Indian hostility, and the many effects of European wars.

The Dutch colonies in Guiana were not very important during the days of the Old West India Company. The real prosperity for the Dutch on the Wild Coast came only in the late seventeenth and in the eighteenth centuries. All that was accomplished earlier, however, was a very important foundation for future growth.

NEW WALCHEREN

Een vergeten Nederlandsche kolonie.[1]

From 1628 to 1678 the island of Tobago, called New Walcheren by the Dutch, had been a colony of the West India Company under the supervision of the Chamber of Zeeland, albeit it with some interruptions and not uncontestedly. It probably received its name when, on Columbus' third voyage, the natives were found smoking the dry leaves of the soon well-known tobacco plant which grew in abundance in the fertile soil on the southern half of the island. Its history from 1628 to 1678 is one of the most dramatic of any area in the Caribbean archipelago.

The English gave a fairly accurate description of the island, its geography, and its history during the first years of European colonization.[2] From the early seventeenth century onward, descriptions multiplied. The Dutch chronicler de Laet, who had never seen the island, wrote, "It is all good soil, but it is uninhabited because of the malicious natives of the island of Dominica."[3]

The combination of climate, soil, and excellent harbors made the island an attractive target for the English in the sixteenth century. While, of course, Spain never abdicated her claim on Tobago, during the seventeenth century the site was occupied alternately, and sometimes simultaneously, by English, French, Dutch, and Courlandian colonists. Spain had nominal title to the island and tried but failed during the Truce to take possession *de facto*. Thereafter, Tobago changed masters several times, but the Dutch were permanently driven out in 1678.

Much romance surrounding the island still depends upon the possibility that Tobago was the haven for Robinson Crusoe, Daniel Defoe's immortal hero. Some believe that Defoe visited the island and had it in mind when he published his novel in 1719. Van Kampen, already quoted various times, thinks this probable; his conclusions were shared by several contemporary authors.[4] Historical evidence, however, establishes the fact that in 1659, the year in which Crusoe was supposed to have begun his life as a hermit, there were European colonists on Tobago. "I came here on shore September 30, 1659," begins Robinson Crusoe's diary; but we know from the journal of the *St. Jan* ("St. John"), a Dutch slave trader, that his ship had refreshed at Tobago three days earlier.[5]

As referred to before, English, French, Dutch, and Courlandian colonists all played an important role in the colonization of the island. It was first called Asunción; Spanish writers soon tried to approximate the Indian word for the leaf growing there and arrived at "tobaco."[6] The island does not appear on the oldest maps of the Caribbean, and the earliest Spanish accounts do not mention it. Las Casas' *History of the Indies* does not indicate that the island was known. Of course, it may have been one of the *islas inútiles* where the *indieros* or slave hunters sought Indians for the labor markets of the Greater Antilles.

Although no certain date can be given, Spanish interest in the island may have begun around 1535. The English became concerned about it in the 1580's, but when Keymis came there in 1596 he found it deserted except for a few Indians. A report of English activity on Tobago in 1608 must be in error and most likely refers to Trinidad, which was a thriving colony by that date.[7] In 1614, according to the account of John Scott, Tobago was the site of a colonizing attempt by Juan Rodríguez, who wished to raise tobacco for the rapidly expanding European market, a project which he abandoned after four months.[8]

The status of the island in 1628, when the Dutch first arrived there, is not known.[9] Rumors were circulated in the United Provinces that Thomas Warner had claimed the island for James I in 1626. This king orally granted all the Caribbean islands to James Hay, Earl of Carlisle. Somewhat later, however, possibly forgetting the previous grant, he gave the same islands, or at least most of them, to Philip Herbert, Earl of Pembroke. It seems possible that Tobago was also among King James' christening gifts to Jakob, son of William, Duke of Courland, in 1610.[10]

The Dutch were latecomers to the Caribbean; when they finally did arrive, however, they came in such numbers that the Spanish governor of Trinidad was complaining regularly about them by the turn of the century. When they came to refresh and to trade, they brought textiles and hardware which were exchanged for tobacco, hides, and cacao. They presumably founded, before the Truce, a trading post on Tobago, although no clear evidence for this assumption is available. Tobago remained for them a side interest, while their main efforts were concentrated on the Wild Coast.

Although England and France lead the way in colonizing the Caribbean, the Dutch soon followed their example. The English had previously founded an unsuccessful colony at Santa Lucia in the southern Lesser Antilles in 1605 and another similarly brief settlement on Grenada in 1609. In the twenties the English attempts were continued. As noted earlier, Thomas Warner made several efforts and ultimately earned such a reputation for himself on St. Christopher that he was named governor of the island. The English also settled on Barbados, which, like St. Christopher, formed part of the Carlisle grant that was presently confirmed by Charles I. The Barbados colony in its first difficult years of existence received various kinds of aid from Groenewegen of the Dutch Essequibo settlement.

Meanwhile, Zeelanders began to take a more permanent interest in the islands near Guiana, and especially Tobago. One of their first expeditions was made by Jan de Moor, probably the most important agent for Dutch, and especially Zeelandian, colonial enterprises.[11] His action may well have been prompted by an abortive Amsterdam venture to Tobago a year earlier.[12] Whatever the reason, de Moor, acting through Jacob Maerssen, sent a request to the Chamber of Zeeland for permission to transport sixty to eighty colonists to the West Indies "in order to render themselves to the island of Tobago, situated close to Trinidad."[13] This request was granted on condition that a certain bail be paid. For reasons now obscure, de Moor's expedition never sailed, and the grant was revoked in 1628. A similar grant to Pieter van Corselles, one of the partners of the first one, was likewise not undertaken and, consequently, unsuccessful.[14]

In the midst of these developments Jan de Moor did dispatch a ship with sixty-eight colonists for Tobago in 1628. This ship is later found among the vessels which were assigned to Admiral Ita for the pursuit of a Spanish silver fleet.[15] Ultimately it did reach Tobago, and a Dutch colony was founded there as a consequence.[16] The sixty-eight colonists survived and were reinforced the next year, 1629, by another Zeelandian ship sailing under Admiral Pater. In that same year, Admiral Loncq's secret instructions ordered him to return home by way of the Caribbean and New Netherland to provide these colonies —among which Tobago was specifically mentioned—with any Negroes he had managed to capture.[17] Tobago had by now obviously become a matter of the utmost concern to the Heren XIX as well as to the Chamber of Zeeland.

In 1632, even more Dutch colonists reached Tobago from Flushing.

The island's population had now increased to two hundred.[18] Ships destined for Brazil thereafter occasionally received specific instructions which ordered them to stop at Tobago en route home. The commander of a squadron leaving New Holland in 1634, for instance, was instructed to pause at Tobago and to send two yachts from there to cruise between St. Vincent, Matitino, and Guadeloupe to gather information about the Tierra Firme fleet. Tobago was, geographically speaking, better situated than Curaçao for action against this fleet because ships arriving from Brazil or from the United Provinces could drop anchor at Tobago without being sighted by the Spaniards. This was not true, however, of ships which penetrated the Caribbean to Curaçao.

The Zeelandian colony on Tobago was eliminated between 1634 and 1637, probably on New Year's Day of the latter year. No one knows what really happened. Kesler maintains that the colonists were massacred in 1634 and that the few survivors returned to Zeeland.[19] Massacre no doubt best describes what happened to the settlers, but other evidence argues that it did not occur until late in 1636 or early in 1637. Jacques Onsiel, secretary and treasurer of Tobago, at that time offered to attack the Spaniards on Trinidad, on condition that the colonists themselves muster sixty to eighty musketeers and four hundred Indians.[20] This action was delayed and, with the help of an Indian spy, the Spaniards who might have been warned struck first, presumably on January 1, 1637.

The Spanish raid on Tobago, involving some four hundred Spaniards and three thousand Indians, simply overwhelmed the settlers. Their small fort soon had to surrender. The members of its garrison, only forty-five men and twenty boys, were promised life and transportation to St. Christopher or elsewhere at their own choice; they were instead carried off to Margarita. The Spanish governor there ordered them all hanged. The Franciscans, however, intervened and saved the lives of boys under sixteen and of a few others, probably the Catholics among them. Those who were spared were compelled to work on the plantations. The two leaders, Onsiel and Cornelis de Moor, the latter a son of Jan de Moor, were taken via Cartagena and Havana to Spain.[21] They somehow made their way home from there to the United Provinces.

Report of this outrageous breach of the surrender conditions and *buena guerra* principles—the latter idea had been tacitly adopted by both belligerents since the Truce—aroused great indignation in the Low Countries. The Spaniards soon found that they were going to pay for this action. Although the Prince of Orange and the States

General discussed many means of retaliation, actual orders to Groenewegen of Essequibo can no longer be found. Groenewegen certainly
acted, however, and led the Dutch and their Indian allies in ransacking
the Spanish town of San Tomé on the Orinoco. A similar fate befell
the island of Trinidad. Such drastic measures can only have been
authorized by the States General.

During this same period, the middle thirties, another series of
events was to affect Tobago. William Usselinx, though frustrated in
Holland and Zeeland, had tried to interest the Duke of Courland in a
colonizing project in the Caribbean as early as 1627. Duke Frederick
was then involved in the Thirty Years' War, however, and had resisted
Usselinx' overtures. An English diplomat Thomas Roe, sent by Charles
I, had more success with the duke. The influence of a Courlandian
soldier, Captain Joachim Deniger, probably did the rest.[22] Deniger
had served in Brazil under the Dutch, and, like Roe, he was familiar
with the tropics. Presumably it was Deniger who, in addition,
suggested that the United Provinces was the best place to gain financial
support for colonizing plans. Indeed, in 1634 Frederick sent his heir
Jakob to Amsterdam where the necessary connections with Dutch
merchant houses were made. Duke Frederick then sent a ship to the
Caribbean with 212 colonists who settled on Tobago. However, the
Courlandian settlers, many of them from Zeeland, left because they
could not adapt to the tropical climate.[23]

The question remains whether Jakob was involved in this enterprise.
The names of Amsterdam merchants and bankers have been linked
with young Jakob's. Evidently, Amsterdam capitalists were not unwilling to support claims in those areas where Zeeland had previously
held a monopoly.

Although documentation does not exist for a Courlandian expedition in 1634 or shortly thereafter, it is highly probable that such
an expedition did take place in 1637. But it can only have ended in
failure. There is no doubt, however, that since the middle of
the thirties, Jakob and others had successfully allied the Duchy
of Courland with Dutch commercial interests. This alliance has
become evident from the fact that a certain Henryck Momber, a
prominent Amsterdam merchant, became the chief official agent for
Courland's colonizing ventures. The mystery surrounding these
Courlandian expeditions may be attributed to conflicting claims on
the island which the duke wished to avoid. Jakob, however, might
certainly have been directly involved in a venture which took place
after his return to Courland.[24]

The 1630's were confusing years in the history of Tobago. Several authors of the seventeenth and eighteenth centuries, Exquemeling, for example, mention a Courlandian expedition after 1632. As Anderson has shown, however, none of these sources can be relied upon for accurate chronology. Although John Scott describes a later Courlandian colonial venture in 1639, which was another failure, to be sure, it can no longer be determined whether this was the second or third expedition to Tobago which was sponsored by the ducal house of modern Latvia.

In 1639 the English also made a renewed effort to settle on Tobago,[25] when a certain Captain Massam was instrumental in bringing a group of dissatisfied Barbados settlers to its shores. Like all other such early ventures, however, the continuous attacks by Indians from St. Vincent drove the colonists away within a year. Massam's group, in this case, fled to Trinidad. Although the latter island was under nominal Spanish control, it actually had several English developments along its northern coast, and these clandestine settlers welcomed the refugees from Tobago.

Captain Marshall led the next English attempt to settle Tobago with colonists from Barbados. This group arrived in 1642, and despite murderous attacks by the Caribs, the English managed to plant tobacco and indigo, and lived for some time on the island. Eventually, however, these colonists were driven away to settle in Surinam where they met a disastrous end a few years later.[26]

At this juncture the young Duke of Courland decided that the right moment had come to make another effort at colonizing Tobago. Jakob—too poor for a king and too rich for a duke because his country was quite prosperous during these years—had built a fleet and had undertaken several colonial ventures based on certain mistaken ideas about the importance of colonies as commercial pursuits. His first venture had led to the occupation of some small islands controlling the mouth of the Gambia River in West Africa. These islands were strategically located and made it possible for the enterprising duke to engage in the highly profitable trade in African slaves. Tobago now became the ideal site to expand these activities. In order to avoid open opposition from the powerful United Provinces, however, Jakob first offered the States General the patronage of the island. Their High Mightinesses did not deign to accept his proposition.[27]

Warned, however, by earlier failures, Duke Jakob employed two Dutchmen, Otto Heye and Cornelis Caron. Caron had previously been employed by the Dutch West India Company, and his reputation was questionable, although Scott calls him "a gentleman of good conduct."[28] The colonists, perhaps as many as three hundred, were largely Zeelanders. They must have reached Tobago shortly after Captain Marshall and his followers had been driven off to Surinam. The Caribs did not wait long to attack, and many members of the expedition were killed. Seventy survivors escaped to Trinidad. Aided by the Arawaks, the determined foes of the Caribs, this sad remainder proceeded to the Wild Coast. There, at the Pomeroon River, it found a haven. A very prosperous colony was soon established.[29]

In the forties, civil strife lessened English colonizing attempts to a certain extent, but Robert Rich, Earl of Warwick, did make another effort to colonize Tobago. He had already earned an excellent reputation for himself as commander of the Parliamentary marine, and was rewarded with the governor-generalship of the English colonies in the Americas. Despite all of the fruitless earlier undertakings, Tobago was still attractive to investors and adventurous pioneers. Warwick's propaganda to "divers Gentlemen of the English Nation" led to another voyage in 1647.[30] The colony must have met with almost immediate disaster, however, and no record of the venture has survived. Some months later Tobago was offered for sale. There were no buyers, but the Pembroke-Courteen-Warwick patent thereafter disappeared from the political field.[31]

During the forties, then, no permanent settlement can be traced in Tobago. As Anderson has pointed out, however, at the close of this period there may have been a small and illegal Zeelandian station engaged in smuggling and the slave trade. This settlement may have been composed of Zeelanders who had earlier participated in Duke Jakob's last enterprise, and who had somehow survived the Indian massacres. Such a base would also have fitted into Duke Jakob's scheme to turn Tobago into a center for the slave trade. If this dream were to come true, he expected to be able to provide the Spanish colonies with a thousand or more slaves a year.[32] However, because of the hostility of the Dutch West India Company, which was building up its own slave market on Curaçao, the Courlandian scheme was doomed to fail. Duke Jakob was also unsuccessful in finding the necessary financial backing in spite of the repeated efforts of his representative in Amsterdam, Momber.[33] The Dutch capital was too closely linked to Curaçao.

In 1653, Duke Jakob decided to undertake the venture on his own. Since the United Provinces were engaged in the first Anglo-Dutch War, a treaty of neutrality with the Dutch favored Courlandian aims. Eighty families were induced to sail to Tobago, and they were to be accompanied by 124 soldiers and 25 officers for their protection. The leader of this expedition was a Dutchman, Willem Mollens,[34] proof that the duke needed Dutch knowledge and experience even if he did proceed without Dutch money, which was not very probable. On May 20, 1654, their ship dropped anchor at what has since been called Great Courland Bay, on the southwestern coast of the island. Mollens took official possession of Tobago in the name of Duke Jakob and renamed the island New Courland. His report to the duke reveals that the island had been deserted for many years. For example, the Dutch fort of 1628, Fort Flushing, had been almost completely overgrown by tropical vegetation. Another fort and a few houses built by the Dutch in 1634 were in advanced states of deterioration.

The Courlanders immediately embarked upon the construction of Fort Jacobus. A letter from Matthias Beck, later vice-governor of Curaçao but then leader of a group of Dutch fugitives from Pernambuco, describes the situation he found on Tobago shortly after the Courlanders had settled there. Each colonist was eligible to receive at least 630 acres as private property which was to be free of taxes for the first three years. Beck expressed proper amazement at this magnanimity.[35]

Avoiding Duke Jakob, refugees from Brazil, together with colonists from the Wild Coast who were largely Jewish, petitioned the States General in July, 1654, for permission to found a separate colony on Tobago. Their High Mightinesses did not respond to this request because the de Moor heirs, Adriaen and Cornelis Lampsins, were then pressing claims to the island. "These two generous brothers," as de Rochefort calls them,[36] were members of a well-known Zeelandian family. Cornelis, as burgomaster of Flushing and deputy of Zeeland at the States General, showed special interest in the West Indies. Anderson describes him as a man of great abilities, and he certainly was, yet he also seems to have been *ein grosser Spitzbube* (a big crook).[37]

As early as 1648, the Lampsins had already had their eyes on Tobago. At the end of April, 1650, they received permission to go ahead, but the first Anglo-Dutch conflict interrupted their colonizing efforts. Immediately after the war, they sent a ship with fifty Zeelanders to Tobago to establish *de facto* control over the island. The leader of this expedition, Pieter Becquard, with the approval of the States General had been appointed commander of the island, now known as New Walcheren; he anticipated a heavy flux of Dutch settlers from St. Eustatius and the Guianas.[38]

The Zeelanders arrived in the middle of September, 1654, four months after the Courlanders. Becquard seems to have founded his colony on the opposite side of the island and, for some time, remained unaware of the presence of the Courlanders. He made a trip to St. Eustatius in order to persuade former Tobago inhabitants to return to strengthen his little colony. He also allied himself with the Carib chieftain of the island and sent him three hostages as proof of his friendship. After belatedly discovering that his colony was not the only one, however, he wrongly informed his patrons that he and his group had arrived a few months *before* the Courlanders.[39] The reverse was true, although it is not difficult to see why he did this, since priority in settlement almost always meant priority in claims.

The Courlanders learned of the Dutch presence in a peculiar way, namely, when they came upon the miserable Dutch captives of the Carib chieftain. These hostages were released and all three took an oath of allegiance to Duke Jakob. When Becquard returned from his trip to St. Eustatius and met the Courlanders, he agreed to a treaty because he realized his own vulnerability. Both parties divided the island until such time as their respective governments could come to an understanding. The Courlanders were to pay dearly for this agreement.[40]

Although the Lampsins' colony was a patronship, the States General was much interested in it. Patents of this era reveal that the government of the United Provinces was determined to keep some sort of official control over all colonial ventures. The Lampsins received certain exemptions from the XIX in 1655 and the right to appoint magistrates for their colony, but the States General had not only to approve the patent but also the selected administrators. No mention was made of Courlandian or English claims.[41] Requests to found colonies within the charter of the WIC were regularly brought to the attention of Their High Mightinesses, although these requests might be directed to one of the chambers and discussed in the meetings of the Heren XIX. Cornelis Caron's repeated petitions to found a colony on Tobago, for example, did not meet the final approval of the States General, and were returned to the Heren XIX with the statement that "this Caron is absolutely untrustworthy because he has committed many notorious crimes, at home as well as in Brazil."[42]

During the Commonwealth period, Duke Jakob could no longer expect support from his Stuart friends. He protested to Cromwell about the Zeelandian settlement on Tobago. The United Provinces, in a delicate position vis-à-vis the Protector, were hesitant to support the Lampsins' claim wholeheartedly. Cromwell, however, had too many irons in the fire to concern himself with Stuart allies. The Lampsins were thus free to develop their colony without interference.

New Walcheren now became the scene of fast expanding activities. The patrons built warehouses for commodities they intended to send there. Indeed, the island was soon to become a place for colonists of every nation to buy what they needed. The stores included everything from nails to slaves.

The Zeelanders were masters of only a part of the island, but with patrons like the Lampsins, it was easy to predict that they would not confine themselves to a limited section. The Courlandian colony had continuously received large numbers of reinforcements. But the Baltic war proved to be an advantage to the Dutch. When Duke Jakob, one of the participants, was taken captive by the Swedes, his colony in the Caribbean suffered accordingly. Ships setting out for the West Indies from Courland were intercepted by Swedish vessels, and no supplies reached the colony at Great Courland Bay. The Dutch colony, New Flushing, situated at Lampsins Bay, received all it needed, by contrast.

Conflict between the neighbors was inevitable. Each colony was a small settlement along the coast. The Caribs held the middle and northern part of the island, and their raids, often with help from St. Vincent, were more harmful to the Courlanders who could not replace lost supplies or men. A ship did reach Tobago with 120 Courlanders in 1657, just before Duke Jakob was imprisoned. It was one of the last to reach the island from Courland. But the new governor Joachim Deniger never arrived, since he preferred to chase the mysterious Ophir in Africa. At this most crucial moment, the colony was left without leadership.[43]

Tensions between the settlements continued to increase. The Lampsins, encouraged by the Provincial States of Zeeland and by the local chamber of the wic, began to capture those Courlandian ships which had escaped the Swedes. The situation for Duke Jakob's colonists grew progressively worse. The Dutch were expanding so rapidly, moreover, that the Courland settlement was soon no more than an enclave in Dutch territory. In 1658 this situation worsened and a Dutch report referred to it as "miserable."[44] According to this report, there were no more than forty Courlanders capable of carrying arms, while there were at least five hundred Dutchmen, most of them Zeelanders. Their number was increased by the same amount of Frenchmen who had settled under the Dutch.[45]

In 1659, the Amsterdam Chamber of the wic requested of Duke Jakob's representative Momber the surrender of his master's islands in the Gambia River. Being a Dutchman himself, Momber succumbed to pressure from his fellow-countrymen and signed an agreement with the chamber. The Dutch at Tobago, no doubt advised of this move, now took the initiative to annihilate the Courland settlement. They surrounded the colony and blockaded the bay, and Mollens, the Dutch governor of the Courland group, was persuaded to leave the island. After he had left, the colony entered a series of crises because of lack of leadership, and its situation soon became unbearable.

The Dutch, more familiar with the European background, now began a campaign to convince the Courlandian colonists that, with Duke Jakob in custody, their situation was hopeless. The latter were inclined to agree, but Holtzbruch, their commander and Mollen's successor, refused to cooperate. The Courlanders then mutinied against Holtzbruch; he was replaced by a new leader, and the latter surrendered the colony to the Dutch on December 11, 1659.

The new Dutch governor, Huybrecht van Beveren, who had relieved Becquard, promised the captives free transportation to Courland and the restoration of the enclave to the duke upon the latter's release.[46] Some time after the surrender, the Lampsins amended the treaty to the effect that Fort Jacobus had surrendered voluntarily. Some attempt was made to pacify curious onlookers by the claims that the Dutch had purchased the Courlandian colony, but no Dutch document exists to prove this.[47] In May, 1660, with the Peace of Oliva, Duke Jakob was set free.

The Dutch, meanwhile, had complete control over Tobago, and the colony was prospering. Under Dutch protection a large number of French planters had also founded a colony named *Le Quartier des Trois Rivières* (The Quarter of the Three Rivers) at a place not far from Little Courland Bay and to the southwest of the Courland settlement. The two groups cooperated in all matters. There were, by now, annual crops of tobacco, dye, indigo, sugar, and cotton.

Duke Jakob, advised of the events on Tobago, now opened negotiations with the United Provinces to carry out the letter of the treaty. He instructed Momber to take certain steps in that direction. Of course, Momber did not accomplish anything. In order to intimidate the duke, the West India Company continued to rob him of his ships. A new representative, Jean de Wicquefort, was able, however, to convince the Lampsins to sell Tobago; they asked 200,000 guilders. The Zeelanders, to be sure, had their reasons, the most important the fact that their patent was due to expire in 1665 and there was no assurance of a renewal. Not blind to the pecuniary advantages, however, they tried to make the best possible bargain in every investment.[48] Yet the parties were unable to come to an agreement, and the project was soon abandoned.

Cornelis Lampsins, for unknown reasons, now appealed to Louis

XIV for the protection of his colony.[49] Perhaps he believed that French support would strengthen his position. The 1662 treaty between Louis and the United Provinces may have originated Lampsins' move. As a result, however, the merchant from Flushing, no doubt for a price, found himself elevated to the French aristocracy as the Baron of Tobago; his military rank was *Chevalier de l'Accolade*.[50] The tiny Caribbean island was reborn as a French barony, while still dependent on the Dutch States General—a strange political phenomenon. It developed into a very important trade center in the Antilles as well as a major producer of sugar and rum. At the beginning of the second Anglo-Dutch war, New Walcheren boasted 1,000 to 1,500 colonists and a slave population estimated at 7,000.[51]

The Dutch settlement at Lampsins Bay was protected by three forts, the main fort Lampsinsberg, and two smaller ones Van Beveren and Bellavista. The Caribs had been banished to St. Vincent. By 1660 there were six sugar mills operating on the island, all of them owned by either the Lampsins, the governor, or other high officials. In addition to the sugar, the island produced cacao and rum, "which is as much valued as it is needed in these hot countries."[52] Trade continued to be brisk, and the population grew both with those who paid thirty guilders for transport from the Low Countries, and those who came as the Dutch counterpart of "indentured servants" under three-year contracts.

In September, 1664, a month after he submitted a request for a renewal of his charter and on the eve of the second Anglo-Dutch war, Cornelis Lampsins died, leaving the colony to his two sons and to his brother Adriaen. These heirs were soon to have the greatest difficulty in retaining the island barony. A war with England meant great danger for New Walcheren, and the new patrons appealed to the United Provinces. Van Campen's fleet, currently being equipped to restore Dutch possessions in Guinea, was now requested by Cornelis' heirs to protect Tobago. A second petition soon followed.[53] There was no response.

Charles II of England, in the throes of his most vigorous anti-Dutch campaign, suddenly decided to forget his long-standing refusal of Duke Jakob's demands and to use him against the Netherlanders. In November, 1664, the two signed a treaty in which the Duke of Courland was awarded Tobago in exchange for his islands in the Gambia River.[54] At that time the latter were probably already in English possession because of Holmes' actions. This arrangement ultimately cost the Courlander all of his colonial possessions. For the moment, though, Charles implemented the treaty by ordering the governor of Barbados to lend all possible assistance to the duke's subjects. He also advised the Dutch that he regarded Tobago as English property and as a Courlandian fief. The Dutch, although aware of Charles' hostile policies, were not impressed. They renewed the Lampsins' patent and approved the appointment of Johan Bolle as the new governor of Tobago.

In another chapter it has been shown how Tobago had been attacked by Modyford's buccaneers during the second Anglo-Dutch war, and how the island's colony, no longer supplied from Zeeland, had been driven to desperation and surrender. The island then went through a bewildering array of owners, Willoughby and the French, only to be found deserted by Crijnssen in 1667. Crijnssen rebuilt the main fort and garrisoned the island with twenty-nine men and four cannon.[55] The Peace of Breda restored Tobago to the Dutch, but did not eliminate French and Courlandian claims.[56]

The history of the early postwar years on Tobago is not well known. A Dutch colony was established there. In 1668, a new governor named Abel Tisso, a Frenchman who could not speak Dutch, arrived from Surinam with a small detachment of soldiers. Little is to be discovered, however, about the colony's numbers or prosperity. In 1670 the settlement withstood a foray of Indians. A request to the States of Zeeland from the inhabitants informed the provincial government that nineteen persons had been killed during that attack. They asked that two well-armed ships be sent to patrol the coastal waters in order to prevent Indian raids staged from the nearby islands. The petitioners, who were all former inhabitants of Tobago from prewar days, had endured the evils of the war only to return to abject poverty on their island.

Duke Jakob, because of his treaty with Charles II, still considered Tobago as his fief and did not relinquish his claim. In December, 1668, a Courlandian ship came to the old site and disembarked some soldiers,[57] but the commanding officer did not occupy the fort. The Dutch then intimidated the leader of the Courlanders by presenting him with two alternatives, either to join them or to leave the island; he departed.[58] Duke Jakob, meanwhile, initiated the long legal process of reclaiming the island by advising his agent in The Hague to open proceedings against the Lampsins.[59] This suit lasted through the Anglo-French war against the Dutch and was then abandoned; its only tangible result was the Dutch government's promised support to the Lampsins, and this in spite of a Courlandian contingent which aided the Dutch in their war against France and England. Shortly thereafter the Zeeland Chamber awarded Tobago to the

Lampsins as a hereditary fief "under a patent which would last until 1700."[60]

Charles II, however, now decided to assist Duke Jakob, and renewed his orders to Barbados to seize Tobago from the Dutch.[61] By the summer of 1672, the English plans were laid. The Lampsins, in the meantime, had reinforced their colony with five hundred new members. The ships which had brought the new settlers, however, had captured some English merchantmen while en route to the island. The English at Barbados were sufficiently provoked by these captures so that they scarcely needed the orders of Charles II to attack the Dutch on New Walcheren.[62]

The English force, equipped on Barbados, could be measured in pounds of sugar since its members were to be paid in that commodity.[63] Governor William Willoughby contributed heavily to the expenses. Although the English did not underestimate the Dutch strength, they knew that there were Quakers on the island who would not bear arms. One English man-of-war, the *King David*, and six ships carrying six hundred men reached Tobago on December 18. Three days later the English commander, Tobias Bridge, wrote to Willoughby that the "conquest" was over.[64] Even though the *King David* had been badly damaged in the fight which had lasted five to six hours, the Dutch governor, "meinheer Constant," soon sent two colonists to negotiate peace. Together with some other officials the governor was taken to Curaçao after having ordered the colonists to abandon fighting. The conquest of Tobago was the first Caribbean action in the war that started in 1672 with the United Provinces opposing England and France.

Tobias Bridge's orders were to destroy whatever he could lay his hands on. Only the lives of the four hundred colonists were saved; they were transported to Barbados together with their slaves and cattle.[65] Many escaped into the woods which covered a large part of the island. Two days after the surrender, a French frigate arrived, sent by the governor of Martinique who intended to take advantage of the prevailing confusion to capture the island for Louis XIV. The French captain could barely contain his displeasure when he learned that the English had beaten him to it, but there was little he could actually do.[66]

The epilogue of the "Tobago plunder," as it is called in the minutes of the Council of Barbados,[67] dragged on for several years. In May, 1673, neither the booty of the expedition nor the sugar allotments had been divided among the participants. The island was deserted by the English, and the Council of Barbados refused to garrison the site because, as it claimed, the men were needed at home.[68] The Lampsins' request to the States General to reconquer the island at their own expense was denied in 1673.[69]

The second Peace of Westminster, however, which ended the third Anglo-Dutch war—hostilities against the French continued—awarded Tobago to the Dutch. The Zeeland Chamber of the WIC once again became the supervisor of the island. In May, 1676, the Lampsins' heirs sold New Walcheren to the Provincial States of Holland for 36,000 guilders.[70] Zeeland's reaction to that sale is not known. Holland then placed the island under the direction of the admiralty board of Amsterdam. The New West India Company, founded in 1674, was thus completely left out of the transaction. The deed for Tobago explicitly stated that the Lampsins' title had not been investigated.[71] The barons of Tobago retained four plantations on their island and the right to trade there for the ensuing six years.

The plans to repopulate and restore the defenses of New Walcheren seem to have been suggested by Hendrick Carloff, an impoverished Swedish planter, who had a pathological hatred for the French and a burning desire to drive the instigators of his loathing from the West Indies.[72] Carloff had served the WIC in Africa, and later he had joined the Swedish African Company. At a still later date he became the Danish agent for the same area. In 1665, he had signed a six-year contract with the French West India Company to transport a certain number of slaves annually to the French Antilles, to be paid for with sugar which was to be sold in France. He had made a voyage in 1669, and brought 750 Negroes to Martinique; in 1672, he delivered 350 Negroes to Guadeloupe.[73] He insisted that the heavy losses he had suffered during the last Anglo-French war were wholly due to indiscriminate action on the part of his archfoes the French. Colbert's West India Company had forced him out of the slave market and ruined his assets in this trade.

For Carloff, a Dutch expedition to the Caribbean meant a chance to recoup. He contacted the secretary of the Amsterdam admiralty board, Hiob de Wildt, and the two schemers won the support of the grand pensionary and of the Prince of Orange. The Amsterdam Chamber of the New West India Company was also eager to cooperate, and the Zeelandian States protested in vain. On September 20, the States General reached a decision based on the plan submitted by one former commander of the Cayenne colony before it was lost to the French. The latter proposed to make New Walcheren a densely colonized and fortified trade center, and to populate it with Dutch and French fugitives from Brazil, Cayenne, and the Lesser Antilles, all accustomed to a tropical climate. The plan also proposed to expand this activity toward the Wiapoco River. The consequence of this idea was a virtually unanimous decision to send a Dutch squadron to the West Indies.[74]

The squadron was placed under the leadership of Jacob Binckes, a distinguished Frisian naval commander who had earned his merits under both famous Dutch admirals, Tromp and de Ruyter.[75] Binckes seemed to be the right man for the job, for he knew the area, was brave, and had excellent qualities as a leader. In the following chapter, his 1673 voyage to the West Indies will be discussed, as well as his raids against the French at Cayenne. The idea behind these attacks was twofold: first, to cause the French as much damage as possible, and second, to acquire prospective settlers for Tobago.

After a battle at St. Martin against the French, the victorious Binckes divided his fleet into two squadrons. He sailed with the larger squadron to Puerto Rico and Hispaniola and sent the smaller squadron under Jan Bont to Tobago to found the planned colony. Bont was accompanied by Hendrick Carloff, the appointed governor of the island. In addition, the ships carried more than one hundred recruited settlers and a few hundred slaves, as well as the captured loot.[76]

Bont never arrived at the island. The reason for his subsequent desertion has originated another mysterious tale in the colorful spectrum of Caribbean history. While sending the rest of his ships to New Walcheren, he turned the rudder of his ship and sailed to Cadiz, Spain, and from there to the Low Countries. He was arrested there, and, after a court-martial, publicly beheaded in the capital.[77] No explanation exists for his strange behavior, for he had courageously fought in both the second and third Anglo-Dutch wars, and had proven his gallantry in an attack on Guadeloupe (see Chapter XVIII).

By weakening the Dutch fleet, his action indirectly contributed to its defeat at Tobago. The rest of his squadron arrived, although near Guadeloupe it had run into some French men-of-war under the Marquis de Grancey. The latter followed the Dutch ships for some time, constantly keeping them under fire. The Dutch, according to the French version of the battle, did not respond because the decks of their ships were cluttered with Binckes' loot.[78]

The other squadron arrived at Tobago on September 1, 1676, and Binckes immediately organized the island's defense. A new fort called *Sterreschans* was built at Klip Bay (Rockly Bay), and a smaller bulwark was erected nearby. Work had to be done quickly, for the French knew the Dutch intended to make an armory of Tobago,[79] as well as a base for attacking French islands and settlements on the Wild

Coast. In February, 1677, their morale was boosted by the arrival of a large *secours* from home with 150 soldiers, more colonists, and many provisions.[80]

In the meantime the Count d'Estrées, finding himself without employment, petitioned Louis XIV, who was preparing an attack on the Dutch colonies in the Caribbean with the idea of permanently eliminating the Netherlanders from the area. Louis remained cool to d'Estrées' suggestions until reports of Binckes' actions against Cayenne and the French Antilles reached Versailles. Tobago, as a Dutch stronghold, was a perpetual menace to the French.

At this time, d'Estrées was commissioned to sail to the Caribbean. He began with the recapture of Cayenne and then secured the French Antilles for replacements and supplies. He left Martinique on February 17 with ten men-of-war, six lighter ships, a fire ship, some provision ships, and more than four thousand men.[81] His target was Tobago.

On February 18, Binckes received reports that two small French ships were approaching Klip Bay. He rightly understood these to be the reconnoitering units of d'Estrées' fleet.[82] That night Jan Erasmus Reining, a privateer who had sailed with Binckes from Holland and who had been sent to the Leeward Islands for scouting purposes, arrived at New Walcheren with a letter from the governor of Nevis concerning d'Estrées' successful recapture of Cayenne and his recruiting in the French Antilles.[83] On February 19 the Dutch sighted nine sails, the following day fourteen sails. They worked frantically to complete their fort, while Binckes sent a detachment of one hundred soldiers to Palmyt Bay to prevent French debarkation. He soon realized, however, that Tobago's excellent harbors were simply too numerous to attempt to defend them all.

The Dutch commander, convinced the French would not dare enter a bay which contained dangerous rock formations as well as ten Dutch men-of-war and the guns of *Sterreschans*, concentrated his defenses around the fort. His ships were drawn up in a half-moon parallel to the shore beneath the fort. Between these vessels and the shore, he placed two unarmed merchantmen and his provision ship, the *Sphera Mundi*. The women and children of the island, more than two hundred, were removed to the latter ships—the *Sphera Mundi* received the majority—as well as the sick and the slaves. Only a fool would now attack the fort from the sea, Binckes thought. The Dutch commander and his war council did not know it, but d'Estrées turned out to be just such a fool.

The Dutch premise of defensive organization led Binckes to make a rather unfortunate move. He decided to strengthen his garrison at the expense of his ships. His men-of-war, having approximately the same tonnage as the French fleet, were now stripped of sailors; the flagship *Bescherming* ("Protection") was left with only 153 men, the others with even fewer.[84] As a direct consequence, the Dutch were unable to concentrate their naval fire power as d'Estrées' fleet entered the harbor to attack, and the Dutch fleet was almost completely destroyed.

Binckes organized a corps of grenadiers and used his remaining time to complete the fort. An incomplete bastion of the main fort was fabricated from barrels interspliced with forty-two guns. All the houses around the fort were burned. He also decided to surrender command of the fleet to his subcommander and to assume responsibility only for the fort. This proved to be a wise decision, for Carloff, the governor, soon demonstrated his incompetence.[85] The resolution was based, however, on another factor; among the defenders of the fort were a number of Frenchmen from Marie Galante whom the Dutch commander did not quite trust. Finally, Binckes hoped that his personal presence in what he expected to become the center of danger would favorably influence discipline and bolster morale. As an incentive to bravery, he promised three months' extra pay.[86]

The French landed a thousand men under the command of de Hérouard de la Piogerie, who was seconded by the Chevalier de Grand'Fontaine on February 21. In order to reach the fort they had to hack their way through the island's vegetation. On February 23, a French officer disguised as a drummer approached the *Sterreschans*, demanded its surrender to the Count d'Estrées, and asked the French members of the garrison not to fight their compatriots. Binckes declined to surrender, and advised the officer that no soldier would be required to fight against his own nation.[87]

Skirmishes between French and Dutch reconnoitering units persisted for several days. Generally speaking, these were disadvantageous to the Dutch because of their fewer numbers. Everything pointed to a tremendous French assault. D'Estrées' navy, however, made no move after a single French man-of-war had floundered soon after it arrived on one of the hidden rocks at the mouth of the bay. Many of the French captains believed that the fort had to be taken before a naval engagement could be dared. D'Estrées now personally inspected the troops he had landed and placed near the fort. From this site on a hill, the French guns fired at the fort but failed to inflict damage.

The first French attack occurred on the evening after the inspection. D'Estrées ordered de Grand'Fontaine to charge the fort between 9 and 10 P.M., while he himself would distract the Dutch with some action at sea. From his flagship the *Glorieux* he sent fourteen sloops to attack Reining at the entrance of the bay where the latter had stationed himself. What happened next is not clear—Dutch and French reports conflict—but one fact is certain: Reining made good his escape into the bay.[88]

At the scheduled time for the attack on the fort, the French soldiers found the brook which they had to cross swollen into a raging river and impassable. A second reason for their failure to act was the French commander's realization that his forces were much too weak to launch a successful assault on an enemy who occupied such a strong position. To all appearances the French upper command now moved into a crisis. The count and his staff had a sharp dispute about how an attack could be mounted, by land or by sea. D'Estrées, whose provisions would not survive a protracted siege, favored a simultaneous assault from both sides. The Dutch position, however, dismayed the more experienced officers, and they were reluctant to follow the count's risky plan. The humiliation of leaving without any gesture, however, was what finally propelled the French to agree to d'Estrées' audacious project to hit the Dutch from both land and sea at once. The attack was set for dawn of March 3 and was vastly helped by the capture of a Dutch vessel whose pilot agreed to betray his countrymen and to lead the French ships into Klip Bay in return for his freedom after the battle.

So it came about that the French fleet entered the bay in two columns on the appointed morning "against our conjectures," as Binckes wrote to the Prince of Orange.[89] One column was headed by d'Estrées himself on the *Glorieux*, the other by his Vice-Admiral Louis de Gabaret on the *Intrépide*. The French naval guns launched a withering fire, and the Dutch responded in kind. The ensuing fracas was described by de la Roncière as "not a battle, but a slaughter."[90] On land the French made three unsuccessful attacks against the fort. They were finally forced to retire to a safer position with nearly two hundred casualties, leaving behind their battering rams and other arms. The retreat left Binckes free to concentrate his attention on the attack from the sea (see map).

In the bay a murderous encounter was taking place. Perhaps as many as one thousand shots were fired by the French while their fleet was entering, and they succeeded in disabling the one Dutch fire ship almost at once. In spite of heavy counterfire the French did not falter and, once inside Klip Bay, each man-of-war threw itself against a Dutch warship anchored there. D'Estrées engaged the Dutch rear admiral on the *'t Huis te Kruiningen*, the biggest and strongest ship in

Binckes' fleet. Although threatened by the disabled fire ship, d'Estrées managed to board the 't Huis te Kruiningen, and there he raised the French flag. A thunderous Vive le Roi greeted this action. The Intrépide and the Marquis were engaged in a fight with the Dutch left wing. During this encounter the men of the Marquis boarded the Dutch Leyden where hand-to-hand fighting resulted. Shortly afterwards both ships caught fire. The fire spread rapidly and engulfed three other Dutch vessels in addition to the provision ships and the Sphera Mundi, which housed the colonists' wives, children, and slaves. Continuing to spread, the fire touched off a blaze near the powder magazine of d'Estrées' recent prize the 't Huis te Kruiningen. The count made various efforts to rid himself of this dangerous captive, but he was barely two fathoms away when the powder exploded and turned his own ship into a fiery prison. Although wounded in the head, d'Estrées was rescued, but many members of his crew were not so fortunate.

Next, the sloop bearing the injured count was hit by a gunshot, and the only hope lay in reaching shore before the boat sank. But there some Dutch sailors who had escaped their burning ships lay in wait. D'Estrées, despite his wounds, now demonstrated his ability by organizing his few French followers and demanding the Dutch surrender for promised quarter. The few Dutch sailors acceded to his demands, and the count returned to one of his own remaining ships. Both fleets were now in shambles.

Sterreschans, after having beaten off several French attacks, then opened vigorous fire on the crippled French ships. Two of them lost their masts, and a fireball from the fort started a blaze on board the Glorieux, which soon lost control. When the ship exploded, most of its 445 men died. Some of the Dutch ships had caught fire also, and seemed to resemble torches. Consequently, the scene at Klip Bay was comparable to Dante's hell. Nowhere, however, was the misery and tragedy more evident than on board the Sphera Mundi and on the two merchantmen where on that bloody day two hundred women, children, and an unknown number of slaves perished in the engulfing flames.

Of the thirteen Dutch ships only three survived the battle, yet these had also been hit below the waterline and were slowly sinking. The French losses were heavy, too; too weak to inflict any real danger on the battered but undefeated enemy, no ships remained undamaged of the fleet that had sailed proudly into the bay. Two of d'Estrées' biggest units were burned and were total losses; two more had been wrecked on the beach while the others had either lost their masts or had become unmaneuverable because of some other mishap. One hour before sunset the count ordered a cease-fire, but the fort continued to fire at the French fleet until well into the night.

In the ensuing three days d'Estrées sent another demand for surrender to the fort. He threatened to string all the inhabitants on his sword if this ultimatum were to be refused. His terms also called for the extradition of all French prisoners. Both of his requests were turned down. In all probability, d'Estrées acted to stall for time until he could rescue two French men-of-war, the *Intrépide* and the *Précieux*, which were then stranded on the beach. In vain the French struggled to get them afloat. An infamous plan to burn them, which would have sacrificed the wounded aboard who could not be gotten ashore, was foiled. The firing parties sent by d'Estrées were repulsed by the few remaining able-bodied men and were forcibly thrown into the bay. Another of the count's efforts to destroy both ships in order to prevent their falling into Dutch hands failed when a French deserter warned Binckes of this intention. Both ships were easy prey for the Dutch and were taken without a loss. The French withdrew to Palmyt Bay, boarded their land troops, and left Tobago.[91]

D'Estrées made for Grenada to treat his many wounded and to caulk his battered ships. He sailed from there to Martinique and then on to France to give an account of what had happened. The French, "as usual," observes Dutch naval historian de Jonge, claimed a great victory despite their obvious losses in men and ships. Bonfires filled the streets of Paris, and, in the traditional way, medals were struck which bore the image of the *Roi Soleil* and the proud inscription *Incensa Batavorum Classe ad Insulam Tabago*.[92]

Was it a French victory? D'Estrées went to great lengths to make it seem so. The reports of his officers, "we only tried to save ourselves . . . we had lost everything," are perhaps a closer approximation of the facts. French demoralization at Tobago was most evident when the mutiny which broke out aboard the *Précieux* prevented its burning. The French had fought valiantly against overwhelming odds and in a general atmosphere of unrelieved tropical heat, but what had they gained? Retreating to Grenada every man must have been aware of the facts: four of His Majesty's finest men-of-war were missing, hundreds of his bravest men had been killed or wounded, and the remainder of this once proud fleet had been mutilated beyond recognition. If they had really achieved a victory, why did not d'Estrées, when he met a contingent of two hundred troops dispatched by Colbert, return to Tobago to finish the job? It was clear that this so-called victory would protect the French Antilles only very temporarily from further Dutch attacks. The two hundred French troops were sent, instead, to harass the Dutch settlements at the Wiapoco and in Surinam.[93]

It was equally true, of course, that Dutch offensive power had been decisively curtailed by the French attack. Binckes had lost seven ships and many men, and the Dutch struck no victory medals. Indeed, the Dutch commander found himself criticized for his actions at Tobago and for the losses he had sustained. Why had he not sent his ships to sea before the French arrival? "If I had done so," he replied, "I would have been the greatest fool and never have dared to return. We would have given the enemy an opportunity to take the fort without striking a simple blow, and I would like to ask those who propose this, what they would have done at sea with a squadron so weakly manned."[94]

Binckes' full attention was now needed to restore Dutch losses. In addition, he had to feed colonists, soldiers, and slaves from scanty provisions and an unproductive island economy. Of the one hundred colonists and six hundred to seven hundred soldiers, only three hundred to four hundred men were likely to have survived.[95]

While Binckes waited for help from the United Provinces, Louis XIV, humiliated by this Pyrrhic victory, acted quickly. What had begun as a matter of commercial defense had suddenly become an affront to national dignity. Colbert realized only too well that a Dutch-held Tobago provided Dutch privateers, roaming in the Caribbean, with an excellent port—a haven, furthermore, that was conveniently located close to the French Antilles. D'Estrées, as Colbert knew, had simply destroyed a Dutch fleet, not a Dutch stronghold.

A new fleet was therefore equipped by the French government: eleven men-of-war, six flutes, and fire ships. This new fleet lay in readiness at Brest in the fall of 1677. D'Estrées was once again appointed commander. The ships reached the Caribbean in November of that year. Before proceeding to the West Indies, however, d'Estrées successfully seized the Dutch island of Goree on the West African coast.

Binckes, meanwhile, had sent urgent requests for help via a repaired French man-of-war under Pieter Constant, who had been seriously wounded during the battle.[96] But two valuable months passed without any action. Not before they were sure that the French were equipping a new fleet did the responsible authorities in the United Provinces appear to lose their lethargy. The Amsterdam admiralty board then equipped a squadron of three ships under Commander Hals, one man-of-war and two provision ships. Binckes and his men were granted leave and replaced by four hundred soldiers who would follow with three other well-armed ships.[97] Much time, however, had been lost in fruitless discussions, and Hals arrived too late.

While Binckes' urgent pleas for assistance made their way through the cumbersome machinery of governmental and company regulations, the French fleet arrived at Tobago reinforced with four frigates from Martinique. When d'Estrées closed on the island on December 6, 1677, he heard to his delight that Binckes was still there. Consequently, he disembarked 1,500 men at Palmyt Bay and left them to hack their way across the vegetation barrier to *Sterreschans*. The Dutch commander had sent two hundred men to hamper the French landing, but because of the overwhelming French strength these troops had to retreat.

Binckes' forces, although reinforced from other Dutch settlements, could not have numbered more than six hundred or seven hundred men. Two hundred of them manned the derelict fleet of two men-of-war in Klip Bay; one, the former *Précieux*, was placed under Reining, and the other was Binckes' own flagship the *Bescherming*. Besides these two ships Binckes had three other smaller vessels, although they were of little fighting value. The odds were undeniably against them.

After his last encounter with the Dutch, however, d'Estrées had learned his lesson. In spite of the fact that the Dutch fleet was much weaker than the one in March, he attacked the fort from the land side only. Before actual fighting began, the count advised Binckes that if the Dutch compelled French colonists on the island to fight, he, d'Estrées, would use the greatest severity on the four hundred Dutch prisoners taken at Goree and elsewhere. Binckes replied that he would not compel any Frenchmen to fight against their own king and asked, "Why did not *Monsieur le vice-amiral* call upon him to surrender the fort, as he had done last time?" This ironic query can only have been posed because Binckes believed the Dutch to have a secret ally, the rainy season, which could save them from the French.

Rain did delay the French attack, but only for one or two days. On December 12 their guns opened fire on the *Sterreschans*; the Dutch rejoinder was fierce. But d'Estrées also had a secret weapon: he had brought with him the celebrated French engineer de Combes. The latter, with the aid of an inventor of a new type of "fire-balls," placed his mortars and adjusted their aim. The first of these balls went over and past the fort; the second fell short. The third, however, landed near the littered path which led to the gunpowder supply precisely when Binckes and his staff were having their lunch in the dining hall directly above the powder magazine of the fort. The

French "fire-ball" ignited some powder that had been spilled on the path and the impromptu "fire" traversed the short distance to the magazine in a matter of minutes.

The resulting explosion killed Binckes, his staff, and half the fort's garrison, more than 250 men. Mass confusion reigned. The one surviving Dutch officer was unable to restore order. The French, quick to take advantage of such incredible good fortune, immediately sent five hundred men to take the dilapidated fort. Reining, the Dutch privateer, and one other captain who acted almost as quickly managed to escape in their ships.

The French seized the other Dutch ships and imprisoned the survivors of the garrison. The Dutch relief squadron under Captain Hals, which arrived after the disaster, found some soldiers who had escaped and fled into the island's hills. Yet the French booty only amounted to two flimsy men-of-war—one of which had been French anyway—and some three hundred to four hundred prisoners. Medals were nevertheless struck again to commemorate this French triumph in the Caribbean—*Tabagum expugnatum*.[98] D'Estrées dismantled the *Sterreschans*, or what remained of it, and departed for Martinique to plan his attack on Curaçao. Tobago, the scene of these violent human clashes, was once more abandoned to the melodic interplay of Caribbean sea and breeze.

With the tragic death of Jakob Binckes the Dutch lost "a cautious soldier, a brave captain, a faithful commander and a merciful Christian."[99] He was, indeed, the last Dutch representative of aggressive naval strength, and he influenced decisively the precarious balance of power in the Caribbean. After his death, Dutch expansion in the West Indies ceased to be a matter of concern. The Dutch fight was over, not only for Tobago but for the entire Caribbean archipelago as well. Their century of glory was past, their decline imminent.

The Peace of Nijmegen in 1678 between the United Provinces and France stipulated that each party was to keep what it held outside Europe at the moment when hostilities ended. Tobago, although deserted, thus remained French. The victors, after having expended such effort and blood to gain control over the island, never even bothered to settle a colony there. No further attempt to reconquer the island was ever made by the Dutch, although a certain Laurentius Fabri in 1680 requested Their High Mightinesses "to populate and cultivate the island."[100] The Dutch were content to consolidate their hold on what they had: the Curaçao group and the three Leeward Islands. Asunción, Tobago, New Courland, New Walcheren—whatever its name, the island's colorful history was over.

18

THE LAST DUTCH STAND

Nec pluribus impar.

With the Peace of Breda in 1667 the Dutch international position appeared strong. They had not been defeated; on the contrary, the "Medway disaster" had forced England to accept the Dutch possession of Surinam and the rest of the Wild Coast, and to make some mitigating amendments to the Navigation Laws. The English did acquire New Netherland, but at that time this colony was considered of lesser importance than Surinam. The Dutch also maintained their footing both in the Caribbean and on the African coast. But peace for the United Provinces, which would last only until 1672, was accompanied by a peculiarly hectic internal struggle; *pax in terris* did not coincide with domestic tranquility.

There were two political parties in the United Netherlands: the Orangist, or pro-stadhouder, and the "true-freedom" or anti-Orangist faction, the republicans. The latter had ruled the country since 1650. Their talented leader Grand Pensionary Johan de Witt was a capable politician, a man of recognized qualities, an *"oprecht Hollander."*[1] De Witt's policy was one of balance and, if possible, of abstention. He was well aware that the United Provinces was neither economically nor militarily self-sufficient. His one failing, if it was one, was that his concentration on the European entanglements of his little nation excluded major concern for her involvement in the East and West Indies.

De Witt had become grand pensionary shortly after the sudden death of the stadhouder Prince William II of Orange. The stadhouder's heir, an infant, had at the time offered no threat to the republicans and anti-Orangists. During de Witt's prolonged administration, however, the young Prince of Orange had grown into a man of outstanding talents with supporters who became increasingly articulate about the grand pensionary's "neglect" of international Dutch prestige. Indeed, opposition to the rule of "King John"[2] existed within his own party, where there was growing resentment about the leader's dictatorial regime and his flagrant nepotism.

In de Witt's view the postwar Netherlands had more to fear from its late ally France than from its late enemy England. A vigorous anti-Dutch faction still existed in the latter country, but Charles II was temporarily disposed to ignore it. Meanwhile, France, under Louis XIV, was espousing a doctrine of "natural frontiers" which implied French occupation of the Spanish Netherlands. Within the framework of this philosophy, the Rhine River was to be France's eastern and northern border. De Witt's policy in the seventeenth century was to isolate this potential menace to Dutch independence. *Galla amica non vicina* best portrays the official attitude in the United Provinces. Louis' military adventurism seemed to make the grand pensionary's policy all the easier.

In 1667 Louis XIV sent his troops to invade the Spanish Netherlands, the so-called *Guerre des Droits de la Reine* or War of Devolution. They won an easy victory. Although duly alarmed, Spain's incapable monarch Charles II took no action. But French aggression frightened the Dutch and the English into a mutual pact aimed at stopping Louis. The result is known as the Triple Alliance of 1668 among England, Sweden, and the United Provinces. The alliance halted Louis' advance but Spain had to make territorial concessions to France. It also forced Colbert, Louis' astute and crafty minister, to intensify his mercantile system for the purpose of excluding the Dutch from trade with France and with the French colonies. This policy was to have far-reaching repercussions in the Caribbean.

It is well known that, while tensions mounted between France and the United Provinces, Charles II of England cautiously sought a rapprochement with Louis XIV. The latter was delighted when he found this Stuart peer for sale.[3] The English king may have been acting with the additional intention of destroying de Witt for the benefit of his nephew William of Orange, but his alliance with France proved to be disastrous for the United Provinces as a whole. In 1670 Charles succumbed to the tempting offer of both a subsidy and a mistress, the charms of the latter far exceeding those of his Portuguese wife.[4] The ensuing contract, the secret Treaty of Dover, laid the foundation for a joint Anglo-French onslaught upon the Dutch at home and abroad.

The years which followed the Peace of Breda witnessed a sharp decrease in Dutch activity in the Caribbean. Willemstad, the capital of Curaçao, which was considered impregnable because of its Fort Amsterdam, constituted the only major fortified Dutch station in the

West Indies. For the moment Zeelanders still occupied Tobago, and there were Dutch settlements at St. Martin, St. Eustatius, Saba, Tortuga, and on the Wild Coast. For the most part these colonies had converted to sugar production, while Curaçao was specializing in the slave trade. Although the English and French islands were increasingly poor markets for Dutch traders, the slave trade with Spanish settlements prospered.

In 1670, the year of the Treaty of Dover, Charles II of England also concluded a treaty with Madrid. This agreement, reaffirming a former one which had been concluded three years earlier, granted the English approximately the same privileges the Dutch had previously obtained in 1648, i.e., the right to navigate and trade in the Caribbean in those areas where the Spanish king had not taken actual possession. The agreement, of course, implied official Spanish recognition of the English ownership of some West Indian islands.[5]

In accordance with the new English policy towards Spain, Charles II also made some significant changes in personnel among his Caribbean administrators. Governor Thomas Modyford of Jamaica, whose anti-Spanish sentiments were widely known, was the first of these to be replaced. He was recalled to England and imprisoned in the Tower for alleged misconduct which included "many depredations upon the territories of the Catholic king,"[6] but the real reason was, of course, to mollify Spain. Tacitly recognized in the Treaty of Madrid as an English possession, Jamaica now received as governor Thomas Lynch, former member of the army that seized the island in 1655.

The second man to fall victim to the new English policy in the Caribbean was Colonel Henry Morgan of buccaneer fame. Although Lynch recommended the erstwhile pirate as "an honest, brave fellow," Morgan was arrested and sent to England. The circumlocutions in Charles II's policy are evident in Morgan's future career; he quickly secured again the favor of the king. The obvious conclusion to be reached here is that as the third Anglo-Dutch war approached, the English king became disinclined to pacify Spanish sentiment. It is certain, however, that the earlier replacements were designed to effect a rapprochement with Madrid. But such an understanding grew less mandatory if, in the event of war, the United Provinces' predictable ally was to be Spain.

The French policy in the years between 1667 and 1672 was confined to the general harassment of Spain and the United Provinces. After the Treaty of Dover this policy was brought into the open. Louis XIV realized only too well that such harassment could not be accomplished by French naval strength alone—thus his understanding with Charles Stuart, whose marriage ties with Portugal were expected to keep England not very pro-Spanish, in spite of the Treaty of Madrid. Louis sincerely believed that henceforth he would be able to rely on Charles' acquiescence to France's anti-Spanish designs. The secret Treaty of Dover provided the cornerstone for this new French policy line.

Although Louis had no such intention, the Treaty of Dover gave England the means to establish political superiority in the Caribbean. The decline of Dutch eminence, which was caused by both nations, did not benefit France but England. Despite England's clear advantage in an alliance with France, the tortuous realities of European power politics soon convinced Charles' ministers that England's real competitor was not the United Provinces but France, and the hinge on which Louis' policy hung, the Treaty of Dover, became a *cause célèbre* against the Stuart monarch.

Thus France's *renversement des alliances* intimidated Charles II and at the same time worked on behalf of England. Stuart unpopularity, which is sometimes wrongly attributed to difficulties growing out of stipulations of the Peace of Breda and French intransigence about the restoration of the English base on St. Christopher, had its real source in the tangled negotiations that paired England with her future rival France, and excluded her erstwhile foe the United Provinces.[7]

Meanwhile, Charles II continued to reorganize his colonial administration. The French had returned Antigua and Montserrat; only St. Christopher remained a problem. In 1671 Charles Wheler was appointed governor-in-chief over the Leeward Islands—Nevis, Montserrat, Antigua, Barbuda, Anguilla, St. Christopher, and others. The appointment meant that these islands, which had been traditionally supervised from Barbados, were now to have a separate administration. There were, thereafter, three English colonial units in the Caribbean—Jamaica, Barbados, and the Leeward Islands—and each had its own vocal interest in policies which affected the Western hemisphere. In 1672 Colonel William Stapleton succeeded Wheler.

Locked in an internecine political struggle, Dutch survival in the Caribbean was questionable. Although their islands in the Lesser Antilles had only barely survived the disasters of the second Anglo-Dutch conflict, they were recovering satisfactorily. Mention has already been made of Dutch diplomatic efforts to restore St. Eustatius and Tobago. St. Martin had never been involved in the second Anglo-Dutch war because, perhaps, it had the able commander John Simpson. During this same period, however, so many French settlers had moved into the Dutch half of the island that the English considered the whole of St. Martin as French. After the war a band of five hundred Englishmen under Captain Thomas Malet looted the island and then deserted it. Shortly afterwards Commander Simpson occupied Saba in 1667. The Curaçao islands stayed firmly in Dutch hands. And, in spite of the losses suffered to the Portuguese in the late forties, the Dutch position in West Africa likewise remained strong.

This brief review of the position of the three major parties in the ensuing conflict shows that the situation in the Caribbean had a certain explosive potential. Events in Europe were to add fuel to this incipient conflagration.

The war of 1672 was, as far as the Caribbean was concerned, not so much a third Anglo-Dutch war as it was a Franco-Dutch conflict. In the first place, although England and the United Provinces concluded peace in 1674, French hostilities against the Dutch were not terminated until four years later. Second, even though Europe provided the stage for a relentless fight between the English and Dutch naval powers, the Caribbean area was almost exclusively restricted to French-Dutch combat. This twofold attack on the United Provinces resulted in closing the Dutch Golden Age at home as well as in the Caribbean. It opened a century-long Anglo-French conflict in that area. But this end was, of course, inconceivable at the beginning.

French aggression against the Dutch in the West Indies began as soon as Louis XIV had secured English complicity following the Treaty of Dover. A "cold war" against the Dutch, however, had actually begun even before the second Anglo-Dutch conflict. Nicolas Fouquet, the one-time heir apparent to Mazarin, had, at the time, instituted a duty of fifty sous per ton on all foreign ships that entered and left French ports. The treaty of 1662 between France and the United Provinces had not allayed French anti-Dutch feeling. Colbert, Fouquet's successor, was particularly outraged at Amsterdam's important role in European affairs generally, and in anti-French alliances specifically. "That town," a French agent reported to the minister, "has taken over our navigation in the East Indies, on the Guinea coast and in South America; it has ruined the fisheries of our Basques in whales, and was willing to make peace with Spain to plunge us into a civil war." The peace referred to was the Westphalian treaty of 1648. In a previous *traité de partage*, concluded in 1635, the Dutch had promised not to make peace without their French ally.[8] Inflammatory comments of the French ambassador in The Hague did nothing to appease the general attitude in France: The "Roi Soleil" had cast the die: It would be war.[9]

Colbert continued Fouquet's policy. He estimated the Dutch commercial fleet to be sixteen thousand ships as compared to England's three thousand to four thousand and France's five thousand to six thousand.[10] "As we have crushed Spain on land, so we must crush the Dutch at sea."[11] This "cold war," a purely commercial conflict, became the preliminary skirmish to the ensuing Anglo-Franco-Dutch war of 1672. Twice, in 1664 and 1667, French customs tariffs were altered to the detriment of the Dutch. Grand Pensionary de Witt, fully conscious of growing anti-Dutch sentiment in France, countered Colbert's moves with the Triple Alliance and by reciprocal tariff increases that culminated in a total prohibition of French imports in 1672. The anticipated war grew closer.

The smouldering hostility between these two former allies was instigated, primarily, by French jealousy about Dutch successes in commerce. The Dutch simply outdid the French everywhere.[12] Vessels from the Netherlands dominated not only the North and Baltic seas, but also, to the great annoyance of the French, the Bay of Biscay. The Dutch flag had supplanted the French banner in the Mediterranean, and there was no French port in or outside of Europe where Dutch ships were not to be found.

This Dutch hegemony was a matter of utmost concern to French-men everywhere. In the *Mémoires de Gourville* an amusing story is told to illustrate the prevailing anxious mood. Louis XIV's minister de Lionne is reported to have asked the diplomat de Gourville why the Dutch were so rich. The latter explained that the Dutch had a marvelous economy and illustrated his analysis by pointing out the small amount of meat in the Dutch diet. De Lionne persisted with a query about how the French might destroy Dutch commercial preponderance. De Gourville's answer: "Take Holland." De Lionne laughed,[13] but the French were deadly serious about ending Dutch commercial power.

While tensions were mounting in Europe, events followed a parallel course in the Caribbean and on the West African coast. In the spring of 1670 a French man-of-war captured two Dutch ships that were subsequently towed to the harbor of Martinique. To all appearances, this was the first, but certainly not the only, overtly hostile act of the French against the United Provinces in the area. The growing split between the two recent allies undoubtedly pleased the English. At that time jealousy was stronger than fear. Christopher Codrington, deputy-governor of Barbados, wrote to Willoughby, "We are well pleased to see the great animosity between the French and the

Dutch."[14] It was a perfect expression of English sentiment, a sentiment which further encouraged the English to proclaim certain rights to St. Eustatius and Saba. Charles Wheler, for instance, Stapleton's predecessor, wrote at the end of 1671 that the king should purchase St. Eustatius because "it lies on the back of the French quarter at Sandy Point within an hour's rowing,"[15] while he stated in the same letter that Saba was "the King's by right and should be demanded of the Dutch ambassador." It was taken by the Dutch, Wheler said, on the same day the English recaptured Surinam.[16]

The English government was reluctant to admit that growing French power was the real rival to its Caribbean aspirations. French power annoyed the English, but Charles and his advisors did not think it dangerous and, instead, were more immediately concerned with their century-old competition with the Dutch. Yet there were certain troubling signs, as, for example, the French employment of buccaneers, which should have warned the English about the future. At the same time, the importance of such French-held colonies as Tortuga and the northern coast of Hispaniola was steadily increasing. Lastly, French colonial resistance to Colbert's stringent policy designed to cease trade with the Dutch lulled England into ignoring French advances while delighting in Dutch setbacks.

And setbacks the Dutch had in plenty. In the Caribbean the stricter application of the Navigation Laws made trade relations with the English islands almost impossible, if not nonexistent. Although some smuggling still occurred, of course, its extent is not known. Colbert's West India policy similarly afflicted Dutch commerce with the French Antilles. His special creature, the French West India Company, employed regular squadrons of frigates under Louis de Gabaret to prevent the Dutch from infringing upon French territory. Indeed, in one instance already cited pertaining to the Lampsins, the French, in pursuing Colbert's policy, successfuly captured two Dutch ships while they were trading in the northern coastal ports of French Hispaniola.[17]

Dutch presence on that island also provoked other difficulties. At approximately the same time, the colonists had broken in open rebellion against the mother country, as Governor d'Ogeron wrote to Colbert, "by reason of the regulation which forbade trade with foreigners."[18] Although Newton may have exaggerated the role of the Dutch in this revolt—it happened "under Dutch prompting,"[19] he writes—the Dutch certainly were not the innocent bystanders they claimed to be. Henceforth, complaints about the seizure of their ships were met by French outcries against Dutch presence in French ports.

By 1671 all the nations involved in the Caribbean were poised to strike, and the French were the most eager. Colbert advised de Baas, his governor-general there, to cause as much damage to the Dutch as possible "without breaking openly." He added that de Baas could not please Louis XIV more than by "hampering their trade" and driving the Netherlanders from their islands "if this was possible without infringing directly the treaties His Majesty has with them."[20]

By now, the French had also taken the initiative in asserting their prior rights to West Africa. They allegedly discovered the area between 1364 and 1410. They also employed, for purposes of disturbing and antagonizing the Dutch, the former West India Company employee Hendrick Carloff. Through this new agent, who had concluded friendship pacts with certain Negro chiefs, Colbert hoped to be able to provide the French colonists in the Caribbean with that one special product they needed most—slaves. The lack of slaves was the basis of persistent colonial opposition to Colbert's anti-Dutch policy, since Dutch activities as slave traders were thus curtailed in French colonies.

Colbert took a calculated risk in this African adventure. The Dutch were certain to be offended and to break their alliance with France. The French minister wrote to d'Estrées, therefore, to ascertain the count's estimate of the consequences his policy was likely to evoke. The latter responded that the Dutch be hanged; with six men-of-war and three smaller ships he, Count d'Estrées, could take the lightly defended Dutch fortress at Elmina and climax the adventure by crossing the Atlantic to seize Curaçao and St. Eustatius.

D'Estrées, indeed, sailed at once to reconnoiter the Dutch defenses around Goree, 36 guns and 250 men, he wrote. In the meantime, subordinates were dispatched to seek information about other Dutch strongholds along the Guinea coast. On January 2, 1671, a treaty the French concluded with the ruler of Commenda pledged eternal friendship between the two nations. France received permission to build a fort at Commenda and a promise of aid against the Dutch. The African coast thus became another potential area of friction between France and the United Provinces.

De Witt, however, remained confident, but he did not know about the secret Treaty of Dover. Louis XIV's threat to bring the Dutch to reason on land and at sea was met with a cynical "At sea, Sire?"[21] The grand pensionary, though, did require the Dutch ambassador at Paris to keep him informed on all French forces, and particularly those at sea.[22] War did not seem a realistic solution to de Witt, however, since France must know that the Dutch were able to count on the support of the cosignatories of the Triple Alliance. No one informed him, however, of the feelings of Charles II of England who loathed the Dutch "republicans" as much as Louis XIV did. Nor did he know that the anti-Dutch faction at Louis' court made adroit use of the Sun King's sister, the Duchess of Orléans, to further its designs. "France, in her big negotiations, has always found herself well served by women because they are insinuating and easier to flatter than men," de la Roncière wrote, with obvious satisfaction.[23]

The Dutch were certainly not innocent in augmenting French antagonism. Adding insult to the threat of the Triple Alliance, they struck a medal, though the government denied having endorsed it, which pictured a Dutchman as the principal negotiator of a league between both branches of the House of Hapsburg and the United Provinces. A radiant sun shone above the Dutchman's head and the legend read, "At my sight the sun halts."[24]

The allusion was obvious to everyone. An even more offensive medal had appeared at the conclusion of the Triple Alliance; on one side a sun rose over England, the Netherlands, France, and Spain and the question was inscribed, *Ecquis cursum inflectet?* (Who will stop her course?). On the reverse of the medal was Joshua, staring at the sun, and the legend, *Stetit sol in medio caeli* (And the sun stood still in the middle of heaven).[25] France thus enshrined in the Treaty of Dover what she took to be Dutch offenses and Batavian ingratitude for her "magnificent" gestures on behalf of Dutch independence.

A formidable attack upon the United Provinces was thus coiled and ready to strike. Last minute negotiations to bring Portugal into the Dover arrangement failed, and the Portuguese, fearful of Dutch naval prowess, chose to remain neutral. The French and English combination, though, was challenge enough to Dutch shipping lanes all over the world. Indeed, there was serious doubt in the United Provinces, after the war had started, whether the Dutch fleet could possibly resist a combined Anglo-French maritime assembly. The Dutch, moreover, were not very numerous, and they were thus particularly vulnerable to land invasions. Only the relatively easy inundation of the western part of the country could save them, and they could resort to this only at the risk of great personal and material loss.

The northern Netherlands, however, did have more positive assets for the coming fray. She retained a latent friendship with Spain, even though this country was deteriorating rapidly under Charles II. The Hapsburgs of Austria and the Elector of Brandenburg might yet be encouraged to join against the English and the French. The grand pensionary had for some time taken their goodwill for granted. In addition to all of these assets was the fact that the United Provinces was indisputably the richest country in the world.

Lastly, in spite of internal strife and years of crises, the Low Countries had produced remarkably capable leaders. One such was de Witt, the grand pensionary, who became the architect of Dutch courage in the face of overwhelming odds. It is true that he had made some undeniable blunders; he had trusted England's adherence to the Triple Alliance, while not totally unaware of Charles' peculiar attitude. In March, 1671, for instance, he had written, "We hear from England nothing else than vacillation and wrong inclinations."[26] He had known that Parliament and the English people were in favor of the Triple Alliance, and this knowledge had made him utterly confident of Charles Stuart's cooperation. As late as December, 1671, he had still hoped that England, in the event of a Franco-Dutch conflict, would choose the Dutch side. Later, when the Franco-English alliance had become a fact, he still nurtured the hope that it meant English neutrality in case of a conflict.[27] Not before late February, 1672, did Johan de Witt finally realize that a *renversement des alliances* had taken place. Only then did he fully understand the fact that the French had neatly drawn Charles II to their side.

Public announcement of the Treaty of Dover hung like a thundercloud over the tiny Dutch republic. A new arrangement, the 1672 Treaty of Whitehall, strengthened the earlier secret one and stipulated that the French fleet would be reinforced with English units. Even more ominous were the articles in the treaty concerning the Roman Catholic Church in England. The reasons for war against the United Provinces were made clear: the Ambon "atrocities," the "Medway disaster," compounded by a famous Dutch painting and an audacious medal,[28] and Dutch resistance to lowering their flag to English ships in British seas. Taken individually or collectively, however, the English obviously had no *casus belli*.

The Dutch were spared what appeared to be their inevitable destruction by the combined heroism of de Witt, de Ruyter, and the young William III. The grand pensionary, although too long committed to his Triple Alliance, played the first part in dramatically saving his country,[29] and did not deserve his tragic death at the hands of a mob in The Hague in 1672. Admiral Michiel Adriaenszoon de Ruyter, already justly famed for his role in the second Anglo-Dutch war, rose to even greater prominence. William III, called to lead his country when the French invaded the United Provinces, was soon to show ample evidence of his military, diplomatic, and political abilities. "I know of one way in which one does not have to witness the fall of his country," he proudly answered the English envoys who brought him the humiliating terms for peace, "and that is to die while defending the last trench." Thanks to these men and to her allies the United Provinces survived—the Hapsburgs (Spain and the emperor) and Brandenburg aligned with the Dutch. Charles Stuart was forced to make peace in 1674.

From the outset the Dutch were well aware of their vulnerable position in the Caribbean and on the Wild Coast. De Witt's correspondence gives evidence of concern about an Anglo-French attack. In April, 1672, the grand pensionary wrote a letter to de Huybert, his Zeelandian colleague, to ask the latter's advice about defending Surinam;[30] both men agreed that ships must be sent. The grand pensionary probably knew of English and French animosity toward each other in their colonial territories, and he counted somewhat on a lack of cooperation between them. Such was certain to occur in the case of the English seizure of St. Eustatius and Tobago; both actions chagrined the French more than they were willing to admit.[31]

De Huybert of Zeeland, stimulated by de Witt's interest, wasted no time equipping an expedition to protect Zeelandian interests in the Caribbean and on the Wild Coast. After the successful naval battle of Solebay in June, 1672, the Dutch were able to mount an offensive outside European waters. As in the earlier war the States General, who were preoccupied with the European battlefield, allowed the various admiralty boards to determine the destination of their squadrons, as long as injury was inflicted on the enemy. De Huybert, well pleased with this arrangement, persuaded the States of Zeeland to outfit a provincial fleet in order to defend her colonies in the Western hemisphere and to begin belligerencies against French and English possessions in the New World.[32]

War also reopened the possibilities of privateering. No lack of finances delayed the preparation of the squadron destined to cripple Anglo-French units operating in the Caribbean, to privateer on the enemy's trade, as well as to open long-closed colonial ports to Dutch merchandise. Merchants from both Holland and Zeeland were quick to grasp a chance for easy money, and they offered generous contributions to what was rightly called a perilous exploit.[33] Since Crijnssen had died a few years earlier, the squadron of six ships was placed under the command of Cornelis Evertsen the Younger. The latter's son Evert joined the expedition as captain of one of the frigates. The Evertsens, like the Crijnssens, were a well-known Zeelandian family with an excellent record in the service of their country.[34] Although the admiralty of Amsterdam declined help to this Zeelandian adventure, it did not waste any time in equipping a squadron of its own.

The Zeelandian squadron was still in its home port when an English fleet with seven or eight men-of-war was reported off the nearby coast. Leaving port was thus going to be perilous.[35] Despite the danger, however, the squadron lifted anchor on December 15, and departed in the company of a few privateers who, as soon as it was safe, went their own way.[36] Evertsen's ships had shortly passed through the channel and reached the Atlantic. Unknown to the commander, an Amsterdam squadron led by Jakob Binckes had left Texel three days later and was right behind him. The two squadrons would meet accidentally in the Caribbean.

Although the plans for this Zeelandian venture were strictly reminiscent of the earlier Crijnssen mission during the previous conflict, Evertsen's instructions were in no way as involved as Crijnssen's had been. The new mission called for the seizure of St. Helena and an attack on the English East Indian return fleet. From St. Helena, Evertsen was to sail to Cape Orange near Cayenne to meet a Dutch yacht which would be carrying further orders and perhaps bringing along supporting units for the squadron. The Zeelander was to consider an attack on Cayenne, then proceed to Surinam to provide supplies to that outpost if it were still in Dutch hands. In case the enemy held the site, however, he was to recapture it. These same orders applied to all the Dutch settlements on the Wild Coast.[37]

If the conquest of St. Helena and the English return fleet failed, according to the supplementary instructions, the Zeelandian commander was to sail on to the area between Cape Orange and Newfoundland to capture and damage what he could. He was also ordered to investigate the situation at Barbados and at other enemy-held islands. The fleet was ordered to return home via Virginia and New Netherland.

Evertsen sailed for the Cape Verde Islands where, in an engagement with the English fleet, he took two prizes and incorporated them into his squadron. He then continued toward St. Helena, an island which had a long history of European interest. The Dutch had occupied it in 1632 because of its strategic value but had abandoned it in 1650 to settle shortly afterwards at the Cape of Good Hope. A year later the English had transformed the island into an important intermediate station for their ships sailing to and from the East Indies.[38] Evertsen arrived in February, 1673, soon after the Dutch had captured the island from Capetown. An informed English contingent, however, awaited the Dutch squadron with a blockade off the St. Helena coast. The English were obviously too strong to be attacked,[39] and Evertsen proceeded across the Atlantic to the Wild Coast.

Arriving at Cayenne in March, the Dutch commander consulted with his fleet council and decided not to storm or besiege the fort since no member of the expedition knew the configuration of the currents or the depths in the area. The squadron moved on to Surinam and anchored below Fort Zeelandia on March 25. Necessary repairs delayed it for almost two months, but Evertsen meanwhile satisfied himself that the colony was in good condition. Commander Claes Reyniersen told him that the enemy had not yet started hostilities and that the situation was under control. The fort was well provided, and the plantations had recovered from Henry Willoughby's malicious activities.

The Zeelandian ships left Surinam for Martinique late in May. In that area the squadron engaged a small fleet of six ships carrying French flags—only to discover that the "enemy" was the Amsterdam squadron of Jacob Binckes. With Evertsen and Binckes alternating in command on a weekly basis, the two fleets now merged their forces for combined operations.

Binckes had unexpectedly come upon two English men-of-war and seven or eight merchantmen at Barbados. Unable to attack at the time with his tiny force, he had sailed away. Now, however, the odds favored the Dutch, and the two commanders mutually agreed to a plan. Unfavorable winds and weather combined with the fact that the enemy ships were anchored too close to the fort doomed the exploit. The Dutch sailed north, took a few French and English prizes, and arrived at St. Eustatius on June 8.

A year before the arrival of the combined Dutch squadrons, Governor Stapleton of the English Leeward Islands had arrived at St. Eustatius. Negotiations for a truce with the island's garrison had just begun when French forces arrived from St. Christopher. The Dutch, however, preferred to surrender to the English, and the French were forced to withdraw. A few days later, on July 4, 1672, Saba was likewise occupied and the two islands were left under the protection of English garrisons. Tortola and Virgin Gorda, two of the Virgin Islands, hitherto under Dutch rule, were also taken by the English.

St. Martin, which had escaped conquest and destruction in the second Anglo-Dutch conflict, was not so fortunate during this third set of hostilities. When news of the war reached the inhabitants, the French governor invaded the Dutch part of the island and captured it without loss to himself. Thus, within a few months after the war had started, all the Dutch islands in the Leeward group had fallen to the enemy. The Curaçao islands, however, escaped this fate, and two French expeditions against the main island—in 1673 and 1678—proved abortive.

This was the situation when Binckes and Evertsen dropped anchor at St. Eustatius. When this island's English governor, John Pognon, refused to surrender, the Dutch opened fire on the fort and disembarked six hundred men. The English then yielded. Part of the Dutch population of this island and of Saba—which surrendered a few days later—was sent to Curaçao for having sided with the enemy. The English prisoners were transported to St. Christopher. In addition there were two hundred slaves. The Dutch tried first to sell them to the Spaniards at Puerto Rico. The governor there, however, acting under strict orders, refused to consider the purchase proposal. Subsequently, the slaves were also sent to Curaçao. Two captured ships netted the Dutch conquerors some 37,000 pounds of sugar.

Despite a long tradition of Dutch ownership of the islands, Binckes and Evertsen destroyed the fort, demolished all the houses, and abandoned the sites. As soon as they had lifted anchor, however, the English and French from the neighboring islands raced back to reoccupy the ruined settlements. The former won by four hours and held them until they were reluctantly returned to the Dutch by the second Peace of Westminster, although actual Dutch occupation was postponed for reasons previously explained. The English retained at the peace table the two Virgin islands already mentioned.

Although it had not accomplished much, the combined Dutch fleet now left the Caribbean. Its only conquest, St. Eustatius, was deserted, and its booty and prizes were soon lost because of bad weather. No effort was made to attack any of the French or English Antilles, nor was any investigation made of the situation at Tobago. Its one accomplishment was attained only after the fleet had left the area. Evertsen and Binckes then sailed to New Amsterdam (New York since 1664) and demanded its surrender. After a polite exchange of legal niceties, the colony was turned over to the Dutch on August 9, 1673. Later diplomatic arrangements at the second Peace of Westminster, however, returned the settlement to the English.

Upon his return Evertsen found the States of Zeeland very much displeased with his performance; Cayenne had not been taken, St. Eustatius had not been kept, and New Netherland was only of interest to Amsterdam.[40] Although feelings in the capital were slightly better, no one in the United Netherlands was overjoyed. There were even suggestions that Evertsen be suspended, but, luckily for the Zeelandian commander, these proposals were not carried out.

The show of offensive force, however, had bolstered Dutch morale, and the impressive defeat of the French at Curaçao contributed even more to the Dutch posture. The French attack, which was launched while Evertsen and Binckes were in the Caribbean but unaware of Curaçao's danger, had been led by Jean Charles de Baas, governor-general in the French West Indies and "an experienced veteran."[41]

Evertsen and Binckes were still operating independently when de Baas, who had obtained royal permission,[42] left Martinique in March, 1673, with three men-of-war sent by Colbert and three transportation ships.[43] Expecting to have the assistence of d'Ogeron and his buccaneers, de Baas had arranged for a rendezvous at St. Croix. But d'Ogeron and his men never arrived, for their ships had disappeared in bad weather off the northern coast of Puerto Rico. Those who were lucky enough to escape drowning had fallen into the hands of the Spaniards. D'Ogeron himself had managed to reach Hispaniola.[44]

De Baas arrived at St. Croix after having drafted a few hundred men at Guadeloupe and St. Christopher. He waited a few days, but after learning of the fate that had befallen d'Ogeron and his men, he decided, notwithstanding, to launch the attack on Curaçao. So he left with a fleet of at least seven and perhaps as many as 22 sails and 1,200 to 2,000 men. He was sighted by the Dutch on March 13.

Meanwhile, the governor of Curaçao Jan Doncker had organized the defense of the island by calling all free inhabitants to arms and sending part of the island militia to the small Fort Tolcksburg on St. Barbara Bay at the eastern side of the island. While the guns of the main fort were trained on the entrance of the *Schottegat*, a captured English fire ship was stationed in St. Ann Bay. Other ships were placed so that their guns controlled the road leading from St. Barbara to Willemstad.

On the day after their appearance, the French landed their troops at St. Barbara. These soldiers engaged in some skirmishes with Doncker's men, who withdrew. In the meantime, however, de Baas' scouting parties were bringing back information which suggested that the French commander's estimates of Curaçao's defenses were distinctly incorrect. Besides, Doncker ignored a summons to surrender; indeed, the Dutch leader refused all negotiations, despite his former friendship with de Baas. Instead Doncker harassed the French by spying on their movements and stalling for time to let their provisions run out. Four days later a dispirited army and a humiliated French leader left Curaçao.

When de Baas reported his defeat to Colbert, he blamed it on the faulty information he had received about the fortification of the Dutch stronghold. The French naval historian de la Roncière blames the defeat on d'Ogeron's failure to join the expedition. Colbert chose to be understanding, however, as did Louis XIV. "His Majesty," wrote the French minister to de Baas, "was easily consoled that you had failed in this enterprise."[45] Official tolerance, however, was not reflected at the popular level, and rumors were soon bruited about that de Baas had fled from the island because of cowardice or, worse yet, that he had accepted a bribe from Doncker to arrange the withdrawal of his troops.[46]

The war took a new turn when Charles II quarreled with Parliament and was forced to disregard his solemn pledges to Louis XIV. Since diplomatic contact had continued between the United Provinces and England, the Dutch were soon aware—and delighted—that the Anglo-French entente was crumbling. Parliament was most distressed because Charles accepted his brother's marriage to a Catholic princess "which would disturb Your Majesty's Protestant subjects," especially since Charles had no immediate heirs.[47] Aware of the fact that Parliament disapproved of the Anglo-French alliance, the Dutch now chose to be conciliatory about lowering their flag to English ships in "British waters." This was not enough of a concession. But a later offer to restore New Netherland and the promise of a huge indemnity pacified the English and led to the conclusion of the second Treaty of Westminster in February, 1674. The treaty was ratified and made public on March 6, 1674.

Yet this second Peace of Westminster was far from a victory for the Dutch. Their diplomacy had only succeeded in separating England and France. But this came about largely because of Parliamentary support for breaking the alliance and English popular opposition to a war with the Protestant Dutch. The two-year struggle with the English, though, had driven the United Provinces to the wall in their attempt to preserve status as a first-rate naval power. The peace consequently was, as Innes has written, acknowledgment by the Dutch that they were no longer able to hold out against the combined might of their enemies.[48] The Dutch relinquished their claim to naval superiority by the terms of the peace. England was now to gain what the United Provinces had lost.

The peace did, however, alleviate a great financial burden in limiting Dutch naval operations and it also provided Louis XIV with his first serious check. The young Prince of Orange was free now to consolidate an anti-French coalition in Europe proper. The treaty confirmed the stipulations of the Peace of Breda and, moreover, served to govern the diplomatic relations between England and the United Provinces in the future. The Dutch acknowledged English naval supremacy, but the English recognized a Dutch *mare clausum* in the East Indies and agreed to restore St. Eustatius and Tobago to the Dutch when peace with France was concluded. The diplomacy which led to the second Peace of Westminster and culminated in an Anglo-Dutch alliance against the French was the last instance in which the United Provinces were to play the part of a leading European power.

The Dutch at once began a concerted effort against France and her possessions in the Caribbean. Although the situation was different on land, at sea the Dutch still had a numerical majority as well as superior leadership. De Ruyter had no French counterpart; d'Estrées tried hard, but he did not enjoy the confidence of his men nor did he have much need for their council.[49]

In late 1673, when the Evertsen-Binckes expedition reached home, the States General ordered the admiralty boards to study a new naval action against the French.[50] Although a massive program was sent to Their High Mightinesses in December, 1673, which requested the equipment of sixty ships with more than twenty thousand sailors and soldiers, it was radically modified when peace with England was achieved. The new project called for eighteen huge ships, twenty-four of middle size, and twelve of small size, twelve frigates, eighteen fire ships, twelve large and twelve small galliots, and a landing force of nine thousand soldiers. The total cost for this assemblage was estimated at 5,730,000 guilders.[51]

William of Orange and Admiral de Ruyter were now brought into the discussions about the best possible use of the fleet. A Dutch assault on the French coast was planned, preferably where a Huguenot population would help the invaders. Moreover, part of this fleet, under de Ruyter, was to make for the Caribbean. The parties responsible for this plan all agreed on its execution.

From the very beginning the conquest of the French Antilles had seemed feasible. "It is with Martinique that de Ruyter wants to begin the conquest," wrote de la Roncière,[52] and de Ruyter set out directly to Martinique, the center of French power in the Caribbean. Aside from Dominica, it was the strongest of France's ten colonies in the area, with a population of five thousand Frenchmen—not counting the slaves—and a very prosperous sugar industry. Like the rest of the French Antilles it was a perpetual menace to the tiny Dutch possessions in the northern part of the Caribbean archipelago. Martinique was the base, for instance, from which de Baas had launched his attack against Curaçao. It was also the key island in controlling the buccaneer strongholds at Dominica and Tortuga. Besides, the capture of Martinique would facilitate the seizure of Cayenne and would result in Dutch control of the Wild Coast. Finally, the Dutch counted on support from the population. In previous years there had been pro-Dutch demonstrations against Colbert's policy on the French islands.

De Ruyter received broad instructions. Although he was authorized to use his own judgment concerning Cayenne, he was not to delay his attack on Martinique lest the French discover his presence and have time to organize their defenses. Aiding de Ruyter was a French fugitive, a Huguenot officer named Charles de Birac, a former resident of Martinique and now a guide to the Dutch landing party on the island. De Birac advised the Dutch admiral that he would need five hundred men for his attack. A victory, assuming this was the case, would net the Dutch an annual 4,000,000-guilder sugar production. Although the French deserter was never fully trusted by the Dutch admiral, de Ruyter agreed to make him the new governor-general of the French Antilles and to grant him some private property on Martinique.

On May 28, 1674, an enormous Dutch fleet passed through the English Channel under the commands of admirals Cornelis Tromp and de Ruyter, the two finest Dutch naval leaders. The French *vedettes* of the governor of Calais counted sixty-six ships, eighteen fire ships, and fifty-eight transportation and service ships. Their count was mistaken; the Dutch fleet was even larger. Three regiments of landing troops, batteries of a new invention, special cars which were to be used by musketeers against any attack of cavalry, separate battalions of grenadiers, and companies of ordinary infantry gave this expeditionary corps the aspect of a modern army. The fleet had been delayed in sailing, and, thanks to an adequate system of spies, all the French Atlantic ports had been warned of its approach—Le Havre, Cherbourg, Saint Malo, Brest, and particularly Rochefort. Tromp's orders were to disembark his troops at Belle Isle and Noirmoutier which were centers of French Protestantism. These religious dissenters were expected to join the Dutch and further inconvenience Louis XIV.

The French soon saw that when the Dutch fleet reached the Atlantic, it separated into two parts. The smaller segment, led by de Ruyter, consisted of seventeen large men-of-war and three smaller ships in that category, six fire ships and eighteen transportation and provision vessels. It left the main body, together with 3,400 sailors, 4,000 soldiers, and 1,100 pieces of artillery.[53]

De Ruyter crossed the Atlantic via the Azores, Madeira, and the Canaries. His orders to the Dutch consul at Santa Cruz (one of the Canaries) indicate that he had given up an attack on Cayenne in favor of a direct assault on Martinique; stragglers were to head straight for this island. The Dutch admiral, an old hand in the Caribbean, must almost certainly have concluded that he had to attend to the French Antilles before the hurricane season arrived. One miscalculation, however, crept into his plans. His hopes that the expedition had remained a secret were dashed when French money found its way surreptitiously into official government circles where the fleet's destination had been revealed.

By July 19, the Dutch were off Martinique planning their landing and drawing up an exhortation to French colonists on the island to cooperate with the invaders. A calm immobilized the movements of the latter's fleet for an entire day.[54] Martinique did not need time to get ready. Its defenses were set, and Colbert had dispatched men, munitions, and other provisions about one month earlier. A French yacht had arrived a few days before with additional information about the Dutch, and a few merchantmen carrying precious sugar had left hurriedly for France. The garrisons were well manned and occupied the two main forts of the island, Fort Saint Pierre and Fort Royal, although the "colic of fear" had caused some desertions.[55] Expendable ships were sunk in order to thwart a Dutch landing at Cul-de-Sac. Only one man-of-war lay in the harbor, and it was fatigued by a long campaign and was virtually useless.

A shore party sent by de Ruyter captured several planters and slaves, who provided the admiral with the disturbing news that his fleet had been expected for a month and its numbers known exactly.[56] Despite this discouragement, the admiral, in view of the great power at his disposal and against the advice of de Birac, decided to attack at Cul-de-Sac. The captured French settlers, however, encouraged de Ruyter by pointing to the lack of essential wood and water at the landing site which de Birac proposed. They knew, as de Ruyter did not, that Cul-de-Sac was heavily defended by 20 guns, barricades, and a battalion of 160 planters, sailors, and soldiers.

The assault began on the morning of July 20. A fiery duel between naval and shore guns preceded the landing of one thousand Dutch troops under Colonel Uytenhove. These troops were caught in fierce firing from well-concealed French gun emplacements, and many casualties resulted, especially among the commanding officers. Governor Antoine André de Sainte-Marthe had posted his men well. In spite of the spirited defense, however, the Dutch took the beach and its immediate surroundings. Although the French drew back into the hills, they managed to take up positions that prevented any Dutch progress. Continuous French fire was accompanied by the displacement of huge stones sent hurling down on the invading forces. These stones, more than the guns, caused many to panic, and some of the Dutch soldiers fled to the shore and drowned. Of those who remained many were incapacitated for fighting because the Dutch had captured wine warehouses. They got drunk. Since not a few Dutch officers had fallen in the assault, a morale problem also developed that especially affected the troops fighting on the beach, who were caught in a cross fire from the hills, from the French man-of-war in the harbor, and from the nearby fort.

De Ruyter, stranded beyond the harbor by the sunken ships, was unable to reach the French with his guns. He paced the deck of his flagship and watched the debacle unfolding before him. Although de Birac's offer to go on shore to organize the troops was welcomed by the admiral, his Dutch subordinates on the beach refused to cooperate with the Frenchman. De Birac returned without having achieved anything. As evening approached de Ruyter realized he had lost the battle. The *Zeven Provinciën* ("Seven Provinces"), his flagship, signaled a cease-fire. When a white flag ordered the return of his troops, their retreat resulted in mass confusion, because of the enemy's murderous fire. The panic-stricken Dutch soldiers, caught in this slaughter, fled back to the boats, leaving behind their dead and wounded with their weapons and other implements of war. The re-embarkation lasted far into the night. The French had lost fewer than 20 while Dutch casualties were 143 dead and 318 wounded. Small consolation for de Ruyter was the fact that his fleet was left intact—it had been beyond the range of French guns.[57]

Where the Dutch had expected an easy victory, they had found an unassailable citadel, and an enemy determined to fight and well prepared for defense. De Birac, however, blamed de Ruyter because he had told the admiral not to land at Cul-de-Sac and because his warnings had not been heeded once the landing had been made.

After the withdrawal de Ruyter summoned his surviving fleet council members to discuss the situation. He wasted no time in revealing to them the brutal fact that the enterprise had been a dismal failure. The Dutch admiral, without glorifying his own role, was inclined to attribute much of the resulting fiasco to two facts, that the French had been amply warned of his approach and that the Dutch had lost so many officers during the early part of the battle. The council unanimously agreed to sail toward Guadeloupe to refresh, repair, and gather new supplies.[58] Only as the Dutch departed did the French realize the extent of their success.[59]

The French victory at Martinique ended the Dutch intention to destroy the French colonial empire in the Caribbean. De Ruyter remained for some time at Guadeloupe, but only for the purposes mentioned. Every suggestion to seize another island was rejected by the admiral because, as he said, the Dutch occupation of a single island in the midst of the French Antilles could not be protected. The real reasons for de Ruyter's withdrawal from the Caribbean may never be known. Was he demoralized? Had he lost confidence in himself? Was it fear of the hurricanes or the timidity that comes with old age? He had served his country well. Now, with this defeat at the end of his career, he was even loathe to react when a French corsair took one of his ships before his eyes.[60]

The main reason for de Ruyter's failure must, however, be found in other directions: the miscalculation of French strength, the demoralization of the Dutch troops under heavy French fire, their drunkenness, and above all their deep disappointment when the secret of the expedition had leaked out.

For two years it was impossible for the States General or provincial governments to undertake any other action of importance in the West Indies. Dutch naval forces were, however, fully occupied in European waters, specifically in the Mediterranean where de Ruyter covered himself once more with glory in several historic battles. The great admiral died a hero's death in the battle of Etna in 1676.

The Dutch West India Company was no longer able to equip a fleet to attack the French in the Caribbean. It not only persisted in its fiscal problems but also faced imminent dissolution. When it came, in 1674, it may have been an act of mercy. A new company was established, which bore the old name, but this New West India Company never acquired any power or glory to compare with the old one. After a quarter of a century of narrow survival in the slave trade, it led for almost a hundred years a dreary and unremarkable existence. The new WIC, however, started issuing letters of marque to Dutch privateers who dared to prey on French shipping in African and American waters. The story of the next two years of what had become a Franco-Dutch war revolves around the surprisingly success-ful exploits of these privateers against the French in the Caribbean.

A detailed account of these ventures can no longer be constructed because data are very often missing. One of the more spectacular privateers, however, was Jan Erasmus Reining, a man met earlier in this narrative.[61] The latter's relation with Jan Doncker probably brought him a commission with the New West India Company. By staging an attack on St. Eustatius in early 1674, he learned that the English were holding the island in trust for the Dutch until the war with France was over.[62] The next year, Reining and another Dutch privateer, Jurriaen Aernouts, took Grenada but found themselves prisoners of a French man-of-war that had come in behind them and had caught them off guard. As a result of this kind of warfare the island of Curaçao prospered. In 1673, for instance, more than twenty-five prizes were brought to the island, among them six so-called Barbados sailers.[63]

In 1676, the Dutch had finally pulled themselves up sufficiently to turn their attention once more to the Caribbean. A new expedition was dispatched under the command of Jacob Binckes. Although this expedition's activities at Tobago have already been noted, Binckes' earlier actions in the venture deserve attention since they serve as evidence of a renewed Dutch offensive in the West Indies. Reining was an important member of this expedition.

Binckes' squadron crossed the Atlantic and first went to Cayenne, a familiar bone of contention between the Dutch and the French in that area. Near the fort, Binckes landed nine hundred men virtually without any French attempt to stop him. The Dutch troops ap-proached the fort carefully, and a trumpet sounded to demand surrender.[64] Governor de Lézy, the French commander of the fort, decided to cover himself with glory and refused. Before the Dutch had reached the fort, however, he had already hoisted the white flag and had surrendered his 300-man garrison. Within two days the entire colony had been returned to the authority of the WIC.[65] Binckes left a garrison under Quirijn Spranger and made for Marie Galante.

The latter island was taken with very little effort; many French colonists, unhappy under Colbert's regulations, agreed to settle at Tobago. The Dutch then sailed to Guadeloupe where they arrived on June 16. The attack on this island was abandoned, however, as soon as a small French squadron—two men-of-war and an advice-boat—was sighted. The opportunity seemed too good for Binckes to lose, and he immediately gave orders to attack the enemy's ships. The French men-of-war escaped into Guadeloupe's port, however, and anchored under the protection of the fort's guns. Captain Jan Bont almost took one of the smaller French ships,[66] but a fortunate shot bereft him of his foresail, and the Frenchman escaped.

Binckes next sailed to St. Martin, an island long shared by French and Dutch colonists but which had been consolidated under French rule at the outbreak of hostilities. Its governor de Magne had reinforced the island's defenses with a parapet and a fort near the great salt pan. The parapet was to provide excellent protection for the French against the five hundred attacking Dutchmen whom Binckes landed on the island. The fighting was heavy, and during the battle the French seem to have shot at Dutch noncombatants who had been sent to negotiate the conditions for surrender. Binckes, furious at this treachery, then ordered that no quarter was to be given to the enemy. The Dutch eventually managed to occupy a hill above the parapet and fired into it. Victory was theirs; de Magne was killed, but most of the French settlers disappeared into the hills. Binckes seized, however, a hundred slaves and a large number of cattle. When he left with most of the Dutch colonists, the French resumed control of the island (see Chapter XIII).[67]

While the recruited French and Dutch settlers under Jan Bont now headed straight for Tobago, Binckes himself, with the larger part of the fleet, sailed on to Hispaniola. Knowing of the tensions which existed on that island between the buccaneers and the French officials, he, together with Pieter Constant, the former governor of Tobago, importuned the French population of the north coast "to shake off the unbearable yoke of the king."[68] There was no response. Then Binckes met seven French merchantment at Petit Goâve. The ensuing battle between the two fleets lasted an entire day and night. The French fought bravely, but ultimately were worsted. The Dutch kept three of their ships; the others were too badly damaged to bother salvaging.[69] The Dutch were now masters of the port. They abandoned hope of taking the town, however, when French reinforcements arrived the next day from Tortuga. Binckes sent some of the French ships, the ones full of tobacco, to the Low Countries. He proceeded to Tobago and the exploits that ended both his career and Dutch possession of that island.

Word of Binckes' feats reached Paris in September, 1676. D'Estrées was at once commissioned to the Caribbean with orders to drive the Netherlanders from the area and to recapture everything taken by the Dutch.[70] When he arrived at Cayenne in December, the

French triumph which followed paralleled the course of the Dutch victory six months earlier. He immediately disembarked eight hundred men, and the former governor de Lézy, who had accompanied d'Estrées, demanded surrender. The Dutch leader, Quiryn Spranger, refused. Two days later the French successfully attacked the fort during the night and, within an hour, their flag once again flew over the island. D'Estrées now restored de Lézy to his former post and allowed him to reap most of the honors. The Dutch survivors, some 260 of them, were sent to France and were, against solemn promises, badly mistreated. All France was delirious about the victory, and Colbert wrote exultantly to d'Estrées, "We must chase the Dutch from America and Africa."[71]

D'Estrées' abortive attempt at Tobago now occurred together with subsequent victory there (see Chapter XVII). The two missions were divided by a successful French venture on the West African coast that greatly harmed the Dutch slave trade in the Guinea region. Covered with glory, the count then determined to give the Dutch the *coup de grâce* by attacking their last stronghold, Curaçao. Consequently, he spent some time at Martinique while ships from his fleet sailed throughout the French Antilles recruiting assistance. Finally, d'Estrées himself appeared at St. Christopher leading eighteen royal ships and twelve corsairs prepared for an enterprise he firmly believed could not fail.

A Frenchman who had been imprisoned on the island assured the count that Curaçao's defense consisted of only one infantry company, which was composed of forty planters and as many poor Jews.[72] Adapting his plan of attack to this information he decided to follow de Baas' procedure of five years earlier, to land troops at St. Barbara Bay. A battery and two mortars placed on top of a hill that dominated the town and the fort would force the Dutch to surrender within a few days.

At Curaçao, however, Governor Jan Doncker was fully aware of the French plans and was awaiting the coming of the attack with confidence. Counting on the services of the redoubtable Reining as captain of all fortifications, he was, in any event, prepared to offer the enemy a warm welcome. Reining became impatient while waiting for the French attack, though, and sailed for Holland shortly before the French left Martinique for the final encounter.

On May 7, 1678, almost five months after the conquest of Tobago, d'Estrées judged himself strong enough to sail against Curaçao.[73] Subsequently, his fleet set its course toward the Dutch stronghold. His flag-captain rightly pointed out that the fleet did not have an experienced pilot, but the count, whose haughtiness made him a hated commander, impatiently brushed aside the warning and ordered the fleet to make for Orchilla, an island east of Bonaire.

On the evening of May 11, when the French arrived west of Orchilla, d'Estrées believed that he was twenty miles north of it and ignored his pilot's corrections. He ordered the fleet to sail south-southwest. Even the warnings of high fleet officials did not produce any result. "Those who came to these regions for the first time," the count fumed, "had no pilot either."[74] The sad comments of French historians are eloquent enough; indeed, there is something worse than temerity, it is incapacity.[75]

Before long, at nine o'clock in the evening, cannon fire alerted d'Estrées that one of his ships was stranded. More ships soon struck the hidden reefs and broke their keels. No land was in sight and heavy clouds overhead added to the gravity and horror of the situation. It was, in the words of de la Roncière "a disaster without parallel."[76] D'Estrées did not even know where he was. He had to ask to learn that his fleet had been marooned on an archipelago which stretched between Bonaire and Orchilla, an oversize reef formation that was inhabited only by birds that gave the dangerous hazard its name, the Aves Islands. This reef, which is hidden at high tide, caught the fleet, held it prisoner until the ships broke up, and then offered little in the way of sanctuary for the hundreds of men thrown into the sea.

Of the French fleet, seven huge men-of-war, three transportation ships, and three ships belonging to the buccaneers were destroyed without the Dutch having to lift a hand. According to the Dutch, an act of divine intervention had come to their aid. Only a few sloops and some smaller ships of d'Estrées and his privateers had survived the mishap, but these ships proved unable to prevent the episode from becoming a colossal tragedy. Many sailors were saved only because of great personal heroism and individual courage, but more than five hundred drowned. A humiliated d'Estrées sailed sadly home to France with what could be called an embryo of a squadron.[77]

D'Estrées alone was responsible for the disaster which had befallen the French fleet in the Caribbean. One of the French captains wrote in his report, "The loss of the squadron caused by the vice-admiral, is too big to let pass in silence as I did last year at Tobago." Another captain refused to sign the official account, which had been, in all probability, altered to cover d'Estrées' mistakes because "it did not contain the truth."[78] The count, even despite such bitter attacks on his leadership, had influential friends; he was eventually elevated to *maréchal de France* in 1681.

The war was over. France had gained some advantages in Europe, although she returned territory to the Dutch that her troops had occupied for several years. William III of Orange had lost some battles, but he had won the war. More significantly, he had also won the hand of Mary Stuart, the daughter of the Duke of York who would become James II in 1685. This marriage would next catapult the Dutch stadhouder to the English throne and would strengthen considerably the bond between the United Provinces and England.

Although France restored all Dutch territory in Europe, the Dutch had to suffer the loss of several posts on the West African coast, leaving France in command of trade there. The Dutch, however, soon won a suspension of the high tariffs, which had precipitated the war. In addition, they achieved a measure of free trade with France in flat contradiction to Colbert's protective system. The Dutch had survived, moreover, and that in itself was quite worthwhile.

The Peace of Nijmegen, signed on August 10, 1678, meant the end of the Dutch as a major factor to be reckoned with in the Caribbean. Dutch military and naval offensive power was finished, and Dutch supremacy in trade was soon to be a thing of the past. For half a century the United Provinces had been an arbiter in the destiny of the Caribbean, a power in its development, and a force for change. Those decades were now gone. The old Dutch West India Company —the real competitor in American seas—was also gone, and its successor would never be able to recover the role its parent had played. The Caribbean remained a theater of struggle and national rivalry, but the Dutch, after 1678, became only interested albeit impotent bystanders.

APPENDIXES

APPENDIX I

Report to the States General of a Dutch voyage to the coast of Guiana (December 3, 1597—October 28, 1598); written by A. Cabeliau, clerk of the expedition, and submitted by him February 3, 1599.

Account of the unknown and unsailed course of America, from the river Amazon as far as the island of Trinidad.

In the name of our Lord Jesus Christ, amen, and in the year thereof fifteen hundred and ninety-seven, on the third of December, in the morning, we set sail from Briel with two ships, the one named *den Zeeridder* of about eighty double-tons, whose skipper is Jacob Cornelisz alias Oom, the other named *den Jonas*, of about sixty double-tons, whose skipper is Marten Willemsz, of Schiedam, and so we ran out to sea together and sailed in company until the seventh of the same month, and from that time our ship was separated from the other, being about 44 degrees off the channel, and did not see each other again (during the whole voyage), although it had been agreed to wait for each other, if we separated, at the island of Palma, one of the Canary Islands.

On the twenty-seventh of the same month the island of Palma came in sight and we lay there. Not having sighted Marten Willemsz, on the same day we arrived off the city of Palma and lay there to procure wine for ourselves until the fifteenth of January in the year 1598, and inasmuch as Marten Willemsz aforesaid did not come, we, the aforesaid, set sail and laid our course for the island of Teneriffe.

There we arrived on the sixteenth and lay off there with our ship, in order to speak several ships which were drifting under the lee of the land, to ask whether they had seen or heard of Marten Willemsz; but, learning nothing of him, we laid our course on the seventeenth between the island of the Great Canary and Teneriffe to the islands of Cape Verde and so to Cape North. On the ninth of February we caught sight of the land at about five degrees north of the equator, where we cast anchor on the same day and lowered our ship's boat and with it sailed around the islands, seeking whether there was no convenient spot where we could beach our yacht, or sloop, but found it ill-suited and very craggy, so that we were obliged to take the yacht on board of the ship and there repair and caulk it as was needful, not without great danger.

On the fifteenth we sighted a boat, named by the Indians *canoe*, which had come from the mainland, a distance of about two miles, from the river Caurora, wherein were six men, one woman, and a little child of the Carib or Yao tribe, and they were entirely naked. It was long before they ventured to come on board, but at last they emboldened themselves by means of drums and in other ways and came on board and called out to us "Anglees," and we answered "Si, Si," and so they came over [the rail] and we led them into the cabin and made it clear to them that we were from Holland, and said "Hollandees," and treated them very well, so far as we were able, so that they next day went off gayly, and after this evinced much friendship for us. On the seventeenth day there came to our ship from the mainland, out of the aforesaid river, three more canoes, in which were men, women and children to the number of about sixty persons, and this aforesaid tribe, together with the Hebaio and Arawak tribes, continued to come on board with their wares and provisions as long as we lay in the aforesaid islands and also during the time that we lay in the river Cayana, next following.

On the twenty-seventh of March we set sail for the river Cayani, and that with great opposition on the part of the skipper, although he was assured by us and by an Englishman named Captain John Meysinge, of London, and also knew himself that he could enter the aforesaid river without danger; and through persuasion from us and his sailors we entered the before-mentioned river on the thirty-first by God's help, without any hindrance, and anchored by the aforesaid English Captain.

On the following day we sent our yacht up stream to the river Cauwo and there we found the tribe Yao dwelling, and thence with their own consent we brought these Indians here present, one named Arymowacca, aged about forty years, so far as we can understand, and the other Cayariwara, aged about twenty years, together with a yachtful of wood having a substance and color like Brazil wood, besides tobacco and other drugs (unknown to me). And on the eighth of April the yacht came to the ship and we traded on this river Cayani and lay there until the twenty-seventh of June.

On the sixteenth of April the aforesaid Englishman set sail.

On the twenty-ninth of the same month two ships from Amsterdam joined us, through our help, whereof the skippers were Dierck Jansz Roomschkerck and Wouter Syvertsz, and sailed off again on the tenth of May to the island of Margarita.

On the third of June two ships from Amsterdam joined us, named the Great and Little *Sphera Mundi*, the skippers whereof were Jan Cornelisz van Leyen and Adriaen Reyndertssoen before mentioned. And we joined forces with them in order to visit together the entire coast as far as the river called Orinoco by the Indians, Raliana by the English, and Rio El Dorado by the Spaniards. And all that might fall to us upon the aforesaid coast was to be shared, three eighths for our company and five eighths for the company of Jan van Leyen aforesaid. And we visited the following rivers: Wyapoco, Curassawini, Cunanamae, Juraco, Mavary, Amano, Marawini, Carapi, Surinamo, Saramo, Coupanama, Waycara, Curetini, Orinoco. In the river Orinoco, Rio Barima and Amacura, and in these we bartered and traded. The rivers between the Amazon and Wiapoco are as follows: Aroway, Arafioco, Maycary, Cassipoura, Arrocava. These rivers we neither visited nor traded in, because we could not get there, on account of the regular current which always flows westerly along the coast. The rivers between the Wiapoco and the Caurora are as follows: Wanary, Apperwacca, Cawo, Wya, Cayany, Macuria. These in particular we ourselves visited and traded in, except the rivers Wanary and Apperwacca. Between Mamiamanory and Synamary are two little streams named Owapary and Paurama, upon which no tribe dwells. The river, or the mouth, of the Surinam is forked. The Cammawini lies to the east and the Surinam to the west, and they empty into the sea together. Between the rivers Corentyn and Orinoco are these rivers: Berbice, Abary, Mahaicony, Mahaica, Demerara, Essequibo, Pomeroon, Moruca, Waini. These we have not visited or traded in, either singly or in company, since our time was far spent and there was not so much to be found there, as the Indians informed us, and, moreover, our provisions were very low; so we did no more than to coast along the land, in order to have some idea of it, as far as the river Orinoco, which we entered on the twenty-seventh of July and anchored by each other, about two miles from the mouth of said river.

On the twenty-eighth we prepared to visit the river Orinoco with the ship of Jan van Leyen, of about 36 double-tons burden, our yacht of about 9 double-tons, and the yacht, or row-boat, of Adriaen Reynderssen, our whole force being about fifty persons.

On the twenty-ninth, the aforesaid boats and people sailed up the river together, against the strong current which always runs there at this time of the year. And we traveled, with the direction of these Indians here present, not more than about forty [Dutch] miles in the space of twenty days, up to the place or settlement where the Spaniards are, which is named St. Thomé, whereof Don Fernando de Berreo is Governor and also Marquis of Guiana, the river Orinoco and all the coasts being still unconquered as far as the river Maranon, or Amazon. Their strength consists of about sixty horsemen and one hundred musketeers, who daily seek to conquer the gold-land Guiana, but do not yet succeed either by means of the expeditions made thither up to this time nor by any means of friendship, because the tribe called Caribs violently opposes them every day with their weapons. These are bows, and they shoot with them poisoned arrows, which are so deadly that if anyone is hit therewith so that blood flows, he must perforce die within twenty-four hours, unless a remedy be instantly applied, and all his flesh would drop from his bones. Therefore the Spaniards greatly fear that tribe and their arrows. Moreover they [the tribe] stand firm in battle and will not yield, and up to now they have always been victorious; and the Spaniards, seeing that they can gain nothing there, have begun, about six days' journey to the south of the river Orinoco, at the mountains of Guiana, to make a road through the rocks and hills about 1,600 stadia long and wide enough for five horses to march abreast, and by these means they hope to conquer it.

From St. Thomé the yacht of our ship and the sloop of Adriaen Reyndertsen, with Jan van Leyen's two herring-scows, sailed up to the river Caroni, which has a terrible and mighty cataract, and falls down out of the mountains and makes such a noise that it can be heard about four [Dutch] miles away. In this neighborhood we sought (following our description made by Sir Walter Raleigh) certain gold mines, but found none, whether it be from oversight or because there were none there we know not which, but we did our best in it all, nevertheless, as it seemed to us. We are the more confident of this because the Governor, Don Fernando, gave us his miner to help us investigate, who took us to all the places where, in his opinion, Sir Walter Raleigh had been and whence his minerals were taken. And in all the places that we have seen we could find no proofs that gold was underneath, but understand from our Indians that there is a place about six [Dutch] miles up stream where there are said to be certain mines; but the water had overflowed there to such a degree that it was impossible for us to visit it. The Spaniards also said that there was much gold up stream, but they dared not go thither on account of the war with the aforesaid Caribs. To sum up briefly, there is up that river in the kingdom of Guiana certainly much gold, as we were told by the Indians from there as well as by our own Indians here present, and the Spaniards themselves say so; but for people busied with trade it is not feasible to expect any good therefrom unless to that end considerable expeditions were equipped to attack the Spaniards. This is the only means of learning the whereabouts of any gold mines from the Indians; for whosoever are enemies, and bear enmity to the Spaniards, are friends with the Indians, and they hope steadily that they shall be delivered from the Spaniards by the Dutch and the English, as they told us. When a captain of the Indians, taken prisoner by the Spaniards, was going to be hanged, he said that he had spoken with the spirit Wattopa and she had prophesied deliverance through us and through the English. I could wish to help in this, in case it could be brought about and succeed to the profit and advantage of the country. Having traded in this river to no great extent with the Indians, as also with the Spaniards, we departed from the town of St. Thomé, by common consent, for the ships, and came on board on the thirtieth of August, with express promises from the Spaniards that they would come to trade with us at Trinidad.

On the first of September we sailed together to the island of Trinidad, and on the seventh we arrived off the west coast of Trinidad and there anchored. This is a rich and beautiful island, adorned with many sorts of merchandise and wares useful for many things, and we traded off to the Spaniards all our remaining merchandise and wares, except a few which we brought back, since we could not trade among the Indians with such articles.

On the twenty-first of the said month Jan van Leyen and Adriaen Reynderssen left us and sailed for the island of Margarita.

On the thirtienth of October we set sail for these provinces and took our course, on account of lack of provisions, through the Pragonis and Aeso between the islands of St. Lucia and Grenada, and on the sixteenth of the same month spoke there with the galley of Sir Walter Raleigh, of London, of about twenty-five tons, and coming from the coast of Barbary. On the same day sailed on between the aforesaid islands and on the twenty-second of the same month again between the islands of Dominica and Poorebano, and so laid our course to the islands of the Azores, and on the twenty-first of November came in sight of the island of Fayal and sailed by it, and in the evening sighted an English pinnace, and on the twenty-second spoke it near the island of Graciosa, and thence laid our course for the Channel and on the eleventh of December ran into Plymouth in England on account of contrary winds, and lay there until the twenty-fifth of the same month and set sail for these provinces with divers ships, and on the twenty-eighth arrived at Middelburg in Zeeland.

So that, in this voyage, we have discovered, found, and navigated more than twenty-four rivers, many islands in the rivers, and divers other harbors, which have hitherto neither been known in these provinces nor sailed to therefrom. Aye, more, in no chart and by no geographer down to this time has our route been described or pointed out. All of which, I, the undersigned, as supercargo of this voyage, declare to be true, being ready (if need be) to explain the same to Your High Mightinesses more fully either by word of mouth or in writing. In witness of the truth I have signed this on the third of February, in the year 1599.

Your obedient servant,

A. CABELIAU

English translation of the Dutch original in *ARA* from *U.S. Commission on Boundary between Venezuela and British Guiana. Report and Accompanying Papers of the Commission*, II, *Extracts*, pp. 13-22; also J. K. J. de Jonge, *De Opkomst van het Nederlandsch Gezag in Oost-Indië*, I, 153-60.

APPENDIX II

Effects of the West India Company, 1626.

Effects of the Incorporated West India Company, as they are found at present, after it was determined, as it indeed is true, that the Sailors and Soldiers of the Fleets of General Boudewyn Hendrixsen, the Admiral t'Lam, be paid, and can be forthwith paid out of the Company's previous funds, and all moneys on interest be paid, which are very trifling. Estimated this 4th Sept^r, 1626.

	9 ships from 150 to 200 a. 230 lasts, well equipped.	
	3 large yachts.	
In all,	12 ships and yachts destined for the African trade in Guinea, Benin, Angola, Greyn, and Quaqua coasts, with the exported cargoes and expected returns, as more fully can be shown, amount to, according to cost	fl. 1,709,000
	1 ship of Dordrecht to Cape Verde, with cargo	60,000
	1 ship 〉 destined for the trade of the Amazon 2 yachts 〈 and the Coast of Guiana, with the cargoes,	80,000
	1 ship of about 130 lasts 〉 well equipped, destined for the 1 yacht 〈 trade and colonization of New 〉 Netherland, estimated, at least, at	120,000
Total,	18 ships and yachts trading to all quarters where the Company hath any free trade, amounting to	1,969,000
	9 large ships of 200 to 300 lasts, 〉 despatched in May, 1626, 5 large and small yachts, 〈 under Admiral Pieter Pieterzen Heyn, (whose plan promises to be successful) victualled for 18 months, having full 1800 men, furnished with metal and iron guns, amounting, with the equipage, to	700,000
	8 ships and yachts on divers expeditions, under Thomas Sickes' flag, victualled for 18 months, amounting to .	200,000
In all 73 ships	33 ships of 200, a. 300, a. 350 lasts, including 9 or 10 big and little yachts which the company hath still lying here in port, provided with metal and iron guns, and all sorts of supplies of ammunition of war, powder, muskets, arms, sabres, and whatever may be necessary for the equipment, which can be fitted for sea at the fourth	

part of their former cost, estimated, as more fully can be seen, at	1,100,000
The sugar prize lately by Thomas Sickes, and the goods freighted through the fleet by General Boudewyn Hendrixen, will amount fully to	300,000
The wages of the 1600 soldiers allowed to the Company by your High Mightinesses, and the expense incurred thereupon by the refusal to pay anything	180,000
That your High Mightinesses still owe, on the promised 1500^m guilders, to be paid before you can derive any advantage as partners.	150,000
These following moneys are still to be received in cash, which being in the Treasury, will be applied to keep the foregoing ships at sea, not only to injure the King of Spain, but also by God's blessing to do your High Mightinesses and the Company much service, and the Partners good profit:	
From the shareholders what is yet unpaid of the 3^d installment, estimated at	488,000
From the shareholders for the 4th installment, all which is forthcoming, amounting to	1,467,000
Your High Mightinesses still remain indebted on the 1500^m guilders, besides the 150^m guilders before stated, ...	750,000
Total, ...	fl. 7,304,000

Further 5 ships ⎱ which your High Mightinesses promised to in-
and   3 yachts ⎰ demnify the Company for in guns, powder, and
    other munitions of war; as these are still wanting to
    complete the subsidy promised by the 40th article of
    the Charter, and by divers acknowledgements made by
    your High Mightinesses, as to be seen in resolutions.
    It remains to be stated, that the valuation of the ships and
    necessaries of war hereinbefore entered in gross, is not
    taken at the highest value, but will doubtless bring
    more when minutely reëxamined. Then, as to what re-
    lates to the state of the trade and the pay of shareholders,
    they think they are sufficiently well informed thereof.

N.B. When the Assembly of the XIX. resolved to send the expedition under Admiral Willekens, the capital of the shareholders of all the chambers, added together, amounted to	fl. 4,300,000
To which is added what your High Mightinesses promise by the Charter, ...	1,000,000
In all, ...	fl. 5,300,000

Thus, the Company's capital is greater at this time, by two millions, than it was at that period; besides, experience has given it more knowledge as to the condition of the places situated in the West Indies and the Brazils; what are useful or useless to the Company in that country; what can, and what cannot, be defended; all which is of great advantage to the Company and this country.

English translation from the original in *ARA* from *Documents Relative to the Colonial History of the State of New York*, ed. E. B. O'Callaghan, I, 35-37.

APPENDIX III

Conditions for Colonies, adopted by the West India Company (the Nineteen), June 12, 1627.

Extract from the minutes of the meeting of the Chamber of the Nineteen, held on June 12, 1627, in the name of the chartered West India Company.

Of the colonists to be carried over by the participants.

1.

To all directors, chief or minor shareholders, it is hereafter permitted to send colonists to the Wild Coast and adjacent islands, to such places as they shall see fit, on condition that the first comer shall have the command in that river or island, under the supreme directorship of the Commandeur and Council of that coast, [and] on condition that the colonies which come later to that river or island shall have the right to place beside him one or more councilors, in order jointly to care for the interests of the colonies on the river or island.

2.

These colonists shall be carried over in the Company's ships, on condition that, from the proceeds of the first commodities which they shall send over, there be paid to the Company for every individual six stivers per day, from the time of their coming on board until their landing and their leaving the Company's table; in return for which the Company shall for the space of the voyage supply them with food and drink together with the sailors, and transport their necessary outfit.

3.

Each colonist shall be required to show to the directors or to those commissioned by them, that he is provided with the following necessaries, these to be in good condition: One pea-jacket, three collars, three shirts, one night-gown, two suits of duck clothes, one suit made of cloth, three pairs of stocking, four pairs of shoes, two pairs of bedsheets, seven yards of duck from which to make a mattress when over, one bag for [use] on board, wares enough to buy food yonder for one whole year.

Each household: one musket, one half-pike, one sword with a hanger, two axes, one pickaxe, one handsaw, three shovels, three spades, one kettle, one pan.

4.

These goods, first having been shown to the directors or to those commissioned by them, shall remain in the keeping of the agent or shipper, until the ship or ships shall be at sea, and then be handed to the owners for better keeping and airing.

5.

The colonists shall take care to be on board when the crew is mustered, and shall swear to the articled letter in so far as this concerns them; they shall agree to aid in the ship's service when required, and particularly in case of defence or offence to carry arms, in the same way as the others, though without being entitled to wages from the Company; but, in case they should take a ship or ships of the enemy, the colonists shall receive their share *pro rata* with the other shipfolk, every one according to his rank.

6.

The colonies must consist of at least 20 households, each of at least three persons.

7.

A colony having planted itself, no other shall be allowed to approach it within 7 or 8 miles, except in case the condition of the land thereabout should be such that for good reasons the Commandeur and Council ordain otherwise; these shall also decide and settle such questions as may arise concerning the limits.

8.

Each colony must [have] a good yacht of from 12 to 20 tons, fit for sailing and rowing, provided with 4 swivel-guns and six stone-pieces, and one herring-boat, barber, and smith.

9.

Those who send over this colony shall provide it with proper instructions, in order that it may be governed and ruled in accordance with the law of the land; which instructions they shall beforehand submit to the directors of the respective chambers, and they shall moreover be subject to the civil and criminal code made by the Company or hereafter to be made.

10.

The colonies which in course of time shall be situated on the respective rivers and islands shall have the right (namely, each river for itself) to designate one deputy, who shall report to the Commandeur in Cayenne and shall further in the Council the interests of the colonists; these shall be replaced every two years, and all the colonies shall be bound to send to the Commandeur and the Council in Cayenne, at least once in every six months, a full report concerning their colonies and adjacent lands.

11.

The colonists shall for a fair price yield to the Company the commodities which they have raised or gained by trade, or, in case they should not find this advisable, they may send them over to their patroons in the Company's ships, on condition that they pay, for articles of which a hundredweight is worth above fifty florins, one fair fifth part, and for those which are worth from twenty-five up to fifty one fourth part, and for those which are worth less than 25 florins one half; this to be for the space of seven years, counting from now on.

12.

Likewise there may be sent from here thither to the colonists by their patroons all articles and manufactures, on condition that, for transportation thereof, there be paid to the Company one fourth part of what they shall have cost here, to be collected by the Company from the first return-cargoes which shall come in from the settlers.

13.

But, in case any of the Company's ships should go to those regions empty and in ballast, in that case the patroons of the colonists shall be allowed to send over therein some horses or cattle, on condition that they pay the expenses for the wooden partitions and other conveniences, and put on board the necessary fodder, and that for those whom they send along they pay as above, and no more.

14.

The patroons shall through their colonists see to it that the lands which they take into possession be, *within the first three years* after their taking possession, brought under cultivation to their utmost ability, and in case they in the absence of serious obstacle fail to do so, *such lands shall be taken away from them by the Commandeur and Council after previous admonition and shall be assigned to others.*

15.

However, should it become evident that the colonists had been deceived in the choosing of the ground, and that it did not suffice to maintain them or give them profit, in that case they shall be allowed to select another locality after having addressed a complaint and petition to the Commandeur and his Council.

16.

The colonists shall have the right to carry on the inland trade for their own benefit, on condition that they do with the commodities as above.

17.

They shall also be allowed to practice all kinds of sport, such as netting, hunting, fishing, in the rivers and waters situated in their territory.

18.

And if any one of these colonists by his exertion and application should come to discover any minerals, precious stones, crystals, marble, or anything of that sort, these shall remain the property of the patroon or patroons of that colony, on condition that he grant to the finder such a reward as does the Company to its colonists, and that he give to the Company as a tax and fee twenty per cent of the aforesaid minerals, when it is seen that the thing is a success.

19.

The colonists shall not be at liberty to weave there any cloth of woolen, linen, or cotton, or to make any other kind of cloth, on penalty of being excluded and as perjurers fined at the discretion of the company.

20.

Lastly, they shall take pains to find among themselves at the earliest date some funds wherewith to *maintain a preacher and schoolmaster*, in order that worship and religious zeal may not lose vigor in them.

21.

And the Company shall take pains to furnish to the colonists as many negroes as shall be possible, on condition that it receive therefore as above, namely, two and a half fares [?], without its being required to clothe them after having delivered them over.

Notice, that these conditions, by resolution of the Board of Nineteen of November 22, 1628, were made easier, according to the revised conditions granted to the colonists, and entered hereinafter on Fol. 54.

English translation from the Dutch original in *ARA* from *U.S. Commission on Boundary between Venezuela and British Guiana. Report and Accompanying Papers of the Commission*, ii, *Extracts*, pp. 47-52.

APPENDIX IV

The *Oficiales Reales* of Vera Cruz to His Majesty, July 19, 1628.

Señor.

En esta flotta, General don Juan de Venauides, registramos por quentta de Vuestra Magestad de lo que se nos a rremitido de las Caxas Reales de Vuestra Magestad de la Ziudad de Mexico, Guatemala, Yucatan, y de la de nuestro cargo de esta çiudad de la Nueua Veracruz, 738,941 pesos 5 tomines 6 granos de oro comun, en plata y reales, los 100,768 pesos 2 tomines 3 granos dellos que ban a entragar en la Hauana para el situado de aquel presidio y los 638,173 pesos 3 tomines 3 granos restantes consignados al presidente y juezes de la Casa de Contrataçion de Sevilla, para que guarden la orden de Vuestra Magestad, que lo que ba de cada una de las dichas Caxas y porque quentta, se dira en esta manera:

De la Caxa Real de Mexico, 524,357 pesos 2 tomines 2 granos, por las quenttas siguienttes.

Por el çituado de la Hauana	100,768 pesos 2 tomines 3 granos
para San Lorenço el Real	1,343 pesos 3 tomines
para salarios de los consejeros del consejo de Yndias	18,218 pesos 1 tomin
para don Juan de Villela	1,378 pesos 5 tomines 5 granos
para Pedro de Valencia	797 pesos 4 tomines 4 granos
para Antonio de Herrera y su muger	1,155 pesos – tomines
por quentta de condenaçiones cobradas en Philiphinas	1,460 pesos 6 tomines
por quentta de la condenaçion de don Juan Velazquez	3,025 pesos 6 tomines 9 granos
por quentta de los 10,000 ducados de los nouenos	13,787 pesos – tomines
por quentta de mesada de Philiphinas	5,265 pesos 4 tomines 5 granos
Por quentta de mesada de Guadalaxara	526 pesos 1 tomin 6 granos
por quentta de mesada de Mexico	1,808 pesos – tomines
prestamo cobrado del Lizençiado Medrano	744 pesos 4 tomines

por quentta de donatiuo de Guadalaxara	500 pesos – tomines
Donatiuo de Mexico	310 pesos 5 tomines
por quentta del real de seño-raje	58,080 pesos 4 tomines
por quentta de libros del Conçilio Mexicano	1,066 pesos 4 tomines
La mitad del ualor del offiçio de depositario general de Mexico	25,000 pesos – tomines
por quentta de la Santa Cru-çada	125,000 pesos – tomines
Resto de Real Hazienda de Mexico	164,120 pesos 6 tomines 6 granos

524,357 pesos 2 tomines 2 granos	524,357 pesos 2 tomines 2 granos

De la Caxa Real de Guatemala: 103,453 pesos 7 tomines 9 granos de oro comun por las quentas siguientes.

para don Fernando Ruiz de Contreras	2,460 pesos 4 tomines
de offiçios vendidos	3,872 pesos – tomines
por quentta de nouenos del obispado de Guatemala	2,778 pesos 4 tomines
Condenaçion del Consejo de Yndias	5,508 pesos – tomines
derechos de esclauos negros de Guatemala	4,424 pesos 2 tomines
Composision de estrangeros de Guatemala	919 pesos 4 tomines
Por arrendamientos de las casas de aposento de los Conseje-ros del Consejo de Yndias	1,000 pesos – tomines
por quentta de Real Haçienda de Guatemala	82,491 pesos 1 tomin 9 granos

103,453 pesos 7 tomines 9 granos	103,453 pesos 7 tomines 9 granos

De la Real Caxa de la prouinçia de Yucatan 20,662 pesos 5 to-mines	20,662 pesos 5 tomines
De la Real Caxa de nuestro cargo de esta çiudad de la Nueua Veracruz 90,467 pesos 6 tomines 7 granos en esta manera.	

Real Hazienda de la Veracruz   81,221 pesos – tomines
   por quentta de derechos de   9,246 pesos 6 tomines
esclauos negros   7 granos

—————————————

         90,467 pesos 6 tomines   90,467 pesos 6 tomines
         7 granos   7 granos

—————————————   —————————————

                                 738,941 pesos 5 tomines
                                 6 granos.

—————————————

Que son los dichos 738,941 pesos 5 tomines 6 granos.

Los que remitimos a Vuestra Magestad registrados en capitana y almiranta por las quenttas referidas, como comsta de sus rregistros.
   Quarde Dios la Catholica Real persona de Vuestra Majestad como la christiandad a menester.
   Veracruz, 19 de Julio 1628.

Es copia de la carta que escribimos a Su Magestad en la ultima fflota, y asi lo çertificamos en la Nueua Veracruz a veinte de Henero de mill y seisçientos y veinte y nuebe años.

Don Juan Blazquez Maioral
Diego de Valle Almarado   (Rubricados)

Palo campeche	Purga	Camanguan	Chocolate y Regalos	Çarparrilla
615 quintales	—	150 lbs.	15 caxas	—
1,000 quintales	68 arrobas	—	20 caxas	—
758 quintales	98 arrobas	260 lbs.	26 caxas	—
920 quintales	—	750 lbs.	47 caxas	—
1,350 quintales	—	750 lbs.	12 caxas	24 arrobas
—	—	—	—	—
1,250 quintales	—	—	—	—
—	—	—	—	—
800 quintales	—	—	—	—
—	—	—	—	—
330 quintales	—	—	—	—–
7,023 quintales	166 arrobas	1,910 lbs.	120 caxas	24 arrobas
apreciasse este jenero por el aualio	apreciasse este xenero por el aualio	apretiasse este genero por el aualio	apreciasse este xenero por el aualio	apreciasse este xenero por el aualio
3,511 pesos 4 tomines	512 pesos 4 tomines	955 pesos	8,000 pesos	75 pesos

General Account of all the Silver and Gold—and also how many hundreds of thousands these amount to—which on September 8, 1628 were happily captured, through the graceful blessing of God, by the brave General Pieter Pietersz Heyn, and the valiant Admiral Heyndric Lonc...in the service of the chartered West India Company...about Havana and the Bay of Matanses, under the Island of Cuba in the West Indies...

177,329¼ pound Silver, a 44 guilder the pound	f. 7,802,487
606 cases and bales of Cochineal, a 3000 gld.	1,818,000
114 cases Cochineal Silvestre, a 400 gld.	45,600
154 bales of silk, a 2000 gld.	308,000
2112 cases of Indigo, a 400 gld.	844,800
361 chests of Sugar, a 250 gld.	90,250
382 various goods, a 400 gld.	152,800
37,375 hides, a 12 gld.	448,500
	f. 11,510,437

Historian Nicolaes van Wassenaer also mentions some curiosities: a Head, said to have been a Head of the Martyrs who were killed in Japan by the King,[1] a crucifix of ivory,[2] a silver church-lamp,[3] etc.

---

[1] Van Wassenaer, *Historisch Verhael*, XVI, 102.

[2] L'Honoré Naber and Wright, *Piet Heyn en de Zilvervloot*, p. 155; a crucifix in the R. C. church of St. Antonius-Abt in Rotterdam (before World War II) was said to come from the Spanish silver fleet; also L. J. Rogier, *Het zoogenaamde Piet Heynskruis*, in *Rotterdamsch Jaarboekje* (Rotterdam, 1926).

[3] Van Wassenaer, *Historisch Verhael*, XVI, 102.

From De Laet/Naber, II, 72-73.

APPENDIX V

Remonstrance of the West India Company against a Peace with Spain, 1633.

To the Great and Mighty Lords, the States of Holland and Westfriesland.

Great and Mighty Lords.

Your Great Mightinesses were pleased to summon this day the Directors of the Incorporated West India Company, namely those of the Chamber at Amsterdam; and to explain to them what was done, or would still likely be done in this negotiation with the enemy concerning the Company, and to ask their opinion thereupon. We had truly wished that all the opinions of the respective Chambers in these United Netherlands, could be heard on this subject at the same time, and so considered by the High and Mighty Lords States General and his Highness the Prince of Orange, that both might thereby advance the interest of the Fatherland and the prosperity of the Company; and that the Company might be maintained, as we herefore have humbly set forth in divers Deductions and Remonstrances; and particularly in the year 1629, when like deliberations were held.

But as Your Great Mightinesses have been pleased to call on us specially on the subject, we shall not remain in default, but well and thoroughly inform Your Great Mightinesses of everything that must be considered in this connection, for the interest of this State, according to our limited abilities and good disposition.

And, lay before Your Great Mightinesses, first of all, the vast services this Company hath, from its inception until now, conferred on this State, and what it can further perform hereafter.

For, howbeit, we trust that the enemy's persevering endeavors to be freed from the arm of this Company in the West Indies, is a clear and irrefragible argument of the service which it is daily conferring on this State, whilst the latter seems, nevertheless, not to greatly esteem or consider it; yet the following Deduction will serve more strongly to confirm those who have duly comprehended the importance of the Company to this State, and afford better information to those who may entertain a doubt thereupon.

Brief Deduction of the advantages the Commonwealth derives from the Company.
First: As regards what it consumes.

The Company hath yearly, on an average, one year with another, equipped, victualled and dispatched over fifty ships.

Hath employed over six thousand, as well soldiers as seamen, and over eight or nine thousand during the last year.

And for the support thereof, purchased and slaughtered a large quantity of cattle, made great store of biscuit, hard bread, flour, beans, peas, groats, dried codfish, butter and cheese, and such like supplies.

Hath, also, sent large quantity of wines, brandies, oil, vinegar, and similar liquors.

Item, a large amount of powder, lead, bullets, and other munitions of war.

Secondly: Regarding duties.

The Company imported an excessively large amount of costly wares, such as Cocheneal, Silk, Indigo, an innumerable quantity of Sugars, Hides, Ginger, and other spices. Cotton, Elephants' teeth, Tobacco, Brazil and other woods, Salt, Gums, etc., from the exportation of which to other countries the State had the benefit of large duties.

Thirdly: By the increase of the Trade and Wealth of the Commonwealth.

The said Company brought into the Country a very large amount of gold and silver, both coined and uncoined; exported a vast quantity of all sorts of manufactures, most of which were made here; for the Trade to Guinea alone requires, for all descriptions of manufactures, an annual outlay of above five tons of gold, and returns yearly into the country over ten tons of gold.

In like manner, a large quantity of goods was shipped to other parts of Africa and America, in return for which many other goods were imported, whereby the inhabitants of this country obtained trade and employment.

Fourthly: By strengthening the Country.

The Company hath, at present, about one hundred and twenty well built ships, some of 400 and some of 300 lasts; several of 250, 200 and 150 lasts and the remainder of smaller dimensions; all as well supplied with metal and iron pieces, and suitable ammunition, as any of the enemy's best and largest vessels.

One third, or in case of need, fully one-half of those can almost always be employed in the public service.

The Company maintains and employs a large number of seamen, who, otherwise, would not find any work, and fits them for divers situations, even the highest in the State.

Fifthly: Regarding the aid afforded to the Company.

Particularly, when the enemy invaded the Veluwe, the Company supplied the common people with ammunition and provisions, so that its fleet, destined for Brazil, was thereby detained over three months, whilst it had to maintain above three thousand men abroad doing nothing, to the great damage and obstruction of its designs.

The Company aided the State, in its necessity, with a handsome sum of ready money.

And so strengthened it by the rich distribution of public and private wealth, that it became much better able to bear the public charges, and more promptly to discharge them.

Sixthly: Seeing that it had inflicted such excessive damage on the enemy, and caused an indescribable diversion.

Laid waste Bahia, which, independent of the incurred damages, cost the King of Spain over ten millions to recover it; and, also, captured, plundered and destroyed Porto Rico, Margarita, Sancta Martha, St. Thomas, Guiana, and sundry other places.

Took and retained Pernambuco and Tamarica, whereby the King of Spain hath lost over a million and a half of yearly revenue.

Forced the said King to great expence of fleets, to be sent to Brazil, whence his sugars used heretofore to be brought home without any trouble, and whilst he lay asleep; and his revenue collected without any cost.

Item. Prevented the Portuguese, by the continual cruizing of our ships on the coast of Brazil, from bringing over their sugars and other produce; twenty-three per cent of which, when imported, went to the King; and as much when exported, amounting together to forty-six per cent, nearly half the sugar; without the loss which is suffered in Brazil wood from shrinkage.

Also, captured his fleet from New Spain, and thrice made prize of the rich Honduras ships; took, moreover, in divers parts of Africa and America, over a hundred of his vessels, most of which had full freights, including several of his best galleons; and burnt and destroyed nearly as many, if not more, that had ran ashore.

Forced him to dispatch a greater number of galleons and armed ships, than he was formerly accustomed to send, to convoy the fleet from Terra firma and New Spain.

Obliged him to change his usual seasons, and to let the ships come over at unusual and unfavorable periods of the year, whereby a rich fleet from New Spain was, last year, almost entirely lost; and (as far as we can ascertain) his last year's fleet, which otherwise ought to have been in before the winter, hath not yet arrived up to the present time; by all which his treasury is so exhausted, and his credit so damaged, that it can with difficulty be repaired, and he is, in consequence, obliged to apply to this country even for the Truce.

It is also to be considered, that this State hath paid and still pays to foreign princes, heavy yearly subsidies, the money whereof goes and remains out of the country; and nothing was obtained in return, except what was effected last year by the Company, who expend the subsidies in this country.

From all this, and from what can be more fully set forth, if necessary, your Great Mightinesses will easily perceive what services the Company hath rendered this State, and what advantages the country hath derived from it. And more especially this province of Holland and Westfriesland, because thither flowed six-ninth of the Company's capital, and here most of the equipments were made; besides all that is above enumerated, the Company can hereafter effect still more for the public service, and to the enemy's prejudice.

And that with greater ease and much more effectually than heretofore, first, because it now possesses, in Brazil, the most important points in that country, and the most convenient that could be selected in all America; as the entire world, and even the enemy best knows.

Secondly, because it has ascertained by great outlay and long experience, where the King's power in America is weakest, and how easily he can be deprived of the most valuable of his revenues.

Whether these services which the Company can confer on the country, and which this State hath undoubtedly a right to expect for its preservation and for the humbling of the enemy, ought still be continued and encouraged; or rather whether, on the contrary, such favorable advantages ought to be thrown away, are considerations which we leave to commend themselves to your Great Mightinesses' wise deliberations.

For your Great Mightinesses will easily perceive the advantage the King of Spain hath to expect if the Company's ships, and power be lifted off his neck. And how soon he, unobstructed in the arrival of his fleets, will be able to recruit his battered finances and credit, and become, ere long, more formidable to this State and its Allies than he ever hath been before; and how easily he will be able to fortify the places which now lie open to us and to strengthen those already fortified, so that all our power and knowledge will hereafter profit us nothing.

We can herein prescribe in no wise to your Great Mightinesses, nor be of use any longer than is agreeable to this State.

But this we must, in virtue of our office, lay in all submission, before your Great Mightinesses, that the Company, so far as the interest of its stockholders is concerned, can without great loss, be easily brought to this negotiation, by money or goods for its contracts, such as the case deserves. That the stockholders also would easily forget their losses, if the State might, by that means, be much benefitted; but that the Company would thereby, in time, come to ruin, and be unable to do the State any further service.

For unless the war with the King of Spain continue, and liberal subsidies be received from the State, it can derive scarcely any benefit from the Company, even if any essential injury done the enemy; for, it will be of no consequence to this State, whether the Company, by negotiation, retain its possessions in Brazil, or restore them to the King for a sum of money.

We willingly acknowledge that this Company was, in the beginning, designed principally for the augmentation of trade and navigation, without which the great multitude of seafaring people, with which God hath blessed this country, could not be employed, nor the several trades kept in continual action and prosperity.

Also, that those who, in that operation, pretended to have been most clear sighted, were of the opinion that the countries of the West Indies were not so thickly settled and planted by our enemies, but that trade could be established with divers people and Nations; colonies carried over, plantations of divers profitable products promoted, and emoluments derived therefrom similar to what our enemies have now for many years drawn from their's to the manifest strengthening of the King's finances; and in case of delay or ill success, it was expected to make good a part of the loss, by return cargoes of salt; but in consequence of the tedious negotiations with those of the North Quarter, the enemy hath wholly destroyed our Salt Trade at Punta del Rey.

And in regard to trade, experience hath by degrees, made us wiser, and taught us, that it is very meager and indifferent with the people and nations who are still independent of the King of Spain; also, that the countries still unoccupied, are for the most part unproductive and of little value, and those which have been found good and productive, being greatly encumbered by timber, &c., are very difficult of cultivation, especially for our nation, who, being unaccustomed to so hot a climate, find it difficult to apply themselves to labor, and being unprovided with slaves and also not in the habit of making use of them, cannot supply their own inefficiency by the labor of others, as the Spaniards and Portuguese easily do by that of the Blacks and Indians.

However, the peopling of such wild and uncleared lands, demands more inhabitants than our country can supply; not so much for want of population, with which our provinces swarm, but because all those who will labor in any way here, can easily obtain support, and, therefore, are disinclined to go far from home on an uncertainty.

To which can be added, the uncertainty of being able to protect themselves, unless at a greater expence than the apparent gains to be derived therefrom, seem to justify. But in order that your Great Mightinesses may be thoroughly informed herein, and understand the condition of the countries, yet unoccupied by our enemies, we shall, with this view, explain to you, Great and Mighty, more minutely our limits in the West Indies, together with the extent and condition thereof.

The limits granted to us by their High Mightinesses begin, on the North, at New France, the bounds whereof were extended so very far by the French that they would call in question over New Netherland, which is the first country occupied by our people. Though this district, in point of climate, ought to be as warm and suitable for fruit culture as the confines of France joining Spain, yet it was found to be nearly colder than the latter, yes, than more northerly countries. For this reason, then, the people conveyed thither by us have as yet been able to recover only scanty means of subsistence, and have been no advantage, but a drawback to the Company. The trade there in peltries is, indeed, very profitable, but one year with another only fifty thousand guilders, at most, can be brought home. South of this follow Virginia, settled by the English, and Florida, so far as it is adapted to trade, by the Spaniards.

The large Islands are occupied by the Spaniards; the small are difficult of access; their condition as yet but little known, and some of the best of all the roadsteads are in the possession of the French and English; in addition to this, the English lay claim to all the Caribbean islands, by virtue of a certain grant made to the Earl of Carlisle. Moreover, from the cape of Florida, which runs out opposite Cuba, to the beginning of New Spain, there is still more land adapted for settlement, and people to trade with. Now, from New Spain, eastward, the whole coast of Incanata, Honduras and Terra Firma (as the Spaniards call it) to beyond Trinidad, and not only the coasts, but also the islands, are all settled by Spaniards; except next to these, the Guiana country, which we call the Wild Coast; this Coast and divers rivers are inhabited by free Indians, and still unsettled; in these countries are many products which might be advantageously brought hither; but what of them? Those people are so barbarous, and have so few wants (inasmuch as they feel no desire for clothing, and require no necessaries for their subsistence) that all the trade which exists there, can be easily carried on with two or three ships a year, and be maintained with trifling Capital. The country is bounded by the great river of the Amazons, which also, is not free from Spanish settlements, as our people have experienced to their damage. Next follows again, an extensive coast unto Brazil, the greatest part of which possessing any capability of producing articles of trade or cultivation, is altogether settled by the Portuguese. Brazil, wholly settled by them, extends beyond the Tropic of Capricorn, and from thence onward to the straits of Magellan, and is of no value.

Across the Strait, in the South sea, nothing remains unsettled, except the west part of Magellianica and a part of Chili, and finally the isolated (*geunageneerde*) wealthy countries of Terra Australis.

Thus, your Great Mightinesses see what remains, within such great limits, in the West Indies, open to the Company for trade or cultivation; wherefore, from the commencement of our administration, we preferred to proceed in a warlike manner against the common enemy; the rather, because we found that even the few nations (whether situate far or near) who are independent of the King of Spain, could be brought to trade with us in no other way than by declaring themselves in our favor, and showing themselves to be, in fact, enemies of the Spaniards; but principally because we found that the expected service, for the welfare of our Fatherland and the destruction of our hereditary enemy, could not be accomplished by the trifling trade with the Indians, or the tardy cultivation of uninhabited regions; but in reality, by acts of hostility against the ships and the property of the King of Spain and of his subjects; surprizing his possessions and preserving them for the public service; which plan has been so graciously blessed by God, during these latter years, that great wealth has thereby been brought to this State, and the enemy's finances thrown into such arrears and confusion, that no improvement is to be expected therein, except from the cessation of our arms and retaining our fleets at home, out of these countries. But this prosecution of war, instead of commerce, hath not been undertaken by us, of our own mere motion, but principally by the advice of the High and Mighty Lords States General, and the concurrence of his Serene Grace, the Prince of Orange; for your Great Mightinesses will well remember, that from the very inception of the Company, we have all been solicited by their High Mightinesses' Commissioners, not only to undertake some hostile expedition against the enemy, but even to dispatch our fleet to reinforce that which a short time before had been ordered out under the command of Admiral L'Hermite, and to send the ships we had then by us ready equipped in the Zuyder Zee, which from good motives and with their High Mightinesses' concurrence, were dispatched to Bahia de Todos los Sanctos. From these beginnings have we proceeded farther and farther into war; and undertaken, with their High Mightinesses'

advice and the approbation of his Serene Grace, divers expeditions which, to the astonishment of the universe, have been crowned, from time to time, with such success;
and neglected to plant colonies and to settle countries, from which as great trade
might have followed as we at present possess, or in all probability, could speedily
establish; so that there remains only the trade to Guinea and Africa, which is trifling
in comparison with the Company's large Capital, and had been already diverted and
spoiled by other nations; and, in season of truce, still greater hazard is to be expected
in that quarter. We, therefore, confidently, and of our certain knowledge, do assert,
that the entering into a Truce, must be the ruin of this Company; and that your
High Mightinesses will for ever lose the fortunate prop of this State, and the great
decrease of your hereditary enemy's finances; for, let us by means of commerce be
much greater than we can yet imagine, not a straw can the enemy be weakened thereby; nor can the sixth part of our ships be employed; and consequently, only a small
portion of the Seamen kept in service. We cannot oblige the Indians to trade with
us; nor can we trade with them, without circumspection, if we show ourselves the
friends of the Spaniards, and to have intimate relation with them. It were idle to
court the Chileans and to spare the Spaniards. In fine, nothing will remain for us,
save a meager scum of a well fed body; for the Company will be obliged to sell a
great portion of their largest ships and many of their guns, at a heavy sacrifice, and
to send the people away empty or sick; and then, nevertheless, to make further
reductions. The stockholders will be discouraged; the shares will fall in value; many
will sell out; as some have already done, and daily continue to do; even those who,
up to this time, have conferred lustre on this Company.

We earnestly trust that neither their High Mightinesses, nor his Serene Grace,
will suffer this, nor unnecessarily surrender so great an advantage to the enemy; but
rather, that they will adopt a laudable and firm resolution to maintain the Company
in their Charter, and aid them in prosecuting the war; and that your Great Mightinesses will, herein, set them an example of zeal equal to what you formerly ex-
hibited.

For, as we have lately at some length submitted to their High Mightinesses,
affairs in Brazil are so shaped that by sending a some what stronger force and an
experienced chief thither (as we now propose to do, if properly encouraged) that
place will not only be secured to this State, but rendered so profitable that its expenses will disappear, and it will produce great trade and prosperity to this country.

Your Great Mightinesses can determine that the subsidies we have hereunto
demanded are not so great as to embarrass this State; some provinces make no
difficulty about them; but where those subsidies appear to be a little heavier than
present circumstances can well justify, the profit to be reaped therefrom is also so
great, and the security which this State will obtain thereby, so evident, that there
ought not to be a moment's hesitation about it.

Foreign princes, whose good success were both to be desired and feared, were
voted these past years heavier subsidies; these were not grudged to those from whom
this State hath heretofore derived but little advantage, all for the purpose of creating a
diversion, and weakening the enemy; with what excuse then will men be able to
cover their neglect or disregard of a Company, which, out of its own private means,
hath wrought such good for the commonwealth, and which nestles here under your
Great Mightinesses' wings, and cannot be dreaded except by its enemies?

If your Great Mightinesses please to examine the deliberations previous to the
complete establishment of the Company; the Charter which their High Mightinesses
offered, unsolicited by their subjects; the circumstances which occurred in the
course of the Administration, it is a very questionable point, whether the Directors

are not better able to vindicate themselves before their stockholders for having expended their property so lavishly in the public service, than the rulers of this State to excuse themselves to posterity for having had such little regard for the services of the Company, which they had hitherto assisted, as to abandon it at last on the appearance of the enemy.

It depends on the determination of the Lords to continue the war, or to terminate it by a peace, or even to suspend it for some years, by a truce. Whichever be resolved upon, the Company must necessarily come into consideration. The enemy who intrudes herein, seems not disposed to come to any conclusion, before and until the Company be taken off his neck, and the captured places restored on certain conditions.

We are not afraid that their High Mightinesses will concur with the foe in this; but, indeed, that those who most affect the truce, may charge us with being an obstruction to its full accomplishment. And, although it were in no wise to be tolerated, the consequence will be, that the resolution of subsidies will be passed late, and carried slowly into effect, so that, in conclusion, we shall have to pray your Great Mightinesses seriously to consider, first: whether this State hath to expect any notable relief and profit from the war which the Company is to continue in the countries of America; or, if it be better to oblige the King so far as to surrender such considerable advantages, obtained at so great an expense, and to abandon the Company.

And, meanwhile, your Great Mightinesses are humbly requested to take into consideration the Charter the High and Mighty Lords States General have granted us, which attracted stockholders not only in this country, but also among many of the confederates, and how it will be possible to answer the one or the other before the world; also to pay due attention to the placards lately promulgated in Brazil, in the name of their High Mightinesses, according to which the natives and likewise some of the Portuguese, as we are informed, have already begun to regulate themselves, and cannot be abandoned without marked infamy and loss of credit. We pray God, that He be pleased to inspire your Great Mightinesses in such wise, as shall tend to the dissemination of His honor, and the prosperity of our fatherland.

English translation of the Dutch original in *ARA* from *Documents Relative to the Colonial History of the State of New York*, ed. E. B. O'Callaghan, I, 62-68.

APPENDIX VI

Letter of the Governor of Cartagena to the King, December 23, 1634.

Señor.

Francisco Nuñez Melian, gobernador de la provincia de Venezuela en carta de dos de septiembre me escribo, como el enemigo se ha apoderado de la ysla de Curaçao y que esta fortificado de que remite la relaçion que V.Mag.^d vera por los papeles que remito. El puerto es a barlovento desta çiudad y toda su costa y a donde bienen a reconocer todas las fregatas y nauios que desembocan la canal de Bahama, y los de essos Reinos que es ymportantissimo y da asta cuidarlo, al comercio por los daños que puede causar. V.Mag.^d determinara lo que fuere servido, que guarde Dios. Cartaxena a 23 de diziembre de 1634.

Pedro Francisco de Suarez

(A.G.I. Indiferente 2568)

APPENDIX VII

Letter of Peter Stuyvesant to Ruy Fernández de Fuenmayor, Curaçao, October 16, 1642.

Nobilissime Generalis.

Lectis et intellectis vestris literis haec paucula in responsum valebunt quod minarum et repitum non veremur sed adjutore Deo ter opt. max. propugnaculum hoc a generossimo principe Arausio et Indiae Occidentalis Societatis illustrissimis Directoribus nobis commissum summis viribus defendere et ad mortem usque protegere conemur adventrimque ante trimestrem nobis significatum expectemus, et more bellico tormentis gratulemur confidentes in Deum opt. max. illud nunquam in potestatem regis Hispaniae reducturum.

Quod de venificatis aquis vestra Claritas scribit Deum assumo testem illas de nostris contra omnem belli usum non esse infectas neque generosi militis mori positum est, huius modi tortis auxiliis in insidiis hostem nostrum contravenire sed Batavico more apertis et strenuis armis.

Quod ad captivos en Barbaratta acceptos, eos iam antea demisi et nostris navibus ad ripam terrae firmae portari curavi, interim obsecro ut nostri siqui sint alqui bonique tractentur quod in vestris recompendere non negligam.

Hisce vale. Festinantor in propugnaculo nostro.

Amstelerdamo Curassovice Adij 16 octobris 1642

P. Stuyvesant

Generoso ac nobilissimo generali Rooijs Fernandez.

I. A. Wright and C. F. A. van Dam, eds., *Nederlandsche zeevaarders op de eilanden in de Caraïbische Zee en aan de kust van Columbia en Venezuela*, II, 109 (159), Doc. 113.

APPENDIX VIII

Market quotations of the West India Company, 1628-1650.

1628	Nov. 15	115		1640	May 17	130
1629	January	206		1640	May 26	120
1629	beginn. Sept.	165 a 166		1641	Jan. 22	104 a 106
1630	Jan. 19	130 a 131		1641	June 12	117
1630	Febr. 15	133		1642	April 24	102$^1/_2$
1630	April	138 a 149		1642	June 13	102$^1/_4$
1630	June 13	120 a 123		1643	Febr. 7	92
1630	July 9	140		1643	March 5	85
1630	July 22	134		1643	June 3	92
1630	July 28	142		1643	Sept. 15	79 a 80
1630	Aug. 16	121 a 122		1643	Sept. 25	76
1630	Sept. 11	120		1643	Sept. 27	83$^1/_2$a 84
1630	Dec. 30	99 a 100		1644	March 14	68
1631	April 2	102		1644	May 1	55$^1/_4$
1631	April 30	103		1644	Oct. 1	47
1631	May 10	101		1644	Nov. 23	50 a 51
1631	June 21	95		1645	June 28	44
1633	Febr. 2	61		1645	Aug. 8	46
1634	May 6	93		1645	Sept. 13	38
1634	Oct. 30	112		1645	end Sept.	46
1635	Aug. 16	120		1646	June 9	36$^3/_4$
1635	Aug. 23	120 a 121		1647	Jan. 16	36
1635	Nov. 19	98		1648	beginn. Jan.	36 a 36$^1/_2$
1635	Nov. 23	97$^1/_2$		1648	June 15	33$^1/_2$a 34
1635	Dec. 3-5	104		1648	Sept. 14	31$^3/_4$
1636	March	105		1648	Dec. 14	31$^1/_2$
1637	Jan. 19	93		1648	Dec. 29	28
1637	March 6	94 a 95		1649	Jan. 1	28$^3/_4$a 29
1637	Nov. 4	97 a 98		1649	Febr. 8	26$^1/_4$
1640	May 4	134		1650	March 21	14$^1/_4$
				1650	Aug. 11	16

J. G. van Dillen, "Effectenkoersen aan de Amsterdamsche beurs," pp. 9-10.

APPENDIX IX

Orders for the combined Franco-Dutch fleet engaged in the Battle of Nevis, May 20, 1667.

Ordres que tiendra la flote, tant pour sa route & marche, que pour le combat.

La flote partant de cette Isle, fera sa route droit à la Guadeloupe, dans laquelle tous les vaisseaux observeront de suivre la manoeuvre de l'Amiral, & ne s'en point écarter: Et afin qu'aucun navire n'ayt pretexte de s'en tenir éloigné, l'Amiral reglera ses voiles sur le moindre voillier de la flote, & les meilleurs voilliers se regleront sur l'Amiral.

L'Amiral François portera deux feux de nuit, & l'Amiral de Messieurs les Estats un, afin que chacun puisse reconnoistre son escadre. Toute la flote sera divisée en deux escadres; la premiere de l'Amiral François, sera composée de son Vice-Amiral & Contr'-Amiral, du Florissant, des Armes d'Angleterre, de l'Armonie, de la Nostre-Dame, du Marsoüin, du Saint Christophle, & du bruslot le Cher amy.

La seconde escadre sera composée des quatre navires de guerre de Messieurs des Etats, du Levrier, & des navires François le Saint Jean, l'Hercule, le Mercier, l'Hirondel, & le Soucy.

Allant d'icy à la Guadeloupe, la flote marchera avec ordre, & à la pointe du jour, la Nostre-Dame se détachera de l'escadre de l'Amiral, & . . . se détachera pareillement de l'escadre de Messieurs des Estats, pour aller une lieuë devant la flote à la découverte, & se rejoindront à la flote sur le soir.

Toute la flote partant de la Guadeloupe, tâchera de passer au vent de Mont Sarra, & reglera sa marche, en sorte qu'elle puisse arriver au petit jour à la pointe du Sud-Est de Nieve.

Si les ennemis demeurent à la Rade, et ne mettent pas sous voile, lors que la flote sera à la pointe du Sud sur ou Est, elle changera son ordre de marche: & chaque vaisseau à la file, serrera la terre, la sonde à la main, le plus près de la baye qu'elle pourra, pour passer au plus loin à la portée du pistolet des navires mouïllez, afin de les pouvoir empécher en mettant à la voille, de tenir le vent sur nous. Tous les navires passants de file, donneront leur bordée & iront le plus avant qu'ils pourront dans la baye de Nieve. Les Armes d'Angleterre tiendra la teste de tout, suivi du Florissant, puis de l'Amiral & du reste de son escadre: celle de Messieurs des Estats suivis aussi de file; & dans cette manoeuvre, les deux bruslots prendront le dessous du vent, & dans cette marche, les navires iront serré beaupré sur poupe avec le moins de distance qu'ils pourront.

Que si dans le temps de cette manoeuvre, les ennemis mettoient à la voille pour tomber à vaut le vent de la seconde escadre, la premiere escadre reviendra sur les ennemis, faisant ses efforts pour tomber entre la terre & eux, & les mettre sous le vent; ce qui ne se fera qu'après que l'Amiral aura reviré.

Que si les ennemis mettent à la voile avant que la flote eust doublé la pointe de Nieve du Sud sur ou Est, chaque navire serrera la terre le plus proche qu'il pourra, pour l'oster avec le vent aux ennemis.

Que si la flote venoit à passer sous le vent de la nostre, pour tâcher de nous gagner le vent à la seconde bordée, chacun fera ses efforts pour aborder le navire ennemi le plus proche, & si-tost qu'un navire sera à bord, il sera secouru par le navire qui le pourra faire le plus commodement, lequel rabordera nostre vaisseau pour jetter son monde dedans, & dans cette manoeuvre, les bruslots feront leurs efforts pour afin de border les navires ennemis s'il se peut.

En cas que les ennemis demeurent mouïllez, ou se tirent sous leurs bateries, la flote ira le plus loin qu'elle pourra dans la baye de Nieve, où elle tiendra Conseil.

Separation et ordre de la marche des vaisseaux.

L'Amiral aura pour ses deux matelots les Armes d'Angleterre et le Florissant.

Le Vice-Amiral aura pour son matelot le Saint Christophle.

Le Contre-Amiral aura pour son matelot l'Harmonie.

Ordre de la Marche.

Les Armes d'Angleterre & le Florissant tiendront la teste, & sur tout, ils seront suivis de l'Amiral.

Le Vice-Amiral suivra l'Amiral avec son matelot; il sera suivi de la Nostre-Dame & du Marsoüin.

Le Contr'Amiral avec son matelot fera l'arriere-Garde de l'Escadre Françoise.

Le bruslost le Cher Ami, se tiendra au vent de l'Amiral, proche & un peu sur son arriere.

L'Amiral de Messieurs des Estats, fera la marche & la division de son escadre.

Les barques armées & autres bastiments se tiendront un peu sous le vent de la flote, s'ils n'ont ordre au contraire.

Signaux pour la Marche.

L'Amiral voulant faire voile de jour defreslera son artimon, & tirera un coup de canon; chacun des vaisseaux defreslera son artimon, & se mettra en estat de le suivre. Si c'est de nuit, tirera un coup de canon, & allumera deux feux à son arriere; chacun des vaisseaux en allumera un qu'il esteindera lors que tous les vaisseaux seront en route et hors d'estat de s'aborder, à l'exception de l'Amiral de Messieurs des Estats qui tiendra son feu allumé.

S'il arrive que l'Amiral veuïlle mouïller de nuit, il tirera deux coups de canon à peu de temps l'un de l'autre, mettra trois feux à l'arriere & un sur son beaupré, afin d'éviter les abordages; chacun des navires en mettra à l'arriere & un sur le beaupré, et mouïllera avec ordre.

Si un des navires de la flote apperçoit quelques navires, il mettra pavillon rouge, & tirera un coup de canon.

Lors que l'Amiral voudra que l'on donne chasse à quelques navires qui auront esté reconnus, mettra son pavillon rouge, & sa flamme blanche au dessus.

Si l'Amiral veut rappeller un ou plusieurs navires de la chasse, il mettra pavillon blanc & tirera un coup de canon.

S'il arrive accident de jour à quelque navire, il mettra coste en travers & son pavillon blanc, & carguera sa grande voille, auquel signal les vaisseaux les plus proches arriveront sur luy pour le secourir.

Que s'il arrivoit accident de nuit, ou que par le mauvais temps ou autrement, un navire se trouvast trop éloigné de sa flote, il tirera un coup de canon & mettra plusieurs feux dans ses hauts bancs, auquel signal toute la flote arrivera sur luy.

Si un navire estant écarté de sa flote la rencontroit, pour la reconnoistre sans estre connu, il arisera les deux huniers tout bas mettra pavillon blanc, & luy sera respondu par le navire le plus proche de luy en carguant ses deux basses voilles, mettra un pavillon rouge; & sera observé que si la flote est au vent, un de ses vaisseaux fera le premier le signal; que si le vaisseau écarté est au vent, il le fera le premier.

S'il se mesloit de nuit quelque navire dans la flote; pour le reconnoistre, il sera demandé d'où est le navire: à quoi il doit répondre *d'Orleans trever*, & à la demande qu'il fera, sera répondu *Daparis Roterdam*; que si le navire ne donnoit cette réponse, il sera tenu pour ennemi & suspect; & pour le faire connoistre à la flote, tirera un coup de canon, mettra un feu à sa poupe.

Signaux pour le combat.

Le signal du combat sera le pavillon rouge à l'arriere de l'Amiral, auquel chacun des vaisseaux, mettant pavillon rouge, prendra son poste pour suivre les ordres qu'il doit tenir dans le combat, observant exactement le matelotage.

Lors que l'Amiral mettra la flamme rouge au haut de son mats d'artimon, les bruslots appresteront leurs artifices, & celuy qui doit suivre l'Amiral s'approchera de luy, tenant le vent, afin de pouvoir aborder sous son feu le navire ennemi que l'Amiral attaquera; & lors que l'Amiral voudra qu'il aborde ledit navire, il ostera sadite flamme du haut mats d'artimon, & la fera mettre au haut de la vergue d'artimon.

Lors que l'Amiral mettra sa flamme rouge au haut de sa vergue d'artimon, le Vice-Amiral, le Florissant & le Saint Christophle envoyeront leurs chaloupes à bord bien équipées armées de soldats avec piques & armes à feu, pour soûtenir le bruslot, et empécher que les chaloupes ennemies ne luy deffendent l'abordage.

Que si dans le combat un navire apperçoit un brûlot ennemi venant sur luy, il mettra son pavillon rouge en berne, & en ce moment les chaloupes des vaisseaux les plus proches, iront à eux en toute diligence avec leurs gafes & grapins pour tâcher de détourner le brûlot, et le faire arriver, & empécher qu'il ne puisse aborder nostre navire.

Lors que l'Amiral voudra que les navires aborderont ceux des ennemis, il mettra sa flamme rouge au haut de son pavillon de grand mats, auquel signal chacun des vaisseaux fera son devoir d'aborder son ennemi, et les matelots de l'Amiral le seconderont de tout leur pouvoir, ainsi que les autres matelots des pavillons.

Si un navire estoit blessé dans le combat en ses mats & vergues, en sorte qu'il fust en estat de tomber sous le vent il mettra la flamme à la vergue de fougue, auquel signal le plus prochain navire luy donnera le cap d'ermorgue, pour l'oster d'entre les mains de l'ennemi.

Que si un navire est blessé au corps & qu'il fasse trop d'eau, & soit en peril de couler bas, il mettra en pavillon aux hauts bancs d'artimon, auquel signal les plus prochains navires envoyront leurs chaloupes équipées de matelots et charpentiers, le plus prochain navire donnant pareillement le cap d'ermorgue.

Lors que l'Amiral voudra les barques pour venir à luy recevoir ses ordres, il mettra sa flamme blanche au haut du mats de misane, auquel signal toutes les barques viendront pour recevoir ses ordres.

Lors que l'Amiral voudra tenir Conseil, il mettra sa flamme blanche au perroquet d'artimon, auquel signal tous les Capitaines de la flote se rendront à bord.

Que si dans le combat, l'Amiral juge à propos de faire retraite, il ostera son pavillon de la poupe, & mettra pavillon blanc, auquel signal chacun des vaisseaux suivra la manoeuvre de l'Amiral, se retirant sans confusion, & arrivant sans fuite; ensorte que les ennemis ne puissent prendre avantage de nostre retraite.

The aforesaid orders were amended four days later, on May 18, as follows:

Les Capitaines des navires sont avertis, que dans le commencement du combat, chacun doit mettre pavillon blanc pour combattre sous iceluy.

Que le signal lors que l'on appercevra un brûlot, sera du pavillon blanc en berne, au lieu du pavillon rouge.

Et que le signal de retraite sera la flamme rouge à l'Amiral sous le pavillon blanc.

From Dutertre, *Histoire générale des Ant-Isles*, IV, 221-27.

APPENDIX X

Agreement to deliver 4,000 slaves to the island of Curaçao, May 18, 1668.

In the Name of the Lord, Amen. In the year of Our Lord Jesus Christ 1668, on the 18th day of May, there appeared before me Pieter Panhuysen, public notary, admitted by the Court of Holland, residing at Amsterdam, the undermentioned witnesses Nicolaes van Beeck and Jan Erpecum, Directors of the Chartered West India Company of the Chamber of this town, committed by its honorable college especially for this purpose, which college is also authorized to make this agreement by the Board of XIX, on the one side, and Francisco Ferony, merchant within the aforesaid town, as proxy and agent of Mr. Domingo Grillo and Mr. Ambrosio Lomelin, residing at Madrid, together with their successive orders, shown to me notarized in the original, on the other side, and declared the aforementioned parties to have agreed and accorded with each other in the following way, to wit:

That the aforementioned Directors, residing here, from time to time will equip and send off successively a sufficient number of ships with sufficient cargoes in order to trade on the coast of Africa, to gather a number of 4000 deliverable slaves, namely pieces of India, to be transported within this current year 1668, and the next year 1669, to Curaçao before December 31 of that same year, to be delivered by the order of the aforementioned Grillo and Lomelin; which aforesaid 4000 Negroes will be received and paid by said Grillo and Lomelin on said island (if they are delivered within the aforementioned period of December 31 1669 and otherwise not) in a way that will be explained hereafter.

That, in addition, the aforementioned gentlemen Directors may deliver above the aforesaid 4000 Negroes another 500, who must be received and paid for at the same price and conditions as the aforesaid 4000.

That among the aforesaid slaves there will be no one bought in the Rio Calbary, del Rey or Camaronis, and that all those who have no considerable defect and are healthy, not blind, lame nor broken, will be considered as deliverable slaves.

That, in regard to age, the calculation will be made in such a way that those who are from 15 to 36 years old will be considered to be a deliverable piece of India, and those who are under 15 years of age to 8 years, three persons will be considered for two pieces of India, and those who are under 8 years to 4 years old will be considered 2 persons for one piece of India, and those under 4 years of age will follow the mother. And said Grillo and Lomelin will not be compelled to receive any Negroes or slaves older than 36 years, while also the Company will not be compelled to deliver these.

That, in regard of sex, three-quarters of the slaves to be delivered have to be men, and the other one-quarter women in such a manner that the said Grillo and Lomelin will not be compelled to receive above the aforesaid fourth part any more women, it being the condition that if the said Directors would deliver some more men above the aforesaid three fourth part, that in such a case, for each man (piece of India) who will be delivered above the aforesaid three fourth part, they will be paid 7 pieces of eight more than for the others.

That the said Grillo and Lomelin must provide their factors with sufficient orders and establish them on the aforementioned island of Curaçao to receive the aforesaid slaves and to pay them, which factors are compelled to visit, within fourteen days after the arrival of each ship, the newly arrived slaves and to separate the deliverable from the undeliverable; which being done the aforesaid Directors will be compelled to maintain the said Negroes who are found to be deliverable for another twenty-four days, being together 38 days after the arrival of each ship at their cost and risk, without being permitted to pretend anything for this, not in regard to death or provisions or support from the aforesaid Grillo and Lomelin, but will be permitted to have the disposal of those who were not considered to be deliverable immediately after the separation, to send them away or to sell them, as they will find most convenient for their profits.

That said Directors, after the aforementioned 38 days, if necessary, will be compelled to support the aforesaid deliverable slaves, who are separated, with food and drink and take upon them the risk of death for a period of three months, thus will the said Grillo and Lomelin, at the time that the aforesaid separated slaves will be delivered to them, pay (in addition to the purchase price of every deliverable piece of India after the said thirty-eighth day after the arrival of each ship) for board, six nickels daily and continue to pay this fee until the expiration of three months if these slaves are not delivered within the said three months; and after the expiration of those three months being delivered until the day of delivery, as hereunder further it shall be described, being it understood that Grillo and Lomelin will not have to pay, any longer, the board of those Negroes who will have died up to the day of each death, nor be compelled to pay any compensation for the deceased Negroes; wherefore the Vice-Director of the Company at Curaçao, each time one of the said Negroes dies, will notify the factors of said Grillo and Lomelin and prove this, so that pertinent notice of this can be given; and, in case of the absence of said factors, the notice of the aforementioned Vice-Director, if sufficiently verified, shall be warranted by two or three witnesses.

Thus, that after the expiration of the said three months, and in case the said separated deliverable Negroes are not picked up or paid for, the said Directors, if they think it advisable, will be obligated no longer to keep those Negroes for Grillo and Lomelin on the island of Curaçao, but will be permitted to dispose of them at their pleasure and at their highest profit with this understanding: that after the aforesaid three months, if a ship of said Grillo and Lomelin arrives at the island with enough cash, before said Directors will have disposed of those Negroes by sale or transportation, said Grillo and Lomelin will be compelled to receive those Negroes, and said Directors to deliver them, on the conditions as mentioned in this contract; then Grillo and Lomelin will be compelled to pay board, at the price given previously, from the thirty-eighth day until the delivery, and the Directors will be compelled to prove that they have disposed of the Negroes after the expiration of three months if they are asked to do so by Grillo and Lomelin.

That said Directors are permitted to employ the said separated deliverable Negroes for the whole said period on the island of Curaçao to their profit, as they will judge advisable, without, however, receiving said board, provided that, if the factors of Grillo and Lomelin require delivery and pay the purchase and board, the said Vice-Director will release the Negroes immediately.

That said Grillo and Lomelin, for each Negro of India, i.e. the Negroes separated on the fourteenth day and found deliverable at the time of the delivery and which are delivered, as above, must pay to the Company, or at its order, besides the delivery, 107$^{1}/_{2}$ pieces of eight of full value; thus said Grillo and Lomelin will be exempt and free of the recognition for every out going slave, ordered by the meeting of the Nineteen, that must be paid and of all other taxes imposed by the Company in respect to the blacks.

That the aforementioned Directors will not sell any of the slaves separated by the factors of Grillo and Lomelin, nor any others, to the crews of the ships of said Grillo and Lomelin, and further, that the Directors will order the aforementioned Vice-Director to prohibit, by publication, all and every one of the inhabitants of the island of Curaçao, on heavy penalty, to sell or deliver any slave to the crews of said ships.

That the aforesaid Directors will prohibit explicitly all skippers of ships, namely those who have not yet sailed from this town before this date and who will be employed for the transportation of the aforesaid Negroes, to touch upon the Caribbean islands unless there is great necessity, and only after this shall have been approved by the whole ship's council; much less may they trade some Negroes or disembark them there. The skippers, for the sake of more security, will have signed a bill of lading by which these slaves will be consigned to the Vice-Director of the island of Curaçao, which bill of lading, at the arrival of the ships at Curaçao, will be handed to the aforesaid factor; and all the aforesaid skippers will especially affirm the usual certificate of the Company's employees (of which, at the bottom of this contract a copy will be added) that they will commit themselves further, by special deed, to do nothing against the aforesaid order and law on penalty of loss of the aforesaid slaves, their monthly payments, their part in the ship and part in the cargoes on behalf of the aforesaid Directors and Grillo and Lomelin half and half to pay out of this as far as it will go the expenses, damages and interests and because of the indemnization and payment of further expenses, damages and interests the aforesaid skippers will commit themselves and their further goods.

That the Directors will be compelled, each time a ship, in compliance with the aforesaid contract departs, to give notice here to the agent of aforesaid Grillo and Lomelin and make known the names, in order to take with them instruction to the aforesaid factors on Curaçao, especially those ships which depart from this town after this date; to give notice to the aforesaid agent of those which have already departed.

That, further, all differences and questions which will rise between the Vice-Director and the factors of Grillo and Lomelin, because of the quantity and the quality of the Negroes and the aforesaid board money will be arranged amicably by four good men, to be chosen two by each side, with authority if necessary to assume a super-arbiter, who must terminate the aforesaid differences within the period of 14 days and decide them, without it being permitted, because of the aforesaid differences, to hold up the already delivered Negroes or ships of the aforesaid Grillo and Lomelin; but, if in addition to the aforementioned specified points some other differences on the present contract may arise—though it is hoped not—these points will be sent over to be decided here by good men as arbiters chosen by both parties or in the absence of this by the honorable court of this town, to whose decision both parties will submit themselves, because of which the aforesaid Grillo and Lomelin, not making the necessary order to their defense, will be summoned by writs of sub-poena and then the problem may be proceeded upon by the aforesaid arbiters.

That the honorable Directors will order the Vice-Director of Curaçao, to receive and treat the factors of the aforesaid Grillo and Lomelin with all proper courtesies as well as assist them in all in which they might require his assistance, such as to promote their business as well as to maintain their respect and authority to everyone, even to their own people, if need be with force, and generally to contribute everything to their persons which is required by civility and may serve to the conservation of good relations and friendship.

And so that everything may proceed with better confidence and mutual accord it is further agreed that the slaves of the ship St. Jago, departed in November from Zeeland and not reported by the aforesaid Grillo and Lomelin through an oversight before it had left port, in settlement of the contract of May 16, will be received by the factors on the island of Curaçao, as if it had been reported at the apropriate time, and that for that purpose, after signing, this order from the aforesaid Francino Ferony will be handed to the aforesaid Directors to be sent by different ways as soon as possible, with this understanding, however, that such orders arrive in time and before (by way of contract or otherwise) the Negroes of said ship St. Jago might have been disposed of at Curaçao or the same have already been bought by the factors of Grillo and Lomelin.

Finally, it has been agreed upon between the contracting parties in this, namely the Directors of the aforesaid Chartered West India Company's Chamber here, on approval of the XIX and Mr. Francisco Ferony on approval of Grillo and Lomelin, that the aforesaid Directors will deliver from December 31, 1669 and before December 1670 another party of 4000 or 4500 slaves to the place aforementioned, and on conditions as in this contract, and that the said Grillo and Lomelin will receive them, and that within 2 months after this date the contracting parties must declare themselves to each other in terms of approval of this or that their silence will be accepted as a total consent.

And in fulfillment of what is written above both parties aforesaid commit themselves, namely the aforesaid Directors with all the effects and means of the aforesaid Company and the aforesaid Ferony and Co. because of his aforesaid power of attorney and successive orders, effects and means of the aforesaid Grillo and Lomelin, putting all those under the jurisdiction of all justice and courts in good confidence.

Thus done within Amsterdam, present Johannes Voordaege and Jan . . . van Collen, as witnesses asked for this purpose.

From van Brakel, "Bescheiden over den slavenhandel der West Indische Compagnie," pp. 66-73.

NOTES

(Some of the titles are abbreviated. We refer to the bibliography.)

ABBREVIATIONS

ABA	Admiralty Board Amsterdam
ABZ	Admiralty Board Zeeland
AGI	Archivo General de Indias, Seville
AHA	American Historical Association
AJHS	American Jewish Historical Society
ARA	Algemeen Rijksarchief, The Hague
Aud.	Audiencia
BH	Baltische Hefte
BHPR	Boletín Histórico de Puerto Rico
BMHG	Bijdragen en Mededelingen van het Historisch Genootschap
BVGO	Bijdragen voor Vaderlandsche Geschiedenis en Oudheidkunde
CC	Casa de Contratación
Col.	Colección
Doc.	Documentos or documents
EA	Estudios Americanos
EHR	English Historical Review
EIC	(Dutch) East India Company
GTLVG	Geschied-, Land-, Taal- en Volkenkundig Genootschap, Curaçao
HAHR	Hispanic American Historical Review
IG	Indiferente General
Inéd.	Inéditos
Inv.	Inventaris or inventory
KHG	Kroniek van het Historisch Genootschap
NC	Nieuwe Compagnie (New Company)
OC	Oude Compagnie (Old Company)
PHR	Pacific Historical Review
PK	Knuttel's Pamphlets' Collection (see bibliography)
Res. Holl.	Resolutions of the Provincial States of Holland (and West Friesland)
Res. Zeel.	Resolutions of the Provincial States of Zeeland
RH	Revue Historique
RSG	Resolutions of the States General
SAA	Stedelijk Archief (City Archives) of Amsterdam
S. Dom.	Santo Domingo
St. Gen.	States General
TvG	Tijdschrift voor Geschiedenis
WIC	West India Company
WIG	West Indische Gids

INTRODUCTION

1 S. Muller's *Mare clausum. Bijdrage tot de geschiedenis der rivaliteit van Engeland en Nederland in de zeventiende eeuw* (Amsterdam, 1872) is one of the few Dutch studies on this subject. French ambassador de Buzanval wrote an interesting memorandum on the freedom of commerce of neutral nations. See G. W. Vreede, *Lettres et négociations de Paul Chouart* (Utrecht, 1846), pp. 365 ff. (hereafter cited as Vreede, *Lettres*). Cf. Charles R. Boxer, *The Dutch Seaborne Empire, 1600-1800* (New York, 1965), pp. 84-112.

2 "Mare Liberum" is Chapter XII of a larger study entitled *De Iure Praedae* to defend the commercial interests of the Dutch East India Company. There were Calvinist merchants whose consciences were burdened by the piratical aspects of this company's activities. See A. Hyma, "Hugo Grotius on the Freedom of the Seas," *Michigan Academy of Science, Arts and Letters*, XXVII (1941), 615-23.

3 Of the many authors who analyze this development and its results for the Iberians we mention José Honório Rodrigues and Joaquim Ribeiro, *Civilização holandesa no Brasil* (São Paulo, 1940).

4 Emanvel van Meteren, *Belgica. Historie der Nederlandscher ende haerder na-buren oorlogen ende geschiedenissen tot den iare mvi⁰xii* ('s Graven-haghe, 1614), fol. 357.

5 "...des Pausen donatie is idel ende teghens de leeringhe Christi ende teghens de religie." See J. H. de Stoppelaar, *Balthasar de Moucheron* ('s-Gravenhage, 1901), p. 131 and note 3 of Chapter xvi.

6 "Die Niederländer haben sich groszen Ruhm erworben durch den Kampf für das Mare Liberum gegen das Mare Clausum," observes E. Laspeyres in *Geschichte der volkswirtschaftlichen Anschauungen der Niederländer und ihrer Literatur zur Zeit der Republik* (Leipzig, 1863), p. 159. The Dutch ideals, however, were dictated by the purse.

7 W. J. M. van Eysinga, "Een onuitgegeven nota van de Groot," *Mededelingen der Koninklijke Nederlandsche Academie van Wetenschappen. Afdeling Letterkunde* (Amsterdam, 1955), p. 4. It was not the first nor the last time that Grotius became confused. A striking example is his *De veritate religionis christianae*, in which he, an Arminian, tried to prove his puritanism and orthodox faith. See Conrad Busken Huet, *Het Land van Rembrand* (Haarlem, 1886), II, 1, 66, 73.

8 "If to make a sale I had to sail through hell, I would risk the fire in my sails," a Dutch businessman must have said while he sold war material to Antwerp when this town was under siege by Frederik Hendrik, the stadhouder. See J. H. Kernkamp, *De handel op den vijand* (Utrecht, 1931-34).

NOTES TO CHAPTER I

1 J. C. de Jonge, *Geschiedenis van het Nederlandsche zeewezen* (Zwolle, 1869), I, 42 (hereafter cited as De Jonge, *Zeewezen*). Its income was derived from two sources: a convoy and a license tax.

2 For further details see Joseph Lecler, *Histoire de la tolérance au siècle de la Réforme* (Aubier, 1955), II, 163.

3 There is an abundance of literature on this subject. We quoted Cecil J. Cadoux, *Philip of Spain and the Netherlands. An Essay on Moral Judgments in History* (London, Redhill, 1947), p. 133.

4 Santiago Nadal, *Las cuatro mujeres de Felipe II* (Barcelona, 1944), p. 168.

5 There is an abundance of literature on Philip. Rafael Altamira y Crevea, *Ensayo*

sobre Felipe II, hombre de estado; su psicología general y su individualidad humana (México, 1950), probably gives the fullest treatment.

6 A. J. Namèche, *Guilleaume le Taciturne, Prince d'Orange et la révolution des Pays-Bas au XVIe siècle* (Louvain, 1890), I, 48.

7 We chose the expression of John W. Mears, *The Beggars of Holland and the Grandees of Spain* (Philadelphia, 1867), p. 114.

8 Guilleaume Groen van Prinsterer *et al.*, eds., *Archives ou correspondance inédite de la Maison d'Orange-Nassau* (Leide, Utrecht, 1835-1915). Although an ardent Calvinist the editor is probably the most impartial in his judgment. See the introductions to the first volumes of this work.

9 "...van vernuftheyt oft verstande en was hij bij sijnen Vader ofte Voorouders niet the ghelycken...gheneycht tot melancolie, afgunstich, nydich, seer diep ghe-veynst." Van Meteren, fol. 418.

10 "Car ne désirons oultre chose de vous que le seul exercice de la foi et Religíon Catholique Romaine," he wrote to the magistrates of Bourbourg. See Ph. A. Kervyn de Volkaersbeke and J. Diegerick, *Documents inédits concernant les troubles des Pays-Bas, 1577-1584* (Gand, 1847-50), I, 82.

11 Cardinal de la Cueva to the king's grandson, Philip IV, observes this fact again: "...y siendo, como es certisimo, que la mayor paıte destos paises consideran a Vuestra Magestad por estrangero." Cf. S. P. L'Honoré Naber and Irene A. Wıight, eds., *Piet Heyn en de Zilvervloot* (Utrecht, 1928), p. *113 (hereafter cited as Naber/Wright, *Piet Heyn*).

12 Cadoux, p. 159.

13 R. H. Tawney, *Religion and the Rise of Capitalism* (London, 1944), p. 100.

14 L. J. Rogier, *Eenheid en Scheiding* (Nijmegen, 1952), p. 62. Vol. II in *Geschiedenis der Nederlanden*, L. G. J. Verberne *et al.*, eds.

15 "Dès l'an 1527, la Hollande et la Zélande étaient sans le savoir entachées d'hérésie," writes D. Stern, *Histoire des commencements de la République des Pays-Bas, 1581-1625* (Paris, 1872), p. 44.

16 *Ibid.*, p. 80.

17 *Ibid.*, p. 81.

18 Lecler, II, 168.

19 Rogier, p. 88. Another Catholic historian called him "le grand Duc d'Albe." See J. B. M. C. Kervyn de Lettenhove, *Les Huguenots et les Gueux* (Bruges, 1883-85), II, 21, 22; W. Kirchner, "The Duke of Alva Reconsidered," *PHR*, XIV (1945), 64-70.

20 Jean P. E. Jurien de la Gravière, *Les gueux de mer* (Paris, 1893), p. 7.

21 Johan van den Sande, *De waeckende leeuw der Nederlanden* (Amsterdam, 1663), p. 15.

22 Pieter C. Bor, *Oorsprongk, begin ende vervolgh der Nederlandsche oorlogen, beroerten en borgerlyke oneenigheden* (Amsterdam, 1679-84), I, 114.

23 The presentation of a petition for moderation by the League of Nobles in 1566 frightened the governess Margaret, but her advisor Barlaimont soothed her with the observation "Que s'alarme-t-on d'un tas de gueux?" The word *gueux*—in Dutch *geuzen*, in English beggars—became a title of honor.

24 Busken Huet, II, 1, 38.

25 De Jonge, *Zeewezen*, p. 119.

26 "Un seul élément de résistance à la domination espagnole reste debout et va grandir jusqu'à devenir le plus efficace et le plus redoutable: ce sont les Gueux de mer." Lettenhove, II, 408.

27 A. Renaudet, *Les Pays-Bas espagnols et les Provinces-Unies de 1508 à 1714* (Paris, 1960), p. 13.

28 Gravière, p. 107.

29 "Il faut infiniment mieux conserver par la guerre pour Dieu et pour le roi un royaume appauvri et même ruiné que, sans la guerre, l'avoir entier pour le démon et les hérétiques ses sectateurs." See Lecler, II, 171. Philip and Alva were more intransigent than the pope, Gregory XIII, who "aurait même voulu comprendre dans l'amnestie le Prince d'Orange et les autres chefs de la révolte, mais se heurta sur ce point à l'intransigeance du roi." *Ibid.*, p. 173.

30 Margriet, Jeroons huisvrouwe en Janneken op Dexterlaer,
Claerken was oock getrouwe, Op den Steen verdronken, niet openbaer,
In de Scheldt geworpen, daernaer. Daer heeft men se sien drijven
Op 't water, met schoone witte lijven. Dat bleeck wel alsoo claer.
Geuzenliedtboeck, many editions, with an abundance of Beggar songs.

31 L. P. Gachard, *Correspondance de Philippe II sur les affaires des Pays-Bas* (Bruxelles, 1848-79), I, cxlvii.

32 Stern, pp. 61, 62.

33 Gerard van Loon, *Beschrijving der Nederlandsche Histori-penningen* ('s-Gravenhage, 1723-31), II, 104. See also Pieter C. Hooft, *Nederlandse historien*, M. Nijhoff, ed. (Amsterdam, 1947), p. 118.

34 Onno Zwier van Haren, *De Geuzen*, edited by Arnold Stakenburg (Santpoort, 1943).

35 Hooft, p. 169.

36 For contemporary authors: Bor, Van Meteren, Hooft.

37 Roger Avermaete, *Guilleaume le Taciturne, 1533-1584* (Paris, 1939), p. 8.

38 Henri Pirenne, *Histoire de Belgique*, Vol. IV (Bruxelles, 1911), p. 26. Thus we translated *finesse* and *ténacité*.

39 *Ibid.*, IV, 26 ff.

40 "Hij hadde alle gaven om een Ghemeente te leyden," Everhard van Reyd, *Historie der Nederlantscher oorlogen* (Amsterdam, 1644), p. 81. The Calvinist preacher Dathenus called the Prince an atheist. Cf. Van Meteren, fol. 229: "Een bequaem instrument van den hooghen Godt."

41 Hooft, p. 358: "Immers, dit zal niemand loochenen, dat geen vorst onder de zon ooit vuriger bemind en hoger geacht mocht worden van zijn onderdanen dan Zijne Doorluchtigheid geweest is van de Hollanders en Zeeuwen."

42 Pieter de la Court (and Johan de Witt), *The True Interest and Political Maxims of the Republick of Holland and West Friesland* (n.p., 1702) expresses this feeling on several pages of this work.

43 A. P. van Groningen, *Geschiedenis der Watergeuzen* (Leiden, 1840), pp. 39, 57-60.

44 The fall of Brielle is an important landmark in the history of the Dutch war of independence; it electrified the country into open rebellion against Spain.

45 This is maintained by such authorities as P. L. Muller, *De Staat der Vereenigde Nederlanden in de jaren zijner wording 1572-1594* (Haarlem, 1872) and denied by others like J. van Vloten, *Nederlands opstand tegen Spanje in zijn eerste wording en ontwikkeling, 1567-1572* (Haarlem, 1858), who in II, 212, talks of "de steeds toenemende krachten der Geuzen."

46 Muller, *De Staat*, p. 165.

47 Said by the pope after the battle of Lepanto and repeated in 1576. Cf. Hooft, p. 231, Van den Sande, p. 29.

48 Lettenhove, IV, 496 ff.

[49] Lecler, II, 174.

[50] *Ibid.*, p. 177.

[51] Avermaete, *Guilleaume le Taciturne*, p. 249.

[52] Stern, p. 164.

[53] The role played by the Sea-Beggars in the defeat of the Armada has escaped many historians. Cf. de Jonge, *Zeewezen*, I, 137 ff.

[54] P. Bizot, *Histoire métallique de la république de Hollande* (Paris, 1687), p. 61: "You God are great and You do great things." See also Van Loon, I, 390-92.

[55] L. Pfandl, *Philip II. Gemälde eines Lebens und einer Zeit* (München, 1938), p. 457.

[56] Robert J. Fruin, *Tien jaren uit den tachtigjarigen oorlog, 1588-1598* (Amsterdam, 1861).

[57] Vreede, *Lettres*, pp. 50, 120, 139, *et passim*.

[58] José de Viera y Clavijo, *Noticias de la historia general de las islas de Canaria* (Madrid, 1772-83), III, 179-88, gives a romantic account of the Dutch attack. The best Dutch account is from Ellert de Jonghe, *Waerachtigh verhael van de machtighe scheeps-armada...onder het ghebiet en gheleyt van Joncker Pieter van der Does* (Amsterdam, 1600). Good Dutch accounts are in Bor, III, 565 ff., Van Meteren, fol. 426 ff., De Jonge, *Zeewezen*, I, 204 ff., and J. H. Abendanon, "De vlootaanval van Jhr. Pieter van der Does op de Canarische eilanden en het eiland Santo Thomé," *BVGO*, v, 8 (1921), 14-63.

[59] Strangely enough he found aboard one of the prizes taken by him an Amsterdam merchant, Laurens Bicker, who two years earlier had outfitted two ships to Guinea and the Río de la Plata and was imprisoned while his crew was killed. Bicker himself was on his way to Lisbon for an *auto da fe*. Van Reyd, p. 604.

[60] De Jonge, *Zeewezen*, I, 208 ff. Cf. *ARA*, *ABA*, 1353/1607, Jan. 22 and Nov. 28.

[61] R. Avermaete, *Les gueux de mer et la naissance d'une nation* (Bruxelles, 1944), p.164.

NOTES TO CHAPTER II

[1] Busken Huet, II, 1, 54.

[2] Bor, I, 664. Psalm 118:23.

[3] Busken Huet, II, 1, 65.

[4] Irene A. Wright, "The Dutch and Cuba," *HAHR*, IV (1921), 609.

[5] Pierre Chaunu, "Les crises au XVIIe siècle de l'Europe réformée," *RH*, LXXXIX (Janvier-Mars, 1965), 23-60.

[6] Busken Huet, II, 1, 47.

[7] A. Hyma, *The Dutch in the Far East* (Ann Arbor, Mich., 1942), pp. 16, 17. Population figures are, of course, estimates and lack accuracy.

[8] P. J. Blok, "De handel op Spanje en het begin der groote vaart," *BVGO*, v, 1 (1913), 119.

[9] Theodorus Velius, *Chronijck van Hoorn* (Hoorn, 1740), as quoted by Blok, p. 104.

[10] Bor, II, 623.

[11] In 1595 when commercial relations with Spain, in spite of the rebellion, were flowering again, a new arrest of the aging Philip II caused consternation in the United Provinces. More than 400 ships with their crews were seized. The Archduke Albert of the Southern Netherlands offered mediation and the arrest was canceled. In 1598, under Philip III, a third arrest was tried to give the rebels "quelque goust de son gouvernement."

12 J. K. J. de Jonge, *De opkomst van het Nederlandsch gezag in Oost-Indië* (s-'Gravenhage, 1862-95), I, 70 ff.

13 *Ibid.*, p. 162. Frisius' work was published in 1550.

14 This very interesting field is, as far as Dutch participation goes, not much explored. Florentinus van Langeren, Jodocus Hondius and Adriaen Veen were among the most prominent Dutch investigators. *Ibid.*, pp. 56-90, 161-200.

15 The allegation of the Belgian refugees that the North became what it was through the invasion of the "Brabanders" is discussed in J. L. M. Eggen, *De invloed door Zuid-Nederland op Noord-Nederland uitgeoefend op het einde der XVIe en het begin der XVIIe eeuw* (Gent, 1908).

16 Pirenne, IV, 407-44.

17 Our authority was S. P. L'Honoré Naber, *Reizen van Willem Barentsz, Jacob van Heemskerck, Jan Cornelisz de Rijp en anderen naar het noorden* ('s-Gravenhage, 1917).

18 A. J. van der Aa, *Biographisch woordenboek der Nederlanden* (Haarlem, 1852-78), II, 5, p. 42.

19 P. A. Tiele, *Mémoire bibliographique sur les journaux des navigateurs néerlandais* (Amsterdam, 1867), pp. 184-85.

20 For the various expeditions all over the globe the "Linschoten Vereniging"—the Dutch equivalent of the Hakluyt Society—has published an abundance of material. See on Pomp, J. W. IJzerman, *Dirck Gerritsz Pomp, alias Dirck China, de eerste Nederlander die China en Japan bezocht* ('s-Gravenhage, 1915).

21 Paludanus, the latinized form of the Dutch *broek* (*moeras*-swamp).

22 *ARA, ABA*, 1343/1597, September 2. Cf. J. K. J. de Jonge, *Opkomst*, I, 4. See also Jan Huyghen van Linschoten, *Itinerario voyage ofte schipvaert van Jan Huyghen van Linschoten naer Oost ofte Portugaels Indien, 1579-1592*, H. Kern, ed. ('s-Gravenhage, 1910), pp. lxvii-lxxi. The cited lines are from Th. Velius: *Per te nunc Batavis Indos lustramos ab orbis*, p. xciv.

23 We have already mentioned Ellert de Jonghe's *Waerachtigh verhael*. The Dutch titles of the other journals are: Joris van Spilbergen, *'t Historiael Journael van tghene ghepasseert is van weghen dry schepen ghenaemt den Ram, Schaap ende het Lam* (Delft, 1601); Hendrick Ottsen, *Journael oft daghelycx register van de voyagie na Rio de Plata, ghedaen met het schip ghennoemt de Silveren Werelt...* (Amstelredam, 1603); and Willem Lodewijcksz, *De eerste schipvaert naer Indien*, and a second edition *Historie van Indien, waer inne verhaelt is de avonturen die de Hollandtsche schepen bejeghent zijn...* (Amsterdam, 1598).

24 S. P. L'Honoré Naber, ed., *Dierick Ruyters, Toortse der zeevaert* ('s-Gravenhage, 1913).

25 *Ibid.*, pp. xiii.

26 "Ende dewijl Dirck Ruyter hier eenige daghen gheweest heeft zijnen dienst offrerende hebben een bequaem boeck ten dienste van de Compagnie ghemaect..." *ARA, WIC, OC*, 1, Minutes of the XIX 1623-24, Nov. 3, 1623.

27 Ioannes de Laet, *Nieuwe Wereldt ofte beschrijvinghe van West Indien* (Leiden, 1625) (cited as De Laet, *Nieuwe Wereldt*).

28 Grotius in his *Dissertatio de origine gentium Americanarum* sees the Indians as emigrants from Scandinavia. De Laet disagreed.

29 *RSG*, July 29, 1623. The resolutions of the States General from 1576 to 1609 are quoted from Nicolaas Japikse, ed., *Resolutiën van de Staten Generaal, 1576-1609* ('s-Gravenhage, 1915-41). Later resolutions are cited from the *RSG* collections in *ARA*.

30 See on *pichelingues* or *frejelindes* P. A. Euwens, "Wat zijn 'Frejelindes' en 'Frechlingas'?" WIG, XIII (1931), 337-64, and Engel Sluiter, "The Word Pichelingue: Its Derivation and Meaning," *HAHR*, XXIV (1944), 683-98.

31 H. J. Koenen, "Pavonia. Eene bijdrage tot de kennis der voormalige Nederlandsche koloniën," *BVGO*, I, 5 (1847), 120 ff.

32 Wissel means "bill of exchange."

33 French Ambassador Jeannin must have had men like van der Veken in mind when he wrote his remonstrance in favor of the Dutch Catholics: "Ils ont travaillé avec vous, exposé leurs vies et moyens aux mesmes dangers, et toujours gardé une immuable fidélité à l'Estat tant que la guerre a duré." Vreede, *Lettres*, p. 289. Cf. R. Bijlsma, "De opkomst van Rotterdams koopvaardij," *BVGO*, V, 1 (1913), 56-87.

34 Otto van Rees, *Geschiedenis der koloniale politiek van de republiek der Vereenigde Nederlanden* (Utrecht, 1868), p. 10.

35 Johan E. Elias, *Schetsen uit de geschiedenis van ons zeewezen* ('s-Gravenhage, 1916-30), II, 9 (hereafter cited as Elias, *Schetsen*).

36 Van der Aa, III, 8, pp. 28, 29: "Brandende van ijver om de luister en roem zijns vaderlands te bevorderen." There is no biography on these remarkable brothers. For detailed information the printed sources are G. Brandt, *Het leven en bedrijf van den Heere Michiel de Ruiter* (Amsterdam, 1701), and P. J. Blok, *Michiel Adriaenszoon de Ruyter* ('s-Gravenhage, 1947) (cited as Brandt, *De Ruiter*, and Blok, *De Ruyter*).

37 An excellent biography of this gifted merchant given by the South to the North by Stoppelaar, *Balthasar de Moucheron*.

38 See *Reizen van Jan Huyghen van Linschoten naar het noorden, 1594-1598*, S. P. L'Honoré Naber, ed. ('s-Gravenhage, 1914), pp. lxvii and 33.

39 Some details are given in N. G. van Kampen, *Geschiedenis der Nederlanders buiten Europa* (Haarlem, 1831-32), I, 46 ff. (cited as Van Kampen, *Nederlanders*).

40 Willem Usselinx or Usselincx probably is the most exciting and interesting personality of the Belgian refugees. C. Ligtenberg wrote his biography *Willem Usselinx* (Utrecht, 1914). Outstanding and far from outdated is the article written by J. Franklin Jameson, "The Life of Willem Usselinx, Founder of the Dutch and Swedish West India Companies," *AHA*, II (1887), 14. See also Van Rees, pp. 72-143.

41 Van Meteren, fol. 562 ff.

42 Ligtenberg, pp. 20 ff.

43 Van Meteren, fol. 591.

44 See on Francken the biography written by Jan Huges, *Het leven en bedrijf van Mr. Franchois Vranck* ('s-Gravenhage, 1909), and the information given by G. M. Asher, *A Bibliographical and Historical Essay on the Dutch Books and Pamphlets Relating to New Netherland and to the Dutch West India Company* (Amsterdam, 1854-67), p. xviii.

45 Ligtenberg, pp. 24, 25. The most important pamphlets are *PK* 1438: *Bedenckingen Over den staet van de Vereenichde Nederlanden: Nopende de Zeevaert, Coophandel ende de gemeyne Neeringhe in deselve. Ingevalle den Peys met de Aerts-hertogen in de aenstaende Vrede-handelinge getroffen wert* (n.p., 1608); *PK* 1441: *Naerder bedenckingen* (n.p., 1608); and *PK* 1442: *Vertoogh, hoe nootwendich, nut ende profijtelick het sij voor de Ver-eenichde Nederlanden te behouden de Vryheyt van te handelen op West-Indien, In den vrede met den Coninck van Spangien* (n.p., 1608). "Vertoogh" was translated as "Remonstrance."

46 Johan E. Elias, *De vroedschap van Amsterdam, 1578-1795* (Haarlem, 1903-5), I, xliii ff., lxix (cited as Elias, *Vroedschap*).

47 Laspeyres, p. 59.
48 Ligtenberg, p. 27. Cf. Van Rees, p. 99.
49 Van Rees, pp. 102 ff.
50 This was the military budget of the United Provinces for one year before the Truce was concluded.
51 Ligtenberg, pp. 30, 31. Van Rees, pp. 103, 104, 106, 107. Another promotor of the West India Company was not very successful, either. This was Frederick L'Hermitte (or L'Hermite) whose relationship with the well-known Admiral Jacques L'Hermitte could not be established. Frederick L'Hermitte was the author of an anonymous pamphlet entitled *Fin de la Guerre* (see note 55); his request "Points of Discussion" was brought by van Oldenbarnevelt to a meeting of the Provincial States of Holland in 1600, long before Usselinx thought of this method to attract the authorities. It contained a proposal for a company composed of the three already in existence: the East India and Guinea companies and the combination of the Brazil and Caribbean navigators. The result of this official discussion is not known. See *ARA*, WIC, OC, Inv. St. Gen. (West Indië), 5751; the request mentions the author as a "burgher" of Amsterdam. Cf. Ligtenberg, p. 61.
52 Eggen, pp. 42 ff. See also P. Geyl, *The Revolt of the Netherlands, 1555-1609* (London, 1958).
53 Information of a general character is provided by H. Brugmans, *Opkomst en bloei van Amsterdam*, (Amsterdam, 1911); for detailed information see J. G. van Dillen, "Amsterdam's Role in Seventeenth-Century Dutch Politics and its Economic Background," in John S. Bromley and Ernst H. Kossmann, eds., *Britain and the Netherlands* (London, 1960-64), II, 133-48. See also van Dillen, "De West Indische Compagnie, het calvinisme en de politiek," *TvG*, LXXIV (1961), 145-71, and A. Hallema, "Friesland en de voormalige compagnieën voor den handel op Oost en West," *WIG*, XV (1933), 81-96. Investments Aug. 31, 1623: f. 7,108,106,50 of which Amsterdam contributed f. 2,846,582.
54 S. van Brakel, *De Hollandsche handelscompagnieën der zeventiende eeuw, hun ontstaan, hunne inrichting* ('s-Gravenhage, 1908), p. 33. See also Appendix v.
55 PK 3428, *Fin de la guerre* (Amsterdam, n.d.). This pamphlet must have been published in 1608, just before the Truce. It begins with the advice of P. Scipio Africanus to the Romans to cross the sea to Africa to fight against the Carthagians, "dienende tot een exemplaer of spiegel om te bewijsen dat de West Indische interprinse d'eenige ende beste middel is...omdat sijn *nervus belli* macht ende kracht bestaet in sijn rijcke gout ende silver mijnen ende andere rijkdommen in West Indien."
56 Ligtenberg, p. 61. Cf. Van Rees, pp. 305 ff. These is another interesting pamphlet, published fifty years later by an anonymous author, *'t Verheelickte Nederland door d'herstelde zeevaert* (n.p., 1659), in which the suggestion is made to bestow alms on invalids and children but to compel all men who are in good health and still depend on charity to emigrate. PK 8176.
57 These paragraphs summarize the ideas given in Usselinx' pamphlets mentioned before, and what Jameson, Ligtenberg, and Van Rees wrote about this subject. Interesting information is found in Otto Keye, *Het waere onderscheyt tusschen koude en warme landen* ('s-Graven Hage, 1659). We used a German translation: *Kurtzer Entwurff von Neu-Niederland und Guajana, einander entgegengesetzt umb den Unterschied zwischen warmen und kalten Landen herausz zu bringen* (Leipzig, 1672), p. 141.

58 Van Rees, pp. 140-41. See also Ligtenberg, pp. 235-36. C. R. Boxer, *The Dutch in Brazil* (Oxford, 1957), p. 2, rightly pointed out that Usselinx' basic idea was sound: that Dutch agricultural colonies should be settled in the New World, giving the mother country a valuable and expanding market.

59 R. C. Bakhuizen van den Brink, *Studiën en schetsen over vaderlandsche geschiedenis en letteren* (Amsterdam, 1860-1913), IV, 290. Elias, *Vroedschap*, I, xliv, introduces the term *mercator sapiens* for the type of merchants discussed in this chapter. Cf. R. J. Fruin's *Verspreide geschriften* ('s-Gravenhage, 1900-1905), III, 279.

NOTES TO CHAPTER III

1 G. Arciniegas, *Caribbean, Sea of the New World* (New York, 1946), pp. 3 ff.

2 G. Freyre, *The Masters and the Slaves* (New York, 1964), p. 83.

3 Stefan Zweig, *Amerigo Vespucci* (Stockholm, 1944), p. 121.

4 Juan de Castellanos, *Elegías de varones ilustres de Indias* (Bogotá, 1955), I, 152.

5 There are many confusing and contradictory statements on these first visits. See Pedro J. Guiteras, *Historia de la isla de Cuba* (Havana, 1865-66), I, 233 ff.; Ramón Guerra y Sánchez, *Manual de historia de Cuba* (Habana, 1938), pp. 61 ff.; and Pierre X. de Charlevoix, *Histoire de l'ile Espagnole ou de S. Domingue* (Paris, 1730-31), I, 404 ff. According to Irene A. Wright, *Documents Concerning English Voyages to the Spanish Main, 1569-1580* (London, 1932), the French made their first appearance in the Caribbean in 1528. See p. xviii, note 1.

6 Wright, *Documents*, passim. Miss Wright's works have the excitement of being directly based on studies in the Spanish archives. Cf. Arturo Morales Carrión, *Puerto Rico and the Non-Hispanic Caribbean* (Puerto Rico, 1952), p. 17, and Richard Hakluyt, *The Principal Navigations, Voyages, Traffiques & Discoveries of the English Nation* (London, 1927-28), x, 6 ff.

7 *CSP*, Colonial Series, West India, I, 1574-1660, p. xi.

8 A. P. Newton, *The European Nations in the West Indies, 1493-1688* (London, 1933), p. 82.

9 C. Fernández Duro, *Armada española desde la unión de los reinos de Castilla y de León* (Madrid, 1895-1903), II, 462 (cited as Duro, *Armada española*); M. Fernández de Navarrete, *Biblioteca marítima española* (Madrid, 1851), II, 586-88 (cited as Navarrete, *Bibl. Mar.*).

10 But he finds defenders like Charles de Lannoy and Herman van der Linden, *Histoire de l'expansion coloniale des peuples européens. Portugal et Espagne* (Bruxelles, Paris, 1907), pp. 315-16.

11 Duro, *Armada española*, III, 184.

12 Newton, p. 82.

13 I. A. Wright, "Rescates, with Special Reference to Cuba, 1599-1610," *HAHR*, III (1920), 333-61.

14 Van Meteren, fol. 11, 12.

15 J. Reygersbergh van Cortgene, *De oude chronijcke ende historien van Zeelandt* (Middelberch, 1634), pp. 286-87.

16 Charles de Lannoy and Herman van der Linden, *Histoire de l'expansion coloniale des peuples européens. Néerlande et Danemark* (Bruxelles, 1911), p. 5.

17 Velius, p. 467.

18 Engel Sluiter, "Dutch-Spanish Rivalry in the Caribbean Area, 1594-1609," *HAHR*, XXVIII (1948), 165-96. They resumed trade and navigation on the Iberian

peninsula under false passports, and Philip II was aware of this but he was forced to admit them in his ports. On this trade, see Kernkamp, *De handel op den vijand*.

19 Vreede, *Lettres*, p. 202, Letter of de Buzanval to Villeroy, June 12, 1598.

20 It is said that the Prince of Orange was fully aware of the fact that the American waters could become an excellent substitute for the North Sea, once his Sea-Beggars' services were no longer required at home. "Der erwähnte Gedanke, der zuerst bei den Franzosen im Zeitalter Franz I auftauchte, wurde während des niederländischen Freiheitskrieges von dem Leutnant-Admiral von Seeland, Willem Blois van Treslong, wieder erlebt." See F. Graefe, "Beiträge zur Geschichte der See-Expeditionen von 1606 und 1607," *BVGO*, VII, 3 (1933), 202.

21 The Cape Verde Islands.

22 Some original dates on these relations are given by J. Nanninga Uitterdijk, *Een Kamper handelshuis te Lissabon, 1572-1594* (Zwolle, 1904), pp. 351 *et passim*. See W. S. Unger, "Nieuwe gegevens betreffende het begin der vaart op Guinea," *EHJ*, XXI (1940), 194-217, and Reygersbergh, p. 286.

23 That this route was the normal one is illustrated by the patent granted to Jacob Floris van Langeren in 1592: "...from these countries to Cabo de Fernambuco in Brazil, to St.Thomé under the equator and Isola del Principe," J. K. J. de Jonge, *Opkomst*, p. 36. See also by this same historian *De oorsprong van Neerlands bezittingen op de kust van Guinea* ('s-Gravenhage, 1871).

24 Stoppelaar, p. 138.

25 G. Brandt, *Historie der vermaerde zee- en koop-stadt Enkhuisen* (Hoorn, 1747), p. 262.

26 J. K. J. de Jonge, *Opkomst*, p. 37.

27 Velius, p. 493. See also Bor, III, 337.

28 Pieter de Marées, *Beschrijvinghe ende historische verhael van het Gout Koninckryck van Gunea anders de Gout-Custe de Mina genaemt leggende in het deel van Africa*, S. P. L'Honoré Naber, ed. ('s-Gravenhage, 1912), p. lvii.

29 J. K. J. de Jonge, *Opkomst*, p. 40.

30 The Dutch knew that Drake's raids on those countries had yielded more than two million guilders (see Bor, III, 336). The resolutions of the States General give interesting details on these enterprises. For instance, *RSG* 1597, Jan. 24, request of Pieter Verhagen (Van der Haghen); March 24, request of Hans van der Veken and Captain Jacob Hendricksz; July 5, request of Hendrick Anthonisz Wissel and company; Sept. 5, request of Gerrit Bicker of Amstelredam; Oct. 14, request of Nicolaes de Haen, merchant of Rotterdam; Dec. 23, request of Johan van Veken and Pieter van der Hage; Dec. 24, request of Olivier van Oirt, Jacob Claesz, Balthasar de Moucheron, and Adriaen Hendricksz ten Haeff. All these merchants asked the States General permission to trade and navigate on the African coast, the East Indies, or the West. This was the prelude of the Dutch outward thrust which started in 1598 and continued in the following years. See also J. H. Kernkamp, *Johan van der Veken en zijn tijd* ('s-Gravenhage, 1952).

31 Appendix 1 gives a report of such a voyage.

32 J. K. J. de Jonge, *Opkomst*, I, 15 ff., 38, 46 ff.

33 Our authority was the biography of Stoppelaar. Details are found in the works of Bor, Van Meteren, and Van Reyd. J. K. J. de Jonge, *Opkomst*, I, 234 ff., Ligtenberg, *passim*, and Lannoy and Van der Linden, pp. 48, 49, summarize the older authors and add details from research in the archives. Joris van Spilbergen took the "Ile d'Elisabeth" close to the Cape of Good Hope and the "Iles de Moucheron" in the Gulf of Guinea.

34 *ARA, ABA,* 1334/1587 to 1344/1598 gives the information on this shipping. See also J. W. IJzerman, "Amsterdamsche bevrachtingscontracten, 1591-1602," *EHJ,* XVII (1931), 163-291.

35 *RSG,* Oct. 2, 1600.

36 *ARA, ABA,* 1351/1605, Feb. 15; 1352/1606, May 9 and Sept. 9; *RSG,* March 10, 1605, and April 14, 1606.

37 Navarrete, *Bibl. Mar.,* I, 450, 470; II, 267-68.

38 *AGI,* CC, 4991, "Autos en dos ramos de la presa que hizo en 10 filibotes el General Francisco Coloma," July 16, 25, 1593. The captains were hanged; most, perhaps all, of the crews ended on the galleys.

39 *Res. Zeel.,* March 11, 1595. Sluiter, "Dutch-Spanish Rivalry," p. 172.

40 *Res. Zeel.,* Nov. 18, 1595. J. K. J. de Jonge, *Opkomst,* I, 33.

41 Hakluyt, VII, 175.

42 J. K. J. de Jonge, *Opkomst,* I, 46, 47. Sluiter, "Dutch-Spanish Rivalry," p. 173.

43 Dionisio Alcedo y Herrera, *Piraterías y agresiones de los ingleses y de otros pueblos de Europa en la América española desde el siglo XVI al XVIII* (Madrid, 1883), maintains that Margarita lost its "pesquería de las perlas" because of the hostilities and robberies of the corsairs and pirates (p. 450). See Sanford A. Mosk, "Spanish Pearl-fishing Operations on the Pearl Coast in the Sixteenth Century," *HAHR,* XVIII (1938), 392-400. G. F. Kunz and Ch. H. Stevenson, *The Book of the Pearl* (New York, 1908), p. 233, maintain that by 1597 the production of Cubagua had already decreased drastically. *AGI,* Aud S. Dom., 187, has a letter of Suárez de Amaya, dated Jan. 2, 1601, mentioning the case of a Dutch ship that carried off a value of 30,000 *pesos* of *lindísimas perlas.*

44 *RSG,* Nov. 23, 1596.

45 *Ibid.,* July 5, 1597.

46 *Ibid.,* March 24, 1597.

47 PK 1435, *Le Plaidoyer de l'Indien hollandois* (n.p., 1608), p. 2: "Le traffique que l'on fait avec vint navires et quinze cent hommes nous apporte bien huit cent mille florins." See Van Meteren, fol. 588.

48 Sluiter, "Dutch-Spanish Rivalry," p. 182.

49 Van Meteren, fol. 588.

50 Sluiter, "Dutch-Spanish Rivalry," pp. 170-79.

51 W. Usselinx, *Remonstrance* (PK 1442, n.p., 1608), p. 14: "...so de West Indische handel van t'Zout ende huyden die...bij de hondert schepen in de vaert houden...."

52 *Le Plaidoyer,* p. 2: "...les cent navires qui ont esté envoyées au sel au Puncto del Rey..."

53 H. G. Dalton, *The History of British Guiana* (London, 1855), I, 105.

54 *U.S. Commission on Boundary between Venezuela and British Guiana. Report and Accompanying Papers* (Washington, 1896-97), II, *Extracts from Archives,* pp. 4 ff. (hereafter cited as *USC,* II, *Extracts*). Detailed information is also found in *Res. Holl.,* June 10, 14, July, 7, 1581; Robert Schomburgk, *A Description of British Guiana* (London, 1840), p. 81; and J. J. Hartsinck, *Beschrijving van Guiana of de wilde kust in Zuid-Amerika* (Amsterdam, 1770), I, 206.

55 *RSG,* Nov. 16, Dec. 8, 1598, *et passim.*

56 The Dutch title of this report is: "Verclaringe van de onbekende ende de onbeseylde voiage van America, beginnende van de reviere Amasonis tot het eylant van de Trinidat toe"; see Appendix I.

57 *RSG*, Dec. 10, 22, *et seq.*, 1599.
58 As mentioned by Hartsinck, I, 207, 262.
59 "Memorial on the colonization of Guiana," 1603. See *USC*, II, *Extracts*, pp. 27 ff.
60 *RSG*, Feb. 25, 1603.
61 *Ibid.*, July 10, 1602, Jan. 12, 1604, *et passim*.
62 Wright, "Rescates," p. 339.
63 *Ibid.*, pp. 338-39, Letters of Váldez to the king, Dec. 15, 1605, July 18, 1603.
See also *AGI*, Aud. S. Dom., 187, Letters of Suárez de Amaya to the king, July 2,
Dec. 10, 14, 1600, Jan. 2, Feb. 13, May 27, 1601, June 15, 1602, May 13, 1603,
and May 22, 1604. In 1602: 96 salt carriers, 5 *barcos de rescate*. For 1603 the
numbers are 172 and 13; for 1604, 96 and 11.
64 *AGI*, Aud. S. Dom., 52, Antonio Osorio to the king, Sept. 27, 1602: "Los nabios
de enemigos...cada dia bienen a estas partes y dame notable pena no las poder
castigar."
65 Wright, "Rescates," p. 344.
66 *Ibid.*
67 *AGI*, Aud. S. Dom., 100, "Relaçion de lo sucedido en la ysla de Jamaica della
India del Mar Oceano contra la armada ynglessa..." Jan. 26, 1603. Cf. Wright,
"Rescates," p. 347, Váldez to the king, July 11, 1604.
68 Sluiter, "Dutch-Spanish Rivalry," p. 188.
69 *AGI*, IG 1867, Aug. 1, 1605. The informer was a certain Cornelis Guillermo
(Willemsz). *RSG*, April 15, 27, 1605.
70 *AGI*, IG 1867, April 10, 1606, Spanish War Council to the king. There is an
extensive collection of documents in this *legajo* under the title "Consultas desde
el año de 1603 hasta el de 1607 sobre cegar la salina de Araya." See also *AGI*, IG
2535, March 18, 28, 1605, Spanish War Council to the king.
71 Sluiter, "Dutch-Spanish Rivalry," p. 186.
72 Duro, *Armada Española*, III, 157: "...corriendo voz de ir a Flandes."
73 Conflicting numbers on the smugglers' fleet are given by Sluiter, "Dutch-Spanish
Rivalry," p. 190, and Duro, *Armada Española*, III, 157. It counted probably 31
ships; at least 17 were Dutch, 6 were French. In the battle the flagship of Admiral
Du Verne boarded the Spanish *almiranta*. The latter exploded; both ships went
to the bottom.
74 PK 1304, *Waerachtigh verhael van de Spaensche vloot...*(Amsterdam, 1605):
"...ander de Vredevane opstekende werden alle soldaten ghevanckelick over-
ghenomen ende over t' boort gheworpen bevelende de selve aenroepende hare
Santen ende Santinnen ende Lipsius' Lieve Vrouwe van Halle..." ARA, ABA,
1351/1605, May 15, 1605, 1353/1607, Jan. 22, March 11, 1607. The blockade
was conducted by a Dutch fleet under Lambrecht Hendricksz.
75 *AGI*, IG 1867, the Spanish War Council to the king, Dec. 29, 1606: "...contri-
buyendo para ello entre todos y con ellos el Rey de Francia hasta la suma de
800,000 ducados, cuatro mil francos cada dia..."
76 *Ibid.*, May 22, 1607.
77 Duro, *Armada Española*, III, 258. Sluiter, "Dutch-Spanish Rivalry," p. 191.
78 Sluiter, "Dutch-Spanish Rivalry," p. 192.
79 A. Arellano Moreno, *Orígenes de la economía venezolana* (Caracas, 1947), pp. 37,
63, 214, *et passim*. The stimulating effect of an outlet for the colonial produce was,
of course, lost.
80 *AGI*, Aud. S. Dom., 100, Royal cédula of Dec. 2, 1606: "...tratado y contratado

con enemigos de nuestra santa fe catolica, ynglesses, francesses, flamencos y de otros naciones que han acudido a aquellas costas llevandoles las mercadurias que en aquella provincia ay falta..."

[81] Sluiter, "Dutch-Spanish Rivalry," p. 195.

NOTES TO CHAPTER IV

[1] Jameson, *Usselinx*, pp. 22 ff., gives an excellent exposé. Holland was Holland and West-Friesland.

[2] Busken Huet, II, 1, 65.

[3] H. Lonchay and J. Cuvelier, *Correspondance de la Cour d'Espagne sur les affaires des Pays-Bas au dix-septième siècle* (Bruxelles, 1923-37), I, 266-67, Louis Verrycken, "Rapport de sa mission en Hollande, Août 15, 1607."

[4] Die mijnheer Vader in den zetel geholpen hebben.

[5] Vreede, *Lettres*, p. 52, letter of de Buzanval to Villeroy, Jan. 4, 1599. Van Meteren, fol. 593: "...diverse discoursen op dit stuck gemaeckt ende in Druck laten uytgaen."

[6] Sirach 12:10.

[7] PK 1438, *Bedenckingen over den Staet van de Vereenichde Nederlanden* (n.p., 1608), and PK 1441, *Naerder bedenckingen* (n.p., 1608). See note 45, Chapter II. We translated "Bedenckingen" as "Considerations." Cf. Laspeyres, Van Rees, and Ligtenberg.

[8] Nahum 3:16. *Naerder Bedenckingen*, p. 5.

[9] *Ibid.*, p. 18.

[10] *Ibid.*, p. 28.

[11] *ARA*, Inv. St. Gen. (West Indië, Loketkas, Lit. L, no. 8), March 31, 1609: "...solemnelijck sijn ghemaeckt contracten met verscheyden Coningen en volckeren die met eede ende stercke beloften bevesticht sijn..."

[12] Laspeyres, p. 59n1.

[13] *Remonstrance*, pp. 6, 10, *et passim.*

[14] Lonchay and Cuvelier, I, 135-36, "Edit de Philippe III réglementant le commerce extérieur de l'Espagne," Feb. 27, 1603.

[15] *Ibid.*, pp. 135-36, 241. See also Luis de Cabrera de Córdoba, *Relaciones de las cosas sucedidas en la corte de España desde 1599 hasta 1614* (Madrid, 1857), p. 312.

[16] Cabrera, p. 367.

[17] The alarm is illustrated by the report presented to Philip III by Iñigo de Brizuela, envoy of the archdukes, in Lonchay and Cuvelier, I, 304 ff.: "Si les provisions mensuelles sont insuffisantes la perte des provinces obéissantes est certaine, car les rebelles verraient leurs puissance renforcée et ils menaceraient les Etats mêmes du Roi ainsi que les Indes occidentales et orientales..."

[18] J. P. Arend and Otto van Rees, *Algemeene geschiedenis des vaderlands* (Amsterdam, 1840-79), III, 2, 260.

[19] The *uti possidetis* principle, according to Spain, applied only in Europe and the West Indies. See Duro, *Armada Española*, III, 322: "Se escribió en términos tan oscuros y ambiguos que los mismos tratantes no les entendían." In our opinion this statement hits the nail on the head. Cf. Newton, p. 128.

[20] Busken Huet, II, 1, p. 65.

[21] H. C. Diferee, *De geschiedenis van den Nederlandschen handel tot den val der Republiek* (Amsterdam, 1908), pp. 176, 177.

22 J. F. Bense, *Anglo-Dutch Relations from the Earliest Times to the Death of William the Third* (The Hague, 1924), pp. 142, 146, 157 ff.

23 Lieuwe van Aitzema, *Saken van staet en oorlogh in ende omtrent de Vereenigde Nederlanden* ('s Graven-Haghe, 1669-72), I, 2. Aitzema's extensive work gives a detailed, although perhaps biased, and always very interesting account of events from 1621 to 1668 in which he was personally involved as a diplomat of the United Provinces. For the English point of view see David Hume, *The History of England* (many editions), and Percy M. Thornton, *The Stuart Dynasty* (London, 1890).

24 J. J. Poelhekke, *'t Uytgaen van den Treves* (Groningen, 1960), Bijlage I, pp. 186-88. Cf., Arend-Van Rees, III, 2, pp. 599-601: 600,000 pounds asked, 250,000 paid.

25 J. A. Williamson, *English Colonies in Guiana and on the Amazon, 1604-1668* (Oxford, 1923,) pp. 60, 61 (hereafter cited as Williamson, *English Colonies*).

26 G. N. Clark and W. J. M. van Eysinga, *The Colonial Conferences Between England and the Netherlands in 1613 and 1615* (Leiden, 1940-51), I, 4.

27 Arend-Van Rees, III, 2, p. 390. Cf. J. K. J. de Jonge, *Opkomst*, II, 36, and Hyma, *The Dutch in the Far East*, p. 30.

28 J. G. Doorman, "Die Niederländische West-Indische Compagnie an der Goldküste," *Tijdschrift voor Indische Taal-, Land- en Volkenkunde*, XL (1897), 440. Nikolaus Hadeler, *Geschichte der holländischen Colonien auf der Goldküste* (Bonn, 1904), pp. 33, 34. The Guinea Company pointed out the importance of Dutch trade there: twenty ships yearly with six hundred men amounting to one million guilders. See also *ARA*, St. Gen. 3224, Resolutions of the States General concerning the EIC and other Companies, 1602-12, and *RSG*, Aug. 25 and Oct. 22, 1611.

29 Marées/Naber, p. lxvii. Van Wassenaer, VI, 68: "...en veel van onse ingesethenen die de hitte niet verdraghen conden daer legghende over de duysent van d'onse begraven."

30 V. T. Harlow, *Colonising Expeditions to the West Indies and Guiana, 1623-1667* (London, 1925), pp. lxxv-lxxix, 139 ff. (hereafter cited as Harlow, *Col. Expeditions*).

31 De Laet, *Nieuwe Wereldt*, pp. 460-77, gives the description. G. Edmundson, "The Dutch on the Amazon and Negro in the Seventeenth Century," *EHR*, XVIII (1903), 642-63; XIX (1904), 1-25.

32 Appendix I.

33 Hartsinck, I, 207; *USC*, I, *Historical*, pp. 154 ff.

34 *AGI*, Aud. S. Dom. 179, "Relaçion del estado de las cosas de la Isla de Trinidad," Dec. 9, 1614.

35 Forts were built not only to protect the colonists against the Indians but also against the Spaniards. Cf. *USC*, IX, *Brief for Venezuela*, pp. 117-18.

36 There is some literature on this settlement: Harlow, *Col. Expeditions*, p. 139; Williamson, *English Colonies*, pp. 63 ff.; Herbert I. Bloom, *The Economic Activities of the Jews in Amsterdam in the Seventeenth and Eighteenth Centuries* (Williamsport, Penn., 1937), p. 152; *Coll. Navarrete*, XXV, 328, report of Feb. 21, 1615. See also Edmundson, "The Dutch in Western Guiana," *EHR*, XVI (1901), 640-75, and "The Dutch on the Amazon."

37 Edmundson, "The Dutch in Western Guiana," pp. 672-73. Harlow, *Col. Expeditions*, pp. 139-40.

38 M. Jiménez de la Espada, *Viaje del Capitán Pedro Texeira aguas arriba del río de las Amazonas* (Madrid, 1889), p. 110, quoting one of the "Avisos tocantes á la India Occidental, 6 noticias interesantes que explican los progresos que holandeses, franceses é ingleses hacían en las riberas y tierras del río de las Amazonas en el

Marañon," of April 4, 1615, continues: "Por la Haya de Olanda ha parecido Pedro Luis, un capitán de la armada naval residente en Ulissinga, con su hijo Juan Pedro Atar ambos de vuelta de la India Occidental de la ribera de Uiapoco en donde han fabricado dos casas y han cogido el tabaco."

39 The reliability of this document is sufficiently proven by Edmundson, "The Dutch on the Amazon," p. 647.

40 Williamson, *English Colonies*, p. 68. Edmundson, "The Dutch on the Amazon," p. 648.

41 Information on the "Golden Cocq" expedition in Edmundson, "The Dutch on the Amazon," pp. 647-48; Williamson, *English Colonies*, p. 68; Jiménez de la Espada, pp. 115-19.

42 Edmundson, "The Dutch on the Amazon," p. 2.

43 This hostile attitude was very different from the one stated by Cabeljau in his report of 1599. See Appendix I.

44 Jiménez de la Espada, pp. 109, 122-31: "Relaçam de varios successos acontecidos no Maranham e Gram Para Assim de paz como de guerra contra o rebelde Olandes, Ingreses & Franceses & outras nações." Information is also given in Joaquim Caetano da Silva, *L'Oyapoc et l'Amazone* (Paris, 1861), I, 11, 12.

45 See also *AGI*, Aud. S. Dom. 179, Juan de Tostado to the king, June 13, 1618, and Edmundson, "The Dutch on the Amazon," pp. 649-50.

46 Edmundson, p. 650. Cf. Williamson, *English Colonies*, pp. 95-96.

47 *AGI*, Aud. S. Dom. 177, Letter of the Governor of Jamaica, June 8, 1610.

48 R. Bijlsma, *Rotterdams welvaren 1580-1650* ('s-Gravenhage, 1918), pp. 168 ff.

49 J. J. Reesse, *De suikerhandel van Amsterdam van het begin der 17de eeuw tot 1813* ('s-Gravenhage, 1908), I, 30.

50 Wright, "The Dutch and Cuba," p. 601. The lack of Dutch activity during the first years of the Truce is, in a negative way, confirmed by the omission of the *rebeldes* or *flamencos* in the many complaints on piracy of Spanish governors who continue to mention the French and English intruders. See also A. Montanus, *De nieuwe en onbekende weereld: of beschryving van America en 't zuid-land* (Amsterdam, 1671), p. 549, where this Dutch historian mentions the fact that Dutch navigation on the salt pan of Araya was *resumed* after the Truce.

51 *AGI*, Aud. S. Dom. 180, Letter of the Governor of Margarita to the king, March 29, 1611; 179, Letter written by the officials of the cc to the king, July 8, 1610: "despues que cessaron los rescates con los enemigos padecen mucho los vecinos por que no tienen ni se les lleva lo necessario para su provision y sustento." The royal *cédula* against tobacco raising was of August 7, 1606.

52 *Groot Placaetboeck*, I, 563. "Generael Octrooy voor die geene, die eenige nieuwe passagien, havenen, landen of plaetsen sullen ontdecken. In date den 27 Maert 1614." See also J. Tjassens, *Zee-politie der Vereenichde Nederlanden* ('s Graven-Hage, 1670), pp. 281 ff.

53 Lonchay and Cuvelier, I, 523, Letter of the Archduke Albert to Philip III, Jan. 24, 1614. Cf. Edmundson, "The Dutch on the Amazon," p. 646. The Orellana River is the Amazon.

54 *Col. Navarrete*, xxv, 325-30, Information brought to the attention of the king, dated Nov., 1614, Feb. 2, April 15, Aug. 12, 1615. It reveals the strength of the Dutch: "En Amsterdam 38 navios, unos a 300 toneladas; en Rotterdam 20 navios, unos a 300 toneladas; en Eschusa (Enkhuizen) 6 navios, unos a 500 o 600 toneladas; en Horn 4 navios; en Fregelingen (Flushing) 3 navios, algunos a 1000 toneladas,"

adding the frightening conclusion: "Tienen los ojos en Puerto Rico y Puerto Velo."

55 A. Canovas del Castillo, *Historia de la decadencia de España desde el advenimiento de Felipe III al trono hasta la muerte de Carlos II* (Madrid, 1910), p. 20.

56 P. and H. Chaunu, *Séville et l'Atlantique, 1504-1650* (Paris, 1955-59), VIII, 2, 2, p. 1419.

57 *Ibid.*, VIII, 2, 1, p. 25 gives the following cycles in Spanish economic development: 1540-50, 1550-62, 1562-1563-1592, 1593-1622, 1623-50. The last one is called *la grande dépréssion*.

58 Lonchay and Cuvelier, I, 532; Poelhekke, *Treves*, p. 37. Cf. G. Fagniez, "Le commerce extérieur de la France sous Henry IV," *RH*, XVI (Mai-Août, 1881), 4.

59 Navarrete, *Bibl. Mar.*, I, 606-11. Lonchay and Cuvelier, I, 550.

60 Wright, "The Dutch and Cuba," p. 603.

61 PK 3189, *Propositie van den Ambassadeur P. Peckius* (n.p., 1621), p. 2: "... voorsz propositie is erroneus ende onverdraechelijck in heuren staet treckende in dispuut de selve souvereyniteyt."

62 Aitzema, I, 3-5.

63 Ioannes de Laet, *Historie ofte Iaerlijck Verhael van de verrichtinghen der Geoctroyeerde West-Indische Compagnie*, Samuel P. L'Honoré Naber, ed. ('s-Gravenhage, 1931-37), I, 2 (hereafter cited as De Laet/Naber). Cf. PK 1466 to 1473, and W. van Ravensteyn, *Onderzoekingen over de economische en sociale ontwikkeling van Amsterdam gedurende de 16de en het eerste kwart der 17de eeuw* (Amsterdam, 1906), pp. 212 ff.

64 Aitzema, I, 39.

65 Arend-Van Rees, III, 3, p. 427.

66 *RSG*, Aug. 23, Sept. 2, 3, 21, Oct. 15, Dec. 7, 27. Arend-Van Rees, III, 3, p. 428.

67 Van Ravensteyn, p. 236.

68 Arend-Van Rees, III, 3, p. 428: "Dat het groote werk in Godes naam aangevangen zou mogen worden."

69 Van Wassenaer, IV, 21.

NOTES TO CHAPTER V

1 De Laet/Naber, I, 1, 2,

2 Lannoy and Van der Linden, *Néerlande et Danemark*, p. 73. Pierre (L. J. P. M.) Bonnassieux, *Les grandes compagnies de commerce: étude pour servir à l'histoire de la colonisation* (Paris, 1892), pp. 69 ff., and Eleazar Córdoba Bello, *Compañías holandesas de navegación* (Sevilla, 1964), give a wrong picture.

3 P. Geyl, *Geschiedenis van de Nederlandse stam* (Amsterdam, Antwerpen, 1948-49), I, 480; van Dillen, "De West Indische Compagnie," p. 152; Ligtenberg, p. 216; Van Ravensteyn, pp. 237 ff.

4 Slightly different versions of the first charter are found in *ARA*, WIC, OC, 1322, Octrooien WIC; in De Laet/Naber, I; in *Groot Placaetboeck*, I, and Aitzema, I.

5 Numerous sources confirm this. We have used Ernst Baasch, *Holländische Wirtschaftsgeschichte* (Jena, 1927), p. 374.

6 Van Wassenaer, VII, 11, 12. These colonists arrived just in time to stop a Frenchman from taking possession of this region.

7 Aitzema, I, 61: "... tot meerder afbreuck van Spaignien; welcke Compagnye haer rolle wel heeft ghespeelt inde volghende jaren, hoewel meer tot schade van de Spaensche ende Portugesen, als tot haer eighen voordeel."

8 K. R. Andrews, *Elizabethan Privateering. English Privateering during the Spanish War* (Cambridge, 1964), p. 15.

9 A. Zimmermann, *Die Europäischen Kolonien:* v, *Die Kolonialpolitik der Niederländer* (Berlin, 1903), pp. 40, 74-79. Cf. Laspeyres, p. 64, and Van Kampen, *Nederlanders*, I, 312.

10 G. J. van Grol, *De grondpolitiek in het Westindisch domein der Generaliteit* ('s-Graven-hage, 1934-47), I, 10 ff., Memorial of May 26, 1628.

11 Jameson, *Usselinx*, pp. 62 ff. Usselinx had suggested 200,000 guilders. Of the first seventy-four directors Amsterdam had twenty, Zeeland twelve, the other chambers fourteen each. See *Groot Placaetboeck*, I, 570 ff. The EIC had a similar board, called the Heren XVII.

12 Usselinx, in general, had suggested more democratic procedures; see his concept in Van Rees, pp. 387 ff. See also *Encyclopaedie van Nederlandsch West-Indië* ('s-Gra-venhage, Leiden, 1914, 1917), p. 215.

13 "Geen beter bewijs dat buit- en kaapvaart het doel der Compagnie was dan deze bepalingen," is the reaction of Diferee, p. 265.

14 Asher, p. xix, is certainly wrong in his statement that "the new company...adapted the democratic principle of the Belgian party and allowed a very complete control of the shareholders to whose approval the accounts and affairs had to be submitted."

15 Diferee, p. 266: "Het oorlogsbedrijf, dat de Compagnie zou gaan voeren, maakte velen huiverig." Van Rees, p. 121, calls both companies "oorlogvoerende Mo-gendheden." See also Van Rees, p. 124.

16 Van Rees, p. 124.

17 Van Wassenaer, I, 44. Cf. Van Rees, p. 125.

18 *Groot Placaetboeck*, I, 589-90.

19 The best known of the pamphlets published in these days are PK 3348, *Nootwendigh discours* (n.p., 1621), PK 3360, *Anderder discours* (n.p., 1621), and PK 3362, *Levendich discours* (n.p., 1621).

20 *RSG*, April 13, 1622, *et seq.*

21 PK 3362, *Levendich discours* (Vivid discussion) probably by Usselinx. He expected an expansion of industry, especially the textile industry as a result of trade with the West Indies and the conditions of colonization which prevented the weaving of anything. See Appendix III, Article 19.

22 *Groot Placaetboeck*, I, 579-82. Aitzema, I, 66, 67.

23 *ARA*, WIC, OC, 18, Chamber of Amsterdam, "Lijst van inteekenaren in het kapitaal der West Indische Compagnie met opgave der ingelegen bedragen," Feb. 10, 1656.

24 Asher, p. xix. See also Van Dillen's article on the West India Company, cited earlier. More information in PK 5112, *Twee deductien aengaende de Vereeninge van d'Oost ende West Indische Compagnien* ('s-Gravenhaghe, 1644).

25 *ARA*, WIC, OC, 1, Minutes of the XIX 1623-24, March 27, 1624. Dordrecht wanted its own chamber and offered 500,000 guilders; towns or private persons in the other provinces without a chamber could subscribe in one of the existing chambers. This was done by Deventer, Zwolle, and Arnhem. The latter town, capital of the province of Gelderland, did so on the condition that it would receive a director's seat. See also R. Bijlsma, "Rotterdams Amerikavaart in de eerste helft der zeventiende eeuw," *BVGO*, v, 3 (1915), 105-7.

26 See Bloom, pp. 124 ff., and H. Wätjen, *Das holländische Kolonialreich in Brasilien* (Haag, 1921), pp. 36, 37. Amsterdam Jews subscribed 36,100 guilders in the initial capital, or 0.5 per cent. In 1658 their contribution had risen to 4 per cent.

In 1674 it was 10 per cent. See also Hk. Brugmans and A. Frank, eds., *Geschiedenis der Joden in Nederland* (Amsterdam, 1940), p. 565.

27 *Groot Placaetboeck*, I, 586-87, "Accoordt tusschen de Bewinthebberen ende Hooft-participanten van de West Indische Compagnie," June 21, 1623. Cf. Aitzema, I, 69-71.

28 *ARA*, WIC, OC, I, Minutes of the XIX 1623-24, May 20, 1624, *et seq.*

29 *ARA*, WIC, OC, Inv. St. Gen. (West Indië), 5751, April 17, 1624. *RSG*, March 23, 1624. E. B. O'Callaghan, ed., *Documents Relative to the Colonial History of the State of New York* (Albany, 1853-57), I, 29, 30 (hereafter cited as O'Callaghan, *Documents*).

30 *Groot Placaetboeck*, I, 589-92. *RSG*, Sept. 5, 1624.

31 See De Laet/Naber, I, with a list of the first directors of the WIC.

32 See Appendix III for such a patent. A similar one in J. M. J. Hamelberg, *De Nederlanders op de West-Indische eilanden* (Amsterdam, 1901-3), II, Documenten, pp. 13-16, "Vrijheden en exemptien bij de gecommitteerde bewinthebberen van de respectieve Cameren der geoctroyeerde West-Indische Compagnie als represen-teerende de vergaderinge van de XIX, toegestaen ende geaccordeert aen d'Heeren Adriaen ende Cornelis Lampsins, als patroonen van een colonie op het eylant Tobago, alles getrocken en geformeert wt de notulen der voorn. vergad., in dato 30 Augusti, 1655."

33 P. M. Netscher, *Geschiedenis van de koloniën Essequibo, Demerary en Berbice* ('s-Gravenhage, 1888), pp. 53 ff.

34 See Appendix III, article 9.

35 See, for example, Jacobo de la Pezuela y Lobo, *Historia de la isla de Cuba* (Madrid, 1868-78), II, 35.

36 *Groot Placaetboeck*, I, 578-84.

37 Bijlsma, "Rotterdams Amerikaart in de eerste helft der zeventiende eeuw," p. 113.

38 Alan C. Burns, *History of the British West Indies* (London, 1954), p. 238. Cf. R. H. Schomburgk, *The History of Barbados* (London, 1848), p. 268, and J. A. Williamson, *The Caribbee Islands under the Proprietary Patents* (London, 1926), pp. 131, 155, 174.

39 *ARA*, WIC, OC, St. Gen. 3535, Plakaet Boeck 1631-40, pp. 72, 98. Cf. PK 3998, *Articulen met approbatie van de Hoogh Moghende Heeren Staten Generael der Vereenichde Nederlanden provisionelyck beraemt by bewinthebberen van de generale geoctroyeerde West Indische Compagnie ter vergaderinghe van de XIX over het openstellen van den handel ende negotie op de Stadt Olinda de Pernambuco ende custen van Brasil* (Amsterdam, 1630). Cf. Van Rees, p. 184.

40 PK 3998. See also Elias Luzac, *Hollands rijkdom* (Leyden, 1780-83), I, 327-38; II, 256 ff., bijlage K.

41 Luzac, II, 256 ff., bijlage K. Cf. *Groot Placaetboeck*, I, 603-6. See also Van Rees, p. 184.

42 *ARA*, WIC, OC, 39, Chamber of Zeeland, Resolutien van de Staten Generael rakende de West Indische Compagnie, enz., 1623-46, Jan. 30, 1637. Amsterdam's arguments were entitled: "Corte redenen bij die van Amsterdam overge-geven om te bewijsen de nodigheyt van vrije handel." Cf. Van Rees, p. 185: "...het odieuste dinck van de werelt ende het schandelijckste bedrijff van alle Staten." The other quote is from Boxer, *The Dutch in Brazil*, p. 80.

43 *ARA*, WIC, OC, 39, Chamber of Zeeland, Resolutien van de Staten Generael rakende de West Indische Compagnie, enz., 1623-46, Jan. 30, 1637. Redenen

waeromme de bewinthebberen van de Compagnie ter Camere Zeelant, Maze met de Stadt en Lande susteneeren dat de particuliere handel niet en can noch behoorde toegestaen te worden.

44 *Ibid.*, "Discours onder vrage ende antwoorde hoe de West Indische Compagnie sal comen gestabiliseert werden buyten coste vant Landt tot merckelijcke voordeel van de participanten," July 25, 1636. *RSG*, Dec. 27, 1636.

45 Aitzema, II, 445; PK 4514, 4515, 4580, 4581. *ARA*, WIC, OC, Chamber of Zeeland, 39, "Resolutiën van de Staten Generaal rakende de West Indische Compagnie, enz., 1623-46; Corte redenen...enz."

46 *Ibid.*, "Memorial of the Chamber of Zeeland," March 18, July 22, 1638; see also *Groot Placaetboeck* I, 609-18. Cf. Boxer, *The Dutch in Brazil*, p. 76.

47 Wätjen, *Holl. Kolonialreich*, p. 298.

48 Lonchay and Cuvelier, II, 4, Philip IV to the Archduke Albert, April 22, 1621. It is impossible to quote here all the letters exchanged between the King and the Archduke or other Spanish officials in the Southern Netherlands. The observations of A. Waddington, *La République des Provinces-Unies, la France et les Pays-Bas espagnols de 1630 à 1650* (Paris, 1895-97), I, 64 ff. are interesting.

49 Lonchay and Cuvelier, II, 429. In a letter of Carlos Coloma to Juan de Villela, Jan. 24, 1629, the former calls Piet Heyn "that barbarian."

50 *Ibid.*, II, 431, Isabella to Philip, Feb. 13, 1629.

51 Aitzema, I, 897 ff. Of the many pamphlets PK 3917 is perhaps the most interesting: *Discours over den Nederlandtschen vredehandel* (Leeuwarden, 1629).

52 Aitzema, I, 901, 903-5.

53 Jameson, "Usselinx," p. 149.

54 Lonchay and Cuvelier, II, 509, Philip IV to Isabella, Jan. 8, 1630, and p. 526, Isabella to Philip IV, April 6, 1630.

55 *Ibid.*, p. 628, Philip IV to Isabella, June 24, 1632. See also pp. 653, 654.

56 Aitzema, I, 967.

57 *Ibid.*, II, 20 ff. "He can but little who can only damage."

58 Arend-Van Rees, III, 5, p. 73.

59 Lonchay and Cuvelier, III, 350, Philip IV to the Cardinal Infante, Nov. 26, 1639, p. 380, Philip IV to the Cardinal Infante, Oct. 3, 1640, pp. 391-92, *et passim*.

NOTES TO CHAPTER VI

1 The salmon may be beautiful, the herring surpasses all.

2 The *Tractaet van de haringvisscherij* by Meindert Semeyns was not available. We quoted from Brandt, *Historie der vermaerde zee- en koop-stadt Enkhuisen*, p. 289.

3 There is much material in Dutch to prove this. We refer to the works of Stoppelaar, J. K. J. de Jonge, *Opkomst*, and Marées/Naber.

4 Rudolf Häpke, *Niederländische Akten und Urkunden* (München, 1913-23), II, 428-29.

5 J. K. J. de Jonge, *Opkomst*, I, 40. Brandt, *Enkhuisen*, p. 272.

6 Kernkamp, *De handel op den vijand*, II, 197.

7 Velius, p. 505. Van Meteren, fol. 562 ff. Newton, p. 125, is wrong in stating that the salt deposits were worked with Negro slaves.

8 Laspeyres, p. 57.

9 Lonchay and Cuvelier, I, 10, 11, 58, 59.

10 Pablo Ojer, *Las salinas del oriente venezolano en el siglo XVII* (Caracas, 1962), p. 4.

11 PK 3362, *Levendich discours* (n.p., 1622), p. 11. See also Van Meteren, fol. 588.
12 Häpke, II, 428-29: "Ordre gheraemt voor de schepen die welcke van nu voortaen ut dese landen nae Westindien in Punto Rey om sout sullen navigeren ende waernae de schipperen ende 't scheepsvolck van de voors. schepen aldaer leghende ende aen lant tot conservatie van haer persoonen ende schepen zullen hebben te reguleren."
13 De Laet, *Nieuwe Wereldt*, pp. 494-95.
14 Navarrete, *Bibl. Mar.*, I, 222-27; AGI, IG 1867, Nov. 23, 1604: "Relaçion y disposiçion de la gran Salina de Araya y de la manera que se podia anegar y de la horden que se ha de tener en ello esta dicha salina en diez grados de altura entre el Tropico de Cancer y la Equinoccial."
15 Sluiter, "Dutch-Spanish Rivalry," p. 176.
16 AGI, Aud. S. Dom. 187, Letter of Suárez de Amaya to the king, July 2, 1600: "...que es tan fertil que pueden cargar della mil urcas."
17 *Ibid.*, Suárez de Amaya to the king, June 19, 1601. Cf. Velius, p. 275: "...als dat in t' sieden overvloedigh wel uytleverde."
18 AGI, Aud. S. Dom. 187, Letters of Suárez de Amaya to the king, Dec. 10, 14, 1600, Jan. 2, 1601 *et seq.* The *Col. Navarrete*, XXVII, has three letters copied of this governor to the king: July 2, 1600, June 19, 1601, and June 15, 1602.
19 AGI, Aud. S. Dom. 187, "Informaçion" by Pedro de Fajardo, governor of Margarita, to the king, Oct. 20 to Nov. 6, 1599. See also Brandt, *Enkhuizen*, p. 272, and Van Reyd, p. 399.
20 J. B. Antoneli gave a good description of the pan in 1604: "Relaçion y disposiçion de la gran salina de Araya," in AGI, IG 1867. In the *Col. Navarrete*, VIII, 233-42 is a slightly different report, the differences probably caused by the copyist. Excellent information is also given by I. A. Wright and C. F. A. van Dam, *Nederlandsche zeevaarders op de eilanden in de Caraïbsche Zee en aan de kust van Colombia en Venezuela gedurende de jaren 1621-1648* (Utrecht, 1934-35; hereafter cited as Wright/Van Dam). A third source is the letters of Suárez de Amaya to the king in AGI, Aud. S. Dom. 187. In a letter dated Dec. 14, 1600, the Spanish governor writes on these disturbing activities that they are performed "con tanta libertad y desberguencia como si estubieron en sus tierras," and in another letter of May 27, 1601: "de la gran desorden, atrevimiento y libertad que tenian los estrangeros." See also Ojer. Ojer visited the pan in 1958 and observed that the salt was carried away in much the same way as in 1600.
21 AGI, Aud. S. Dom. 187, Letters of Suárez de Amaya to the king, May 23, July 2, Nov. 14, Dec. 8, 1600, and June 19, 1601.
22 AGI, Aud. S. Dom. 180, Letters of the Governor of Margarita to the king, the last one dated July 24, 1601. See also IG 1867, "Consultas desde el año de 1603 hasta el de 1607 sobre cegar la Salina de Araya."
23 AGI, Aud. S. Dom. 187, Suárez de Amaya to the king, June 15, 1602.
24 *Ibid.*; in 1602, 96 salt carriers; in 1603, 172; in 1604, 96.
25 *Ibid.*, Letters of Governor Fadrique de Carcer to the king. He made an inspection with Jorge Veneciano and another engineer. An undated letter to the Duke of Medina reports the inspection. Suárez de Amaya, in a letter to the king, July 10, 1604, calls Veneciano "un mercador...que no tiene platica de este sino de sus mercaderias." The other man was called "yn piloto de la mar de no mvcho entendimiento a lo que dizen por cegar la salina."
26 Diego Angulo Iñiguez, *Bautista Antoneli. Las fortificaciones americanas del siglo XVI*

(Madrid, 1942), p. 80. Of the same author: *Historia del arte hispanoamericano*, I (Barcelona, Buenos Aires, 1945), Chapter X (written by Enrique Marco Dorta), pp. 496-522. See also *AGI*, Aud. S. Dom. 187, Suárez de Amaya to the king, July 10, 1604.

27 *Ibid.*, "...costara mas de trezientos mill ducados y mas de cinquenta mill cada año en sustentar dozientos soldados de presidio." See also *Col. Navarrete*, VIII, 234 ff., "Relaçion y disposiçion...etc."

28 *AGI*, Aud. S. Dom. 187, Suárez de Amaya to the king, May 24, 1605.

29 *AGI*, IG 1867, Meeting of the Spanish War Council, June 16, 1605.

30 *AGI*, Aud. S. Dom. 187, Suárez de Amaya to the king, Nov. 22, 1605; Duro, *Armada Española*, III, 256; Van Meteren, fol. 546; Cabrera de Córdoba, p. 272, says that Fajardo hanged 400 men; 53 Zeelanders sent to the galleys were released in 1608. The Dutch leader was Daniel de Moucheron, defined by Suárez de Amaya as "un atrevido y maldito cosario y que ha diez o doze años que anda haziendo dano en estas costas," letter to the king of Nov. 22, 1605. Duro, *Armada Española*, III, 257, calls him "Príncipe de las Salinas."

31 Velius, p. 524-25.

32 *AGI*, IG 1867, War Council to the king, April 10, 1606.

33 Velius, p. 529.

34 *AGI*, Aud. S. Dom. 187, P. Suárez Coronel's letters to the king, written between August, 1606, and June, 1608.

35 As early as 1606 Fadrique de Carcer, the Governor of Margarita, who at first had disagreed with Antoneli, came back to the latter's proposals of inundation to convert the lagoon into an "ensenada." See Ojer, p. 14.

36 *ARA*, WIC, OC, Inv. St. Gen. (West Indië), 5760, Report of the Heren XIX to the States General, April 29, 1648, in which Their High Mightinesses stated: "the salt navigation on Puncta del Rey was carried on by the inhabitants of these countries for many years, during the Truce also." This statement had to serve political and economic purposes.

37 Asher, p. 46.

38 Häpke, II, 382. Die *Vroedschap* von Edam nimmt Stellung gegen Errichtung einer Westindischen Kompagnie.

39 Van Rees, pp. 127, 128, and appendices IV and V (pp. 433-40).

40 *ARA*, WIC, OC, Inv. St. Gen. (West Indië), 5768: "Nootsaeckelycke Poincten om de West Indische Compagnie te doen voortgaen," Nov. 23, 1621, in which Usselinx stated: "Erstelyck dient geresolveert dat de Soutvaert van de West Indische Compagnie moet annex aen deselve blijven."

41 *Ibid.*, 5751, Letter of the Northern Quarter to the States General, Oct. 23, 1623: "...waerop door de Edele Heeren Burgemeesteren [van Hoorn] tot antwoort gegeven is, dat syluiden nopende t'halen van t'sout altijdt hadden verstaen en noch verstonden dat sulcx moest blijven buyten de Compagnie." See also letters of Aug. 12, Nov. 21, 1623. Dordrecht sent Jacob Cats, Delft Geraerdt van Santen and Amsterdam Dirck Bas. Information also in *ARA*, WIC, OC, 1, Minutes of the XIX 1623-24, Oct. 13, 1623, and 19, Chamber of Zeeland, Extract resolutien Staten van Hollandt ende West Vrieslandt, Dec. 19, 1626, Jan. 21, 1627.

42 Wright/Van Dam, I, *13-15. Letter of Arroyo Daza to the king, Sept. 25, 1621. The Dutch ships were 200, 300, and 400 tons with 20 or more guns.

43 *Ibid.*, I, *15-20, Letters of Sept. 30, Oct. 14, 1621, Jan. 13, 1622. The exact amount was 13,773 *reales*.

44 *Ibid.*, I, *15-20, 23-25, and p. 17. See also *AGI*, Aud. S. Dom. 180, Andrés Rodríguez de Villegas to the king, Nov. 6, 1623. A sketch of the fort is printed in *Estudios Americanos, Historiografía y bibliografía americanista* (Sevilla, 1964), pp. 28-30.

45 Ojer, p. 15.

46 Full details are given in the *Relaçion de las vitorias qve Don Diego de Arroyo y Daça tuvo*... (Biblioteca Nacional, Madrid, MSS 2353), printed in *Boletín de la Academia Nacional de Historia* (Caracas), XXXVIII, 150 (Abril-Junio de 1955), 166-71. See also Wright/Van Dam, I, *23-26. A Dutch prisoner pointed the admiral out among the dead.

47 Wright/Van Dam, I, 32n2.

48 *Ibid.*, *23-26, Arroyo Daza to the king, April 15, 1623: "...no se qve aya abido tan grande vitoria en el mundo." Van Wassenaer, V, 105 ff.: "...en quamen thuys met een verloren reyse." *ARA*, WIC, OC, I, Minutes of the XIX 1623-24, Oct. 12, 1623, contains the story of a Dutch interloper who visited the pan at about that time.

49 Wright/Van Dam, I, *24: "...que se les a quitado dos millones de prouecho de la sal que auian de cargar." The loss of salt was more than 30,000 tons. See Van Wassenaer, VIII, 123.

50 The history of the fort is eloquently told by Ojer, pp. 15 ff., and by Pedro Fernández del Pulgar in *Trofeos gloriosos de los Reyes Cattolicos de España* (Biblioteca Nacional, Madrid, MSS 2995, fol. 468 ff.). Cf. Van Wassenaer, IV, 125: "...soo heeft de Coninck op de welstant syns Rhycks ghelet en dien plaets met een Fort op een plaets het Galghevelt ghenaemt ghesterckt."

51 De Laet/Naber, I, 119.

52 De Laet, *Nieuwe Wereldt*, pp. 26 ff. Many salt carriers were used to convey merchantmen through the Strait of Gibraltar. Afterwards they wandered off and sailed to the West for salt—a not uncommon procedure.

53 *ARA*, WIC, OC, Inv. St. Gen. (West Indië), 5751: Directors of the Chamber of Amsterdam to the States General, Jan. 27, 1624.

54 We must limit ourselves to a few examples. *ARA*, WIC, OC, 2, Secret minutes, copies, and outgoing letters, instructions, etc. 1629-45 (quoted as Secret minutes), Sept. 5, 1630: Request of Abraham van Pere "that 34 skippers would go with their ships to carry salt within the limits of the charter if in relation to their ships they could get up to 50 soldiers." *ARA*, WIC, OC, 8, Copybook of outgoing letters: Instruction to Admiral Loncq to send the hired ships back to Holland via the Caribbean to go to "the Tortugas, Bonos Ayres [Bonaire] other good places to get wood and salt." June 4, 1630.

55 De Laet/Naber, II, 24. The director who visited the island was Samuel Godijn. See also Johan E. Elias, *Het voorspel van den eersten Engelschen oorlog* ('s-Gravenhage, 1920), II, 159.

56 Wright/Van Dam, I, *123-24, Núñez Melián to the king, Aug. 22, 1630. See also Elias, *Voorspel*, II, 159.

57 Wright/Van Dam, I, *136-40, Report of Juan Bautista Antoneli, Nov. 20, 1633, pp. *125-29, Declarations of witnesses who saw the pan in 1630.

58 *Ibid.*, I, *134-35, Declarations of witnesses, 1632.

59 A *fanega* is 55 1/2 liters; an *arroba* is 11 1/2 Kg.

60 Wright/Van Dam, I, *140-46, Arias Montano to Ruy Fernández de Fuenmayor, June 10, 1638, Francisco Núñez Melián to the Marqués de Cadereyta, Oct. 15,

1633. See also the reports of Arias Montano to the king, Oct. 1, 12, 1630, pp. *129-32. See also pp. 210-24.

[61] *Ibid.*, *129-32. One of the ships was later sent to Spain with a load of brazil wood. This was cut by Dutch prisoners on the island of Curaçao. One of them, Jan Ottsen, got the idea that the Dutch should take the island. See also *AGI*, Aud. S. Dom. 194, Núñez Melián to the king, Oct. 5, 1632.

[62] Wright/Van Dam, I, 229-30, Juan de Eulate to the king, Nov. 20, 1633, and Report of Antoneli, pp. *136-40.

[63] *Ibid.*, I, *161-62, Enrique de Sotomayor to the king, Feb. 12, 1632: "...en San Martin...se han descubierto por los olandeses tres ensenadas de sal de minas qve pueden en vn ano cargar mas de quatrocientos nauios."

[64] *Ibid.*, "...qve antes de ocho meses abra en San Martin pasados de trescientos olandeses, muy vien fortificados."

[65] *Ibid.*, I, *163-66, Declaration of William Guine made in Puerto Rico, Nov. 23, 1632. See on St. Martin also Thomas G. Mathews, "The Spanish Domination of Saint Martin," *Caribbean Studies*, IX, 3-23.

[66] *AGI*, IG 2568, Letter of the governor of Puerto Rico to the king, Dec. 16, 1632: "...una gruessa armada con muy bvena artilleria y gente para echarla a tierra."

[67] Wright/Van Dam, I, *166-68, Spanish War Council to the king, March 8, 1633; letter of Pedro Coloma to Fernando Ruiz de Contreras, March 10, 1633.

[68] We follow the account written by Lope de Hoces to the king, July 13, 1633, Wright/Van Dam, I, *168-70, and a letter by Cadereyta to the king, July 15, 1633, *ibid.*, I, *171-77. Careful research in *ARA* did not reveal Dutch information on this conquest. Extensive information, however, is available in the "Relaçion verdadera de la famosa vitoria que ha tenido el Marques de Cadereyta, capitan general de los galeones en la Isla de San Martin contra el enemigo olandes que estaba apoderado della," *Col. Navarrete*, XXIV, 234-39.

[69] Wright/Van Dam, I, 286-91.

[70] *ARA*, WIC, OC, Inv. St. Gen. (West Indië), 5753, March 18, 1634.

[71] *ARA*, WIC, OC, St. Gen. 3535, *Plakaet Boeck* 1631-40, Aug. 22, 1634.

[72] Wright/Van Dam, I, 295, Cibrián de Lizarazu to the king, Aug. 30, 1634.

[73] Ojer, p. 23, "Relaçion çierta y verdadera del famosa suceso y vitoria que tuvo el capitan Benito Arias Montano contra los enemigos olandeses que estavan fortificados en una salina que esta riberas del rio Unare."

[74] Wright/Van Dam, I, *146-47, Arias Montano to the king, Nov. 5, 1633, and *147-49, the bishop of Puerto Rico to the king, Dec. 10, 1633.

[75] *Ibid.*, I, *152-56, Spanish War Council to the king, Oct. 7, 1641, and report of Orpín.

[76] *Ibid.*, I, p. 253.

[77] In a letter to the king Orpín was accused by the inhabitants of Cumanagoto of incompetency in his attack on the Dutch fort and asking too much money for his inundation project (he had asked 50,000 pesos), June 29, 1644, *ibid.*, *156-58.

[78] *ARA*, WIC, OC, St. Gen. 3535, *Plakaet Boeck* 1631-40, Resolution of the Heren XIX, March 24, 1634. The expert was the former commander of St. Martin, Jan Claeszoon van Campen.

[79] *Calendar of Historical Manuscripts; Dutch Manuscripts*, Vol. XVII, *Curaçao Papers, 1640-65* (New York State Library, Albany, N.Y.) gives the Dutch account. The correspondance between Stuyvesant and Fajardo and the declarations of witnesses in Wright/Van Dam, II, *133-53.

80 Wright/Van Dam, II, 210, 211, Spanish War Council to the king, Sept. 7, 1644: Advice to abandon the island. See also J. B. Dutertre, *Histoire générale des Antilles habitées par les François* (Paris, 1667-71), I, 408 ff. According to Dutertre the Spaniards left the island because of the high expenses.

81 *ARA*, WIC, OC, 21, Chamber of Zeeland, Minutes 1629-33. July 15, 1633, "Ordre en reglement van de Hoog Moghende Heeren Staten Generael der Vereenichde Nederlanden waer op ende waer naer alle ghemonteerde schepen uyt deese respectieve Provintien sullen vermoghen te vaeren in seecker ghedeelte van de limiten van t'Octroy van de West Indische Compagnie," art. IV. These instructions were many times repeated.

82 Aitzema, III, 261 ff.

83 *Ibid.*, III, 51, 52, 246 ff., 259-66. *RSG*, April 20, 26, 29, May 26, June 3, 1648.

84 Wright/Van Dam, II, *163-64, Memorial of the Dutch plenipotentiaries to the Spanish embassy.

85 Ojer, p. 29.

86 *Ibid.*, p. 30.

87 Aitzema, IV, 285.

88 *Ibid.*, IV, 774. See also L. Sylvius (Lambert van den Bos), *Vervolgh van Saken van staat en oorlogh in ende ontrent de Vereenigde Nederlanden en in geheel Europa voorgevallen* (continuation of Aitzema, Amsterdam, 1685-99), I, 1, 67.

89 Ojer, pp. 31, 32.

90 *Ibid.* Ojer's story is probably correct. Research in *ARA* did not reveal anything contradictory or supplementary to Ojer's account.

NOTES TO CHAPTER VII

1 Wright, "The Dutch and Cuba," p. 602.

2 Lonchay and Cuvelier, I, 525, Philip III to the Archduke Albert, March 14, 1619; also pp. 531, 532, letters of May 23, 25, 1619.

3 Wright, "The Dutch and Cuba," p. 603.

4 *Ibid.*, p. 604.

5 *Ibid.*, p. 605, Suggestion of the Spanish War Council, Oct. 28, 1621.

6 *Ibid.*, p. 605, Report of Cardinal de la Cueva, March 5, 1622.

7 *Ibid.*, p. 607, the king to Venegas, Nov. 24, 1622.

8 Pezuela, II, 23.

9 Wright/Van Dam, I, 32n2. Letters of Juan Ribera y Quesada and Garcia Girón to the king, Dec. 29, 1622. Gómez de Sandoval to the king, Jan. 29, 1623.

10 Van Wassenaer, VI, 61, 62. Jaricks brought home samples of wood and seeds which were given to the University of Leyden.

11 Aitzema, I, 489.

12 De Laet/Naber, I, 5, 6.

13 H. Winkel Rauws, *Nederlandsch-Engelsche samenwerking in de Spaansche wateren, 1625-1627* (Amsterdam, 1947), p. 1.

14 Pezuela, II, 35.

15 Chaunu, *Séville et l'Atlantique*, VIII, 2, 2, p. 1524: "Ni l'Armada ni la flotte de Terre Ferme ne sont de retour avant 1623. Les trésors de Terre Ferme comme ceux de Nouvelle Espagne arriveront en Espagne avec neuf mois pleins de retard. D'où tension, d'où dangers qui portent en eux l'échec complet de 1623."

16 Duro, *Armada Española*, IV, 43. They probably were the Schouten squadron.

544

17 De Laet/Naber, I, 4 ff. *ARA*, WIC, OC, 1, Minutes of the XIX 1623-24, Aug. 3, 1623. See also K. Ratelband, *De Westafrikaanse reis van Piet Heyn, 1624-1625* ('s-Gravenhage, 1959), pp. li, lii (hereafter cited as Ratelband, *Piet Heyn*).

18 Ratelband, *Piet Heyn*, pp. l-lxi. *ARA*, WIC, OC, 1, Minutes of the XIX, 623-24, July 31, 1623.

19 Ratelband, *Piet Heyn*, pp. lii, lvi.

20 *Ibid.*, pp. l-lvi, lxvi-lxxi. See also A. Oliveira de Cadornega, *História geral das guerras angolanas*, José Matias Delgado and Alves da Cunha, eds. (Lisboa, 1940-42), I, 99-111.

21 On the Van Zuylen expedition we followed De Laet/Naber, I, 50 ff., and Wright/ Van Dam, I. Ratelband, *Piet Heyn*, gives valuable information. Interesting details on the trade are given by Marées/Naber, and Boxer, *Salvador de Sá and the Struggle for Brazil and Angola, 1602-1686* (London, 1952).

22 *ARA*, WIC, OC, 1, Minutes of the XIX 1623-24, Aug. 17, 1623. Cf. De Laet/ Naber, I, 7 ff.

23 De Laet/Naber, I, 8.

24 PK 3541, *Redenen waeromme de West Indische Compagnie dient te trachten het landt van Brasilie den Coninck van Spaignien te ontmachtigen* by Jan Andries Moerbeeck (Amsterdam, 1624).

25 Wätjen, *Holl. Kolonialreich*, p. 38.

26 Sluiter, "Dutch Maritime Power and the Colonial Status Quo," *PHR*, XI (1942), 35.

27 Boxer, *The Dutch in Brazil*, p. 15. See also PK 3539 and 3540.

28 Boxer, *Salvador de Sá*, p. 44.

29 The ideas of Usselinx are best explained in the pamphlets already mentioned. See also Van Rees, pp. 408-32, Bijlage III; Boxer, *The Dutch in Brazil*, p. 16; Ligtenberg; Jameson; Ratelband, *Piet Heyn*, p. lxvi.; and António Cordeiro, *Historia insulana das ilhas a Portugal sujeitas no oceano occidental* (Lisboa, 1866), II, 361.

30 *ARA*, WIC, OC, 1, Minutes of the XIX 1623-24, Aug. 17, Oct. 11, 14, Nov. 1, 1623. There are different numbers on this fleet. In *ARA*: 24 ships, 3 yachts; Aitzema, I, 336 ff.: 23 ships, 3 yachts; De Laet/Naber, I, 8, 9: 22 ships, 4 yachts. For the appointments see *ARA*, WIC, OC, St. Gen. 3310, Eedt-Boeck 12528, Oct. 8, Nov. 7, 1623. For the artillery, *ABZ*, 2455/1624, Feb. 5, and *ABA*, 1369/1623, May 19.

31 Aitzema, de Laet, van den Sande, and van Wassenaer were contemporary Dutch historians of this conquest. Of the modern historians we mention Varnhagen, Netscher, Wätjen, and Boxer.

32 *ARA*, WIC, OC, 1, Minutes of the XIX 1623-24, Sept. 10, 1624: "Alsoo Godt de Almachtighe de Compagnie ghesegent heeft met de veroveringhe van de Bahia de Todos os Sanctos soo sullen de gecomitteerden insonderheyt ghelast comen om ter sulckx op de spoedighste ende beste middelen [te beramen] om deselve plaetse te conserveeren ende de negotie aldaer te stabiliseren."

33 *Ibid.*, March 30, April 1, 15, Sept. 23, 1624. It is difficult to conclude how many yachts were sent. We came to three.

34 *Ibid.*, April 15, 1624. Aitzema, I, 336-43.

35 Wätjen, *Holl. Kolonialreich*, p. 42. An eyewitness account is printed in the *Colección de documentos inéditos para la historia de España*, Martín Fernández de Navarrete *et al.*, eds. (Madrid, 1842-95), LV, 43-200, "Compendio historial de la Jornada del Brasil," by Juan de Valencia y Guzmán.

36 On the Schouten expedition see *ARA*, WIC, OC, 1, Minutes of the XIX 1623-24, and De Laet/Naber, I, 36 ff. See also Van Wassenaer, VII, 154-55.

37 *Col. Navarrete*, XXIII, 226 ff. "Carta que escribio al Rey el Dr. Alonso Criado

de Castilla, gobernador de la Provincia de Guatemala," June 28, 1606, followed by a "Segunda Relaçion."

38 "...eveneens werdt ter kennis ghebracht het inbrengen van het schip bij Hilbrant Jacobszoon Jansen ontrent de Honduras verovert." *ARA*, WIC, OC, 1, Minutes of the XIX 1623-1624, Sept. 21, 1624.

39 Van Zuylen left Luanda in August. Piet Heyn arrived at the end of October. See De Laet/Naber, 1, 60 ff. Cf. Ratelband, *Piet Heyn*, pp. lxxiv-lxxviii.

40 *ARA*, WIC, OC, Inv. St. Gen. (West Indië), 5752. Report of Piet Heyn. This report is one of the few documents signed by Heyn himself. Other information on the Piet Heyn expedition of 1624-25 in Ratelband, *Piet Heyn*, De Laet/Naber, 1, and Van Wassenaer. Boxer, *The Dutch in Brazil*, gives an interesting account. Cf. M. G. de Boer, "De val van Bahia," *TvG*, LVIII (1943), 38-49.

41 *ARA*, WIC, OC, 1, Minutes of the XIX 1623-24, Sept. 23, 1624.

42 The information of this paragraph was provided by *ARA*, WIC, OC, 1, Minutes of the XIX 1623-24, Oct. 1, Nov. 8, 9, 11, 12, 14, Dec. 26, 1624. Hendrick Corneliszoon Loncq was the first choice, as he had been for the Bahia expedition. Again his demands were too high. Five other candidates were seriously discussed: Lam, Rebel, Swartenhondt, Veron, and Hendricksz. Lam was appointed and took the oath Nov. 17, 1624. *ARA*, WIC, OC, 3310, Eedt-Boeck 12528.

43 Boxer, *Salvador de Sá*, Chapter 6.

44 It is not clear where Lam's place was in these changing plans. Did he sail with Hendricksz to Brazil? It is possible, not probable. Naber/Wright, *Piet Heyn*, p. 26: "Ick en hebbe niet connen vernemen off de Heer Jan Dircksz Lam in de West Indies gheweest is."

45 De Laet/Naber, 1, 85 ff., 104 ff. Aitzema, 1, 420 ff., copies de Laet almost literally. Cf. Van Wassenaer, XII, 54 ff.

46 Our information concerning the attack on Puerto Rico rests mainly on four sources: De Laet/Naber, 1, 92 ff., Wright/Van Dam, 1, *31 ff. and two articles by Cayetano Coll y Toste in *BHPR*, IV (1917), 229-43: "Relaçion de la entrada y cerco del enemigo Boudoyno Henrico, general de la armada del Principe de Orange, en la ciudad de Puerto Rico de las Yndias por el licenciado Diego de Larrasa, teniente auditor general que fue de ella"; and XII (1925), 193-204, "Ataque de los Holandeses a la isla. Rectificaciones históricas." See also Juan Manuel Zapatero, *La guerra del Caribe en el siglo XVIII* (San Juan de Puerto Rico, 1964), pp. 301-7.

47 De Laet/Naber, 1, 95.

48 "Relaçion de la Entrada," p. 232: "...he visto [en Flandes] las bravatas de aquella tierra..." De Laet's reaction: "De Gouverneur gaf een spottelyck antwoorde." De Laet/Naber, 1, 97.

49 "Relaçion de la Entrada," p. 236. In Coll y Toste's article Hendricksz is called "el enemigo fanfarrón" (*BHPR*, XII [1925], 199).

50 In Jan., 1626, the States General, not yet knowing that Hendricksz had withdrawn from the island, was requested by the XIX, also ignorant of the defeat, to support the WIC to keep the island. See *ARA*, WIC, OC, Inv. St. Gen. (West Indië), 5752, and *RSG*, Jan. 24, 29, 31, Feb. 13, 24, 1626. *Res. Holl.*, April 2, 1626.

51 Francisco Morales Padrón, *Jamaica española* (Sevilla, 1952), p. 247.

52 Wright/Van Dam, 1, *52-54, Declaration of Pedro Angola, March 1, 1626.

53 De Laet/Naber, 1, 115-18. Wright/Van Dam, 1, 94, *57-63, Andrés Rodríguez de Villegas to the king, June 4, 1626.

546

54 See on this construction the letter written by Rodríguez de Villegas mentioned in note 53.
55 De Laet/Naber, I, 118, 119. Wright /Van Dam, I,* 72-74, Declaration of Juan Matias de la Carrera, Nov. 20, 1626.
56 De Laet/Naber, I, 123 ff.
57 Wright, "The Dutch and Cuba," p. 610. Royal cédula of March 16, 1625.
58 Ibid., Velásquez de Contreras to the king, July 30, 1625.
59 Ibid., p. 611. See also De Laet/Naber, I, 127, 128, and Wright/Van Dam, I, *77-79.
60 De Laet/Naber, I, 130. See also Duro, Armada Española, IV, 96.
61 Wright, "The Dutch and Cuba," p. 613.
62 De Laet/Naber, I, 130: "Door dit ontydich verseylen van dese Vloote van den Generael Boudewijn Hendricksz uyt dese Ghewesten ontrent de Havana, quam niet alleen te passe dat de Compagnie dese schoone Vloote ghenoechsaem leedich en schadeloos t'huys kreegh, maer wierde mede verloren de alderschoonste occasie die de Compagnie oyt hadde ghehadt om den vyandt afbreuck te doen..."
63 ARA, WIC, OC, Inv. St. Gen. (West Indië), 5752, March 27, 1626. RSG, March 28, 1626. Sources differ in the number of ships: Aitzema, I, 535 ff. follows de Laet as we did. Van Wassenaer, xv, 53, mentions eight ships and five yachts.
64 Naber/Wright, Piet Heyn, p. lxxiii.
65 Ibid., p. lxxvi. This mysterious "Green Island" was mentioned by a certain Cornelis Adriaenszoon Ackersloot. The two yachts had a most interesting voyage but failed to locate the island. They never joined Heyn's fleet again, and arrived home in February, 1627.
66 Ibid., p. lxxvii. Letter written by Piet Heyn to the XIX, Nov. 10, 1626. Cf. Duro, Armada Española, IV, 96.
67 Wright, "The Dutch and Cuba," p. 613. Cabrera to the king, April 19, 1627.
68 Naber/Wright, Piet Heyn, pp. lxxxi ff. ARA, WIC, OC, Inv. St. Gen. (West Indië), 5752. Cf. Izaäk Commelin, Frederick Hendrick van Nassauw, Prince vâ Orangien, zyn leven en bedrijf (Amsterdam, 1651), I, 20.
69 De Laet/Naber, II, 4, 5. Van Wassenaer, XIV, 53.
70 Van Wassenaer, XIV, 54-57. Commelin, I, 20. The two ships lost in this daring attack—including his own flagship the "Amsterdam"—as well as the two yachts lost on the expedition to "Green Island" were replaced by five of the eighteen Spanish prizes. The other thirteen were burnt.
71 J. W. IJzerman, Cornelis Buysero te Bantam, 1616-1618 ('s-Gravenhage, 1923), pp. 223-25. Lam had been defeated by the Spaniards in 1616 as commander of a fleet of eleven sails. In another encounter he had lost his ship. In 1621 he had safely brought home two ships from the East Indies. The Chamber of Amsterdam awarded him a golden chain and a sum of money.
72 On the Lam-Veron disaster we followed De Laet/Naber, I, 104 ff., Van Wassenaer, XII, 54 ff., and ARA, WIC, OC, Inv. St. Gen. (West Indië), 5752 which contains an extensive report of this enterprise and its disastrous end.
73 De Laet/Naber, I, 144-49.
74 Ibid., I, 159-61.
75 Wright/Van Dam, I, *101-3. Cristóbal Aranda to the king, July 16, 1627; p. 171, Report written by Tomás de Larraspuru, Nov. 10, 1627, and report of the president of the Council of the Indies, Madrid, Nov. 22, 1627.
76 De Laet/Naber, II, 31-33.

77 De Laet/Naber, IV, 282 ff.

78 Andrews, p. 224.

79 Chaunu, *Séville et l'Atlantique*, VIII, 2, 2, pp. 1643-46, 1462-63, *et passim*.

NOTES TO CHAPTER VIII

1 Piet Heyn, his name is small, his actions were great; he took the silver fleet. From a Dutch popular song.

2 Simon Stijl, *De opkomst en bloei der Vereenigde Nederlanden* (Amsterdam, 1778), p. 267.

3 De Laet/Naber, II, 47 ff., gives a substantial account of this exploit. See also Van Wassenaer, XV, 28. The fleet stood under the command of Dirck Simonsz van Uytgeest.

4 De Laet/Naber, II, 34.

5 *Ibid.*, p. 39: "...een Portugees Schip met Swarten gheladen, door een onghe-luckighe scheut onder water te gronde doen gaen..."

6 Andrews has two interesting chapters (IV and V) on the amateurs and professionals in privateering. We adopted his terminology without accepting fully Andrews' implications.

7 De Laet/Naber, II, 42-46, gives a captivating picture of this fight. So do the documents which give the Spanish side in Wright/Van Dam, I, *103-9.

8 De Laet/Naber, II, 46, gives the list of the cargo. See also Commelin, I, 36.

9 Guerra y Sánchez, *Manual de historia de Cuba*, p. 100: "...dio lugar a un error funesto para los españoles."

10 Our sources on the equipment and composition of this fleet are Naber/Wright, *Piet Heyn*, pp. 55 ff.; De Laet/Naber, II, 56 ff.; Van Wassenaer, XV, 54, and the following resolutions of the States General and the Provincial States of Holland: *RSG*, Feb. 29, March 27, 28, 31, 1628; *Res. Holl.*, March 3, 1628.

11 Van Wassenaer, XV, 54: "...tot generael was de vaillante en vermaerde Pieter Heyn van Delfshaven; als admirael de voorsichtighe Hendrick Loncq gestelt." Cf. De Laet/Naber, II, 56.

12 Naber/Wright, *Piet Heyn*, pp. xli, xlii. The father died Sept. 14, 1624. Piet Heyn's mother survived her son; so did his wife. There were no children.

13 Aitzema, I, 720. Aitzema was a member of the Frisian nobility.

14 PK 3867, Dionysius van Spranckhuysen, *Tranen over den doodt van den Grooten Admirael van Hollandt, loffelycker ende onsterffelicker ghedachtenisse, Pieter Pietersz Heyn* (Delft, 1629). The Spanish evaluation is interesting. Duro, *Armada Española*, IV, 98, calls him "antiguo corsario, vencido y prisionero en una de las correrías, fue sentenciado á galeras, sirviendo quatro años al remo en las de España, tiempo que aprovechó en completar el conocimiento de nuestra lengua y costumbres." His epitaph confirms this statement: *Indiam, Hispaniam, Flandriam, captivitatis suae, mox libertatis ac victoriae testes habuit.* See Aitzema, I, 822.

15 PK 3867.

16 Naber/Wright, *Piet Heyn*, pp. xlv, xlvi, *41: "...que havia estado en la Havana quatro años," and p. 88: "...porque dixo avia sido prisionero en el Morro, y en las galeras de Santa Marta."

17 *Ibid.*, p. li. See also R. Bijlsma, "Rotterdamsche akten betreffende Pieter Pietersz Heyn," *De Navorscher*, LXV (1916), 130-32. Some information in Dirck van Bleyswyck, *Beschryvinghe der Stadt Delft* (Delft, 1667), pp. 178 ff.

18 *Recopilación de leyes de los Reinos de las Indias* (5th ed., Madrid, 1841), IV, Book 9, tit. XXXVI, ley XIV, 80. See also "The Naval Tracts of Sir William Monson," M. Oppenheim, ed., *Publications of the Navy Record Society*, XXIII, (1902) 2, 309-40, and Morales Padrón, *Jamaica española*, pp. 302 ff.

19 Naber/Wright, *Piet Heyn*, pp. *3-8. The Spanish titles of these reports are: "Memoria de las flotas del Rey que salen cada año, assi de Sevilla como de Cadiz, para Tierra Firme, Nueua España, Honduras, La Hauana, y otras partes" and "Memoria de la flota de Nueua España y Honduras que sale cada año para México."

20 From the first memorial, p. *5.

21 Piet Heyn's report on these two ships is printed in Naber/Wright, *Piet Heyn*, pp. 20-27. Heyn's suggestions were followed in the attack of Van Uytgeest in 1627, mentioned above and by Ita in Aug., 1628, a month before the attack of Heyn on the silver fleet from New Spain.

22 *Ibid.*, p. cvi.

23 Conflicting numbers are given by Aitzema, I, 720, 721; Van Wassenaer, XV, 54; De Laet/Naber, II, 56, 57; Naber/Wright, *Piet Heyn*, p. 55. The differences, however, are minor and not important. Duro, *Armada Española*, IV, 98, gives "29 galeones armados con 623 piezas de artillería."

24 Naber/Wright, *Piet Heyn*, pp. 166, 167. Van Spranckhuysen quoted Proverbs 28:1.

25 Van Wassenaer, XV, 58: "...opdat niemant van sijn doens of cours kennisse soude hebben." See map.

26 Banckert, alias Joost van Trappen, of a well-known Zeelandian family of sailors. See E. B. Swalue, *De daden der Zeeuwen gedurende den opstand tegen Spanje* (Amsterdam, 1846), pp. 292 ff., and Pieter de la Rüe, *Staatkundig en heldhaftig Zeeland* (Middelburg, 1736), pp. 127-31.

27 Naber/Wright, *Piet Heyn*, pp. *17, 18. Letter of Francisco Terril to Tomás de Larraspuru, July 27, 1628.

28 *Ibid.*, p. 18. Letter of Domingo Vázquez to Tomás de Larraspuru, Aug. 9, 1628. Copies of this and the other letter (note 27) were sent to Cabrera, who sent them to the king.

29 *Ibid.*, pp. *37-45; cxv-cxvi.

30 The information on this organization of the Dutch fleet is taken from Naber/Wright, *Piet Heyn*, pp. 74-88; p. 77.

31 Van Wassenaer, XVI, 95 ff.

32 Spanish accounts of the New Spain fleet under Benavides in *Col. Navarrete*, XXIV, 240-43: "Relaçion del suceso de Don Juan de Benavides, General de la flota de Nueua España de que se apoderaron los olandeses en el Puerto de Matanzas el dia 8 de Septiembre de 1628 y de su prision y muerte en Sevilla que se ejecuto Jueves 18 de Mayo de 1634," and Naber/Wright, *Piet Heyn*, pp. 19-23, Doc. IV.

33 *Ibid.*, p. *xii. Benavides himself stated that his fleet was composed of four galleons, fourteen or fifteen merchantmen, and six sloops.

34 Van Wassenaer, XV, 107: "...there was a strong wind blowing south." Commelin, I, 41, follows Piet Heyn's report. So do Aitzema, I, 723, and De Laet/Naber, II, 64. See also this report in Naber/Wright, *Piet Heyn*, pp. 95 ff.

35 J. de Solórzano Pereira, *Obras varias postumas* (Madrid, 1776), "Discurso, y alegación en derecho sobre la culpa que resulta contra el General Don Juan de Benavides Bazán, el Almirante Don Juan de Leoz, ambos cavalleros de la Orden de Santiago, y otros consortes," pp. 245-334.

36 Naber/Wright, *Piet Heyn*, pp. *26-29. This testimony of one of his captains, Hernando Guerra, was very damaging for Benavides.
37 *Ibid.*, pp. *xvi ff., cxxi. ff. We followed the sources mentioned, although it is not always possible to mention with each sentence or paragraph which source was cited. Many times they overlap. Spanish and Dutch accounts are remarkably similar. See also pp. *31, 32, Declaration of Benavides.
38 *Ibid.*, p. *xix, note 1.
39 Solórzano y Pereira, p. 318: "...les hizo entrar con amenazas."
40 PK 3858, D. van Spranckhuysen, *Triumphe van weghen de Gheluckighe ende Over-rijcke Victorie welcke de Heere onse Godt op den 8en Septembris des Iaers 1628 verleent heeft aen de Vloote van de West-Indische Compagnie, onder het beleyt van den Heer Generael Pieter Pietersz Heyn teghen de Silver vlote onser vijanden, komende van Nova Hispania, in en ontrent de haven van Matance* (Delft, 1629).
41 Naber/Wright, *Piet Heyn*, pp. *33-36. Admiral Juan de Leoz to the president and judge of the "Casa Real de Contratación de Indias," Oct. 7, 1628.
42 *Ibid.*, pp. *86-88, Declaration of Diego Ordóñez, Doc. IX.
43 Van Wassenaer, XVI, 97.
44 M. G. de Boer, *Piet Heyn en de Zilveren vloot* (Amsterdam, 1946), p. 95.
45 Van Wassenaer, XVI, 98, gives the following losses for the Dutch: 150 dead including the 34 men lost on the Lesser Antilles and 54 men lost by Banckert on Tobago.
46 De Laet/Naber, II, 66 ff. Van Wassenaer, XVI, 100, 101. Naber/Wright, *Piet Heyn*, pp. 128-58. See also Appendix IV.
47 Van Wassenaer, XVI, 102. Piet Heyn took four Franciscan monks with him.
48 We followed Piet Heyn's report in *ARA*, WIC, OC, 17, Chamber of Amsterdam: Letters to the Chamber. The report, probably written by Heyn himself, is dated Dec. 8, 1628 and printed in Naber/Wright, *Piet Heyn*, pp. 103 ff. It was probably sent from Falmouth.
49 Heyn's letters to the units of his fleet in English ports are published in Naber/Wright, *Piet Heyn*, pp. 107 ff. The important articles of the Treaty of Southampton were XV, XVI, and XVII. See Van Wassenaer, XVI, 98-99. Heyn's distrust of the English was misplaced.
50 *RSG*, Nov. 25, 28, Dec. 1, 1628. Arend-Van Rees, III, 4, p. 353.
51 Arend-Van Rees, III, 4, p. 353.
52 Naber/Wright, *Piet Heyn*, pp. 118 ff., Doc. xxxi-xxxiv.
53 The Zeelandian admiral Evertsen was ordered to protect the incoming ships. *RSG*, Dec. 5, 10, 12, 16, 19, 1628. *Res. Holl.*, Dec. 19, 1628. Not one ship was lost to the Dunkirkers.
54 A. van der Capellen, *Gedenkschriften, 1621-1654* (Utrecht, 1777-78), I, 492.
55 His statue was inaugurated in Delfshaven, Oct. 17, 1870. In 1965 it was removed from its original beautiful site. Instead of looking over the Maas River, Heyn now faces a modern bridge. The Latin inscription says: Silver and gold gave way to his courage.
56 De Laet/Naber, II, 66: "Siet hoe het volck nu raest, omdat soo grooten Schat t'huys brenghe, daer weinich voor hebbe ghedaen; ende te voren als ick der voor hadde ghevochten, ende verre grooter daden ghedaen als dese, en heeft men sich naewlijcks aen my ghekeert."
57 Van Wassenaer, XVI, 89: "Volgens dien heeft men in alle frontierplaetsen der Vereenichde Provincien de ghewende teeckenen van vreucht ghetoont, opdat de parthye sulcks bekent soude worden."

58   THE INDIAN FLEET INTERCEPTED
AND WITHOUT BLOODSHED A VERY RICH BOOTY TAKEN
AT CUBA'S PORT
NOW MORE FAMOUS BECAUSE OF THE HARM SUFFERED BY THE SPANIARDS
THAN BEFORE BECAUSE OF THEIR DEFEAT
THE STATES OF THE UNITED NETHERLANDS
HAVE STRUCK FROM THE CONQUERED TREASURE
THIS MEDAL, 1629.

The other side reads: Despoiled Matanzas shortly ago tasted the courage of Heyn's men. Van Loon, II, 174, 175.

59 PK 3858; see note 40.

60 PK 3860. *Loffdicht ter eeren van den manhaftigen zee-heldt Pieter Pietersz Heyn over het ver-overen van de rijcke Silver-vloot. En vermaninghe tot danckbaerheyt daerover* (Delft, 1629).

61 PK 3861. *Protest ofte scherp dreyghement, 't welck den Coninck van Spagnien is doende d'Heeren Staten Generael...* (Middelburg, 1629).

62 PK 3862. *Practycke van den Spaenschen aes-sack* (s' Graven Haghe, 1629).

63 PK 3864. *Oratio panegirica* (Lugdunum Batavorum, 1629): *Tu aeterne Deus, victor noster ac stator, custos ac vindex huyus Reipublicae, cuyus unicum auxilium in hac victoria agnoscimus, colimus, veneramur...*

64 See Appendix IV. De Laet/Naber, II, 72-73: 11,509,524 guilders. "Het buytgeldt voor elck bijsonder soude beloopen sesthien maenden en twee derde part maents, doch door tusschen sprake van den Heer Generael, d'Admirael, Vice-Admirael en andere Scheeps officieren wierdt het op seventhien maenden ghestelt." Cf. Van Wassenaer, XVI, 102, 103. See also Naber/Wright, *Piet Heyn*, p. cxxxviii.

65 Aitzema, I, 725.

66 De Laet/Naber, IV, 282, mentions 50 per cent for war revenues in 1628 and 25 per cent for revenues in 1629. See also Van Wassenaer, XVI, 100.

67 De Boer, *Piet Heyn en de Zilveren vloot*, p. 113. Naber/Wright, *Piet Heyn*, pp. cxxxix, cxix.

68 Naber/Wright, *Piet Heyn*, pp. lii, cxxxix.

69 Spain was not capable of taking an active part in the Thirty Years' War.

70 "Uyt Romen wordt geadviseert, dat geheel Romen, soo paus als andere, sich vroolyck hebben ghemaeckt met d'victorie van Piet Heyn; jae, dat de Paus sal geseit hebben, dat haer die tyding soo smaeckelick was als het euangelium selve," J. S. van Veen, "Brief aan het Hof van Gelderland over de vernietiging der zilver-vloot (1628)," *De Navorscher*, LXIII (1914), 49-50.

71 Naber/Wright, *Piet Heyn*, pp. cxxxvi, cxxxvii. The value of the cargoes captured was perhaps as high as 13 to 14 million. It is not known what Heyn thought of his 7,000 guilders. See also F. Graefe, "Beiträge zur Lebensgeschichte Piet Heyns," *BVGO*, VII, 1 (1931), 145-51; and "Piet Heyn als Leutnant-Admiral von Holland," *BVGO*, VII, 6 (1935), 174-204.

72 Aitzema, I, 822: To die is not shameful but a shameful death.

73 Duro, *Armada Española*, IV, 102.

74 Naber/Wright, *Piet Heyn*, pp. *37-45.

75 For the trial our source of information was J. de Solórzano Pereira. The author was a former *oidor* of the *Audiencia* of Lima and a member of the Council of the Indies, *una lumbrera del foro.* See Duro, *Armada Española*, IV, 103-5.

76 Solórzano Pereira, p. 318: "...á unos hombrecillos hechos andrajos, sin personas, sin lustres."

77 Wright, "The Dutch and Cuba," p. 616.
78 *Col. Navarrete*, XXIV, 240, "Relaçion del suceso de Don Juan de Benavides, General de la flota de Nueva España de que se apoderaron los olandeses en el Puerto de Matanzas." See also Pezuela, II, 57 ff.
79 Naber/Wright, *Piet Heyn*, p. *xxxiii, Dudley Carlton to the Home Office, Nov. 18, 1628.

NOTES TO CHAPTER IX

1 Wright, "The Dutch and Cuba," p. 618.
2 *Ibid.*, pp. 618-19.
3 Dutertre, I, 5. Besides Dutertre we used Charles de Rochefort, *Histoire naturelle et morale des iles Antilles de l'Amérique* (Rotterdam, 1658).
4 Dutertre, I, 28. Harlow, *Col. Expeditions*, p. xx.
5 W. R. Menkman, "Aanteekeningen op Hamelbergs Werken," WIG, XXIII (1941), 11, writes that a fortress was built in 1635.
6 Harlow, *Col. Expeditions*, p. xxiii, xxiv.
7 Accounts of this action in Duro, *Armada Española*, IV, 109 ff., Dutertre, I, 28 ff., De Laet/Naber, II, 98 ff., *ARA*, WIC, OC, Inv. St. Gen. (West Indië), 5752, Extract from Spanish letters; and Harlow, *Col. Expeditions*, xxiv.
8 *CSP*, I, 1574-1660, no. 100, July 29, 1630.
9 Wright, "The Dutch and Cuba," pp. 620-22.
10 Our sources on this expedition were *ARA*, WIC, OC, 2, Minutes of the XIX, 1629-45; 20, Chamber of Zeeland, Minutes 1626-29; Van Wassenaer, XV, XVI; De Laet/Naber, II, 83 ff.; and *Res. Holl.*
11 The Flemish Islands were the Azores. On his instructions see *ARA*, WIC, OC, 2, Minutes of the XIX 1629-45. Aug. 1, Nov. 8, 12, 1629. Van Wassenaer, XV, 90, gives the following details: 11 ships, well provided (for 16 months), 842 sailors, 326 soldiers, 117 bronze and 506 iron pieces. Pater took the oath July 12, 1628; see *ARA*, WIC, OC, St. Gen. 3310, Eedt-Boeck 12528.
12 There is a suggestion in Arend-Van Rees, III, 4, p. 355, that the venture was inspired by a traitor from the Spanish Netherlands, who was compensated by the States General (*RSG*, March 10, 1629).
13 Guerra y Sánchez, *Manual*, p. 100.
14 *Ibid.*, "... en pos de ellos una nube de barcos menores traficantes y piratas, completaban la obra de destrucción."
15 Pater was probably cleaning his ships at Ile à Vache when Fadrique de Toledo entered the Caribbean area and sailed to Nevis. See Wright/Van Dam, I, 198n, and Pezuela, II, 69 ff.
16 *ARA*, WIC, OC, 2, Minutes of the XIX 1629-45, Nov. 8, 1629. In this meeting earlier resolutions (from minutes which have disappeared) are repeated.
17 De Laet/Naber, II, 91 ff., gives an account of these problems. Pater's pilots, arriving at Grenada, had made a longitude mistake of one hundred miles.
18 Wright/Van Dam, I, *113, Cabrera to Fadrique de Toledo, Nov. 26, 1629. An odd circumstance in the movements of the Spanish and Dutch fleets was the fact that they did not know about each other for some time. Another interesting detail is that, as in the case of Piet Heyn, this Dutch fleet also stood under the command of a former prisoner of the Spaniards. Pater had been taken prisoner in Fajardo's

actions at Araya in 1605: "...que el General se llama Juan Pater y le tomo en Araya Don Luis," Wright/Van Dam, I, *118.

¹⁹ De Laet/Naber, II, 97.

²⁰ ARA, WIC, OC, 2, Minutes of the XIX 1629-45, Nov. 12, 1629: "De Heere heeft de tijden en plaetsen besloten op welcke en in welcke hij ons sal gelieven weder te segenen."

²¹ De Laet/Naber, II, 102: "Daer quamen verscheyden Ghewesten in bedenken, doch naer dat alles wel hadden overleght..."

²² Wätjen, Holl. Kolonialreich, pp. 45, 46.

²³ Casparus Barlaeus, Rerum per Octennium in Brasilia (Amstelodami, 1647). A Dutch translation by S. P. L'Honoré Naber, Nederlandsch Brazilië onder het bewind van Johan Maurits, grave van Nassau, with the author's Dutch name Kaspar van Baerle ('s-Gravenhage, 1923) will be cited as Van Baerle. In the Latin edition (cited as Barlaeus) Loncq is called militiae maritimae veteranus (p. 17), "een ervaren zeeman van den ouden stempel."

²⁴ Rear-admiral under Piet Heyn, vice-admiral under Loncq, "the terror of the enemy," in Swalue's romantic account. Swalue, pp. 292 ff.

²⁵ PK 3909, Consideratien ende redenen der Edele Heeren Bewinthebberen van de Geoctroyeerde West Indische Compagnie... nopende de teghenwoordige deliberatie over den Treves met den Coninck van Hispanjen (Haarlem, 1629).

²⁶ Arend-Van Rees, III, 4, 430 ff. See also O'Callaghan, Documents, I, 62-68, and Ligtenberg, pp. 137-38. We call this the fourth "Great Design," while Piet Heyn's expedition of 1628 is considered to be the third.

²⁷ Van Baerle, p. 22: "De Compagnie ondersteunt het benarde Vaderland." Cf. Arend-Van Rees, III, 4, pp. 395 ff., 435.

²⁸ "Hoe veel Schepen tot dese Vloot onder den Generael ter Zee ende Colonel; hoeveel Matrosen ende Krijchslieden bij dese twee Oversten gedestineert sijn is niet te beschrijven," Van Wassenaer, XVII, 62.

²⁹ De Laet/Naber, II, 115. There was a St. Vincent (São Vicente) in the Cape Verde archipelago and also one among the Windward Islands.

³⁰ ARA, WIC, OC, 2, Minutes of the XIX 1629-45, Nov. 8, 1629. Loncq's secret instruction is dated Aug. 1, 1629.

³¹ Ibid., Aug. 1, 1629.

³² Van Loon, II, 193: He initiated the Golden Age.

³³ ARA, WIC, OC, 2, Minutes of the XIX 1629-45, Nov. 12, 1629. Pater's instruction is dated Sept. 23, 1629. Van Hoorn's letter Dec. 2, 1629.

³⁴ Following his instruction of June 13, 1630. ARA, WIC, OC, Inv. St. Gen. (West Indië), 5752, 1630-34. De la Rüe, pp. 257-62, gives information on Thijsz.

³⁵ De Laet/Naber, II, 178-82.

³⁶ Duro, Armada Española, IV, 111: "...echaron en tierra cosa de mil hombres." Cf. Netscher, Les Hollandais au Brésil (La Haye, 1853), pp. 51 ff.

³⁷ Wright/Van Dam, I, *114, 115, 198. Gerónimo de Quero to Francisco de Murga, Feb. 27, March 5, 1630. Report of the Dutch attack on Santa Marta.

³⁸ Ibid., I, 187. Wright, "The Dutch and Cuba," pp. 622-23.

³⁹ ARA, WIC, OC, Inv. St. Gen. (West Indië), 5752, 1630-34, June 13, 1630: "Ende voorts dat niet alleen een eerste secours van 15 soo Schepen als jachten, volck, vivres en admonitien, t'gent wij den Admirael Pater om den alarm in West Indien te continueren."

⁴⁰ Ibid. The XIX requested support from the States General, pointing out that both

fleets (of Loncq and Pater) consisted of 106 ships and yachts, 13,230 men, 2613 bronze and iron pieces and "powerfully equipped." They added to this: "Zo ist dat wij ons keeren tot de gewoonlijcke liberaliteyt van Uwe Ho: Mo: met onder-danich versouck dat deselve favorabel gelieve te considEREN hoe alle de exploiten van de Compagnie sijn ghelycke functien als die van de oorlogsschepen deeser Landen op alle zeehavenen ende scheepen des Conincks van Spagnien...de oorlogen ghebracht ter plaetse daer den vijant al sijne schatten versamelt."

41 ARA, WIC, OC, 2, Minutes of the XIX 1629-45, Instruction for Loncq, Aug. 1, Nov. 8, 1629. See also Boxer, The Dutch in Brazil, p. 46. This author bases his opinion on J. A. Gonsalves de Mello, Tempo dos Flamengos (Rio de Janeiro, 1947). Cf. Van Wassenaer, XIX, and RSG, June 18, Oct. 5, 1630.

42 He was appointed general of a fleet destined for Brazil.

43 RSG, Aug. 1, 2, Sept. 23, 1630. Van Wassenaer, XIX, 89: "alwaer de Burghers ende Inghesetenen verstaen hebbende dat den Heer Generael de stadt naerderde hem met ontallijcke Jachten, Chaloupen ende Speelschuyten zijn te ghemoet ghevaren."

44 Wright/Van Dam, I, 211. Fadrique de Toledo to the king, July 30, 1630.

45 ARA, WIC, OC, Inv. St. Gen. (West Indië) 5752, 1630-34, June 13, 1630; 21, Chamber of Zeeland, Minutes 1629-33, Instruction of Booneter, June 4, 1630.

46 ARA, WIC, OC, 2, Minutes of the XIX 1629-45, March 23, 1630.

47 De Laet/Naber, II, 144 ff.

48 Ibid., II, 163: "Alwaer den Admirael Pieter Adriaensz haer achterhaelde, ende onder sijn Vlagghe nam."

49 "...te cruyssen bedachterwijse tussen Santa Martha ende Rio Grande de la Mag-dalena om aldaer te passen op de Spaensche schepen en barquen comende van Santo Domingo die wy verstaen dat nu iaerlycks in de maent van February ofte Maert van Santo Domingo naer Cartagena loopen." From Booneter's instruction (see note 45).

50 ARA, WIC, OC, 2, Minutes of the XIX 1629-45. Letter of the XIX to Booneter, Sept. 2, 1630.

51 De Laet/Naber, II, 173: "...geboodt den Admirael dat yeder Schipper hem soude brenghen de monsterrolle van sijn volck, by de welcke bevonden wierdt dat in de vloote waren 1888 koppen, ende daeronder 237 soldaten."

52 Wright, "The Dutch and Cuba," p. 623.

53 Duro, Armada Española, IV, 112.

54 "...te gaen naer de Eylanden benoorden Cuba ghelegen om ons van de ghelegent-heyt derselver grondig rapport te connen doen." See the instruction of Booneter. In a letter of September 2, 1630 (see note 50) this is repeated. Careful research in ARA, WIC, OC, did not reveal such report.

55 ARA, WIC, OC, 8, Copybook of outgoing letters 1629-42. Letter to Booneter, June 4, 1630: "...alle Uwe schepen en jachten wederom bij den anderen komen tot half Mey 1631 aen Isle de Vacq [Ile à Vache] ende soo daer enighe t'niet beseylen conden aen Cabo Tybron."

56 ARA, WIC, OC, 21, Chamber Zeeland, Minutes 1629-33. Instructions for de Neckere, Jan. 8, 1631. A secret resolution of Feb. 13 added to the former a new article to use the squadron "op seker exploit."

57 G. W. Kernkamp, "Zweedsche archivalia," BMHG, XXIX (1908), 143. Letter of Samuel Blommaert to Oxenstierna, Nov. 18, 1637.

58 ARA, WIC, OC, 21, Chamber Zeeland, Minutes 1629-33. Letter of the XIX to Booneter, Feb. 3, 1631.

59 *ARA*, WIC, OC, 8, Copybook of outgoing letters 1629-42. Letter of the XIX to Booneter, Feb. 15, 1631: "...dat Ued. sich wacht met deselve inde havenen van Engelandt in te loopen op dat weghens den teghenswoordighen vrede tusschen de twee Croonen van Spanje en Engelandt..."

60 Wright, "The Dutch and Cuba," p. 624. Bitrián to the king, June 30, 1631.

61 De Laet/Naber, III, 4.

62 Guerra y Sánchez, *Manual*, p. 101.

63 There is extensive literature on this battle: Netscher, Wätjen, and Boxer are most prominent non-Portuguese authors. Of Dutch historians we mention de Laet, van Wassenaer, Commelin.

64 Wätjen, *Holl. Kolonialreich*, p. 56. Wätjen quotes here de Laet.

65 Van Loon, II, 196: Dulcia sic meruit—Thus he earned the sweetness.

66 George Edmundson, "The Dutch Power in Brazil," *EHR*, XV (1900), 46 ff.

67 *ARA*, WIC, OC, 2, Minutes of the XIX 1629-45, Dec. 29, 1631. Appointment of Marten Thijsz as admiral of the fleet which would sail from Pernambuco to the West Indies. De Laet/Naber, III, 89: "...ende besloten den Ammirael Marten Thijsz met een stercke Vloote naer West-Indien te senden om aldaer den vijandt te beschadigen."

68 Larraspuru, arriving at Havana Aug. 24, 1631, had not seen any but insignificant enemies. Wright, "The Dutch and Cuba," p. 624.

69 *ARA*, WIC, OC, 2, Minutes of the XIX 1629-45, April 9, 1632: "...dat voor eerst dient ghelet datter op de Custe van Brasil ende te Pernambuco..."

70 *ARA*, WIC, OC, 45, Chamber of Zeeland, Resolutions of Admiral Marten Thijsz and his councils. Instructions, 1631-32. Thijsz divided his fleet into three squadrons to operate separately. See also De Laet/Naber, III, 117-19.

71 *Ibid.*, Instruction for Galeyn van Stapels, June 14, 1632, signed by Thijsz.

72 *ARA*, WIC, OC, 2, Minutes of the XIX 1629-45, Nov. 3, 1632. Orders to equip a squadron of "twee jachten ende drij chaloupen" plus an instruction for van Hoorn.

73 *Ibid.*, 4 ships, 3 yachts, 3 sloops, 518 sailors, 420 so-called old soldiers, i.e. soldiers whose contracts with the company had expired and who were going home. See also De Laet/Naber, III, 187-96.

74 De Laet/Naber, III, 191.

75 *Ibid.*, III, 195. For this venture we followed the accounts of De Laet/Naber, III, 188 ff. Cf. Duro, *Armada Española*, IV, 115-16.

76 A few years later an Anglo-Dutch expedition under Nathanael Butler, departing from Providence, had better luck. San Francisco was surprised and a ransom of 16,000 pieces of eight extorted from its citizens. See Burns, p. 210. In 1659 Captain (afterwards Sir) Christopher Myngs returned to Port Royal after having destroyed the towns of Campeche, Coro, Cumaná, and Puerto Cabello. The loss for the Spaniards amounted to £300,000. *Ibid.*, p. 261.

77 De Laet/Naber, IV, 116.

78 M. G. de Boer, "Een memorie over den toestand der West Indische Compagnie in het jaar 1633," *BMHG*, XXI (1900), 343-62. This memorial was preceded by two letters sent by the WIC, without date, but with an *exhibitum* of Oct. 11 and Dec. 23, 1632. De Laet/Naber, IV, 283 and 284 gives the following list of ships taken in the Caribbean and Brazil:

Year	Caribbean	Brazil
1629	12	6
1630	9	36
1631	13	16
1632	8	14
1633	27	63
	69	135

J. B. van Overeem, *De Reizen naar de West van Cornelis Cornelisz Jol 1626-1640* ('s-Gravenhage, 1942), also as an article in the WIG, XXIV (1942), 1-19, 33-49, gives slightly different numbers. If we estimate the average ship at 10,000 guilders, the damage caused by the Dutch amounts to 7,000,000 guilders in ships in the Caribbean. To this must be added the losses in cargoes and lives.

NOTES TO CHAPTER X

1 The noise of his stump sounds in Aragon's ears as a thunder. From a poem by Dutch poet Jan Vos.
2 Barlaeus, p. 91: Van Baerle, p. 111. Cornelius Iölus, à teneris mari fluctibusque innutritus, coeli ac sali, quibus adsueverat, indole acrior, promptae, ad omne facinus audaciae, quiete nullus, navalibus studiis erectus & suus, silentio fortis, impetu vehemens, laboris ac fidei capacissimus, caetera rudis. See also Ratelband, *Piet Heyn*, xliii, lxxiii.
3 Kernkamp, "Zweedsche archivalia," p. 143. Letter of Blommaert to Oxenstierna, Nov. 18, 1637.
4 Aitzema, II, 539. Duro, *Armada Española*, IV, 191, calls Jol "uno de los más hábiles y osados marineros que tenían [los holandeses]."
5 "...omdat d'eene been in een scheepsgevecht verloren hebbende, op een houten soo wel gingh, dat men het quaelijck konde mercken ende soo rap selver scheep was als andere die haer beyde beenen hebben." De Laet/Naber, II, 48.
6 Only Van der Aa gave Jol some attention, III, 7, pp. 50-51. Cf. Brandt, *De Ruiter*, p. 5. Commelin, I, 95, 180-83; II, 25, 26, 60, 125. Van der Aa's sketch formed the model for the studies of J. C. M. Warnsinck in his introduction to De Laet/Naber, IV, and van Overeem (see note 78, Chapter IX). K. Ratelband completed Overeem's study with "De expeditie van Jol naar Angola en São Tomé," *WIG*, XXIV (1942), 320-44.
7 De Laet/Naber, II, 49, 50.
8 *Ibid.*, II, 113.
9 The Dutch name for the Caribbean Sea; from the Spanish *corral* or the Portuguese *curral*.
10 "...een scheepken...gheladen met cacaonooten, ende wilde haer naer Nova Hispania. De onse, de waerde van dit ghewas niet wetende lieten t' scheepken weder los." De Laet/Naber, II, 175.
11 ARA, WIC, OC, 2, Minutes of the XIX 1629-45, Jan. 6, Feb. 10, 11, 1631. Cf. Overeem, p. 9.
12 "...alwaer hij een schip hadde ghenomen met vierhondert Swarten, komende van Catschieu uyt het welcke alleen hadde ghenomen...ende hadde t' schip voorts laten varen." A few days later Jol took another slave ship and did the same "omdat met de Swarten niet wisten te verrichten." De Laet/Naber, III, 59 ff.

13 *Ibid.*, IV, 284, gives van Hoorn (plus Jol) 27 ships in 1633. Jol, in 1634, took 3 more ships on this same expedition. On this expedition see De Laet/Naber, III, 186 ff.

14 Hamelberg, I, 21.

15 Van Grol, I, 94.

16 The story is well told by De Laet/Naber, IV, 187-93. Menkman wrote an article on the flags in *WIG*, "Aantekeningen op Hamelsberg werken," pp. 161-76. The Spanish side is represented by the letters of the Governor Juan de Amexquita Quijano, of May 12, 1635, and Francisco Riaño y Gamboa, May 25, 1635: Wright/Van Dam, II, *3-5, 6-9. The governor describes Jol's ships as follows: "...dos naues poderosas con color que eran de escolta diciendolo assi a las personas que con mi horden estauan en la uoca, con uanderas de quadra, con auitos de Cristo y Santiago."

17 De Laet/Naber, IV, 188.

18 "Hanse despachado de todo esto auisos a Nueba España y Cartagena por triplicado, a Honduras, Campeche, Puerto Rico, Santo Domingo, Caracas y Maracaybo, y demas partes...y a las çentinelas que ay en cauo de Corrientes y en isla de Pinos se les ha auisado para que den notiçia de estos enemigos a las nauios y fregatas que por aquellas parajes pasaron," wrote Francisco Riaño y Gamboa to the king, May 25, 1635, Wright/Van Dam, II, *9.

19 *Ibid.*, p. *7, "...se auian de estar en estas costas y sobre este puerto hasta hazer buenas presas de plata, cochenilla y sedas para boluer a Olanda." Cf. De Laet/Naber, IV, 189-90.

20 Accounts of this battle in De Laet/Naber, IV, 190, and in Wright/Van Dam, II, *9 ff. Letter of Francisco Riaño y Gamboa to the king, Sept. 26, 1635. Overeem, p. 18.

21 Wright/Van Dam, II, *9-13, 20n.

22 De Laet/Naber, IV, 192 ff. De Laet called this ship the "admirael van Cartagena."

23 *Ibid.*, IV, 193. Cf. De Jonge, *Zeewezen*, I, 264, and Arend-Van Rees, III, 5, p. 54.

24 *ARA*, WIC, OC, 14, Chamber of Amsterdam, Minutes 1635-36, Nov. 12, 19, 21, 1635. On a letter received by this Chamber March 17, 1636, the comment was: "Op de requeste van Cornelis Cornelisz Jol tot Bourborch in Vlaenderen gevangen daer hij seer miserabelick getracteert versoucken dit door beneficie van dese camer syne ontslaginge by dese occasie van de gevangenen van admirael Collaert mocht worden gecoruceert, is geresolveert dat Heeren Preses Van Poorte, Becker en Biscop den President van de Admiraliteyt sal spreecken om te sien watter geschieden kan."

25 *ARA*, WIC, OC, 22, Chamber of Zeeland, Minutes 1634-36, March 17, 1636. Cf. Overeem, p. 19.

26 Lonchay and Cuvelier, III, 117. Letter of Jean de Gavarelle to the Cardinal Infant, June 2, 1635: "On ne saurait dès lors satisfaire à l'ordre du Roi d'envoyer en Espagne un corsaire hollandais appelé Pie de Palo, récemment capturé."

27 *ARA*, WIC, OC, 14, Chamber of Amsterdam, Minutes 1635-36, Aug. 21, 1636, and 2, Minutes of the XIX 1629-45, July 18, 1636. See Overeem, p. 33, and De Laet/Naber, IV, 261-76.

28 *ARA*, WIC, OC, 50, Letters and Papers from Brazil. Van Walbeeck to the XIX, Dec. 4, 1635.

29 *ARA*, WIC, OC, 2, Minutes of the XIX 1629-45, July 18, 1636, and 42, Commissions, conditions, etc., July 18, 1636: "De Heeren Commissarissen met Cornelis Cornelisz Jol gebesoigneert hebbende, refererende dat hy oordeelt voor dese tydt ghenoegh te syn een schip met twee jachten."

30 *ARA*, WIC, OC, 2, Minutes of the XIX 1629-45, Secret instructions for Commander

Jol, July 18, Aug. 15, 1636. If Jol died, his brother Siebert, captain of one of the ships of this squadron, would succeed him.

31 De Laet/Naber, IV, 263: "...om dat ontrent de Havana in die tijdt van t'jaer niet te doen en was."

32 *Ibid.*, IV, 265: "Merckt hier hoe dat alle ghelegentheden metter tijdt werden uytghevonden, ende hoe dat dese twee schepen inde tijdt van minder als twintigh daghen uyt de Strate van Bahama sijn weder gecommen aen de Caribische Eylanden." It took Booneter almost 50 days.

33 *Ibid.*, IV, 271: "...telden ses en twintigh zeylen."

34 "Daer waren wel negen particuliere kapers, soo dat niet wisten naer wie te jaghen." *Ibid.*, IV, 274. Ten years earlier Piet Heyn had already complained about this kind of competition. Most privateers were licensed by the Chamber of Zeeland.

35 Kernkamp, "Zweedsche archivalia," p. 143, Letter of Blommaert to Oxenstierna, Nov. 18, 1637: "...en verclaert, indien hy ses goede schepen by hem hadde gehadt, dat hy deselve vermeestert soude hebben."

36 "Dit concept op de zilvervloot is meest door my beleyt en hebbe alle instructien daertoe gemaect, is oock alleen by vier ofte vijf bewinthebberen bekent," *ibid.*, pp. 148-59, Letter of Blommaert to Oxenstierna, Sept. 4, 1638. A similar statement in a letter of Nov. 13, 1638. In the letter to Oxenstierna of Nov. 18, 1637, Blommaert wrote: "Had de Compagnie mynen raedt willen volgen, dat is dat men in Brazil ordre op het voorleden voorjaer gegeven hadde dat alle schepen die van tyt tot tyt thuis gecomen syn, dat die tesamen in de maend Mey over West Indië thuys gecomen souden hebben en hen onder de vlagghe van Houtebeen vervoecht om volgens myn aenwysinge den 20 Juny op seeckere plaetse te wesen, wy souden voorseecker met Godes hulpe de vlote vermeestert hebben." In other letters, Blommaert expresses the same ideas.

37 "Die van Zeelandt syn nu de presidiale Camer...haer Ho: Mo: hebben ons verbot gedaen dat wy op de vergaderingen niet en sullen verschynen voor en aleer die van Zeelandt de notulen van de voorgaende vergaderinge in Den Hage gehouden hebben geteeckent en datse uyt de poincten van beschryvinge die daer off gehandelt syn toucherende het openstellen van den handel op Brazil," *ibid.*, pp. 153-54. Cf. Aitzema, II, 538 ff.

38 Barlaeus, p. 91: *Designatus huic operi fuit Cornelius Iölus.*

39 *Ibid.*, p. 92. Van Baerle, p. 112.

40 Boxer, *The Dutch in Brazil*, p. 84. Cf. Stoppelaar, note 6, chapter xvii. The conquest was the work of Colonel Coen or Koin. The count commented: "Chose inoye et incroyable quand on veut considérer la force de cette place."

41 Commelin, II, 25.

42 Kernkamp, "Zweedsche archivalia," pp. 155 ff. Blommaert to Oxenstierna, Sept. 4, 1638.

43 De Laet/Naber, IV, lxxxiii.

44 *ARA*, WIC, OC, 53, Letters and Papers from Brazil. Letter of Johan Maurits to the XIX, June 29, 1638. Also 23, Chamber of Zeeland, Minutes 1637-39. Report on the exploit by Cornelis Cornelisz Jol, Feb. 16, 1638.

45 *ARA*, WIC, OC, 53, Letters and Papers from Brazil. Letter of Johan Maurits to Abraham Roozendael, June 10, 1638.

46 *ARA*, WIC, OC, 53, Letters and Papers from Brazil, Letter of Johan Maurits to the XIX, June 29, 1638.

47 D. F. Scheurleer, *Onze mannen ter zee, in dicht en beeld* ('s-Gravenhage, 1912-14), I, 140.

48 Spain was frightened. *Col. Navarrete*, XXIV, 258-59: "Real cédula expedida por el Rey con fecha de 8 de Mayo de 1638 a Don Carlos de Ybarra, Almirante General de su Armada Real de las Grandes Islas de Yndias a cuyo cargo estaba su gobierno avisandole las noticias del Armada que habia salido de Olanda y por cabo de ella el cosario Pie de Palo."

49 *ARA*, WIC, OC, 53, Letters and Papers from Brazil. Second instruction for Jol, June 19, 1638. Cf. Netscher, *Les Hollandais au Brésil*, p. 99.

50 Besides the sources quoted there is detailed information on the movements of the Spanish fleet in *Col. Navarrete*, VII, 7-23: "Los sucesos maritimos acaecidos con la Armada de Galeones del Gen¹. Don Carlos de Ybarra," and PK 4620, *Waerachtigh Verhael t'welck de Heere Don Carlos Ibarra Visconde van Centera, Capᵗ. Generael van de Konincklicke Armada dienende tot bewaringhe van de vaert van West-Indien. Translaet uyt den Spaenschen weghens t'gevecht tusschen des Conincx Silvervloot, en den Admirael Houtebeen in West-Indien op den 31 augustus 1638, 12 mylen van de Havana* (Amsterdam, 1639). See also Duro, *Armada Española*, IV, 189-96.

51 "Cartas atrasadas," they were called by Duro, *Armada Española*, IV, 192.

52 Interesting, although not always correct details of this battle are furnished by some manuscripts of the Biblioteca Nacional of Madrid: MSS 2369, f. 80, *Relaçion verdadera de la refriega que tuvieron nuestros galeones de la Plata en el cabo de San Anton, con catorce navios de que era General Pie de Palo* (Madrid, 1638), and MSS 2639, f. 177, *Muerte de Pie de Palo. Segunda relaçion, y muy copiosa de una carta que embio el señor Duque de Medina a la Contrataçion de Sevilla. Da secuenta de la batalla que han tenido los Galeones con 40 navios de Olandeses, siendo General de ellos Pie de Palo. Assi mismo se da cuenta de su muerte* (Madrid, 1638). Cf. Wright/Van Dam, II, 47, 48.

53 Wright/Van Dam, II, 47n1.

54 Van Baerle, pp. 113-14. Barlaeus, p. 93.

55 Kernkamp, "Zweedsche archivalia," pp. 168-69, Blommaert to Oxenstierna, Nov. 13, 1638. Cf. *RSG*, Nov. 17, 1638.

56 Van Baerle, pp. 115-16. Barlaeus, p. 95.

57 Wright/Van Dam, II, *31-33. Sancho de Urdanivia to the king, Nov. 15, 1638. This Spanish captain had fought a brave rearguard action which, as Irene A. Wright ("The Dutch and Cuba," p. 625) poetically writes, "stood forth among the more prosaic documents of the Archives of the Indies like a highly colored painting of a vigorous seafight touched by a ray of sunlight fallen into a darkened picture gallery." The poetry of the story looses, perhaps, some of its glamor if one realizes that it was the brave captain himself who described his own actions. Cf. Wright/Van Dam, II, *34-36.

58 PK 4620, closing sentence.

59 *Ibid*. Cf. Duro, *Armada Española*, IV, 193, and Van Baerle, p. 115.

60 Kernkamp, "Zweedsche archivalia," p. 168, Blommaert to Oxenstierna, Nov. 13, 1638.

61 *RSG*, Nov. 18, 25, 1638. Aitzema, II, 539.

62 Aitzema, II, 591.

63 *Encyclopedia Universal Ilustrada Europea-Americana*, XXVIII (Barcelona, 1925), p. 812.

64 Boxer, *The Dutch in Brazil*, p. 94. See also *KHG*, V, 5 (1869), 515-29: "Kort en waarachtig verhaal van de komst en het vertrek van de Spaansche vloot in Brazilië, Pernambuco, 25 Febr. 1644."

65 Van der Aa, III, 8, 126. *RSG*, Dec. 24, 1639.

66 *ARA*, WIC, OC, 55, Letters and Papers from Brazil. Letter of Johan Maurits to the XIX, May 9, 1640. Cf. Overeem, p. 31.

67 *ARA*, WIC, OC, 55, Letters and Papers from Brazil. Instruction of Johan Maurits for Jol, July 10, 1640.

68 Wright/Van Dam, II, *36-46. Also *ARA*, WIC, OC, 55, Letters and Papers from Brazil. Declaration of Lucas Gilles, Oct. 6, 1640; Jol to the XIX, Oct. 6, 1640; Bartel Wouters to the XIX, Oct. 9, 1640.

69 Wright/Van Dam, II, *36-46. Alvaro de Luna Sarmiento to the king, Nov. 6, 1640: "Aviendose entendido de algunos prissioneros qve dichos enemigos echaron en tierra en diferentes tiempos, qve todos los vajeles qve auia en estas costas, y otros qve andauan en la de Cartaxena, esperauan a Pie de Palo, qve auia ydo de socorro al Brasil con sessenta naos, y qve auia de venir a juntarsse con ellos a los fines de agosto..."

70 *Ibid.*, II, *38-46. Alvaro de Luna Sarmiento to the king, Nov. 6, 1640: "...antes de ameneçer auia hallandosse tan empeñado el General Juan Cornieles en la entrada deste puerto qve le auia dicho a uno de los religiosos: 'Padre, si me entre en el Puerto de Havana, haranme buen quartel?'"

71 Wright, "The Dutch and Cuba," pp. 628-29.

72 Van Baerle, p. 257; Barlaeus, p. 196: *Una in Belgium praemissa infelicis coepti nuntia fuit.*

73 Wright/Van Dam, II, *45. Alvaro de Luna Sarmiento to the king, Nov. 6, 1640: "En todo hara vuestra señoria lo qve mas gustare, teniendo por çierto me holgara yo qve la armada de España le hallara muy sobrado de todo lo qve falta, para qve el buen suceso qve de la mano de Dios esperamos tubiera mas luçimiento en la mayor preuençion de vuestra señoria."

74 *ARA*, WIC, OC, 55, Letters and Papers from Brazil, Jol to the XIX, Oct. 6, 1640.

75 *Ibid.*, Instruction of Johan Maurits for Jol, July 10, 1640.

76 "Nicht Bahia, sondern Angola müsse man angreifen. Keine Expedition würde Neuholland gröszere Vorteile bringen als die Eroberung dieser afrikanischen Kolonie! Denn Angola sei der erste Sklavenmarkt an der Westküste des dunklen Kontinents." Wätjen, *Holl. Kolonialreich,* p. 106. Cf. *ARA*, WIC, OC, 42, Commissions, conditions, etc., Feb. 2, March 7, 1642.

77 Ratelband, "De expeditie van Jol," pp. 323-24. Barlaeus, pp. 342-47.

78 Dutch literature on this expedition is far from abundant. We used *ARA*, WIC, OC, 55, 56, Letters and Papers from Brazil, and St. Gen. 8275 (new 9410), "Besogne ende rapport van saecken voorgevallen op de vergaderinge vande XIX den 5 Feb. 1642," with "Eene Beschrijvinge van de Reise naer Angola en resolutien op deselve genomen onder den Admirael Jol beginnende de 30 Mey ende eindigende 25 Augusti 1641"; Inv. St. Gen. (West Indië), 5756, 1641-42, Johan Maurits to the XIX, Oct. 29, 1641; Jan. 17, Feb. 28, March 4, 12, 19, April 30, 1642, resolutions of the XIX; a "Report of the conquest of S. Thomé," Dec. 2, 1642, signed by Jan Claessen Cock. Printed sources: Ratelband, "De expeditie van Jol," pp. 320-44; Boxer, *The Dutch in Brazil*; Cadornega; Cordeiro; Ralph Delgado, *História de Angola* (Benguela, 1948-55).

79 *ARA*, WIC, OC, 56, Letters and Papers from Brazil. Letter of Cornelis Hendricx Ouwman, Feb. 28, 1641. Cf. Ratelband, "De expeditie van Jol," pp. 328-29.

80 Jol followed instructions. See *ARA*, WIC, OC, 56, Letters and Papers from Brazil, May 25, 1641, Instruction for Huygen, Aug. 11, 1641.

81 Cordeiro, II, 361: "...estão expostas ao commercio de hereges, nações estrangeiras."

82 ARA, WIC, OC, 56, Letters and Papers from Brazil, Instruction of Aug. 23, 1641.

83 ARA, WIC, OC, 8275 (new 9410), Minutes of the meetings of the XIX in 1641 and 1642. "Eene beschrijvinge..." p. 2. Cf. Ratelband, "De expeditie van Jol," p. 333.

84 Van Baerle, p. 267. Barlaeus, p. 204.

85 ARA, WIC, OC, 56, Letters and Papers from Brazil, Letter of Jol to Johan Maurits, Sept. 16, 1641. See also Inv. St. Gen. (West Indië), 5760, Oct. 16, 1641: "Articulen geaccordeert by den Heer Admirael met de Inwoonderen."

86 Van Baerle, pp. 268-69, Barlaeus, pp. 205-6. See also RSG, Jan. 19, 1648: "...voor date van de publicatie aldaer gedaen van den gemaecten Treves."

87 Van Baerle, pp. 269-70. Barlaeus, pp. 206-7.

88 ARA, WIC, OC, Inv. St. Gen. (West Indië), 5756, "Report of the Conquest of São Thomé." 5760, Articles accorded to the inhabitants. They were approved by the XIX, Nov. 2, 1641. Cf. Ratelband, "De expeditie van Jol," pp. 337-41.

89 Barlaeus, p. 209. "It was not a victory for Mars but for Death." Van Baerle, p. 271.

90 ARA, WIC, OC, 56, Letters and Papers from Brazil, Dec. 12, 1641, Jan Claessen Cocq's report: "...den hr. Admirael de 25 sieck geworden sijnde is den 31 godsalichlyck in den Heere gerust...seer magnifelyck naer onse gelegentheyt in de groote kercke begraven."

91 ARA, WIC, OC, 58, Letters and Papers from Brazil, Protest of the Governor of São Thomé, Jan. 1, 1643.

92 Barlaeus, p. 93. *Haec vitae, haec mortis area.* Van Baerle, p. 114.

93 Barlaeus, p. 209, *Non ad apparatum & aulicas elegantias factus vir erat, sed simplicem coepti pertinaciam, & Hispanorum internecionem.*

NOTES TO CHAPTER XI

1 Our soil is barren. Line of the national anthem of the present Dutch Antilles, Aruba, Curaçao, and Bonaire in their local dialect, Papiamento.

2 From De Laet/Naber, I, 16-30, 48 *et passim;* II, 24 *et passim.*

3 ARA, WIC, OC, 46, Reports and accounts concerning Brazil, Angola, etc., "Description of the 'Wilde Eylanden,' Tobago, St. Christopher, St. Eustatius, Saba, St. Martin, while also of other islands, Isla de Vacq, etc." 1627. See also Wright/Van Dam, I, *193-95, Declaration of Alonso Díaz in Coro, Jan. 3, 1635. In this declaration Díaz testified that the Dutch had visited the Curaçao islands many times before the conquest in 1634.

4 Dutertre, I, 34-35.

5 ARA, WIC, OC, Lias West Indië, 1631, Letter of Marcus van Valckenburch to the Chamber of Amsterdam, May 27, 1631. Cf. Hamelberg, "Historische schets van de Nederlandsche bovenwindsche eilanden tot op het einde der 17e eeuw," in GTLVG, II (1899), 109 (hereafter cited as Hamelberg, "Hist. Schets.").

6 David Pieterszoon de Vries, *Korte historiael ende journaels aenteyckeninge van verscheyden voyagiëns,* ed. H. T. Colenbrander ('s-Gravenhage, 1911), pp. 151 ff. See also Hartog, *Bovenwindse eilanden.*

7 ARA, WIC, OC, 22, Chamber of Zeeland, Minutes 1634-36, Dec. 27, 1635.

8 *Ibid.,* Report of Jan Snouck, Aug. 11, 1636.

9 Hamelberg, *Nederlanders*, II, 11: "...door de natuur van zelf geleverde zaken," and *ibid.*, II, Doc., 13-16: "Vrijheden en exemptiën bijde gecommitteerde bewinthebberen vande respective Cameren der geoctroyeerde West Indische Compagnie...toegestaan aen d'Heeren Adriaen en Cornelis Lampsins." Aug. 30, 1655.

10 Excellent research concerning governmental organization is done by Van Grol, II, 18 ff. *et passim*.

11 Wright/Van Dam, II, 110.

12 Hamelberg, II, Doc., 21-22, gives examples of the trade in red slaves.

13 ARA, WIC, OC, 23, Chamber of Zeeland, Minutes 1637-39, Oct. 3, 1639.

14 Hamelberg, "Hist. Schets," p. 115.

15 ARA, WIC, NC, 1160, Letters and Papers from Curaçao, May 1, 1752. Letter of Willem Kock to the X. Information given to me by M. A. Visman. Besides *ARA* information is given mainly by three historians. Hamelberg and Van Grol are already quoted. Both did extensive and systematic research in *ARA*. J. Hartog's *Geschiedenis van de Nederlandse Antillen* is more a compilation of printed secondary sources and very disorganized. It must be observed, that the Dutch call the islands in the St. Martin group *bovenwindse eilanden*, i.e., windward islands. The English call all the islands in this region Leeward islands. We followed the English denomination.

16 On Alonso de Ojeda there is much information. See Demetrio Ramos, "Alonso de Ojeda en el gran proyecto de 1501 y en el tránsito del sistema de descubrimiento y rescate al de poblamiento," *Boletín de la Academia Nacional de Historia*, L, 197 (enero-marzo, 1967), 34-85, with many sources in the footnotes; Alberto Harkness, "Alonso de Hojeda y el descubrimiento de Venezuela," *Revista Chilena de Historia y Geografía*, CIII (1943), 197-213; Cornelis Ch. Goslinga, "Ojeda en Vespucci. Opmerkingen bij een ontdekking," in *Voor Rogier* (Hilversum, 1964), pp. 19-36. There is an abundance of literature on Rodrigo de Bastidas, especially in German studies on the Welsers.

17 ARA, WIC, OC, 2, Minutes of the XIX 1629-45, April 6, 1634. Discussions on point 5 of the deliberations (*Poincten van beschrijvinghe*): "...het bemachtighen van het eylant Curazao om te hebben een bequaeme plaetse daer men sout, hout ende andere mocht becomen ende van deselve plaetse den viant in West Indië te infesteren."

18 De Laet/Naber, IV, 94. Cf. Wright/Van Dam, I, *181, 182, Declaration of Diego Gómez, Aug. 10, 1632.

19 Wright/Van Dam, I, *183-85, Instructions for Pedro de Llovera; declaration of Pedro Navarro Villavicencio, public notary.

20 ARA, WIC, OC, 2, Minutes of the XIX 1629-45, April 6, 1634. "Verclaringe van Cornelis Rijmelandt, gevaren hebbende op t' Schip Domburch ende gevangene in Cartagena." This declaration contained ten points. Rijmelandt was well aware of intercolonial navigation.

21 Information on van Walbeeck and le Grand in Hamelberg, *Nederlanders*, I, and Hartog, *Curaçao*, I.

22 ARA, WIC, OC, 2, Minutes of the XIX 1629-45, April 6, 1634: "...om den viant beter t'abuseren de vlaggen van de Compagnie worden afgeslagen ende achter op de spiegel een Cruys gestelt, laetende tien of elf mannen in Spaensche habiten boven staen; men sal daertoe sien waer te nemen eenen Sonnendach ofte heylighendach op dat men des viants schepen onversien van volck soude moghen vinden."

23 Wright/Van Dam, I, 310n4.

24 Van Grol, I, 89.

25 Our information of the conquest comes from the reports of van Walbeeck and le Grand, sent to the XIX, both dated Aug. 27, 1634, and reprinted in De Laet/ Naber, IV, 301-11, and Hartog, Curaçao, I, 134-42. The Spanish point of view is given by Wright/Van Dam, I, *183-247, and A. Maduro, Spaanse documenten uit de jaren 1639-1640 (Scherpenheuvel, Curaçao, 1961).

26 Wright/Van Dam, I, *187-93, López de Morla to Francisco Núñez Melián, Sept. 2, 1634. Hartog's arguments that Morla was not the governor but Juan Mateo are weak. Morla wrote a report in which he stated that there were only seven Spaniards. He probably limited himself to those capable of carrying arms: "El qual me adelante algunos passos de los yndios y de los siete españoles que en mi compañia estauan..." This letter gives an excellent account of events from the Spanish point of view. Morla had just become governor of the island and the former governor, Juan Mateo, was still on the island. Hartog, Curaçao, I, 111, discusses the titles of the Spanish authorities.

27 De Laet/Naber, IV, 99 ff. The account of the Dutch actions is mainly taken from De Laet/Naber and Wright/Van Dam.

28 Wright/Van Dam, I, *187-93, Lope López de Morla to Francisco Núñez Melián, Sept. 2, 1634.

29 Ibid., I, *201-4, Declaration of Anton in Valencia, Feb. 9, 1635: "...los primeros olandeses que binieron luego entendieron a haçer la fuerça de la boca y de la poblaçion a la cual acudian los soldados..."

30 "Soo uwe E.E. resolveren mochten dit eylant tegens den viant te maintineren, soo sullen boven de 200 soldaten die hier nu sijn, noch een 300 dienen gesonden te worden, want de havens van St. Anna ende St. Barbara ende haer waterplaetsen dienen met vasticheden bewaert ende voorsien te wesen, alsoo opt verlies vant water de Fortressen moeten volgen." Report Van Walbeeck in Hartog, Curaçao, I, 134-39.

31 Le Grand's report (in Hartog, Curaçao, I, 140-42, dated Aug. 27, 1634) agrees with Van Walbeeck's but emphasizes the defense more.

32 ARA, WIC, OC, 2, Minutes of the XIX 1629-45, Aug. 30, 1634, Equipment of a Brazilian fleet of three ships and three yachts. Dec. 6, 1634, Secret instruction for this fleet.

33 Res. Holl., Nov. 10, 1634.

34 De Laet/Naber, IV, 182. See also Hamelberg, Nederlanders, and Hartog, Curaçao, I.

35 Van Grol, I, 94, 95. ARA, WIC, OC, 22, Chamber of Zeeland, Minutes 1634-36, Nov. 30, Dec. 1, 1634, Jan. 4, June 30, 1635.

36 Wright/Van Dam, I, *185-87. Juan Mateos to Francisco Núñez Melián, Aug. 31, 1634.

37 The Dutch prisoner's name, misspelled in the Spanish documents as Maripitersen, was probably Martin Petersen. Ibid., I, *199-201, Núñez Melián to the king, Feb. 11, 1635. See also Spanish War Council to the king, Jan. 22, 1635, ibid., I, *196-99.

38 Ibid., I, 347n.

39 Ibid., I, *205-10, Special Council for Curaçao to the king, March 8, 1635.

40 Ibid., I, *226-39, Declaration of Juan Mateos, Oct. 19, 1635, and Mathias Herman, Jan. 31, 1636.

41 The Portuguese refused to add Portuguese ships to this squadron. Ibid., I, 404n3

and *241-47, Minutes of the War Council, May 30, 1636.

42 *Ibid.*, II, *53, 54, Iñigo de la Mota Sarmiento to the king, July 25, 1636: "...es este puerto tan perniciosso para estas yslas de vuestra magestad..."

43 "...seis vageles que aprecian en mas de 400,000 pesos, y de las demas yslas se vien las mismas malas nuebas, siendo los que obran estos daños vageles que en Curaçao tienen los olandeses," *ibid.*, II, 54.

44 Burns, p. 214.

45 Wright/Van Dam, II, *59, Ruy Fernández de Fuenmayor to the king, June 24, 1638: "Uno y otro, señor, despierta al cuydado mas perozosso..."

46 *Ibid.*, II, *61, 62, Information given by the scouts sent by Iñigo de la Mota Sarmiento, April 6, 1639.

47 *Ibid.*, II, *63, Iñigo de la Mota Sarmiento to the king, Oct. 3, 1639: "Ocuparon los ynglesses con mayor preuencion la ysla de Tortuga en la vanda del norte de Santo Domingo...Repartieronse los Estados de Olanda las piraterias de aquella costa..."

48 "...queriendo boluer a poblar la dicha ysla el Capitan Galo, corsario llamado comunmente Pie de Palo..." *ibid.*, II, *64-67, Francisco de Tajagrano and Diego Núñez de Peralta to the king, June 24, 1640.

49 *Ibid.* The guns and some other arms taken by Fuenmayor were estimated at 2,812 *reales*.

50 Maduro, *Spaanse documenten uit de Jaren 1639 en 1640*, gives the correspondence, requests, and complaints of those years.

51 Wright/Van Dam, I, 415n. See also pp. *248-56, Memorandum of the War Council, July (n.d.), 1641. In this memorandum Curaçao is called "mas una ladronera que fortificacion principal."

52 *Ibid.*, Memorandum of the War Council: "Y todos reconocieron la importancia grande de esta materia, y que estauan promptos de ir a hazer esta empressa, hauiendo polbora y muniçiones bastantes para ello, y particularmente bastimientos, sobre que tambien se confirmio. Y viendo que no hauia sufiçiente cantidad para el intento en las çinco naos del cargo de Francisco Diaz Pimienta quardase las ordenes que tenia de su general, y que el governador de Cumana socoriesse al de Veneçuela con lo que pudiesse para el intento referido." In the same *legajo* a letter of the governor of Cumaná, Benito Arias Montano, dated March 3, 1640, insists on action to be taken against the Dutch.

53 *Ibid.*, II, *68, 69, Declaration of José de Vergara, May 19, 1640.

54 Hamelberg, *Nederlanders*, I, 30 ff. Hartog, *Curaçao*, I, 164-71.

55 *ARA*, WIC, OC, 14, Chamber of Amsterdam, Minutes 1635-36, Jan. 4 and Feb. 1, 1635. Objections of Zeeland in 22, Chamber of Zeeland, Minutes 1634-36, Jan. 4, 1636. In a meeting of June 30, 1635, the Zeeland Chamber agreed "Beter gedaen als gelaten is goetgevonden dat dese Camer part sal houden int eylant Curakau." See also Hamelberg, *Nederlanders*, I, Doc., pp. 42-43.

56 Thus he is called in the Spanish documents and in the Memorandum of the War Council (see note 52). Van Walbeeck was called Balbecque.

57 *ARA*, WIC, OC, St. Gen., 3310, Eedt-Boeck 12528, Dec. 23, 1638.

58 Hartog, *Curaçao*, I, 151. The source of information is not mentioned.

59 Luis Alberto Sucre, *Gobernadores y capitanes generales de Venezuela* (Caracas, 1928), p. 131.

60 Hamelberg, *Nederlanders*, I, 38.

61 Sucre, p. 134. Wright/Van Dam, II, *81-100.

⁶² Wright/Van Dam, pp. *81-100, Manuel de Velasco to Ruy Fernández de Fuen-mayor, Oct. 18, 1641; Diego Ruiz Maldonado to Fuenmayor, Oct. 22, 1641; Francisco Cornelio Briceño to Fuenmayor, Oct. 29, 1641; Juan Pacheco Maldo-nado to Fuenmayor, Oct. 31, 1641. Governors and other officials along the coast listed their complaints like Fuenmayor in his letter to the king, Dec. 18, 1641: "El enemigo de Curaçao ha comenzado mouimientos si recelados siempre desde que se apodero de aquella ysla, dettenidos quiça para mas asigurarlos."

⁶³ On this Spanish counteraction, *ibid.*, ɪɪ, *105-15. Fuenmayor's War Council at Bonaire, Sept. 1-Oct. 9, 1642. The Dutch fortress had a garrison of 40 soldiers, 13 Negroes, 4 Indians, and 3 Indian women. See also Sucre, p. 134.

⁶⁴ The literature in English on Peter Stuyvesant is not very appreciative of his charac-ter. We used M. Eerdmans, *Pieter Stuyvesant; an Historical Documentation* (Grand Rapids, 1957), B. Tuckerman, *Peter Stuyvesant, Director-General for the West India Company in New Netherland* (New York, 1893), the article of J. H. P. Kemperink, "Pieter Stuyvesant: waar en wanneer werd hij geboren?" *De Navorscher*, xcvɪɪɪ (1959), 49 ff.; S. Kalff, "Iets over Peter Stuyvesant," *WIG*, vɪɪɪ (1926), 517-30. Anglo-American interest centered, of course, on his New Netherland career.

⁶⁵ *ARA*, wɪc, oc, St. Gen., 3310, Eedt-Boeck 12528, July 28, 1646.

⁶⁶ Kemperink, p. 49, quotes Maud Wilder Goodwin, "The Dutch and English on the Hudson," *The Chronicles of America*, v, and W. R. Shepherd, *The Story of New Amsterdam*.

⁶⁷ W. Irving, *A History of New York* (New York, 1848), p. 180.

⁶⁸ See Appendix vɪɪ.

⁶⁹ The interesting details of this encounter are given in the Spanish documents published in Wright/Van Dam, ɪɪ, *109-15, and 164n.

⁷⁰ Miss Wright's observation: "Who is capable, after three centuries, to give an explanation of this mysterious smile of Peter Stuyvesant?" *Ibid.*, ɪɪ, 164nɪ.

⁷¹ *Ibid.*, ɪɪ, *119 ff., 168n. The information is given in the letters of the bishop of Caracas to the king, Nov. 4, 1642, and of the Dutch raiding in the letters of the governor of Puerto Cabello to Fuenmayor, Nov. 30, 1642, and Joaquín de Belgarra to Peter Stuyvesant, Dec. 11, 1642.

NOTES TO CHAPTER XII

¹ Figures from De Laet/Naber, ɪv, 280 ff.

² Wätjen, *Holl. Kolonialreich*, p. 35.

³ Van Dillen, "De West Indische Compagnie," p. 155.

⁴ See the *Catalogus van de pamfletten-verzameling berustende in de Koninklijke Bibliotheek*, W. P. C. Knuttel, ed. ('s-Gravenhage, 1889-1920) over those years.

⁵ Willem J. van Hoboken, "The Dutch West India Company; the Political Back-ground of its Rise and Decline," in John S. Bromley and Ernst H. Kossmann, eds., *Britain and the Netherlands* (London, 1960), ɪ, 41-42.

⁶ *Ibid.*, p. 42.

⁷ In the *Geschiedenis van Nederland*, H. Brugmans, ed. (Amsterdam, 1935-38), ɪv, the author of this volume, Dr. J. C. H. de Pater, does not pay attention to Amster-dam's role in this field.

⁸ *Joost van den Vondel's hekeldichten*, J. Bergsma, ed. (Zutphen, 1920), pp. 36-38.

⁹ PK 6783, *Hollandts rommelzootje, vertoonende de gantsche ghelegentheyt van het benaudt, ontzet en gewapent Amsterdam* (n.p., 1650), p. 7.

10 Laspeyres, p. 82.

11 Bromley and Kossmann, p. 55. Resolution of the vroedschap of Amsterdam, April 23-27, 1627.

12 Boxer, *The Dutch in Brazil*, pp. 255-58.

13 PK 6469, *Copie van de resolutie van de Heeren burgemeesteren ende raden tot Amsterdam op t'stuk van de West Indische Compagnie genomen in Amsterdam 1649* (n.p., 1649).

14 Aitzema, I, 900, 902. Arend-Van Rees, III, 4, 687. See Appendix v.

15 Aitzema, II, 22: "In the midst of a victorious course."

16 M. G. de Boer, *Die Friedensunterhandlungen zwischen Spanien und den Niederlanden in den Jahren 1632 und 1633* (Groningen, 1898), pp. 102 ff.

17 *Ibid.*, p. 96. His Excellency said: "da diese [die West-Indische Kompagnie] dem Spanischen König in fremden Weltteilen so groszen Schaden zufügen kontte."

18 Aitzema, II, 36: "...belangende de West Indische, dat men deselve soude conserveeren, t'sy by oorlogh ofte by andere bequaeme expedienten met communicatie ende bewilliginge van de West Indische Compagnie te beramen, doch dat men in geenderlei maniere de forten van Pernambuco soude verlaten, overgeven, ofte jeghens gelt verwisselen."

19 Van Wassenaer, XVI, 28: "De staet van de West Indische Compagnie was deser tyt dat het eene gheluk het andere volchede." Cf. de Boer, "Een memorie." See for the memorial of 1629 PK 3909 and Chapter IX, note 25.

20 "De groote eylanden sijn bij de Spaignaerden beset; de kleine periculeus om aen te tasten ende... eenighe van de alderbeste alreede bij de Francoisen ende Engelsche beslagen, behalve dat de Engelsche op alle de Caraibische Eylanden wegen seecker octroy aen den grave van Carliel vergunt actie te pretenderen," De Boer, "Een memorie," p. 356. See Appendix v.

21 PK 3909. Cf. Wätjen, *Holl. Kolonialreich*, p. 45.

22 Netscher, *Les Hollandais au Brésil*, p. 82.

23 PK 3869, *Verhooginge der capitalen van de West Indische Compagnie voor een derde part* (n.p., 1629), and *RSG*, July 13, 1629.

24 *ARA*, WIC, OC, 2 Minutes of the XIX 1629-45, April, 1632.

25 *SAA*, WIC, 55, "Memorie over de agterstallige subsidien bij den Staet geconsenteert aen de West Indische Compagnie" (no date). This document is part of an "Extract uyt het register van de resolutien ghenomen by de Provinciale Staten van Holland en Westfriesland."

26 *Ibid.*, "...meynende daermede ghenoechsaem verseeckert te syn...ende verder in lasten inghewickelt heeft."

27 *Ibid.* Res. Holl. May 24, 1639.

28 *ARA*, WIC, OC, 39, Res. of the St. Gen. concerning the WIC 1623-46, Feb. 1, 1639, Conference of the States General, the directors of the WIC and the Prince of Orange; March 22, 1639, Missive of the States General to the Zeeland States inviting them to agree with the decisions; April 6 and May 24, 1639, Remonstrances of the WIC for subsidy.

29 On the situation created by the Portuguese rebellion and its relation to the United Provinces we used Aitzema, II, III, IV; Abraham van Wicquefort, *L'histoire des Provinces-Unies confirmée et éclairée par des preuves authentiques* (La Haye, 1719-1745); Edgar Prestage, *The Diplomatic Relations of Portugal with France, England, and Holland from 1640 to 1668* (Watford, 1925); and Cornelis van de Haar, *De diplomatieke betrekkingen tussen de Republiek en Portugal, 1640-1661* (Groningen, 1961). For the Portuguese point of view we consulted Luis de Menezes, Conde da Ericeira,

História de Portugal restaurado (Lisboa: Vol. 1, 1751; Vol. 2, 1698); M. Bensabat Amzalak, *As relações diplomáticas entre Portugal e a França no reinado de D. João IV* (Lisboa, 1934); and A. Botelho de Sousa, *Subsidios para a história das guerras da restauração no mar e no além-mar* (Lisboa, 1940).

30 PK 4767, *Manifest vant Koninckryck van Portugal* (Dutch trans., n.p., 1641).

31 Van de Haar, p. 15.

32 H. Handelmann, *Geschichte von Brasilien* (Berlin, 1860), p. 179. See also M. de Jong, "Holland en de Portugese restauratie van 1640," *TvG*, LV (1940), 225-53.

33 *ARA*, WIC, OC, Inv. St. Gen., WIC (Loketkas, Lit. L), 9, "Stucken van den Ambassadeur van Portugael. Concepten van antwoorden. Item, stucken van de Oost ende West-Indische Compagnien, etc.," May 8, 1641: Opinion of the EIC on a peace or truce. "Wat is dienstiger, Vrede of Trefves of Oorlog met de Portugesen?"

34 *Archives ou correspondance inédite de la Maison d'Orange-Nassau*, G. Groen van Prinsterer *et al.*, eds. (Leide, Utrecht, 1835-1915), 2d. série, III, 413-14, François van Aerssen to the Prince of Orange, March 28, 1641. *RSG*, March 25, 1641. Aitzema, II, 754: "De nieuwe Koningh schickte terstont Ambassadeurs aen alle kanten..." and Menezes, I, 153 ff.

35 Arend-Van Rees, III, 5, 307-9, 372 ff. See also "Origineele brieven van H. Doedens aan A. van Hilten betreffende de West Indische Compagnie, 1641-1648," *KHG*, V, 5 (1869), 396-97, *et passim*.

36 Prestage, pp. 176-77.

37 Aitzema, II, 754. The EIC dropped from 500 per cent to 400 per cent.

38 *Conclusum est verum, firmum, sincerum ac inviolabile Induciarum pactum.* *ARA*, WIC, OC, 19, Chamber of Zeeland, Treaty of a Truce between the States General and Portugal. See also PK 4775, *Extract uyt d'Articulen van het Tractaet van Bestant ende ophoudinge van alle Acten van Vyantschap, als oock van Traffycq ende Commercie* ('s-Graven-Haghe, 1641).

39 Van de Haar, pp. 40-41.

40 Menezes, I, 296 ff. See on Sousa Coutinho Menezes, I, 538 ff.

41 Boxer, *The Dutch in Brazil*, pp. 109 ff.

42 G. T. F. Raynal, *A Philosophical and Political History of the Settlements and Trade of the Europeans in the East and West Indies*, trans. (London, 1798), III, 289.

43 "De ervarendheyt heeft gheleert, dat don Philippe den Tweeden, Koninck van Castiliën, met kracht ende ghewelt van wapenen hier bevorens heeft gheinvadeert de Croone van Portugal..." Aitzema, II, 756.

44 *Ibid.*, II, 832.

45 *Ibid.*, II, 866.

46 *RSG*, Dec. 3, 16, 1642. *Res. Holl.*, Dec. 5, 18, 1642, March 3, 7, April 22, 27, 28, 1643. See also Boxer, *The Dutch in Brazil*, p. 160.

47 Boxer, *The Dutch in Brazil*, p. 160.

48 G. do Couto Ribeiro Villas, *História colonial de Portugal* (Lisboa, 1938), p. 251.

49 Menezes, I, 440. Sousa, I, 23, 27.

50 Menezes, I, 641: "Propoem-se meyos de se ajustar com os Olandezes a compra das Praças do Brazil." See also Prestage, p. 190, and Van de Haar, p. 60.

51 See on the deteriorating relations Aitzema, III, 30-35, 103, 210, *et passim*. Appendix VIII.

52 Asher, p. 59.

53 PK 5112, *Twee deductien aengaende de vereeninge van d'Oost ende West-Indische Compagnien aen de Ed. Gr: Mo: Heeren Staten van Holland ende West-Friesland van de West-*

Indische Compagnie overgelevert ('s Gravenhaghe, 1644), and PK 5114, *Remonstrantie ende consideratien aengaende de vereeninghe van de Oost ende de West Indische Compagnien* ('s Graven Haghe, 1644) give good information on the subject. PK 5115 gives the considerations of the EIC in detail.

54 PK 5122, *Kort discours ofte naerdere verklaringe* (n.p., 1644).

55 *ARA*, WIC, OC, 26, Chamber of Zeeland, Minutes 1644-46, June 16, July 11, 1644.

56 Aitzema, II, 976: "Die van de Oost-Indische seyden dat die van de West vijftigh tonnen gouts als niet hadden."

57 Arend-Van Rees, III, 5, p. 448. The exact amount was f. 874,190.

58 *Ibid.*, III, 5, pp. 448-49. See also *Res. Holl.*, March 17, *et passim*, April 3, May 15, 1643.

59 They used the same argument the Heren XVII had used years ago during the Twelve Years' Truce. See *ARA*, WIC, OC, St. Gen., 3224, Resolutions of the States General concerning the East India and other companies, 1602-12; and *RSG*, Nov. 16, 1610: "...dat de navigatie van Oost-Indien niet en is een particulier werck, maer een groot important stuck van State, ende dat de remonstranten niet anders en sijn als dienaers ende uytvoerders van Uw principaelste desseynen."

60 Van Rees, pp. 195 ff.

61 "Memorie. Aenwijsende tot wat eynde de West Indische Compagnie opgeweckt ende tot haeren aenvanck gebracht is door verscheyden omstellingen en aenmaningen aen hare Ho: Mo:, den Prinse Maurits hoogh loffelycker ghedachtenis ende de Provincien van Hollandt en Zeelandt gedaen tsedert tjaar 1592 tot 1623," *ARA*, WIC, OC, Inv. St. Gen. (West Indië), 5758, 1645-46, Oct. 3, 1644. Cf. Van Rees, pp. 461 ff.

62 PK 5514, *Remonstrantie ende consideratien aengaende de vereeninghe van de Oost ende Westindische compagnien* ('s Graven Hage, 1644), p. 25.

63 Arend-Van Rees, III, 5, pp. 449 ff. Some "blue books" or pamphlets approach the problem from the humorous point of view. Cf. PK 5225, *Uytvaert van de West Indische Compagnie* (n.p., 1645). Its author offers the following solution to the king of Spain: Buy 50 seats of head-participants in the Chamber of Amsterdam at 6,000 guilders a seat. This will obstruct and paralyze the company's activities effectively.

64 This was the Hendrik Brouwer expedition. *RSG*, March 15, 1644, *et passim*.

65 *ARA*, WIC, OC, St. Gen., 8276 (new 9411), "Extract uyt het Register der Resolutien van de gecommitteerden wegens de generale Geoctroyeerde West Indische Compagnie ter vergaderinge van de XIX te Amsterdam," Oct. 19, 1643: "...soo hebben de Cameren eenpaerlijck geresolveert die conqueste van dit eylant voor desen Staet ende de Compagnie te conserveren."

66 Van Rees, p. 209. Proposal of Feb. 25, 1645.

67 *ARA*, WIC, OC, 2, Minutes of the XIX 1645-46, Nov., 1645. Balthazar van Voorde was the mouthpiece of the High Council of Brazil in the meetings of the XIX and also in the States General. Cf. Aitzema, III, 30, 31, and Arend-Van Rees, III, 5, pp. 599 ff.

68 *Res. Holl.*, Oct. 12, 13, Nov. 23, 24, 1645.

69 *ARA*, WIC, OC, 2, Minutes of the XIX 1629-1645, March 3, 1645, *et passim*. Letter of the XIX to the States of Holland, April 30, 1646.

70 *Res. Holl.*, Nov. and Dec., 1645. *RSG*, Dec. 23, 1645. Aitzema, III, 89, 204.

71 Aitzema, II, 1009, 1010. Cf. *RSG*, March 18, *passim*, June 25, 1647.

[72] *Res. Holl.*, Jan., Feb., March 21, May 22, 25, 1647. Aitzema, III, 175, 210, ff. *R.S.G.* March, 1647, *passim*.

[73] Wätjen, *Holl. Kolonialreich*, p. 37.

[74] *Groot Placaetboeck*, II, 1235-48, "Ordre van Regieringe soo in Policie als Justitie in de plaetsen verovert ende te veroveren in West-Indien," issued Oct. 13, 1629.

[75] This instruction is in *Curaçao Papers, 1640-65*.

[76] Van Grol, I, 26, 98. Because of the fact that the Chamber of Amsterdam took care of the Curaçao islands the governors of this colony often directed themselves to the directors of this chamber.

[77] Fred Oudschans Dentz, "Hoe het eiland St. Maarten werd verdeeld," *WIG*, XIII (1931), 163-64. See also Rochefort, p. 44, and Hartog, *Bovenwindse eilanden*.

[78] Dutertre, I, 409 ff.

[79] Violet Barbour, *Capitalism in Amsterdam in the Seventeenth Century* (Baltimore, 1950), gives some details on Dutch trading methods in the Caribbean.

NOTES TO CHAPTER XIII

[1] "Thus, because of the weakness, incapacity and cowardice of two or three men, and because of the little care and money the Hollanders had to support her, the State and the West India Company lost that great and beautiful country." Wicquefort, *Histoire des Provinces Unies des Païs Bas*, II, 325-26.

[2] *Ibid.*, II, 279, "Les affaires du Brésil estoient dans un très deplorable estoit..." See also I, 379.

[3] W. J. van Hoboken, *Witte de With in Brazilië, 1648-1649* (Amsterdam, 1955), p. 8.

[4] Menezes, I, 190-91.

[5] Van Hoboken, *Witte de With*, pp. 8 ff. We refer also to the works of Portuguese historians like Menezes, mentioned before.

[6] PK 5547, *Brasilische Gelt-sack, waer in dat klaerlyck vertoont wort waer dat de participanten van de West Indische Compagnie haer gelt ghebleven is* (Reciff, 1647). Cf. Arend-Van Rees, III, 5, p. 48, who mentions f. 3,030,000.

[7] Boxer, *The Dutch in Brazil*, pp. 188 ff., calls him "Double With."

[8] PK 5786, *Brandt in Brasilien* (n.p., 1648). Translation of the letter of Juan Fernandes Vieira to the merchants of Recife, Sept. 11, 12, 1646.

[9] PK 6467, *Ses Poincten welck by de Ho: Mo: Heeren Staten Generael ende alle de steden vastgestelt* (n.p., n.d.). Van de Haar, p. 116; Aitzema, III, 338.

[10] "...de saecken van de West Indische Compagnie sijn dit jaer noch al weder den kreeftenganck gegaen." Aitzema, III, 338. Wicquefort, I, 233, comments: Les affaires de la Compagnie y estoient en fort mauvais estat."

[11] Wicquefort, I, 380: He was treated as a ridiculous being.

[12] Aitzema, III, 340.

[13] Our sources of the development of Dutch-Portuguese relations are those mentioned in the preceding chapter. See also *ARA, WIC, OC*, 5, Minutes of the XIX 1651-54.

[14] Aitzema, II, 648: "I am a little man but I have a big heart."

[15] Prestage, pp. 212 ff.

[16] *RSG*, Feb. 18, 1652. See also Burns, pp. 238-39.

[17] "Wij kennen den aert van die Superbe natie, God betert, maer al te wel." *ARA*,

WIC, OC, 5, Minutes of the XIX 1651-54. Memorial of the WIC to the States General, no date.

18 "...raeckende de forme ende maniere van te doene equipage van 50 cloecke welgemonteerde oorlogsschepen in minderinge van 150 gelycke schepen van oorlog den 3 dezes gearresteert tot nadere beveylinge van de zee ende conservatie van de navigatie ende commercie dezer Vereenigde Nederlanden." *RSG*, March 8, 1652.

19 *Ibid.*, July 21, Sept. 3, Nov. 26, 1652. In the November meeting Zeeland requested "dat een notabel secours van schepen van oorlogh tot conservatie van de navigatie op de Caraibische Eylanden voor de inghesetenen van desen Staet ende affbreuck van de Engelschen ten spoedighste derwaerts mocht worden ghesonden."

20 *Ibid.*, March 21, 26, 1653.

21 "Le Conseil de Lisbonne vouloit traitter pour les Indes Orientales aussi bien que pour le Brésil, mais les Deputés n'avoient ny pouvoir ny ordres pour cela, et Ainsy ils ne purent rien conclurre." Wicquefort, II, 279.

22 Aitzema, III, 1, 116-24. The loss of Brazil was, according to Wicquefort, II, 279, 323, "une des mauvaises suittes de la funeste guerre d'Angleterre." Boxer, *The Dutch in Brazil*, p. 235, maintains: "In point of fact the Anglo-Dutch war of 1652-4 did not sever communications between the United Provinces and Netherlands Brazil, as is often asserted." In spite of this statement we are more inclined to accept Aitzema's and Wicquefort's observations.

23 Van de Haar, p. 143. *RSG*, July 28, 1655.

24 Aitzema, IV, 107-16.

25 *Ibid.*, IV, 268-72. Louis' answer: "I am absolute in my seas."

26 PK 8730, *Articulen van vrede ende confederatie geslooten tusschen den Doorluchtigsten Coninck van Portugael ter eenre ende de Ho: Mo: Heeren Staten Generael der Vereenigde Nederlanden ter andere zijde* (Haag, 1663). See also Aitzema, IV, 764-74.

27 As early as 1655 creditors began to distrain the company's property. The States General stopped this action.

28 Wicquefort, II, 198: "...blessoit l'honneur et la reputation de la Republique."

29 *RSG*, Feb. 13, 1648. See note 36.

30 *Ibid.*, March 11, 1649. There is another account in *SAA*, WIC, 55, "Staet aengaende de West Indische Compagnie," Nov. 20, 1648, that comes to a total of f. 7,697,615-11-7¹/₂ in arrears. The "Summary Report" of 1648 comes to f. 7,400,000. The differences, if not caused by the periods involved, are hard to explain.

31 *ARA*, WIC, OC, Inv. St. Gen. (West Indië), 5758, 1645-46, "Extract uit het Reces des Landtdaghs des vorstendoms Gelre en Graefschap Zutphen, Anno 1646 binnen Arnhem gehouden."

32 *ARA*, WIC, OC, 4, Book of remonstrances, extracts, etc., 1647, "Adres van de Camer van West Frieslandt ende Noorder Quartier over den teghenwoordigen noot van de West Indische Compagnie ende hoe deselve geholpen ende herstelt zijnde behoort gedirigeert ende behandelt te worden." This address was discussed in the meeting of the XIX with members of the States General of May 25, 1647, and was probably influenced by the request of Feb. 6, 1647.

33 *ARA*, WIC, OC, Inv. St. Gen. (West Indië), 5759, 1647-48. Letter from Angola to the XIX, Feb. 5, 1647: "Belangende onsen toestant is droevig te verhaelen ende bevinden ons inde uyterste armoede en becommeringen, gantsch verlaten, van alle hulp gedestitueert en soo verre in gebreck van vivres vervallen dat bij aldien cortelick en weynigh daghen hier niet ontset werden dese conqueste de ruine van onse eygene soldaten ghenoegsaem onderworpen sal sijn."

34 *ARA*, WIC, OC, 4 Book of remonstrances, extracts, etc., 1647, "Consideratien van bewinthebberen ende hooft-participanten der West Indische Compagnie ter Kamere Zeelandt," March 30, 1647.

35 *ARA*, WIC, OC, Inv. St. Gen. (West Indië), 5759, 1647-48. Letter of the XIX to the States General, Aug. 23, 1647.

36 This report is printed in O'Callaghan, *Documents*, I, 216-21.

37 A fund, already suggested in *RSG*, Feb. 27, 1637, was recommended in which the participants would be invited to subscribe for one million guilders. This fund would function as a catalyst in the trade on the West African coast, especially Guinea and São Thomé (for Angola was a special arrangement) which trade had to be open and free for two years. See *ARA*, WIC, OC, 3, Collection of minutes... etc., 1647, 1648, 1653, and 1654; Feb. 3, 1648.

38 This address is already mentioned in note 32.

39 *RSG*, Jan. 2, 1649, "Verclaringhe van Gelderland raeckende de subsistentie en t' maintien van de West Indische Compagnie."

40 *SAA*, WIC, 55, Jan. 19, 1649.

41 J. G. van Dillen, "Effectenkoersen aan de Amsterdamsche beurs," *EHJ*, XVII (1931), pp. 9-10.

42 *ARA*, WIC, OC, 40, Res. of the St. Gen. concerning the WIC, 1640, 1644-52, "Voorslag tot Redres vant Verval der West Indische Compagnie," Oct. 1, 1650.

43 PK 6627, *Amsterdamsche Veerman op Middelburgh* (Vlissingen, 1650).

44 Aitzema, III, 338, 513. See also Van de Capellen, II, 253, "Voorslagen om te formeren een Raedt van Indien."

45 *RSG*, July 21, 1651.

46 *ARA*, WIC, OC, 40, Res. of the St. Gen. concerning the WIC, 1640, 1644-52, Sept. 5, 1651: "...seer beweeght voor ogen stellen de desolate toestant van de West Indische Compagnie."

47 *RSG*, Jan. 31, 1652.

48 *ARA*, WIC, OC, 40, Res. of the St. Gen. concerning the WIC, 1640, 1644-52, Aug. 17, 1652, "Advijs van Coopluyden vergadert uit last van Ed. Mo: Heeren Gecommitteerde Schepenen over de Negotie op de Caribische Eylanden."

49 In PK 7454, *West Indisch Discours* (n.p., 1653) the suggestion is made to revoke the WIC charter and create four new companies: a Guinea Company, a Brazil Company, a Caribbean Company and a New Netherland Company.

50 Luzac, II, 131 ff.

51 *ARA*, WIC, OC, 15, Chamber of Amsterdam, Minutes 1668-71, July 16, 1668.

52 *RSG*, July 19, 1668.

53 *ARA*, WIC, OC, 15, Chamber of Amsterdam, Minutes 1668-71, Sept. 23, 1669.

54 *Ibid.*, Nov. 27, 1670.

55 *ARA*, WIC, OC, 17, Chamber of Amsterdam, Minutes of the meetings of the head-participants, 1646-74, Nov. 16, 1671.

56 *Ibid.* See also Boxer, *The Dutch Seaborne Empire 1600-1800*, p. 48.

57 For the many renewals see *RSG*, Aug. 27, 1672, Nov. 28, Dec. 8, 1673, March 12, 28, 1674.

58 *ARA*, WIC, OC, 16, Chamber of Amsterdam, Minutes 1671-74, April 19, 1674. *RSG*, April 2, 1674.

59 Van Rees, p. 219. Netscher, *Geschiedenis van de koloniën Essequibo, Demerary en Berbice*, pp. 83 ff., mentions f. 630,000.

60 PK 8176, *'t Verheerlickte Nederland door d'Herstelde Zee-vaert* (n.p., 1659).

61 D. Hannay, *The Great Chartered Companies* (London, 1926), pp. 196 ff.

62 Burns, p. 232.

63 *Ibid.*, p. 237.

64 *Ibid.*, p. 238.

65 N. M. Crouse, *French Pioneers in the West Indies, 1624-1664* (New York, 1940), pp. 209 ff. See also Dutertre, I, 436 ff., and Rochefort, pp. 305-9.

66 Hartog's *Geschiedenis van de Nederlandse Antillen* gives in the five volumes here and there good chronological information. On the Virgin Islands see Waldemar C. Westergaard, *The Danish West Indies under Company Rule, 1671-1754 with a Supplementary Chapter: 1755-1917* (New York, 1917). On Tortola, there was a small Dutch colony in those days for some time see *CSP*, VII, 1668-74, 1109, and W. R. Menkman, "Tortola," *WIG*, XX (1938), 178-92.

67 Another reason might have been the increasing importance of Curaçao as a slave market.

NOTES TO CHAPTER XIV

1 "Inhuman practice, wicked rascality, that human beings are peddled like animals..."Dutch poet Bredero in his "Moortje." H. Bolingbroke, *A Voyage to Demerary*, (Philadelphia, 1813), p. 86. We used new edition, Georgetown, 1947.

2 Luis M. Díaz Soler, *Historia de la esclavitud negra in Puerto Rico* (Río Piedras, 1965), p. 27.

3 Elizabeth Donnan, *Documents Illustrative of the History of the Slave Trade to America* (Washington, 1930-35), I, 16. See also F. Brito Figueroa, *Ensayos de historia social venezolana* (Caracas, 1960), p. 101.

4 Donnan, I, 17.

5 Arthur Helps, *The Spanish Conquest in America and its Relation to the History of Slavery and to the Government of Colonies* (New York, 1856-58), III, 152. See also Donnan, I, 17.

6 Marian Goslinga, "The End of an Epoch in Venezuelan History" (Master's thesis, University of California, Berkeley, 1967), p. 8. Figueroa, p. 106.

7 Díaz Soler, p. 83.

8 *Col. Navarrete*, XXVII, 290, Letter of Diego Suárez de Amaya to the King, July 2, 1600: "...por muchas calamidades que han tenido...como de viruelas que se les han muerto muchos negros, y por estar el enemigo tan al ojo de todo lo qual envio informacion a V.M. y le suplico les socorra de Negros..."

9 W. S. Unger, "Bijdragen tot de geschiedenis van de Nederlandse slavenhandel," *EHJ*, XXVI (1956), 135.

10 Stoppelaar, p. 134, note 2, chapter xvii. The Negroes all died within a year because of the rough climate. They were caught at sea.

11 J. A. Goris, *Etude sur les colonies marchandes méridionales à Anvers de 1488 à 1567* (Louvain, 1925), pp. 31 ff. See also Unger, "Bijdragen," p. 136.

12 We refer for this expedition to the works of Stoppelaar and J. K. J. de Jonge cited before. Research in *ARA* did not reveal details.

13 De Laet/Naber, I, II, *passim*.

14 Burns, p. 203, gives an example.

15 Unger, "Bijdragen," p. 137.

16 *Ibid.*, p. 138. See also Netscher, *Geschiedenis*, p. 354. Just before the departure of Van Pere's expedition to Berbice, this patron had received permission to send

six blacks to his colonists at the Wild Coast (*Res. Zeel.*, Sept. 6, 1627). Similar permission was granted to Jan de Moor for his colony at Tobago.

17 Van Grol, I, 110.

18 Swalue, pp. 313-17.

19 *ARA*, WIC, OC, 22, Chamber of Zeeland, Minutes 1634-36, Oct. 13, 1635.

20 *ARA*, WIC, OC, 34, Chamber of Zeeland, Minutes of the head-participants 1623-40, Oct. 7, 1636: "...instantelicken aen te houden dat den handel van de swarten werde in t' werck gestelt..." See also Unger, "Bijdragen," pp. 138 ff.

21 Unger, "Bijdragen," pp. 138-39.

22 K. Ratelband, ed., *Vijf dagregisters van het kasteel São Jorge da Mina aan de Goudkust 1645-1647* ('s-Gravenhage, 1953), p. lxvii, Report of Pompeius de la Sale on the "Stant ende gelegentheyt vant Casteel de Mina." Ratelband is the only Dutch authority of today on the history of the WIC on the West African coast. His works have, like those of Irene A. Wright, the excitement of being based on a careful study of the archives.

23 De Laet/Naber, IV, 124-25.

24 Unger, "Bijdragen," p. 139. The evaluation of slaves varied in the course of the century. Van Walbeeck recommended, for instance, in 1634, Negroes from Elmina and Angola. In 1670 the Curaçao market refused to accept Negroes from Calabar (Goldcoast). Thirty years later, however, these Negroes were very much in demand. See Menkman, "Aanteekeningen op Hamelbergs werken," pp. 321-29. See also L. C. Vrijman, *Slavenhalers en slavenhandel* (Amsterdam, 1937), pp. 69, 70, 84, *et passim*; and S. van Brakel, "Eene memorie over den handel der West-Indische Compagnie omstreeks 1670," *BMHG*, XXXV (1914), 96-98.

25 Boxer, *The Dutch in Brazil*, pp. 138 ff. See also Unger, "Bijdragen," p. 140.

26 Van Brakel, "Memorie," p. 96.

27 Ratelband, *Dagregisters*, p. xxvii. The last settlement was the island of Annabón. Only the insignificant Portuguese fort at Cachou, though twice attacked by the Dutch, remained in Portuguese hands.

28 Donnan, I, 76.

29 Ratelband, *Dagregisters*, p. xxviii.

30 J. H. Parry, *Europe and a Wider World, 1415-1715* (London, 1966), p. 153.

31 J. C. Nettelbeck, *Eine Lebensbeschreibung von ihm selbst aufgezeichnet* (Leipzig, 1845), p. 127. Menkman, "Nederlandsche en vreemde slavenvaart," *WIG*, XXVI (1944-45), 103. Gaston Martin, *Nantes au XVIIIe siècle: II, L'ère des négriers, 1714-1774* (Paris, 1928-31), 27 ff. *ARA*, WIC, OC, Inv. St. Gen. (West Indië), 5768, gives some information and mentions ships of 340 tons with 18 to 20 pieces of artillery, crews of 30 and more men, depth $13^1/_2$ feet, length 125 feet, wide 24 feet. See also *ibid.*, 5754 and 5755, Extract minutes of the XIX, June 3, 1638, with different requirements.

32 *ARA*, WIC, OC, Inv. St. Gen. (West Indië), 5768, 1638, Cargo of a ship destined for Ardra. Unger, "Bijdragen," p. 28, gives a similar list.

33 Ratelband, *Dagregisters*, p. xcv. The slaves were bought by the planters for 1,250 to 1,500 pounds of sugar. The sugar was sold by the Dutch for 380 to 450 guilders.

34 Hermann Wätjen, "Der Negerhandel in West-Indien und Süd-Amerika bis zur Sklavenemanzipation," *Hänsische Geschichtsblätter*, XIX (1913), 426.

35 Ratelband, *Dagregisters*, p. xcvi.

36 Vrijman, *Slavenhalers*, p. 100. A second or third printing was published in Middelburg in 1675.

37 *Ibid.*, pp. 101 ff. See also Menkman, "Sprokkelingen op het terrein der geschiedenis van de Nederlandsche Antillen," *WIG*, XVII (1935), 65-115 with additional information.

38 Dieudonné Rinchon, *La traite et l'esclavage des Congolais par les Européens* (Bruxelles, 1929), p. 199.

39 Unger, "Bijdragen," p. 141. Unger mentions also a report by Pieter Mortamer, first Dutch governor of Angola, which report exaggerated the profits but was pessimistic in that it stated that the Portuguese could better transport 500 slaves in a caravel of small size than the Dutch could carry 300 slaves in a larger ship.

40 Wätjen, "Negerhandel," p. 431. The exact amount was f. 6,714,423:12.

41 Boxer, *The Dutch in Brazil*, pp. 138, 139.

42 *ARA*, WIC, OC, 23, Chamber of Zeeland, Minutes 1637-39, Aug. 25, 1639.

43 *Ibid.*, Aug. 31, 1639.

44 *ARA*, WIC, OC, 24, Chamber of Zeeland, Minutes 1640-41, Feb. 14, 1641.

45 Menkman, "Nederlandsche en vreemde slavenvaart," pp. 97 ff.

46 Unger, "Bijdragen," p. 142.

47 This report is discussed in Menkman, "Nederlandsche en vreemde slavenvaart."

48 *ARA*, WIC, OC, 25, Chamber of Zeeland, Minutes 1642-44, Advice of Cornelis Janssen Oudeman, Feb. 24, 1643; also 36, Chamber of Zeeland, Minutes head-participants, 1643-45, March 14, 1644.

49 *ARA*, WIC, OC, 36, Chamber of Zeeland, Minutes head-participants 1643-45, Sept. 5, 1645.

50 *ARA*, WIC, OC, 27, Chamber of Zeeland, Minutes 1658-63, June 29, 1662.

51 "Over den slaeffschen handel zijn wij dapper becommert of Ued. in dese stant van Brasil sijt genegen deselve te onderhouden ofte niet," *ARA*, WIC, OC, 26, Chamber of Zeeland, Minutes 1644-46, Dec. 3, 1646. See also Unger, "Bijdragen," p. 143.

52 On trade with the Dutch see Schomburgk, *The History of Barbados*, pp. 72, 76, 268.

53 Burns, p. 232. See also Hamelberg, *Nederlanders*, II, Doc. p. 22.

54 Kalff, "Iets over Peter Stuyvesant," p. 517.

55 *ARA*, WIC, OC, 25, Chamber of Zeeland, Minutes 1642-44, May 21, 1644, and 26, Chamber of Zeeland, Minutes 1644-46, March 9, 1645. See also Hamelberg, *Nederlanders*, II, Doc. pp. 21, 22.

56 *ARA*, WIC, OC, 26, Chamber of Zeeland, Minutes 1644-46, Jan. 19, 1645.

57 *Ibid.*, Feb. 2, 1645.

58 S. van Brakel, "Bescheiden over den slavenhandel der West Indische Compagnie," *EHJ*, IV (1918), 49.

59 SAA, WIC, 55, "Korte remonstrantie van bewinthebberen der West Indische Compagnie," n.d.

60 *ARA*, WIC, OC, 15, Chamber of Amsterdam, Minutes 1668-71, March 25, 1669.

61 *ARA*, WIC, OC, 16, Chamber of Amsterdam, Minutes 1671-74, "Verslag van conditien waarop de West Indische Compagnie deser landen Negros soude connen leveren van Ardra in Guinea," Oct. 4, 1673.

62 *Hollandtze Mercurius*, XIII (1662), pp. 49, 50. Cf. Hamelberg, *Nederlanders*, I, Doc., pp. 75-76.

63 Menkman, "Nederlandsche en vreemde slavenvaart," pp. 97 ff. Already in 1642 a memorial had been sent to the XIX discussing "how and in what way the trade of Negroes from Loanda de St. Paulo to Curaçao could be directed."

64 *USC*, II, *Extracts*, 133-38.

574

65 Samuel Oppenheim, "An Early Jewish Colony in Western Guiana, 1658-1666, and its Relation to the Jews in Surinam, Cayenne, and Tobago, "*AJHS*, XVI (1907), 186. For the grant see pp. 182-86.

66 *Ibid.*, 114. Netscher, *Geschiedenis*, p. 73.

67 Oppenheim, "An Early Jewish Colony," and Keye, pp. 10 ff., 93 ff.

68 Keye, pp. 122-23. We summarized the original text.

69 The problem continues to harrass the Spanish. See Irene Wright, "The Coymans Asiento, 1685-1689," *BVGO*, VI, 1 (1924), 29 ff. See also G. Scelle, *La traite negrière aux Indes de Castille* (Paris, 1906), I, 505-49.

70 *CSP*, V, 1660-68, no. 744, the governor of Jamaica to Arlington.

71 *ARA*, WIC, OC, 15, Chamber of Amsterdam, Minutes 1668-71, Dec. 13, 1668. See Appendix X and Van Brakel, "Bescheiden," pp. 66-78.

72 Van Brakel, "Bescheiden," p. 51. Scelle, I, 551-97, 599-640.

73 Unger, "Bijdragen," pp. 144-46. *ARA*, WIC, OC, Inv. St. Gen. (West Indië), 5768, 1665-70. Request Nov. 14, 1668. "...ontrent de 3000 stuck Negros sijn blijven leggen...welcker coop en costpenningen...ontrent een millioen comen te bedragen."

74 Hamelberg, *Nederlanders*, I, Doc., p. 70. Scelle, I, 829-31, Doc. 32.

75 *ARA*, WIC, OC, Inv. St. Gen. (West Indië), 5768, 1665-70. Request Nov. 14, 1668.

76 Fill out the name of the agent or the *asentista*.

77 *ARA*, WIC, OC, 6, Minutes of the XIX 1660-65, Sept. 18, 1660, April 15, 16, 1662.

78 Unger, "Bijdragen," p. 141. Cf. Netscher, *Geschiedenis*, p. 58.

79 Van Brakel, "Bescheiden," pp. 81-83. *ARA*, WIC, OC, 16, Chamber of Amsterdam, Minutes 1661-74, Oct. 4, 1673. "Verslag," see note 61.

80 *ARA*, WIC, OC, 6, Minutes of the XIX 1660-65, Oct. 2, 1664.

81 Van Brakel, "Bescheiden," p. 54. See Appendix X.

82 Van Brakel, "Bescheiden," p. 56.

83 *ARA*, WIC, OC, 16, Chamber of Amsterdam, Minutes 1671-74, Nov. 16, 1671, Oct. 4, 1673. See also Hamelberg, *Nederlanders*, I, Doc., p. 84.

84 *ARA*, WIC, OC, 16, Chamber of Amsterdam, Minutes 1671-74, Nov. 16, 1671.

85 Van Brakel, "Bescheiden," p. 58.

86 Cornelis Ch. Goslinga, *Emancipatie en Emancipator* (Assen, 1956), p. 17.

87 Hamelberg, *Nederlanders*, I, Doc., p. 107, Letter to the governor of Curaçao, Dec. 24, 1694.

88 *Ibid.*, I, 96.

89 *Ibid.*, I, 99, 100.

90 Hartsinck, II, 898 ff. Hamelberg, *Nederlanders*, I, 100-102.

NOTES TO CHAPTER XV

1 N. Japikse, *Johan de Witt* (Amsterdam, 1915), pp. 166-67.

2 J. Thurloe, *A Collection of the State Papers of John Thurloe Exp.* (London, 1742), I, 179 ff. Cf. Charles Firth, *Oliver Cromwell and the Rule of the Puritans in England* (London, 1900), pp. 312-13.

3 Burns, p. 238.

4 V. T. Harlow, *A History of Barbados, 1625-1685* (Oxford, 1926), pp. 84-86. Cf. Clarence H. Haring, *The Buccaneers in the West Indies in the XVIIth Century* (New York, 1910), Chapter III.

5 Burns, p. 260.
6 *ARA, ABZ*, 2496/1670, Jan. 13: "Want de Schippers dezer Landen handelende op Barbados terwijle buyten de Engelsche geen vreemde natie off schepen mogen traffiqueren, varen voor eerst nae Engelandt oft Ierlant alwaer sij middel vinden om voorts na de Barbados op Engelsche namen te varen, sich aldaer uytgevende voor Engelsche Schepen en Coopluyden." The first protest of the so-called Caribbean navigators signed by 49 merchants and skippers had already occurred in 1651. See Chapter XIII.
7 A. D. Innes, *The Maritime and Colonial Expansion of England under the Stuarts, 1603-1714* (London, 1932), pp. 231-32. Hume, *The History of England*, IV, 199: "The Duke of York, more enterprising and active, pushed the war more eagerly with Holland."
8 *CSP*, v, 1661-68, no. 618. See also K. G. Davies, *The Royal African Company* (London, New York, 1957), pp. 291-343.
9 Parry, *Europe and a Wider World*, p. 153.
10 The opinions on Downing do not vary much. T. H. Lister in his *Life and Administration of Edward, First Earl of Clarendon* (London, 1837-38), II, 231, calls him "keen, bold, subtle, active and observant, but imperious and unscrupulous," and p. 262: "who labored heartily to incense the English and to provoke the Dutch." Cf. John Beresford's biography *The Godfather of Downing Street* (London, 1925), and Hume, IV, 188, 199.
11 "Frivole practijquen." *ARA*, WIC, OC, 6, Minutes of the XIX 1660-1665, Sept. 4, 1664. See also Aitzema, v, 356-68.
12 *ARA*, WIC, OC, Inv. St. Gen. (West Indië), 5767, 1658-1664, Jan. 10, 1662.
13 *RSG*, Aug. 14, 1664. Memorial of Downing.
14 *CSP*, v, 1660-68, pp. xxiv, xxv, and nos. 593, 603, 622, *et passim*.
15 *Ibid.*, v, 1660-68, no. 788. Aitzema, v, 64-65.
16 *CSP*, v, 1660-68, no. 618. Dutch historian Japikse's statement is rather strange. See his *De verwikkelingen tusschen de Republiek en Engeland van 1660-1665* (Leiden, 1900), thesis II, in which he defends Charles II's attitude: "The action of Holmes on the coast of Cabo Verde in 1661, and his conquest of Cabo Verde in 1664, was not done on orders of Charles II." Cf. David Ogg, *England in the Reign of Charles II* (Oxford, 1934), and G. M. Trevelyan, *England under the Stuarts* (London, 1925). Valuable information came also from Ancil N. Payne, "The Relations of the English Commercial Companies to the Government, 1660-1715" (Ph.D. dissertation, University of Illinois, 1930), pp. 11-13.
17 *ABZ*, 2483/1664, May, 19 1664. *ARA*, WIC, OC, 6, Minutes of the XIX 1660-65, June 19, 1664.
18 *RSG*, July 21, 23, Aug. 9, 1664. Cf. Aitzema, v, 90.
19 Aitzema, v, 92: "...ghewelt tegen ghewelt te opposeren." Holmes, it was said, "found the English and Portuguese factors eloquent on the subject of Dutch usurpation, violence, rapine, and treachery." He acted accordingly with "judgment, prudence, skill, and courage." See *Dictionary of National Biography*, IX (Oxford, 1937-38), 1088-91.
20 Aitzema, v, 265, 275. Cf. Dutertre, III, 17-24.
21 Detailed information in Brandt, *De Ruiter*, pp. 292 ff.
22 *Ibid.*, p. 319.
23 Boxer, *The Dutch Seaborne Empire*, p. 89.
24 P. Verhoog and L. Koelmans, *De reis van Michiel Adriaenszoon de Ruyter in 1664-1665*

('s-Gravenhage, 1961), pp. 69 ff. See also Brandt, *De Ruiter*, pp. 319-62, and Blok, *De Ruyter*, Chapter x. *CSP*, v, 1660-68, no. 986.

25 Harlow, *Col. Expeditions*, pp. 103-8. *CSP*, v, 1660-68, no. 986. It may be pointed out here that the Province of Friesland, abstaining for several years in affairs concerning the wic, now cooperated rather fullheartedly with the other provinces. See Hallema, "Friesland en de voormalige compagnieën voor den handel op Oost en West."

26 Besides the Dutch sources mentioned there is much material in *CSP*, v, 1660-68, pp. lxxx, lxxxi, and nos. 408, 737, 780, 954. See also J. C. de Jonge, *Zeewezen*, I, 606 ff., and Payne, pp. 95-97.

27 Brandt, *De Ruiter*, pp. 356-58.

28 Aitzema, v, 351.

29 Pepys' effusions are from *The Diary of Samuel Pepys*, ed. Henry B. Wheatley (New York, 1893-99), I, 986, Oct. 6, 1664; 995, Oct. 29, 1664; 1005, Dec. 21, 1664.

30 *RSG*, Dec. 27, 1664.

31 Pepys, I, 1005, Nov. 22, gives the yearly war budget during the first Anglo-Dutch conflict; the other quotes are from pp. 1018-19, Dec. 22, 1664; p. 1051, Feb. 23, 1665; p. 1053, Feb. 27, 1665.

32 *ARA*, wic, oc, 6, Minutes of the xix 1660-65, Oct. 4, 1664. *RSG*, Oct. 8, 10, Nov. 14, 1664.

33 Japikse, *Verwikkelingen*, p. 407.

34 *Ibid.*, p. 412.

35 Boxer, *The Dutch Seaborne Empire*, p. 92.

36 Aitzema, v, 352, 374-75. R. J. Fruin, G. W. Kernkamp, and N. Japikse, eds., *Brieven van Johan de Witt*, III (1665-69) (Amsterdam, 1912), pp, 42-43; cited as Fruin/Japikse). Japikse publishes in *Verwikkelingen* a concept treaty proposed by England on the basis of the exchange (Bijlage ivc, pp. vi ff.). See also Payne, pp. 90-91.

37 Japikse, *Verwikkelingen*, pp. 446-47, 462-63.

38 Pepys, I, 1037, Jan. 24, 1665.

39 *Ibid.*, I, 1032, Jan. 15, 1665.

40 For information on de Ruyter's youth, see Brandt, *De Ruiter*, and Blok, *De Ruyter*. Dutertre, II, 28, mentions a visit of de Ruyter to St. Martin in 1648.

41 Verhoog/Koelmans, p. 90.

42 For the account of the battle we followed Harlow, *Col. Expeditions*, pp. 109-11, including a letter of an eyewitness, George Cartwright, to Col. Nicholls, June 5, 1665. See also *CSP*, v, 1660-68, nos. 1008, 1016, 1023, *et passim*. Dutch sources: Verhoog/Koelmans, Brandt, *De Ruiter*, pp. 362-66, and Blok, *De Ruyter*, pp. 225-29.

43 Harlow, *Col. Expeditions*, p. 110.

44 Blok, *De Ruyter*, p. 227. Dutertre, III, 175 ff.

45 Verhoog/Koelmans, p. 92.

46 *CSP*, v, 1660-68, nos. 830, 843, 942, 944, *et passim*.

47 *Ibid.*, v, no. 938.

48 *Ibid.*, v, no. 954.

49 *Ibid.*, v, no. 979. Cf. Newton, p. 237.

50 *CSP*, v, 1660-68, no. 1042. Cf. Burns, p. 305, and Hartog, *Bovenwindse eilanden*, pp. 94-104.

51 *CSP*, v, 1660-68, nos. 1042, 1088.

52 *Ibid.*, v, nos. 1085, 1124. Cf. Haring, *Buccaneers*, pp. 134-36.

53 *CSP*, v, 1660-68, nos. 1079, 1169, 1188.

54 Charles de la Roncière, *Histoire de la marine française* (Paris, 1899-1923), v, 441-42.

55 *Ibid.*, v, 443.

56 Léon Guérin, *Histoire maritime de France* (Paris, 1862-63), III, 180.

57 *CSP*, v, 1660-68, no. 1166.

58 Burns, p. 310.

59 *CSP*, v, 1660-68, nos. 1209, 1213.

60 *Ibid.*, nos. 1188, 1224.

61 Because of the social structure of the French nation Colbert was limited in his choice and could appoint only members of the nobility. This limitation caused the appointment of some inefficient men. See P. Clément, *Histoire de Colbert et de son administration* (Paris, 1874) I, 497 ff.

62 Dutertre, III, 201, 278 ff. Cf. Stewart L. Mims, *Colbert's West India Policy* (New Haven, 1912), p. 284.

63 On the English expedition see *CSP*, v, 1660-68, nos. 1244, 1245, 1267. French accounts in Guérin, III, 181 ff., J. Ballet, *La Guadeloupe* (Basse Terre, 1890-96), I, 1, pp. 56-58, 62 ff. See also Harlow, *Col. Expeditions*, pp. 196-98, Letter from Captain William Porter to Sir Robert Harley, being an account of the last expedition and death of Francis Lord Willoughby.

64 On this strange event there are two sometimes contradictory Dutch reports, one of Gerart Bogaert, and another of Ferdinand van Overschelde. *ARA*, WIC, OC, 17, Chamber of Amsterdam, Letters to the Chamber, 1626, 1628, 1637, 1666, has Bogaert's report, dated Dec. 19, 1666. The other one is in Lias West Indië, 1665-70, dated Dec. 21, 1666. Both reports are written at St. Christopher and published in Hamelberg, *Nederlanders*, II, Doc., 38 ff. Dutertre, IV, 153-55, gives the French version. For the English point of view see *CSP*, v, 1660-68, and VII, 1668-74.

65 *ARA*, WIC, OC, Inv. St. Gen. (West Indië), 5783, 1665-70. Letter written by L. van Vrijberge, member of the States of Zeeland, from St. Christopher, Dec. 21, 1666, about the conquest of Surinam by Willoughby came too late to influence the decision already taken. It is possible that earlier letters exercized influence in the decision of P. de Huybert and the Provincial States of Zeeland.

66 The Dutch source for the Zeelandian expedition was J. C. M. Warnsinck, *Abraham Crijnssen, de verovering van Suriname en zijn aanslag op Virginië* (Amsterdam, 1936), p. 7. The quote is from a letter of de Huybert to Jan de Witt, Nov. 9, 1665.

67 Van Kampen, *Nederlanders*, I, 170. Cf. de la Rüe, pp. 190-92.

68 Warnsinck, *Crijnssen*, p. 10. See also *ARA*, *ABZ*, 2492/1666, Oct. 19, Dec. 18, 1666.

69 Warnsinck, *Crijnssen*, pp. 105-23, Bijlage B, "Instructie voor Abraham Crijnssen van den 23sten December 1666 met de daarbij behoorende aanvullende documenten" and a "Naarder instrucktie voor den Capiteyn Abraham Crijnssen commanderende een esquader van zeven zeylen." See also *ARA*, *ABZ*, 2492/1666, Sept. 5, with a somewhat summarized instruction.

70 Warnsinck, *Crijnssen*, pp. 125-26, Letter of the Zeelandian States to de la Barre, Jan. 26, 1666. This enormous program Crijnssen had to carry out with only three frigates of the smallest size and four other small ships. The instruction emphasized not to loose time but to follow the time schedule it suggested.

71 Harlow, *Col. Expeditions*, pp. 199-222. Besides Byam's report contained in these

pages there is a Dutch account written by minister Abraham à Westhuysen, *Waerachtich verhael van de heerlijke overwinning van Pirmeriba ende de reviere van Serename* ('s Gravenhage, 1667). Westhuysen wrote his story May 29, 1667 "seylende tusschen Guardeloupe en Antigoa." It is reprinted in Warnsinck's *Crijnssen*, pp. 131-40. A third source of information was *CSP*, v, 1660-68, no. 1421, "Narrative of the Taking of the English Colony of Surinam by the Zeeland fleet," together with the articles of surrender.

72 Harlow, *Col. Expeditions*, p. 209. Cf. Warnsinck, *Crijnssen*, pp. 143-44, Bijlage E.
73 Harlow, *Col. Expeditions*, p. 213.
74 *Ibid.*, p. 218. See also *Hollandtze Mercurius*, 1667, pp. 41-43.
75 Harlow, *Col. Expeditions*, p. 222.
76 Warnsinck, *Crijnssen*, p. 43.
77 Netscher, *Geschiedenis*, pp. 78-79.
78 *CSP*, v, 1660-68, nos. 1400, 1477.
79 Newton, p. 247.
80 Clarence H. Haring, *Trade and Navigation Between Spain and the Indies in the Time of the Hapsburgs* (Cambridge, Mass., 1918), p. 256.
81 La Roncière, v, 459.
82 Warnsinck, *Crijnssen*, p. 55.
83 *Ibid.*, Bijlage F 1. See also Dutertre, IV, 218-37. See Appendix IX.
84 Our sources of information on this battle were La Roncière, v, 466 ff.; Dutertre, IV, 218-37. Warnsinck, *Crijnssen*, especially Bijlage F, pp. 148-58, with "Le récit du Combat de Nieve et de tout ce qui le concerne," and "Ordres que tiendra la flote tant pour sa route, que pour le combat" (see Appendix IX). See also J. C. de Jonge, *Zeewezen*, II, 161 ff., and *CSP*, v, 1660-68, nos. 1484, 1488. Some information also in *ARA, ABZ*, 2492/1667.
85 La Roncière, v, 466-68. Warnsinck, *Crijnssen*, pp. 156-58, Bijlage F 3.
86 La Roncière, v, 466, "Plaintes et griefs de M. de Cloderé."
87 Crijnssen's report to the Admiralty Board of Zeeland. See Warnsinck, *Crijnssen*, pp. 156-58, Bijlage F 3.
88 *Ibid.*, p. 161, Letter of de Huybert to de Witt, July 31, 1667.
89 Newton, p. 250.
90 Harlow, *Col. Expeditions*, pp. 222-57, "An exact Narrative Concerninge the Takinge of The Island of Cayenne from the French, and the Fort & Collony of Surrynam from the Dutch," July, 1667.
91 Japikse, *De Witt*, p. 252.

NOTES TO CHAPTER XVI

1 Show me first that as a man you have good courage. And travel first to Surinam, As from old times every serious young Zeelander ought to do, Who falls for a beautiful Zeelandian maiden.
2 Van Kampen, *Nederlanders*, II, 171, perhaps is right in observing that the Dutch had already a settlement on the Essequibo as early as 1596.
3 Menkman, "Tobago," *WIG*, XXI (1939), 229. Edmundson, "The Dutch on the Amazon," p. 14. Groenewegen, as mentioned, sent Indians to Barbados.
4 G. Edmundson, "The Dutch on the Amazon," pp. 644-51.
5 *ARA*, WIC, OC, 1, Minutes of the XIX 1623-24, Nov. 4, 1623.
6 Edmundson, "The Dutch on the Amazon," p. 651.

7 *Ibid.*, pp. 652 ff. See also Williamson, *English Colonies in Guiana and on the Amazon*, pp. 100 ff. The fort was perhaps founded by Ita.

8 De Laet/Naber, II, 16 ff. Edmundson, "The Dutch on the Amazon," p. 657.

9 Caetano da Silva, *L'Oyapoc et l'Amazone*, I, 7. The story of this settlement is also told by Hartsinck, I, 210 ff., and by Swalue, pp. 283 ff. Other authorities: Van Kampen, I, 316 ff., Netscher, *Geschiedenis*, pp. 55-56, Edmundson, "The Dutch on the Amazon," pp. 658-60, Williamson, *English Colonies*, pp. 103 ff.

10 Williamson, *English Colonies*, pp. 112-13. James Purcell, not to be confused with Philip Purcell, was released in 1627, back in England in 1628, where he organized another expedition. His colony at Tocujos was soon reinforced by Irish and English colonists from Holland but attacked again by Teixeira and destroyed.

11 ARA, WIC, OC, 42, Commissions, conditions, etc. 1627-71, July 22, 1627. Van Grol, II, 25.

12 ARA, WIC, OC, 42, Commissions, conditions, etc. 1627-71. Dec. 9, 1626, Commission for Captain Claude Prevost, Jan. 16, 1627, Commission for Jan van Ryen. See also *USC*, II, *Extracts*, pp. 41 ff., and De Laet/Naber, II, 16 ff. Cf. Netscher, *Geschiedenis*, pp. 54-55.

13 Netscher, *Geschiedenis*, pp. 56-57. This story is also told by Swalue, p. 54, J. K. J. de Jonge, *Opkomst*, I, and Hartsinck, I.

14 Harlow, *Col. Expeditions*, pp. 139 ff. *USC*, II, *Extracts*, p. 43. Edmundson, "The Dutch in Western Guiana," p. 659.

15 *USC*, II, *Extracts*, pp. 78-83. *Nederlandsche Jaarboeken*, 1750, pp. 1492 ff., and Edmundson, "The Dutch in Western Guiana," p. 661, "The Dutch on the Amazon," pp. 12, 13.

16 Edmundson, "The Dutch in Western Guiana," pp. 669 ff.

17 Espada, p. 105. L. Storm van 's Gravensande, *The Rise of British Guiana* (London, 1911), I, 12. Edmundson, "The Dutch in Western Guiana," pp. 669 ff.

18 Espada, pp. 104-5.

19 Edmundson, "The Dutch in Western Guiana," p. 668.

20 Edmundson, "The Dutch on the Amazon," p. 13.

21 Edmundson, "The Dutch in Western Guiana," p. 669. Harlow, *Col. Expeditions*, pp. 139-40.

22 ARA, WIC, OC, 21, Chamber of Zeeland, Minutes 1629-34, April 8, 1632.

23 *Nederlandsche Jaarboeken*, 1750, pp. 1491-1520; 1751, pp. 179-201, 427-51, 1079-1135. See also *Res. Zeel.* May 21, June 23, 1635.

24 Netscher, *Geschiedenis*, p. 64.

25 *Ibid.*, p. 62.

26 *Res. Zeel.*, July 29, 1634.

27 De Vries, pp. 187-225.

28 L. C. Vrijman, "Iets over de Nederlandsche volksplantingen in 'Cayanen' gedurende de 17de eeuw," *WIG*, XVIII (1936), 13-24. See also PK 11389, *Pertinente beschrijving van Guiana* (Amsterdam, 1676), pp. 2-3, and Netscher, *Geschiedenis*, p. 67.

29 De Vries, p. 192. Dalton, *The History of British Guiana*, I, 139-40.

30 Scott does not mention this colony. There is nothing known about it. See Hartsinck, I, 209, and De Vries, p. 192.

31 Hartsinck, I, 209, and Harlow, *Col. Expeditions*, p. 141.

32 Hartsinck, I, 209.

33 *USC*, I, *Historical*, p. 65. De Vries, pp. 202, 207-8.

34 *USC*, ii, *Extracts*, pp. 96 ff. *ARA*, wic, oc, 23, Chamber of Zeeland, Minutes 1637-39, Feb. 21, April 18, 1639; 24, *ibid.*, 1640-42, Dec. 20, 1640.

35 *ARA*, wic, oc, 26, Chamber of Zeeland, Minutes 1644-46, May 29, 1645. See also *USC*, ii, *Extracts*, p. 104.

36 *ARA*, wic, oc, 50, Letters and Papers from Brazil 1633-35, Feb. 21, 1634, Galeyn van Stapels to the Chamber. Van Stapels sailed with two ships for the Chamber of Zeeland and the patron of Berbice. Cf. Van Grol, ii, 110.

37 *USC*, ii, *Extracts*, p. 81. The seven colonies mentioned are Wiapoco, Cayenne, Suriname, N (nomen, name forgotten), Serrano, Essequibo, and Berbice.

38 *USC*, i, *Historical*, pp. 74-117, "Report as to the Meaning of Articles v and vi of the Treaty of Münster," by George L. Burr.

39 *Ibid.*, pp. 191-92.

40 *Ibid.*, p. 194. *Nederlandsche Jaarboeken* 1750, p. 1504n. *USC*, ii, *Extracts*, pp. 120-23.

41 *USC*, ii, *Extracts*, pp. 113-14. *ARA*, wic, oc, 27, Chamber of Zeeland, Minutes 1658-63, Sept. 20, 1658, Sept. 3, 1659.

42 *ARA*, wic, oc, Inv. St. Gen. (West Indië), 5767, 1658-64, Letter of the xix to the States General, Nov. 15, 1658. Cf. Van Grol, ii, 90.

43 On Spranger see an article of L. C. van Panhuys, "Quyrin Spranger," *WIG*, xii (1930), 535-40. See also J. B. Wolbers, *Geschiedenis van Suriname* (Amsterdam' 1861), pp. 31 ff.; Dutertre, iii, 17 ff., tells the story from the French point of view. Fort Nassau was the former Fort Céperou.

44 See on Gerbier and his projects the article of M. G. de Boer, "Een Nederlandsche goudzoeker. Een bijdrage tot de geschiedenis onzer nederzettingen aan de Wilde Kust," *TvG*, i (1886), 1-18.

45 Harlow, *Col. Expeditions*, p. 142. See also *USC*, i, *Historical*, pp. 214 ff., and Netscher, *Geschiedenis*, pp. 73-74.

46 Luzac, ii, pp. 158-59. Williamson, *English Colonies*, p. 153, and Dalton, *British Guiana*, i, 131.

47 The provisional contract is in Hartsinck, ii, 938-40. An English translation is in *USC*, ii, *Extracts*, pp. 125 ff. The date was Dec. 24, 1657.

48 *USC*, ii, *Extracts*, pp. 125 ff.

49 *Ibid.*, p. 126.

50 Netscher, *Geschiedenis*, p. 72; Dalton, *British Guiana*, i, 141; Hartsinck, i, 207. The latter erroneously states that this name was already given before 1613, a statement copied by Netscher, *Geschiedenis*, p. 40. See also *ARA*, wic, oc, 33, Chamber of Zeeland, Minutes concerning Essequibo 1657-1713, Dec. 16, 1661; Inv. St. Gen. (West Indië), 5767, Chamber of Zeeland to the States General, Oct. 1, 1661.

51 *USC*, ii, *Extracts*, pp. 127-28. From the proceedings of the chamber governing the colony of Nova Zeelandia for the three Walcheren cities, Dec. 24, 1657.

52 *Ibid.*, pp. 125-29. See also i, *Historical*, pp. 214-17, 227-29.

53 *USC*, i, *Historical*, p. 172. Dalton, *British Guiana*, p. 128. Netscher, *Geschiedenis*, pp. 73-75. Bloom, pp. 150-51. The Hebrew nation was allowed "liberty of conscience as well as exercise of its religion, practices and ceremonies." Van Grol, ii, 88. The Dutch minister who was sent back was Johannes Urseleus. Cf. Netscher, *Geschiedenis*, p. 73.

54 Hartsinck, ii, 940-46, gives the Nassy charter. See also Max Kohler, "Some Early American Zionist Projects," *AJHS*, viii (1900), 75-118, and G. Herbert Cone, "The Jews in Curaçao," *AJHS*, x (1902), 141-58.

55 The American Jewish Historical Society published some good articles on Jewish colonization in the Guianas in which the Dutch and the WIC were involved. In the previous note we mentioned two. In another context the article of S. Oppenheim was mentioned. See also J. Zwarts, "Eene episode uit de Joodsche kolonisatie van Guyana," *WIG*, IX (1927), 519-30.

56 Oppenheim, "An Early Jewish Colony," p. 122; Netscher, *Geschiedenis*, pp. 74-75. The grant for Curaçao is dated Feb. 22, 1652. The earliest Jewish colony on the Wild Coast probably dates from the year 1639. See Zwarts, pp. 521 ff.

57 Harlow, *Col. Expeditions*, pp. 141-42. Oppenheim, "An Early Jewish Colony," p. 129. Netscher, *Geschiedenis*, pp. 74-75.

58 Oppenheim, "An Early Jewish Colony," pp. 129 ff. See also Hartsinck, I, 163, and *Hollandtze Mercurius*, 1665 (July, 1664), p. 127.

59 Oppenheim, "An Early Jewish Colony," pp. 135 ff. See also Dutertre, III, 22 ff., and Netscher, *Geschiedenis*, pp. 74-75.

60 Oppenheim, "An Early Jewish Colony," pp. 183-86. Cf. *Calendar of Historical Manuscripts. Dutch Manuscripts*, XVII, Curaçao Papers, p. 329, and D. Nassy, *Essai historique sur la colonie de Surinam* (Paramaribo, 1788), II, 113-22.

61 *USC*, I, *Historical*, p. 196, and II, *Extracts*, pp. 133-38. See also *Nederlandsche Jaarboeken*, 1751, pp. 1093 ff.

62 Van Grol, II, 90. The loan was at 6¹/₄ per cent. Cf. Netscher, *Geschiedenis*, p. 75.

63 Oppenheim, "An Early Jewish Colony," p. 124. Bloom, p. 152. Information is also found in H. J. Koenen, *Geschiedenis der Joden in Nederland* (Utrecht, 1843), pp. 284 ff.

64 *USC*, II, *Extracts*, p. 137. The prosperity of the English settlement is confirmed by Sylvius, *Vervolgh van saken van staat en oorlogh* I, 2, 92, and Williamson, *English Colonies*, p. 160. See also Luzac, II, 160.

65 *USC*, I, *Historical*, p. 197.

66 *CSP*, V, 1660-68, nos. 1710 and 1746, ii "Protest of Wm. Hendricksen, Captain of the Shakerloo, against Lieutenant-General Henry Willoughby." See also *RSG*, Feb. 17, 18, June 9, 20, 22, July 9, Aug. 6, 1668. Cf. Harlow, *Col. Expeditions*, p. 257, and *Barbados*, pp. 186 ff.

67 *CSP*, V, 1660-68, no. 1759, "Memorial of J. Meerman and Joh. Boreel, Dutch Ambassadors, to the King." See on Crijnssen's mission Warnsinck, *Crijnssen*. Some information in Harlow, *Barbados*, p. 187, and *RSG*, Dec. 1, 10, 15, 1668, Feb. 2, 3, March 20, 1669.

68 *CSP*, VII, 1668-74, nos. 18, 27, 41, *et passim* on this unsavory affair. Hartsinck, II, 589 ff., publishes the letters of Charles II to Willoughby and the governor of Surinam, July 8, and 29, 1668. Crijnssen carried with him a letter of the States General, dated Feb. 17, 1668. See also Sylvius, II, 10, pp. 6 ff., 13, 302.

69 *USC*, I, *Historical*, p. 197. Hartsinck, I, 224-27.

70 *RSG*, Oct. 15, 1670. Van Grol, II, 112-13 tells the story of the dissension between Holland and Zeeland. Holland maintained that as a conquest Surinam fell under the jurisdiction of the States General. Zeeland disagreed. See Netscher, *Geschiedenis*, p. 79.

71 [The Dutch] "... have called off their small colonies at Banrooma and other places to reinforce Surinam," wrote Byam to William Willoughby, *CSP*, VII, 1668-74, no. 508.

72 Netscher, *Geschiedenis*, p. 80, and *USC*, II, *Extracts*, p. 138. Also *ARA*, WIC, OC, 29, Chamber of Zeeland, Minutes 1669-71, Aug. 26, 1669.

73 *ARA*, WIC, OC, 18, Chamber of Amsterdam, Patent to Count Friedrich Casimir von Hanau for the foundation of a Colony situated on the Wild Coast "tusschen Rio d'Orinoque ende Rio de las Amazonas," June 9/19, 1669. See also F. M. Jaeger, "Over Johan Joachim Becker en zijne relaties met de Nederlanden," *EHJ*, v (1919), 60-135, and *USC*, I, *Historical*, pp. 114-15.

74 Netscher, *Geschiedenis*, p. 80. *Res. Zeel.* July 17, 1670.

75 Edmundson, "The Dutch on the Amazon," p. 15.

76 *USC*, I, *Historical*, pp. 204-5.

77 *Ibid.*, I, 204-5, and II, *Extracts*, pp. 138-43, 150-55.

78 Netscher, *Geschiedenis*, p. 80.

79 Adriaan van Berkel, *Amerikaansche voyagien, behelzende een reis na rio de Berbice...mits-gaders een andere na de colonie van Suriname...*(Amsterdam, 1695), pp. 43-49. See also F. E. Baron Mulert, "Eene episode uit den Indianen oorlog in Suriname in den Zeeuwschen tijd," *WIG*, I (1919), 221-25.

80 *ARA*, WIC, OC, 28, Chamber of Zeeland, Minutes 1663-66, March, 1664, has a list of 36 Carribbean navigators of which 14 had not paid their recognition. The ships used in this trade were between 200 and 400 tons. See Netscher, *Geschiedenis*, p. 82.

81 Dalton, *British Guiana*, I, 144, mentions a rebellion of the troops under Dirk Rosenkrans.

82 C. A. van Sypesteyn, *Beschrijving van Suriname* ('s-Gravenhage, 1854), p. 10. *USC*, I, *Historical*, p. 374. Wolbers, pp. 46-47.

83 M. G. de Boer, "Een Nederlandsche nederzetting aan de Oyapok, 1677," *TvG*, XIV (1899), 321-42. There is an interesting pamphlet on this venture written by G. de Myst, *Kortbondigh vertoogh van de colonie in de lantstreke Guiana, aan de vaste kuste van Amerika op de Rivier Wiapoca, desselfs verkiesinge, bebouwinge, versterckinge, mitsgaders oneenigheden, disordres en verlies* (Thysiana 9602; Amsterdam, 1677). See also *Res. Holl.*, July 28, 1677, Decision to maintain the colony. The Chamber of Amsterdam sent provisions worth 350,000 guilders. It was all in vain and made this little poem true:

Met sorg en cost en moeyt bevaren een nieuw lant,
Bevolkt, bebout, versterckt, gesuyvert en beplant,
Doch naar vijf maanden, laas, verovert en beschreyt,
Wat is dit anders als verloren arrebeyt?

With worries, expenses, and difficulties they sailed to a new land,
Populated, cultivated, defended, cleaned, and planted it,
But after five months, alas, conquered, and mourned for,
What is this all but lost work?

Cf. Netscher, *Geschiedenis*, p. 364, Van Grol, II, 98, and Hartsinck, I, 923 ff.

84 PK 11390, *Beschrijvinge van Guiana* (Hoorn, 1676). The subtitle gives an indication of the content of this booklet: "Discourerender wijze voorgestelt tusschen een boer ofte landt-man, een burger ofte stee-man, een schipper ofte zee-man, een Haagsche bode."

85 *USC*, II, *Extracts*, pp. 56, 60, 113, *et passim*; I, *Historical*, pp. 358-59. See also *RSG*, Sept. 3, 1659.

86 *Groot Placaetboeck*, II, 1235-48, "Ordre van Regieringe soo in Policie als Justicie

in de plaetsen verovert ende te veroveren in West-Indien," issued Oct. 13, 1629, and pp. 1248-64, "Instructie van de Ho: Mo: Heeren Staten Generael deser Ver-eenighde Nederlanden voor de hooge en lage regieringe der Geoctroyeerde West-Indische Compagnie, naer de welcke voorts aen beleyt ende gederigeert sullen worden, alle het bewint ende saecken, met den aenkleven van dien, ver-vallende ende noch voor te vallen inde geconquisteerde capitanien, steden, forten ende plaetsen in Brazil, ende die noch naemaels geconquisteert sullen worden. In date den 23 Augusti 1636." Cf. Van Grol, II, 28, et passim.

87 Van Grol, II, 85. USC, II, Extracts, pp. 113-17: Conditions for Colonists provi-sionally adopted by the West India Company (Zeeland Chamber), Oct. 12, 1656.

88 ARA, WIC, OC, Lias West Indië 1671-75. Van Grol, II, 85, 94.

89 Laspeyres, p. 99: "Die Colonien sind den Niederländern niemals in ausgedehntem Maasse geglückt."

NOTES TO CHAPTER XVII

1 "A forgotten Dutch colony," as Hamelberg called it.

2 Harlow, Col. Expeditions, pp. 114 ff.

3 De Laet, Nieuwe Wereldt, p. 490: "...en seer goede grondt: dat teghenwoordigh niet wa sbewoont [in 1596] door de quade nae-ghebueren van het Eylandt Dominica."

4 Van Kampen, Nederlanders, I, 209.

5 Menkman wrote a historical essay on Tobago that has many merits, although it is now outdated. The other Dutch authority is Hamelberg, "Tobago. Een vergeten Nederlandsche kolonie," GTLVG, IV (1900), 13-93.

6 J. F. Dauxion-Lavaysse, Description of Venezuela, Trinidad, Margarita, and Tobago (London, 1820), p. 341.

7 Menkman, "Tobago," p. 223.

8 In 1626 the Spanish probably had a fortress on the island. See Harlow, Col. Ex-peditions, p. 114, and Burns, p. 224. See also CSP, XII, 1685-88, no. 1033.

9 Non-Dutch authorities on Tobago history consulted for this chapter are: Alex. V. Berkis, The Reign of Duke James in Courland 1638-1682 (Lincoln, Neb., 1960); Walter Eckert, Kurland unter dem Einfluss des Merkantilismus, 1561-1682 (Marburg, 1926); Otto H. Mattiesen, Die Kolonial- und Uberseepolitik der kurländischen Herzöge im 17. und 18. Jahrhundert (Stuttgart, 1940), the standard work; Ernst and August Seraphim, Aus vier Jahrhunderten. Gesammelte Aufsätze zur baltischen Geschichte (Reval, 1913); Ernst Seraphim, Geschichte von Livland (Gotha, 1906); A. Bilmanis, A History of Latvia (Princeton, 1951); and the articles of Edgar Anderson, "Die ersten kurländischen Expeditionen nach Westindien im 17. Jahrhundert," BH, VIII (1961), Heft 1, 13-35, and "Die kurländische Kolonie Tobago," BH, VIII (1961), Heft 3, 129-55, Heft 4, 216-32.

10 Mattiesen, p. 437, calls the gift of James I a legend. See Anderson, p. 13; C. K. Kesler, "Tobago, een vergeten Nederlandsche kolonie," WIG, X (1928), 527-34. See also information in CSP, V, 1661-74, passim.

11 On the de Moors see de la Rüe, pp. 194-98. The first request for settlement in the Caribbean and on the Wild Coast was in 1624. The request for settlement on Tobago is not dated, but it was discussed in the meeting of the XIX of June 21, 1627, after the canceling of a previous request by Jacob Maerssen. The relationship between Maerssen and de Moor is not clear. See ARA, WIC, OC, 42, Chamber of Zeeland, Commissions, conditions, etc., and 1, Minutes of the XIX, June 21, 1627.

12 Menkman, "Tobago," p. 231. It was the yacht "De Kater" from the Chamber of Amsterdam.

13 *ARA, ABZ*, 2457/1627-29, Feb. 20, 1627, April 10, May 31, 1628, and WIC, OC, 20, Chamber of Zeeland, Minutes 1626-29. The petitioners requested the Zeeland-ian States to deliver the guns and the ammunition for the fortress (Feb. 1, 1629); 21, Chamber of Zeeland, Minutes 1629-33, April 29, 1630, this was granted on condition that the petitioners would pay for it.

14 *ARA*, WIC, OC, 20, Chamber of Zeeland, Minutes 1626-29, June 27, 1627.

15 De Laet/Naber, II, 46: "Het Schip de Fortuyn...d'welck den 3den Martij [1628] uyt Zeeland vertrock, hadde op boven sijn Bootsvolck 63 coloniers met last deselve...te landen aen t'Eylandt Tabago."

16 *ARA*, WIC, OC, 20, Chamber of Zeeland, Minutes 1626-29 gives in its meetings of Jan. 13, 17, 20, 1628, some information on this expedition. See also De Laet/Naber, II, 46, and Menkman, "Tobago," p. 231.

17 *ARA*, WIC, OC, 2, Minutes of the XIX 1626-45, Aug. 1, 1629: Secret instructions for Loncq.

18 Dauxion-Lavaysse, p. 342. See also Rochefort, pp. 7-8.

19 Kesler, "Tobago," p. 530.

20 *ARA*, WIC, OC, 46, Reports and accounts concerning Brazil, Angola, etc., 1637, Report of Jacques Onsiel: "Relatie van de Staet ende de ghelegentheyt van de resp. Landen en Eylanden van Trinidad, Parra, Margarita, Punta Araya, Cumana, Carracas, Cartagena ende de Havana, metsgaders van de Oyape van de patache van Margarita ende de silvervlooten van Terra Firme." This report was sent to the directors of the Amsterdam Chamber and written on their request.

21 *Ibid.*, Letter of the governor of Trinidad, Diego López de Escobar, to the king, May 28, 1637 (Dutch translation). Cornelis de Moor is called by the Spaniards Cornelio de Morg de Frechilingues. *USC*, II, *Extracts*, pp. 73-83, and Van Grol, I, 45n.

22 Deniger had served the Dutch WIC in Brazil and thus acquired experience in the tropics. On Roe and Deniger see Anderson, pp. 14-15. See also Mattiesen, pp. 289 ff.

23 Probably for this reason Bilmanis calls the colonial enterprises of Duke Jakob "exotic" (p. 189). Cf. Anderson, p. 16.

24 E. and A. Seraphim, p. 53, mention the "höchst mangelhaftes Menschenmaterial das dem Herzoge für seine kolonialen Unternehmungen zur Verfügung stand." See also Edmundson, "The Dutch in Western Guyana," p. 642.

25 Edmundson, p. 642. Cf. Harlow, *Col. Expeditions*, p. 115. E. and A. Seraphim are probably right in attributing the Courlandian failures to the lack of men experienced in the field (pp. 53 ff.). See on Massam also Menkman, "Tobago," pp. 234-35.

26 On the English ventures see Harlow, *Col. Expeditions*, which gives first hand in-formation from the Scott manuscript. The articles of Edmundson, quoted before, add valuable material. See also the introduction to Harlow's work, pp. lix-lxiv.

27 Menkman, "Tobago," p. 307.

28 "A gentleman of good conduct," Caron is called by John Scott. Cf. Edmundson, "The Dutch in Western Guyana," p. 642. Dutch authorities had not such a high regard for Caron. See *ARA*, WIC, OC, St. Gen. WIC (Secrete kas), 10, Missive of the Chamber of Zeeland, Feb. 15, 1657. They wanted him back in the United Provinces, and Crijnssen was commissioned to find him but failed.

29 Harlow, *Col. Expeditions*, p. lx. See also Edmundson, "The Dutch in Western Guyana," pp. 642-43, and Menkman, "Tobago," p. 235.

30 *CSP*, v, 1660-68, nos. 1368, 1657. See also Mattiesen, pp. 428-29, and Anderson, p. 26.

31 Mattiesen, p. 430.

32 *Ibid.*, p. 117. On the duke's colonial dreams: *ibid.*, pp. 95 ff., 118 ff., and Chapter II, pp. 6, 12-14. Cf. Eckert, pp. 160 ff.

33 *ARA*, WIC, OC, 40, Resolution of the States General concerning the WIC, 1640, 1644-52, Dec. 15, 1651, "Extract uyt de propositie van den afgesant van den Hertog van Coerland, "read in the meeting of Dec. 1, 1651. See also Eckert, p. 167.

34 Anderson, pp. 126 ff. Cf. Ewald von Klopman, "Abrégé de l'histoire de Tobago," in the article of J. Kleyntjens, "De Koerlandsche kolonisatiepoging op Tobago," *WIG*, XXX (1949), pp. 193-97.

35 Beck arrived at the island from Brazil with a ship full of fugitives at the beginning of June, 1654, a few weeks after the Courlanders had arrived. His ship had lost its rudder and the repair took a few weeks. After six weeks the Dutch were brought to Europe on a Courlandian ship. See Anderson, p. 113.

36 Rochefort, p. 8. The best information on the Lampsins brothers is given by de la Rüe, pp. 72, 73, and Van der Aa, III, 8, pp. 28-29.

37 Anderson, p. 136.

38 *ARA*, WIC, OC, 42, Chamber of Zeeland, Commissions, conditions, etc., 1626-71, Sept. 1655.

39 Menkman, "Tobago," p. 312.

40 Menkman's story in "Tobago," pp. 310 ff., is confusing. See Anderson, p. 137.

41 The first patent was dated May 5, 1655. A renewal was requested Aug. 21, 1664. See *ARA*, WIC, OC, 28, Chamber of Zeeland, Minutes 1663-66.

42 Anderson, p. 139. *RSG*, Aug. 21, 1656.

43 Hamelberg, "Tobago," p. 18. See, on Deniger, Mattiesen, pp. 289 ff. Cf. Mattiesen, pp. 511 ff.

44 Mattiesen, p. 477. *ARA*, WIC, OC, Coll. Fagel, no. 445.

45 Hamelberg, "Tobago," p. 18, comes to 1,200 men. Dutertre, III, 218-20, writes: "Cette Isle estoit au rapport de ce même auteur [Rochefort] dès l'an 1655 munie de trois forteresses, dont il y en avoit deux presque imprenable, & habitée par douze mille habitans." Becquard was replaced by Huybrecht van Beveren.

46 There are different versions of what really happened and what was promised. See Berkis, p. 80, and Mattiesen, pp. 511 ff. The latter mentions a letter, called by him a "masterpiece of intrigue," sent by the Dutch, May 10, 1658, to the Netherlands giving their view. Research in *ARA* failed to discover this letter. Cf. E. and A. Seraphim, pp. 56-57, Klopman, p. 200, and Anderson, p. 148.

47 E. and A. Seraphim, p. 57: "Die Lampsins hätten den kurländischen Söldner vorgespiegelt, dasz der Herzog Jakob niemals mehr in den Besitz seines Landes gelangen würde, und sie dadurch zu einer Meuterei bewogen." This same author states that the Dutch bought the Courlandian colony for the sum of 300 R. Thaler, what seems to be an awfully small sum. It is more probable that the Dutch gave money to the corrupt leaders of the Courlandian colony. Cf. Anderson, p. 149.

48 Anderson, p. 218.

49 "Die Lampsins hatten sich in der Meinung dasz die Generalstaaten sie in ihrem Besitz nicht genügend schützen würden, an Ludwig XIV gewandt der denn die Insel zu einer französchen Baronie und Cornelius Lampsins zum Baron von Tobago erhob," is probably not such a bad explanation — E. and A. Seraphim, p. 60. Van Grol, I, 54, adds the following detail: "... werd baron van Tobago voor veel geld

en goede woorden door de bemiddeling van Justus de Huybert, de Zeeuwsche afgevaardigde bij de onderhandelingen tusschen de Republiek en Frankrijk."

50 See Rochefort, pp. 18-19.

51 Anderson, p. 217. The English captured in 1667, after the attack of the buccaneers, 500 Dutchmen and 500 Negro slaves.

52 Berkis, p. 78, mentions 120 plantations, 7 sugarmills, 2 rum distilleries, and 3 churches in 1658; Menkman, "Tobago," mentions 18 sugarmills. See also *ARA*, WIC, OC, 28, Chamber of Zeeland, Minutes 1663-66, Aug. 21, 1664.

53 *RSG*, Oct. 11, Nov. 14, 15, 1664.

54 *CSP*, v, 1660-68, no 854. Cf. Harlow, *Col. Expeditions*, p. lxi.

55 *ARA*, WIC, OC, 42, Chamber of Zeeland, Commissions, conditions, etc., 1626-71, Sept. 17, 1665. Two buccaneer captains, Searles and Stedman, with commissions of Modyford, took the island and handed it over a few days later to the men sent by Francis Lord Willoughby. Dutertre, III, 220 ff., tells the story from the French point of view. *CSP*, v, 1660-68, adds details in nos. 861, 1412, *et passim*. So does Abraham à Westhuysen, *Waerachtigh verhael*.

56 *RSG*, Feb. 15, March 3, June 9, 16, July 19, 28, Aug. 16, 1667. Cf. Anderson, p. 219.

57 There is some confusion in Courlandian historiography because authors disagree on what ship was sent. Mattiesen, p. 617, says *Der Isländer*, Eckert, p. 189, *Der Islandfahrer*. Cf. E. and A. Seraphim, pp. 57 ff., and Klopman, "Abrégé," p. 199.

58 Mattiesen, p. 620. Cf. Anderson, p. 219, and Menkman, "Tobago," p. 35.

59 Kleyntjes, "Koerlandsche kolonisatiepoging," p. 196. Cf. Ernst and August Seraphim, pp. 60-61. The States General referred the Courland representative Melchior Folckersamb (perhaps the same as Pieter van Volckershofen, representative of the Duke of Courland) to the civil judge because it was a claim against a private person, i.e. the Lampsins. See *ARA*, WIC, OC, 15, Chamber of Amsterdam, Minutes 1668-71, Sept. 16, 1669, and *RSG*, Sept. 29, 1669, May 28, June 8, 17, July 10, 29, Aug. 21, 1671.

60 *ARA*, WIC, OC, 30, Chamber of Zeeland, Minutes 1669-71, March 16, 1671: "Bij forme van onsterffelyck erfleen."

61 *CSP*, VII, 1668-74, nos. 901, 995-97, *et passim*.

62 *Ibid.*, nos. 885, 901, 940, 955, 956, 967, 969. The last number gives the minutes of the Council of Barbados.

63 *Ibid.*, no. 1018, Minutes of the Council of Barbados, Jan. 4-8, 1673; 80,000 lbs. plus 40,000 lbs. for the cost of the expedition plus additional expenses. Added to this was 30,000 lbs. for victuals and other necessities.

64 The story of this expedition is well told in *CSP*, VII, 1668-74, nos. 989, 997, 1000, 1021, 1029, 1131. Cf. Sylvius, I, 8, pp. 583-84. Menkman, "Tobago," pp. 37 ff. contributes the weak defense to the strong possibility that there were quite a few "Friends" and also many Frenchmen among the population who stayed neutral, or sympathized with the invaders. The latter were in this war allies of the French.

65 There is some confusion as to who was Tobago's commander or governor. *CSP*, VII, 1668-74, no. 1030, mentions "meinheer Constant." See Tobias Bridge's letter to Arlington, Feb. 10, 1673. *ARA*, WIC, OC, 46, Commissions, conditions, etc., 1626-71, mentions the appointment of Wouter Hendricx as commander. What ever happened to Hendricx is not known.

66 *CSP*, VII, 1668-74, no. 1029.

67 *Ibid.*, VII, 1668-74, nos. 1084, 1091, 1094, 1333. iii

68 *Ibid.*, VII, 1668-74, nos. 1030, 1031.

69 *RSG*, July 10, Aug. 2, 1673.

70 Menkman, "Tobago," p. 40. Anderson, p. 220.

71 Anderson, p. 220.

72 Menkman, "Tobago," p. 41. See also Westergaard, *The Danish West Indies*, p. 21.

73 Donnan, I, 77-78. In 1654 the Dutch had brought 600 to 700 Negroes to Martinique; by 1655 there were 12,000 to 13,000 blacks in the French Antilles. In 1664 the Dutch brought at least 300 slaves to Martinique. In 1654 they sold for 2,000 pounds of sugar; ten years later they asked 3,000 pounds, but Governor de Tracy arbitrarily reduced this price to 2,000 pounds, which price the Dutch accepted. Throughout 1668 Dutch vessels were freely admitted to French ports if they carried slaves. De Baas, governor-general of the French Antilles, was explicitly instructed in 1668 to admit Dutch vessels bringing slaves. See also Donnan, I, pp. 98-99, and J. C. de Jonge, *Zeewezen*, II, 687, on Carloff.

74 De Jonge, *Zeewezen*, II, 687 ff. *SAA*, WIC, 55, Nov. 15, 1675. The former governor was Quiryn Spranger.

75 G. W. Kernkamp, *Baltische archivalia* ('s-Gravenhage, 1909), p. 78.

76 "…enlève les moulins, les chaudières et les nègres…afin d'établir plus vite la nouvelle colonie qu'il voulait fonder à Tabago," Eugène Sue, *Histoire de la marine française* (Paris, 1835-38), III, 409-10.

77 J. C. de Jonge, *Zeewezen*, II, 703.

78 Sue, III, 410.

79 La Roncière, V, 650.

80 Sylvius, I, 15, p. 39. Sue, III, 420: "D'Estrées…impatient de prévenir l'arrivée de la flotte hollandaise qui faisait voile pour Tabago…"

81 For the preparation of d'Estrées' expedition see Sue, III, 407 ff., La Roncière, V, 652, Guérin, III, 302 ff. For the Dutch view J. C. de Jonge, *Zeewezen*, II, 705 ff. For the following two battles our main sources of information were the works of the following French naval historians: Guérin, III, 302-15; O. Troude, *Batailles navales de la France* (Paris, 1867-68), I, 166-71; A. Jal, *Abraham Du Quesne et la marine de son temps* (Paris, 1873), II, 282-309; La Roncière, V, 652-62; Sue, III, 420 ff. The Dutch sources were Sylvius, XV; J. C. de Jonge, *Zeewezen*, II; A. O. Exquemelin, *De Americaensche zee-roovers* (Amsterdam, 1678). Information also in *SAA*, WIC, 55, and in Claude Farrère, *Histoire de la marine française* (2d ed., Paris, 1962), pp. 154-56. See also *Hollandtze Mercurius*, 1677, pp. 77-88.

82 Sylvius, I, 15, p. 37. "Missive van den Commandeur Binckes, geschreven aen sijne Hoogheyt den Heere Prince van Orange, in s' Lants Schip de Bescherminge, ten anker leggende in de Rode Klips Bay, aen t'Eylant Tabago, den 22 Maart, 1677."

83 *Ibid.*, XV, 39-41: "Frans verhael van de zee-slag aen t' Eylant Tabago." Cf. Sue, III, 420 ff.

84 Binckes' report in Sylvius, I, 15, p. 39.

85 Hamelberg, "Tobago," p. 23.

86 *SAA*, WIC, 55. Extract *Res. Holl.* (no date).

87 La Roncière, V, 653, mentions the fact that Binckes had, among his soldiers, 200 French colonists from Marie Galante "résolus de se défendre à toute extrémité pour échapper à leur juste châtiment."

88 Sue, III, 421, says that the French attacked Reining's yacht "avec une intrépidité extra-ordinaire." What really happened is not clear because of conflicting reports.

89 Sylvius, I, 15, p. 38. Report of Binckes.

90 La Roncière, v, 654. Farrère, p. 155: "une tuerie sans art."
91 Sue, III, 428 ff., gives the official reports of many French officers engaged in the battle.
92 Van Loon, III, 221-22. The fleet of the Bataves burnt at the island of Tobago.
93 Sue, III, 426.
94 De Jonge, *Zeewezen*, II, 730.
95 *CSP*, IX, 1675-76, nos. 1152 and 1174; X, 1677-80, no. 422.
96 Hamelberg, "Jan Erasmus Reining," *GTLVG*, III (1899), 88, writes that Binckes had first appointed Reining for this mission, then changed his mind and appointed Constant. Binckes, somehow, had received some reinforcements from local sources and had presumably as many as 700 men of whom probably 500 manned the *Sterreschans* while the rest served on the ships in Klip Bay. The urgent request of Binckes brought by Constant to the attention of the States General met the lackadaisical attitude characteristic of institutions in decline.
97 *SAA*, WIC, 55, Sept. 29, 1677: "Missive van afschrijvinge over t'afsenden van ses schepen naer Tobago," and Oct. 13, 1676: "...tot wiens lasten de kosten van de equipage na Tabago gedaen of noch te doen mochten komen." Cf. *RSG*, Aug. 16, 1677.
98 Van Loon, III, 223. Another medal had the legend *Ignibus Ictus Congeminat* (p. 224). Cf. *Hollandtsche Mercurius*, 1677, pp. 263-64.
99 De Jonge, *Zeewezen*, II, 735.
100 Van Grol, II, 103.

NOTES TO CHAPTER XVIII

1 Thus Johan or Jan de Witt was called by William Temple, English ambassador in The Hague. Cf. Japikse, *De Witt*, p. 60.
2 Another denomination of de Witt. *Ibid.*, p. 161.
3 The expression is Renier's in *The Dutch Nation* (London, 1944), p. 189. See also A. T. Mahan, *The Influence of Sea Power upon History*, p. 138.
4 Renier, p. 189.
5 Haring, *Buccaneers*, p. 141.
6 *CSP*, VII, 1668-74, no. 452. Cf. Burns, p. 327.
7 Frémy Elphège, "Causes économiques de la guerre de Hollande, 1664-1672," *Revue de l'Histoire Diplomatique*, XXVIII/XXIX (1914-15), 523-51. See also Simon Elzinga, *Het voorspel van den oorlog van 1672* (Haarlem, 1926), and H. H. Rowen, *The Ambassador prepares for War. The Dutch Ambassy of Arnault de Pomponne, 1669-1671* (The Hague, 1957).
8 This treaty included the partition of the Southern Netherlands into Dutch and French halves. To understand French feelings see Clément, *Histoire de Colbert*, I, 346, 354 ff., and II, 425 ff.
9 The correspondance of Johan de Witt with the Dutch ambassadors in France and England gives good information. See Fruin/Japikse, IV. Starting with p. 140 this volume contains some interesting letters to Pieter de Groot, Dutch ambassador at Louis XIV's court.
10 *The New Cambridge Modern History*, V, *The Ascendancy of France* (Cambridge, 1960), 213-14. Cf. Mims, pp. 3 ff., and Nellis M. Crouse, *The French Struggle for the West Indies, 1665-1713* (New York, 1943), Chapter IV. Cf. John B. Wolf, *Louis XIV* (New York, 1968), p. 214, who comes to a much lower estimate.

11 Clément, *Histoire de Colbert*, I, 402, admits the inferiority of the French navy as compared with the Dutch.

12 Ballet, I, 2, pp. 28-30, III, 16, gives examples.

13 *Mémoires de Gourville*, Léon Lecestre, ed. (Paris, 1894-95), I, 256-57.

14 *CSP*, VII, 1668-74, no. 388.

15 *Ibid.*, no. 680.

16 *Ibid.*

17 *RSG*, Oct. 15, 1670. Memorial handed to the States General by French ambassador de Pomponne complaining about two Zeelandian ships belonging to the Lampsins. See also *RSG*, Dec. 17, 18, 1670, and Barbour, pp. 100-101, on trading methods of the Dutch around 1670.

18 La Roncière, V, 489. It was "meinheer Constant," future governor of Tobago, who tried to push the population into rebellion.

19 Newton, p. 291: "If the Dutch had not come to trade and made strong appeals to the inhabitants to do so the revolt would not have occurred." This statement does not take into consideration the insolent and rebellious spirit of the people there who made better deals with foreigners (the Dutch) than with the French merchants to whom the French government wanted to restrict their trade. Newton even asserts that the Dutch WIC had an agent established in Jamaica who offered good prices to the inhabitants of Hispaniola for their produce. This seems incredible (and we found no confirmation in *ARA*) in view of the general attitude of the English. Lynch, at that time governor, certainly was not the man to compromise with the strict Navigation Laws. True, he was eager to observe peace with Spain; more, he was willing—in agreement with the general line of English policy—to grant the Spaniards certain privileges. He was not willing to do the same for the Dutch.

20 *Lettres, instructions et mémoires de Colbert*, Pierre Clément, ed. (Paris, 1861-1873), III, 487, July 3, 1670.

21 La Roncière, V, 526.

22 Fruin/Japikse, IV, 150.

23 La Roncière, V, 529.

24 Guérin, III, 218.

25 Van Loon, III, 18-19. In 1673, when Louis XIV failed with his campaign against the Dutch who stopped him at the inundation line, the latter struck a new medal: the French sun obscured by a Dutch cheese: Sta Sol. Fromage d'Hollande (p. 126).

26 Fruin/Japikse, IV, 160 ff., Letter to de Groot, March 5, 1671.

27 *Ibid.*, IV, 204. Letter to Johan Boreel, Dutch ambassador in London, Dec. 4, 1671.

28 Van Loon, II, 557: *Sic Fines Nostros Tutamur et Undas* struck after the Medway disaster. (Thus we protect our rights and the sea.)

29 Fruin/Japikse, IV, 259-60. Letter to Boreel, Feb. 19, 1672.

30 *Ibid.*, IV, 317. Letter to de Huybert, April 19, 1672.

31 On St. Eustatius *CSP*, VII, 1669-74, nos. 891, 940, 1109. On Tobago, *ibid.*, 995-97.

32 *Res. Zeel.*, Oct. 12, 13, 1672.

33 *Ibid.*, Nov. 9, 10, 11, Dec. 5, 1672.

34 On Evertsen J. C. de Jonge, *Levensbeschrijving van Johan en Cornelis Evertsen* ('s-Gravenhage, 1820), with information on this famous Zeelandian family of sailors. Also de la Rüe, pp. 150-52, 162-71.

35 There is a good Dutch account of this expedition by C. de Waard, *De Zeeuwsche*

expeditie naar de West onder Cornelis Evertsen de Jonge, 1672-1674 ('s-Gravenhage, 1928).

[36] De Waard, pp. xxiv, xxv.

[37] The "Secrete Instructie voor het esquader uyt te senden in voldoeninge vande secrete resolutie van de Ed: Ho: Mo: Heeren Staten van Zeeland, genomen op den 12 October, 1672" and the "Tweede secrete Instructie voor het esquader uyt te senden in voldoeninge vande secrete resolutie van de Ed: Ho: Mo: Heeren Staten van Zeeland, genomen op den 12 October, 1672," the first having 19 articles, the second 8 in De Waard, pp. 91 ff. De Waard gives also the "Journael gehouden opt Lants Schip Swanenburgh gedestineert na de West, begonnen in de maent December 1672."

[38] On St. Helena, J. de Hullu, "De Oost Indische Compagnie en St. Helena in de 17de eeuw," *De Indische Gids*, LXVIII (1913), 877 ff.

[39] De Waard, p. xxxi. Cf. De Jonge, *Zeewezen*, II, 450 ff.

[40] *Res. Zeel.*, July 20, 25, Aug. 3, Sept. 21, 22, 1674.

[41] Crouse, *The French Struggle for the West Indies*, p. 62. Cf. Hartog, *Curaçao*, I, 258.

[42] They left the area in June. See *CSP*, VII, 1668-74, no. 583, and Ballet, I, 2, p. 95.

[43] On the attack on Curaçao there is a pamphlet, PK 10827, probably an eyewitness account *Omstandigh verhael van de Fransche rodomontade voor het Fort Curassau* (n.p., 1673), discussed by Fred Oudschans Dentz in *WIG*, VII (1925), pp. 279 ff., and B. de Gaay Fortman in *WIG*, VII (1925), 501 ff. *CSP*, VII, 1668-74, no. 1082, gives additional information. From the French side we have the naval historians already mentioned before. Letters of de Baas in Hamelberg, *Nederlanders*, I, Doc., pp. 92-94. Some information found in *ARA*, WIC, OC, St. Gen. (West Indië), 5768-69, 1671-78.

[44] La Roncière, V, 587-88.

[45] *Lettres, instructions et mémoires de Colbert*, III, 564, Sept. 5, 1673.

[46] Ballet, I, 2, p. 95: "...il avait acheté du gouverneur hollandais la reddition de Curaçao," and "le gouvernement hollandais l'avait immédiatement remplacé." This statement that blames Doncker's predecessor Dirck Otterinck for treason is not proven by the facts. Otterinck died just before de Baas attacked.

[47] Sylvius, I, 9, p. 687.

[48] Innes, p. 239.

[49] La Roncière, V, 549.

[50] "Les Hollandais, délivrés de la crainte des flottes d'Angleterre, se flattèrent d'avoir raison de celles de la France abandonnées à elles mêmes, et préparèrent deux armements considérables," Guérin, III, 251.

[51] See on this huge venture Brandt, *De Ruiter*, pp. 897 ff., and Blok, *De Ruyter*, pp. 376 ff.

[52] La Roncière, V, 589.

[53] Brandt, *De Ruiter*, pp. 895 ff., gives a list of the ships and an abundance of details. Blok, *De Ruyter*, pp. 376-82, follows Brandt.

[54] The Dutch sources we used for the account of this attack are, besides the works of Brandt and Blok, the following: Sylvius, I, 11, pp. 136 ff.; PK 11109, *Journael uyt t'schip de Prins te Paert van wegen het gepasseerde op t'eylant Martenique* (Amsterdam, 1674); "Extract uyt het Journael gehouden op s'Lants schip de Jupiter, gecommandeert door den Capiteyn Willem van Ewijck" (in Sylvius, I, 11, p. 137); and ARA, WIC, OC, Inv. St. Gen. (West Indië), 5768-5769, 1671-76. This folder contains the orders written by de Ruyter for this expedition, dated from May 18 to July 17,

1674. The most important are those dated July 15, 1674: "Eigenhandig door den Lt. Admirael de Ruyter onderteekende order aen den Schout bij Nacht Engel de Ruyter omtrent het doen van de eerste landing," and July 17: "Eigenhandig door den Lt. Admirael de Ruyter onderteekende order aen den Schout bij Nacht de Ruyter nopende de bewapening bij de landing," written aboard "s' Landts schip de Seven Provincien." Our French sources were the naval historians mentioned before.

55 La Roncière, v, 591.

56 *Lettres...de Colbert*, III, 2, pp. 590-94.

57 For this battle we followed Brandt, *De Ruiter*, p. 901, and La Roncière, v, 590-97.

58 *ARA*, WIC, OC, Inv. Gen. (West Indië), 5768-5769, 1671-76, War Council, July 21, 1674.

59 "Une médaille fut frappée à la gloire de l'île triomphante. On y lisait d'une côté: 'Colonie française victorieuse en Amérique' et de l'autre: 'Les Bataves défaits et mis en fuite à la Martinique, 1674," Guérin, III, 254-55.

60 Sylvius, I, 11, p. 136, *RSG*, Oct. 5, 1674. Report of de Ruyter. There is perhaps nothing more frustrating for a soldier on a secret mission than to find out that the enemy is informed. Hence miscalculation and demoralization.

61 The exploits of Jan Erasmus Reining are described by his biographer D. van der Sterre, *Zeer aanmerckelijke reysen gedaan door Jan Erasmus Reining* (Amsterdam, 1691).

62 *CSP*, IX, 1668-74, no. 1152, Answers to inquiries sent to Col. Stapleton...by Sir Robert Southwell.

63 *ARA*, WIC, NC, 52, Chamber of Amsterdam, Copybook of remonstrances, memorials, etc., 1674-89, Aug. 3, 1675: "Tis ons onsmakelijck geweest te verstaen den ongeluckigen aenslagh van de Capiteynen Erasmus ende Jurian Aernouts opt eylant Grenades, ende willen hopen, dat de voorn. capiteynen met haer onderhorigh volck respective albereyts wederom aen Curaçao sullen sijn gecomen." Hamelberg, *Nederlanders*, I, Doc., p. 98. There were more of these comic opera capers operating in the area.

64 We followed the information given by Sylvius, I, 14, Exquemelin, pp. 176-77, Sue, III, 408 ff., La Roncière, v, 648 ff., Farrère, pp. 156 ff., Hartsinck, I, 165 ff. and C. K. Kesler, "Twee rooftochten met tragischen afloop," *WIG*, III (1921), 609-29. Details are added by *SAA*, WIC, 55, and de Jonge, *Zeewezen*, II, 691 ff.

65 *SAA*, WIC, 55, Aug. 1, 1676, "Extract Res. Holl. Missive van Binckes aen S.H. den Prince van Orange," dated May 13, 1676 with "een omstandigh verhael van... de veroveringe van Cayenne." In the same collection is a similar "Extract" also dated Aug. 1, 1676.

66 De Jonge, *Zeewezen*, II, 694.

67 Sylvius, I, 14, pp. 348 ff. The colony remained under French rule until 1690.

68 La Roncière, v, 649. The Dutch probably expected support of the population; in 1671 there had been pro-Dutch demonstrations against Colbert's colonial policy. See Barbour, p. 101; Donnan, I, 98-99.

69 La Roncière, v, 649-50. Cf. Sylvius, I, 14, pp. 355 ff., and 15, pp. 36-37.

70 Extensive information of this exploit is given in Guérin, III, La Roncière, v, Farrère, Sue, III, and *Lettres...de Colbert*, III. The Dutchs ide is represented by Sylvius, I, 15, Hartsinck, *ARA*, WIC, NC, 52, Chamber of Amsterdam, and *SAA*, WIC, 55.

71 *Lettres... de Colbert*, III, 2, p. 612, April 6, 1677. Sue, III, 411 ff., gives a "Relation de la navigation de l'escadre des vaisseaux de Sa Majesté depuis Brest jusqu'à

Cayenne, de la descente de l'Ile et de l'attaque du port et des travaux ainsi que ceux de la prise de la dite ville, le 21 décembre, 1676." Martinique, Jan. 21, 1677, written by d'Estrées.

72 La Roncière, v, 662.

73 See on this expedition Troude, I, 172 ff., La Roncière, v, 662-67, Guérin, III, 315 ff., Jal, II, 309-11, Sue, III, 453 ff., and Sylvius, I, 16, pp. 128-29.

74 Sue, III, 453-54. Cf. La Roncière, v, 663, Farrère, p. 160.

75 Farrère, p. 156, Jal, II, pp. 309-10, La Roncière, v, 663.

76 The best account of this disaster is given by Sue, III, 451-61, with an additional "Relation du naufrage de l'escadre des Iles, arrivé à l'île des oiseaux au mois de mai 1678, par le sieur de Méricourt et avec sa lettre du 5 juin 1678." See also CSP, x, 1677-80, no. 1646, Jonathan Atkins, governor of Barbados, to Coventry, Aug. 1, 1678; and de Jonge, Zeewezen, II, 736 ff. Roncière, v, 665, calls it "l'horrible malheur."

77 Guérin, III, 315, La Roncière, v, 664. It is interesting to know that during the peace negotiations of Nijmegen, Colbert, anticipating a return of the island of Curaçao to the Dutch, wrote to d'Estrées "...que Sa Majesté seroit obligé de restituer les forts de l'isle de Curaçao en cas que vous l'ayez pris, et qu'il seroit d'un grand avantage pour elle que ces forts fussent rasés, elle m'ordonne de faire... et transporter les habitants." Lettres...de Colbert, III, 2, p. 637.

78 Sue, III, 451-61. Cf. La Roncière, v, 665 ff., Hollandtze Mercurius, 1678, pp. 226-28, CSP, x, 1677-80, nos. 604, 605, 665, 687-90, et passim.

BIBLIOGRAPHY

Unprinted Sources.

AGI   Archivo General de Indias, Seville.
        Santa Fe (de Bogotá), nos. 20, 38, 223.
        Indiferente General, nos. 1867, 1871, 2535, 2568, 2569, 2766, 2795, 2796, 2829.
        Casa de Contratación, nos. 4991, 4995.
        Audiencia de Santo Domingo, nos. 52, 72, 100, 155, 177, 179, 180, 187, 194, 215, 272.
Instituto Histórico de Marina, Madrid.
        Colección Navarrete, 30 v. Martín Fernández de Navarrete, ed.
Biblioteca Nacional, Madrid.
        Colección de manuscritos.
ARA Algemeen Rijksarchief (General Archives of the Government), The Hague.
    West Indische Compagnie, Oude Compagnie.
        Meetings of the XIX,   nos. 1-13.   Minutes, secret minutes, deductions, copy-books, patents.
        Chamber of Amsterdam,   nos. 14-18.   Minutes, copy-books, patents, etc.
        Chamber of Zeeland,   nos. 19-38.   Minutes, commissions, instructions, resolutions, etc.
                                  nos. 39-40.   Resolutions of the States General concerning the WIC, OC.
                                  nos. 41-47.   Commissions, conditions, instructions, reports, etc.
                                  nos. 48-76.   Letters and papers from Brazil, 1635-54.
                                  nos. 77-80.   Subscription lists, etc.
        Inventory Collection Maps, p. 12, MS "X."
        Chamber of Stadt en Lande, nos. 1322, 1323. Charters WIC.
        States General,   nos. 3224-32. (new numbers 4841-49), resolutions concerning the WIC, OC.,
                                  no. 3310.   ect. (new numbers 12528-30), Eedtboeck.
                                  nos. 3534-35. Plakaet Boecken.
                                  no. 5746a.   Letters concerning the EIC.
                                  nos. 5784-88. (new numbers 5768-72), Letters from West India.

nos. 8275-76. (new numbers 9410-11), Reports, etc.

    Secrete kas.

Inventaris Staten Generaal (West Indië).

    nos. 5751-69.

    Loketkas.

Lias West Indië, 1621-78.

Aanwinsten West Indië, 1890-1906. In (printed) reports of *ARA*.

Verspreide West Indische stukken.

    no. 501.

    Nieuw Nederland, nos. 2-6.

    Brazilië, nos. 730-1408.

    St. Eustatius, St. Martin en Saba, no. 172.

    Suriname, nos. 463, 764, 766, 767, 768, 769, 770, 973, 1177.

Collectie Rademaeker. Zaken Oude WIC, 1621-74, nos. 77-84.

Collectie Fagel.

West Indische Compagnie, Nieuwe Compagnie.

    Chamber of Amsterdam, nos. 52, 452, 467.

    Letters and Papers from Curaçao, no. 1160.

Resolutieboeken van de Staten Generaal, 1580-1680.

    (The resolutions of the years 1580-1609 are all quoted from *Resolutiën van de Staten Generaal, 1576-1609*, Rijks geschiedkundige publicatiën. Grote serie, 's-Gravenhage, 1915-41, Nicolaas Japikse, ed. Nos. 26, 33, 41, 43, 47, 51, 55, 62, 71, 85, 92, 101.)

Resolutieboeken van de Staten van Holland en West-Friesland, 1580-1680.

Resolutieboeken van de Staten van Zeeland, 1580-1680.

Archieven der Admiraliteits Colleges.

    Admiralty Board of the Maze, nos. 411-19, 548-50.

    Admiralty Board of Amsterdam, nos. 1333-1415, 1528-63, 1626-28, 2865.

    Admiralty Board of Zeeland, nos. 2424-2738.

SAA Stedelijk Archief (City Archives), Amsterdam.

    West Indische Collectie, nos. 54, 55.

New York State Library, Albany, N.Y.

    Calendar of Historical Manuscripts. Dutch Manuscripts, vol. XVII, Curaçao Papers, 1640-65.

PRINTED SOURCES

Aa, A. J. van der. *Biographisch woordenboek der Nederlanden.* Haarlem, 1852-78. 12v.

Abbad y Lasierra, Iñigo. *Historia geográfica y natural de la Isla San Juan de Puerto Rico.* José J. de Acosta y Calbo, ed. Puerto Rico, 1866.

Abendanon, J. H. "De vlootaanval van Jhr. Pieter van der Does op de Canarische eilanden en het eiland Santo Thomé in 1599 volgens Nederlandsche en Spaansche bronnen." *Bijdragen voor Vaderlandsche Geschiedenis en Oudheidkunde*, V, 8 (1921), 14-63.

Abreu e Lima, José de. *Synopsis ou deducção chronologica dos factos mais notaveis da historia do Brazil.* Pernambuco, 1845.

Acosta, José de. *Historia natural y moral de las Indias.* Edmundo O'Gorman, ed. México, 1962.

Acuña, Cristoval de. *Nuevo descubrimiento del gran rio de las Amazonas.* Madrid, 1641.

Aitzema, Lieuwe van. *Saken van staet en oorlogh in ende omtrent de Vereenigde Nederlanden.* 's Graven-Haghe, 1669-72. 6 v.

Alcedo y Herrera, Dionisio. *Piraterías y agresiones de los ingleses y de otros pueblos de Europa en la América española desde el siglo XVI al XVIII.* Madrid, 1883.

Algemeene geschiedenis der Nederlanden. J. A. van Houtte *et al.*, eds. Utrecht, 1949-58. 12 v.

Altamira y Crevea, Rafael. *Ensayo sobre Felipe II, hombre de estado; su psicología general y su individualidad humana.* México, 1950.

————. *Historia de España y de la civilización española.* 3rd ed. Madrid, 1913-30. 4v.

Anderson, Edgar. "Die ersten kurländischen Expeditionen nach Westindien im 17. Jahrhundert." *Baltische Hefte,* VIII, 1 (1961), 13-35.

————. "Die kurländische Kolonie Tobago." *Baltische Hefte,* VIII (1961), 3, 129-55; 4, 216-32.

Andrews, K. R. *Elizabethan Privateering. English Privateering during the Spanish War, 1585-1603.* Cambridge, 1964.

Angulo Iñiguez, Diego. *Bautista Antoneli. Las fortificaciones americanas del siglo XVI.* Madrid, 1942.

————. *Historia del arte hispanoamericano.* Barcelona, Buenos Aires, 1945-56. 3 v.

Arbusow, L. *Grundriss der Geschichte Liv, Est- und Kurlands.* Riga, 1908.

Arcila Farías, E. *El regimen de la encomienda en Venezuela.* Sevilla, 1957.

————. *Economía colonial de Venezuela.* México, 1946.

Arciniegas, Germán. *Biografía del Caribe.* Buenos Aires, 1945.

————. *Caribbean, Sea of the New World.* New York, 1946.

Arellano Moreno, Antonio. *Orígenes de la economía venezolana.* Caracas, 1947.

Arend, J. P., and O. van Rees. *Algemeene geschiedenis des vaderlands.* Amsterdam, 1840-79. 4 v.

Asher, G. M. *A Biographical and Historical Essay on the Dutch Books and Pamphlets Relating to New Netherland and to the Dutch West India Company.* Amsterdam, 1854-67.

Avermaete, Roger. *Guilleaume le Taciturne, 1533-1584.* Paris, 1939.

————. *Les gueux de mer et la naissance d'une nation.* Bruxelles, 1944.

Azevedo J. Lúcio d'. *Épocas de Portugal económico. Esboços de história.* 2d ed. Lisboa, 1947.

Baasch, Ernst. *Holländische Wirtschaftsgeschichte.* Jena, 1927.

Bakhuizen van den Brink, R. C. *Studiën en schetsen over vaderlandsche geschiedenis en letteren.* Amsterdam, 1860-1913. 5 v.

Ballet, J. *La Guadeloupe.* Basse Terre, 1890-96. 3 v.

Barbour, Violet. *Capitalism in Amsterdam in the Seventeenth Century.* Baltimore, 1950.

————. "Privateers and Pirates of the West Indies." *American Historical Review,* XVI (1910-11), 529-66.

Barlaeus, Casparus. *Rerum per Octennium in Brasilia.* Amstelodami, 1647. Trans. and ed. Samuel P. L'Honoré Naber: *Kaspar van Baerle. Nederlandsch Brazilië onder het bewind van Johan Maurits, grave van Nassau.* 's-Gravenhage, 1923.

Becht, H. E. *Statistische gegevens betreffende den handelsomzet van de republiek der Vereenigde Nederlanden gedurende de 17de eeuw. 1637-1644.* 's-Gravenhage, 1923.

Bensabat Amzalak, M. *As relações diplomáticas entre Portugal e a França no reinado de D. João IV.* Lisboa, 1934.

Bense, J. F. *Anglo-Dutch Relations from the Earliest Times to the Death of William the Third.* The Hague, 1924.

Benson, M. *Histoire des colonies françaises.* Paris, 1931.

Beresford, John. *The Godfather of Downing Street*. London, 1925.

Bergsma, J., ed. *Joost van den Vondel's hekeldichten*. Zutphen, 1920.

Berkel, Adriaan van. *Amerikaansche voyagien, behelzende een reis na rio de Berbice, gelegen op het vaste land van Guiana, aan de wilde-kust van America, mitsgaders een andere na de colonie van Suriname, gelegen in het noorder deel van het gemelde landschap Guiana*. Amsterdam, 1695.

Berkis, Alexander V. *The Reign of Duke James in Courland, 1638-1682*. Lincoln, Neb., 1960.

Berns, E. *Die Wirtschaftsethik der calvinistischen Kirche der Niederlande, 1565-1650*. Haag, 1933.

Bethencourt, C. de. "Notes on the Spanish and Portuguese Jews in the U.S., Guiana, and the Dutch and British West Indies during the Seventeenth and Eighteenth Centuries." *Publications of the American Jewish Historical Society*, XXIX (1925), 7-38.

Biet, Antoine. *Voyage de la France équinoxiale en l'isle de Cayenne entrepris par les François en l'année MDCLII*. Paris, 1664.

Bijlsma, R. "Rotterdams Amerikavaart in de eerste helft der zeventiende eeuw." *Bijdragen voor Vaderlandsche Geschiedenis en Oudheidkunde*, V, 3 (1915), 97-142.

———. "Rotterdamsche akten betreffende Pieter Pietersz Heyn." *De Navorscher*, LXV (1916), 130-32.

———. "De opkomst van Rotterdams koopvaardij." *Bijdragen voor Vaderlandsche Geschiedenis en Oudheidkunde*, V, 1 (1913), 56-87.

———. "De stichting van de Portugeesch-Joodsche gemeente en synagoge in Suriname." *West Indische Gids*, II (1920), 58-60.

———. *Rotterdams welvaren, 1580-1650*. 's-Gravenhage, 1918.

Bilmanis, Alfreds. *A History of Latvia*. Princeton, 1951.

Bizot, P. *Histoire métallique de la république de Hollande*. Paris, 1687.

Black, John B. *Elizabeth and Henry IV. Being a Short Study in Anglo-French Relations, 1589-1603*. Oxford, 1914.

Blanche, Lénis. *Histoire de la Guadeloupe*. Paris, 1938.

Bleyswyck, Dirck van. *Beschryvinghe der Stadt Delft*. Delft, 1667.

Blok, Pieter J. *History of the People of the Netherlands*. Trans. New York, 1898-1912. 5 v.

———. *Michiel Adriaenszoon de Ruyter*. 3rd ed. 's-Gravenhage, 1947.

———. "De handel op Spanje en het begin der groote vaart." *Bijdragen voor Vaderlandsche Geschiedenis en Oudheidkunde*, V, 1 (1913), 102-20.

Bloom, Herbert I. *The Economic Activities of the Jews in Amsterdam in the Seventeenth and Eighteenth Centuries*. Williamsport, Penn., 1937.

Boer, Michael G. de. "Een Nederlandsche goudzoeker. Een bijdrage tot de geschiedenis onzer nederzettingen aan de Wilde Kust." *Tijdschrift voor Geschiedenis*, I (1886), 1-18.

———. *Die Friedensunterhandlungen zwischen Spanien und den Niederlanden in den Jahren 1632 und 1633*. Groningen, 1898.

———. "Een Nederlandsche nederzetting aan de Oyapok, 1677." *Tijdschrift voor Geschiedenis*, XIV (1899), 321-42.

———. "Een memorie over den toestand der West Indische Compagnie in het jaar 1633." *Bijdragen en Mededelingen van het Historisch Genootschap*, XXI (1900), 343-62.

———. "De verovering der Zilvervloot." *Tijdschrift voor Geschiedenis*, XXXI (1916), 1-16, 65-74.

———. "De val van Bahia." *Tijdschrift voor Geschiedenis*, LVIII (1943), 38-49.

———. *Piet Heyn en de Zilveren vloot*. Amsterdam, 1946.

Bolingbroke, Henry. *A Voyage to Demerary. Containing a Statistical Account of the Settlements there, and of those on the Essequibo, the Berbice, and other Contiguous Rivers of Guyana.* Philadelphia, 1813. The new edition (Georgetown, 1947) was used here.

Bonnassieux, Pierre (L. J. P. M.). *Les grandes compagnies de commerce; étude pour servir à l'histoire de la colonisation.* Paris, 1892.

Bor, Pieter C. *Oorsprongk, begin ende vervolgh der Nederlandsche oorlogen, beroerten en borgerlycke oneenigheden.* 2d ed. Amsterdam, 1679-84. 4 v.

Borde, P. G. L. *Histoire de l'île de Trinidad sous le gouvernement espagnol.* Paris, 1876-82. 2 v.

Bosman, Willem. *A New and Accurate Description of the Coast of Guinea, divided into the Gold, the Slave, and the Ivory Coasts.* In *A General Collection of the Best and Most Interesting Voyages and Travels,* XVI, 337-547. London, 1814.

Botelho de Sousa, A. *Subsídios para a história das guerras da restauração no mar e no além-mar.* Lisboa, 1940. 2 v.

———. *O período da restauração nos mares da metrópole no Brasil e em Angola.* Lisboa, 1940.

Boxer, Charles R. *Salvador de Sá and the Struggle for Brazil and Angola, 1602-1686.* London, 1952.

———. *The Dutch in Brazil, 1624-1654.* Oxford, 1957.

———. *The Dutch Seaborne Empire, 1600-1800.* New York, 1965.

———. "Padre António Vieira S. J. and the Institution of the Brazil Company in 1649." *Hispanic American Historical Review,* XXIX (1949), 474-97.

———. "Piet Heyn and the Silver-Fleet." *History Today,* XIII (June, 1963), 398-406.

Boyer de Peyreleau, Eugène E. *Les Antilles françaises, particulièrement la Guadeloupe.* Paris, 1825. 3 v.

Brakel, S. van. "Eene memorie over den handel der West-Indische Compagnie omstreeks 1670." *Bijdragen en Mededelingen van het Historisch Genootschap,* XXXV (1914), 87-104.

———. "Bescheiden over den slavenhandel der West Indische Compagnie." *Economisch Historisch Jaarboek,* IV (1918), 47-83.

———. "Een Amsterdamsche factorij in Paramaribo in 1613." *Bijdragen en Mededelingen van het Historisch Genootschap,* XXXV (1914), 83-86.

———. *De Hollandsche handelscompagnieën der zeventiende eeuw, hun ontstaan, hunne inrichting.* 's-Gravenhage, 1908.

Brandt, Geeraert. *Historie der Reformatie en andere kerkelijke geschiedenissen in en ontrent de Nederlanden.* Amsterdam, 1674, 1677; Rotterdam, 1704. 4 v.

———. *Het leven en bedryf van den Heere Michiel de Ruiter, hertog, ridder, &c. lt. admiraal generaal van Hollandt en Westvrieslandt.* Amsterdam, 1701.

———. *Historie der vermaerde zee- en koop-stadt Enkhuisen.* 2d ed. Hoorn, 1747.

Brau, Salvador. *Puerto Rico y su historia.* Valencia, 1894.

Bredius, A., H. Brugmans, and C. Kalff, eds. *Amsterdam in de zeventiende eeuw.* 's-Gravenhage, 1897-1904. 3 v.

Brito Figueroa, Federico. *Ensayos de historia social venezolana.* Caracas, 1960.

Bromley, John S., and Ernst H. Kossman, eds. *Britain and the Netherlands.* London, 1960-64. 2 v.

Brown, Vera L. "Contraband Trade: a Factor in the Decline of Spain's Empire in America." *Hispanic American Historical Review,* VIII (1928), 178-89.

Brugmans, H. *Opkomst en bloei van Amsterdam.* Amsterdam, 1911.

Brugmans, Hk., and A. Frank, eds. *Geschiedenis der Joden in Nederland.* Amsterdam, 1940.

Brunschwig, Henri. "Le nègre hors d'Afrique: planteurs et esclaves (Indes occidentales, Mascareignes, Madagascar)." *Revue Historique,* LXXXVII (Juillet-Septembre, 1963), 149-70.
Bueno de Mesquita, J. A., and Fred. Oudschans Dentz. *Geschiedkundige tijdtafel van Suriname.* Paramaribo, 1924.
Burn, W. L. *The British West Indies.* London, 1951.
Burnet, G. *History of his Own Time.* London, 1724-34. 2 v.
Burney, James. *History of the Buccaneers of America.* Many editions. London, 1891, edition used here.
Burns, Alan C. *History of the British West Indies.* London, 1954.
Busken Huet, Conrad. *Het Land van Rembrand.* Haarlem, 1886. 3 v. (referred to as I, II,1, II,2).
Cabrera de Córdoba, Luis de. *Relaciones de las cosas sucedidas en la corte de España desde 1599 hasta 1614.* Madrid, 1857.
Cadornega, A. Oliveira de. *História geral das guerras angolanas.* José Matias Delgado and Alves da Cunha, eds. Lisboa, 1940-42. 3 v.
Cadoux, Cecil J. *Philip of Spain and the Netherlands. An Essay on Moral Judgments in History.* London and Redhill, 1947.
Caetano da Silva, Joaquim. *L'Oyapoc et l'Amazone, question brésilienne et française.* Paris, 1861. 2 v.
Calendar of State Papers. Colonial Series (America and West Indies). I, 1574-1660; V, 1660-68; VII, 1668-74; IX, 1675-76; X, 1677-80; XI, 1681-85; XII, 1685-88; XIII, 1689-92; XIV, 1693-96; XV, 1696-97; XVI, 1697-98.
Canovas del Castillo, Antonio. *Historia de la decadencia de España desde el advenimiento de Felipe III al trono hasta la muerte de Carlos II.* Madrid, 1910.
―――. *Estudios del reinado de Felipe IV.* Madrid, 1888.
Capellen, Alexander van der. *Gedenkschriften van Jonkheer Alexander van der Capellen, 1621-1654.* R. J. van der Capellen, ed. Utrecht, 1777-78. 2 v.
Cassou, Jean. *La vie de Philippe II.* Paris, 1929.
Castellanos, Juan de. *Elegías de varones ilustres de Indias.* Many editions. Bogotá, 1955, edition used here.
Charlevoix, Pierre X. de. *Histoire de l'ile Espagnole ou de S. Domingue.* Paris, 1730-31. 2 v.
Chaunu, Pierre. "Les crises au XVIIe siècle de l'Europe réformée." *Revue Historique,* LXXXIX (Janviers-Mars, 1965), 23-60.
―――― and Huguette. *Séville et l'Atlantique, 1504-1650.* Paris, 1955-59. 8 v.
Cheyney, Edward P. *A History of England from the Defeat of the Armada to the Death of Elizabeth.* London, 1914-26. 2 v.
Chijs, J. A. van der. *Nederlandsch-Indisch plakaatboek 1602-1811.* Batavia, 1885-1900. 17 v.
―――. *Geschiedenis der stichting van de Vereenigde Oost Indische Compagnie en der maatregelen van de Nederlandsche regering betreffende de vaart op Oost-Indië, welke aan deze stichting voorafgingen.* 2d ed. Leiden, 1857.
Clark, George N. *The Seventeenth Century.* Oxford, 1927.
―――. *The Later Stuarts.* Oxford, 1934.
―――― and W. J. M. van Eysinga. *The Colonial Conferences Between England and the Netherlands in 1613 and 1615.* Leiden, 1940 and 1951. 2 v.
Clément, Pierre, ed. *Lettres, instructions et mémoires de Colbert.* Paris, 1861-73. 7 v.
―――. *Histoire de Colbert et de son administration.* Paris, 1874. 2 v.
Cloderé, J. *Relation de ce qui s'est passé dans les iles & Terre Ferme de l'Amérique.* Paris, 1671. 2 v.

Colección de documentos inéditos para la historia de España. Madrid, 1842-95. 112 v.

Colección de documentos inéditos para la historia de Hispano-América. Madrid, 1927-32. 14 v.

Colenbrander, Herman T. *Koloniale geschiedenis.* 's-Gravenhage, 1925-26. 3 v.

Coll y Toste, Cayetano. "Relaçion de la entrada y cerco del enemigo Boudoyno Henrico, general de la armada del Principe de Orange, en la ciudad de Puerto Rico de las Yndias por el licenciado Diego de Larrasa, teniente auditor general que fue en ella." *Boletín Histórico de Puerto Rico,* IV (1917), 229-43.

———. "Ataque de los Holandeses a la isla. Rectificaciones históricas." *Boletín Histórico de Puerto Rico,* XII (1925), 193-204.

Collins, Edward D. "Studies in the Colonial Policy of England, 1672-1680. The Plantations, the Royal African Company and the Slave Trade," *Annual Report of the American Historical Association, 1900.* Pp. 139-92. Washington, 1901.

Commelin, Izaäk. *Frederick Hendrick van Nassauw, Prince vâ Orangien, zyn leven en bedrijf.* Amsterdam, 1651. 2 v.

Cone, G. Herbert. "The Jews in Curaçao." *Publications of the American Jewish Historical Society,* X (1902), 141-58.

Corbett, J. S. *Drake and the Tudor Navy. With a History of the Rise of England as a Maritime Power.* London, 1899.

Cordeiro, António. *Historia insulana das ilhas a Portugal sujeitas no oceano occidental.* Lisboa, 1866. 2 v.

Córdoba, Pedro T. *Memorias geográficas, históricas, económicas y estadísticas de la isla de Puerto Rico.* Puerto Rico, 1831-33. 6 v.

Córdoba Bello, Eleazar. *Compañías holandesas de navegación.* Sevilla, 1964.

Coreal, Francisco. *Voyages aux Indes occidentales, 1666-1669.* Amsterdam, 1722.

Costa Quintella, I. da. *Annaes de marinha portugueza.* Lisboa, 1839-40. 2 v.

Court, Pieter de la (and Johan de Witt). *The True Interest and Political Maxims of the Republick of Holland and West Friesland.* N.p., 1702.

Couto Ribeiro Villas, G. do. *Os Portugueses na colonização.* Lisboa, 1929.

———. *História colonial de Portugal.* Lisboa, 1938. 2 v.

Crouse Nellis M. *French Pioneers in the West Indies, 1624-1664.* New York, 1940.

———. *The French Struggle for the West Indies, 1665-1713.* New York, 1943.

Dalton, H. G. *The History of British Guiana.* London, 1855. 2 v.

Dampierre, Jacques de. *Essai sur les sources de l'histoire des Antilles françaises, 1492-1664.* Paris, 1904.

Dapper, Olfert. *Naukeurige beschrijvinge der Afrikaensche gewesten van Egypten, Barbaryen, Lybien, Biledulgerid, Negroslant. Naukeurige beschrijvinge der Afrikaense eylanden.* Amsterdam, 1668.

Dauxion-Lavaysse, J. F. *A Statistical, Commercial and Political Description of Venezuela, Trinidad, Margarita, and Tobago.* Trans. M. Lavaysse. London, 1820.

Davies, D. W. *A Primer of Dutch Seventeenth Century Overseas Trade.* The Hague, 1961.

Davies, K. G. *The Royal African Company.* London, New York, 1957.

Davies, Reginald T. *Spain in Decline, 1621-1700.* London, 1957.

Deer, Noël. *The History of Sugar.* London, 1950. 2 v.

Delarbre, Jules. *Tourville et la marine française de son temps.* Paris, 1889.

Delgado, Ralph. *História de Angola.* Benguela, 1948-55. 4 v.

Depons, François R. J. *Voyage à la partie orientale de la Terre Firme de l'Amérique meridionale, fait pendant les années 1801, 1802, 1803 et 1804.* Paris, 1806. 3 v.

Deventer, Marinus L. van. *Gedenkstukken van Oldenbarnevelt en zijn tijd.* 's-Gravenhage, 1860-65. 3 v.

Díaz Soler, Luis M. *Historia de la esclavitud negra in Puerto Rico.* 2d ed. Río Piedras, 1965.

Diferee, Hendrik C. *De geschiedenis van den Nederlandschen handel tot den val der Republiek.* Amsterdam, 1908.

Dillen, Johannes G. van. "Effectenkoersen aan de Amsterdamsche beurs." *Economisch Historisch Jaarboek,* XVII (1931), 1-46.

————. "De West Indische Compagnie, het calvinisme en de politiek." *Tijdschrift voor Geschiedenis,* LXXIV (1961), 145-71.

Donnan, Elizabeth, ed. *Documents Illustrative of the History of the Slave Trade to America.* Washington, D.C., 1930-35. 4 v.

Doorman, G. *Patents for Inventions in the Netherlands during the 16th, 17th, and 18th Centuries, with notes on the historical development of technics.* The Hague, 1942.

Doorman, J. G. "Die Niederländische West-Indische Compagnie an der Goldküste." *Tijdschrift voor Indische Taal-, Land- en Volkenkunde,* XL (1897), 395-478.

Duarte Level, Lino. *Cuadros de la historia militar y civil de Venezuela desde el descubrimiento y conquista de Guayana hasta la batalla de Carabobo.* 2d ed. Madrid, 1917.

Dutertre, Jean B. *Histoire générale des Antilles habitées par les François.* Paris, 1667-71. 4 v.

Eckert, Walter. *Kurland unter dem Einfluss des Merkantilismus, 1561-1682.* Marburg, 1926.

Edmundson, George. "The Dutch Power in Brazil." *English Historical Review,* XI (1896), 231-59; XIV (1899), 676-69; XV (1900), 38-57.

————. "The Dutch in Western Guiana." *English Historical Review,* XVI (1901), 640-75.

————. "The Dutch on the Amazon and Negro in the Seventeenth Century." *English Historical Review,* XVIII (1903), 642-63; XIX (1904), 1-25.

Edwards, Bryan. *The History, Civil and Commercial, of the British Colonies in the West Indies.* 3rd ed. London, 1793-1801. 3 v.

Eerdmans, Marian. *Pieter Stuyvesant; an Historical Documentation.* Grand Rapids, Mich., 1957.

Eggen, J. L. M. *De invloed door Zuid-Nederland op Noord-Nederland uitgeoefend op het einde der XVIe en het begin der XVIIe eeuw.* Gent, 1908.

Elias, Johan E. *De vroedschap van Amsterdam, 1578-1795.* Haarlem, 1903-5. 2 v.

————. *Schetsen uit de geschiedenis van ons zeewezen.* 's-Gravenhage, 1916-30. 6 v.

————. *Het voorspel van den eersten Engelschen oorlog.* 's-Gravenhage, 1920. 2 v.

————. *Geschiedenis van het Amsterdamsche regentenpatriciaat.* 's-Gravenhage, 1923.

————. *De vlootbouw in Nederland in de eerste helft der 17e eeuw.* Amsterdam, 1933.

Elout van Soeterwoude, W. *Onze West.* 's-Gravenhage, 1884.

Elphège, Frémy. "Causes économiques de la guerre de Hollande, 1664-1672." *Revue de l'Histoire Diplomatique,* XXVIII-XXIX (1914-15), 523-51.

Elzinga, Simon. *Het voorspel van den oorlog van 1672. De economisch-politieke betrekkingen tusschen Frankrijk en Nederland in de jaren 1660-1672.* Haarlem, 1926.

Emmanuel, Isaac S. *Precious Stones of the Jews of Curaçao. Curaçao Jewry 1656-1957.* New York, 1957.

Encyclopaedie van Nederlandsch West-Indië. H. D. Benjamins and Joh. Snelleman, eds. 's-Gravenhage-Leiden, 1914, 1917.

Ericeira, Luis de Menezes, Conde da. *História de Portugal restaurado.* (Lisboa: Vol. 1, 1751; Vol. 2, 1698). 2 v.

Euwens, P. A. "De eerste jood op Curaçao." *West Indische Gids,* XII (1930), 360-66.

————. "Wat zijn 'Frejelindes' en 'Frechlingas'?" *West Indische Gids,* XIII (1931), 337-64.

Exquemelin, Alexander O. *De Americaensche zee-rovers. Behelsende een pertiente en waerachtige beschrijving van alle de voornaemste rooverijen en onmenschelijcke wreedheden, die de Engelsche en Fransche roovers tegens de Spanjaerden in America gepleeght hebben.* Amsterdam, 1678. English translation under John Exquemeling, *The Buccaneers of America.* Many editions.

Eysinga, Willem J. M. van. "Een onuitgegeven nota van de Groot." *Mededelingen der Koninklijke Nederlandse Academie van Wetenschappen. Afdeling Letterkunde.* Amsterdam, 1955.

Fagniez, Gustave C. "Le commerce extérieur de la France sous Henri IV." *Revue Historique,* XVI (Mai-Août, 1881), 1-48.

Farrère, Claude. *Histoire de la marine française.* 2d ed. Paris, 1962.

Felice Cardot, Carlos. "Algunas acciones de los Holandeses en la región del oriente de Venezuela, primera mitad del siglo XVII." *Boletín de la Academia Nacional de Historia,* XLV (Julio-Sept., 1962), 179, pp. 349-72.

Fermin, Philippe. *Nieuwe algemeene historische, geographische en natuurkundige beschrijving van de colonie Suriname.* Amsterdam, 1795. 2 v.

Fernández de Navarrete, Martín, *et al.,* eds., *Colección de documentos inéditos para la historia de España.* Madrid, 1842-95. 112 v.

————. *Biblioteca maritima española.* Madrid, 1851. 2 v.

Fernández Duro, Cesareo. *Armada española desde la unión de los reinos de Castilla y de León.* Madrid, 1895-1903. 9 v.

Firth, Charles H. *Oliver Cromwell and the Rule of the Puritans in England.* London, 1900.

Freyre, Gilberto. *The Masters and the Slaves.* Trans. Samuel Putman. Abridged edition. New York, 1964.

Fruin, Robert J. *Tien jaren uit den tachtigjarigen oorlog, 1588-1598.* Amsterdam, 1861.

————. *Robert Fruin's Verspreide geschriften met aanteekeningen, toevoegsels en verbeteringen uit des schrijvers nalatenschap.* Pieter J. Blok and Pieter L. Muller, eds. 's-Gravenhage, 1900-1905. 11 v.

————, G. W. Kernkamp, and N. Japikse, eds. *Brieven van Johan de Witt.* Amsterdam, 1906-13. 4 v.

———— and N. Japikse, eds. *Brieven aan Johan de Witt.* Amsterdam, 1919-22. 2 v.

Gachard, Louis P. *Correspondance de Philippe II sur les affaires des Pays-Bas.* Bruxelles, 1848-79. 6 v.

Gedenkboek Nederland-Curaçao, 1634-1934. Amsterdam, 1934.

Geigel Sabat, Fernando J. *Balduino Enrico. Estudio sobre el General Balduino Enrico y el asedio de la ciudad de San Juan de Puerto Rico por la flota holandesa en 1625, al mando de dicho general y del almirante Andrés Verón; con otros episodios de las empresas de estos dos caudillos en aguas antillanas.* Barcelona, Araluce, 1934.

Geschiedenis der Nederlanden. L. G. J. Verberne *et al.,* eds. Vol. II: L. J. Rogier. *Eenheid en Scheiding.* Nijmegen, 1952.

Geschiedenis van Nederland. H. Brugmans *et al.,* eds. Amsterdam, 1935-38. 8 v.

Geyl, Pieter. *The Netherlands Divided, 1609-1648.* London, 1936. 2 v.

————. *The Revolt of the Netherlands, 1555-1609.* 2d ed. London, 1958.

————. *Geschiedenis van de Nederlandse stam.* 2d ed. Amsterdam, Antwerpen, 1948-49. 3 v.

Gittée, August. "Wat heeft Noord Nederland aan het Zuiden te danken?" *Tijdschrift voor Geschiedenis,* IX (1894), 333-49.

Goris, Johannes A. *Etude sur les colonies marchandes méridionales à Anvers de 1488 à 1567; contribution à l'histoire des débuts du capitalisme moderne.* Louvain, 1925.

Goslinga, Cornelis Ch. *Emancipatie en emancipator.* Assen, 1956.

————. "Juan de Ampués, vredelievende Indianen jager." *West Indische Gids,* XXXVII (1956), 169-87.

———. "Ojeda en Vespucci. Opmerkingen bij een ontdekking." *Voor Rogier*, pp. 19-36. Hilversum, 1964.

———. "Rodrigo de Bastidas. Tien jaar Caribische geschiedenis, 1532-1542." *Nieuwe West Indische Gids*, XLIV (1965), 185-215.

Goslinga, Marian. *March 24, 1854: The End of an Epoch in Venezuelan History*. Master's thesis, University of California, Berkeley, 1967.

Graefe, Friedrich. "Beiträge zur Lebensgeschichte Piet Heyns." *Bijdragen voor Vaderlandsche Geschiedenis en Oudheidkunde*, VII, 1 (1931), 145-51.

———. "Beiträge zur Geschichte der See-Expeditionen von 1606 und 1607." *Bijdragen voor Vaderlandsche Geschiedenis en Oudheidkunde*, VII, 3 (1933), 201-30.

———. "Piet Heyn als Leutnant-Admiral von Holland." *Bijdragen voor Vaderlandsche Geschiedenis en Oudheidkunde*, VII, 6 (1935), 174-204.

Groen van Prinsterer, Guilleaume, *et al.*, eds. *Archives ou correspondance inédite de la Maison d'Orange-Nassau*. Leide, Utrecht, 1835-1915. 24 v.

Grol, G. J. van. *De grondpolitiek in het Westindisch domein der generaliteit*. 's-Gravenhage, 1934-47. 3 v.

Groningen, A. P. van. *Geschiedenis der Watergeuzen*. Leiden, 1840.

Groot-Placaetboeck, inhoudende de placaten ende ordonnantien vande Hoogh-Mog: Heeren Staten Generael der Vereenighde Nederlanden ende vande Ed. Groot Mog: Heeren Staten van Hollandt ende West-Vrieslandt. Mitsgaders van de Ed. Groot Mog: Heeren Staten van Zeelandt. Vols. I, II, III. 's-Graven Hage, 1658, 1664, 1683.

Grose, Clyde L. "The Anglo-Portuguese Marriage of 1622." *Hispanic American Historical Review*, X (1930), 313-52.

Guérin, Léon. *Histoire maritime de France*. Paris, 1862-63. 6 v.

Guerra y Sánchez, Ramón. *Manual de historia de Cuba (económica, social y política)*. Habana, 1938.

———. *Azúcar y población en las Antillas*. 3rd ed. Habana, 1944.

Guiteras, Pedro J. *Historia de la isla de Cuba*. Havana, 1865-66. 2 v.

Gumilla, Joseph. *El Orinoco ilustrado. Historia natural, civil y geográfica de las naciones situadas en las riveras del río Orinoco*. New ed. Barcelona, 1791. 2 v.

Gunsteren, W. F. *Kalvinismus und Kapitalismus. Ein Beitrag zur Erkenntnis der Beziehungen zwischen kalvinistischer Sozial-Ethik und kapitalistischen Wirtschaftsgeist*. Amsterdam, 1934.

Haar, Cornelis van de. *De diplomatieke betrekkingen tussen de Republiek en Portugal, 1640-1661*. Groningen, 1961.

Hadeler, Nikolaus. *Geschichte der holländischen Colonien auf der Goldküste, mit besonderer Berücksichtigung des Handels*. Bonn, 1904.

Häpke, Rudolf. *Niederländische Akten und Urkunden zur Geschichte der Hanse und zur deutschen Seegeschichte*. München, Leipzig, 1913-23. 2 v.

Hagedoorn, B. *Die Entwicklung der wichtigsten Schiffstypen bis ins 19. Jahrhundert*. Berlin, 1914.

Hakluyt, Richard. *The Principal Navigations, Voyages, Traffiques & Discoveries of the English Nation, made by Sea or Overland to the Remote & Farthest Distant Quarters of the Earth at any Time within the Compasse of these 1600 years*. London, New York, 1927-28. 10 v.

Hallema, A. "Friesland en de voormalige compagnieën voor den handel op Oost en West." *West Indische Gids*, XV (1933), 81-96.

Hamelberg, J. H. J. *De Nederlanders op de West-Indische eilanden*. Amsterdam, 1901-3. 2 v. (with additional documents).

———. "Historische schets van de Nederlandsche bovenwindsche eilanden tot op het einde der 17e eeuw." Tweede jaarlijksch verslag van het Geschied-, Taal-, Land- en Volkenkundig Genootschap. Willemstad, Curaçao, 1899.

———. "Jan Erasmus Reining." Derde jaarlijksch verslag van het Geschied-, Taal-, Land- en Volkenkundig Genootschap. Willemstad, Curaçao, 1899, pp. 13-93.

———. "Tobago. Een vergeten Nederlandsche kolonie." Vierde jaarlijksch verslag van het Geschied-, Taal-, Land- en Volkenkundig Genootschap. Willemstad, Curaçao, 1900.

Handelmann, Heinrich. Geschichte von Brasilien. Berlin, 1860.

Hannay, David. The Great Chartered Companies. London, 1926.

Harcourt, Robert. A Relation of a Voyage to Guiana. C. Alexander Harris, ed. London, 1928.

Haren, Onno Zwier van. De Geuzen. Arnold Stakenburg, ed. Santpoort, 1943.

Haring, Clarence H. The Buccaneers in the West Indies in the XVIIth Century. New York, 1910.

———. Trade and Navigation Between Spain and the Indies in the Time of the Hapsburgs. Cambridge, Mass., 1918.

Harkness, Alberto. "Alonso de Hojeda y el descubrimiento de Venezuela." Revista Chilena de Historia y Geografía, CIII (1943), 197-213.

Harlow, Vincent. A History of Barbados, 1625-1685. Oxford, 1926.

———, ed. Colonising Expeditions to the West Indies and Guiana, 1623-1667. London, 1925.

———, ed. The Discoverie of the Large and Bewtiful Empire of Guiana by Walter Ralegh. London, 1928.

Hartog, Johannes. Geschiedenis van de Nederlandse Antillen. Oranjestad, 1956-64. 5 v. I, Aruba; II, Bonaire; III and IV, Curaçao; V, De bovenwindse eilanden.

Hartsinck, Jan J. Beschryving van Guiana of de wilde kust in Zuid-Amerika. Amsterdam, 1770. 2 v.

Hazewinkel, Hendrik C. Geschiedenis van Rotterdam. Amsterdam, 1940-42. 3 v.

Helps, Arthur. The Spanish Conquest in America and its Relation to the History of Slavery and to the Government of Colonies. New York, 1856-58. 4 v.

Heredia Herrera, Antonio M. "Las fortificaciones de la isla de Margarita en los siglos XVI, XVII y XVIII." Anuario de Estudios Americanos, XV (1958), 1-84 (429-512).

Hilfman, P. A. "Notes on the History of the Jews in Surinam." Publications of the American Jewish Historical Society, XVIII (1909), 179-207.

Hoboken, Willem J. van. Witte de With in Brazilië, 1648-1649. Amsterdam, 1955.

———. "The Dutch West India Company; the political background of its rise and decline." In J. S. Bromley and E. H. Kossmann, Britain and the Netherlands, 1. London, 1960, pp. 41-61.

———. "Een wederwoord inzake de West Indische Compagnie." Tijdschrift voor Geschiedenis, LXXV (1962), 49-53, with a postscript of J. C. van Dillen, pp. 53-56.

Hollander, Jacob H. "Documents Relating to the Attempted Departure of the Jews from Surinam in 1675." Publications of the American Jewish Historical Society, VI (1897), 9-29.

Hollandtze Mercurius. Haarlem, 1651-91. 41 v.

Hooft, Pieter C. Nederlandse historien. M. Nijhoff, ed. Amsterdam, 1947.

Hoyer, W. M. "De naam Curaçao." West Indische Gids, XX (1938), 225-27.

———. "De naam Aruba." West Indische Gids, XX (1938), 370-71.

Huges, Jan. Het leven en bedrijf van Mr. Franchois Vranck. 's-Gravenhage, 1909.

Hullu, J. de. "De Oost-Indische Compagnie en St. Helena in de 17de eeuw." De Indische Gids, LXVIII (1913), 877 ff.

Hume, David. *The History of England from the Invasion of Julius Caesar to the Abdication of James the Second*. Many editions. London, 1816, used here.

Hussey, Roland D. *The Caracas Company, 1728-1784; a Study in the History of Spanish Monopolistic Trade*. Cambridge, 1934.

———. "Spanish Reaction to Foreign Aggression in the Caribbean to about 1680." *Hispanic American Historical Review*, IX (1929), 286-302.

———. "Antecedents of the Spanish Monopolistic Trading Companies (1624-1738)." *Hispanic American Historical Review*, IX (1929), 1-30.

Hyma, Albert. *The Dutch in the Far East; a History of the Dutch Commercial and Colonial Empire*. Ann Arbor, Mich., 1942.

———. "Calvinism and Capitalism in the Netherlands, 1550-1570." *Journal of Modern History*, X (1938), 321-43.

———. "Hugo Grotius on the Freedom of the Seas." *Papers of the Michigan Academy of Science, Arts and Letters*, XXVII (1941), 615-23.

IJzerman, Jan W. *Dirck Gerritsz Pomp, alias Dirck China, de eerste Nederlander die China en Japan bezocht (1544-1604)*. 's-Gravenhage, 1915.

———. *Cornelis Buysero te Bantam, 1616-1618*. 's-Gravenhage, 1923.

———. "Amsterdamsche bevrachtingscontracten, 1591-1602." *Economisch Historisch Jaarboek*, XVII (1931), 163-291.

Innes, Arthur D. *The Maritime and Colonial Expansion of England under the Stuarts, 1603-1714*. London, 1932.

Irving, Washington. *A History of New York from the Beginning of the World to the End of the Dutch Dynasty*. New York, London, 1848.

Jaeger, F. H. "Over Johan Joachim Becker en zijne relaties met de Nederlanden." *Economisch Historisch Jaarboek*, V (1919), 60-135.

Jal, Auguste. *Abraham Du Quesne et la marine de son temps*. Paris, 1873. 2 v.

Jameson, J. Franklin. "The Life of Willem Usselinx, Founder of the Dutch and Swedish West India Companies." *Papers of the American Historical Association*, II (1887), [149-382], 1-234.

Japikse, Nicolaas. *De verwikkelingen tusschen de Republiek en Engeland van 1660-1665*. Leiden, 1900.

———. *Johan de Witt*. Amsterdam, 1915.

———, ed. *Resolutiën van de Staten Generaal 1576-1609*. Rijks geschiedkundige publicatiën. Grote serie. 's-Gravenhage, 1915-41. Nos. 26, 33, 41, 43, 47, 51, 55, 62, 71, 85, 92, 101.

Jiménez de la Espada, Marcos. *Viaje del Capitán Pedro Texeira aguas arriba del río de las Amazonas*. Madrid, 1889.

Jones, J. R. *Britain and Europe in the Seventeenth Century*. New York, 1966.

Jong, M. de. "Holland en de Portugese restauratie van 1640." *Tijdschrift voor Geschiedenis*, LV (1940), 225-53.

Jonge, Johannes C. de. *Levensbeschrijving van Johan en Cornelis Evertsen, luitenant-admiralen van Zeeland*. 's-Gravenhage, 1820.

———. *Geschiedenis van het Nederlandsche zeewezen*. 3rd ed. Zwolle, 1869. 5 v.

Jonge, Johan K. J. de. *De opkomst van het Nederlandsch gezag in Oost-Indië*. 's-Gravenhage, 1862-95. 13 v.

———. *De oorsprong van Neerlands bezittingen op de kust van Guinea*. 's-Gravenhage, 1871.

Jonghe, Ellert de. *Waerachtigh verhael van de machtighe scheeps-armada...onder het ghebiet en gheleyt van Joncker Pieter van der Does*. Amsterdam, 1600.

Jurien de la Gravière, Jean P. E. *Les gueux de mer*. 2d ed. Paris, 1893.

Juste, Théodore. *Les Pays-Bas sous Philippe II, 1555-1565*. 2d ed. Bruxelles, 1884.

Kalff, S. "West Indische gedenkpenningen." *West Indische Gids*, VI (1924), 223-37.
————. "Joden op het eiland Curaçao." *West Indische Gids*, VIII (1926), 69-84.
————. "Uit de geschiedenis van St. Eustatius." *West Indische Gids*, VIII (1926), 405-20.
————. "Iets over Peter Stuyvesant." *West Indische Gids*, VIII (1926), 517-30.
Kampen, Nicolaas G. van. *Geschiedenis der Nederlanders buiten Europa of verhaal van de togten, ontdekkingen, oorlogen, veroveringen en inrigtingen der Nederlanders in Aziën, Afrika, Amerika en Australië.* Haarlem, 1831-32. 3 v.
————. *Levens van beroemde Nederlanders.* Haarlem, 1838-40. 2 v.
Kemperink, J. H. P. "Pieter Stuyvesant; waar en wanneer werd hij geboren?" *De Navorscher*, XCVIII (1959), 49-59.
Kernkamp, Gerard W. *Baltische archivalia. Onderzoek naar archivalia, belangrijk voor de geschiedenis van Nederland, in Stockholm, Kopenhagen en de Duitse Oostzeesteden.* 's-Gravenhage, 1909.
————. "Zweedsche archivalia. Brieven van Samuel Blommaert." *Bijdragen en mededelingen van het Historisch Genootschap*, XXIX (1908), 3-196.
Kernkamp, Johannes H. *De handel op den vijand, 1572-1609.* Utrecht, 1931-34. 2 v.
————. *Johan van der Veken en zijn tijd.* 's-Gravenhage, 1952.
Kervyn de Lettenhove, Joseph B. M. C. *Les Huguenots et les Gueux.* Bruges, 1883-85. 6 v.
————. *Relations politiques des Pays-Bas et de l'Angleterre sous le règne de Philippe II.* Bruxelles, 1882-85. 6 v.
Kervyn de Volkaersbeke, Ph. A. C., and J. Diegerick. *Documents inédits concernant les troubles des Pays-Bas, 1577-1584.* Gand, 1847-50. 2 v.
Kesler, C. K. "Willem Usselincx en de oprichting van de West-Indische Compagnie." *West Indische Gids*, III (1921), 65-78.
————. "Twee rooftochten met tragischen afloop." *West Indische Gids*, III (1921), 609-29.
————. "Zeventiende eeuwse concurrenten der Nederlanders in de West." *West Indische Gids*, VIII (1926), 437-50.
————. "Het asiento." *West Indische Gids*, X (1928), 65-88.
————. "De verovering van de Zilvervloot." *West Indische Gids*, X (1928), 193-213.
————. "Tobago, een vergeten Nederlandsche kolonie." *West Indische Gids*, X (1928), 527-34.
————. "Uit de eerste dagen van den West-Indischen slavenhandel." *West Indische Gids*, XXII (1940), 175-85.
Kessler, Henry H., and Eugene Rachlis. *Pieter Stuyvesant and his New-York.* New York, 1959.
Keye, Otto. *Kurtzer Entwurff von Neu-Niederland und Guajana, einander entgegengesetzt umb den Unterschied zwischen warmen und kalten Landen herausz zu bringen.* Leipzig, 1672. Translation of *Het waere onderscheyt tusschen koude en warme landen.* 's-Graven Hage, 1659.
Kirchner, W. "The Duke of Alva Reconsidered." *Pacific Historical Review*, XIV (1945), 64-70.
Kleyntjes, J. "De Koerlandse kolonisatiepoging op Tobago." *West Indische Gids*, XXX (1949), 193-97.
Klopman, Ewald von. "Abrégé de l'histoire de Tobago." *West Indische Gids*, XXX (1949), 197-216.
Knuttel, Willem P. C., ed. *Catalogus van de pamfletten-verzameling berustende in de Koninklijke Bibliotheek.* 's-Gravenhage, 1889-1920. 9 v.

Koenen, Hendrik J. *Adriaen Pauw. Eene bijdrage tot de kerk- en handels-geschiedenis der zestiende eeuw.* Amsterdam, 1842.

——. *Geschiedenis der Joden in Nederland.* Utrecht, 1843.

——. "Pavonia. Eene bijdrage tot de kennis der voormalige Nederlandsche koloniën." *Bijdragen voor Vaderlandsche Geschiedenis en Oudheidkunde,* I, 5 (1847), 114-32.

Kohler, Max J. "Some Early American Zionist Projects." *Publications of the American Jewish Historical Society,* VIII (1900), 75-118.

Kok, Jacobus. *Vaderlandsch woordenboek.* Amsterdam, 1785-99. 38 v.

Kooy, Tjalling P. van der. *Hollands stapelmarkt en haar verval.* Amsterdam, 1931.

Krafft, Arnoldus J. C. *Historie en oude families van de Nederlandse Antillen. Het Antilliaans patriciaat.* 's-Gravenhage, 1951.

Kunz, George F., and Charles H. Stevenson. *The Book of the Pearl. The History, Art, Science, and Industry of the Queen of the Gems.* New York, 1908.

Laet, Ioannes de. *Nieuwe Wereldt ofte beschrijvinghe van West Indien.* Leiden, 1625.

——. *Historie ofte Iaerlijck Verhael van de verrichtinghen der Geoctroyeerde West-Indische Compagnie.* Samuel P. L'Honoré Naber, ed. 's-Gravenhage, 1931-37. 4 v.

Langemeyer, C. I. "Het zoutbedrijf op St. Maarten." *West Indische Gids,* IV (1922), pp. 243-65.

Lannoy, Charles de, and Herman van der Linden. *Histoire de l'expansion coloniale des peuples européens. Portugal et Espagne.* Bruxelles-Paris, 1907. *Néerlande et Danemark.* Bruxelles, 1911.

Laspeyres, Etienne. *Geschichte der volkswirtschaftlichen Anschauungen der Niederländer und ihrer Literatur zur Zeit der Republik.* Leipzig, 1863.

Lecestre, Léon, ed. *Mémoires de Gourville.* Paris, 1894-95. 2 v.

Lecler, Joseph. *Histoire de la tolérance au siècle de la Réforme.* Aubier, 1955. 2 v.

Leclerc, Jean. *Négociations secrètes touchant la paix de Munster et d'Osnabrug; ou recueil général des préliminaires, instructions, lettres, mémoires &c. concernant ces négociations, depuis leur commencement en 1643, jusqu'à leur conclusion en 1648.* La Haye, 1725-26. 4 v.

Lefevre Pontalis, Germain A. *John de Witt, Grand Pensionary of Holland or Twenty Years of a Parliamentary Republic.* London, 1885. 2 v.

Leupe, Pieter A. *Inventaris der verzameling kaarten berustende in het Rijksarchief.* 's-Gravenhage, 1867.

Levasseur, Emile. *La France et ses colonies (géographie et statistique).* Paris, 1890-93. 3 v.

L'Honoré Naber, Samuel P., ed. *Pieter de Marées: Beschrijvinghe ende historische verhael van het Gout Koninckryck van Gunea anders de Gout-Custe de Mina genaemt leggende in het deel van Africa.* 's-Gravenhage, 1912.

——, ed. *Dierick Ruyters. Toortse der zee-vaart en Samuel Brun's Schiffahrten.* 's-Gravenhage, 1913.

——, ed. *Reizen van Jan Huyghen van Linschoten naar het noorden, 1594-1598.* 's-Gravenhage, 1914.

——, ed. *Reizen van Willem Barentsz, Jacob van Heemskerck, Jan Cornelisz de Rijp en anderen naar het noorden.* 's-Gravenhage, 1917.

——, ed. *Kaspar van Baerle. Nederlandsch Brazilië onder het bewind van Johan Maurits, Grave van Nassau, 1637-1644.* 's-Gravenhage, 1923.

——, ed. "Het dagboeck van Hendrik Haecx, lid van den Hoogen Raad van Brazilië, 1645-1654." *Bijdragen en Mededelingen van het Historisch Genootschap,* XLVI (1925), 126-311.

————, ed. "'t Leven en bedrijf van Vice-Admiraal de With zaliger." *Bijdragen en Mededelingen van het Historisch Genootschap*, XLVII (1926), 47-169.

————, ed. *Reisebeschreibungen von deutschen Beamten und Kriegsleuten im Dienst der niederländischen West- und Ostindischen Kompagnien, 1602-1797.* 's-Gravenhage, 1930-32. 13 v.

————, ed. "Rapport van Piet Heyn aan de bewindhebbers van de Kamer Amsterdam der West Indische Compagnie dd. 11 Augustus 1627," and "Nalezingen en verbeteringen op de uitgave Piet Heyn en de Zilvervloot." *Bijdragen en Mededelingen van het Historisch Genootschap*, LI (1930), 22-34.

———— and Irene A. Wright, eds. *Piet Heyn en de Zilvervloot. Bescheiden uit Nederlandsche en Spaansche archieven.* Utrecht, 1928.

Ligtenberg, Catharina. *Willem Usselinx.* Utrecht, 1914.

Linschoten, Jan Huygen van. *Itinerario, voyage ofte schipvaert van Jan Huygen van Linschoten naer Oost ofte Portugaels Indien, 1579-1592.* H. Kern, ed. 's-Gravenhage, 1910.

Lister, Thomas H. *Life and Administration of Edward, First Earl of Clarendon.* London, 1837-38. 3 v.

Lonchay, Henri. *La rivalité de la France et de l'Espagne aux Pays-Bas, 1635-1700. Etude d'histoire diplomatique et militaire.* Bruxelles, 1896.

Lonchay, Henri, and Joseph Cuvelier, eds. *Correspondance de la Cour d'Espagne sur les affaires des Pays-Bas au XVIIe siècle, 1598-1700.* Bruxelles, 1923-37. 6 v. (Vol. II-VI, J. Cuvelier and J. Lefèvre, eds.).

Loon, Gerard van. *Beschrijving van Nederlandsche Histori-penningen.* 's-Gravenhage, 1723-31. 4 v.

Loon, Hendrik W. van. *Life and Times of Pieter Stuyvesant.* New York, 1928.

Lugo, A. *Edad media de la isla Española. Historia de Santo Domingo desde el 1556 hasta 1608.* Ciudad Trujillo, 1952.

Luzac, Elias. *Hollands rijkdom.* (Translation and revision of Acarius de Sérionne, *Tableau du commerce des Hollandais dans les quatre parties du monde.* Amsterdam, 1768. 3 v.) Leyden, 1780-83. 4 v.

Lydius, Jacobus. *'t Verheerlikte ofte verhoogde Nederland.* Dordrecht, 1668.

Maduro, Antonio J. *Spaanse documenten uit de jaren 1639 en 1640.* Scherpenheuvel, Curaçao, 1961.

————. *Spaanse documenten uit de jaren 1641 en 1642.* Scherpenheuvel, 1963.

Mahan, Alfred T. *The Influence of Sea Power upon History, 1660-1783.* Many editions. Boston, 1941, used here.

Malouet, Pierre V. *Collections de mémoires et correspondances officielles sur l'administration des colonies et notamment sur la Guiane française et hollandaise.* Paris, 1802.

Markham, Clements R. *Expeditions into the Valley of the Amazon, 1539-1540, 1639.* London, 1859.

Martin, Gaston. *Nantes au XVIIIe siècle.* Paris, 1928-31. 2 v. (Vol. II: *L'ère des négriers, 1714-1774*).

Mathews, Thomas G. "The Spanish Domination of Saint Martin." *Caribbean Studies,* IX (1969), 1, 3-23.

Mattiesen, Otto H. *Die Kolonial- und Überseepolitik der kurländischen Herzöge im 17. und 18. Jahrhundert.* Stuttgart, 1940.

Mauro, Frédéric. *Le Portugal et l'Atlantique au XVIIe siècle, 1570-1670. Etude économique.* Paris, 1960.

Mears, John W. *The Beggars of Holland and the Grandees of Spain. A History of the Reformation in the Netherlands, from A.D. 1200 to 1578.* Philadelphia, 1867.

Menezes, Luis de. See Ericeira, Luis de Menezes, Conde da.

Menkman, W. R. *De Nederlanders in het Caraïbisch zeegebied*. Amsterdam, 1942.
———. *De West-Indische Compagnie*. Amsterdam, 1947.
———. "Slavenhandel en rechtsbedeling op Curaçao op het einde der 17de eeuw." *West Indische Gids*, XVII (1935), 11-26.
———. "Sprokkelingen op het terrein der geschiedenis van de Nederlandsche Antillen." *West Indische Gids*, XVII (1935), 65-115.
———. "Curaçao, zijn naam en zijn taal." *West Indische Gids*, XVIII (1936), 38-50.
———. "Van de verovering van Curaçao tot de Vrede van Munster." *West Indische Gids*, XVIII (1936), 161-83.
———. "Tortola." *West Indische Gids*, XX (1938), 178-92.
———. "Tobago." *West Indische Gids*, XXI (1939), 218-36, 305-14, 369-81; XXII (1940), 33-46, 97-110, 129-33.
———. "Aanteekeningen op Hamelbergs werken." *West Indische Gids*, XXIII (1941), 1-22, 33-50, 65-77, 97-111, 161-76, 203-24, 321-29.
———. "Suriname in Willoughby's tijd." *West Indische Gids*, XXVI (1944, 1945), 1-18.
———. "Nederlandsche en vreemde slavenvaart." *West Indische Gids*, XXVI (1944-45), 97-110.
Merriman, Roger B. *The Rise of the Spanish Empire in the Old World and in the New*. New York, 1918-34. 4 v.
Meteren, Emanuel van. *Belgica, Historie der Nederlandscher ende haerder na-buren oorlogen ende geschiedenissen tot den iare* MVI⁰XII. 's Graven-haghe,1614.
Millares Torres, Agustín. *Historia general de las islas Canarias*. Agustín M. Carlo y Antonio Santana, eds. La Habana, 1945.
Mims, Stewart L. *Colbert's West India Policy*. New Haven, 1912.
Miramón, Alberto. "Los negreros del Caribe." *Boletín de Historia y Antigüedades* (Bogotá), XXXI (1944), 168-87.
Montanus, Arnoldus. *De nieuwe en onbekende weereld: of beschryving van America en 't zuid-land, vervaetende d'oorsprong der Americanen en zuid-landers, gedenkwaerdige togten derwaerts, gelegendheid der vaste kusten, eilanden, steden, sterkten, dorpen, tempels, bergen, fonteinen, stroomen, huisen, de natuur van beesten, boomen, planten en vreemde gewasschen, Gods-dienst en zeden, wonderlijke voorvallen, vereeuwde en nieuwe oorlogen*. Amsterdam, 1671.
Morales Carrión, Arturo. *Puerto Rico and the Non-Hispanic Caribbean. A Study in the Decline of Spanish Exclusivism*. Puerto Rico, 1952.
Morales Padrón, Francisco. *Jamaica española*. Sevilla, 1952.
Morón, Guillermo. *Los orígenes históricos de Venezuela*. Madrid, 1954.
Mosk, Sanford A. "Spanish Pearl-fishing Operations on the Pearl Coast in the Sixteenth Century." *Hispanic American Historical Review*, XVIII (1938), 392-400.
Motley, John L. *History of the United Netherlands, from the Death of William the Silent to the Twelve years' Truce—1609*. New York, 1868. 4 v.
———. *The Rise of the Dutch Republic. A History*. New York, 1883. 3 v.
Mulert, F. E. Baron. "Eene episode uit den Indianen oorlog in Suriname in den Zeeuwschen tijd." *West Indische Gids*, I (1919), 221-25.
Muller, Pieter L. *Onze gouden eeuw; de republiek der Vereenigde Nederlanden in haar bloeitijd*. Leiden, 1896-98. 3 v.
———. *De Staat der Vereenigde Nederlanden in de jaren zijner wording, 1572-1594*. Haarlem, 1872.
Muller, Samuel. *Mare clausum. Bijdrage tot de geschiedenis der rivaliteit van Engeland en Nederland in de zeventiende eeuw*. Amsterdam, 1872.
Nadal, Santiago. *Las cuatro mujeres de Felipe II*. Barcelona, 1944.

Namèche, Alexandre J. *Guilleaume le Taciturne, Prince d'Orange et la révolution des Pais-Bas au XVIe siècle.* Louvain, 1890. 2 v.

———. *Le règne de Philippe II et la lutte religieuse dans les Pays-Bas au XVIe siecle.* Louvain, 1885-87. 8 v.

Nanninga Uitterdijk, Johanna. *Een Kamper handelshuis te Lissabon, 1572-1594.* Zwolle, 1904.

Nassy, D. *Essai historique sur la colonie de Surinam.* Paramaribo, 1780. 2 v.

Nederlandsche Jaarboeken. Leiden, Amsterdam, 1766-90. 25 v.

Nederlandsche reizen tot bevordering van den koophandel na de meest afgelegene gewesten des aardkloots. Doormengd met vreemde lotgevallen en menigvuldige gevaaren die de Nederlandsche reizigers hebben doorgestaan. Amsterdam, 1784-87. 14 v.

Netscher, Pieter M. *Les Hollandais au Brésil. Notice historique sur les Pays-Bas et le Brésil au XVIIe siècle.* La Haye, 1853.

———. *Geschiedenis van de koloniën Essequibo, Demerary en Berbice.* 's-Gravenhage, 1888.

Nettelbeck, Joachim C. *Joachim Nettelbeck, Bürger zu Kolberg; eine Lebensbeschreibung, von ihm selbst aufgezeichnet.* Leipzig, 1845.

Newton, Arthur P. *The European Nations in the West Indies, 1493-1688.* London, 1933.

Nierop, Leonie van. "Rensselaarswijck, 1629-1704." *Tijdschrift voor Geschiedenis,* LXI (1948), 70-123, 305-47.

Nijhoff, W. *The Hollanders in America. A Choice Collection of Books, Maps and Pamphlets relating to the Early Colonization, Voyages, Exploration &c. by the Hollanders in Different Parts of North and South America.* The Hague, 1925.

Núñez Ponte, José M. *Estudio histórico acerca de la esclavitud y de su abolición en Venezuela.* 3rd ed. Caracas, 1954.

Nuyts, David. "Brieven betreffende de belangen van de Oost- en West-Indische Compagnie." *Kroniek van het Historisch Genootschap,* V, 5 (1869), 110-57.

Ober, Frederick A. *Crusoë's Island; a bird-hunter's story.* New York, 1898.

O'Callaghan, Edmund B., ed. *Documents Relative to the Colonial History of the State of New York.* Albany, 1853-57. 15 v.

———, ed. *Voyages of the Slavers St. John and Arms of Amsterdam, 1659, 1663; together with Additional Papers Illustrating the Slave Trade of the Dutch.* Albany, 1867.

———, ed. *The Records of New Amsterdam from 1653-1674.* Berthold Fernow, co-ed. New York, 1897. 7 v.

Ogg, David. *England in the Reign of Charles II.* Oxford, 1934. 2 v.

Ojer, Pablo. *Las salinas del oriente venezolano en el siglo XVII.* Caracas, 1962.

Oppenheim, Michael, ed. "The Naval Tracts of Sir William Monson." *Publications of the Navy Record Society,* XXIII (1902), 309-40.

Oppenheim, Samuel. "An Early Jewish Colony in Western Guiana, 1658-1666, and its Relation to the Jews in Surinam, Cayenne, and Tobago." *Publications of the American Jewish Historical Society,* XVI (1907), 95-186; Supplement in XVII (1909), 53-70.

Ottley, C. R. *Trinidad, 'Capital of the West Indies,' and Tobago, 'Robinson Crusoe isle.'* Port of Spain, 1959.

Oudschans Dentz, Fred. "Historische monumenten in Britsch Guyana." *De Navorscher,* LXV (1916), 314-20.

———. "Suriname vóór de verovering door Abraham Crijnssen." *Bijdragen en Mededelingen van het Historisch Genootschap,* XXXIX (1918), 173-213, 411-12.

———. "Stukken over de verovering van Suriname." *Bijdragen en Mededelingen van het Historisch Genootschap,* XL (1919), 1-9.

———. "De aanval op Curaçao in 1673." *West Indische Gids,* VII (1925), 279-88.

————. *De kolonisatie van de Portugeesch Joodsche natie in Suriname en de geschiedenis van de Joden Savanne.* 2d ed. Amsterdam, 1927.

————. "Tobago." *West Indische Gids*, X (1928), 527-34.

————. "Lucien Wolf en de Joodsche kolonisatie in West-Indië." *West Indische Gids*, XII (1930), 590-91.

————. "Hoe het eiland St. Maarten werd verdeeld." *West Indische Gids*, XIII (1931), 163-64.

————. "De inbezitneming van het Fransche gedeelte van St. Maarten door de Nederlanders." *West Indische Gids*, XV (1933), 280-81.

————. "De Crijnssen herdenking in 1917." *West Indische Gids*, XVIII (1936), 276-83.

————. "De kolonisatie van Guyana." *West Indische Gids*, XXV (1943), 248-54.

Overeem, J. B. van. "De reizen naar de West van Cornelis Cornelisz Jol, 1626-1640." *West Indische Gids*, XXIV (1942), 1-19, 33-49.

Ozinga, Murk D. *De monumenten van Curaçao in woord en beeld.* Willemstad, 1959.

Pahlow, E. W. "Anglo-Dutch Relations, 1671-1672." *Annual Report of American Historical Association*, I (1911), 123-27.

Panhuys, L. C. van. "Quyrin Spranger." *West Indische Gids*, XII (1930), 535-40.

Parry, John H. *Europe and a Wider World, 1415-1715.* New ed. London, 1966.

————. *The Spanish Seaborne Empire.* New York, 1966.

———— and P. M. Sherlock. *A Short History of the West Indies.* London, New York, 1956.

Payne, Ancil N. "The Relations of the English Commercial Companies to the Government, 1660-1715." Ph.D. dissertation, University of Illinois, 1930.

Paz, Julián. *Catálogo de la colección de documentos inéditos para la historia de España.* Madrid, 1930-31. 2 v.

Pepys, Samuel. *The Diary of Samuel Pepys.* Henry B. Wheatley, ed. London, New York, 1893-99. 2 v.

Petit, Louis D. *Bibliotheek van Nederlandsche pamfletten. Verzamelingen van de bibliotheek van Joannes Thysius en de bibliotheek der Rijksuniversiteit te Leiden.* 2d ed. Leiden, 1882-1934. 4 v.

Pezuela y Lobo, Jacobo de la. *Historia de la isla de Cuba.* Madrid, 1868-78. 4 v.

Pfandl, Ludwig. *Philip II. Gemälde eines Lebens und einer Zeit.* München, 1938.

————. *Karl II. Das Ende der spanischen Machtstellung in Europa.* München, 1940.

Pigeonneau, Henri. *Histoire du commerce de la France.* Paris, 1885-97. 2 v.

Pirenne, Henri. *Histoire de Belgique.* Bruxelles: Vol. IV, 1911.

Poelhekke, J. J. *De vrede van Munster.* 's-Gravenhage, 1948.

————. *'t Uytgaen van den Treves. Spanje en de Nederlanden in 1621.* Groningen, 1960.

Prestage, Edgar. *The Diplomatic Relations of Portugal with France, England, and Holland from 1640 to 1668.* Watford, 1925.

Rainsford, Marcus. *An Historical Account of the Black Empire of Hayti: comprehending a view of the principal transactions in the revolution of Saint Domingo; with its antient and modern state.* London, 1805.

Ramos, Demetrio. "Alonso de Ojeda en el gran proyecto de 1501 y en el tránsito del sistema de descubrimiento y rescate al de poblamiento." *Boletín de la Academia Nacional de Historia*, L, 197, enero-marzo. Caracas, 1967, pp. 34-85.

Ratelband, K. "De expeditie van Jol naar Angola en São Tomé." *West Indische Gids*, XXIV (1942), 320-24.

————, ed. *Reizen naar West Africa van Pieter van den Broecke, 1605-1614.* 's-Gravenhage, 1950.

————, ed. *Vijf dagregisters van het kasteel São Jorge da Mina aan de Goudkust, 1645-1647.* 's-Gravenhage, 1953.

————, ed. *De Westafrikaanse reis van Piet Heyn, 1624-1625.* 's-Gravenhage, 1959.

Ravensteyn, Willem van. *Onderzoekingen over de economische en sociale ontwikkeling van Amsterdam gedurende de 16de en het eerste kwart der 17de eeuw.* Amsterdam, 1906.

Raynal, G. T. F. *A Philosophical and Political History of the Settlements and Trade of the Europeans in the East and West Indies.* Trans. J. O. Justamond. London, 1798. 6 v.

Recopilación de leyes de los Reynos de las Indias. 5th ed. Madrid, 1841. 4 v.

Rees, Otto van. *Geschiedenis der koloniale politiek van de republiek der Vereenigde Nederlanden.* Utrecht, 1868.

Reesse, J. J. *De suikerhandel van Amsterdam van het begin der 17de eeuw tot 1813, een bijdrage tot de handelsgeschiedenis des vaderlands.* 's-Gravenhage, 1908. 2 v.

Renaudet, A. *Les Pays-Bas espagnols et les Provinces-Unies de 1598 à 1714.* Paris, 1960.

Renier, Gustaaf R. *The Dutch Nation; an Historical Study.* London, 1944.

Reyd, Everhard van. *Historie der Nederlantscher oorlogen.* Amsterdam, 1644.

Reygersbergh van Cortgene, Jan. *De oude chronijcke ende historien van Zeelandt.* Middelberch, 1634.

Rinchon, Dieudonné. *La traite et l'esclavage des Congolais par les Européens.* Bruxelles, 1929.

Rivas, Raimundo. "El corso y la piratería en Colombia." *Boletín de Historia y Antigüedades* (Bogotá), XXXI (Feb. de 1944), 118-67.

Rochefort, Charles de. *Histoire naturelle et morale des iles Antilles de l'Amérique.* Rotterdam, 1658.

Rodrigues, José Honório, and Joaquim Ribeiro. *Civilização holandesa no Brasil.* São Paulo, 1940.

Rodway, James. *Guiana: British, Dutch, and French.* New York, London, 1912.

———— and T. Watt. *Chronological History of the Discovery and Settlement of Guiana, 1493-1668.* Georgetown, 1888.

Roever, N. de. "Twee concurrenten der eerste West-Indische Compagnie." *Oud Holland,* VII (1899).

Romein, Jan M. *Erflaters van onze beschaving. Nederlandse gestalten uit zes eeuwen.* 8th ed. Amsterdam, 1959.

Romero, Fernando. "The Slave Trade and the Negro in South America." *Hispanic American Historical Review,* XXIV (1944), 368-86.

Roncière, Charles de la. *Histoire de la marine française.* Paris, 1899-1923. 6 v.

Roos, J. S. "Additional Notes on the History of the Jews in Surinam." *Publications of the American Jewish Historical Society,* XIII (1905), 127-36.

Rowen, H. H. *The Ambassador prepares for War; the Dutch Ambassy of Arnault de Pomponne, 1669-1671.* The Hague, 1957.

Rüe, Pieter de la. *Staatkundig en heldhaftig Zeeland.* Middelburg, 1736.

Sande, Johan van den. *De waeckende leeuw der Nederlanden. Historie 't begin ende voortgangh der Nederlandsche oorlogen ende beroerten tot den vrede van Munster.* Amsterdam, 1663.

Savary, Jacques. *Le parfait négociant; ou instruction générale pour ce qui regarde le commerce des marchandises de France & des pays étrangers.* Paris, 1767-70. 2 v.

Scelle, Georges. *La traite négrière aux Indes de Castille.* Paris, 1906. 2 v.

Scheurleer, Daniel F. *Onze mannen ter zee, in dicht en beeld.* 's-Gravenhage, 1912-14. 3 v.

Schiller, J. Ch. Friedrich von. *Geschichte des Abfalls der Vereinigten Niederlande.* Many editions. *Schiller's Werke* used here. Berlin, Stuttgart, 1882-90.

Schomburgk, Robert H. *A Description of British Guiana, Geographical and Statistical.* London, 1840.

————. *The History of Barbados.* London, 1848.

Seraphim, Ernst. *Geschichte von Livland.* Gotha, 1906.

————. *Geschichte Liv-, Est- und Kurlands.* Reval, 1895-96. 2 v.

———— and August Seraphim. *Aus vier Jahrhunderten. Gesammelte Aufsätze zur baltischen Geschichte.* Reval, 1913.

Sluiter, Engel. "Dutch Maritime Power and the Colonial Status Quo." *Pacific Historical Review,* XI (1942), 29-41.

————. "The Word Pichelingue: Its Derivation and Meaning." *Hispanic American Historical Review,* XXIV (1944), 683-98.

————. "Dutch-Spanish Rivalry in the Caribbean Area, 1594-1609." *Hispanic American Historical Review,* XXVIII (1948), 165-96.

Solórzano Pereira, Juan de. *Obras varias postumas.* Madrid, 1776.

Stern, D. *Histoire des commencements de la République des Pays-Bas, 1581-1625.* Paris, 1872.

Sterre, Dionysius van der. *Zeer aanmerckelijke reysen gedaan door Jan Erasmus Reining, meest in de West-Indien en ook in veel andere deelen des werelds.* Amsterdam, 1691.

Stijl, Simon. *De opkomst en bloei der Vereenigde Nederlanden.* 2d ed. Amsterdam, 1778.

Stoppelaar, Johannes H. de. *Balthasar de Moucheron; een bladzijde uit de Nederlandsche handelsgeschiedenis tijdens den tachtig-jarigen oorlog.* 's-Gravenhage, 1901.

Storm van 's Gravensande, Laurens. *The Rise of British Guiana.* C. A. Harris and J. A. J. de Villiers, eds. London, 1911. 2 v.

Sucre, Luis A. *Gobernadores y capitanes generales de Venezuela.* Caracas, 1928.

Sue, Eugène. *Histoire de la marine française.* Paris, 1835-38. 5 v.

Supan, Alexander G. *Die territoriale Entwicklung der europäischen Kolonien.* Gotha, 1906.

Swalue, Edelhardus B. *De daden der Zeeuwen gedurende den opstand tegen Spanje.* Amsterdam, 1846.

Sylvius, Lambertus (Lambert van den Bos). *Vervolgh van Saken van staat en oorlogh in ende ontrent de Vereenigde Nederlanden en in geheel Europa voorgevallen.* Amsterdam, 1685-99. 3 v.

Sypesteyn, Cornelis A. van. *Beschrijving van Suriname.* 's-Gravenhage, 1854.

Tapia y Rivera, Alejandro. *Biblioteca histórica de Puerto Rico.* San Juan de Puerto Rico, 1854.

Tawney, Richard H. *Religion and the Rise of Capitalism; a historical study.* London, 1944.

Ternaux Compans, Henri. *Notice historique sur la Guyane française.* Paris, 1843.

Thornton, Percy M. *The Stuart Dynasty; Short studies of Its Rise, Course, and Early Exile.* London, 1890.

Thurloe, J. *A Collection of the State Papers of John Thurloe Exp.* London, 1742. 7 v.

Tiele, Pieter A. *Mémoire bibliographique sur les journaux des navigateurs néerlandais, réimprimés dans les collections de de Bry et de Hulsius et dans les collections hollandaises du XVIIe siècle et sur les anciennes éditions hollandaises des journaux de navigateurs étrangers.* Amsterdam, 1867.

Tjassens, J. *Zee-politie der Vereenichde Nederlanden.* 2d ed. 's Graven-Hage, 1670.

Trevelyan, George M. *England under the Stuarts.* Many editions. The 12th ed. revised, being Vol. V of the *History of England,* C. Omen, ed. (London, 1925), used here.

Troude, O. *Batailles navales de la France.* Paris, 1867-68. 4 v.

Tuckerman, Bayard. *Peter Stuyvesant, Director-General for the West India Company in New Netherland.* New York, 1893.

Unger, W. S. "Nieuwe gegevens betreffende het begin der vaart op Guinea." *Economisch-Historisch Jaarboek,* XXI (1940), 194-217.

————. "Bijdragen tot de geschiedenis van de Nederlandse slavenhandel." *Economisch Historisch Jaarboek*, XXVI (1956), 133-74.

United States Commission on Boundary between Venezuela and British Guiana (*Commission to Investigate and Report upon the True Divisional Line between Venezuela and British Guiana*). *Report and Accompanying Papers of the Commission*. I, *Historical*. II, *Extracts from Archives*. VII, *Official History: The Discussion between Venezuela and British Guiana*. IX, *Brief for Venezuela*. Washington, 1896-97.

Varnhagen, Francisco A. de. *Historia das lutas com os Holandezes no Brazil desde 1624 a 1654*. Lisboa, 1872.

Vela, V. Vicente. *Indice de la colección de documentos de Fernández de Navarrete que posee el Museo Naval*. Madrid, 1946.

Velius, Theodorus. *Chronijck van Hoorn. Daer in verhaelt werden des selven stadts eerste begin, opcomen en gedenckweerdige geschiedenissen tot op den jare 1630*. 4th ed. Hoorn, 1740.

Verhoog, P., and L. Koelmans. *De reis van Michiel Adriaenszoon de Ruyter in 1664-1665*. 's-Gravenhage, 1961.

Vieira, António. *Obras escolhidas*. António Sérgio and Hernâni Cidade, eds. Lisboa, 1951-54. 12 v.

Viera y Clavijo, José de. *Noticias de la historia general de las islas de Canaria*. 2d ed. Madrid, 1772-83. 4 v.

Vloten, Johannes van. *Nederlands opstand tegen Spanje in zijn eerste wording en ontwikkeling, 1567-1572*. Haarlem, 1858. 2 v.

Voor Rogier. Hilversum, 1964. A collection of essays by his students presented to Dr. L. J. Rogier at his retirement.

Vreede, George W. *Lettres et négociations de Paul Chouart, Seigneur de Buzanval, ambassadeur ordinaire de Henry IV en Hollande et de François d'Aerssen, agent des Provinces-Unies en France, 1598-1599*. Utrecht, 1846.

————. *Nederland en Cromwell*. Utrecht, 1853.

Vries, David Pietersz de. *Korte historiael ende journaels aenteyckeninge van verscheyden voyagiën in de vier deelen des wereldtsronds, als Europa, Africa, Asia, ende America gedaen*. H. T. Colenbrander, ed. 's-Gravenhage, 1911.

Vrijman, L. C. *Slavenhalers en slavenhandel*. Amsterdam, 1937.

————. "Iets over de Nederlandsche volksplantingen in 'Cayanen' gedurende de 17de eeuw." *West Indische Gids*, XVIII (1936), 13-24.

Waard, Cornelis de. *De Zeeuwsche expeditie naar de West onder Cornelis Evertsen de Jonge, 1672-1674*. 's-Gravenhage, 1928.

Waddington, Albert. *La république des Provinces-Unies, la France et les Pays-Bas espagnols de 1630 à 1650. Annales de l'université de Lyon*. Paris, 1895-97. 2 v.

————. "Sommaire de la forme du régime des Provinces-Unies des Pays-Bas." *Bijdragen en Mededelingen van het Historisch Genootschap*, XV (1894), 152-79.

Wätjen, Hermann. *Das holländische Kolonialreich in Brasilien*. Haag, 1921.

————. "Der Negerhandel in West-Indien und Süd-Amerika bis zur Sklavenemanzipation." *Hänsische Geschichtsblätter*, XIX (1913), 417-43.

Wagenaar, Jan. *Vaderlandsche Historie, vervattende de geschiedenissen der nu Vereenigde Nederlanden*. 2d ed. Amsterdam, 1752-59. 21 v.

————. *Bijvoegsels en aanmerkingen van het eerste-twintigste deel der Vaderlandsche Historie van Jan Wagenaar*. H. van Wijn, N. C. Lambrechtsen, A. Martini, E. M. Engelberts *et al.*, eds. Amsterdam, 1790-96. 20 v.

Warnsinck, Johan C. M. *Abraham Crijnssen, de verovering van Suriname en zijn aanslag op Virginië in 1667*. Amsterdam, 1936.

————. *Drie zeventiende-eeuwsche admiraals: Piet Heyn, Witte de With, Jan Evertsen.* Amsterdam, 1938.

————, ed. *De reis om de wereld van Joris van Spilbergen, 1614-1617.* 's-Gravenhage, 1943.

Wassenaer, Nicolaes van. *Historisch verhael alder ghedenck-weerdichtste geschiedenisse die hier en daer in Europa, als in Duytsch-lant, Vranckrijck, Enghelant, Spaengien, Hungarijen, Polen, Sevenberghen, Wallachien, Moldavien, Turckijen en Neder-lant, van den beginne des jaers 1621...tot Octobri, des jaers 1632 voorgevallen syn.* Amsterdam, 1622-35. 21 v.

Watson, Robert. *The History of the Reign of Philip the Third, King of Spain.* London, 1786. 2 v.

Weber, Henri. *La compagnie française des Indes.* Paris, 1904.

Westergaard, Waldemar C. *The Danish West Indies under Company Rule, 1671-1754 with a Supplementary Chapter: 1755-1917.* New York, 1917.

Westhuysen, Abraham à. *Waerachtich verhael van de heerlijke overwinning van Pirmeriba ende de reviere Seraname.* 's Gravenhage, 1667.

Wicquefort, Abraham van. *L'histoire des Provinces-Unies confirmée et éclairée par des preuves authentiques.* La Haye, 1719-45. 3 v. A second edition was published under the title *Histoire des Provinces Unies des Païs Bas depuïs le parfait établissement de cet état par la paix de Munster.* L. E. Lenting and C. A. Chais van Buren, eds. Amsterdam, 1861-74. 4 v.

Wieder, Frederik C. *De reis van Mahu en de Cordes door de Straat Magalhäes naar Zuid-Amerika en Japan, 1598-1600.* 's-Gravenhage, 1923-25. 3 v.

————, ed. *Monumenta cartographica; reproductions of unique and rare maps, plans and views in the actual size of the originals; accompanied by cartographical monographs.* 's-Gravenhage, 1925-33. 5 v.

Wiersum, E. van. "Johan van der Veken, koopman en bankier te Rotterdam." *Handelingen van de Maatschappij der Nederlandsche Letterkunde* (1911-12), pp. 165-90.

Williamson, James A. *English Colonies in Guiana and on the Amazon, 1604-1668.* Oxford, 1923.

————. *The Caribbee Islands under the Proprietary Patents.* London, 1926.

Winkel Rauws, H. *Nederlandsch-Engelsche samenwerking in de Spaansche wateren, 1625-1627.* Amsterdam, 1947.

Wittram, Reinhart *Baltische Geschichte.* München, 1954.

Wolbers, J. B. *Geschiedenis van Suriname.* Amsterdam, 1861.

Wolf, John B. *Louis XIV.* New York, 1968.

Wright, Irene A. *Cuba.* New York, 1910.

————. *The Early History of Cuba, 1492-1586, Written from Original Sources.* New York, 1916.

————. "Rescates, with Special Reference to Cuba, 1599-1610." *Hispanic American Historical Review,* III (1920), 333-61.

————. "The Dutch and Cuba." *Hispanic American Historical Review,* IV (1921), 597-634.

————. "The Coymans Asiento, 1685-1689." *Bijdragen voor Vaderlandsche Geschiedenis en Oudheidkunde,* VI, 1 (1924), 23-62.

————, ed. *Documents Concerning English Voyages to the Spanish Main, 1569-1580.* London, 1932.

————, ed. *Further English Voyages to Spanish America, 1583-1594.* London, 1951.

———— and Cornelis F. A. van Dam, eds. *Nederlandsche zeevaarders op de eilanden in de Caraïbische Zee en aan de kust van Colombia en Venezuela gedurende de jaren 1621-*

1648. Documenten hoofdzakelijk uit het Archivo General de Indias te Sevilla. Utrecht, 1934-35. 2 v.

Zapatero, Juan Manuel. *La guerra del Caribe en el siglo XVIII.* San Juan de Puerto Rico, 1964.

Zimmermann, Alfred. *Die europäischen Kolonien. Schilderung ihrer Entstehung, Entwicklung, Erfolge und Aussichten.* Berlin, 1896-1903. 5 v. Vol. v: *Die Kolonialpolitik der Niederländer.* Berlin, 1903.

Zwarts, J. "Eene episode uit de Joodsche kolonisatie van Guyana." *West Indische Gids,* IX (1927), 519-30.

Zweig, Stefan. *Amerigo Vespucci. Die Geschichte eines historischen Irrtums.* Stockholm, 1944.

INDEX